Narrative Of A Voyage To The Pacific And Beering's Strait, To Co-operate With The Polar Expeditions:

Beechey, F[rederick] W[illiam], 1796-1856

1

NARRATIVE

OF A

VOYAGE TO THE PACIFIC

AND BEERING'S STRAIT,

TO CO-OPERATE WITH

THE POLAR EXPEDITIONS:

PERFORMED IN

HIS MAJESTY'S SHIP BLOSSOM,

UNDER THE COMMAND OF

CAPTAIN F. W. BEECHEY, R. N.

F.R.S &c

IN THE YEARS 1825, 26, 27, 28.

PUBLISHED BY AUTHORITY OF THE LORDS COMMISSIONERS
OF THE ADMIRALTY

PHILADELPHIA

CAREY & LEA—CHESNUT STREET

1832

AMHERST.
PRINTED BY J. S. & C. ADAMS.

CONTENTS.

CHAPTER 1.

CHAPTER II

CHAPTER III.

CHAPTER IV.

CHAPTER V.

CHAPTER VI.

CHAPTER VII.

CHAPTER VIII.

CHAPTER IX.

CHAPTER X

CHAPTER XI

CHAPTER XII

CHAPTER XIX

NOTE.

In presenting to the public a new edition of this interesting and popular work, the Publishers feel bound in duty to observe, that some of Captain Beechey's remarks upon the moral condition of the Society and Sandwich Islands, especially upon the nature and effects of the missionary exertions, have been shown to be very defective and unjust. For a more correct account in these particulars, the reader is referred to the " *Journal of Voyages and Travels by Tyerman and Bennett,*" and " *Stewart's Voyages to the South Seas.*"

TO THE KING.

————

In availing myself of Your Majesty's gracious permission to dedicate this work to your Majesty, I feel that I am performing a most pleasing duty.

The claims of Your Majesty's family on the gratitude of the nation, for the efficient patronage they have afforded to maritime discovery, require merely to be alluded to, to ensure the attention of every well-wisher to his country.

Under a less powerful Sovereign than your Royal Father, the voyages of Cook and Vancouver, in all probability, would never have been projected, and could hardly have prospered ; while it is certain that the expeditions of Parry and Franklin owed their chief distinction to the enlightened encouragement of His late Majesty.

But these great enterprises—so productive of national renown—so extensively useful in diffusing the blessings of civilization over distant and savage lands—and so eminently beneficial to the cause of science and of commerce, could never have been successfully accomplished, had not the character of the Navy been habitually maintained at, perhaps, the highest level which human exertion is capable of reaching.

To produce this generous spirit, however, and to preserve it entire when once created, there was required, on the part of the Royal Family, some signal example of personal sacrifice to the popular service of the country. And although it would be very presumptuous in any one to pretend to estimate the advantages which the profession has derived, in our own days, from Your Majesty having condescended to become one of its working members, there can be no doubt, that in all future times, the British Navy will retain the salutary impression, and cherish the remembrance of this high honour.

May it please Your Majesty,

Your Majesty's

most dutiful servant,

most grateful

and most faithful subject,

FREDERICK WILLIAM BEECHEY.

INTRODUCTION.

———

THE discovery of a north-west passage to the Pacific had for some years occupied the attention of the British government and of the public at large, and several brilliant attempts had been made both by sea and by land to ascertain the practicability of its navigation, which, though conducted with a zeal and perseverance that will transmit them to the latest posterity, had, from insurmountable difficulties, failed of success.

In 1824 His late Majesty having commanded that another attempt should be made by way of Prince Regent's Inlet, an expedition was equipped—the last that sailed upon this interesting service—and the command again conferred upon Captain Parry, whose exploits have so deservedly earned him the approbation of his country. At the same time Captain Franklin, undaunted by his former perilous expedition, and by the magnitude of the contemplated undertaking, having with the promptness and perseverance peculiar to his character, proposed to connect his brilliant discoveries at the mouth of the Coppermine River with the furthest known point on the western side of America, by descending the Mackenzie River, and, with the assistance of his intrepid associate, Dr. Richardson, by coasting the northern shore in opposite directions towards the two previously discovered points, His late Majesty was also pleased to command that this expedition should be simultaneously undertaken

From the nature of these services it was nearly impossible that either of these expeditions could arrive at the open sea in Beering's Strait, without having nearly, if not wholly, exhausted their resources, and Captain Franklin's party being, in addition, destitute of a conveyance to a place whence it could return to Europe To obviate these anticipated difficulties, his Majesty's government determined upon sending a ship to Beering's Strait to await the arrival of the two expeditions

As this vessel would traverse, in her route, a portion of the globe hitherto little explored, and as a considerable period must necessarily elapse before her presence would be required in the north, it was intended to employ her in surveying and exploring such parts of the Pacific as were within her reach, and were of the most consequence to navigation

The vessel selected for this service was his Majesty's ship Blossom, of twenty-six guns, but on this occasion mounting only sixteen, and on the 12th of January, 1825, I had the honour of being appointed to the command of her. The following officers, most of them men distinguished for their abilities, were placed under my orders, viz.—

Lieutenant,	George Peard.	*Naturalist,*	George T Lay.
Ditto,	{ Edw. Belcher, *Su-Assistant Surgeon,*	Thomas Neilson.
	{ per numerary and *Clerks,* .	{ John Evans
	{ Assistant Surveyor.	{ Chas. H Osmer
Lieutenant,	John Wainwright.	*Volunt 1st Class*	{ John Crawley
Master, .	Thomas Elson		{ John Hockley.
Surgeon,	Alex. Collie	*Ditto, 2d Class,*	{ J. C Barlow.
Purser, .	George Marsh		{ Charles Lewis.
Admiralty Mates,	{ J. F. Gould,*	*Gunner,*	John Richardson
	{ William Smyth,	*Boatswain,* .	James Clarkson
	{ James Wolfe	*Carpenter,* .	Thos. Garrett.
Midshipmen,	{ John Rendall,		
	{ Richard B. Beechy		

To these were added such a number of seamen, marines, and boys, as, with the exception of the supernumeraries, would form a complement of a hundred and ten persons, but in consequence of the weakness of our crew when collected, I was permitted to discharge ten of the most inefficient; a reduction which, without sensibly diminishing the strength of our crew, materially increased the duration of our stock of provisions, and in the sequel proved of the most happy consequence

The ship was partially strengthened, and otherwise adapted to the service, by increasing her stowage. A boat was supplied, to be used as a tender, and for this purpose she was made as large as the space on the deck would allow. She was rigged as a schooner, decked, and fitted in the most complete manner, and reflected great credit upon Mr. Peake, the master-shipwright of Woolwich dock-yard, who moddelled and built her

*This valuable young officer was obliged to quit the ship at Rio Janerio on account of his health

To the usual allowance of provision was added a variety of anti-
scorbutics Cloth, beads, cutlery, and other articles of traffic, were put
on board ; and two fowling-pieces, embossed with silver, and fitted in
the most complete manner, were supplied as presents to the kings of
the Society and Sandwich Islands. The College of Surgeons sent bottles of spirits for the preservation of specimens, and the Horticultural
Society enhanced our extra stores with a box of seeds properly prepared for keeping.

The seamen were furnished with two suits of clothes gratis, and were
allowed the further privilege of having six months' wages in advance

In the equipment of all the expeditions of this nature it has been the
good fortune of the officers engaged in them to meet with the utmost
courtesy and attention to their wishes from the departments which
have the power so materially to contribute to their comfort ; and I take
this opportunity of expressing my sincere thanks to Sir G Cockburn
and the other Lords Commissioners of the Admiralty, to Sir Thomas
Byam Martin, and the Commissioners of the Navy and Victualling
Boards, for the readiness with which they at all times complied with
my requests.

Being in every respect ready, on the 19th May I received the following instructions from the Lords Commissioners of the Admiralty :—

" By the Commissioners for executing the office of Lord High Admiral of the United Kingdom of Great Britain and Ireland &c

" Whereas it is our intention that his majesty's sloop Blossom, under
your command, should be at Beering's Strait in the Autumn of 1826,
and, contingently, in that of 1827, for the purpose of affording such assistance as may be required, either by Captain Parry or Captain Franklin, should one or both of those officers make their appearance in that
neighbourhood. You are hereby required and directed to put to sea in
the said sloop, so soon as in every respect ready, and observe the following instructions for your guidance :—

" You are to proceed with all convenient expedition to Rio Janeiro,
where you are to complete your provisions and water ; after which you
are to make the best of your way round Cape Horn, and endeavour to
make Easter Island ; from whence you are to take your departure,
steering for the Society Islands, and passing near the spot where Gomez
Island appears in the charts, in order to ascertain whether such island
has any existence ; and, in like manner, whether Ducie's and Elizabeth
Islands be not one and the same. You will then proceed to Pitcairn's
Island at the south-eastern extremity of the groupe of the Society Islands, or, as they are sometimes called, the Georgian Islands, where you
will commence a survey of this groupe, proceeding north-westerly to

Otaheite In the execution of this survey it may be found most advisable to anchor, if practicable, every evening, under one of the islands, in order that the situation of the ship may, by these means, be more secure, and that you may be certain that none of them are passed by you unobserved If, however you should experience any difficulty in pursuing the route herein pointed out from the prevailing winds, you will make the best of your way to Otaheite, and proceed from thence in your survey to Pitcairn's Island

"During your stay among these or any other of the islands of the Pacific which you may visit, you are to use every possible endeavour to preserve an amicable intercourse with the natives, and to caution your officers and ship's company to avoid giving offence or engaging in disputes with them , and you are to show them on all occasions every act of kindness that may be in your power, taking care that when any purchases, by barter or otherwise, are made, an officer of the ship may always be present to prevent disputes and you are particularly to impress on the minds of your officers and men the necessity of being extremely guarded in their intercourse with the females of those places, so as to avoid exciting the jealousy of the men.

" Having completed the survey of this groupe of islands, if you find that your time will admit of it, you are to direct your course to the Navigator's Islands, settling in your way thither the true position of Suwarow's Islands, from whence, in your progress to the northward, you will touch at Owhyhee, to deliver the despatches and packages addressed by the Foreign Office for his Majesty's consul at that island, and to procure refreshments and water

"You are however, to be particularly careful not to prolong your stay at any of those islands, so as to retard your arrival at the appointed rendezvous in Beering's Strait later than the 10th July, 1826 ; which period, together with the rendezvous, has been fixed by Captain Franklin and yourself, by a memorandum, a copy of which is annexed, and we desire and direct you to pay particular attention to the the various matters contained therein

' You are to remain at the said appointed rendezvous until the end of October, or to as late a period as the season will admit, without incurring the risk of being obliged to winter there, provided you shall hear nothing of Captain Franklin or his party ; but in the event of his joining, you are to receive him and his party on board, and convey him either to Kamtschatka, the Sandwich Islands, Panama, or to China, as he may determine, in order to procure a further conveyance to England. If, however, you should receive certain intelligence of Captain Parry having passed through Beering's Strait into the Pacific, you are in that case to proceed with the Blossom round Cape Horn, and bring Captain Franklin and his party to England , touching at Callao, and such other ports on the western coast of South America as you may deem proper for refreshments, intelligence, &c.

" In the former event. namely, of your leaving Beering's Strait with Captain Franklin, but without having obtained any intelligence of Captain Parry, you are to complete your water and provisions at the place to which you convey Captain Franklin, or in the event of your hearing nothing either of Captains Franklin or Parry, previous to the season obliging you to leave Beering's Strait in 1826, you are to proceed to such place as you may deem most eligible and convenient for completing your provisions and water, taking care in either of the last mentioned cases to be again in Beering's Strait by the 1st August, 1827, calling in your way thither again at Owhyhee, at which place Captain Parry has been directed to give the preference of touching in his way homeward, for the purpose of affording you intelligence of him

"If you should find that Captain Parry has passed, or should he pass after joining you, and that you have heard nothing of Captain Franklin, you are, nevertheless, to proceed to, or remain at (as the case may be) Beering's Strait, in the autumn of 1827, as already directed, following in all respects the directions already given for your conduct in the autumn of 1826.

"In order that you may be put in full possession of that part of our instructions to Captain Parry which relates to his arrival in Beering's Strait, we enclose you herewith an extract from them, as also a copy of a ' Memorandum,' drawn up by Captain Parry, and dated 'Hecla, Davis' Strait, June, 1824 ;' to both of which we desire to call your particular attention, in order that you may govern your proceedings accordingly

"Having remained in Beering's Strait as late in the autumn of 1827 as the season will admit, and without risking the chance of being obliged to winter on account of the ice, you are to proceed to England by the route before directed ; reporting to our secretary your arrival, and transmitting the journals of yourself and officers for our information.

"In the prosecution of your voyage out, and during your stay in the Pacific, you are to be particular in noticing the *differences of longitude* given by your chronometers, from any one place to another, which you may visit in succession

"As we have appointed Mr. Tradescant Lay as naturalist on the voyage, and some of your officers are acquainted with certain branches of natural history, it is expected that your visits to the numerous islands of the Pacific will afford the means of collecting rare and curious specimens in the several departments of this branch of science.

You are to cause it to be understood that two specimens *at least*, of each article are to be reserved for the public museums, after which the naturalist and officers will be at liberty to collect for themselves You will pay every attention in your power to the preservation of the various specimens of natural history, and on your arrival in England transmit them to this office ; and if, on your arrival at any place in the course of your voyage, you should meet with a safe conveyance to England, you are to avail yourself of it to send home any despatches you may have, accompanied by journals, charts, drawings, &c, and such specimens of natural history as may have been collected. And you will, on each of your visits to Owhyhee, deliver to his Majesty's consul at that place duplicates of all your previous collections and documents, to be transmitted by him, by the first safe opportunity, to England

"In the event of England becoming involved in hostilities with any other power during your absence, you are, nevertheless, clearly to understand that you are not on any account to commit any hostile act whatsoever, the vessel you command being sent out only for the purpose of discovery and science, and it being the practice of all civilized nations to consider vessels so employed as excluded from the operations of war and, confiding in this general feeling, we should trust that you would receive every assistance from the ships or subjects of any foreign power which you may fall in with.

"On your return home you will proceed to Spithead, informing our secretary of your arrival

"Given under our hands, the 11th of May, 1825

"MELVILLE.
WM JOHNSTONE HOPE.
G. COCKBURN.
G CLERK
W R. K. DOUGLAS

"To Frederick William Beechy, Esq
Commander of his Majesty's Sloop Blossom, at Spithead

"By Command of their lordships.

"J. W. CROCKER."

MEMORANDUM ACCOMPANYING THE INSTRUCTIONS.

" WE deem it advisable that the ship should be in Beering's Strait by the 10th of July, and that she should remain at some appointed rendezvous until the end of October, or to as late a period as the season will admit, without incurring the risk of being obliged to winter there.

" At present we know of but one place on the eastern shore of the strait which we can recommend as a rendezvous for both parties, viz. Kotzebue's Sound, there it appears the ship may remain with all winds. Desirable as it is to take up a more notherly position than this, in order that the voyage of Captain Franklin's party in open boats may be shortened, yet, admitting the possibility of deep inlets on the coast, it is evident that the boats of Captain Franklin would have more difficulty in searching for the ship in them than in proceeding at once to the above-mentioned sound; and the certainty of finding the ship at a fixed point would be more satisfactory to Captain Franklin

" In order, however, to lessen as far as possible the difficulties of the land party (still preserving the fixed rendezvous) it is recommended that a party, well armed, and having a supply of provisions and fuel, shall be left at Chamisso Island with a boat, or, if it be necessary, the defences of the island may be stengthened by the two forecastle guns, which, with a strong boat's crew, will be sufficient to protect the only landing-place in the island against any force the natives can bring, should they be hostile.*

" Leaving this party at the rendezvous, the Blossom may proceed to examine the coast, assisted by her decked launch, keeping in-shore of her, and signals can then be regularly placed on every conspicuous cape or height, according to the mode agreed upon, for the purpose of directing Captain Franklin's attention to bottles containing written information, which will be buried at each station

" In this manner it is proposed, circumstances permitting, to navigate from Kotzebue's Sound northward, and then eastward as far as the state of the ice will allow following up every opening, and never quitting the main shore The distance to which the ship can proceed to the eastward will be limited by the lateness of the season, and the necessity of avoiding the hazard of being beset in the ice and obliged to winter

" Fog-signals and night-lights will of course be established between the launch and the ship; and should the launch part company with the ship, it will proceed to the last formed signal station, and there await the junction of the ship, but if she does not arrive there in five days, the launch is to prosecute the voyage along shore, in search of Captain Franklin, but not to go so far as to put the certainty of returning to Chamisso Island by the 30th of September at any risk, by which date

*This erroneous idea was suggested by Captain Kotzebue's account of the island, arising no doubt from a bad translation

VOL I   2

the ship will also have arrived there, and Captain Franklin will proceed to the same place should he not have met either the ship or launch before

"During the time the Blossom remains in Kotzebue Sound, a party will be directed to proceed inland on a north course, if practicable, in order that should the coast of the Polar Sea be within reasonable distance, signals may be erected upon the heights for Captain Franklin, whose party may by this means be spared a long journey round the N. W promontory of America   At this and every other station where information is deposited of Captain Beechey, it is advisable that a request in the Russian language be also placed, that this information be not taken away, or the signals disturbed

"Since the transmission of the above, Captain Franklin has received his instructions from Earl Bathurst, the contents of which have been made known to Captain Beechey, and the only addition which we think necessary to make is that in the event of Captain Franklin arriving at an early period at Icy Cape, or at the N. W extremity of America, or in the longitude of Icy Cape (161° 42' W) and returning the same season to his former winter quarters, he will, in the above-mentioned meridian, erect, a signal, and bury a bottle containing the information of his having done so for Captain Beechey's guidance

  (Signed) "JOHN FRANKLIN, Captain
        F W BEECHEY, Commander, His
           Majesty's Sloop Blossom.

Woolwich, 10th February, 1825 "

After the receipt of these instructions, I took an early opportunity of communicating to the officers under my command the sentiments of their lordships, contained in the twelfth paragraph.   How satisfactorily these expectations were fulfilled, must appear from the manner in which their lordships have marked their approbation of their conduct As commander of the expedition however I am happy of an opportunity of again bearing testimony to their diligence, and of expressing my thanks for the assistance I derived during the voyage from their exertions.   They are especially due to my first lieutenant, Mr. Peard, upon whom much additional duty devolved, in consequence of my attention being in some measure devoted to other objects of the expedition to Lieutenant Belcher and Mr Elson, the master, for their indefatigable attention to the minor branches of surveying, and to the former, again, for his assistance in geological researches: to Lieutenant Wainwright for his astronomical observations, to Mr Collie for his unremitting attention to natural history, meteorology, and geology, to Mr James Wolfe, for his attendance at the observatory and the construction of charts, and lastly, to Messrs Smyth and Richard Beechey, for the devotion of their leisure time to drawing

On the return of the expedition to England, the journals and papers of the officers were placed in my hands by the Admiralty, with directions to publish an account of the voyage   I found those of Messrs Collie and Belcher to contain much useful information on the above-mentioned branches of science, and in other respects I have derived much assistance from their remarks, and also from those in the journals of Messrs Evans, Smyth, and Beechey I have in general noticed these obligations in the course of my narrative but as this could not always be done without inconvenience to the reader, I take this opportunity of more fully expressing my acknowledgements

In the compilation I have endeavoured to combine information useful to the philosopher with remarks that I trust may prove advantageous to the seaman, and to convey to the general reader the impressions produced upon my mind at the moment of each occurrence. How far I have succeeded in acquitting myself of the task my duty compelled me to undertake, I must leave to the public to decide, and shall conclude with expressing a hope that my very early entry into the service may be taken in extenuation of any faults they may discover.

The collections of botanical and other specimens of natural history have been reserved for separate volumes, being far too numerous to form part of an Appendix to the present narrative His Majesty's government having liberally appropriated a sum of money to their publication, I hope, with the assistance of several eminent gentlemen, who have kindly and generously offered to describe them, shortly to be able to present them to the public, illustrated by engravings by the first artists. The botany, of which the first number has already been published, is in the hands of Dr Hooker, professor, of Botany, at Glasgow, who in addition to having devoted the whole of his time to our collection, has borne with the numerous difficulties and disappointments which have attended the progress of the publication of this branch of natural history, and my thanks on this account are the more especially due to him in particular The department which he has so kindly undertaken will extend to ten numbers 4to , making, in the whole, about 500 pages, and 100 plates of plants, wholly new, or such as have been hitherto imperfectly described

The other branches of natural history are under the care of Messrs N A. Vigors, Edward Bennett, J E Gray, Richard Owen, Dr Richardson, R. N , and Mr T Lay, the naturalist to the expedition, and the geology of Professor Buckland and Captain Belcher, R N ; to all of whom I must express my warmest thanks, for their cordial assistance, and for the ready and handsome manner in which they have taken upon themselves the task of describing and of superintending the delineation of the various specimens Their contributions will form another 4to volume of species entirely new, or, as before, of such as have been imperfectly described The public in general are not aware how much is due to these gentlemen, without whose zeal and aid they would be deprived of much useful knowledge for notwithstanding the liberal assistance of his Majesty's government, there is so little encouragement for works of the above mentioned description, that they could not be published unless the contributions were gratuitously offered to the publishers

VOYAGE

IO THE

PACIFIC AND BEERING'S STRAIT.

CHAPTER I

Departure from England—Teneriffe—Sun eclipsed—Fernanda Norhona—Make the Coast of Brazil—Rio Janeiro—Passage round Cape Horn—Conception—Valparaiso.

On the 19th of May 1825, we weighed from Spithead, and the following afternoon took our parting view of the Devonshire coast, and steered out of the Channel with a fair wind. For several days afterwards our progress was impeded by boisterous weather, for which the approach to the Bay of Biscay has long been proverbial. We however escaped tolerably well, and favorable breezes soon succeeding, we advanced to the southward

On the 30th we ascertained, by running over the spot in a fine clear day, that a reef of rocks, named the Eight Stones, did not exist in the situation which it has for a number of years occupied in our charts the next morning we passed the Desertas, and on the 1st of June were off Teneriffe.

As I purposed touching at Santa Cruz, we immediately hauled up for the land, and it was a fortunate circumstance that we did so, for so strong a current set to the southward during the night, that had we trusted to our reckoning, the port would have been passed, and there would have been much difficulty in regaining it. I mention the circumstance with a view of bringing into notice the great southerly set that usually attends the passage of ships from Cape Finisterre southward. From this cape to Point Naga, our error in that direction, or more correctly S 33° W., was not less than ninety miles I do not stop to inquire into the cause of this great tendency of the water to the equator, which might probably be traced to the remote effect of the trade-wind, but merely mention the fact as a guide to persons who may pursue the same route

We approached the island on a fine sunny day, but from a quarter that was highly unfavorable for a view of the lofty Peak, which was almost hid from us by intervening mountains At four o'clock we came to an anchor in the roads of Santa Cruz, and there found His Majesty's ship Wellesley, Captain, now Admiral Sir G. E. Hamond, Bart., on her way to Rio Janeiro, with his Excellency Sir Charles Stuart, the British Ambassador to the court of Brazil As soon as we had exchanged salutes with the fort, we landed to procure the supplies the ship required, with all despatch, and met with much assistance and civility from Mr. Dupland, who was acting in the absence of the Consul

Santa Cruz, at the time of our arrival, was under the government of Don Ysidore Uriarti, who very obligingly allowed me to pitch a tent in one of the forts for the purpose of making observations, and placed a guard of soldiers to keep watch over the instruments In Santa Cruz there is very little to interest a stranger when he has paraded some inferior gardens which perpetuate the memory of Marquis de Branciforte, cast his eye round the interior of the great church of San Francisco, where a flag that once belonged to Lord Nelson will not be allowed to escape his attention, and scanned a monument erected to the Virgin Mary de la Candelaria, the patroness-saint of the island, he has seen all that can offer an inducement to expose himself to a dusty walk on a hot day, which he will be sure to find in the month of June in this scattered town The Plaza Reale will amuse those persons who wish to indulge their criticism on the manner and costume of the inhabitants, who assemble there in the evening to smoke their cigars, and enjoy the luxurious freshness of the air

At Laguna the capital, visiters will find a better town, a more fertile country, a climate several degrees cooler than that of Santa Cruz, and every species of produce more abundant and forward than at the port; and though the road is bad, few will regret having encountered its difficulties The celebrated Peak of Teyde is the great object of curiosity which engages the attention of travellers to the Canary groupe, and we experienced much mortification at not having it in our power to ascend it To have added our mite toward the determination of its altitude by barometrical measurement, was a consideration not overlooked, but, circumstanced as we were, it was not of sufficient importance to justify the detention of the ship; and we were obliged to console ourselves with the hope that we should shortly visit places less known, and where our time, consequently, would be more usefully employed

Teneriffe is an island which lies in the track of all outward-bound ships from Europe, and most voyagers have touched at it being the first object of interest they meet, their zeal is naturally more excited there, than at any subsequent period of their voyage. it is consequently better described than almost any other island in the Atlantic, and nothing is now left for a casual visiter, but to go over the ground of his predecessors for his own gratification or improvement   My observations for the determination of the latitude and longitude of the place, &c. were made in the Saluting Battery, but they are omitted here, as I propose, throughout these volumes, to avoid, as far as possible, the insertion of figures and calculations, which, by the majority of readers are considered interruptions to the narrative, and are interesting only to a few   On the 3rd, His Majesty's ship Wallesley sailed for Rio Janeiro with His Excellency Sir Charles Stuart, and on the 5th, having procured what supplies we required, we weighed, and shaped our course for the same place

From our anchorage we had been daily tantalized with a glimpse only of the very summit of the Peak, peeping over a nearer range of mountains, and the hazy state of the weather on the day of our departure made us fearful we should pass on without beholding any more of it; but towards sunset, when we had reached some miles from the coast, we were most agreeably disappointed by a fair view of this gigantic cone   The sun set behind it; and as his beams withdrew, the mountain was thrown forward, until it appeared not half its real distance   Then followed a succession of tints, from the glowing colours of a tropical sky, to the sombre purple of the deepest valleys, varying in intensity with every intermediate range, until a landscape was produced, which for beauty of outline, and brilliancy of colour, is rarely surpassed, and we acknowledged ourselves amply repaid for our days of suspense   Night soon closed upon the view, and directing our compass to a well-known headland, we took our last look at the island, which was the only one of the Canary groupe we had seen · not on account of our distance from them, but owing to that mass of clouds which " navigators behold incessantly piled over this Archipelago "   The breeze was fair, and we rolled on, from day to day, with our awnings spread, passing rapidly over the ground with a fresh trade-wind, and daily increasing the heat and humidity of our atmosphere; amused occasionally by day, with shoals of flying-fish starting from our path, followed by their rapacious pursuers, and by night, with the phosphoric flashing of the sea, and the gradual rising of constellations not visible in our native country

Toward the termination of the trade, the wind veered gradually to the eastward, and became fresh until noon of the 15th, when it suddenly ceased, and the sea, foaming like breakers, beneath a black thunder-cloud, warned us to take in our lighter sails.   We weie presently taken aback with a violent gust of wind from the southward, and fiom that time lost the north-east trade   As we approached its limit, the atmosphere gradually became more charged with humidity, and the sky thickened with dark clouds, which, latterly, moved heavily in all duections, pouiing down torrents of iain

On the 16th, the sun was eclipsed, and we made many observations to deteimine the moment of conjunction   In doing this, my attention was arrested by a very unusual appearance. It consisted of a luminous haze about the moon, as if the light had been tiansmitted through an inteivening atmospheie   I made a sketch of it veiy soon afteiwaids, of which I was veiy glad, as a similar phenomenon, I found, had been observed by M Dolland in another eclipse, and as the subject has since ieceived much interest fiom the circumstance of Aldebaran, and Jupiter and his satellites, having been seen projected upon the disc of the moon   About the time of the greatest obscuration, Leshe's photometei stood at 27°, exactly half what it afterwaids showed   Between the inteivals of observation, we amused ourselves with making expeiiments with a burning glass upon differently coloured cloths, in imitation of those recoided in the Memoirs of the Astionomical Society, and which will convey to the general reader a moie intelligible idea of the decrease of intensity in the sun's rays at the time of the gieatest obscuiation, than the obseivations with the photometei, as well as of the ieadiness with which some colours ignite in comparison with otheis : foi instance,

Black	Blue	Scarlet,	Pea-Green
burned instantly,	required 3s. 7,	15s, 7	would not ignite.

After the eclipse, and when the sun was shining bright,

Black	Blue	Scarlet,	Pea-Green,	Yellow,
burned instantly,	instantly,	2s,	7s, 8,	4s, 3

The results are the mean of several observations ; and the intervals, the numbei of seconds between the rays being brought to a focus on the cloth, and its ignition

After losing the tiade-wind, we went through the usual oideal of baffling winds and calms, with oppiessively hot moist weather and heavy rains ; and then, on the 19th, in latitude 5° 30′ N , got the south-east trade, with which we pursued our course towards the equator, and crossed it on the 24th in longitude 30° 2′ West, much further fiom the meridian of Gieenwich than choice would have dictated.   Some anxiety was in consequence felt lest the current, which here ian to the westward at the rate of thirty miles a day, should sweep the ship so far to the leewaid, as to prevent her weathering Cape St Roque, the north-eastern promontory of the Brazilian coast, which would materially protract the passage, by making it necessary to return to the variable winds about the equator in order to regain the easting, as it is almost impossible to make way against the rapid current which sets past Cape St Roque

During the forenoon of the 26th, we observed an unusual number of birds   To our companions, the tropic bird, shearwaters, and Mother Carey's chickens, were added gannets and boatswains: they were conjectured to be the forerunners of land, and, at three o'clock, the island of Fernanda Norhona was seen from the deck, bearing south-west, twelve leagues   When we had neared this island within six leagues, there was an irregular sea, but we had no soundings at 351 fathoms depth   Our observations reduced to the Peak, placed it eighteen miles to the eastward of its position in the East India Directory   Some squally weather, which occasionally broke the ship off her course, increased our anxiety, but we kept clean full, to pass as quickly as possible the current, which here runs with great rapidity

On the 29th we had the satisfaction to find ourselves to the southward of the promontory, and that it would not be necessary to make a tack   The wind, however, led us in with the coast of Brazil, which was seen on the morning of the 8th   The same evening we passed the shoal off Cape St Thomas—a danger which until very lately was erroneously placed upon the charts, and not sufficiently marked to warn ships of the peril of approaching it * Thence, our course was for Cape Frio, a headland which all vessels bound to Rio Janeiro should, on several accounts, endeavour to make.   In fine weather the south-east winds blow home to the cape, and gradually fall into either the land or sea breeze, according to the time of day, though the prevailing wind off it is from the north-east   with either of these winds, a ship can proceed to her port.   The southerly monsoon, which, while it blows, materially facilitates the navigation along the coast to the northward, scarcely affects the wind close in with the cape.   The greatest interruptions to which they are liable are from the pamperos, which in the winter blow with great violence from the River Plate, sweep past Rio Janeiro, extend to the before-mentioned cape, and often beyond it, to a considerable offing.   It was during the influence of one of these gales that we approached Cape Frio, and had no sooner opened the land on the western side of the promontory, than we were met by a long rolling swell from the south-west, gusts of wind,

* A merchant-vessel on her way from Rio Janeiro to Bahia, when about ten miles from the land, struck upon this shoal, and beat over it   fortunately with the loss of her rudder only   She afterwards stood for five hours along the shoal, to the eastward, and her master stated that the sea broke upon it out of sight of land

and unsettled weather, and at noon encountered a violent squall attended by thunder and lightning, which obliged us to take in every sail on the instant. Towards sunset the weather cleared up, and we saw Cape Frio, N W by W, very distant

Calms and baffling winds succeeded this boisterous weather, so that on the morning of the 11th we were still distant from our port, and the daylight was gone, and with it the sea-breeze, before we could reach a place to drop our anchor. It, however, sometimes happens, fortunately for those who are late in making the entrance of the harbour, that in the interval between the sea and land breezes, gusts blow off the eastern shore, and ships, by taking advantage of them, and at the same time by keeping close over on that side, may succeed in entering the port. This was our case; and at nine at night we anchored among the British squadron, under the command of Rear-Admiral Sir George Eyre, who was the following morning saluted with thirteen guns—a compliment which would have been paid by the ships to the authorities of the place, had it not been suspended in consequence of his Imperial Highness requiring certain forms on the occasion, with which his Britannic Majesty's government did not think it right to comply

The ship being in the want of caulking, and the rigging of a refit, previous to encountering the boisterous latitude of Cape Horn, these repairs were immediately commenced, and the few stores expended on the passage were replaced. While these services were going forward, and observations were in progress for determining the geographical position of the port, and for other scientific purposes, excursions were made to the various places of interest in which Rio Janeiro abounds —Bota-Fogo, Braganza, the Falls of Tejuca, and the lofty Corcovado, were successively visited, and afforded amusement to the naturalist, the traveller, and the artist. Few places are more worthy the description that has been given of them by various authors, than those above mentioned; and they have been so frequently described that they are familiar to every reader, and, as well as the picturesque scenery of Rio Janeiro itself, are quite proverbial. Indeed there is little left in the vicinity of this magnificent port, of which the description will possess the merit of novelty

The observations which were made during our stay in Rio Janeiro will be found in the Appendix to the quarto edition. It may, however, be interesting to insert here the height of the Peak of Corcovado, a singularly shaped mass of granite which overlooks the placid waters of Bota-Fogo, as the measurements hitherto given are at variance with each other, and as it is a subject which has caused many discussions among the good people who live in its vicinity

Our first measurement was with barometers, which, calculated by
Mr Daniel's new formula, gave the base of the flag-staff on the
Peak, above half-tide   2308 feet
The next, by trigonometrical measurement, gave   2036

On my return to the same place three years afterwards, I repeated the observations, which gave the height as follows —

By barometrical measurement   2291$\frac{1}{2}$* feet
By trigonometrical measurement   .   2305$\frac{1}{2}$†
The Sugar Loaf by the first base in 1825 was   1286
            by the second base in 1828 was   1299‡

The astronomical observations were made at an observatory
erected in Mr May's garden at Gloria, an indulgence for which I
feel particularly indebted to that gentleman, as well as for other
civilities which I received from him during my stay in the place
On the 13th of August we sailed from Rio Janeiro for the Pacific · a passage interesting from the difficulties which sometimes
attend it, and from its possessing the peculiarity of producing the
greatest change of climate in the shortest space of time   The day
after we left the port, we encountered a dangerous thunder-storm,
which commenced in the evening, and lasted till after midnight
during this time the sheet lightning was vivid and incessant, and
the forked frequently passed between the masts.   The wind varied
so often, that it was with the greatest difficulty the sails were prevented coming aback , and it blew so hard that it was necessary to
lower the close-reefed topsails on the cap   Shortly after midnight,
a vivid flash of lightning left five meteors upon the mast-heads and
topsail yard-arms, but did no damage   they were of a bluish cast,
burnt about a quarter of an hour, and then disappeared.   The
weather almost immediately afterwards moderated, and the thunder cloud passed away
We had afterwards light and variable winds, with which we crept
down to the southward, until the night of the 25th, when being
nearly abreast of the River Plate, a succession of pamperos|| be-
gan, and continued until the 2nd of September, with their usual

* This differs sixteen feet from the first result, which may partly be owing to the
barometers, on this occasion, not being in such good order as at first   the amount,
however, is so small as almost to need no apology, particularly as the observations
were made on days as opposite as possible to each other—the first in drizzling rain,
the last on a clear sunshining day—whereby the formula was put to the severest
trial
† In this operation I was assisted by the late Captain Henry Forster, R N an
officer well known to the scientific world, with whom I had the pleasure to become
acquainted at this place
‡ The difference in these measurements is, no doubt, owing to there being no object on the summit of the hill sufficiently defined for the purpose of observation,
and it is almost impossible to ascend it
|| These are heavy gusts of wind which blow off the heated plains (or pampas)
lying between the foot of the Cordillera Mountains and the sea   In the River Plate,

characteristics, of thunder and lightning, with hail and sunshine between.   On the 9th, soundings were obtained in 75 fathoms off the Falkland Islands; but no land was seen at the time, in consequence of misty weather   We here again experienced a short though heavy gale   As it was against us, we turned our proximity to the land to good account, by seeking shelter under its lee, striking soundings upon a sandy bottom, from 50 to 80 fathoms, the depth increasing with the distance from the coast   The weather moderated on the day following, and we saw the land, from S. 25° W. to S. 56° W , eight or nine leagues distant   the wind, at the same time, became favourable, and carried us past the Islands during the night   The eastern point of these Islands (Cape St Vincent), by such observations as we were able to make, appears to be correctly placed in the charts.   The position I have assigned to it will be seen in the table at the end of the work

From the Falkland Islands we stood to the southward , and after two short gales from the westward, made Cape Horn on the 16th, bearing N 40° W six or seven leagues   This was quite an unexpected event, as a course had been shaped the day before to pass it at a distance of seventy miles   It appeared, however, by the noon observation, that a current had drifted the ship fifty miles to the northward in the twenty-four hours, a circumstance which might have been attended with very serious consequences had the weather been thick ;   and ships in passing the Strait le Maire will do well to be on their guard against a like occurrence *   The view of this celebrated promontory, which has cost navigators, from the earliest period of its discovery to the present time, so much difficulty to double, was highly gratifying to all on board; and especially so to those who had never seen it before ; yet it was a pleasure we would all willingly have exchanged for the advantage of being able to pursue an uninterrupted course along the shore of Tierra del Fuego, which the flattering prospect of the preceding day led us to expect, and which, had it not been for the northerly current, would have been effected with ease   The disappointment was of course very great, particularly as the wind at the moment was more favourable for rounding the cape than it usually is

In the evening, the Islands of Diego Ramirez were seen on the weather bow , and nothing remained but to pursue the inner route, at the risk of being caught upon a lee-shore with a gale of wind, or stand back to the south-eastward, and lose in one day what it

and near the coast, they are very violent and dangerous, from the sudden manner in which they occur   Their force diminishes as the distance from the coast increases

* For remarks on the currents, and observations on the winds, in the vicinity of Cape Horn, the reader is referred to the Nautical Remarks in the quarto edition

would require perhaps a week to recover   We adopted the former alternative, and passed the Islands as close as it was prudent, in a dark night, striking soundings in deep water upon an uneven bottom.

The next morning, the small groupe of Ildefonzo Islands was distant six miles on the lee-beam, and the mainland of Tierra del Fuego appeared behind it, in lofty ranges of mountains streaked with snow.   The cape mistaken for Cape Horn by Lord Anson bore N. 49° E , and the promontory designated York Minster by Captain Cook, W by N   The coast was bold, rocky, and much broken, and every here and there deeply indented, as if purposely to afford a refuge from the pitiless gales which occasionally beat upon it   The general appearance of the landscape was any thing but exhilarating to persons recently removed from the delightful scenery of Rio Janeiro, and we were particularly struck with the contrast between the romantic and luxurious scenery of that place and the bleak coast before us, where the snow, filling the valleys and fissures, gave the barren projections a darker hue and a more rugged outline than they in reality possessed

As we drew in with the land, the water became discoloured, and specifically lighter than that in the offing, whence it was concluded that some rivers emptied themselves into the sea in the vicinity. In the evening it became necessary to stand off the coast , and we experienced the disadvantages of the offing, by getting into the stream of the easterly current, and by the increase of both wind and sea.*   We stood to the westward again as soon as it could be done , and on the 26th were fifty leagues due west of Cape Pillar, a situation from which there is no difficulty in making the remainder of the passage

We now, for a time at least, bade adieu to the shores of Tierra del Fuego, whose coast and climate we quitted with far more favourable impressions than those under which they were approached.   This, I think, will be the case with every man-of-war that passes it, excepting the few that may be particularly unfortunate in their weather, for early navigation has stamped it with a character which will ever be coupled with its name, notwithstanding its terrors are gradually disappearing before the progressive improvement in navigation   It must be admitted we were much favoured. few persons, probably, who effect the passage, will have it in their power to say they were only a week from the meridian of Cape Horn to a station fifty leagues due west of Cape Pillar, and that

* It is a curious fact, that on this day, at a distance of only fifty leagues from where we were, it blew a strong gale of wind, with a high sea, which washed away the bulwark of a fine brig, the Hellespont commanded by Lieutenant Charles Parker, R N , to whom I am indebted for this and other interesting information on the winds and currents encountered by him in his passage

during that time there was more reason to complain of light winds and calms, than the heavy gales which proverbially visit these shores

Navigators distinguish the passages round Cape Horn by the *outer* and *inner*, some recommending one, some the other, and doubtless both have their advantages and disadvantages It would be very uninteresting here to discuss the merits of either, as the question has been sufficiently considered elsewhere; and it would, in my opinion, be equally useless as very few persons follow the advice of their predecessors in a matter of this nature, but pursue that course which from circumstances may seem most advantageous at the moment; and this will ever be the case where such difference of opinion exists What I had to say on this subject has been published in the Nautical Remarks to the quarto edition

In describing the passage round Cape Horn, I have omitted to mention some particulars on the days on which they occurred, in order that they may not interrupt the narrative. As we approached the Falkland Islands from Rio Janeiro, some penguins were seen upon the water in latitude 47° S., at a distance of three hundred and forty miles from the nearest land; a fact which either proves the common opinion, that this species never stray far from land, to be in error, or that some unknown land exists in the vicinity As their situation was not far from the parallell in which the long-sought Ile Grande of La Roche was said to have been seen, those who are wedded to the common opinion above alluded to, may yet fancy such an island has existence; although it is highly improbable that it should have escaped the observation, not only of those who purposely went in search of it, but of the numerous ships also which have of late made the passage from the Atlantic to the Pacific Another opinion, not quite so general, (but which I have heard repeatedly expressed with reference to the coast of California), is, that of aquatic birds confining their flight within certain limits, so that a person who has paid attention to the subject will know by the birds that are about him, without seeing the land, what part of the coast he is off My own experience does not enable me to offer any remarks on the subject, except in the instance of the St. Sawrence Islands, in Beering's Strait, the vicinity to which is always indicated by the Crested Auk (*alca crestatella*). But the following fact may be serviceable in adding weight to the opinion, provided it were not accidental; and if so, it may still be useful in calling the attention of others to the subject. Off the River Plate, we fell in with the dusky albatross (*diomedia fulginosa*), and as we proceeded southward, they became very numerous; but on reaching the latitude of 51° S they 'all quitted us. We rounded the cape, and on regaining the same parallel of 51° S on the opposite side, they again came round us, and accompanied the ship up the Chili coast. The pintadoes were our constant attendants the whole way.

From the time of leaving England, the temperature of the surface of the sea had been registered every two hours. Off Cape Horn, I caused it to be tried every hour, under an impression that it might apprise us of our approach to floating ice, when, from the darkness of the night, or foggy weather, it could not be seen; a plan I would recommend being adopted, as it may be useful, notwithstanding its fallibity, for though ice in detached masses, when drifting fast with the wind. extends its influence a very short way in the direction of its course yet on the other hand, its effect may be felt a considerable distance in its wake. We had only one warning of this nature, by a decrease of temperature of four degrees which lasted about an hour. The temperature of the sea, at the greatest depth our lines would reach, was not below 39°, 2 Off the Falkland Islands, it was the same at 854 fathoms as at 603 fathoms. The lowest temperature of the air was 26° The current, which at a distance from the land runs fast to the eastward to the discomfiture of ships bound in the opposite direction, near the coast to the westward of Cape Horn, at first entirely ceased, and afterwards took a contrary course. There is much reason to believe that it continues this north-westerly course, and ultimately falls into the northerly current so prevalent along the coast of Chili.

The wind was now favorable for making progress to the northward. My instructions did not direct me to proceed to any port on the coast of Chili, but circumstances rendered it necessary to put into one of them, and I selected Conception as being the most desirable for our purpose.

The weather had for a long time been cloudy; but on this night a clear sky presented to our view a comet of unusual magnitude and brilliancy, situated to the southeast of the square formed by επσρ Ceti The head had a blueish cast towards its nucleus, where indeed it was so bright, that with our small telescopes it appeared to be a star; but this was evidently a deception, as Mr Herschell, who made some interesting and satisfactory observations on the same comet, found on turning his twenty feet reflector upon it, that the star-like appearance of the nucleus was only an illusion * The tail extended between 9° and 10° of arc in a N W. direction, and gradually increased in width from the nucleus till near its termination. We made a number of measurements to ascertain its place, and continued them every night afterwards on which the comet appeared, but as its orbit has been calculated from far more accurate

* See Memoir Ast. Soc vol II p 2

observations, and ours were necessarily made with stars unequally
affected by refraction, which involves a laborious reduction besides
the abstruse calculation for determining its orbit, I have not given
them a place.

On the following night we noticed distinctly the bifurcation of
the tail represented in the Memoirs of the Astronomical Society
The branches were of unequal length, and the lower one diverged
from the nucleus at an angle of about 40°

On the 6th we made the island of Mocha, on the coast of
Chili, a place once celebrated as a resort of the Buccaneers, who
anchored off it for the useful supplies which in their days it furnished   Its condition was then certainly very different from the
present   several Indian chiefs and a numerous population resided
there, and it was well stocked with cattle, sheep, hogs, and poultry
At present it is entirely deserted, except by horses and hogs, both
of which, Captain Hall states, are used as fresh stock by whaling
ships in the Pacific   The Indians appear to have been generally
very cordial with their visiters, exchanging the produce of the
island for cutlery and trinkets   They, however, apparently without provocation, attacked Sir Francis Drake, and wounded him and
all his boat's crew   In 1690 the island was found deserted by
Captain Strong, and it has since remained uninhabited.   The cause
of this is not known, though I was informed in Chili, that it was in
consequence of the frequent depredations committed by vessels
that touched at the island.

We quitted Mocha, passed the island of St Mary, which must
not be approached on account of sunken rocks, and anchored at Talcahuana, the sea-port of Conception, on the 8th, fifty-six days from
Rio Janeiro   Here we found the British squadron, under the command of Captain Maling, from whom I received every assistance
and attention   Our arrival off the port was on one of those
bright days of sunshine which characterize the summer of the
temperate zone on the western side of America. The cliffs of
Quiriquina, an island situated in the entrance of the harbour, were
covered with birds, curiously arranged in rows along the various
strata, and on the rocks were numberless seals basking in the sun,
either making the shores re-echo with their discordant noise, or so
unmindful of all that was passing, as to allow the birds to alight upon them and peck their oily skin without offering any resistance.

The sea-port of Conception is a deep, commodious bay, well
protected from northerly winds by the fertile little island above-mentioned, lying at its entrance   there is a passage on either side of it,
but the eastern is the only one in use, the other being very narrow
and intricate   The land on the eastern and western sides of the
bay is high, well wooded, and on the latter very steep, on the

formei it slopes from the mountains towaid the sea with gentle un-
dulations   Several villages aie situated along the shoie on both
sides, but principally on the eastein   Aiound these hamlets, some
diminutive patches of a more lively green than the surrounding
country, show the veiy limited extent to which cultivation is cai-
ried, of which we had fuither proof as we proceeded up the bay,
by witnessing gioups of both sexes up to thei middle in the sea,
collecting their daily subsistence fiom beds of choros and othei
shell-fish

Talcahuana we found to be a miseiable little town, extending
along the beach, and up a once fertile valley ; divided into streets
and squaies, but much dilapidated, dusty, and in some places overgrown with glass.   A thousand inmates occupied these wretched
dwellings, who acknowledged the supremacy of a governor, poor,
but independent, and intrusted their spiritual concerns to the care
of a patiiot piiest.   In the principal squaie stood a church, in
chaiacter with the iest of the buildings ; and in fiont of it a belfry,
which for some time past must have endangered the life of the
bellman.   His occupation, however, was less laborious than in other
catholic countries, as it was here called into action but once in seven
days, and was then attended to only by the female part of the inhabitants.

It was painful to compare the present circumstances of this place
with the prospeiity that once prevailed, and impossible to look upon
the unhappy inhabitants without feelings of pity at the state to
which they were reduced   The other villages in the bay were in
a veiy similar condition ; and one, Tombé, wheie there was formerly an extensive saltpetie manufactoiy, was entiiely deserted.

The day aftei my arrival, I accompanied the captains of the
squadron, and Mr Nugent the consul general, to Conception, pur-
suant to an invitation we received from the Intendente to visit that
city   Its distance from Talcahuaila is about thiee leagues   The
road, at first, leads ovei a steep hill to the eastward of the town,
the summit of which commands an excellent view of the natural
advantages of defence which the peninsula of Talcahuana possesses, and shows how formidable it might become under judicious
management   The royalists weie not ignorant of this, and during
the tuibulent times of emancipation, sought shelter amongst them,
cut ditches, and thiew up temporary works of defence, all of which
are now nearly effaced by the heavy iains that visit this country at
particular periods of the yeai   At the back of this range of hills,
the country is flat and occasionally swampy, and continues so, with
very little interruption, to the Collé de Chepé, a small eminence,
whence a stranger obtains the first view of the river Bio Bio and
the city   The intendente met us about a mile outside the town,

and accompanied us to his residence, where we experienced a most
cordial and hospitable reception

Conception, during its prosperity has been described by the
able pens of Juan de Ulloa, La Perouse, and others, and since its
misfortunes, by a well-known naval author, who has admirably pictured the ruin and desolation which the city at that time must have
presented   Much of his description would have correctly applied
to the time of our visit, but generally speaking, there was a decided
improvement in every department   The panic occasioned by the
daring associates of the outlaw Benavides, Peneleo, and Pinche-
ro, was beginning to subside.   These chiefs, unable to make head
against the people when united, had of late confined their depredations to the immediate vicinity of their strong-holds among the
mountains   the peasants had returned to the cultivation of the soil,
looms were active in various parts of the town; and dilapidations
were gradually disappearing before cumbrous brickwork and mason-
ry   Commerce was consequently beginning to revive, there were
several merchant-vessels in the port; and the Quadra, once " silent
as the dead," now resounded with the voices of muleteers conducting the exports and import of the country.

The tranquil and improving condition of the state was further
evinced by the equipment of an expedition against the island of
Chiloe, which still maintained its allegiance to the mother country.
The preparations appeared to give general satisfaction in Conception, and recruits were daily enlisting. and training in the Presidio.
I peeped through the gate one morning, and saw these tyros in
arms going through the ordeal of the awkward squad   They were
half Indians, without shoes or stockings, and with heads like mush-
rooms.   Their appearance, however, was immaterial   they were
the troops on which the people placed their dependence, which the
result of the expedition did not disappoint; and the effect upon
their minds was equally exhilarating.   Hitherto obliged to act on
the defensive against a few piratical Indian chiefs, they now found
themselves lending their troops to carry on a warfare in a distant
province.   Such was the prosperous state of affairs at the time of
our arrival, and the highest expectations pervaded all classes of
society.

The town of Conception occupies nearly a square mile of ground.
It is situated on the north side of the river Bio Bio, and is distant
from it about a quarter of a mile   Its site was chosen in 1763,
about twelve years after the old city of Penco was destroyed by an
earthquake or rather by an inundation, occasioned by a tremendous
reaction of the sea   Such a catastrophe, it might be supposed,
would be sufficient to deter the inhabitants from again building on
low ground; nevertheless, the present city is erected on a spot

scarcely more elevated than the other, and the river, when high, washes the threshold of the nearest houses. It has no defences; and is also very badly situated in this respect, being commanded by a range of hills close behind it. Benavides was fully aware of this, and constructed a battery upon the eminence, which still bears his name: but the guns are spiked, and the fort is in ruins.

During the late incursions, we were told, that the mode of repelling an attack was to collect the inhabitants into squares, and barricade the streets leading out of them, with whatever came first to hand: the musketry and the muzzles of the field-pieces were then thrust through these temporary bulwarks, and a fire opened upon the assailants. This was a sufficiently secure defence against the Indians: but it is easy to imagine what would have been the effect of a few well-placed cannon upon a crowd of persons so collected.

In the selection of the site of the new city, the advantage of the river Bio Bio was, no doubt, the great consideration; and when inland navigation is as well understood in that country as in some others, it will be of the greatest importance, though its numerous shoals must occasion serious difficulties. Part of the produce of the interior is now brought down upon rafts, which, not being able to return, are broken up and sold for timber. There is a ferry-boat over the river for the accommodation of persons who wish to pass from Conception to the Indian country, and sufficiently large to carry cattle or horses. The natives cross in punts, but have so much difficulty in stemming the current and avoiding banks and shallows, that, though the extreme distance is only a mile, they are sometimes an hour and a half performing the passage. Although the Spaniards nominally possessed territory far to the southward of this river, yet it in reality formed their boundary, and until very lately it was unsafe for an European, to venture far upon that side, on account of straggling parties of the Indians.* The mouth of the Bio Bio is circumscribed by banks, which have progressively risen, to 210 yards; and even this narrow stream is divided by a rock one-third of the way across it. If the plan of the entrance be correct in the chart annexed to La Perouse's Voyage, the formation of these banks has been very rapid, and has altered the channel of the river.

The population of Conception is about 6500 persons. The inhabitants, the labouring class at least, have a particularly healthy look. The men have hard features and strong sinewy limbs, and the women and children are fatter than would be agreeable to most persons: short stature, dark hair and eyes, and pretty Indian features,

---

* I have been informed that since this period (1825), the Intendente has a magnificent estate on that side of the river, that the Indians are quiet, and that Conception has undergone great improvement.

are the characteristics of their persons. They are subject to but few diseases, and for these they have their own remedies, consisting principally of medicinal herbs, with which the country abounds, and in the preparation of which they are well skilled   Fevers, occasioned by cold and dampness, are the most common complaints.

In the streets of Conception I did not see a single cripple, a very rare circumstance in Spanish towns ; nor were we molested by beggars, beyond a few troublesome boys beseeching alms ; and this arose more from impudence, and a determination to try their luck, than from any real necessity : in secret, however, there are not wanting persons who, if opportunity offered, would not only solicit charity, but enforce their demand with a pistol or a stiletto   On meeting the Indians in an unfrequented part of the country, it is particularly necessary to be on your guard, for these half-civilized barbarians are generally intoxicated and care very little about insulting or maltreating strangers even in the heart of the town, much less when alone in the country.   A regiment of Araucaneans is embodied in the army of the state, and quartered in the town they retain their own weapons, and continue their own tactics   A specimen of their extraordinary and barbarous warfare was exhibited at Conception during our stay.

Since the trade of Chili has been thrown open, a remarkable change in the costume of the inhabitants, and also in the furniture of their houses, has taken place, and an Englishman may now see with pride the inferior manufactures of his own country prized, to the exclusion of the costly gold and silver tissue stuffs of Spain, which, Perouse observes, were entailed in families like diamonds, and descended from the great-grandmother to the children of the third and fourth generation   Even the national musical instrument, the guitar, has fallen into neglect, and has been supplanted by the English piano-forte.   It would have been better for the lower orders of society, of which a large portion of the population of Conception consists, if the use of this simple instrument had been retained, for it is well known, in foreign countries, how many hours of innocent mirth are beguiled in the happy circles it assembles around the cottage doors, and how many idle characters its fascination deters from indulging in less innocent occupations, to which the Chilians are equally prone with other nations, though I am by no means an advocate for its being prized to the extent it once was by the Portuguese, who, after a battle in which they were defeated, left 14,000 guitars upon the field *

The entertainments most frequented in Conception are cock-fighting and billiards   All classes of society assemble at the pit,

* Mengiana, tom 1

and if there be no fight, will light their cigars, and chat whole hours away, in the hope of a match being made up, and are dispersed only by the approach of night   The English cocks are most esteemed, and are sometimes valued at a hundred dollars a-piece (twenty guineas)   The Chilian spurs cut as well as thrust, and greatly shorten the cruel exhibition.   Some of the governors are said to have imposed a tax on these establishments for their own private advantage, but without the authority of the laws

Of the country round Conception I have little to say, except that it has undergone a great change since the days of its prosperity   In the parallel of 37° on the western side of a great continent a luxuriant soil may be expected to produce an abundant vegetation.   This district has, in consequence, been famous for its grain, vines, fruits, esculent roots, &c and for its pasture lands, on which formerly were reared immense herds of cattle, and horses of the finest breed   But the effects of the disturbed state of the country are as manifest here as in the different parts of the city.   At present, as much arable land as is absolutely necessary for the support of the inhabitants is cleared, and no more , and even its produce is but scantily enjoyed by the lower classes on the coast, who are obliged to subsist almost entirely upon shell-fish.   The soil, if attended to, will give an abundant return : wheat, barley, Indian corn, beans, pease, potatoes, and arrow-root, grapes, apples, pears, currants, strawberries, and olives, are the common produce of the country.   From the latter a fine oil is extracted , but the fruit is too rank to be eaten at table, except by the natives   The arrow-root is of a good quality and very cheap   In the ravines and moist places the panque (*gunnera scabra*) grows luxuriantly and strong : it is a very useful root, and serves for several purposes ; a pleasant and cooling drink is extracted from it, which is deemed beneficial in feverish complaints ; its root furnishes a liquid serviceable in tanning, and superior to any of the barks of South America , when made into tarts, it is scarcely inferior to the rhubarb, for which it is sometimes mistaken ; and it is eaten in strips after dinner, with cheese and wine, &c.   Several European shrubs and herbaceous plants grow here, but more luxuriantly than in our own country ; among these were hemlock, flax, chickweed, pimpernel, watercresses, and a species of elder.

The wines which were formerly so much esteemed, and carried along the coast to the northward, are now greatly deteriorated, and in the sea-port much adulterated.   There is a great variety of them, and in general they are very intoxicating.   The only palatable kind I tasted was made from the vines on the estate of General Freire, and for which I was indebted to the liberality of the governor, as there was none to be purchased.   This wine, though agreeable to the English palate, is not in such estimation with the

Chilians as one that has a strong empyreumatic flavour It acquires this in the process of heating, or rather of boiling, the fruit, which is done with a view to extract a larger proportion of the juice than could be obtained by the ordinary means, and to produce a mellowness which age only could otherwise give Cici and mattee are still in use, though less so than formerly, and indeed it appeared to me that the Chilians were fast getting rid of all their old customs, of which the drinking of mattee is one

After passing a very pleasant time in the society of the Intendente, we took our leave, and returned to the port. Our occupations there were divided between astronomical observations, making a survey of the bays of Conception and St. Vincent, and equipping the ship for sea

I had some hesitation in procuring coal for our sea-stock of fuel ; not that the article was become scarce, but on account of the enormous price to which the owner thought proper, on this occasion, to raise it Captain Hall states, that when he was at this place, the Penco coal, which was the best, was sold for twelve shillings a ton, all expenses included, but the same quantity was now valued at nine dollars, besides the labour of digging and carrying This arose from a report that some mines which had been recently discovered were about to be worked, which would occasion a great and permanent demand for the material. The coal is of a very inferior quality, and fit only for the forge Hitherto, however, experiment has been made only upon that which is near the surface : when the mines are worked, if they ever be, a better quality, in all probability, will be obtained Talcahuana and Penco are, I believe, the only places where coal has yet been discovered near Conception. Were this article of a good quality and reasonable, there would be a great demand for it at Valparaiso, and among the several squadrons upon the station, and it would probably be well worth the experiment of the owner to search a little deeper in the earth, and ascertain the nature of the lower strata These veins occur in red sandstone formation, and do not appear at the surface to be very extensive, or to promise any very large supply of fuel. This observation applies only to that part of the coast which lies in the vicinity of Conception and the port, a large proportion of which is composed of diluvial depositions

We are informed by a visiter to this country, that limestone is found at Conception, and is used by the inhabitants for whitewashing their houses ; but this is evidently a mistake, as the natives collect shells, and calcine them for that purpose, besides, in no part of the bay or vicinity of Conception could we perceive limestone, or even hear of its existence. A gentleman pointed out a place to the northward of Tome Bay where, he said, it occurred, but, on examination, only clay-slate, chert, and green-stone were found.

As the geology of Conception will appear in another place, I shall merely observe here, that in the secondary sandstone a variety of petrifactions occur, of wood, shells, and bones, formed by an infiltration of siliceous and calcareous matter.   The little island of Quiriquina presents alternate horizontal strata of pebbles, sandstone, and petrified substances, principally of wood, and vertebral and other bones of the whale.   On the opposite shore a fossil nautilus was found, which measured three feet in diameter   Upon the beach, in several parts of the bay, there are ridges of magnetic iron-sand which the waves have thrown up   they are seen adhering together, apparently by mutual attraction.

The abundance of shell-fish in Conception entices a great many birds within the bay.   The shore is occasionally thronged with them, and the shags sometimes fly in an unbroken line of two miles and more in length.   The quebranta huessos, the black-backed gull, a species of tern, and two or three species of pelican, one of which pursues its food in a very entertaining manner.   It first soars to a great height, and then suddenly darts into the sea, splashing the water in all directions: in a few seconds, it emerges and resumes its lofty flight until again attracted by its prey, when it plunges into the sea as before, and thus the flock, for these birds are gregarious, ranges over the whole bay, performing all its motions in conceit and with a surprising rapidity   The penguin is also here, and a very large species of duck, the female of which has a callosity on the shoulder of each wing, and is very excellent eating ; a species of colymbus with lobed toes ; curlews, sea-pies, horned plovers, a beautiful species of chaverey, with iridescent plumage , the oyster-eater, or razor bill, and sanderlings, turkey buzzards, the condor, several species of hawks, owls, black-birds, and wood-pigeons, the latter of which are very large and good to eat ; a very beautiful species of duck, frequenting the marshes and lakes between Talcahuana and Conception ; partridges, a species of woodpecker, a dark-brown fringilla, with a beautiful scarlet breast, a species of lozia, turdus, hirundo, ampelis, not remarkable for their plumage, and numerous flocks of green parrots, which the Chilian Spaniard, who eats almost every kind of bird, has no objection to place upon his table.   The domesticated fowls are the same here as in Europe.   The reptiles are few, and not venomous. small lizards are extremely common on the rocks, and among the trees.   There are one or two species of snakes, a large one, resembling the common English adder is frequent, and a small green snake was caught by one of the officers

The fish are not very numerous, only coming into the bay with a particular wind   The number of whales which guard the entrance, and the shoals of seals, grampusses, and porpoises, which crowd the bay, must destroy a great many   Shell-fish are an exception to this scarcity, and being very large, form no small portion of the food of those inhabitants who live on the borders of the bay Besides the choros, a large muscle, and locas (*concho lepus*), mentioned by Ulloa, there are several other small species which are more esteemed than the large choros, a number of razor, and some venus-shells   Large sea-eggs are highly prized, and, like the others, eaten raw   The smaller shell-fish are, various sorts of limpets, turbots, neritas, murex, and some others.   there are also a great many crabs

In the survey of the Bay of Conception, a shoal was discovered by Lieutenant Belcher on the Penco side, which is probably that upon which a vessel struck some time previous, but which the boats of the squadron could not afterwards find   It was necessary to make some alteration in the position of Belen bank, from the manner in which it is laid down in the Spanish charts, and the shoal said to occur off the sandy point of Quiriquina does not in fact exist   The western entrance was thoroughly examined, and found to be quite safe, though very narrow, and should only be used in all cases of difficulty in weathering Paxaros Niños, with a northerly wind   The bay of St Vincent does not appear to me to afford security to any vessel of more than a hundred tons with a strong westerly wind, and I would advise no large ship to put in there under such circumstances, if she could possibly avoid it. Further information on the subject will be found among the Nautical Remarks

Conception, as a place of refreshment, in every way answered our expectations   fresh beef, poultry, good water, vegetables, and wood are to be had   they happened to be dear at the time of our visit, but no doubt, if the country remains tranquil, they will be both cheap and more abundant

On the 20th our operations were completed, but a strong northerly wind prevented our putting to sea, and we anchored under the little island of Quiriquina.   This is a very secure stopping place, and, in the winter season, a better anchorage to refit a ship at, than that off Talcahuana.   It is small, and a ship must lie very close to the shore   After two days of contrary wind, we put to sea on the 24th, and three days afterwards anchored at Valparaiso, in the hope of receiving some supplies which we could not procure at Conception; but being disappointed in their arrival, on the 29th we weighed, and took our final leave of the coast

CHAPTER II.

On leaving Valparaiso, my intention was, if possible, to pass
within sight of Juan Fernandez, in order to determine its position;
but finding the wind would not allow us to approach sufficiently
near even to see it, we kept away for the island of Sala-y-Gomez,
and with the view of making this part of the voyage useful, the
ship's course was directed between the tracks of Vancouver and
Malespina on the south side, and many other navigators on the
north, who, engaged in pursuits similar to our own, had run down
the parallels of 27° and 28° S. in search of the land discovered by
Davis These parallels, during the summer months, are subject to
light and variable airs, and we, in consequence, made very slow
progress, particularly as we approached the meridian of the island,
where it became necessary to adopt the precaution of lying-to
every night, that the object of our search might not be passed unobserved

When the nights were clear, we continued our observations on
the comet On the 30th the coma had increased to the enormous
length of 24°; the nucleus was larger and more brilliant than before, and the ray before-mentioned as forming part of the coma,
was more distinct and apparently at a greater angle with it than
when first seen

The day after we quitted the coast of Chili, all the birds left us;
even the pintados, which had been our constant attendants for upwards of 5000 miles, deserted us on this occasion We afterwards
saw very little on the wing, I believe nothing, except a wandering
albatross, until we approached the island of Sala-y-Gomez

In the Pacific, in particular, the navigator should not be inattentive to the presence or absence of birds, as they will generally be
found in the vicinity of islands, and especially of such as are uninhabited and of coral formation On the 14th, several tropic

birds, boatswains, and gannets, flew round the ship, and were hailed as an omen which did not deceive us, for at daylight, on the following morning, the island of Sala-y-Gomez was seen from the mast-head, bearing N N W, fifteen miles distant.

We shortly closed with this isolated spot, and found its extent much less than has been stated   It is, indeed, scarcely more than a heap of rugged stones, which the elements appear to have thrown together, and in a gale of wind would not be distinguished amidst the spray   The rocks, except such as have been selected for roosting places by the sea-gulls, are of a dark-brown colour   Upon a small flat spot there was a moss-like vegetation, and near it a few logs of wood, or planks, which the imagination might convert into the remains of some miserable vessel whose timbers had there found a resting-place.   Though several vessels have been missing in these seas, we have no intelligence of any having been wrecked here   Sala-y-Gomez, when he discovered the island, imagined he found the frame of a vessel upon it, and in all probability the wood which we saw was the same; but whether it was so or not, our curiosity and desire to land were fully awakened, though we were disappointed by the high breakers which rolled over every part of the shore.

We remained some time under the lee of the island, narrowly scrutinizing it with our telescopes, but without adding to our information.   During this time the ship was surrounded by sharks and bonitos, but none were taken, nor were our fishermen more fortunate at the bottom   The feathery tribe,* disturbed from their roost, came fearlessly around us; we shot several, and in the stomach of a pelican a volcanic pebble was found, which some of us conjectured to have been gathered upon the island, and thence inferred its particular formation.

Sala-y-Gomez, when first seen has the appearance of three rocks· its direction is N. W. and S E ; and it is something less than half a mile in length, and a fifth of a mile in width.   Some sunken rocks lie off the N. E and S E. points   in other directions the island may be approached within a quarter of a mile   N 50° W. ⅜ mile there are soundings, in 46 fathoms sand and coral ; and N 33° W. 1½ mile, 140 fathoms gray sand   A reference to the geographical table will show the position of the island, and I shall here only remark, that Captain Kotzebue's latitude is nine miles in error, which perhaps may be a typographical mistake

From hence we bore away to the westward, with the intention

---

* Phæton ethereus, Pelicanus leucocephalus, sterna stolida, and a small dove-coloured tern

of passing near the situation of an island named Washington and
Coffin, reported to have been discovered by an American ship
At sunset we were within four leagues of the spot, with a perfectly
clear sky and horizon, but could see nothing of it, nor had we
any indication of land in the immediate vicinity, but rather the contrary, as the birds which had followed us from Sala-y-Gomez had
quitted the ship some time before   As the night was fine, and the
moon gave sufficient light to discover in time any danger that might
lie in the route of the ship, the course was continued toward Easter Island, and daylight appeared without any thing being seen
Had such an island been in existence, and answered the description of that upon which Davis was so near losing his vessel, geographers would not have been long in reconciling their opinions on
the subject of his discovery, as, in all probability, they would have
waived their objection to its distance from Copiapo, in consideration of its identity

The subject of this supposed discovery has been often discussed :
and where the data are so unsatisfactory as to allow one party to
choose the Islands of Felix and Ambrose for the land in question,
and the other, Easter Island, two places nearly 1600 miles apart,
they are not likely to be speedily reconciled, unless two islands
exactly answering the description given by Davis, and situated in
the proper latitude, shall be found.   Such persons as are curiously
disposed on this subject will find it ably treated by the late Captain Burney, R N., in his account of the Buccaneers.

Without entering into a question which presents so many difficulties, I shall merely observe, that, considering the rapid current
that exists in the vicinity of the Galapagos, and extends, though
with diminished force, throughout the trade wind, the error in Davis's reckoning is not more than might have happened to any dull
sailing vessel circumstanced as his was.   To substantiate this, I
shall advert to four instances out of many others which might be
named   In a short run from Juan Fernandez to Easter Island,
Behrens, who was with Roggewein, was drifted 318 geographical
miles from his supposed situation   The Blossom, in passing over
the same ground, in the short space of eighteen days experienced
a set of 270 miles , and on her passage from Acapulo to Valparaiso of 401 miles   and again M La Perouse, on his arrival at the
Sandwich Islands from Conception, touching at Easter Island on
his way, found a similar error of 300 miles in the course of that
passage   It is fair to presume that the passage of Davis from the
Galapagos to Easter Island was longer than that of either of the
above-mentioned vessels ; and consequently it is but reasonable to
allow him a greater error, particularly as the first part of his route
was through a much stronger current.   But taking the error in the

Blossom's reckoning as a fair amount, and applying it to the distance given by Wafer, there will remain only 204 miles unaccounted for between it and the real position of Easter Island, which from the foregoing considerations, added to the manner in which reckonings were formerly kept, does not appear to me to exceed the limit that might reasonably be ascribed to those causes.

M La Perouse was of opinion that the islands of Felix and Ambrose were those under discussion, and in order to reconcile their distance from Copiapo with that given by Wafer, he has imputed to him the mistake of a figure in his text, without considering that it would have been next to impossible for Davis to have pursued a direct course from the Galapagos to those islands, (especially at the season in which his voyage was made,) but on the contrary that he would be compelled to make a circuit which would have brought him much nearer to Easter Island, and that Davis acquainted Dampier with the situation of his discovery, which agreed with that contained in Wafer's account   The alteration in a figure, it must be admitted, is rather arbitrary, as it has nothing to support it but the circumstance of the number of islands being the same   A mistake certainly might have occurred, but in the admission of it either party may claim it as an advantage by interpreting the presumed error in a way which would support their own opinions

At four o'clock in the afternoon of the 16th of November, Easter Island was seen from the mast-head, bearing N 78° W (Mag) fourteen or sixteen leagues, and we were consequently very nearly in the situation of the long looked for, small, sandy island, which, had it existed within reasonable limits of its supposed place, could not have escaped our observation   Nothing of it however was seen, nor had we any indication of the vicinity of such a spot as we proceeded, though we must have actually passed over the place assigned to it.   Easter Island had at first the appearance of being divided into two, rather flat at the top, with rounded capes, the north-eastern of which is distinguished by two hillocks.   To avoid over-running the distance, the ship was hove-to at night, and at daylight on the following morning we bore up for the northern shore of the island   I preferred that side, as it had been but partially examined by Captain Cook, and not at all by M La Perouse

As we approached, we observed numerous small craters rising above the low land, and near the N E extremity, one of considerable extent, with a deep chasm in its eastern side.   None of these were in action, nor indeed did they appear to have been so for a very long time, as, with the exception of the one above-mentioned, they were covered with verdure   The N. E. promontory, already noticed as having two small hillocks upon it, was composed of horizontal strata, apparently of volcanic origin; and near it, some patches of earth, sloping down to the cliff, were supposed to consist of red scoriæ.   The hills, and exposed parts of the earth, were overgrown with short burnt-up grass, which gave the surface a monotonous and arid aspect, but the valleys were well cultivated, and showed that the island required only a due proportion of moisture and labour to produce a luxuriant vegetation.

Passing along the northern shore, we saw several of those extensive habitations which M. La Perouse has described, situated in a valley surrounded by groves of banana trees and other patches of cultivation.   The larger huts were placed near the wood, and the smaller ones close together outside them   Nearer the sea-shore, which here forms a bay, was a morai, surmounted by four images standing upon a low platform precisely answering the description and representation of one given by Perouse : and also an immense enclosure of stones, and several large piles, which, as well as the images, were capped with something white, a circumstance noticed both by Captain Cook and M Perouse

The greatest attention appeared to be paid to the cultivation of . the soil.   Such places as were not immediately exposed to the scorching rays of the sun were laid out in oblong strips, taking the direction of the ravines, and furrows were ploughed at right angles to them, for the purpose of intercepting the streams of water in their descent.   Near the middle of the small bay just mentioned, there was an extinguished crater, the side of which, fronting the sea, had fallen in   The natives, availing themselves of this natural reservoir for moisture, in which other parts of the island are so deficient, had cultivated the soil in its centre, and reared a grove of banana-trees, which as we passed, had a very pleasing effect The natives lighted fires and followed the ship along the coast, their numbers increasing at every step.   Some had white cloth thrown loosely over their shoulders, but by far the greater number were naked, with the exception of the maro.

When the ship had arrived off the N W point of the island, she was hove-to for the purpose of taking observations; and a boat was lowered to examine the bays, and obtain soundings near the shore   Immediately she put off, the natives collected about the place where they supposed she would land   The sea broke heavily upon the rocks, and some of them apprehending the boat would be damaged, waved their cloaks to caution her against making the attempt to land . while others, eager to reach her, plunged into the sea, and so surrounded her that she was obliged to put about to get rid of them   They all showed a friendly disposition, and we began to hope that they had forgotten the unpardonable

conduct of the American master, who carried several of the islanders away by force to colonize Masafuera

Immediately the noon observation was obtained, we ran along
the western side of the island, towards the bay in which Cook and
Perouse had both anchored   The natives, as before, followed
along the coast, and lighted fires in different directions, the largest
of which was opposite the landing place   With a view to ascertain the feeling of the inhabitants, and, if possible, to establish an
amicable intercourse with them, I desired Lieutenant Peard to
proceed with two boats to the shore, and by presents and kindness
to endeavour to conciliate the people and to bring off what fruit
and vegetables he could.   Lieutenant Wainwright was directed to
accompany him, and though I did not apprehend any hostility,
yet, as a precautionary measure, I armed the boats, and placed two
marines in each   Their strength was further increased by several
of the officers, and the naturalist   Thus equipped, they rowed
for the landing-place in Cook's Bay, while the ship remained at a
short distance   The islanders were collected in great numbers,
and were seen running to and fro, exhibiting symptoms of expectation and delight   Some few, however, were observed throwing
large stones at a mark behind a bank erected near the beach

As the boats approached, the anxiety of the natives was manifested by shouts, which overpowered the voices of the officers:
and our boats, before they gained the beach, were surrounded by
hundreds of swimmers, clinging to the gunwale, the stern, and the
rudder, until they became unmanageable.   They all appeared to
be friendly disposed, and none came empty-handed   Bananas,
yams, potatoes, sugar-cane, nets, idols, &c were offered for sale,
and some were even thrown into the boat, leaving their visiters to
make what return they chose.   Among the swimmers there were
a great many females, who were equally or more anxious to get
into the boats than the men, and made use of every persuasion to
induce the crew to admit them   But to have acceeded to their
entreaties would have encumbered the party, and subjected them
to depredations.   As it was, the boats were so weighed down by
persons clinging to them, that for personal safety the crew were
compelled to have recourse to sticks to keep them off, at which
none of the natives took offence, but regained their position the
instant the attention of the persons in the boat was called to some
other object   Just within the gunwale there were many small
things which were highly prized by the swimmers, and the boats
being brought low in the water by the crowd hanging to them,
many of these articles were stolen, notwithstanding the most vigilant attention on the part of the crew, who had no means of re-

covering them, the marauders darting into the water, and diving the moment they committed a theft   The women were no less active in these piracies than the men , for if they were not the actual plunderers, they procured the opportunity for others, by engrossing the attention of the seamen by their caresses and ludicious gestures

In proceeding to the landing-place, the boats had to pass a small isolated rock which rose several feet above the water   As many females as could possibly find room crowded upon this eminence, pressing together so closely, that the rock appeared to be a mass of living beings   Of these Nereids three or four would shoot off at a time into the water, and swim with the expertness of fish to the boats to try their influence on their visiters   One of them, a very young girl, and less accustomed to the water than her companions, was taken upon the shoulders of an elderly man, conjectured to be her father, and was, by him, recommended to the attention of one of the officers, who, in compassion, allowed her a seat in his boat   She was young, and exceedingly pretty , her features were small and well made, her eyes dark, and her hair black, long and flowing , her colour, deep brunette.   She was tattooed in arches upon the forehead, and, like the greater part of her countrywomen, from the waist downward to the knee in narrow compact blue lines, which at a short distance had the appearance of breeches   Her only covering was a small triangular maro, made of grass and rushes , but this diminutive screen not agreeing with her ideas of propriety in the novel situation in which she found herself, she remedied the defect by unceremoniously appropriating to that use a part of one of the officer's apparel, and then commenced a song not altogether inharmonious.   Far from being jealous of her situation, she aided all her countrywomen who aspired to the same seat of honour with herself, by dragging them out of the water by the hair of the head ; but unkind as it might appear to interfere to prevent this, it was necessary to do so, or the boats would have been filled and unmanageable

As our party passed, the assemblage of females on the rock commenced a song, similar to that chaunted by the lady in the boat , and accompanied it by extending their arms over their heads, beating their breasts, and performing a variety of gestures, which showed that our visit was acceptable, at least to that part of the community   When the boats were within wading distance of the shore, they were closely encompassed by the natives ; each bringing something in his hand, however small, and almost every one importuning for an equivalent in return   All those in the water were naked, and only here and there, on the shore, a thin cloak of native cloth was to be seen.   Some had their faces painted black,

some red, others black and white, or red and white, in the ludicrous manner practised by our clown; and two demon-like monsters were painted entirely black. It is not easy to imagine the
picture that was presented by this motley crowd, unrestrained by
any authority or consideration for their visiters, all hallooing to the
extent of their lungs, and pressing upon the boats with all sorts of
grimaces and gestures.

It was found impossible to land where it was at first intended:
the boats, therefore, rowed a little to the northward, followed by
the multitude, and there effected a disembarkation, aided by some
of the natives, who helped the party over the rocks with one hand,
while they picked their pockets with the other. It was no easy
matter to penetrate the dense multitude, and much less practicable
to pursue a thief through the labyrinth of figures that thronged
around. The articles stolen were consequently as irretrievably
lost here, as they were before in the hands of the divers. It is
extremely difficult on such occasions, to decide which is the best
line of conduct to adopt: whether to follow Captain Cook's rigid
maxim of never permitting a theft when clearly ascertained to go
unpunished, or to act as Perouse did with the inhabitants of Easter
Island, and suffer every thing to be stolen without resistance or remonstrance. Perhaps the happy medium of shutting the eyes to
those it is not necessary to observe, an punishing severely, such as
it is imperative to notice, will prove the wisest policy.

Among the foremost of the crowd were two men, crowned with
pelicans' feathers, who, if they were not chiefs, assumed an authority as such, and with the two demons above-mentioned attempted
to clear the way by striking at the feet of the mob; careful, however, so to direct their blows, that they should not take effect.
Without their assistance, it would have been almost impossible to
land: the mob cared very little for threats: a musket presented
at them, had no effect beyond the moment it was levelled, and was
less efficacious than some water thrown upon the bystanders by
those persons who wished to forward the views of our party.

The gentleman who disembarked first, and from that circumstance probably was considered a person of distinction, was escorted
to the top of the bank and seated upon a large block of lava,
which was the prescribed limit to the party's advance. An endeavour was then made to form a ring about him: but it was very
difficult, on account of the Islanders crowding to the place all in
expectation of receiving something. The applicants were impatient, noisy, and urgent: they presented their bags, which they had
carefully emptied for the purpose, and signified their desire that
they should be filled: they practised every artifice, and stole what
they could in the most careless and open manner: some went even

farther, and accompanied their demands by threats   About this
time one of the natives, probably a chief, with a cloak and
head-dress of feathers, was observed from the ship hastening from
the huts to the landing-place, attended by several persons with
short clubs.   This hostile appearance, followed by the blowing of
the conch-shell, a sound which Cook observes he never knew to
portend good, kept our glasses for a while rivited to the spot   To
this chief it is supposed, for it was impossible to distinguish amongst
the crowd, Mr Peard made a handsome present, with which he
was very well pleased and no apprehension of hostilities was entertained   It happened, however, that the presents were expended
and this officer was returning to the boat for a fresh supply, when
the natives, probably mistaking his intentions, became exceedingly
clamorous, and the confusion was further increased by a marine
endeavouring to regain his cap, which had been snatched from his
head   The natives took advantage of the confusion, and redoubled
their endeavours to pilfer, which our party were at last obliged to
repel by threats, and sometimes by force.   At length they became
so audacious that there was no longer any doubt of their intentions,
or that a system of open plunder had commenced , which, with
the appearance of clubs and sticks, and the departure of the women, induced Mr. Peard, very judiciously, to order his party into
the boats.   This seemed to be the signal for an assault   the chief
who had received the present threw a large stone, which struck
Mr Peard forcibly upon the back, and was immediately followed
by a shower of missiles which darkened the air.   The natives in
the water and about the boats instantly withdrew to their comrades,
who had run behind a bank out of the reach of the muskets, which
former experience alone could have taught them to fear, for none
had yet been fired by us

The stones, each of which weighed about a pound, fell incredi-
bly thick, and with such precision that several of the seamen were
knocked down under the thwarts of the boat, and every person
was more or less wounded, except the female to whom Lieutenant
Wainwright had given protection, who, as if aware of the skilfulness of her countrymen, sat unconcerned upon the gunwale, until
one of the officers, with more consideration for her safety than she
herself possessed, pushed her overboard, and she swam ashore
A blank cartridge was at first fired over the heads of the crowd ,
but forbearance, which with savages is generally mistaken for cowardice or inability, only augmented their fury.   The showers of
stones were if possible increased, until the personal safety of all
rendered it necessary to resort to severe measures   The chief,
still urging the islanders on, very deservedly, and perhaps fortunately, fell a victim-to the first shot that was fired in defence.

Terrified by this example, the natives kept closer under their bulwark, and though they continued to throw stones, and occasioned considerable difficulty in extricating the boats, their attacks were not so effectual as before, nor sufficient to prevent the embarkation of the crew, all of whom were got on board.

Several dangerous contusions were received in the affair, but fortunately no lives were lost on our part; and it was the opinion of the officer commanding the party, that the treacherous chief was the only victim on that of the islanders, though some of the officers thought they observed another man fall. Considering the manner in which the party were surrounded, and the imminent risk to which they were exposed, it is extraordinary that so few of the natives suffered, and the greatest credit is due to the officers and crews of both boats for their forbearance on the occasion.

After this unfortunate and unexpected termination to our interview, I determined upon quitting the island, as nothing of importance was to be gained by remaining, which could be put in competition with the probable loss of lives that might attend an attempt at reconciliation. The disappointment it occasioned was great to us, who had promised ourselves much novelty and enjoyment; but the loss to the public is trifling, as the island has been very well described by Roggewein, Cook, Perouse, Kotzebue, and others, and the people appeared, in all material points, the same now as these authors have painted them. With regard to supplies, nothing was to be gained by staying; for after Cook had traversed the island, he came to the conclusion that few places afford less convenience for shipping "As every thing must be raised by dint of labour, it cannot be supposed the inhabitants plant much more than is sufficient for themselves: and as they are few in number, they cannot have much to spare to supply the wants of strangers."

The population of Easter Island has been variously stated Roggewein declares several thousands surrounded the boats: Cook reckoned it six or seven hundred, Mr. Forster, who was with him, at nine hundred, M. la Perouse, at two thousand my officers estimated it at about fifteen hundred If a mean of these be taken, it will leave 1260, which is, perhaps near the truth; for it may be presumed, that in an island of such limited extent, and which does not increase its productions or personal comforts, and where sexual intercourse is unrestrained, the population will remain much the same.

One of the authors of Roggewein's Voyage represents the inhabitants of this island as giants, which, if his assertion be true, makes it evident that, like the Patagonians, they have degenerated very rapidly Cook remarks that he did not see a man that would measure 6 feet; and our estimate of the average height of the

people was 5 feet 7 1-2 inches   They are a handsome race, the
women in particular   The fine oval countenances and regular features of the men, the smooth, high-rounded foreheads, the rather
small and somewhat sunken dark eye, and the even rows of ivory-
white teeth, impressed us with the similarity of their features to the
heads brought from New Zealand.   The colour of their skin is
lighter than that of the Malays   The general contour of the body
is good : the limbs are not remarkable for muscularity, but formed
more for activity than strength   The hair is jet black, and worn
moderately short   One man of about fifty years of age, the only
exception that was noticed, had his hair over the forehead of a
reddish-ash gray   The beards of such as had any were black ;
but many had none, or only a few hairs on the chin   None of the
men had whiskers, which seemed to be rather a subject of regret
with them, and they appeared envious of such of our party as had
them, who were obliged to submit to the ordeal of having them
stroked and twisted about for the admiration and amusement of
their new acquaintances.   Both sexes still retain the hideous practice of perforating the lobes of the ears, though the custom is not
so general with the men as formerly.   The aperture, when distended, which is done by a leaf rolled up and forced through it, is about
an inch and a quarter in diameter.   The lobe, deprived of its ear-
ring, hangs dangling against the neck, and has a very disagreeable
appearance, particularly when wet.   It is sometimes so long as to
be greatly in the way ; to obviate which, they pass the lobe over
the upper part of the ear, or more rarely, fasten one lobe to the
other, at the back of the head   The lips, when closed, form
nearly a line, showing very little of the fleshy part, and giving a
character of resolution to the countenance.   The nose is aquiline
and well-proportioned ; the eyes small and dark brown or black ;
the chin small and rather prominent ; and the tongue disproportionably large, and, on its upper surface, of a diseased white appearance

Tattooing or puncturing the skin is here practised to a greater
extent than formerly, especially by the females, who have stained
their skin in imitation of blue breeches , copied, no doubt, from
some of their visiters, who frequently tuck up their trowsers to the
knee in passing through the water   The deception, which, at a
short distance, completely deceives the eye, is produced by a succession of small blue lines, beginning at the waist and extending
downward to the knee.   Besides this, some of them tattoo their
foreheads in arched lines, as well as the edges of their ears and the
fleshy part of their lips   The males tattoo themselves in curved
lines of a dark Berlin blue colour upon the upper part of the
throat, beginning at the ear, and sloping round below the under

jaw   The face is sometimes nearly covered with lines similar to those on the throat, or with an uninterrupted colouring, excepting two broad stripes on each side, at right angles to each other   Most of their lips were also stained   Others had different parts of their bodies variously marked, but in the greater number it was confined to a small space   All the lines were drawn with much taste, and carried in the direction of the muscle in a manner very similar to the New Zealanders   These people have had so little communication with Europeans, or have benefitted so little by it, that we did not perceive any European cloth among them ; and the cloth mulberry-tree, which grows upon their island, produces so small a supply, that part of the inhabitants necessarily go naked · the larger portion however wear a maro, made either of fine Indian cloth of reddish colour, of a wild kind of parsley, or of a species of sea-weed

Their weapons are short clubs of a flattened oval form, tapering toward the handle, and a little curved.   The straw hats mentioned both by Cook and Perouse appeared to be no longer used.   One man only had his head covered , and that with a tattered felt hat, which he must have obtained from some former visiters   A ramrod, which had probably been procured in the same way, was also seen among them.   We noticed three boats hauled up on the shore to the northward of the landing-place, resembling the drawing in Perouse's Voyage, but the natives did not attempt to launch them

Roggewein and Perouse were of opinion that these people lived together in communities, a whole village inhabiting one extensive hut, and that property was in common.   The former idea was suggested by the very capacious dwellings which are scattered over the island , and the conjecture may be correct, though it is certain that there are a far greater number of small huts, sufficient to contain one family only ; but with regard to the supposition that property is common, it seems very doubtful whether the land would be so carefully divided by rows of stones if that were the case   Some circumstances which occurred at the landing-place, during our visit, certainly favoured the presumption of its being so.   One of the natives offered an image for sale, and being disappointed in the price he expected, refused to part with it , but a by-stander, less scrupulous, snatched it from him without ceremony, and parted with it for the original offer without a word of remonstrance from his countryman   Others again threw their property into the boats, without demanding any immediate return , taking for granted, it may be presumed, that they would reap their reward when a distribution of the property obtained should take place.   But this state of society is so unnatural that, however appearances may sanction the belief, I am disposed to doubt it.   One strong fact in support of my opinion was the unceremonious manner in which the apparent proprietor of a piece of ground planted with potatoes drove away the mob, who, with very little consideration for the owner, were taking the crop out of the earth to barter with our party

The island, though situated nearer the Continent of America than any other of the archipelago to which it belongs, has been less frequently visited, and unfortunately for its inhabitants, some of those visits have rather tended to retard than to advance its prosperity, or improve its moral condition, and they afford a striking example of an extensive intercourse with mankind, before a limited community can emerge from barbarism to a state of civilization   One consolation for this privation is their exemption from those complaints by which some of the ill-fated natives of these seas have so dreadfully suffered.

The gigantic busts which excited the surprise of the first visiters to the island, have suffered so much either from the effects of time, or maltreatment of the natives, that the existence of any of them at present is questionable   At first they were dispersed generally over the whole island. when Cook visited it, there were but two on the western side near the landing-place · Kotzebue found only a square pedestal in the same place and now a few heaps of rubbish only, occupy a spot where it is doubtful whether one of them was erected or not.   When it is considered how great must have been the labour bestowed upon these images before they were hewn from the quarries with the rude stone implements of the Indians, and before such huge masses of rock could be transported to, and erected on, so many parts of the island, it is nearly positive that they were actuated by religious motives in their construction; and yet, if it were so, why were these objects of adoration suffered to go to decay by succeeding generations?   Is it that the religious forms of the islanders have changed, or that the aborigines have died off, and been succeeded by a new race?—Pitcairn Island affords a curious example of a race of men settling upon an island, erecting stone images upon its heights, and either becoming extinct or having abandoned it; and some circumstances connected with Easter Island occur independent of that above alluded to, in favour of the presumption that the same thing may also have taken place there   The most remarkable of these facts is, that the present generation are so nearly allied in language and customs to many islands in the South Sea, as to leave no doubt of their having migrated from some of them,—and yet in none of these places are there images of such extraordinary dimensions, or indeed in any way resembling them   The Easter Islanders have, besides, small wooden deities similar to those used by the inhabitants of the other islands just mentioned

That there had been recent migrations from some of the islands to the westward, about Roggewein's time, may be inferred from the natives having recognised the animals on board his ship, and from their having hogs tattooed upon their arms and breasts; whereas there was not a quadruped upon the island at the time, nor has any one except the rat ever been seen there. Another curious fact connected with this island is, that when it was first discovered it abounded in woods and forests, and palm branches were presented as emblems of peace; but fifty years afterwards, when visited by Captain Cook, there were no traces of them left. The revolution that has taken place in La Dominica, one of the Marquesa Islands, affords another instance of this kind: when first visited by Mendana, in 1595, it exhibited an enchanting aspect "vast plains displayed a smiling verdure, and divided hills, crowned with tufted woods," &c but in 1774 it was found by Captain Cook to have so completely altered its features that Marchand ascribes the change to one of those great "convulsions of nature, which totally disfigure every part of the surface of the globe, over which its ravages extend." Easter Island is studded with volcanos, and an eruption may have driven the natives into the sea, or have so torn up the soil and vegetation, that they could no longer subsist upon it

I cannot say a word on the success that attended the humane efforts of the much-lamented Perouse, who planted many useful fruit trees and seeds upon the island; but there is every reason to believe they have perished, or shared the fate of the vines at Otaheite, as they brought us no fruits or roots beyond what he found there on his arrival Perhaps a tuft of trees in a sheltered spot at the back of Cook's Bay, which had the appearance of orange-trees, are the offspring of his benevolent care and attention Cook had no opportunity of benefiting the islanders in this way; but he planted in them a warm and friendly feeling towards strangers, and his usual rectitude and generous treatment taught them a lesson of which Perouse felt the good effects, and which possibly might have existed until now, but for the interference of a few unprincipled masters of vessels, who have unfortunately found their way to the island; and I fear these communications are more frequent than is generally supposed

The island is 2000 miles from the coast of Chili, and 1500 from the nearest inhabited islands, Pitcairn Island excepted, which has been peopled by Europeans A curious inquiry therefore suggests itself. in what manner has so small a place, and so distantly situated from any other, received its population? particularly as every thing favours the probability of its inhabitants having migrated from the westward, in opposition to the prevalent wind and current Captain Cook obtained considerable knowledge upon this subject at

Wateo ; and I shall hereafter be able to offer something in support of the theory entertained by that celebrated navigator

Cook and Perouse differ in a very trifling degree from each other, and also from us in the geographical position of Easter Island The longitude by Cook is 109° 46′ 20″ W , and deducting 18′ 30′ , in consequence of certain corrections made at Fetegu Island, leaves 109° 27′ 50″W   That by Perouse, allowing the longitude of Conception to be 72° 56′ 30′ W , is 109° 32′ 10″W. , and our own is 109°24′ 54″W   The island is of a triangular shape · its length is exactly nine miles from N. W, to S E , nine and three quarters from W N. W to E S E , and thirteen from N E to S W.   The highest part of it is1200 feet, and in clear weather it may be seen at sixteen or eighteen leagues distance   The geographical description by M Bernizet, who was engineer in the Astrolabe, is exact . the views of the land are a little caricatured, but the angular measurments are perfectly correct   Further remarks on the coast and anchorage will be found in the Nauctical Memoir

We quitted Easter Island with a fresh N E wind, and bore away for the next island placed upon the chart.   On the 19th, during a calm, some experiments were made on the temperature of the water at different depths   As the line was hauling in, a large sword-fish bit at the tin case which contained our thermometer, but, fortunately, he failed in carrying it off   On the 27th, in lat 25° 36′ S , long. 115o 06′ W , many sea-birds were seen ; but there was no other indication of land   From the time of our quitting Easter Island, light and variable winds greatly retarded the progress of the ship, until the 24th, in lat 26° 20′ S , and long. 116° 30′ W , when we got the regular trade-wind, and speedily gained the parallel of Ducie's Island, which it was my intention to pursue, that the island might by no possibility be passed   In the forenoon of the 28th we saw a great many gulls and tern , and at half-past three in the afternoon the island was descried right a-head. We stood on until sunset, and shortened sail within three or four miles to windward of it

Ducie's Island is of coral formation, of an oval form, with a lagoon or lake, in the centre, which is partly inclosed by trees, and partly by low coral flats scarcely above the water's edge.   The height of the soil upon the island is about twelve feet, above which trees rise about fourteen more, making its greatest elevation about twenty-six feet from the level of the sea   The lagoon appears to be deep, and has the entrance into it for a boat, when the water is sufficiently smooth to admit of passing over the bar   It is situated at the south-east extremity, to the right of two eminences that have the appearance of sand-hills   The island lies in a north-east and south-west direction, is one mile and three quarters long, and one mile wide No living things, birds excepted, were seen upon the island, but its environs appeared to abound in fish, and sharks were very numerous The water was so clear over the coral, that the bottom was distinctly seen when no soundings could be had with thirty fathoms of line, in twenty four fathoms, the shape of the rock at the bottom was clearly distinguished The coral-lines were of various colours, principally white, sulphur, and lilac, and formed into all manner of shapes, giving a lively and variegated appearance to the bottom; but they soon lost their colour after being detached.

By the soundings round this little island, it appeared, for a certain distance, to take the shape of a truncated cone having its base downwards The north-eastern and south-western extremities are furnished with points which project under water with less inclination than the sides of the island, and break the sea before it can reach the barrier to the little lagoon formed within. It is singular that these butresses are opposed to the only two quarters whence their structure has to apprehend danger. that on the north-east, from the constant action of the trade-wind, and that on the other extremity, from the long rolling swell from the south-west, so prevalent in these latitudes. and it is worthy of observation, that this barrier, which has the most powerful enemy to oppose, is carried out much farther, and with less abruptness than the other.

The sand-mounds raised upon the barrier are confined to the eastern and north-western sides of the lagoon, the south-western part being left low, and broken by a channel of water On the rocky surface of the causeway, between the lake and the sea, lies a stratum of dark rounded particles, probably coral, and above it another, apparently composed of decayed vegetable substances A variety of ever green trees take root in this bank, and form a canopy almost impenetrable to the sun's rays, and present to the eye a grove of the the liveliest green.

As soon as we had finished our observations on Ducie's Island, and completed a plan of it, we made sail to the westward The island soon neared the horizon, and when seven miles distant ceased to be visible from the deck. For several days afterwards the winds were so light, that we made but slow progress, and as we lay-to every night. in order that nothing might be passed in the dark, our daily run was trifling On the 30th, we saw a great number of white tern, which at sunset directed their flight to the N W At noon on the 2d of December, flocks of gulls and tern indicated the vicinity of land. which a few hours afterwards was seen from the mast-head at a considerable distance. At daylight on the 3d, we closed with its south-western end. and despatched two boats to make the circuit of the island, while the ship ranged its northern shore at a short distance, and waited for them off a sandy bay at its nort-west extremity.

We found that the island differed essentially from all others in its vicinity, and belonged to a peculiar formation, very few instances of which are in existence   Wateo and Savage Islands, discovered by Captain Cook, are of this number, and perhaps also Malden Island, visited by Lord Byron in the Blonde   The island is five miles in length, and one in breadth, and has a flat surface nearly eighty feet above the sea   On all sides, except the north, it is bounded by perpendicular cliffs about fifty feet high, composed entirely of dead coral, more or less porous, honeycombed at the surface, and hardening into a compact calcareous substance within, possessing the fracture of secondary limestone, and has a species of millepore interspersed through it.   These cliffs are considerably undermined by the action of the waves, and some of them appear on the eve of precipitating their superincumbent weight into the sea : those which are less injured in this way present no alternate ridges or indication of the different levels, which the sea might have occupied at different periods, but a smooth surface, as if the island, which there is every probability has been raised by volcanic agency, had been forced up by one great subterraneous convulsion   The dead coral, of which the higher part of the island consists, is nearly circumscribed by ledges of living coral, which project beyond each other at different depths ; on the northern side of the island the first of these had an easy slope from the beach to a distance of about fifty yards, when it terminated abruptly about three fathoms under water.   The next ledge had a greater descent and extended to two hundred yards from the beach, with twenty-five fathoms water over it, and there ended as abruptly as the former, a short distance beyond which no bottom could be gained with 200 fathoms of line   Numerous *echini* live upon these ledges, and a variety of richly coloured fish play over their surface, while some cray-fish inhabit the deeper sinuosities.   The sea rolls in successive breakers over these ledges of coral, and renders landing upon them extremely difficult   It may, however, be effected by anchoring the boat, and veering her close into the surf, and then, watching the opportunity, by jumping upon the ledge, and hastening to the shore before the succeeding roller approaches   In doing this great caution must be observed, as the reef is full of holes and caverns, and the rugged way is strewed with sea-eggs, which inflict very painful wounds ; and if a person fall into one of these hollows, his life will be greatly endangered by the points of coral catching his clothes and detaining him under water   The beach, which appears at a distance to be composed of a beautiful white sand, is wholly made up of small broken portions of the different species and varieties of coral, intermixed with shells of testaceous and crustaceous animals.

Insignificant as this island is in height, compared with others, it is extremely difficult to gain the summit, in consequence of the thickly interlacing shrubs which grow upon it, and form so dense a covering, that it is impossible to see the cavities in the rock beneath They are at the same time too fragile to afford any support, and the traveller often sinks into the cavity up to his shoulder before his feet reach the bottom The soil is a black mould of little depth, wholly formed of decayed vegetable matter, through which points of coral every now and then project

The largest tree upon the island is the pandanus, though there is another tree very common, nearly of the same size, the wood of which has a great resemblance to common ash, and possesses the same properties We remarked also a species of budleia, which was nearly as large and as common, bearing fruit It affords but little wood, and has a reddish bark of considerable astringency . several species of this genus are to be met with among the Society Islands There is likewise a long slender plant with a stem about an inch in diameter, bearing a beautiful pink flower, of the class and order hexandria monogynia We saw no esculent roots, and, with the exception of the pandanus, no tree that bore fruit fit to eat.

This island, which on our charts bears the name of Elizabeth, ought properly to be called Henderson's Island. as it was first named by Captain Henderson of the Hercules of Calcutta Both these vessels visited it, and each supposing it was a new discovery, claimed the merit of it on her arrival the next day at Pitcairn Island, these two places lying close together But the Hercules preceded the former several months. To neither of these vessels, however, is the discovery of the land in question to be attributed, as it was first seen by the crew of the Essex, an American whaler, who accidentally fell in with it after the loss of their vessel Two of her seamen, preferring the chance of finding subsistence on this desolate spot to risking their lives in an open boat across the wide expanse which lies between it and the coast of Chili, were at their own desire, left behind. They were afterwards taken off by an English whaler that heard of their disaster at Valparaiso from their surviving shipmates.*

---

* The extraordinary fate of the Essex has been recorded in a pamphlet published in New York by the mate of that vessel, but of the veracity of which every person must consult his own judgment As all my readers may not be in possession of it, I shall briefly state that it describes the Essex to have been in the act of catching whales, when one of these animals became enraged, and attacked the vessel by swimming against it with all its strength The steersman, it is said, endeavoured to evade the shock by managing the helm, but in vain The third blow stove in the bows of the ship, and she went down in a very short time, even before some of

It appears from their narrative that the island possessed no spring; and that the two men procured a supply of water at a small pool which received the drainings from the upper part of the island, and was just sufficient for their daily consumption

In the evening we bore away to the westward, and at one o'clock in the afternoon of the 4th of December we saw Pitcairn Island bearing S W. by W. ½ W. at a considerable distance.

the boats that were away had time to get on board   Such of the crew as were in the ship contrived to save themselves in the boats that were near and were soon joined by their astonished shipmates, who could not account for the sudden disappearance of their vessel, but found themselves unprovided with every thing necessary for a sea-voyage, and several thousand miles from any place whence they could hope for relief   The boats, after the catastrophe, determined to proceed to Chili, touching at Ducie's Island in their way   They steered to the southward, and after considerable sufferings, landed upon an island which they supposed to be that above-mentioned, but which was, in fact, Elizabeth Island   Not being able to procure any water here, they continued their voyage to the coast of Chili, where two boats out of the three arrived, but with only three or four persons in them   The third was never heard of, but it is not improbable that the wreck of a boat and four skeletons which were seen on Ducie's Island, by a merchant vessel, were her remains and that of her crew   Had these unfortunate persons been aware of the situation of Pitcairn Island, which is only ninety miles from Elizabeth Island, and to leward of it, all their lives might have been saved.

CHAPTER III

Pitcairn Island—Adams and Natives come off to the Ship—Adams' Account of the Mutiny of the Bounty—Lieutenant Bligh sent adrift in the Launch—Mutineers proceed to Tobouai—Hostile reception there—Proceed to Otaheite—Return to Tobouai—Again quit it and return to Otaheite—Christian determines to proceed to Pitcairn Island—Lands there—Fate of the Ship—Insurrection among the blacks—Murder of Christian and four of the mutineers—Adams dangerously wounded—Fate of the remaining number.

The interest which was excited by the announcement of Pitcairn Island from the mast-head brought every person upon deck, and produced a train of reflections that momentarily increased our anxiety to communicate with its inhabitants : to see and partake of the pleasures of their little domestic circle , and to learn from them the particulars of every transaction connected with the fate of the Bounty but in consequence of the approach of night this gratification was deferred until the next morning, when, as we were steering for the side of the island on which Captain Carteret has marked soundings, in the hope of being able to anchor the ship, we had the pleasure to see a boat under sail hastening toward us. At first the complete equipment of this boat raised a doubt as to its being the property of the islanders, for we expected to see only a well-provided canoe in their possession, and we therefore concluded that the boat must belong to some whale-ship on the opposite side , but we were soon agreeably undeceived by the singular appearance of her crew, which consisted of old Adams and all the young men of the island

Before they ventured to take hold of the ship, they inquired if they might come on board, and upon permission being granted, they sprang up the side and shook every officer by the hand with undisguised feelings of gratification

The activity of the young men exceeded that of old Adams, who was consequently almost the last to greet us He was in his sixty-fifth year, and was unusually strong and active for his age, notwithstanding the inconvenience of considerable corpulency He was dressed in a sailor's shirt and trousers and a low-crowned hat, which he instinctively held in his hand until desired to put it on. He still retained his sailor's gait, doffing his hat and smooth-

ing down his bald forehead whenever he was addressed by the
officers

It was the first time he had been on board a ship of war since
the mutiny, and his mind naturally reverted to scenes that could
not fail to produce a temporary embarrassment, heightened, perhaps, by the familiarity with which he found himself addressed by
persons of a class with those whom he had been accustomed to
obey   Apprehension for his safety formed no part of his thoughts.
he had received too many demonstrations of the good feeling that
existed towards him, both on the part of the British government
and of individuals, to entertain any alarm on that head, and as every person endeavoured to set his mind at rest, he very soon made
himself at home *

The young men, ten in number, were tall, robust, and healthy,
with good-natured countenances, which would any where have procured them a friendly reception ; and with a simplicity of manner
and a fear of doing wrong, which at once prevented the possibility
of giving offence   Unacquainted with the world, they asked a
number of questions which would have applied better to persons
with whom they had been intimate, and who had left them but a
short time before, than to perfect strangers, and inquired after
ships and people we had never heard of   Their dress, made up
of the presents which had been given them by the masters and
seamen of merchant ships, was a perfect caricature   Some had
on long black coats without any other article of dress except
trousers. some shirts without coats. and others waistcoats without
either, none had shoes or stockings, and only two possessed hats,
neither of which seemed likely to hang long together

They were as anxious to gratify their curiosity about the decks, as
we were to learn from them the state of the colony, and the particulars of the fate of the mutineers who had settled upon the
island, which had been variously related by occasional visiters ;
and we were more especially desirous of obtaining Adams' own
narrative ; for it was peculiarly interesting to learn from one who
had been implicated in the mutiny, the facts of that transaction,
now that he considered himself exempt from the penalties of his
crime.

I trust that, in renewing the discussion of this affair, I shall not
be considered as unnecessarily wounding the feelings of the friends
of any of the parties concerned ; but it is satisfactory to show, that
those who suffered by the sentence of the court-martial were con-
victed upon evidence which is now corroborated by the statement

* Since the MS of this narrative was sent to press, intelligence of Adams' death
has been communicated to me by our Consul at the Sandwich Islands

of an accomplice who has no motive for concealing the truth The following account is compiled almost entirely from Adams' narrative, signed with his own hand But to render the narrative more complete, I have added such additional facts as were derived from the inhabitants, who are perfectly acquainted with every incident connected with the transaction In presenting it to the public, I vouch, only, for its being a correct statement of the above-mentioned authorities

His Majesty's ship Bounty was purchased into the service, and placed under the command of Lieutenant Bligh in 1787. She left England in December of that year, with orders to proceed to Otaheite,* and transport the bread fruit of that country to the British Settlements in the West Indies, and to bring also some specimens of it to England Her crew consisted of forty-four persons, and a gardener She was ordered to make the passage round Cape Horn, but after contending a long time with adverse gales, in extremely cold weather, she was obliged to bear away for the Cape of Good Hope, where she underwent a refit, and arrived at her destination in October 1788 Six months were spent at Otaheite, collecting and stowing away the fruit, during which time the officers and seamen had free access to the shore, and made many friends, though only one of the seamen formed any alliance there

In April 1789, they took leave of their friends at Otaheite, and proceeded to Anamooka, where Lieutenant Bligh replenished his stock of water, and took on board hogs, fruit, vegetables, &c , and put to sea again on the 26th of the same month Throughout the voyage Mr. Bligh had repeated misunderstandings with his officers, and had on several occasions given them and the ship's company just reasons for complaint Still, whatever might have been the feelings of the officers, Adams declares there was no real discontent among the crew , much less was there any idea of offering violence to their commander The officers, it must be admitted, had much more cause for dissatisfaction than the seamen, especially the master and Mr Christian The latter was a protegé of Lieutenant Bligh, and unfortunately was under some obligations to him of a pecuniary nature, of which Bligh frequently reminded him when any difference arose Christian, excessively annoyed at the share of blame which repeatedly fell to his lot, in common with the rest of the officers, could ill endure the additional taunt of private obligations ; and in a moment of excitation told his commander that sooner or later a day of reckoning would arrive.

The day previous to the mutiny a serious quarrel occurred be-

---

* This word has since been spelled *Tahiti*, but as I have a veneration for the name as it is written in the celebrated Voyages of Captain Cook—a feeling in which I am sure I am not singular—I shall adhere to his orthography

tween Bligh and his officers, about some cocoa-nuts which were missed from his private stock, and Christian again fell under his commander's displeasure   The same evening he was invited to supper in the cabin, but he had not so soon forgotten his injuries as to accept of this ill-timed civility, and returned an excuse

Matters were in this state on the 28th of April 1789, when the Bounty, on her homeward voyage, was passing to the southward of Tofoa, one of the Friendly Islands   It was one of those beautiful nights which characterize the tropical regions when the mildness of the air and the stillness of nature dispose the mind to reflection Christian, pondering over his grievances considered them so intolerable, that any thing appeared preferable to enduring them, and he determined, as he could not redress them, that he would at least escape from the possibility of their being increased   Absence from England, and a long residence at Otaheite, where new connexions were formed, weakened the recollection of his native country, and prepared his mind for the reception of ideas which the situation of the ship and the serenity of the moment particularly favoured His plan, strange as it must appear for a young officer to adopt, who was fairly advanced in an honourable profession, was to set himself adrift upon a raft, and make his way to the island then in sight   As quick in the execution as in the design, the raft was soon constructed, various useful articles were got together, and he was on the point of launching it, when a young officer, who afterwards perished in the Pandora, to whom Christian communicated his intention, recommended him, rather than risk his life on so hazardous an expedition, to endeavour to take possession of the ship, which he thought would not be very difficult, as many of the ship's company were not well disposed towards the commander, and would all be very glad to return to Otaheite, and reside among their friends in that island   This daring proposition is even more extraordinary than the premeditated scheme of his companion, and, if true, certainly relieves Christian from part of the odium which has hitherto attached to him as the sole instigator of the mutiny *

It however accorded too well with the disposition of Christian's mind, and, hazardous as it was, he determined to co-operate with his friend in effecting it, resolving, if he failed, to throw himself into the sea, and that there might be no chance of being saved. he tied a deep sea lead about his neck, and concealed it within his clothes

* This account, however differs materially from a note in Marshall's Naval Biography, Vol ii Part ii p 778   unfortunately this volume was not published when the Blossom left England, or more satisfactory evidence on this, and other points, might have been obtained   However, this is the statement of Adams

Christian happened to have the morning watch, and as soon as he had relieved the officer of the deck, he entered into conversation with Quintal, the only one of the seamen who, Adams said, had formed any serious attachment at Otaheite, and after expatiating on the happy hours they had passed there, disclosed his intentions Quintal, after some consideration, said he thought it a dangerous attempt, and declined taking a part. Vexed at a repulse in a quarter where he was most sanguine of success, and particularly at having revealed sentiments which if made known would bring him to an ignominious death, Christian became desperate, exhibited the lead about his neck in testimony of his own resolution, and taxed Quintal with cowardice, declaring it was fear alone that restrained him Quintal denied this accusation; and in reply to Christian's further argument that success would restore them all to the happy island, and the connexions they had left behind, the strongest persuasion he could have used to a mind somewhat prepared to acquiesce, he recommended that some one else should be tried—Isaac Martin for instance, who was standing by Martin, more ready than his shipmate, emphatically declared, "He was for it, it was the very thing" Successful in one instance, Christian went to every man of his watch, many of whom he found disposed to join him, and before daylight the greater portion of the ship's company were brought over

Adams was sleeping in his hammock, when Sumner, one of the seamen, came to him, and whispered that Christian was going to take the ship from her commander, and set him and the master on shore On hearing this, Adams went upon deck, and found every thing in great confusion; but not then liking to take any part in the transaction, he returned to his hammock, and remained there until he saw Christian at the arm-chest, distributing arms to all who came for them · and then seeing measures had proceeded so far, and apprehensive of being on the weaker side, he turned out again and went for a cutlass

All those who proposed to assist Christian being armed, Adams, with others, were ordered to secure the officers, while Christian and the master-at-arms proceeded to the cabin to make a prisoner of Lieutenant Bligh They seized him in his cot, bound his hands behind him, and brought him upon deck He remonstrated with them on their conduct, but received only abuse in return, and a blow from the master-at-arms with the flat side of a cutlass He was placed near the binnacle, and detained there, with his arms pinioned, by Christian, who held him with one hand, and a bayonet with the other. As soon as the lieutenant was secured, the sentinels that had been placed over the doors of the officers' cabins were taken off, the master then jumped upon the forecastle, and endeavoured to form a party to retake the ship, but he was quickly secured, and sent below in confinement.

This conduct of the master, who was the only officer that tried to bring the mutineers to a sense of their duty, was the more highly creditable to him, as he had the greatest cause for discontent, Mr. Bligh having been more severe to him than to any of the other officers

About this time a dispute arose, whether the lieutenant and his party, whom the mutineers resolved to set adrift, should have the launch or the cutter, and it being decided in favour of the launch, Christian ordered her to be hoisted out. Martin, who, it may be remembered, was the first convert to Christian's plan, foreseeing that with the aid of so large a boat the party would find their way to England, and that their information would in all probability lead to the detection of the offenders, relinquished his first intention, and exclaimed, "If you give him the launch, I will go with him; you may as well give him the ship" He really appears to have been in earnest in making this declaration, as he was afterwards ordered to the gangway from his post of command over the lieutenant, in consequence of having fed him with a shaddock, and exchanged looks with him indicative of his friendly intentions It also fell to the lot of Adams to guard the lieutenant, who observing him stationed by his side, exclaimed, "And you, Smith, are you against me?"* To which Adams replied that he only acted as the others did—he must be like the rest Lieutenant Bligh, while thus secured, reproached Christian with ingratitude, reminded him of his obligations to him, and begged he would recollect he had a wife and family To which Christian replied, that he should have thought of that before

The launch was by this time hoisted out, and the officers and seamen of Lieutenant Bligh's party having collected what was necessary for their voyage,† were ordered into her. Among those who took their seat in the boat was Martin, which being noticed by Quintal, he pointed a musket at him, and declared he would shoot him unless he instantly returned to the ship, which he did. The armourer and carpenter's mates were also forcibly detained, as they might be required hereafter. Lieutenant Bligh was then conducted to the gangway, and ordered to descend into the boat, where his hands were unbound, and he and his party were veered astern, and kept there while the ship stood towards the island During this time Lieutenant Bligh requested some muskets, to protect his party against the natives; but they were refused, and four

---

* Adams went by the name of Alexander Smith in the Bounty.

† Consisting of a small cask of water, 150lbs of bread, a small quantity of rum and wine, a quadrant, compass, some lines, rope canvas, twine, &c

cutlasses thrown to them instead. When they were about ten leagues from Tofoa, at Lieutenant Bligh's request, the launch was cast off, and immediately 'Huzza for Otaheite!' echoed throughout the Bounty.

There now remained in the ship, Christian, who was the mate, Heywood, Young, and Stewart, midshipmen, the master-at-arms, and sixteen seamen, besides the three artificers, and the gardener; forming in all twenty-five

In the launch were the lieutenant, master, surgeon, a master's mate, two midshipmen, botanist, three warrant-officers, clerk, and eight seamen, making in all nineteen: and had not the three persons above-mentioned been forcibly detained, the captain would have had exactly half the ship's company. It may perhaps appear strange to many, that with so large a party in his favour, Lieutenant Bligh made no attempt to retake the vessel, but the mutiny was so ably conducted that no opportunity was afforded him of doing so; and the strength of the crew was decidedly in favour of Christian. Lieutenant Bligh's adventures and sufferings, until hé reached Timor, are well known to the public, and need no repetition

The ship, having stood some time to the W. N W, with a view to deceive the party in the launch, was afterwards put about, and her course directed as near to Otaheite as the wind would permit. In a few days they found some difficulty in reaching that island, and bore away for Tobouai, a small island about 300 miles to the southward of it, where they agreed to establish themselves, provided the natives, who were numerous were not hostile to their purpose Of this they had very early intimation, an attack being made upon a boat which they sent to sound the harbour She, however, effected her purpose; and the next morning the Bounty was warped inside the reef that formed the port, and stationed close to the beach. An attempt to land was next made. but the natives disputed every foot of ground with spears, clubs, and stones, until they were dispersed by a discharge of cannon and musketry. On this they fled to the interior, and refused to hold any further intercourse with their visitors.

The determined hostility of the natives put an end to the mutineer's design of settling among them at that time; and, after two days' fruitless attempt at reconciliation, they left the island and proceeded to Otaheite Tobouai was, however, a favourite spot with them, and they determined to make another effort to settle there, which they thought would yet be feasible, provided the islanders could be made acquainted with their friendly intentions The only way to do this was through interpreters, who might be procured at Otaheite, and in order not to be dependent upon the natives To-

bouai for wives, they determined to engage several Otaheitan women to accompany them.   They reached Otaheite in eight days,
and were received with the greatest kindness by their former friends,
who immediately inquired for the captain and his officers   Christian and his party having anticipated inquiries of this nature, in-
vented a story to account for their absence, and told them that
Lieutenant Bligh having found an island suitable for a settlement,
had landed there with some of his officers, and sent them in the
ship to procure live stock and whatever else would be useful to the
colony, and to bring besides such of the natives as were willing to
accompany them *   Satisfied with this plausible account, the chiefs
supplied them with every thing they wanted, and even gave them
a bull and a cow which had been confided to their care, the only
ones, I believe, that were on the island   They were equally fortunate in finding several persons, both male and female, willing to
accompany them ; and thus furnished, they again sailed for Tobouai, where, as they expected, they were better received than before, in consequence of being able to communicate with the natives
through their interpreters

Experience had taught them the necessity of making self-defence their first consideration, and a fort was consequently commenced, eighty yards square, surrounded by a wide ditch   It was
nearly completed, when the natives, imagining they were going to
destroy them, and that the ditch was intended for their place of
interment, planned a general attack when the party should proceed
to work in the morning   It fortunately happened that one of the
natives who accompanied them from Otaheite overheard this conspiracy, and instantly swam off to the ship and apprised the crew
of their danger   Instead, therefore, of proceeding to their work
at the fort, as usual, the following morning, they made an attack upon the natives, killed and wounded several, and obliged the
others to retire inland

Great dissatisfaction and difference of opinion now arose among
the crew   some were for abandoning the fort and returning to Otaheite, while others were for proceeding to the Marquesas ; but the
majority were at that time for completing what they had begun,
and remaining at Tobouai   At length the continued state of suspense in which they were kept by the natives made them decide
to return to Otaheite, though much against the inclination of Chris-

---

* In the Memoir of Captain Peter Heywood, in Marshall's Naval Biography, it is
related that the mutineers availing themselves of a fiction which had been created
by Lieutenant Bligh respecting Captain Cook, stated that they had fallen in with
him, and that he had sent the ship back for all the live stock that could be spared,
in order to form a settlement at a place called Wytootacke, which Bligh had discovered in his course to the Friendly Islands.

tian, who in vain expostulated with them on the folly of such a resolution, and the certain detection that must ensue

The implements being embarked, they proceeded therefore a second time to Otaheite, and were again well received by their friends, who replenished their stock of provision. During the passage Christian formed his intention of proceeding in the ship to some distant uninhabited island, for the purpose of permanently settling, as the most likely means of escaping the punishment which he well knew awaited him in the event of being discovered On communicating this plan to his shipmates he found only a few inclined to assent to it, but no objections were offered by those who dissented, to his taking the ship ; all they required was an equal distribution of such provisions and stores as might be useful Young, Brown, Mills, Williams, Quintal, M'Coy, Martin, Adams, and six natives (four of Otaheite and two of Tobouai) determined to follow the fate of Christian Remaining, therefore, only twenty-four hours at Otaheite, they took leave of their own comrades, and having invited on board several of the women with the feigned purpose of taking leave, the cables were cut and they were carried off to sea *

The mutineers now bade adieu to all the world, save the few individuals associated with them in exile But where that exile should be passed, was yet undecided the Marquesas Islands were first mentioned, but Christian, on reading Captain Carteret's account of Pitcairn Island, thought it better adapted to the purpose, and accordingly shaped a course thither. They reached it not many days afterwards ; and Christian, with one of the seamen, landed in a little nook, which we afterwards found very convenient for disembarkation They soon traversed the island sufficiently to be satisfied that it was exactly suited to their wishes. It possessed water, wood, a good soil, and some fruits. The anchorage in the offing was very bad, and landing for boats extremely hazardous. The mountains were so difficult of access, and the passes so narrow, that they might be maintained by a few persons against an army, and there were several caves, to which, in case of necessity, they could retreat, and where, as long as their provision lasted, they might bid defiance to their pursuers With this intelligence they returned on board, and brought the ship to an anchor in a small bay on the northern side of the island, which I have in consequence named " Bounty Bay," where every thing that could be of utility was landed, and where it was agreed to destroy the ship, either by running her on shore, or burning her Christian, Adams,

* The greater part of the mutineers who remained at Otaheite, were taken by his Majesty's ship Pandora, which was purposely sent out from England after lieutenant Bligh's return.

and the majority, were for the former expedient, but while they went to the forepart of the ship, to execute this business, Mathew Quintal set fire to the carpenter's store-room   The vessel burnt to the water's edge, and then drifted upon the rocks, where the remainder of the wreck was burnt for fear of discovery   This occurred on the 23d January, 1790.

Upon their first landing they perceived, by the remains of several habitations, morais, and three or four rudely sculptured images, which stood upon the eminence overlooking the bay where the ship was destroyed, that the island had been previously inhabited   Some apprehensions were, in consequence, entertained lest the natives should have secreted themselves, and in some unguarded moment make an attack upon them; but by degrees these fears subsided, and their avocations proceeded without interruption.

A suitable spot of ground for a village was fixed upon with the exception of which the island was divided into equal portions, but to the exclusion of the poor blacks, who being only friends of the seamen, were not considered as entitled to the same privileges   Obliged to lend their assistance to the others in order to procure a subsistence, they thus, from being their friends. in the course of time became their slaves   No discontent, however, was manifested, and they willingly assisted in the cultivation of the soil   In clearing the space that was allotted to the village, a row of trees was left between it and the sea, for the purpose of concealing the houses from the observation of any vessels that might be passing. and nothing was allowed to be erected that might in any way attract attention   Until these houses were finished, the sails of the Bounty were converted into tents; and when no longer required for that purpose, became very acceptable as clothing   Thus supplied with all the necessaries of life, and some of its luxuries, they felt their condition comfortable even beyond their most sanguine expectation, and every thing went on peaceably and prosperously for about two years, at the expiration of which, Williams, who had the misfortune to lose his wife about a month after his arrival, by a fall from a precipice while collecting birds' eggs. became dissatisfied, and threatened to leave the island in one of the boats of the Bounty, unless he had another wife, an unreasonable request, as it could not be complied with, except at the expense of the happiness of one of his companions. but Williams. actuated by selfish considerations alone, persisted in his threat, and the Europeans not willing to part with him, on account of his usefulness as an armourer, constrained one of the blacks to bestow his wife upon the applicant   The blacks, outrageous at this second act of flagrant injustice, made common cause with their companion, and matured a plan of revenge upon their aggressors, which, had it succeeded, would have proved fatal to all the Europeans   Fortu-

nately, the secret was imparted to the women, who ingeniously communicated it to the white men in a song, of which the words were,
" Why does black man sharpen axe ? to kill white man.'   The instant Christian became aware of the plot, he seized his gun and went
in search of the blacks, but with a view only of showing them that
their scheme was discovered, and thus by timely interference endeavouring to prevent the execution of it   He met one of them (Ohoo)
at a little distance from the village, taxed him with the conspiracy,
and, in order to intimidate him, discharged his gun, which he had
humanely loaded with powder only   Ohoo, however, imagining
otherwise, and that the bullet had missed its object, derided his un-
skilfulness, and fled into the woods, followed by his accomplice
Talaloo, who had been deprived of his wife   The remaining blacks,
finding their plot discovered purchased pardon by promising to murder their accomplices, who had fled, which they afterwards performed
ed by an act of the most odious treachery . Ohoo was betrayed and
murdered by his own nephew; and Talaloo, after an ineffectual
attempt made upon by poison, fell by the hands of his friend and
his wife, the very woman on whose account all the disturbance
began, and whose injuries Talaloo felt he was revenging in common
with his own

Tranquillity was by these means restored, and preserved for
about two years; at the expiration of which dissatisfaction was again
manifested by the blacks, in consequence of oppression and ill treatment, principally by Quintal and M'Coy   Meeting with no compassion or redress from their masters, a second plan to destroy their
oppressors was matured, and, unfortunately, too successfully executed

It was agreed that two of the blacks, Timoa and Nehow, should
desert from their masters, provide themselves with arms, and hide
in the woods, but maintain a frequent communication with the other
two, Tetaheite and Menalee, and that on a certain day they should
attack and put to death all the Englishmen, when at work in their
plantations   Tetaheite, to strengthen the party of the blacks on this
day, borrowed a gun and ammunition of his master, under the pretence of shooting hogs, which had become wild and very numerous,
but instead of using it in this way, he joined his accomplices, and
with them fell upon Williams and shot him.   Martin, who was at
no great distance, heard the report of the musket, and exclaimed,
" Well done ! we shall have a glorious feast to-day !" supposing that
a hog had been shot   The party proceeded from Williams' toward
Christian's plantation, where Menalee, the other black, was at work
with Mills and M'Coy , and, in order that the suspicions of the whites
might not be excited by the report they had heard, requested Mills
to allow him (Menalee) to assist them in bringing home the hog

they pretended to have killed   Mills agreed; and the four, being
united, proceeded to Christian, who was working at his yam-plot,
and shot him   Thus fell a man, who, from being the reputed ring-
leader of the mutiny, has obtained an unenviable celebrity, and
whose crime, if any thing can excuse mutiny, may perhaps be considered as in some degree palliated, by the tyranny which led to its
commission. •M'Coy, hearing his groans, observed to Mills, "there
was surely some person dying," but Mills replied, "It is only
Mainmast (Christian's wife) calling her children to dinner" The
white men being yet too strong for the blacks to risk a conflict with
them, it was necessary to conceit a plan, in order to separate Mills and
M'Coy   Two of them accordingly secreted themselves in M Coy's
house, and Tetaheite ran and told him that the two blacks who had
deserted were stealing things out of his house   M'Coy instantly
hastened to detect them, and on entering was fired at , but the ball
passed him   M'Coy immediately communicated the alarm to Mills,
and advised him to seek shelter in the woods ; but Mills, being quite
satisfied that one of the blacks whom he had made his friend would
not suffer him to be killed, determined to remain   M'Coy, less
confident, ran in search of Christian, but finding him dead, joined
Quintal (who was already apprised of the work of destruction, and
had sent his wife to give the alarm to the others), and fled with
him to the woods.

Mills had scarcely been left alone, when the two blacks fell upon
him, and he became a victim to his misplaced confidence in the fidelity of his friend   Martin and Brown were next separately murdered by Menalee and Tenina , Menalee effecting with a maul what
the musket had left unfinished. Tenina, it is said, wished to save
the life of Brown, and fired at him with powder only, desiring him,
at the same time, to fall as if killed , but, unfortunately rising too
soon, the other black, Menalee, shot him.

Adams was first apprised of his danger by Quintal's wife, who,
in hurrying through his plantation, asked why he was working at
such a time ? Not understanding the question, but seeing her
alarmed, he followed her, and was almost immediately met by the
blacks, whose appearance exciting suspicion, he made his escape
into the woods. After remaining three or four hours, Adams, thinking all was quiet, stole to his yam-plot for a supply of provisions;
his movements however did not escape the vigilance of the blacks,
who attacked and shot him through the body, the ball entering at
his right shoulder, and passing out through his throat   He fell
upon his side, and was instantly assailed by one of them with the
butt end of the gun , but he parried the blows at the expense of a
broken finger   Tetaheite then placed his gun to his side, but it
fortunately missed fire twice   Adams, recovering a little from the

shock of the wound, sprang on his legs, and ran off with as much
speed as he was able. and fortunately outstripped his pursuers, who
seeing him likely to escape, offered him protection if he would stop
Adams, much exhausted by his wound, readily accepted their terms,
and was conducted to Christian's house, where he was kindly treated   Here this day of bloodshed ended, leaving only four Englishmen alive out of nine   It was a day of emancipation to the blacks,
who were now masters of the island, and of humiliation and retribu-
tion to the whites.

Young, who was a great favourite with the women, and had, during this attack, been secreted by them, was now also taken to
Christian's house.   The other two, M'Coy and Quintal, who had
always been the great oppressors of the blacks, escaped to the mountains, where they supported themselves upon the produce of the
ground about them

The party in the village lived in tolerable tranquility for about a
week: at the expiration of which, the men of colour began to quarrel about the right of choosing the women whose husbands had been
killed, which ended in Menalee's shooting Timoa as he sat by the
side of Young's wife, accompanying her song with his flute   Timoa
not dying immediately, Menalee reloaded, and deliberately despatched him by a second discharge   He afterwards attacked Tetaheite, who was condoling with Young's wife for the loss of her favourite black, and would have murdered him also, but for the interference of the women   Afraid to remain longer in the village, he
escaped to the mountains and joined Quintal and M'Coy, who,
though glad of his services, at first recieved him with suspicion
This great acquisition to their force enabled them to bid defiance to
the opposite party, and to show their strength, and that they were
provided with muskets, they appeared on a ridge of mountains,
within sight of the village, and fired a volley which so alarmed the
others that they sent Adams to say, if they would kill the black
man, Menalee, and return to the village, they would all be friends
again   The terms were so far complied with that Menalee was
shot; but, apprehensive of the sincerity of the remaining blacks,
they refused to return while they were alive

Adams says it was not long before the widows of the white men
so deeply deplored their loss, that they determined to revenge their
death, and conceited a plan to murder the only two remaining men
of colour   Another account, communicated by the islanders, is
that it was only part of a plot formed at the same time that Menalee was murdered, which could not be put in execution before
However this may be, it was equally fatal to the poor blacks.   The
arrangement was, that Susan should murder one of them, Tetaheite,
while he was sleeping by the side of his favourite, and that Young

should at the same instant, upon a signal being given, shoot the other, Nehow. The unsuspecting Tetaheite retired as usual, and fell by the blow of an axe , the other was looking at Young loading his gun, which he supposed was for the purpose of shooting hogs, and requested him to put in a good charge, when he received the deadly contents

In this manner the existence of the last of the men of colour terminated, who, though treacherous and revengeful, had, it is feared, too much cause for complaint   The accomplishment of this fatal scheme was immediately communicated to the two absentees, and their return solicited.   But so many instances of treachery had occurred, that they would not believe the report, though delivered by Adams himself, until the hands and heads of the deceased were produced, which being done, they returned to the village.   This eventful day was the 3d October, 1793.   There were now left upon the island, Adams, Young, M'Coy, and Quintal, ten women, and some children   Two months after this period, Young commenced a manuscript journal, which affords a good insight into the state of the island, and the occupations of the settlers   From it we learn, that they lived peaceably together, building their houses, fencing in and cultivating their grounds, fishing, and catching birds, and constructing pits for the purpose of entrapping hogs, which had become very numerous and wild, as well as injurious to the yam-crops. The only discontent appears to have been among the women, who lived promiscuously with the men, frequently changing their abode.

Young says March 12, 1794, "Going over to borrow a rake, to rake the dust off my ground, I saw Jenny having a skull in her hand.   I asked her whose it was? and was told it was Jack Williams's   I desired it might be buried   the women who were with Jenny gave me for answer, it should not   I said it should, and demanded it accordingly   I was asked the reason why I, in particular, should insist on such a thing, when the rest of the white men did not?   I said, if they gave them leave to keep the skulls above ground, I did not.   Accordingly when I saw M'Coy, Smith, and Mat. Quintal, I acquainted them with it, and said, I thought that if the girls did not agree to give up the heads of the five white men in a peaceable manner, they ought to be taken by force, and buried " About this time the women appear to have been much dissatisfied; and Young's journal declares that " since the massacre, it has been the desire of the greater part of them to get some conveyance, to enable them to leave the island "   This feeling continued, and on the 14th April, 1794, was so strongly urged, that the men began to build them a boat , but wanting planks and nails, Jenny, who now resides at Otaheite, in her zeal tore up the boards of her house, and endeavoured, though without success, to persuade some others to follow her example.

On the 13th August following, the vessel was finished, and on the 15th she was launched   but, as Young says, "according to expectation she upset," and it was most fortunate for them that she did so; for had they launched out upon the ocean, where could they have gone ? or what could a few ignorant women have done by themselves, drifting upon the waves, but ultimately have fallen a sacrifice to their folly ?   However, the fate of the vessel was a great disappointment, and they continued much dissatisfied with their condition ; probably not without some reason, as they were kept in great subordination, and were frequently beaten by M'Coy and Quintal, who appear to have been of very quarrelsome dispositions; Quintal in particular, who proposed " not to laugh, joke, or give any thing to any of the girls "

On the 16th August they dug a grave, and buried the bones of the murdered people   and on October 3d, 1794, they celebrated the murder of the black men at Quintal's house.   On the 11th November a conspiracy of the women to kill the white men in their sleep was discovered ; upon which they were all seized, and a disclosure ensued ; but no punishment appears to have been inflicted upon them, in consequence of their promising to conduct themselves properly, and never again to give any cause "even to suspect their behaviour." However, though they were pardoned, Young observes, "We did not forget their conduct ; and it was agreed among us, that the first female who misbehaved should be put to death ; and this punishment was to be repeated on each offence until we could discover the real intentions of the women " Young appears to have suffered much from mental perturbation in consequence of these disturbances ; and observes of himself on the two following days, that " he was bothered and idle "

The suspicions of the men induced them, on the 15th, to conceal two muskets in the bush, for the use of any person who might be so fortunate as to escape, in the event of an attack being made On the 30th November, the women again collected and attacked them ; but no lives were lost, and they returned on being once more pardoned, but were again threatened with death the next time they misbehaved. Threats thus repeatedly made, and as often unexecuted, as might be expected soon lost their effect, and the women formed a party whenever their displeasure was excited, and hid themselves in the unfrequented parts of the island, carefully providing themselves with fire-arms   In this manner the men were kept in continual suspense, dreading the result of each disturbance, as the numerical strength of the women was much greater than their own

On the 4th of May, 1795, two canoes were begun, and in two days completed. These were used for fishing, in which employment the people were frequently successful, supplying themselves with rock-fish and large mackarel On the 27th of December following, they were greatly alarmed by the appearance of a ship close in with the island Fortunately for them, there was a tremendous surf upon the rocks, the weather wore a very threatening aspect, and the ship stood to the S. E , and at noon was out of sight Young appears to have thought this a providential escape, as the sea for a week after was " smoother than they had ever recollected it since their arrival on the island "

So little occurred in the year 1796, that one page records the whole of the events; and throughout the following year there are but three incidents worthy of notice The first, their endeavour to procure a quantity of meat for salting; the next, their attempt to make syrup from the tee-plant (*dracœna terminalis*) and sugar-cane; and the third, a serious accident that happened to M'Coy, who fell from a cocoa-nut-tree and hurt his right thigh, sprained both his ancles and wounded his side The occupations of the men continued similar to those already related, occasionally enlivened by visits to the opposite side of the island They appear to have been more sociable, dining frequently at each other's houses, and contributing more to the comfort of the women, who, on their part, gave no ground for uneasiness There was also a mutual accommodation amongst them in regard to provisions, of which a regular account was taken If one person was successful in hunting, he lent the others as much meat as they required, to be repaid at leisure ; and the same occurred with yams, taros, &c , so that they lived in a very domestic and tranquil state

It unfortunately happened that M'Coy had been employed in a distillery in Scotland , and being very much addicted to liquor, he tried an experiment with the tee-root, and on the 20th April 1798, succeeded in producing a bottle of ardent spirit This success induced his companion, Mathew Quintal, to "alter his kettle into a still," a contrivance which unfortunately succeeded too well, as frequent intoxication was the consequence, with M'Coy in particular upon whom at length it produced fits of delirium, in one of which, he threw himself from a cliff and was killed The melancholy fate of this man created so forcible an impression on the remaining few, that they resolved never again to touch spirits ; and Adams, I have every reason to believe, to the day of his death kept his vow

The journal finishes nearly at the period of M'Coy's death, which is not related in it but we learned from Adams, that about 1799 Quintal lost his wife by a fall from the cliff while in search

of birds' eggs, that he grew discontented, and, though there were
several disposable women on the island, and he had already experienced the fatal effects of a similar demand, nothing would satisfy him
but the wife of one of his companions Of course neither of them
felt inclined to accede to this unreasonable indulgence ; and he
sought an opportunity of putting them both to death He was
fortunately foiled in his first attempt, but swore he would repeat it.
Adams and Young, having no doubt he would follow up his resolution, and fearing he might be more successful in his next attempt,
came to the conclusion, that their own lives were not safe while he
was in existence, and that they were justified in putting him to
death, which they did with an axe.

Such was the melancholy fate of seven of the leading mutineers,
who escaped from justice only to add murder to their former
crimes ; for though some of them may not have actually embrued
their hands in the blood of their fellow-creatures, yet all were ac-
cessary to the deed.

As Christian and Young were descended from respectable
parents, and had received educations suitable to their birth, it might
be supposed that they felt their altered and degraded situation much
more than the seamen, who were comparatively well off ; but if so,
Adams says, they had the good sense to conceal it, as not a single
murmur or regret escaped them ; on the contrary, Christian was always cheerful, and his example was of the greatest service in
exciting his companions to labour He was naturally of a happy, ingenuous disposition, and won the good opinion, and respect of all those who served under him ; which cannot be better exemplified than by his maintaining, under circumstances of
great perplexity, the respect and regard of all who were associated
with him up to the hour of his death ; and even at the period of
our visit, Adams, in speaking of him, never omitted to say " *Mr.
Christian* "

Adams and Young were now the sole survivors out of the fifteen males that landed upon the island They were both, and
more particularly Young, of a serious turn of mind ; and it would
have been wonderful, after the many dreadful scenes at which they
had assisted, if the solitude and tranquility that ensued had not
disposed them to repentance. During Christian's lifetime they had
only once read the church service, but since his decease this had
been regularly done on every Sunday They now, however, resolved
to have morning and evening family prayers, to add afternoon service to the duty of the Sabbath, and to train up their own children
and those of their late unfortunate companions, in piety and virtue.

In the execution of this resolution, Young's education enabled
him to be of the greatest assistance, but he was not long suffered

to survive his repentance An asthmatic complaint, under which he had for some time labored, terminated his existence about a year after the death of Quintal, and Adams was left the sole survivor of the misguided and unfortunate mutineers of the Bounty The loss of his last companion was a great affliction to him, and was for some time most severely felt It was a catastrophe, however, that more than ever disposed him to repentance, and determined him to execute the pious resolution he had made, in the hope of expiating his offences.

His reformation could not, perhaps, have taken place at a more propitious moment. Out of nineteen children upon the island, there were several between the ages of seven and nine years ; who, had they been longer suffered to follow their own inclinations, might have acquired habits which it would have been difficult, if not impossible, for Adams to eradicate The moment was therefore most favorable for his design, and his laudable exertions were attended by advantages both to the objects of his care and to his own mind, which surpassed his most sanguine expectations He, nevertheless, had an arduous task to perform. Besides the children to be educated, the Otaheitan women were to be converted ; and as the example of the parents had a powerful influence over their children, he resolved to make them his first care. Here also his labours succeeded ; the Otaheitans were naturally of a tractable disposition, and gave him less trouble than he anticipated · the children also acquired such a thirst after scriptural knowledge, that Adams in a short time had little else to do than to answer their inquiries and put them in the right way. As they grew up, they acquired fixed habits of morality and piety ; their colony improved, intermarriages occurred and they now form a happy and well-regulated society, the merit of which, in a great degree, belongs to Adams, and tends to redeem the former errors of his life.

CHAPTER IV.

Bounty Bay—Observatory landed—Manners, Customs, Occupations, Amusements,
&c of the Natives—Village—Description of the Island—Its produce—Marriage
of Adams—Barge hoisted out—Departure—General description.

Having detailed the particulars of the mutiny in the Bounty, and the fate of the most notorious of the ringleaders, and having brought the history of Pitcairn Island down to the present period, I shall return to the party who had assembled on board the ship to greet us on our arrival.

The Blossom was so different, or to use the expression of our visiters, "so rich," compared with the other ships they had seen,[*] that they were constantly afraid of giving or committing some injury. and would not even move without first asking permission. This diffidence gave us full occupation for some time, as our restless visiters, anxious to see every thing, seldom directed their attention long to any particular object, or remained in one position or place Having no latches to their doors, they were ignorant of the manner of opening ours; and we were constantly attacked on all sides with "Please may I sit down or get up, or go out of the cabin?" or, "Please to open or shut the door" Their applications were, however, made with such good nature and simplicity that it was impossible not to feel the greatest pleasure in paying attention to them They very soon learnt the christian name of every officer in the ship, which they always used in conversation instead of the surname, and wherever a similarity to their own occurred, they attached themselves to that person as a matter of course

It was many hours after they came on board before the ship could get near the island, during which time they so ingratiated themselves with us that we felt the greatest desire to visit their houses, and rather than pass another night at sea we put off in the

---

[*] It was so long since the visit of the Briton and Tagus, that they had forgotten their appearance

boats, though at a considerable distance from the land, and accompanied them to the shore. We followed our guides past a rugged point surmounted by tall spiral rocks, known to the islanders as St. Paul's rocks, into a spacious iron-bound bay, where the Bounty found her last anchorage. In this bay, which is bounded by lofty cliffs almost inaccessible, it was proposed to land   Thickly branched evergreens skirt the base of these hills, and in summer afford a welcome retreat from the rays of an almost vertical sun. In the distance are seen several high pointed rocks which the pious highlanders have named after the most zealous of the Apostles, and outside of them is a square basaltic islet   Formidable breakers fringe the coast, and seem to present an insurmountable barrier to all access.

We here brought our boats to an anchor, in consequence of the passage between the sunken rocks being much too intricate, and we trusted ourselves to the natives, who landed us, two at a time, in their whale-boat   The difficulty of landing was more than repaid by the friendly reception we met with on the beach from Hannah Young, a very interesting young woman, the daughter of Adams   In her eagerness to greet her father, she had outrun her female companions, for whose delay she thought it necessary in the first place to apologize, by saying they had all been over the hill in company with John Buffet to look at the ship, and were not yet returned   It appeared that John Buffet, who was a sea-faring man, ascertained that the ship was a man-of-war, and without knowing exactly why, became so alarmed for the safety of Adams that he either could not or would not answer any of the interrogations which were put to him. This mysterious silence set all the party in tears, as they feared he had discovered something adverse to their patriarch   At length his obduracy yielded to their entreaties   but before he explained the cause of his conduct, the boats were seen to put off from the ship, and Hannah immediately hurried to the beach to kiss the old man's cheek, which she did with a fervency demonstrative of the warmest affection   Her apology for her companions was rendered unnecessary by their appearance on the steep and circuitous path down the mountain, who, as they arrived on the beach, successively welcomed us to their island, with a simplicity and sincerity which left no doubt of the truth of their professions

They almost all wore the cloth of the island: their dress consisted of a petticoat, and a mantle loosely thrown over the shoulders, and reaching to the ancles   Their stature was rather above the common height, and their limbs, from being accustomed to work and climb the hills, had acquired unusual muscularity : but their features and manners were perfectly feminine   Their complexion, though fairer than that of the men, was of a dark gipsy hue, but its deep colour was less conspicuous, by being contrasted with dark glossy hair, which hung down over their shoulders in long waving tresses, nicely oiled . in front it was tastefully turned back from the forehead and temples and was retained in that position by a chaplet of small red or white aromatic blossoms, newly gathered from the flower-tree (*morinda citrifolia*); or from the tobacco plant, their countenances were lively and good natured their eyes dark and animated, and each possessed an enviable row of teeth. Such was the agreeable impression of their first appearance, which was heightened by the wish expressed simultaneously by the whole groupe, that we were come to stay several days with them As the sun was going down, we signified our desire to get to the village and to pitch the observatory before dark, and this was no sooner made known, than every instrument and article found a carrier.

We took the only pathway which leads from the landing-place to the village, and soon experienced the difficulties of the ascent, which the distant appearance of the ground led us to anticipate To the natives, however, there appeared to be no obstacles women as well as men bore their burthens over the most difficult parts without inconvenience ; while we, obliged at times to have recourse to tufts of shrubs or grass for assistance, experienced serious delay, being also incommoded by the heat of the weather, and by swarms of house-flies which infest the island, and are said to have been imported there by H. M. S Briton.

As soon as we had gained the first level, our party rested on some large stones that lay half buried in long grass on one side of a ravine, from which the blue sky was nearly concealed by the overlapping branches of palm-trees Here, through the medium of our female guides, who, furnished with the spreading leaves of the tee-plant, drove away our troublesome persecutors, we obtained a respite from their attacks

Having refreshed ourselves, we resumed our journey over a more easy path, and after crossing two valleys, shaded by cocoa-nut trees, we arrived at the village. It consisted of five houses, built upon a cleared piece of ground sloping to the sea, and commanding a distant view of the horizon, through a break in an extensive wood of palms While the men assisted to pitch our tent, the women employed themselves in preparing our dinner, or more properly supper, as it was eight o'clock at night.

The manner of cooking in Pitcairn's Island is similar to that of Otaheite, which, as some of my readers may not recollect, I shall briefly describe An oven is made in the ground, sufficiently large to contain a good-sized pig, and is lined throughout with stones nearly equal in size, which have been previously made as hot as possible. These are covered with some broad leaves, generally of the tee-plant, and on them is placed the meat If it be a pig, its inside is lined with heated stones, as well as the oven such vegetables as are to be cooked are then placed round the animal the whole is carefully covered with leaves of the tee, and buried beneath a heap of earth, straw, or rushes and boughs, which, by a little use, becomes matted into one mass In about an hour and a quarter the animal is sufficiently cooked, and is certainly more thoroughly done than it would be by a fire

By the time the tent was up and the instruments secured, we were summoned to a meal cooked in this manner, than which a less sumptuous fare would have satisfied appetites rendered keen by long abstinence and a tiresome journey Our party divided themselves that they might not crowd one house in particular: Adams did not entertain, but at Christian's I found a table spread with plates, knives, and forks; which, in so remote a part of the world, was an unexpected sight They were, it is true, far from uniform; but by one article being appropriated for another, we all found something to put our portion upon; and but few of the natives were obliged to substitute their fingers for articles which are indispensable to the comfort of more polished life The smoking pig, by a skilful dissection, was soon portioned to every guest, but no one ventured to put its excellent qualities to the test until a lengthened *Amen*, pronounced by all the party, had succeeded an emphatic grace delivered by the village parson " *Turn to*," was then the signal for attack, and as it is convenient that all the party should finish their meal about the same time, in order that one grace might serve for all, each made the most of his time. In Pitcairn's Island it is not deemed proper to touch even a bit of bread without a grace before and after it, and a person is accused of inconsistency if he leaves off and begins again. So strict is their observance of this form, that we do not know of any instance in which it has been forgotten. On one occasion I had engaged Adams in conversation, and he incautiously took the first mouthful without having said his grace; but before he had swallowed it, he recollected himself, and feeling as if he had committed a crime, immediately put away what he had in his mouth, and commenced his prayer.

Welcome cheer, hospitality, and good humour, were the characteristics of the feast; and never was their beneficial influence more practically exemplified than on this occasion, by the demolition of nearly all that was placed before us With the exception of some wine we had brought with us, water was the only beverage This was placed in a large jug at one end of the board, and, when necessary, was passed round the table—a ceremony at which, in Pitcairn's Island in particular, it is desirable to be the first partaker, as the gravy of the dish is invariably mingled with the contents of the pitcher. the natives, who prefer using their fingers to forks, being quite indifferent whether they hold the vessel by the handle or by the spout. Three or four torches made with doodoe nuts (*aleurites triloba*), strung upon the fibres of a palm-leaf, were stuck in tin pots at the end of the table, and formed an excellent substitute for candles, except that they gave a considerable heat, and cracked, and fired, somewhat to the discomfiture of the person whose face was near them.

Notwithstanding these deficiencies, we made a very comfortable and hearty supper, heard many little anecdotes of the place, and derived much amusement from the singularity of the inquiries of our hosts. One regret only intruded itself upon the general conviviality, which we did not fail to mention, namely, that there was so wide a distinction between the sexes. This was the remains of a custom very common among the South Sea Islands, which in some places is carried to such an extent, that it imposes death upon the woman who shall eat in the presence of her husband; and though the distinction between man and wife is not here carried to that extent, it is still sufficiently observed to exclude all the women from table, if there happens to be a deficiency of seats. In Pitcairn's Island, they have settled ideas of right and wrong, to which they obstinately adhere; and, fortunately, they have imbibed them generally from the best source.

In the instance in question, they have, however, certainly erred; but of this they could not be persuaded, nor did they, I believe, thank us for our interference. Their argument was, that man was made first, and ought, consequently, on all occasions, to be served first—a conclusion which deprived us of the company of the women at table, during the whole of our stay at the island. Far from considering themselves neglected, they very good-naturedly chatted with us behind our seats, and flapped away the flies, and by a gentle tap, accidentally or playfully delivered, reminded us occasionally of the honour that was done us. The conclusion of our meal was the signal for the women and children to prepare their own, to whom we resigned our seats, and strolled out to enjoy the freshness of the night. It was late by the time the women had finished, and we were not sorry when we were shown to the beds prepared for us. The mattress was composed of palm-trees, covered with native cloth; the sheets were of the same material; and we knew by the crackling of them, that they were quite new from the loom or beater. The whole arrangement was extremely comfortable, and highly inviting to repose, which the freshness of

the apartment, rendered cool by a free circulation of air through
its sides, enabled us to enjoy without any annoyance from heat
or insects   One interruption only disturbed our first sleep ; it was
the pleasing melody of the evening hymn, which, after the lights
were put out, was chaunted by the whole family in the middle of
the room   In the morning also we were awoke by their morning
hymn and family devotion   As we were much tired, and the sun's
rays had not yet found their way through the broad opening of the
apartment, we composed ourselves to rest again , and on awaking
found that all the natives were gone to their several occupations,—
the men to offer what assistance they could to our boats in landing,
carrying burthens for the seamen, or to gather what fruits were in
season.   Some of the women had taken our linen to wash ; those
whose turn it was to cook for the day were preparing the oven, the
pig, and the yams ; and we could hear, by the distant reiterated
strokes of the beater,* that others were engaged in the manufacture of cloth.   By our bedside had already been placed some ripe
fruits ; and our hats were crowned with chaplets of the fresh blossom of the nono, or flower-tree *(morinda citrifolia)*, which the
women had gathered in the freshness of the morning dew.   On
looking round the apartment, though it contained several beds, we
found no partition, curtain, or screens ; they had not yet been considered necessary   So far indeed, from concealment being thought
of when we were about to get up, the women, anxious to show
their attention, assembled to wish us a good morning, and to inquire in what way they could best contribute to our comforts, and
to present us with some little gift, which the produce of the island
afforded   Many persons would have felt awkward at rising and
dressing before so many pretty black-eyed damsels assembled in
the centre of a spacious room , but by a little habit we overcame
this embarrassment ; and found the benefit of their services in
fetching water as we required it, and substituting clean linen for
such as we pulled off

It must be remembered, that with these people, as with the
other islanders of the South Seas, the custom has generally been
to go naked, the maro with the men excepted, and with the women the petticoat, or kilt, with a loose covering over the bust,
which, indeed, in Pitcairn's Island, they are always careful to conceal ; consequently, an exposure to that extent carried with it no
feeling whatever of indelicacy ; or, I may safely add, that the Pitcairn Islanders would have been the last persons to incur the charge.

We assembled at breakfast about noon the usual eating hour
of the natives, though they do not confine themselves to that pe-

* This is an instrument used for the manufacture of their cloth

riod exactly, but take their meal whenever it is sufficiently cooked, and afterwards availed ourselves of their proffered services to show us the island, and under their guidance first inspected the village, and what lay in its immediate vicinity.   In an adjoining house we found two young girls seated upon the ground, employed in the laborious exercise of beating out the bark of the cloth-tree, which they intended to present to us, on our departure, as a keepsake. The hamlet consisted of five cottages, built more substantially than neatly, upon a cleared patch of ground, sloping to the northward, from the high land of the interior to the cliffs which overhang the sea, of which the houses command a distant view in a northern direction.   In the N E quarter, the horizon may also be seen peeping between the stems of the lofty palms, whose graceful branches nod like ostrich plumes to the refreshing trade-wind   To the northward, and northwestward, thicker groves of palm-trees rise in an impenetrable wood, from two ravines which traverse the hills in various directions to their summit.   Above the one, to the westward, a lofty mountain rears its head, and towards the sea terminates in a fearful precipice filled with caverns, in which the different sea-fowl find an undisturbed retreat   Immediately round the village are the small enclosures for fattening pigs, goats, and poultry; and beyond them, the cultivated grounds producing the banana, plantain, melon, yam, taro, sweet potatoes, appai, tee, and cloth plant, with other useful roots, fruits, and shrubs, which extend far up the mountain and to the southward; but in this particular direction they are excluded from the view by an immense banyan tree, two hundred paces in circumference, whose foilage and branches form of themselves a canopy impervious to the rays of the sun.   Every cottage has its out-house for making cloth, its baking-place, its sty, and its poultry-house.

Within the enclosure of palm-trees is the cemetery where the few persons who had died on the island, together with those who met with violent deaths, are deposited   Besides the houses abovementioned, there are three or four others built upon the plantations beyond the palm groves.   One of these, situated higher up the hill than the village, belonged to Adams, who had retired from the bustle of the hamlet to a more quiet and sequestered spot, to enjoy the advantages of an elevated situation, so desirable in warm countries; and in addition to these again there are four other cottages to the eastward which belong to the Youngs and Quintals

All these cottages are strongly built of wood in an oblong form, and thatched with the leaves of the palm-tree bent round the stem of the same branch, and laced horizontally to rafters, so placed as to give a proper pitch to the roof   The greater part have an upper story, which is appropriated to sleeping, and contain four beds built in the angles of the room, each sufficiently large for three or four persons to lie on. They are made of wood of the cloth-tree, and are raised eighteen inches above the floor, a mattress of palm-leaves is laid upon the planks, and above it three sheets of the cloth-plant, which form an excellent substitute for linen   The lower room generally contains one or more beds, but is always used as their eating-room, and has a broad table in one part, with several stools placed round it.   The floor is elevated above a foot from the ground, and, as well as the sides of the house is made of stout plank, and not of bamboo, or stone, as stated by Captain Folger; indeed they have not a piece of bamboo on the island; nor have they any mats.   The floor is a fixture, but the sideboards are let into a groove in the supporters, and can be removed at pleasure, according to the state of the weather, and the whole side may, if required, be laid open.   The lower room communicates with the upper by a stout ladder in the centre, and leads up through a trap-door into the bedroom

From the village several pathways (for roads there are none) diverge, and generally lead into the valleys, which afford a less difficult ascent to the upper part of the island than the natural slope of the hills; still they are very rugged and steep, and in the rainy season so slippery that it is almost impossible for any person, excepting the natives, to traverse them with safety. We selected one which led over the mountain to the landing-place, on the opposite side of the island, and visited the several plantations upon the higher grounds, which extend towards the mountain with a gentle slope   Here the mutineers originally built their summer-houses, for the purpose of enjoying the breeze and overlooking the yam grounds, which are more productive than those lower down. Near these plantations are the remains of some ancient morais; and a spot is pointed out as the place where Christian was first buried.   By a circuitous and, to us, difficult path, we reached the ridge of the mountain, the height of which is 1109 feet above the sea; this is the highest part of the island.   The ridge extends in a north and south direction, and unites two small peaks: it is so narrow as to be in many parts scarcely three feet wide, and forms a dangerous pass between two fearful precipices.   The natives were so accustomed to climb these crags that they unconcernedly skipped from point to point like the hunters of chamois; and young Christian actually jumped upon the very peak of a cliff, which was so small as to be scarcely sufficient for his feet to rest upon, and from which any other person would have shuddered even to look down upon the beach, lying many hundred feet at its base   At the northern extremity of this ridge is a cave of some interest, as being the intended retreat of Christian, in the event of a landing being effected by any ship sent in pursuit of him, and where he resolved to sell his life as dearly as he could   In this recess he always kept a store of provisions, and near it erected a small hut, well concealed by trees, which served the purpose of a watchhouse.   So difficult was the approach to this cave, that even if the party were successful in crossing the ridge, as long as his ammunition lasted, he might have bid defiance to any force   An unfrequented and dangerous path leads from this place to a peak which commands a view of the western and southern coasts.   at this height, on a clear day, a perfect map of the bottom is exhibited by the different coloured waters. On all points the island is terminated by cliffs, or rocky projections, off which he scattered numerous fragments of rock, rising like so many black pinnacles amid the surf, which on all sides rolls in upon the shore

We descended by a less abrupt slope than that by which we advanced, and took our way through yam grounds to a ravine which brought us to the village   The path leading down this ravine is, in many places, so precipitous, that we were constantly in danger of slipping and rolling into the depths below, which the assistance of the natives alone prevented.

While we were thus borrowing help from others, and grasping every tuft of grass and bough that offered its friendly support, we were overtaken by a groupe of chubby little children, trudging unconcernedly on, munching a water melon, and balancing on their heads calabashes of water, which they had brought from the opposite side of the island.   They smiled at our helplessness as they passed, and we felt their innocent reproof, but we were still unpractised in such feats, while they, from being trained to them, had acquired a footing and a firmness which habit alone can produce

It was dark when we reached the houses, but we found by a whoop which echoed through the woods, that we were not the last from home.   This whoop, peculiar to the place, is so shrill, that it may be heard half over the island, and the ear of the natives is so quick, that they will catch it when we could distinguish nothing of the kind   By the tone in which it is delivered, they also know the wants of the person, and who it is   These shrill sounds, which we had just heard, informed us, and those who were at the village, that a party had lost their way in the woods.   A blazing beacon was immediately made, which, together with a few more whoops to direct the party, soon brought the absentees home   Their perfection in these signals will be manifest from the following anecdote · I was one day crossing the mountain which intersects the island, with Christian , we had not long parted with their whale-boat on the western side of the island, and were descending a ravine amidst a thicket of trees, when he turned round and said, "The whale-boat is come round to Bounty Bay ," at which I was not a little surprised, as I had heard nothing, and we could not see through the wood , but he heard the signal ; and when we got down it proved to be the case.

In this little retreat there is not much variety, and the description of one day's occupation serves equally for its successor The dance is a recreation very rarely indulged in , but as we particularly requested it, they would not refuse to gratify us   A large room in Quintal's house was prepared for the occasion, and the company were ranged on one side of the apartment, glowing beneath a blazing string of doodoe nuts , the musicians were on the other, under the direction of Arthur Quintal   He was seated upon the ground, as head musician, and had before him a large gourd, and a piece of musical wood (poroo), which he balanced nicely upon his toes, that there might be the less interruption to its vibrations   He struck the instrument alternately with two sticks, and was accompanied by Dolly, who performed very skilfully with both hands upon a gourd, which had a longitudinal hole cut in one end of it , rapidly beating the orifice with the palms of her hands, and releasing it again with uncommon dexterity, so as to produce a tattoo, but in perfect time with the other instrument   A third performed upon the Bounty's old copper fish-kettle, which formed a sort of bass   To this exhilarating music, three *grown-up* females stood up to dance, but with a reluctance which showed it was done only to oblige us, as they consider such performances an inroad upon their usual innocent pastimes   The figure consisted of such parts of the Otaheitan dance as were thought most decorous, and was little more than a shuffling of the feet, sliding past each other, and snapping their fingers, but even this produced, at times, considerable laughter from the female spectators, perhaps from some association of ridiculous ideas, which we as strangers, did not feel , and no doubt had our opinion of the performance been consulted, it would have essentially differed from theirs.   They did not long continue these diversions, from an idea that it was too great a levity to be continued long ; and only the three before-mentioned ladies could be prevailed upon to exhibit their skill   One of the officers, with a view of contributing to the mirth of the colonists, had obligingly brought his violin on shore, and, as an inducement for them to dance again, offered to play some country dances and reels, if they would proceed; but they could not be tempted to do so   They, however, solicited a specimen of the capabilities of the instrument, which was granted, and, though very well executed, did not give the satisfaction which we anticipated   They had not yet arrived at a state of refinement to appreciate harmony, but were highly delighted with the rapid motion of the fingers, and always liked to be within sight of the instrument when it was played.   They were afterwards heard to say, that they preferred their own simple musical contrivance to the violin.   They did not appear to have the least ear for music : one of the officers took considerable pains to teach them the hundreth psalm, that they might not chaunt all the psalms and hymns to the same air, but they did not evince the least aptitude or desire to learn it.

The following day was devoted to the completion of our view of the island, of which the natives were anxious we should see every part   We accordingly set out with the same guides by a road which brought us to "the Rope," a steep cliff so called from its being necessary to descend it by a rope   It is situated at the eastern end of the island, and overlooks a small sandy bay lined with rocks, which render it dangerous for a boat to attempt to land there.

At the foot of "the Rope" were found some stone axes, and a hone, the manufacture of the aborigines, and upon the face of a large rock were some characters very rudely engraved, which we copied ; they appeared to have been executed by the Bounty's people, though Adams did not recollect it.   To the left of "the Rope" is a peak of considerable height, overlooking Bounty Bay. Upon this eminence the mutineers, on their arrival, found four images, about six feet in height, placed upon a platform ; and according to Adams's description not unlike the morais at Easter Island, excepting that they were upon a much smaller scale   One of these images, which had been preserved, was a rude representation of the human figure to the hips, and was hewn out of a piece of red lava.

Near this supposed morai, we were told that human bones and stone hatchets were occasionally dug up, but we could find only two bones, by which we might judge of the stature of these aborigines.   These were an os femoris and a part of a cranium of an unusual size and thickness.   The hatchets, of which we obtained several specimens, were made of a compact basaltic lava, not unlike clinkstone, very hard and capable of a fine polish   In shape they resembled those used at Otaheite, and by all the islanders of these seas that I have seen.   A large stone bowl was also found, similar to those used at Otaheite, and two stone huts.   That this island should have been inhabited is not extraordinary, when it is remembered that Easter Island, which is much more distant from the eastern world, was so, though nothing is known of the fate of the people.

From these images, and the large piles of stones on heights to which they must have been dragged with great labour, it may be concluded that the island was inhabited a considerable time ; and from bones being found always buried under these piles, and never upon the surface, we may presume that those who survived quitted the island in their canoes to seek an asylum elswhere.

Having this day seen every part of the island, we had no further

desire to ramble, and as the weather did not promise to be very fair,
I left the observatory in the charge of Mr Wolfe, and embarked,
accompanied by old Adams. Soon after he came on board it began
to blow, and for several days afterwards the wind prevented any
communication with the shore. The natives during this period were
in great apprehension: they went to the top of the island every
morning to look for the ship, and once, when she was not to be
seen, began to entertain the most serious doubts whether Adams
would be returned to them, but he, knowing we should close the
island as soon as the weather would permit, was rather glad of the
opportunity of remaining on board, and of again associating with his
countrymen   And although he had passed his sixty-fifth year, joined in the dances and songs of the forecastle, and was always
cheerful.

On the 16th the weather permitted a boat to be sent on shore,
and Adams was restored to his anxious friends. Previous to quitting the ship, he said it would add much to his happiness if I would
read the marriage ceremony to him and his wife, as he could not
bear the idea of living with her without its being done. He had
long wished for the arrival of a ship of war to set his conscience at
rest on that point   Though Adams was aged, and the old woman
had been blind and bed-ridden for several years, he made such a
point of it, that it would have been cruel to refuse him. They
were accordingly the next day duly united, and the event noted in
a register by John Buffet

The islanders were delighted at having us again among them, and
expressed themselves in the warmest terms. We soon found, through
our intercourse with these excellent people, that they had no wants
excepting such as had been created by an intercourse with vessels,
which have from time to time supplied them with European articles
Nature has been extremely bountiful to them, and necessity has
taught them how to apply her gifts to their own particular uses.
Still they have before them the prospect of an increasing population,
with limited means of supporting it   Almost every part of the
island capable of cultivation has been turned to account; but what
would have been the consequences of this increase, had not an accident discovered their situation, it is not difficult to foresee. and a
reflecting mind will naturally trace in that disclosure the benign interference of the same hand which has raised such a virtuous colony from so guilty a stock. Adams having contemplated the situation which the islanders would have been reduced to, begged, at our
first interview, that I would communicate with the government upon
the subject, which was done; and I am happy to say that, through
the interference of the Admiralty and Colonial office, means have
been taken for removing them to any place they may choose for

themselves; and a liberal supply of useful articles has recently been sent to them *

Some books of travels which were left from time to time on the island, and the accounts they had heard of foreign countries from their visiters, has created in the islanders a strong desire to travel, so much so that they one day undertook a voyage in their whale-boat to an island which they learnt was not very far distant from their own; but fortunately for them, as the compass on which they relied, one of the old Bounty's, was so rusty as to be quite useless. their curiosity yielded to discretion, and they returned before they lost sight of their native soil

The idea of passing all their days upon an island only two miles long, without seeing any thing of the world, or, what was a stronger argument, without doing any good in it, had with several of them been deeply considered. But family ties, and an ardent affection for each other, and for their native soil, had always interposed to prevent their going away singly. George Adams, however, having no wife to detain him, but, on the contrary, reasons for wishing to employ his thoughts on subjects foreign to his home, was very anxious to embark in the Blossom; and I would have acceded to his wishes, had not his mother wept bitterly at the idea of parting from him, and imposed terms touching his return to the island to which I could not accede It was a sore disappointment to poor George, whose case forms a striking instance of the rigid manner in which these islanders observe their word.

Wives upon Pitcairn Island, it may be imagined, are very scarce, as the same restrictions with regard to relationship exist as in England. George, in his early days, had fallen in love with Polly Young, a girl a little older than himself, but Polly, probably at that time liking some one else, and being at the age when young ladies' expectations are at the highest, had incautiously said, she *never would* give her hand to George Adams He, nevertheless, indulged a hope that she would one day relent; and to this end was unremitting in his endeavours to please her In this expectation he was not mistaken, his constancy and attentions, and, as he grew into manhood, his handsome form, which George took every opportunity of throwing into the most becoming attitudes before her, softened Polly's heart into a regard for him, and, had nothing passed before, she would willingly have given him her hand But the vow of her youth was not to be got over, and the love-sick couple languished on from day to day, victims to the folly of early resolutions

The weighty case was referred for our consideration; and the

---

* I have been informed since that they have changed their mind, and are at present contented with their situation

fears of the party were in some measure relieved by the result, which was, that it would be much better to marry than to continue unhappy, in consequence of a hasty determination made before the judgment was matured, they could not, however, be prevailed on to yield to our decision, and we left them unmarried *

Another instance of a rigid performance of promise was exemplified in old Adams, who is anxious that his own conduct should form an example to the rising generation

In the course of conversation, he one day said he would accompany me up the mountain, if there was nobody else near, and it so happened, that on the day I had leisure to go, the young men were all out of the way. Adams, therefore, insisted upon performing his engagement, though the day was extremely hot, and the journey was much too laborious, in any weather, for his advanced period of life He nevertheless set out, adding, "I said I would go, and so I will ; besides, without example, precept will have but little effect" At the first valley he threw off his hat, handkerchief, and jacket and left them by the side of the path, at the second his trousers were cast aside into a bush ; and had he been alone, or provided with a maro, his shirt would certainly have followed, thus disencumbered, he boldly led the way, which was well known to him in earlier days, but it was so long since he had trodden it, that we met with many difficulties At length we reached the top of the ridge, which we were informed was the place where M'Coy and Quintal appeared in defiance of the blacks. Adams felt so fatigued that he was now glad to lie down The breeze here blew so hard and cold, that a shirt alone was little use, and had he not been inured to all the changes of atmosphere, the sudden transition upon his aged frame must have been fatal

During the period we remained upon the island we were entertained at the board of the natives, sometimes dining with one person, and sometimes with another : their meals, as I have before stated, were not confined to hours, and always consisted of baked pig, yams, and taro, and more rarely of sweet potatoes.

The productions of the island being very limited, and intercourse with the rest of the world much restricted, it may be readily supposed their meals cannot be greatly varied. However they do their best with what they have, and cook it in different ways, the pig excepted, which is always baked There are several goats upon the island, but they dislike their flesh as well as their milk. Yams constitute their principal food ; these are boiled, baked, or made into pillihey (cakes), by being mixed with cocoa nuts, or bruised and formed into a soup Bananas are mashed, and made

* They have since been united, and have two children

into pancakes, or, like the yam, united with the milk of the cocoa-nut, into pillhhey, and eaten with molasses, extracted from the tee-root.   The taro root, by being rubbed, makes a very good substitute for bread, as well as the bananas, plantain, and appai.   Their common beverage is pure water, but they made for us a tea, extracted from the tee-plant, flavoured with ginger, and sweetened with the juice of the sugar-cane.   When alone, this beverage and fowl soup are used only for such as are ill.   They seldom kill a pig, but live mostly upon fruit and vegetables.   The duty of saying grace was performed by John Buffet, a recent settler among them, and their clergyman ; but if he was not present, it fell upon the eldest of the company   They have all a great dislike to spirits, in consequence of M'Coy having killed himself by too free an indulgence in it ; but wine in moderation is never refused.   With this simple diet, and being in the daily habit of rising early, and taking a great deal of exercise in the cultivation of their grounds, it was not surprising that we found them so athletic and free from complaints   When illness does occur, their remedies are as simple as their manner of living, and are limited to salt water, hot ginger tea, or abstinence, according to the nature of the complaint   They have no medicines, nor do they appear to require any, as these remedies have hitherto been found sufficient.

After their noontide meal, if their grounds do not require their attention, and the weather be fine, they go a little way out to sea in their canoes, and catch fish, of which they have several kinds, large and sometimes in abundance ; but it seldom happens that they have this time to spare ; for the cultivation of the ground, repairing their boats, houses, and making fishing-lines, with other employments, generally occupy the whole of each day.   At sunset they assemble at prayers as before, first offering their orison and thanksgiving, and then chaunting hymns.   After this follows their evening meal, and at an early hour, having again said their prayers, and chaunted the evening hymn, they retire to rest, but before they sleep, each person again offers up a short prayer upon his bed.

Such is the distribution of time among the grown people ; the younger part attend at school at regular hours, and are instructed in reading, writing, and arithmetic   They have very fortunately found an able and willing master in John Buffet, who belonged to a ship which visited the island, and was so infatuated with their behaviour, being himself naturally of a devout and serious turn of mind, that he resolved to remain among them ; and in addition to the instruction of the children, has taken upon himself the duty of clergyman, and is the oracle of the community *   During the

* Another seaman has settled amongst them, and is married to one of Adams's daughters , but he is not liked.

whole time I was with them I never heard them indulge in a joke, or other levity, and the practice of it is apt to give offence. they are so accustomed to take what is said in its literal meaning, that irony was always considered a falsehood in spite of explanation. They could not see the propriety of uttering what was not strictly true, for any purpose whatever

The Sabbath-day is devoted entirely to prayer, reading, and serious meditation. No boat is allowed to quit the shore, nor any work whatever to be done, cooking excepted, for which preparation is made the preceeding evening. I attended their church on this day, and found the service well conducted, the prayers were read by Adams, and the lessons by Buffet, the service being preceded by hymns The greatest devotion was apparent in every individual, and in the children there was a seriousness unknown in the younger part of our communities at home In the course of the Litany they prayed for their sovereign and royal family with much apparent loyalty and sincerity. Some family prayers, which were thought appropriate to their particular case, were added to the usual service; and Adams, fearful of leaving out any essential part, read in addition all those prayers which are intended only as substitutes for others. A sermon followed, which was very well delivered by Buffet, and lest any part of it should be forgotten or escape attention, it was read three times The whole concluded with hymns, which were first sung by the grown people, and afterwards by the children. The service thus performed was very long: but the neat and cleanly appearance of the congregation, the devotion that animated every countenance, and the innocence and simplicity of the little children, prevented the attendance from becoming wearisome. In about half an hour afterwards we again assembled to prayers, and at sunset service was repeated; so that, with their morning and evening prayers they may be said to have church five times on a Sunday.

Marriages and christenings are duly performed by Adams. A ring which has united every person on the island is used for the occasion, and given according to the prescribed form The age at which this is allowed to take place, with the men, is after they have reached their twentieth, and with the women, their eighteenth year.

All which remains to be said of these excellent people is, that they appear to live together in perfect harmony and contentment; to be virtuous, religious, cheerful, and hospitable, beyond the limits of prudence; to be patterns of conjugal and parental affection; and to have very few vices. We remained with them many days, and their unreserved manners gave us the fullest opportunity of becoming acquainted with any faults they might have possessed.

In the equipment of the Blossom, a boat was built purposely for her by Mr. Peak of Woolwich dock-yard, upon a model highly

creditable to his professional ability, and finished in the most complete manner.   As we were now about to enter a sea crowded with
islands which rise abruptly to the surface, without any soundings to
give warning of their vicinity, this little vessel was likely to be of
the greatest service, not only in a minute examination of the shore
but, by being kept a-head of the ship during the night, to give notice of any danger that might lie in her route   She was accordingly hoisted out while we were off this island, and stowed and provisioned for six weeks   I gave the command of her to Mr. Elson, the
master, an officer well qualified to perform the service I had in
view, having with him Mr R Beechey, midshipman, and a crew
of eight seamen and marines   Instructions were given to Mr. Elson for his guidance, and proper rendevous appointed in case of separation   We first experienced the utility of this excellent sea-boat,
in bringing off water from the shore through seas which in ordinary
cases would have proved serious obstacles ; and had there not been
so much surf upon the rocks. that the casks could only be got through
it by the natives swimming out with them, we should in a short
time have completed our stock of water   This process, however,
was very harrassing to them, who, besides this arduous task, had to
bring the water from a distance in calabashes , so, that with the utmost despatch, our daily supply scarcely equalled the consumption,
and we were compelled to trust to the hope of being more fortunate
at some other island

During the period of our stay in the vicinity of the island, we
scarcely saw the sun, and I began to despair of being able to fix our
position with sufficient accuracy   On the 20th, however, the clouds
cleared away, and the night was passed in obtaining lunar distances
with stars east and west of the moon   several meridional altitudes,
and transits which, compared with those taken the first night the instrument was put up, gave good rates to the chronometers   Our
labours having thus terminated more successfully than we expected,
we hastened our embarkation, which took place on the 21st   In
return for the kindness we experienced from the islanders, we made
them presents of articles the most useful to them which we could
spare, and they were furnished with a blue cloth suit each from the
extra clothing put on board for the ship's company, and the women
with several pieces of gowns and handkerchiefs, &c

When we were about to take leave, our friends assembled to express their regret at our departure.   All brought some little present
for our acceptance, which they wished us to keep in remembrance
of them, after which they accompanied us to the beach. where we
took our leave of the female part of the inhabitants   Adams and
the young men pushed off in their own boat to the ship. determined
to accompany us to sea as far as they could with safety.   They

continued on board, unwilling to leave us, until we were a considerable distance from land, when they shook each of us feelingly by
the hand, and, amidst expressions of the deepest concern at our departure, wished us a prosperous voyage, and hoped that we might
one day meet again As soon as they were clear of the ship, they
all stood up in the boat, and gave us three hearty cheers, which
were as heartily returned.   As the weather became foggy, the barge
towed them towards the shore, and we took a final leave of them,
unconscious until the moment of separation of the warm interest their
situation and good conduct had created in us.

The Pitcairn islanders are tall, robust, and healthy· Their average height is five feet ten inches, the tallest person is six feet
and one quarter of an inch, and the shortest of the adults is five
feet nine inches and one eighth. Their limbs are well-proportioned,
round and straight: their feet turning a little inwards The boys
promise to be equally as tall as their fathers, one of them whom
we measured was, at eight years of age, four feet one inch ; and another, at nine years, four feet three inches. Their simple food and
early habits of exercise give them a muscular power and activity
not often surpassed It is recorded among the feats of strength
which these people occasionally evince, that two of the strongest
on the island, George Young and Edward Quintal, have each carried, at one time, without inconvenience, a kedge anchor, two sledge
hammers, and and armourer's anvil, amounting to upwards of six
hundred weight, and that Quintal, at another time, carried a boat
twenty-eight feet in length Their activity on land has been already
mentioned. I shall merely give another instance which has been
supplied by Lieutenat Belcher, who was admitted to be the most
active among the officers on board, and who did not consider himself behindhand in such exploits He offered to accompany one of
the natives down a difficult descent, in spite of the warnings of his
friend that he was unequal to the task They, however, commenced the perilous descent, but Mr. Belcher was obliged to confess his
inability to proceed, while his companion, perfectly assured of his
own footing, offered him his hand, and undertook to conduct him to
the bottom, if he would depend on him for safety In the water
they are almost as much at home as on land, and can remain nearly a
day in the sea They frequently swam round their little island, the
circuit of which is at least seven miles When the sea beat heavily on the island they have plunged into the breakers, and swam to
sea beyond them This they sometimes did pushing a barrel of
water before them, when it could be got off in no other way, and
in this manner we procured several tons of water without a single
cask being stove

Their features are regular and well-looking, without being hand-

some. Their eyes are bright and generally hazel, though in one
or two instances they are blue, and some have white speckles on
the iris, the eyebrows being thin, and rarely meeting   The nose,
somewhat flat, and rather extended at the nostrils, partakes of the
Otaheitan form, as do the lips, which are broad, and strongly sulca-
ted.   Their ears are moderately large, and the lobes are invariably
united to the check ; they are generally perforated when young,
for the reception of flowers, a very common custom among the natives of the South Sea Islands   The hair, in the first generation, is,
with one exception only, deep black, sometimes curly, but generally straight, they allow it to grow long, keep it very clean, and always well supplied with cocoanut oil   Whiskers are not common,
and the beards are thin   The teeth are regular and white ; but are
often, in the males, disfigured by a deficiency in enamel, and by being deeply furrowed across.   They have generally large heads, elevated in the line of the occiput.   A line passed above the eyebrows, over the ears, and round the back of the head, in a line with
the occipital spine, including the hair, measured twenty-two inches ; another, twenty-one inches and three-quarters, and in Polly
Young, surnamed Bighead, twenty-three inches,—the hair would
make a difference of about three-quarters of an inch.   The coronal
region is full, the forehead of good height and breadth, giving an
agreeable openness to the countenance, the middle of the coronal
suture is rather raised above the surrounding parts.   Their complexion, in the first generation, is, in general, a dark gipsy hue,
there are, however, exceptions to this ; some are fairer, and others
Joseph Christian in particular, much darker *

The skin of these people, though in such robust health, compared with our own always felt cold ; and their pulses were considerably lower than ours   Mr Collie examined several of them   in the
forenoon he found George Young's only sixty, three others, in the
afternoon, after dinner, were sixty-eight, seventy-two, and seventy-
six ; while those of the officers who stood the heat of the climate
best were above eighty.   Constant exposure to the sun, and early
training to labour, make these islanders look at least eight years
older than they really are

The women are nearly as muscular as the men, and taller than
the generality of their sex.   Polly Young, who is not the tallest
upon the island, measured five feet nine inches and a half   Accustomed to perform all domestic duties, to provide wood for cooking,
which is there a work of some labour, as it must be brought from
the hills, and sometimes to till the ground, their strength is in pro-

* This man was idiotic, and differed so materially from the others in colour, that
he is in all probability the offspring of the men of colour who accompanied the
mutineers to the island, and who, unless he be one, have left no progeny

portion to their muscularity; and they are no less at home in the water than the men

The food of the islanders consists almost entirely of vegetable substances. On particular occasions, such as marriages or christenings, or when visited by a ship, they indulge in pork, fowls, and fish. Although, as has already been mentioned, they discovered a method of distilling a spirit from the tee-root, the miseries it entailed on them have taught them to discontinue the use of it, and to confine themselves strictly to water, of which during meals, they partake freely, but they seldom use it at other times. The spirit, which was first distilled by M'Coy, and led to such fatal consequences, bears some affinity to peat-reeked whisky.

The treatment of their children differs from that of our own country, as the infant is bathed three times a day in cold water, and is sometimes not weaned for three or four years, but as soon as that takes place it is fed upon "popoe," made with ripe plantains and boiled taro rubbed into paste. Upon this simple nourishment children are reared to a more healthy state than in other countries, and are free from fevers and other complaints peculiar to the greater portion of the world. Mr Collie remarks in his journal, that nothing is more extraordinary in the history of the island than the uniform good health of the children, the teething is easily got over, they have no bowel complaints, and are exempt from those contagious diseases which affect children in large communities. He offered to vaccinate the children as well as all the grown persons; but they deemed the risk of infection to be too small to render that operation necessary.

In rainy weather, and after the occasional visits of vessels, the islanders are more affected with plethora and boils than at other periods, to the former the whole population appear to be inclined; but they are usually relieved from its effects by bleeding at the nose, and, without searching for the real cause, they have imbibed a belief that these diseases are contagious, and derived from a communication with their visiters, although there may not be a single case of the kind on board the ship. The result naturally leads to such a conclusion, but a little reflection ought to have satisfied them, that a deviation from their established habits, an unusual indulgence in animal food, and additional clothing, were of themselves sufficient to account for the maladies. They are, however, unaccustomed to trace effects to latent causes. Hence they assert, that the Briton left them headaches and flies; a whaler infected with the scurvy (for which several of her crew pursued the old remedy of burying the people up to the necks in the earth) left them a legacy of boils and other sores, and though we had no diseases on board the Blossom, they fully expected to be affected by some cutaneous disorder

after our departure, and even attributed some giddiness and headaches that were felt during our stay to infection from the ship's
company.

The women have all learned the art of midwifery. parturition
generally takes place during the nighttime; the duration of labour
is seldom longer than five hours, and has not yet in any case proved
fatal   There is no instance of twins, nor of a single miscarriage,
except from accident.

We found upon Pitcairn Island, cocoa-nuts, bread-fruit (*artocar-
pus incisa*), plantains (*musa paradaisaca*), bananas (*musa sapientum*), water-melons (*cucurbita citrullus*), pumpkins (*cucurbita pé-
po*), potatoes (*solanum esculentum*), sweet potatoes (*convolvulus
batatas*), yams (*dioscoria sativum*), taro (*caladium esculentum*),
peas, yappai* (*arum costatum*), sugar-cane, ginger, turmeric, tobacco, tee-plant*(*dracœna terminalis*), doodoe* (*aleurites triloba*),
nono* (*morinda citrifolia*), another species of morinda, parau* (*hibiscus tiliaceus*), fowtoo* (*hibiscus tricuspis*), the cloth-tree (*brous-
soneria papyrifera*), pawalla* (*pandanus odoratissimus*)? toonena*
(?), and banyan-tree.   A species of metrosideros, and several species of ferns.

The first twelve of these form the principal food of the inhabitants.   The sugar-cane is sparingly cultivated; they extract from
it a juice which is used to flavour the tea of such as are ill, by
pounding the cane, and boiling it with a little ginger and cocoanut
grated into a pulp, as a substitute for milk.   In this manner a pleasant beverage is produced.   The tee-plant is very extensively cultivated   Its leaves, which are broad and oblong, are the common
food of hogs and goats, and serve the natives for wrappers in their
cooking   The root affords a very saccharine liquor, resembling
molasses, which is obtained by baking it in the ground; it requires
two or three years after it is planted to arrive at the proper size for
use, being then about two inches and a half in diameter; it is long,
fusiform, and beset with fibres   from this root they also make a tea,
which when flavoured with ginger is not unpleasant.   The doodoe
is a large tree with a handsome blossom, and supplies ornaments for
the ears and hair, and nuts containing a considerable quantity of oil,
which, by being strung upon sticks, serve the purpose of candles.
The porou and fowtoo are trees which supply them with fishing-
lines, rope, and cord of all sorts   The tree is stripped of the bark
while the sap is in full circulation, and dried , a fibrous substance is
then procured from it, which is twisted for use; but it is not strong,
and is very perishable.

* Native names —A more correct account of the botany will be published by Dr
Hooker, Professor of Botany, &c. of Glasgow.

The cloth-tree is pre-eminently useful; and here, as in all places in the South Seas, where it grows, supplies the natives with clothing. The manner in which the cloth is manufactured has been frequently described, and needs no repetition. There is however, a fashion in *the beater*, some preferring a broad, others a very closely ribbed garment, for which purpose they have several of these instruments with large and small grooves. If the cloth is required to be brown, the inner bark of which the cloth is made is wrapped in banana leaves, and put aside for about four days; it is then beaten into a thick doughy substance, and again left till fermentation is about to take place, when it is taken out, and finally beat into a garment, both lengthwise and across. The colour thus produced is of a deep redish brown hue. The pieces are generally sufficiently large to wrap round the whole body, but they are sometimes divided.

The toonena is a large tree, from which their houses and canoes are made. It is a hard, heavy, red-coloured wood, and grows on the upper parts of the island. There was formerly a great abundance of this wood, but it is now become so scarce as to require considerable search and labour to find sufficient to construct a house. The young trees have thriven but partially, arriving at a certain growth, and then stopping. A tree of this kind, which was the largest in the island, measured, at the time of our visit, twelve feet in circumference; another was nine feet seven and a half inches in girth, at five feet from the root; its trunk grew to the height of thirty feet, perfectly straight, and without branching.

The banyan is one of those largest spreading trees common in India. Nature has been so provident to this island, that there are very few trees in it which cannot be turned to account in some way, and this tree, though it yields no fruit and produces wood so hard and heavy as to be unserviceable, still contributes to the assistance of the islanders, by supplying them with a resin for the seams of their boats, &c. This useful substance is procured by perforating the bark of the tree, and extracting the liquor which exudes through the aperture.

We saw dyes of three colours only in Pitcairn Island, yellow, red, and brown. The yellow is procured from the inner bark of the root of the nono tree (*morinda citrifolia*), and also from the root of a species of ginger We did not see this plant growing, but it was described as having leaves broader and longer than the common ginger, a thicker root in proportion to its length, a darker hue, and not so tubercular The red dye is procured from the inner bark of the doodoe tree, and may have its intensity varied by more or less exposure to the rays of the sun while drying These dyes are well coloured, but for want of proper mordants the natives cannot fix them, and they must be renewed every time the linen is washed   The method of producing the brown dye has already been described.

The temperate climate of Pitcairn Island is extremely favourable to vegetation, and agriculture is attended with comparatively light labour   But as the population is increasing, and wants are generated which were before unthought of, the natives find it necessary to improve their mode of culture, and for this purpose they make use of sea-weed as manure.   They grow but one crop in a year of each kind   The time of taking up yams, &c is about April. The land is not allowed time to recover itself, but is planted again immediately   Experience has enabled them to estimate, with tolerable precision, the quantity that will be required for the annual consumption of the island, this they reckon at 1000 yams to each person.   The other roots, being considered more as luxuries, are cultivated in irregular quantities   The failure of a crop, so exactly estimated, must of course prove of serious consequence to the colony, and much anxiety is occasionally felt as the season approaches for gathering it   At times cold south-westerly winds nip the young plants, and turn such as are exposed to them quite black   during our visit several plantations near the sea-coast were affected in this manner.   At other times, caterpillars prove a great source of annoyance

The yam is reproduced in the same manner as potatoes in England.   The taro (*caladium esculentum*) requires either a young shoot to be broken off and planted, or the stem to be removed from the root, and planted after the manner of raising pine-apples   The yappe is a root very similar to the taro, and is treated in the same manner   All the above-mentioned farinaceous roots thrive extremely well in Pitcairn Island ; but this is not the case with English potatoes, which cannot be brought even to a moderate growth Peas and beans yield but very scanty crops, the soil being probably too dry for them, and are rarely seen at the repasts of the natives. Onions, so universally dispersed over the globe, cannot be made to thrive here   Pumpkins and water-melons bear exceedingly well, but the bread-fruit, from some recent cause, is beginning to give very scanty crops   This failure Adams attributes to some trees being cut down, that protected them from the cold winds, which is not improbable, for at Otaheite, where the trees are exposed to the south-west winds, the crops are very indifferent   Having given this short sketch of the soil and vegetation of the island, I shall add a few words on the climate and winds.

The island is situated just without the regular limit of the trade-winds, which, however, sometimes reach it   When this is the case, the weather is generally fine and settled.   The south-west and north-west winds, which blow strong and bring heavy rains, are the chief interruptions to this serenity   Though they have a rainy season, it is not so limited or decided as in places more within the influence of the trade-winds. During the period of our visit, from the 5th of December to the 21st, we had strong breezes from N. E. to S. E., with the sky overcast. The wind then shifted to N. W., and brought a great deal of rain : though in the height of summer, we had scarcely a fine day during our stay.

The temperature of the island during the above period was 70 1-2°   On shore the range from nine A. M. to three P. M. was 76° to 80° : on board at the same time from 74° to 76°   Taking the difference between these comparisons, we may place the mean temperature on shore for the above-mentioned period at 76 1-2°. In the winter the south-westerly winds blow very cold, and even snow has been known to fall.

The number of persons on Pitcairn Island in December, 1825, amounted to sixty-six, and for the information of such as may be disposed to give their particular attention to such an inquiry, I subjoin a notice of the population from the period of its first establishment on the island.

		Males.	Females.
The first settlers consisted of	white	9	0
	coloured	6	12
27 Total		15	12
Of these were killed in the quarrel	white	6	0
	coloured	6	0
by accident	white	1	3
died a natural death		1	3
1 went away	Total deaths	14	6
The original settlers therefore whom we found on the island were		1	5
The children of the white settlers (the men of colour having left none)		10	10
Their grandchildren		22	15
Recent settlers		2	0
Child of one of them		1	0
66 present population.		36	30

The total number of children left by the white settlers was fourteen, of whom two died a natural death , one was seized with fits, to which he was subject, while in the water, and was drowned ; and one was killed by accident, leaving ten, as above   Of the grandchildren. or second generation, there was also another male who died an accidental death. There have, therefore, been sixty-two births in the period of thirty-five years, from the 23d January, 1790, to the 23d December, 1825, and only two natural deaths.

In a climate so temperate, with but few probabilities of infection, with simple diet, cleanly habits, moderate exercise, and a cheerful disposition, it was to be expected that early mortality would be of rare occurrence; and accordingly we find in this small community that the difference in the proportion of deaths to births is more striking than even in the most healthy European nations.

CHAPTER V.

Visit Oeno Island—Description of it—Loss of a boat and one Seaman—Narrow escape of the Crew—Crescent Island—Gambier Groupe—Visited by Natives on Rafts—Discover a passage into the Lagoon—Ship enters—Interview with the Natives—Anchor off two Streams of Water—Visited by the Natives—Theft—Communication with them suspended—Morai—Manner of preserving the Dead—Idols and Places of Worship.

As soon as Adams and his party left us we spread every sail in the prosecution of our voyage, and to increase our distance from a climate in which we had scarcely had the decks dry for sixteen days; but the winds were so light and unfavourable, that on the following morning Pitcairn Island was still in sight. The weather was hazy and moist, and the island was overhung with dense clouds, which the highlands seemed to attract, leaving no doubt with us of a continuation of the weather we had experienced while there. At night there was continued lightning in this direction. Several birds of the pelican tribe (*pelicanus leucocephalus*) settled upon the masts, and allowed themselves to be taken by the seamen.

About ninety miles to the northward of Pitcairn Island there is a coral formation, which has been named Oeno Island, after a whale ship, whose master supposed it had not before been seen; but the discovery belongs to Mr. Henderson of the Hercules. It is so low that it can be discerned at only a very few miles' distance, and is highly dangerous to a night navigation. As this was the next island I intended to visit, every effort was made to get up to it; and at one o'clock in the afternoon of the 23d December it was seen a little to leeward of us. We had not time to examine it that evening, but on the following morning we passed close to the reefs in the ship, in order to overlook the lagoon that was formed within them, and to search narrowly for an opening into it. While the ship took one side of the island, the barge closely examined the other, and we soon found that the lagoon was completely surrounded by the reef. Near the centre of it there was a small island covered with shrubs; and towards the northern extremity, two sandy islets a few feet above the water   The lagoon was in places fordable as far as the wooded island, but, in other parts, it appeared to be two or three fathoms deep   The reef is entirely of coral formation, similar to Ducie's Island, and has deep water all round it   Just clear of the breakers there are three or four fathoms water, the next cast finds thirteen fathoms; then follow rapidly thirty fathoms, sixty fathoms, and no bottom at a hundred fathoms   We found the south-western part of the reef the highest, and the lagoon in that direction nearly filled up as far as the island with growing coral   There were, of course, no inhabitants upon so small a spot, nor should we have been able to communicate had there been any, in consequence of a surf rolling heavily over all parts of the reef, and with such unequal violence that the treacherous smoothness would one moment tempt a landing, while the next wave, as we unfortunately experienced, would prove fatal to any boat that should hazard it

Lieutenant Belcher was sent to ascertain the depth of water round the island, with permission to land if unattended with danger ; and Mr. Collie accompanied him, Mr Barlow being midshipman of the boat   Pulling round the island, they came to a place where the sea appeared tolerably smooth, and where in the opinion of the officers a landing might be effected   The boat was, accordingly anchored, and Messrs. Belcher and Collie prepared to land, by veering the boat into the surf, and jumping upon the reef.   They had half filled two life-preservers, with which they were provided, when Mr Belcher observed a heavy roller rising outside the boat, and desired the crew to pull and meet it, which was done, and successfully passed ; but a second rose still higher, and came with such violence that the sitters in the stern of the boat were thrown into the sea ; a third of still greater force carried all before it, upset the boat, and rolled her over upon the reef, where she was ultimately broken to pieces   Mr Belcher had a narrow escape, the boat being thrown upon him, the gunwale resting upon his neck and keeping him down ; but the next sea extricated him, and he went to the assistance of his companions , all of whom were fortunately got upon the reef, except one young lad, who probably became entangled with the coral, and was drowned   The accident was immediately perceived from the ship, and all the boats sent to the assistance of the survivors.   But the surf rolled so furiously upon the shore as to occasion much anxiety about rescuing them. At last a small raft was constructed, and Lieutenant Wainwright finding no other means of getting a line to them, boldly jumped overboard, with a lead line in his hand, and suffered himself to be thrown upon the reef.   By this contrivance all the people were got off, one by one, though severely bruised and wounded by the coral and spines of the echini

Mr Belcher had here another escape, by being washed off the raft, his trousers getting entangled in the coral at the bottom of a deep chasm. Fortunately they gave way, and he rose to the surface, and by great effort swam through the breakers. Lieutenant Wainwright was the last that was hauled off. To this young officer the greatest praise is due for his bravery and exertions throughout. But for his resolution, it is very doubtful whether the party would have been relieved from their perilous situation, as the tide was rising, and the surf upon the reef momentarily increasing. In the evening we made sail to the westward, and on the 27th saw Crescent Island, and shortly afterwards the high land of Gambier's groupe.

Both these islands were discovered by Mr. Wilson during a missionary voyage, but he had no communication with the natives. The first was so named in consequence of its supposed form, but in fact it more nearly resembles an oblong. It is exactly three miles and a half in length, and one and a half in width, and of similar formation to Oeno and Ducie's Islands. It consists of a strip of coral about a hundred yards or less in width, having the sea on one side and a lagoon on the other. Its general height is two feet above the water. Upon this strip several small islands, covered with trees, have their foundation. The soil, where highest, reaches just six feet above the sea; and the tops of the trees are twenty feet higher. We saw about forty naked inhabitants upon this small spot; but from the mast-head of the boat, which overlooked the land, could perceive no cultivation; and there were no fruit-trees upon the island but the pandanus, which has not been mentioned in any voyage that I am acquainted with as constituting a food for the natives of these seas; indeed, from the fibrous nature of the nut it bears, it did not appear to us possible that it could be serviceable as food. We were consequently curious to know upon what the natives subsisted, independently of the shell-fish which the reefs supplied; but nothing occurred to satisfy us on that head. The surf was too high for the boats to land, and our only communication was by signs and an exchange of sentences unintelligible on both sides.

Upon the angles of the island there were three square stone huts, about six feet high, with a door only to each; they did not appear to be dwelling houses, and were probably places of interment or of worship. Several sheds thatched with the boughs of trees, some open on one side only and others on both, which were seen on different parts of the island, were more appropriate residences in such a climate.

The natives were tall and well-made, with thick black hair and beards, and were very much tattooed. Their signs intimated a disposition to be friendly, and an invitation to land. which we could not do ; but none of them ventured to swim off to the boats, probably on account of the sharks, which were very numerous.

We quitted Crescent Island at day-light on the 29th, and about noon the same day were close off Gambier's groupe. Several of of these islands had a fertile appearance, especially the largest, on which is situated the peak we had seen the day before, and which Mr Wilson, in passing to the northward of the groupe, named Mount Duff. It was probable, that among these islands we should find a stream of water from which our stock might be replenished, provided an opening through the reef which surrounds the volcanic islands could be found, and as it was of the highest importance that our wants in this respect should be supplied, I determined closely to examine every part of the groupe for an entrance, for in the event of not being so fortunate as to succeed here, it would be necessary to alter the plan of operations, and proceed direct to Otaheite, the only place where a supply of that indispensable article could be depended upon On approaching the island, with the ship, we were gratified by perceiving that the coral chain, which to the northward was above water, and covered with trees, to the southward dipped beneath it ; and though the reef could be traced by the light blue-coloured sea, still it might be sufficiently covered to admit of the ship passing over it, and finding an anchorage in the lagoon As we were putting off from the ship in the boats to make this interesting inquiry, several small vessels under sail were observed bearing down to us When they approached we found they were large katamarans or rafts, carrying from sixteen to twenty men each At first several of them were fastened together, and constituted a large platform, capable of holding nearly a hundred persons ; but before they came near enough to communicate they separated, furled their sails, and took to their paddles, of which there were about twelve to each raft. We were much pleased with the manner of lowering their matting sail, diverging on different courses, and working their paddles, in the use of which they had great power, and were well skilled plying them together, or to use a nautical phrase, keeping stroke They had no other weapons but long poles ; and were quite naked, with the exception of a banana leaf cut into strips, and tied about their loins, and one or two persons who wore white turbans Their timidity in approaching both the ship and the barge was immediately apparent, but they had no objection to any of the small boats, which they were probably aware they could. if necessary, easily upset when within their reach, and, indeed, it required considerable caution to prevent any such an occurrence, not from any malicious intention on the part of the natives, but from their thoughtlessness and inquisitiveness I ap-

proached them in the gig, and gave them several presents, for which
they, in return, threw us some bundles of paste tied up in large
leaves   Not knowing at first what it was, I caught it in my arms,
and was overpowered with an ordour that made me drop it instantly   They made signs that it was to be eaten, and we afterwards
found it was the common food of the natives.   It was what is called
mahie at the Marquesas, but with a higher gout than I ever heard
that article possessed in those islands, and very much resembled
the first opening of a cask of sour krout, though considerably more
overpowering   We soon perceived they had a previous knowledge
of iron, but they had no idea of the use of a musket   When one
was presented to induce them to desist from their riotous conduct,
instead of evading the direction of the fatal charge, they approached it, and imagining the gun was offered to them, they innocently
held out their hand to accept it   Before we came close to them,
they tempted us with cocoanuts and roots, performed ludicrous
dances, and invited our approach, but as soon as we were within
reach, the scene was changed to noise and confusion   They seized the boat by the gunwale, endeavoured to steal every thing that
was loose, and demanded whatever we held in our hand, without
seeming in the least disposed to give any thing of their own in return   At length some of them grasped the boat's yoke, which was
made of copper, and others the rudder, which produced a scuffle,
and obliged me to fire my gun over their heads   Upon the discharge, all but four instantly plunged into the sea ; but these, though
for a moment motionless with astonishment, held firmly by the rudder, until they were rejoined by their companions, and then forcibly
made it their prize   We could only have prevented this by the
use of fire-arms, but I did not choose to resort to such a measure
for so trifling an end, especially as the barge was approaching, and
afforded the most likely means of recovering our loss without the
sacrifice of life on their part, or the risk of being upset on our own
As I intended to remain some days at these islands, I wished by all
means to avoid a conflict: at the same time it was essential to our
future tranquillity to show a resolution to resist such unwarrantable
conduct, and to convince them of our determination to enforce a respect of property   As soon, therefore, as we were joined by the
barge, we grappled the raft that contained our rudder, on which
the greater part of the natives again threw themselves into the sea ;
but those who remained appeared determined to resist our attack,
and endeavoured to push the boat off   Finding, however, they
could not readily do this, a man whose long beard was white with
age offered us the disputed article, and we were on the point of receiving it, which would have put an end to all strife, when one of
the natives disengaged the raft, and she went astern   Again free,

the rudder was replaced on the raft, and the swimmers regained their station.   They were followed by the gig and jolly-boat, and a short skirmish ensued, in which Mr Elson fell.   The boat's crew imagining him hurt, and seeing the man he had been engaged with aiming another blow at him, fired and wounded his assailant in the shoulder   The man fell upon the raft, and his companions, alarmed, threw the rudder into the sea and jumped overboard   As this man took a very leading part. he was probably a chief   No other wound was inflicted, nor did this happen before it was merited , for our forbearance had extended even beyond the bounds of prudence , and had less been evinced, we should sooner have gained our point, and probably have stood higher in the estimation of our antagonists   After this rencountre, some of the rafts again paddled towards us, and waved pieces of white cloth , but the evening being far spent, and anxious to find anchorage for the ship, I proceeded to examine the islands   We passed the bar, formed by the chain before-mentioned dipping under water, in five, or seven, and eight fathoms, over a rugged coral bottom, and entered the lagoon, gradually deepening the water to twenty-five fathoms   There was a considerable swell upon the shallow part of the reef, but within it the water was quite smooth.   The first island we approached had a bay formed at its eastern angle, where the ship might ride in safety with almost all winds   Night coming on we anchored the boat upon the bar, and caught a large quantity of fish, consisting of several sorts of perca (vittata, maculata). a labrus, and many small sharks.   After daylight we returned to the ship, and in the evening anchored in the spot we had selected the day before.   As we entered the bay, the natives were observed collected upon a low point, at one extremity of it, hallooing and waving pieces of white cloth   Almost all of them had long poles, either pointed or tipped with bone. Some had mats thrown over their shoulders, and their heads and loins covered with banana leaves cut into strips   They were much startled at the noise occasioned by letting go the anchor, and at the chain-cable running out, and gazed intently at the different evolutions necessary to be gone through in bringing the ship to an anchor, in furling sails, &c.

No person came on board that night ; but daylight had scarcely dawned when one of the natives paddled off to the ship upon a small katamaran · he was quite naked had only a pole and a paddle on the raft   For a considerable time he hesitated to come alongside ; but on our assuring him, in the Oteheitan language, we were his friends he was persuaded to make the attempt   After a little further conciliation he made his raft fast by a rope that was thrown to him, and ascended the side of the ship, striking her several times with his fist, and examining her at every step   His surprise on reaching the deck was beyond all description ; he danced, capered, and threw himself into a variety of attitudes, accompanying them with vehement exclamations , and entered into conversation with every person, not suspecting that his language was unintelligible ; and was so astonished at all he saw, that his attention wandered from object to object without intermission.   He very willingly accepted every present that was offered him ; and having satisfied himself of our friendly disposition, hastened on shore to his companions, who were collected in great numbers upon the low point, anxiously awaiting his return.   The report which he gave was undoubtedly of a favourable nature, as several katamarans, laden with visiters, immediately pushed off, and came fearlessly alongside

The decks were soon crowded with delighted spectators, wondering at every thing they beheld, and expressing their feelings by ludicrous gestures   The largest objects, such as the guns and spars, greatly attracted their attention · they endeavoured to lift them, with a view, no doubt, of bundling them overboard , but finding they could not be moved, the smaller articles became the more immediate subjects of curiosity and desire, and it required a vigilant watch to prevent their being carried off   They were pleased with many articles that were shown them , but nothing made them so completely happy as the sight of two dogs that we had on board. The largest of these, of the Newfoundland breed, was big and surly enough to take care of himself ; but the other, a terrier, was snatched up by one of the natives, and was so much the object of his solicitation that it was only by force he was prevented carrying him away.   To the people who had never seen any quadruped before but a rat, so large an animal as a Newfoundland dog, and that perfectly domesticated and obedient to his master, naturally excited intense curiosity, and the great desire of these people to possess themselves of it is not to be wondered at   Had there been a female dog on board, they certainly should have had them both ; but one would have been of no use, except, probably, to furnish a meal, which is the fate of all the rats they can catch

One of the rafts that came off to the ship, a smaller one than any of the others, brought a person of superior appearance , his complexion was much fairer than his countrymen, and his skin beautifully tattooed , his features were of the true Asiatic character   he had long black mustaches and hair, and wore a light turban, which gave him altogether the appearance of a descendant of Ishmael.   It was natural to infer that this was a person of some authority ; for as yet we had seen no distinction whatever between our visiters   except that some were more unruly than others ; but we found we were mistaken   he mingled indiscriminately with his companions, and was deficient in those little points which are inseparable from a

person accustomed to command   Indeed. by the total disregard
they paid to each other, as also to every person in the ship, we
might have concluded that our visiters were ignorant of any distinctions in society.

Among the many katamarans that came off, not one of them
brought any articles to give or sell, which did not argue much in
favour of the supplies of the place, or the good will of the islanders
A green banana, lying upon one of the rafts, was the only eatable
thing among them, excepting some boiled tee-root, and bundles of
that execrable paste, which they had provided for their own breakfast.   Almost all our visiters were naked, with the exception of a
girdle made of a banana leaf, cut into strips, which by no means answered our idea of the intended purpose.   Maros were worn only
by the aged, and instead of them ligatures of straw were applied in
the manner described at St Christina and Nukahiwa.*   The average height of the islanders was five feet nine; they were, generally speaking, well made, their limbs round, without being muscular, and their figure upright and flexible.   Tattooing was very extensively practised, in which respect, as also in the arrangement of
the lines, they again reminded us of the Marquesans   This general practice in the South Seas, when judiciously executed, besides
having its useful effects, is highly ornamental   In the Gambier Islanders there is a greater display of taste than I have seen or heard
of any where else, not excepting the Marquesans   but the Nuka-
hiwers, as well as the Otaheitans and others, attend principally to
device ; whereas the Gambier Islanders dispose the lines so as materially to improve the figure, particularly about the waist, which at
a little distance, has the appearance of being much smaller than it
really is   Whether this has been accidental or designed we had no
opportunity of learning

The number of visiters on board was considerable, yet there was
very little to interest us beyond the first gratification of our curiosity.   They were so engrossed by their own efforts to purloin some
of the many things which they saw, that it was impossible to engage
their attention in other matters   It was besides necessary to keep
so strict a watch over the stores of the ship, and their conduct was
so noisy and importunate, that our desire for their company was
hourly lessened, and we were not sorry when, on preparing the boats
to land, we saw the rafts put off from the ship, and every man upon
our decks throw himself into the sea and swim ashore.

On approaching the beach, we found the coral animals had reared their structure all round the island, and had brought it so near
to the surface that the large boats could not come within two hun-

* Krusenstern's Embassy to Japan, 4to

died yards of the landing-place, and the smaller ones could approach only by intricate windings between the rocks

The natives were very numerous upon the shore the usual population being greatly increased by parties which curiosity had brought from the other islands The women and children at first formed part of the noisy multitude, all of whom were clamorous for us to effect a landing, but the females shortly retired out of sight, and the men formed themselves into two lines, and ceremoniously proceeded to a place where their katamarans usually disembarked, humming in chorus a sullen tune not devoid of harmony Some of them seeing we were greatly impeded by the coral rocks, waded out and laid hold of the boats, while others pushed off upon rafts, and attempted to drag us in, by fixing their poles under the seats of the boat, and pressing upon the gunwale as a fulcrum; an ingenious contrivance, from which we found it difficult to free ourselves, especially as the poles were very large. Others, again, prepared cords to fasten the boats to their raft, unconscious of our possessing any instrument sufficiently sharp to disengage them In short, they were determined we should land, but as I did not like the place, and as their conduct appeared to be a repetition of what we had experienced outside the harbour, we disappointed their expectations, and went to the next island

We were there joined by some of our visiters who had been on board the ship, who reminded us of our former acquaintance, and greeted us with a hearty rub of their noses against ours This salutation, it was thought by some of us, sealed a friendship between the parties; but we had not sufficient opportunity of ascertaining whether it was considered inviolable The manner of effecting this friendly compact is worthy of description The lips are drawn inward between the teeth, the nostrils are distended, and the lungs are widely inflated, with this preparation, the face is pushed forward, the noses brought into contact, and the ceremony concludes with a hearty rub, and a vehement exclamation or grunt and in proportion to the warmth of feeling, the more ardent and disagreeable is the salutation.

Finding, from communication with our friends, that water was to be had at Mount Duff, we quitted them and crossed to that point, where we had the satisfaction to see two streams trickling down the sides of the hill, either of them sufficiently ample for our purpose, and so situated that the ship could, if necessary be placed near enough to cover the parties sent to procure it This gratifying discovery was of the greatest importance, and the ship was immediately removed to a convenient spot opposite the place

We were late getting across the lagoon from our first anchorage, in consequence of the necessity of proceeding with the utmost caution to prevent striking upon rocks of coral, which were numerous, and in some instances rose from twenty-eight fathoms to within twelve feet of the surface ; so that it was dark before the sails were furled, and we had no communication with the natives that night.   One man only, probably by way of ascertaining whether we kept watch, paddled silently off upon a small katamaran ; but on being hailed, went quietly away.   At daylight, the shore opposite the ship was lined with the natives, and katamarans commenced coming off to her laden with visiters, who, encouraged by their former reception, fearlessly ascended the side, and in a short time so crowded the decks, that the necessary duties of the crew were suspended. Their surprise was, if possible, greater than that of the other islanders , but it did not appear to be excited by any particular object

It is said that as a people become civilized, their curiosity increases   Here, however, it was excited more from a desire to ascertain what was capable of being pilfered than from any thirst for knowledge   Through this propensity every thing underwent a rigid examination   We had taken the precaution to put all the moveable articles that could be spared below, and nothing was stolen from the upper decks , but in the midshipmen's berth, things had not been so carefully secreted, and a soup-tureen, a spyglass, and some crockery were soon missing, the former was detected going over the side, and one of the tea-cups was observed in the possession of a person swimming away from the ship   This afforded a favourable opportunity of showing our determination to resist all such depredations , and indeed it was absolutely necessary to do so as every person appeared to consider he had a right to whatever he could carry away with him , and the number of our visiters amounted to double that of our own crew, so that it was impossible to watch every one of them   Besides, this conduct, if not checked in time, might lead to serious consequences, which I wished by every means to avoid   One of our small boats was consequently sent in pursuit of the thief, who was swimming at a considerable rate towards a raft with his prize in his hand   His countrymen, observing that he was pursued, would not permit him to mingle with them, lest they should participate in the blame . but he eluded detection by diving underneath their rafts, until he became exhausted, when he threw the cup to the bowman of the boat, and made his escape   Immediately the boat was sent off, all the rafts left the ship, and every man upon the decks jumped overboard as if by instinct , but when tranquillity was restored, they returned for fresh plunder   The rapidity with which the news of a theft spreads among such a community has been noticed by Captain Cook, and here it was no less remarkable

I determined, since the main deck was cleared, that it should be

kept so, and placed a marine at each of the ladders, but as the natives tried every method to elude their vigilance, the sentinels had
an arduous task to perform, and disturbances must inevitably have
arisen in the execution of their orders had it not been for our Newfoundland dog   It fortunately happened that this animal had taken
a dislike to our visiters, and the deck being cleared, he instinctively
placed himself at the foot of the ladder, and in conjunction with the
little terrier, who did not forget his perilous hug of the day before,
most effectually accomplished our wishes   The natives, who had
never seen a dog before, were in the greatest terror of them, and
Neptune's bark was soon found to be more efficacious than the point
of a sentry's bayonet, and much less likely to lead to serious disturbances   Besides, his activity cleared the whole of the main deck
at once, and supplied the place of *all* the sentinels   The natives
applied the name of *boa* to him a word which in the Otaheitan language properly signifies a hog   But it may be observed that *boa* is
applied equally to a bull, or to a horse, (which they call *boa-afae-
taata*, literally, man-carrying pig), or to all foreign quadrupeds

Upon one of the rafts which came alongside there was an elderly
man with a grey beard, dressed in white cloth   The paddles of his
raft were of superior workmanship to the others and had the extremity of the handle ornamented with a neatly carved human hand.
He carried a long staff of hard black wood, finely polished, widened at one end like a chisel   But though he was thus distinguished,
he exercised no authority over his unruly countrymen   Several of
the people upon the rafts had provided themselves with food, which
consisted of boiled root of the tee-plant, of pearl oysters, and the
sour pudding before-mentioned   We endeavoured to tempt them
to taste some of our food ; which they willingly accepted, but declined to partake of it, and placed it upon the raft, with nails, rags
and whatever else they had collected.   A piece of corned beef that
was given them passed from hand to hand with -repeated looks of
inquiry, until it was last deposited in the general heap   I took some
pains to explain to them it was not human flesh which they in all
probability at first imagined it to be ; and from their behaviour on
the occasion I think it quite certain they are not cannibals

As the curiosity of one party of our visiters became satisfied, they
quitted the ship, and others supplied their place   One of these favoured us with a song, which commenced with a droning noise, the
words of which we could not distinguish ; they then gave three
shouts, to which succeeded a short recitation, followed by the droning chorus and shouts as before.   In this manner the song proceeded, each recitation differing from the former, until three shouts,
louder than the others, announced the finale   The singers arranged
themselves in a semicircle round the hatchway, and during the per-

formance pointed to the different parts of the ship, to which their song was undoubtedly applicable; but it was impossible to say in what way, though I have every reason to believe it was of a friendly nature.

While the decks were so crowded with visiters, the duty of watering the ship could not be carried on, and it was of the greatest consequence that it should be got through speedily, as the boats were required to survey the groupe upon which I could not bestow many days My hope was that the natives would quit us as their curiosity became satisfied, especially as they had nothing to barter, except some sour paste, which, being extremely unpalatable to every one on board, was not marketable After breakfast, two small boats, the only ones we had in repair, were equipped for landing, and the barge was ordered to be in attendance, for though there was every reason to expect a friendly reception, yet in a country where the language is not understood, and among a barbarous people, whose principal aim is plunder, it is extremely difficult to avoid disputes, especially when the force to which they are opposed is greatly inferior to their own We felt the loss of the cutter at this moment, as she was a boat so much better calculated for the service we had to perform than the gig or whale-boat

As we had anticipated, the boats had no sooner put off from the ship, than all the natives quitted her as before, and joined their companions on shore. who were assembled in a wood skirting the beach. At the approach of the boats, there was much bustle among the trees, every one appeared to be arming himself, and many who had long poles broke them in halves to supply those who had none. These preparations made it necessary to be cautious how the boats were placed in their power, as they were small, and easily upset, and the natives very numerous We found the shore, as at the other island, surrounded by coral rocks, upon which the boats grounded about two hundred yards from the beach, and they could not advance without imminent danger of being stove The natives, whose rafts drew so little water that they could be floated over these impediments. could not understand our motives in delaying, or searching for any other place than that to which they had been accustomed, and kept continually vociferating "Ho-my! Ho-my!" It was natural that they, ignorant of the cause, should suppose we had other things in view than that of landing, and one of them who had received a bottle as a present from some of our people, imagining we were come in search of it, ran into the water as far as he could, holding it up at arm's length, and when he could advance no farther, threw it towards the boat, and, in spite of our signs for him to keep it, he followed the boats, and kept throwing the bottle towards us, until he found it was of no use.

A short distance below the place where the multitude were assembled, the rocks admitted a freer access to the shore than above, and we effected a landing.

Directly the boats touched the beach, one of the natives who was near them took off his turban and waved it to his countrymen, who instantly answered the signal with a shout, and rushed towards the spot   The foremost of their party stopped within a short distance of us until the crowd came up to him, and then advanced and saluted Mr. Belcher, who was unarmed, by rubbing noses.   Observing there was some distrust of a fowling-piece which I held in my hand, I placed it against a rock for an instant among our own party while I advanced a step to salute a person who appeared to be the leading man of the islanders   The opportunity this afforded the natives of indulging their favourite propensity was not overlooked ; and one of them, regardless of all risk, thrust himself between our people, snatched up the gun, and, mingling with the mob with the greatest adroitness, succeeded in making his escape   The crowd instantly fled into the wood, and along the beach, but shortly rallied, and with loud shouts advanced upon us, until the discharge of a carronade from the barge, which was fortunately near, put them to flight.   The man who had sealed the compact of friendship, if so indeed it be, by rubbing noses, sat quietly upon a large stone close to us during this affair, as if he relied upon the pledge that had been given for his security.   It would have been treacherous, and perhaps pregnant with serious evils to them and to ourselves, had any violence been offered, or any thing done that might appear like an infringement of this understanding, or I should certainly have detained his person, in the hope of the gun being returned.   As it was, I allowed him to go quietly away

The boats were at this time unavoidably very awkwardly situated, by being aground upon the rocks, and in a situation from which it would have been extremely difficult to extricate them, had a determined attack been made by the natives.   The consequences in that case would have been very serious , though their weapons consisted only of long poles and bone-headed spears, yet they were sufficiently powerful, from their numbers alone, to have rendered the most determined defence on our part doubtful

As soon as we were free, we followed the natives along the beach, approaching them, whenever the rocks would allow, to offer terms of reconciliation . but our overtures were answered only by showers of stones.   This conduct, which we now began to think was only a part of their general character, rendered it extremely difficult, nay almost impossible, to have any dealings with them without getting into disputes   No time, place, or example, made any difference in the indulgence of their insatiable propensity to theft.   Explanations and threats, which in some instances will prevent the necessity of acting, were unfortunately not at our command, in consequence of our ignorance of their language, and the only option left us was to yield up our goods unresistingly, or inflict a more severe chastisement than the case might deserve. Captain Cook, who managed the natives of these seas better than any other navigator, pursued a system which generally succeeded, though in the end it cost him his life. It was rigid, but I am certain it was better adapted to preserve peace than the opposite plan adopted by Perouse, at Easter Island, who, though one of the most enlightened navigators, was, of all, the most unfortunate.

To seize one of the natives, or upon something that was of more value to them than the goods they had stolen, was the most effectual way of recovering what was lost, and by adopting this mode of proceeding might prevent a recurrence of such a circumstance, I consequently took away a net and some rafts that were lying upon the shore. The net was about forty feet in length, made with the bark of the porou tree (*hibiscus tiliaceus*), precisely in the same manner as our seins are, but weighed with stones and rounded pieces of coral instead of lead. To obtain possession of these articles without strife, it was necessary to drive away a party that was seated upon a large tree near them, and a carronade was fired over their heads but of this they took no notice, probably considering themselves safe at so great a distance, and having had no experience to the contrary, supposed that such weapons were caculated only to intimidate by noise. The next gun dispersing the sand amongst them, they speedily resigned their seats, and with all the inhabitants went to the upper village. After this our communicaton was for a time suspended, as the natives kept aloof, and the boats were required to proceed with the watering.

At daylight on the 2d of January, we commenced filling our casks from two good streams, which supplied water much faster than it could be got off.

We perceived the natives collected in a large body at the village, and soon afterwards some men stole along the beach to reconnoitre the watering party, but they were prevented offering any molestation by a gun being fired from the ship. On this day I observed the old custom of taking possession of the groupe, and hoisted the English ensign upon the shore, turned a turf, and sowed several useful seeds, which it is to be hoped will spring up to the benefit of the natives. I named the island on which Mount Duff stood, after my first Lieutenant, Mr Peard, and the others in succession, Belcher, Wainwright, Elson, Collie, and Marsh, after the other officers, and the lagoon in which the ship was anchored after herself.

Before our party reached the shore the next morning, one of the natives was perceived carrying off a small cask that had been left there the preceding night. We watched him through our telescopes and observed him conceal it with a large mat which he carried with him. He had doubtless no suspicion that his actions could be observed at so great a distance, as he began to retrace his steps along the open beach; but seeing he was not sufficiently quick to escape the boats that were going on the shore, he quitted his prize, and hid himself in the wood. The watering had not long been renewed before a large party collected upon the height above, headed by two men, who appeared to be chiefs, clad in loose white turbans and cloaks · the eldest led the party cautiously down the hill, and made a stand at a large stone, which one of his party ascended, and there waved a banana leaf. We answered this friendly signal by waving in return a white flag from the ship · but here our amity ended, for while this was going forward the other chief stood upon the ridge, and beckoned to the natives on the other side of the hill to join him, which greatly augmented his numbers, and some of them loosened large stones, apparently with a view of annoying our watering party, who were so situated under the hill that a few such fragments precipitated upon them would cause very serious mischief As there was every appearance of treachery, the boats were put upon their guard by signal, but the barge mistaking its purport, fired two shot to dislodge the islanders, both of which, to their great astonishment, fell very close to them, and induced them to retire to the other side of the ridge Some, however, had the curiosity to return and examine the place, and, after a little digging, found one of the shot, which they carried to their comrades, many of whom assembled round the prize, never probably having so large a piece of iron in their possession before.

At noon on the 5th the watering was completed, and without any accident or sickness, which, considering the difficulty of getting the casks off, and the constant exposure of the seamen to a vertical sun while in the water, there was every reason to apprehend. It was further satisfactory to find that this service had been effected without any harm to the natives, except in one instance, when a marine inconsiderately fired at a party who were lurking in the wood, and wounded one of them in the foot From the disposition of the inhabitants, and the superiority of their numbers, there was reason to apprehend a different result; and the quietness with which it was conducted must be attributed to their being kept at a distance during its performance

The boats were now sent to survey the groupe, and were kept constantly employed upon it from daylight to dusk. In the course of this examination every part was visited, and we had frequent communication with the natives, who on such occasions were always civil, and brought such supplies of fruit and food as their scanty means afforded, and generally abstained from the indulgence of their propensity for thieving, which when numerous they so fully indulged   Their behaviour was indeed so different from what it had been, that we must attribute it to the operation of fear, as their numbers were then very small, in consequence of our visits being unexpected and the population of each village very limited   The net we had taken off the shore was carried round to the principal village and offered in return for the articles that had been stolen, but whether our meaning was understood or not, they were not produced

This village is situated in a bay, at the eastern foot of Mount Duff, and is rendered conspicuous by a hut of very large dimensions which we shall describe hereafter, and by a quadrangular building of large blocks of coral erected in the water, at a few yards' distance from the shore, which appeared to us to be a morai   Upon its northern extreme stood a small hut, planted round with trees, which it was conjectured contained images and offerings ; but, as the door was closed, and the natives were watching us, we would not examine it.   Contiguous to it there was a body placed upon boards, wrapped in thick folds of paper cloth   and, not far from it, another enveloped in a smaller quantity of the same material   There was no offensive smell whatever from either of these corpses, though the one last mentioned did not appear to have been long exposed. The heads of both were lying to the N E , both bodies were more abundantly surrounded by cloth than any we had 'seen here ; and from the nature of the platform on which they were placed, which must have required considerable labour to construct, we concluded they were the bodies of chiefs , and we were, on that account, more tenacious of subjecting them to the scrutiny our curiosity prompted, lest the natives should suppose we were offering them some indignity. An old man whom we interrogated as to the nature of the building gave us no information · but looked very serious whenever he was referred to the place, and seemed disposed to believe we were inclined to place his body there to keep the others company

Though we were prevented from examining these mummies by the watchfulness of the natives, we were more successful at the island to the eastward, off which we first anchored   We there found six bodies under a projecting part of a cliff, which overhung them sufficiently to protect them from the inclemency of the weather Above them we noticed a child suspended by a string round its waist tied to a projecting crag   The bodies of the adults were placed parallel, with their heads to the N E , as in the other instance. They were wrapped first in cloth, then in matting, and again covered over with thick folds of cloth secured by a small cord lashing. Mr. Collie, the surgeon, made an incision into the stomach of one of the newest mummies, which appeared the most hardened, and found the membraneous part of the abdomen, dried and shrivelled up, enclosing an indurated earthy substance, which at first induced him to believe it had undergone the process of enbalming, but finding afterwards membranes and earthy matter within a cranium similarly dried, and knowing that there was no way in which any extraneous substance could have been introduced there, except by the vertebral canal, he was induced to alter his opinion, which, he says, had nothing to support it, but the idea that putrefaction must have taken place without some counteracting agent. This complete desiccation of the human frame is not unfrequent in these seas, nor indeed in other places, but requires considerable care and attention to do it effectually. The method formerly pursued at Otaheite, was to keep the corpse constantly wiped dry, and well lubricated with cocoa-nut oil Our intercourse with the Gambier Islanders did not afford us the opportunity of ascertaining if this were their practice also, but we noticed the precaution of exposing the bodies upon frames three or four feet above the ground, that the air might freely circulate about them, and of keeping them well covered with folds of cloth It is remarkable that none of these had any offensive smell, not even those that had been recently exposed upon the drying-board Lieutenant Belcher, whose duty carried him a great deal about the islands, saw some bodies that were exposed to dry, covered with a matted shed to protect them from the rain, and in one he found the head and right arm separated from the trunk, wrapped in separate pieces of cloth, and secured by a lashing to the body On no part of the shore did we see skulls or bones exposed and heaped together, as about the morais common to Polynesia; and although Mr. Belcher found some human bones partly burned lying loose upon a rock together with a body deposited in the grave with a wicker-work frame over it, there is every reason to believe that these exposures are very rare indeed, and that almost all the bodies are wrapped in cloth, and deposited as first described This custom furnishes a satisfactory reason for the cloth being so scarce, and though we cannot commend their policy in clothing the dead at the expence of the living, yet they must be allowed the merit due to their generosity and respect for their departed friends.

On the 7th I visited a village at the south extremity of Belcher Island It was situated in a little bay, at the foot of a ridge of hills which intersected the island We were received by about a dozen men and women, who behaved in a very friendly manner, and brought down cocoa-nuts (some of which, by the by, had been previously emptied of their contents), sugar-cane, tee-roots, one bunch of bananas, and several clusters of pandanus nuts; these they threw into the boat without soliciting any return, and, what is more extraordinary, without evincing any desire to steal. All the men then quitted us, excepting one, who was anxious that we should land. Two of these females behaved in a manner which attracted attention, although we could not account for their conduct; they waded out to the boats, crying most piteously, striking their breasts, and pulling their hair, which hung loose over their shoulders, with every demonstration of the deepest distress, and, to our surprise, threw their arms round our necks, and hugged us so close that we could not disengage ourselves form their embrace without violence. As we were quite unconscious of the nature of their grief, we could offer them no consolation beyond that of kindness, and giving them some beads and trinkets. After a few minutes they disengaged their arms, began dancing, laughing, and saluting us occasionally with a rub of the nose. in the midst of this mirth they would suddenly relapse into grief, and throw their arms about in a frantic way, until I began to fear they might injure themselves, but this paroxysm was as short as that of the mirth by which it was succeeded; they again began to dance, and were afterwards quite cheerful. The only cause to which we could attribute this extraordinary conduct, or at least for the melancholy part of it, was that they might in some way be connected with the man who had been wounded upon the raft. And if this were the case, it affords a presumption that the custom of self-mutilation on such occasions, so common to many of the islands in the Pacific, does not exist here.

As the sun went down the natives pointed to it, and signified to us to be gone, exclaiming "Bobo mai." We got from them a few articles of manufacture, very similar to those of Pitcairn Island. In return for these we made them useful presents, and took our leave with the promise of "Bobo mai," which we understood to mean "come to-morrow." We rowed round the rest of the island, and soon satisfied ourselves of its extreme poverty. There were two villages upon its western side, situated in deep sandy bays, which would form excellent harbours for shipping, if they could be entered; but this is impracticable from the many coral knolls on the outside.

Lieutentant Belcher describes a morai, which he visited, in the following manner. A hut, about twenty feet in length by ten wide, and seven high, with a thatched roof, of which the eaves were three feet from the ground, contained the deity. There were only two apertures, about two feet six inches square, furnished with thatched shutters. In front of the building, a space about twenty feet square was paved with hewn coral slabs, with curbstones at the edges, as neatly fitted as the pavements in England. Along the whole length of the interior of the hut was a trough elevated about three feet from the ground, in the center of which was an idol three feet high, neatly carved and polished, the eyebrows were sculptured, but not the eyes, and from the manner in which the muscles were defined it was evident that these people were not regardless of the anatomy of the figure It was placed in an upright position on the trough or or manger, and fastened by the extremities to the side of the hut: the head was bound with a piece of white cloth, as were also the loins, and those parts which the natives themselves never conceal, the aged excepted In the trough beneath the image were several paddles, mats, coils of line, and cloth, offerings which had been made to the deity, and at his feet was placed a calabash, which the natives said contained water, " *avy* " On each side of the image was a stand, having three carved arms, to the hands of which several articles were suspended, such as carved cocoa-nut shells, and pieces of bamboo, perhaps musical instruments; but Mr. Belcher abstained from trespassing on this sacred ground, for fear of giving offence to the natives, who did not much like this exercise of curiosity. Indeed, the whole time he was there, the women were anxious to get him away, and the men looked serious, and were very glad when he left the place The females accompanied him to the threshold of the morai : but the men studiously avoided treading upon the sacred pavement, and knelt down the whole time he was there, without however, any apparent devotion Mr Belcher endeavoured to purchase this idol, but valuable as his offers must have been to these poor people, the temptation did not prove sufficient. Another image about the same size was found upon one of the coral islands of the groupe, clothed in the same way, but more rudely carved, and deficient in the offerings above-mentioned.

CHAPTER VI

Second interview with the Natives—Visit to the principal Village—Bodies exposed to dry—Areghe or Chief—Lieutenant Wainwright attacked by Natives—Advantage of the Port—Further Description of the Island, its Soil and Productions

On the afternoon of the 8th, we again landed under Mount Duff, to try the feeling of the natives. Our party was not large, and we carefully avoided every thing that might appear offensive, carrying with us a white flag upon a staff One man only, at first, ventured near us, rubbed noses, and received several presents, with which he was highly delighted His companions, who, during the interview, had been peeping from behind the trees, noticing his friendly reception, laid aside their weapons, came out of the wood, and saluted us in their usual manner singing, as they approached, the chorus we had heard on board, which strengthened our opinion of its being a song of welcome

The next day I landed with a party in the bay where the principal village is situated, and was met at the landing-place, which was about half a mile from the village, by two or three men who rubbed noses, and seemed glad to see us They took us by the arm and conducted us to the village along a narrow pathway, through long grass and loose stones, overshadowed by a wood of bread-fruit and cocoa-nut trees In this distance we passed a few patches of cultivation, but they were rare, and indicated very little attention to agriculture The natives increased greatly in numbers as we advanced, and all were officious to pay us attention, and assist us to the village they were armed, yet their manner showed it was, as with us, only a precautionary measure · nothing in appearance could exceed their amicable behavior We had each two or more friends, who officially passed their arms under ours, helped us over the stones, and conducted us along the right pathway to the village ; a species of escort, however, which, by depriving us of the use of our limbs, placed us entirely in their power We passed several huts open on the south side, and one, which was full of fishing-nets, closed up ; near these there were two bodies wrapped in a great many cloths, exposed upon stalls raised about a yard from the ground, and supported upon forked props.

The natives were unwilling that we should touch any of these. and we did not offend them by so doing, but approached within a few feet to ascertain whether there were any offensive smell from the corpse, but none could be discerned

Further on we came to an open area, partly paved with blocks of coral, and divided off from the cultivated land by large slabs of the same material very evenly cut, and resembling those at the Friendly Islands   At one end of this area stood the large hut which had before excited our curiosity. it was about thirteen yards in length by six or seven in width, and proportionably high, with a thatched roof   On the south side it was entirely open, and the gables nearly so, being constructed with upright poles, crossed by smaller ones, forming an open frame-work, through which the sea breeze circulated, and refreshed the area within   Beneath the roof on the open side, about four feet within the eaves, there was a low broad wall well constructed with blocks of coral, hewn out and put together in so workmanlike a style, and of such dimensions, as to excite our surprise, how, with their rude instruments, it could have been accomplished   The blocks were five feet long by three wide, and one foot thick; and were placed upon the narrow edge in a manner in which we traced a resemblance to the walls in Hapae, as described by Captain Cook.   Upon this eminence was seated a venerable looking person about sixty years of age, with a long beard entirely grey; he had well-proportioned features, and a commanding aspect, his figure was rather tall, but lassitude and corpulency greatly diminished his natural stature; he was entirely naked except a maro, and a crown made from the feathers of the frigate-bird, or black tern, his body was extensively tattooed, and from the loins to the ankles he was covered with small lines, which at a distance had the appearance of pantaloons   Long nails, and rolls of skin overhanging his hips, pointed out his exemption from labour, and an indulgence in luxuries which in all probability attached to him in virtue of his birthright.   He was introduced to us as an areghe or chief; he did not rise from his seat, but gave the nasal salutation in his squatting posture, which in the Friendly Islands is considered a mark of respect

An exchange of presents succeeded this meeting   Some scarlet cloth, which I had brought on shore for the purpose, was placed over his shoulders, and closed by a buckle in front, which delighted the subjects as much as the chief, who, in return presented me with his crown, and intimated that I should wear it by placing it upon my hat.   This friendly understanding I endeavoured to turn to our advantage by making him understand, as well as I could by signs and Otaheitan words, that we would barter articles we had brought with us for fruit and vegetables, and in the hope of this being acceded to, we waited longer at the village than we should otherwise have done, but the only answer we got was "Bobo mai," which from the Otaheitan vocabulary we should interpret " Here to-morrow," but its application in the Gambier groupe was so various as to leave us much in doubt whether they were not disposed to turn our imperfect use of it to their own advantage   Our visit to the village brought a great accession to its usual inhabitants, and several hundred people had collected about us, but the greatest order prevailed; nor did their curiosity to scrutinize our persons once lead them to acts of rudeness, notwithstanding we were the first Europeans that had ever landed on their island.   Indeed, throughout this visit, or at least until we were coming away, there was a marked improvement in their behaviour ; not a single act of theft was attempted, while, on the contrary, one of honesty occurred, which, as it is the only instance I have to record, must not be omitted; —it consisted in restoring to one of our officers a handkerchief which he left at a place where he had been sitting   This propriety of conduct no doubt originated in the strictness of the discipline which we observed towards them , It certainly did not proceed from the example of the chief, for the only act of acquisitiveness from which we had reason to apprehend any dispute proceeded from that personage himself   To oblige him, I had consented to his looking into the bag of presents, with which he became so enamoured that he retained it in his grasp, and once or twice endeavoured to appropriate it to himself by force

We had not remained many minutes in the hut where we were first introduced, when the areghe rose, and, taking me with him, went to a large stone, in the centre of the paved area, where we both sat down, and were immediately surrounded by some hundreds of his subjects. The exchange of place was by no means agreeable, as we quitted a cool and refreshing retreat for a spot scarcely screened from a scorching sun by a few scanty leaves of the bread-fruit tree. After being seated here a few minutes, a tall good-looking young man was introduced, also as an areghe, to whom the old chief transferred the cloth I had given him.   I made him in addition a similar present, and distributed others of smaller value to several natives around us, in the hope of quieting their solicitations; but I soon perceived that this generosity had the opposite effect

The young chief was handsomely tattooed; he had a turban of white cloth, and a girdle of bananaleaf as his only covering.   He was more anxious to communicate with us than the old man; pointed to the road leading over the hill to a village on the opposite side, and made many signs, which we interpreted as promising us the restoration of the articles that had been stolen, and also some supplies, at the same time he intimated that a person of superior dignity resided on the other side of the hill   But if this were true, the distance was only half a mile, and we remained long enough in the village for a person to have traversed it five or six times.   We were next introduced, by the chief, to several women, who saluted us in the usual manner, and thankfully accepted our presents.   The chief wished me particularly to notice one of them, a fine tall woman about thirty-five years of age, with sharp black eyes, long black hair, rather sunburnt, white and even teeth, a complexion lighter than the generality of her countrywomen, and with a good-natured countenance which the coarseness of feature only prevented being pretty.   She had an armlet tattooed on each arm, and was without any other ornament whatever, her ears even were not pierced for the reception of rings.   Her dress consisted of a piece of white cloth wrapped round the hips, and another round the waist below the breast, which was exposed.   There was something commanding in her manner, and from her intimacy with the chief she was evidently a person of superior rank.   She addressed her conversation to me with a volubility and earnestness which showed she felt confident of being understood, but I regret that our total ignorance of their language denied me the pleasure of interpreting even one word, and I could only infer from her tears and actions, that her tale was of a serious and distressing nature   She soon however dried her tears, and sat beside us with the greatest composure

While I was engaged with the chief, the officers strolled about, each accompanied by a circle of friends, and were kindly treated. Mr Belcher, in his researches, discovered three drums, very similar to those at Otaheite, as described by Captain Cook.   The largest was about five feet six inches high, and fourteen inches in diameter   It was made of the trunk of a porou tree (*hibiscus tiliaceus*), hollowed out, and covered with a shark's skin, which had been strained over it when wet, the edges were secured with sinnet, neatly made, and finished with pieces of cloth plaited in with fine line, it was otherwise ornamented about the trunk, and stood upon four feet.   It was brought to me, and I offered the areghe some knives in exchange, which he refused until the number was increased.   When the bargain was concluded, the young chief showed the manner of playing upon the instrument, and convinced us that his skill must have been the result of long practice —The art consisted in giving rapid strokes with the palm of the right hand, and placing the left at the same time so nicely as to check the vibrations without stopping them, which produced a harmonic sound, differing from that of any instrument of the kind I had ever heard

The other drums were about three feet and a half in height by

nine inches in diameter, similar in other respects to the large one
The proficiency in execution to which the natives had attained, and
the perfection in the manufacture of these instruments, leave little
doubt of their taking much delight in the amusement of dancing,
though, generally speaking, they do not appear to be a lively people   I used every endeavour, but in vain, to persuade the areghe
to favour us with one of these exhibitions, and among others, I made
the marines go through some of their manœuvres, in the hope that
he would exhibit something in return; this, however, had a very
different effect from what was intended , for the motions of the marines were misinterpreted, and so alarmed some of the bystanders, that
several made off, while others put themselves into an attitude of defence, so that I speedily dismissed the party.

This interview was deficient in those ceremonies which threw
such a lively interest over the voyages of Captain Cook, and, what
was equally mortifying to us, it did not obtain those supplies of fruit
and vegetables which generally attended his visits , although we waited a considerable time in the hope of inducing the chiefs to come on
board the ship, and in the expectation of some supplies before we
quitted them, but to no purpose   I therefore summoned our party
together, and we took leave of the chiefs, both of whom retired,
leaving us in the hands of the mob.   On removing the drum which
had been sold by the areghe. two of the natives laid violent hands
upon it, and demanded something more than had been given.   To
avoid disturbance I complied with their request by doubling the
original sum; but this, so far from securing the drum, rendered the
probability of our obtaining it without force more remote.   I brought
the old chief back to explain the matter to him, but he showed no
disposition to interfere; and foreseeing the consequence of persist-
ing, I left our purchase in the hands of the islanders, disgusted
with their dishonesty and cunning.

On our return, about two o'clock in the afternoon, we observed
the meals of the natives laid out upon tables, made of slabs, raised
about a yard from the ground, and standing in the middle of the paved areas in front of the huts.   These tables again resembled those
in the Friendly Islands, and the execrable sour pudding tied up in
bundles with banana-leaves of which the fare of the ·natives con-
·sisted, is the same as the mahie used there, at Otaheite, and at the
Marquesas, &c , but in flavour it more immediately reminded us of
the Nukahiwans

We found fewer companions in our retreat from the village than
at our introduction to it, and were attended by three individuals
only, who had attached themselves to some officers, though many
followed at a distance   I was a little behind the party, when a man
whom I did not recollect to have seen before, grasped me by the

arm in which I held my gun, with a feigned view of helping me over the rugged path, while a second, putting his arms across, stopped up the road, several others, at the same time, joined in the demand of 'Homy! homy!' and prepared us for what shortly took place I managed to get rid of my unruly assistants without force, and joined the marines, but Lieutenant Wainwright (who, unknown to us all, was left in the village, ignorant of our having quitted it until informed by one of the natives), was not so fortunate. He passed through the village, where the natives were assembled in circles, apparently in debate, without molestation, and in a few minutes would have been among our party: when several of the natives, seeing him alone, assailed him, and endeavoured to throw him down and rob him Finding they could not succeed, they attacked him with their poles. but he was then fortunately within a short distance of us, and we became for the first time apprised of his danger by hearing him call for assistance. Mr Belcher, and those who were nearest, ran to him, but the islanders assailing them with stones, and the attack on their part becoming general, I ordered the marines to fire, which put them to flight, and I am happy to say that we saw only one of them wounded

Thus this interview with the natives terminated in a manner which their general conduct might have led us to expect though the result is much to be deplored It confirmed my opinion, that the natural disposition of the people is highly unfavourable to intercourse, and that they are restrained from acts of violence and aggression by the operation of fear alone With this impression, and finding the island so extremely deficient in supplies, that the natives could not spare us any thing, I was careless about renewing our visit, and we embarked without further molestation, and proceeded to the ship

The bay in which this village is situated lies on the N. E side of Mount Duff, it is bordered by a sandy beach, behind which there is a thick wood of bread-fruit and cocoa-nut trees, above it, to the left, there is a second or upper village, upon a level piece of ground, where the natives retreat in case of necessity The bay would be very desirable for an anchorage, were it not for the coral knolls at its entrance, which make the navigation difficult even for a boat After this visit, the boats were again sent surveying; and on the 12th we had completed all that our time would admit of, by fixing the position of a number of coral knolls which are dispersed over the navigable part of the lagoon, the greater part of which may be seen from a ship's mast-head before she comes upon them Our only want afterwards was a little fire-wood; and having noticed several logs lying upon the shore abreast of the ship, Mr. Belcher was sent to purchase them. The natives readily disposed of their property, and were very friendly as long as they were receiving presents ; but directly he attempted to take away the trees, the islanders collected in the wood, and pelted the boat's crew with stones. Three logs were however got off, and Mr. Belcher was putting in for more, when the natives again beginning to throw stones, he desisted

It is to be regretted that the disposition of the natives obstructed the friendly intercourse we were anxious to establish The task of correcting their evil propensities unfortunately devolved upon us, as the first visiters to the islands ; and we could not prolong our stay, or devote the time that was necessary while we did remain, to conciliate their friendship But though unsuccessful in this respect, it is to be hoped that our visit will prove beneficial to others, by directing them to a port in which ships may be refitted or repaired, and where they may procure a supply of good water, than which nothing is more important to the navigation of these seas · as that indispensable article is not found to exist in a pure state anywhere between Otaheite and the coast of Chili, a distance of 4000 miles, Pitcairn Island excepted, where the difficulty of getting it off has already been mentioned It is also presumed, that the position of the islands having been ascertained, the peaks of Mount Duff, which are high and distinguishable at a great distance, will serve as a guide to the labyrinth of coral islands which the navigator, after passing this groupe, has to thread on his way to the westward.

This groupe was discovered by the ship Duff, on a missionary voyage, in 1797, and named by Mr Wilson, her commander, after Admiral Lord Gambier It consists of five large islands and several small ones, all situated in a lagoon formed by a reef of coral The largest is about six miles in length, and rises into two peaks, elevated 1248 feet above the level of the sea.   These peaks, which were called after the Duff, are in the form of wedges, very conspicuous at a distance, and may be seen fourteen or fifteen leagues All the islands are steep and rugged, particularly Marsh Island, which at a distance resembles a ship The external form of these island at once conveys an impression of their volcanic· origin ; and, on examination, they all appeared to have been subjected to the action of great heat.

" The general basis of the rocks is a porous basaltic lava, in one place passing into a tuffacious slate ; in another, into the solid and angular column of compact basalt, containing the imbedded minerals which characterize that formation, and bearing a close resemblance in this particular to the basaltic formation of the county of Antrim in Ireland There is, however, less of the basalt and more of the porous.   The zealites, soapstone, chalcedony, olivine, and calcareous spar, are formed in, and connect the relationship of these distant formations; whilst the different-coloured jaspers are peculiar to these islands. There is also another obvious distinctive feature produced by the numerous dykes of a formation differing in composition and texture, and marked by a defined line. They are generally more prominent than the common rock: traversing a great many, if not all the islands, in a direction nearly east and west; generally about eighteen inches wide, nearly perpendicular to the horizon, or dipping to the southward. Their texture is sometimes compact, sometimes vesicular, with few if any imbedded minerals, excepting one on Marsh Island, which contained great quantities of olivine. Upon a small island contiguous to this, the harder dyke crosses the highest ridge, and divides on the eastern side into two parts which continue down to the water's edge."*

Lieutenant Belcher, whose scientific attainments also enabled him to appreciate what fell under his observation, noticed every where the trap formation abounding in basaltic dykes also lying N. E. and S. W., and seldom deviating from the perpendicular; or if they did, it was to the eastward. We are indebted to him for specimens of zealite, carbonate of lime, calcareous spar, crystals, an alcine, olivine, jasper, and chalcedony; and had our stay, and his other duties admitted, we should, no doubt, have received from him a more detailed account of this interesting groupe.

There are no appearances of pseudo-craters on any of the islands, nor do they seem to have been very recently subjected to fire, being clothed with verdure, and for the most part with trees. Conspicuously opposed to these lofty rugged formations, raised by the agency of fire, is a series of low islands, derived from the opposite element, and owing their construction to myriads of minute lithophytes endowed with an instinct that enables them to separate the necessary calcareous matter from the ocean, and with such minute particles to rear a splendid structure many leagues in circumference. A great wall of this kind, if we may use the expression, already surrounds the islands, and, by the unremitting labour of these submarine animals, is fast approaching the surface of the water in all its parts. On the N. E. side, it already bears a fertile soil beyond the reach of the sea, sustains trees and other subjects of the vegetable kingdom, and affords even an habitation to man.

In the opposite direction it dips from thirty to forty feet beneath the surface, as if purposely to afford access to shipping to the lagoon within. Whether this irregularity be the consequence of unequal growth, or of the original inclination of the foundation, is a question that has excited much interest. All the islands we subsequently visited were similar to these in having their weather or

* Mr. Collie's Journal.

eastern side more advanced than the opposite one. The outer side of the wall springs from unfathomable depths; the inner descends with a slope to about 120 or 150 feet below the surface. This abruptness causes the sea to break and expend its fury upon the reef without disturbing the waters in the lagoon. The coral animals consequently rear their delicate structure there without apprehension of violence; and form their submarine grottoes in all the varied shapes which fancy can conceive. They have already encircled each of the islands with a barrier, which they are daily extending; and have reared knolls so closely as almost to occupy all the northern part of the lagoon. More independent tribes are in other parts bringing to the surface numerous isolated columns, tending to the same end; and all seem to be going on with such activity, that a speculative imagination migh picture to itself at no very remote period, one vast plain covering the whole surface of the lagoon, yielding forests of bread fruit, cocoa-nuts, and other trees, and ultimately sustenance to a numerous population, and a variety of animals subservient to their use.

The general steepness of the volcaic islands of this groupe is such, that the soil finds a resting place on a comparatively small portion of them; and on the coral islands it is scarcely deep and rich enough, exposed at it is to the sea air, to contribute much to the support of man. A soil formed from the decomposition of the basaltic rocks, irrigated by streams from the mountains, requires nothing but a due proportion of care and labour on the part of the natives to render it very productive. There is, however, a sad neglect in this respect, which is the more extraordinary, as there are no quadrupeds or poultry on the islands, and without vegetable productions the natives have only the sea to depend upon for their subsistence. The wild productions are a coarse grass (*Saccharum fatuum*), which covers such parts of the mountains as are neglected or are too steep for cultivation. Lower down we noticed the capparidia, a procumbent pentandrous shrub, the nasturtium, sesuvium of Pitcairn Island, the eugenia, and scævola kœnigii; and close down to the shore a convolvulus covering the brown rock with its clusters of leaves and pink blossoms. The porou and miroe (*Thespesia popularia*) were more abundant, the nono not common. They must also have the auti and amia, as their weapons are made of it, though we did not see it. The timber of which their rafts are constructed is a red wood, somewhat porous, and of softer grain than the amai. Some of these trunks are so large as at first to excite a suspicion of their having been drifted from a more extensive shore; but the quantity which they possess, several logs of which were newly shaped out, affords every reason for believing that it is the produce of their own valleys. They are not deficient in variety of edible fruits and roots, nor in those kinds which are most productive and nutritious   Besides the tee-plant, sweet potato, appe, sugar-cane, watermelon, cocoa-nut, plantain, and banana, they possess the bread-fruit, which in Otaheite is the staff of life, and the taro, a root which in utility corresponds with it in the Sandwich Islands   Were they to pay but a due regard to the cultivation of the two last of these valuable productions, an abundance of wholesome food might be substituted for the nauseous mixture mahie, which, though it may, as indeed it does, support life, cannot be said to do more.   Rats and lizards were the only quadrupeds we saw upon the islands.   Of the feathered tribe, oceanic birds form the greater part, but even these are rare, compared with the numbers that usually frequent the islands of the Pacific, arising, no doubt, from the Gambier Islands being inhabited.   The whole consist of three kinds of tern, the white, black, and slate-coloured—of which the first is most numerous, and the last very scarce, together with a species of procellaria, the white heron, and the tropic and egg birds.   Those which frequent the shore are a kind of pharmatopus, curlew, charadrine, and totanus; and the woods, the wood-pigeon, and a species of turdus, somewhat resembling a thrush in plumage, but smaller, possessing a similar though less harmonious note   The insects found here were very few, the, common house-fly excepted, which on almost all the inhabited islands in the Pacific is extremely numerous and annoying   Of fish there is a great variety, and many are extremely beautiful in colour; as well those of large dimensions, which we caught with lines, consisting of several sorts of perca, as the numerous family of the order of branchiostigi, which sported about the coral.

The largest portion of the natives of the Gambier Islands belong to a class which Mr. J. R Forster would place among the first variety of the human species in the South Seas   Like the generality of uncivilized people, they are good-natured when pleased, and harmless when not irritated, obsequious when inferior in force, and overbearing when otherwise; and are carried away by an insatiable desire of appropriating to themselves every thing which attracts their fancy—an indulgence which brings them into many quarrels, and often costs them their lives   If respect for the deceased be considered a mark of civilization and humanity, they cannot be called a barbarous people; but they possess no other claims to a worthier designation   In features, language, and customs, they resemble the Society, Friendly, Marquesa, and Sandwich Islanders: but they differ from those tribes in one very important point—an exemption from those sensual habits and indecent exhibitions which there pervade all ranks   It may be said of the Gambier Islanders what few can assert of any people inhabiting the same part of the globe—that during the whole of our intercourse with them we did not witness an indecent act or gesture   There is a great mixture of feature and of colour among them, and we should probably have found a difference of dialect also, could we have made ourselves masters of their language.   It seems as if several tribes from remote parts of the Pacific had here met and mingled their peculiarities.   In complexion and feature we could trace a resemblance even to the widely separated tribes of New Zealand, New Caledonia, and Malacca.   Their mode of salutation is the same as that which existed at the Friendly, Society, and Sandwich Islands: they resemble the inhabitants of the latter almost exclusively in tattooing the face, and the inhabitants of the former in staining their skin from the hips to the knees   Their huts, coral tables, and pavements, are nearly the same as at the Friendly Islands and the Marquesas, but they are more nearly allied to the latter by a custom which otherwise, I believe, is at present confined to them, and without a due observance of which, Krusenstern says, it is in vain to seek a matrimonial alliance at St Christina *   In the preservation of their dead, wrapping them in an abundance of cloth and mats, they copy the Otaheitans and Hapaeans, though in the ultimate disposal of them in caves, and keeping them above ground, they differ from all the other islanders.   Their language and religion are closely allied to several, yet they differ essentially from all the above-mentioned tribes in having no huge carved images surmounting their morais, and no fiatookas or wattas   Unlike them also, they are deficient in canoes, though they might easily construct them; they have neither clubs, slings, nor bows and arrows, and are wanting in those marks of selfmutilation which some tribes deem indispensable on the death of their chiefs or esteemed friends, or in cases when the wish to appease their offended deity

They are for the most part fairer and handsomer than the Sandwich Islanders, but less effeminate than the Otaheitans   The average height of the men is above that of Englishmen, but they are not so robust   One man who came on board measured six feet and half an inch, and one on shore six feet, two and a half inches   The former measured round the thorax, under the arms, three feet two and a half, and a person of less stature three feet one inch.   The thickest part of the middle of this person's arm, when at rest, was eleven inches and three-eighths   These dimensions of girth will, I believe, be found less in proportion than those of the labouring class of our own countrymen, though the general appearance of these islanders at first leads to a different conclusion.   They are upright in figure, and round, but not robust.   In their muscles there is a flabbiness, and in the men a laxity of integument, which allows their

* See Krusenstern's Embassy to Japan

skin to hang in folds about the belly and thighs, to a greater degree than those I afterwards noticed at Otaheite or Woahoo. Two causes may be assigned for this, the nature of their food, and their indolent habits

In general the Gambier Islanders have a fine Asiatic countenance, with mustachios and beards, but no whiskers; and when their heads are covered with a roll of white cloth, common custom, they might pass for Moors. It is somewhat remarkable that we perceived none of the fourth class, or those nearly allied to negroes thus habited, but that it seemed to be confined to those of the lightest complexion The colour of their eyes is either hazel or dark brown: they are small, deep in the head, and have generally an expression of cunning. Their eyebrows are naturally arched, and seldom meet in front, the cheek bones are not so prominent as in the fourth class, and the lips are thinner; the ears are moderately large, and the lobes attached to the cheek, as in all the Pitcairn Islanders, but not perforated: the nose in general is aquiline, the teeth, in the fourth class especially, not remarkable for evenness or whiteness, and seem to fall out at an early period; the hair is turned back and cut straight, and would be quite black, were it less subjected to the sun, or like that of the islanders just mentioned, well oiled; but, exposed as it is to a scorching sun, it becomes dried up and of different hues on the same head, and combs being unknown it is bushy and impervious; the mustachios grow long, but the beards, which are kept from three to four inches in length, are sometimes brought to a point, at others divided into two, one man, however, was observed with a beard which hung down to the pit of the stomach · the hands are large, but the feet small and elegant, and the toes close together, from which it is probable that they pass a great portion of their time upon their rafts, or idly basking in the sun,—perhaps in lying upon their stone pavements like the Hapaeans The women are below the common standard height, and in personal shape and beauty far inferior to the males. The wife of the chief, who has been already described, was the finest woman I saw among them Her dress may be considered a fair specimen of the general covering of the women, who have no ornaments of any kind, and appeared quite indifferent to the beads and trinkets which were offered them

Tattooing is here so universally practiced that it is rare to meet a man without it, and is carried to such an extent that the figure is sometimes covered with small checkered lines from the neck to the ankles, though the breast is generally exempt, or only ornamented with a single device In some, generally elderly men, the face is covered below the eyes, in which case the lines or net-work are more open than on other parts of the body, probably on account of the pain of the operation, and terminate at the upper part in a

straight line, from ear to ear, passing over the bridge of the nose.
With these exceptions, to which we may add the fashion, with some
few, of blue lines, resembling stockings, from the middle of the thigh
to the ankle, the effect is becoming, and in a great measure destroys
the appearance of nakedness   The patterns which most improve
the shape, and which appear to me peculiar to this groupe, are
those which extend from the armpits to the hips, and are drawn
forward with a curve which seems to contract the waist, and at a
short distance gives the figure an elegance and outline not unlike
that of the figures seen on the walls of the Egyptian tombs   It
would be useless to describe the various fanciful attempts to efface
the natural colour of the skin, the most common only will be noticed —A large cross, about eight inches in diameter, left white on
each side, on the latissimus dorsi ; and a smaller one on each shoulder, or on the upper part of the arm : also a narrow stripe passing
from one shoulder to the other in a curved line over the lower part
of the neck, uniting the tattooing over the fleshy part of the deltoid
muscle ; and in many so joined as to leave the natural skin in the
form of a cross in the middle   Imitations of blue pantaloons and
breeches are also very common, and sleeves which divide at the
wrist, and extend along the convexity of the metatarsal bones to
the tips of the fingers and thumbs, leaving a space between the
thumb and forefinger, on which the mark V is punctured   The
chief had this mark, the crosses, the slender waist, and the pantaloons   The women are very little subjected to this torture.   The
wife of the areghe had an armlet on each arm; a female who came
with her had a square upon her bosom, and some few had stockings   From the circumstance of none of the boys being tattooed,
it is probable the practice commences here, as in many other islands, after puberty.

The lines in all cases are drawn with great precision, and almost
always with taste, and bespeak great proficiency   The practice undoubtedly improves the appearance of the figure, and may perhaps,
as in the Marquesas, distinguish certain classes or tribes   At Otaheite it is supposed to harden the skin, and render it less liable to
be blistered by the sun.   Covering the face with lines is very rare
in the South Seas, being almost entirely confined, according to
Cook, to the Sandwich Islanders and New Zealanders.   In no instance did we observe the lips or tongues tattooed, as is the practice with the Sandwich Islanders on the death of an intimate friend.

I have estimated the number of souls inhabiting these islands at
1500, from the number and size of the villages.   Mr. Collie, who
estimates them from other data, says, " On the 1st January, when
the boats went to land, 200 people, for the most part in the prime of
life were counted on the beach.   On the 9th, in the village, we

enumerated 300 persons, men and women   On both these occasions it is highly probable that the men in the vigor of life had come from the adjoining parts of the island, and from the islands contiguous   We may then assume, on the nearest approximation to the truth, that there were between 250 and 300 males between the ages of twenty and fifty—say 275 ; which according to the most accurate census of population and bills of mortality in Sweden and Switzerland, where the modifying circumstances are in all probability not very different, would give 1285 for the total number of inhabitants "

The diseases and deformities of these people are very few.   After we quitted the islands, the surgeon favoured me with the following report —

" Among more than three hundred men, women, and children, who indiscriminately surrounded us at the village on the 9th ; among those who had previously come on board, and at other times, whether upon the shore or on their rafts , we saw very few labouring under any original deformity or annoying disease.   The only case of mal-conformation was a wide fissure in the palate of one man, whose speech was considerably affected by it.   No external mark of cicatrization in the upper lip denoted that the internal defect was the remains of a hare-lip or any injury   One man had a very uneven and jagged stump of the right arm, but without any discharge   Another had a steatomatous tumour over one shoulder-blade, about the-size of a billard ball   One disease was so common that I have no doubt it was endemic   this was, patches of the lepro vulgaris, which being void of any inflammatory appearance, and confined to the back in all who were affected with it, and in a considerable proportion of these to a small space between the shoulders, appeared to create no alarm, and most probably called forth no curative application   The frequent and alternate exposure of the men to the salt water and rays of the sun, with a scanty supply of the anointing oil of the cocoa-nut, would favour the breaking out of this cutaneous affection   The mats which they tied round their necks, and frequently allowed to hang down behind, whether through accident or design, would tend to avert the effects of exposure   A few had lost some of their front teeth , and we saw one man, on the 9th, with two uncicatrized and bare but clean wounds, one before and another behind the middle of the right deltoid muscle, where the flies were feeding without molestation, and the person seemed almost unconscious of them and of the ulcers   No preternatural tumefaction denoted any excess of inflammation   No unhealthy hue in the countenance of man or woman intimated any internal disease lurking within the body "   By far the greater part of the males go entirely naked, except a girdle, which is made of a banana-leaf split into shreds, and tied round the loins, not intended to answer the purpose of concealment; and they differ from all other inhabitants of the Pacific in having no maio. Some wear a turban, others a piece of paper cloth thrown over the shoulders

The huts of the Gambier Islanders are so small that they can only be intended as sleeping-places during bad weather; they are in length from eight or ten feet to fifteen, excepting the larger houses of the areghe; they are built of the porou wood, and covered in with a pointed roof thatched over with the leaves of the palm-tree In some the door is scarcely three feet high, and it is necessary to creep on all-fours to enter. On the inside they are neat, and the floor is covered with mats or grass The larger huts of the village on Mount Duff are so constructed that one side can be conveniently removed, by which means they are rendered cool and comfortable.

The large house, or that of the areghe, was about thirty-nine feet in length by eighteen or twenty in width; the pitch of the roof was about twenty-five feet in height, and that of the perpendicular sides of the house about ten feet; but these dimensions were obtained by estimation only, the natives appearing to have an objection to our pacing the ground for the purpose of measurement. The south side of the house was left open, and the ends were made of an open framework of upright poles traversed at right angles by smaller spars, so that the roof and the north side were the only parts covered in. They served an excellent protection from the sun while the trade-wind traversing every corner of the apartment rendered it agreeably cool On that part of the house where the side was deficient, there was a foundation for the wall about three feet in height thrown up, composed of large blocks of coral, shaped in a very workmanlike style, similar to those mentioned by Cook at the Friendly Islands, and well put together· it stood about three feet within the outer part of the roofing, and served as a seat for the chiefs as well as for many others

We perceived no furniture in their houses, and some of our officers thought it was purposely put out of sight The only utensils were gourds and cocoa-nut shells. The tables were made of slabs of coral, or sometimes of wood, in which case they are carved· they are about a yard long, and are placed upon wooden or stone pedestals sufficiently high to prevent the depredations of the rats. They stand in the middle of the paved areas in front of the houses, from which we infer the practice of eating in the open air Their food has already been described as consisting principally of sour paste (the mahie of the Friendly Islands, Otaheite, Marquesas, &c), made with plantains, bread-fruit, and boiled tee-root The paste or mahie, when fresh and hot, has not a disagreeable taste; a slight flavour of baked apples may be distinguished. but it soon begins to smell very offensively; so much so, that the seamen would not touch it with their hands to throw it overboard The tee-plant (*dracœna terminalis*) is a fusiform root about two feet long, and as thick as the arm, its flavour is not unpleasant, but from its coarseness it must, to ordinary stomachs, be very indigestible The natives collect the fibres in their mouths, and spit them out in round balls. Fish and shell-fish, of which the large pearl oysters and chama are in the greatest abundance, must form a material part of the food of these people. they have, besides, the sweet potato, taro, and the before-mentioned fruits; but these cannot be abundant, as they never brought any of them to us for sale, and frequently deceived us with empty cocoa-nuts

Their method of procuring fish is by lines and nets, and a contrivance still resorted to in Otaheite, consisting of casting into the sea a great many branches of the cocoa-nut tree, and other boughs, tied together, and allowing them to remain some time, during which the small fish become entangled, and are dragged out with them The nets and lines, as well as cord, sinnet, &c, are all made from the bark of the porou, as in all the islands of Polynesia One net which we measured was ninety feet in length. In the manufacture of these, they display a greater proficiency than in their cloth, which is much inferior to that at Pitcairn Island or Otaheite Their implements for this purpose are the same in shape as those at the above-mentioned places; but the one which we got differed in not being grooved

Their weapons consist of spears, and a staff flattened at the end like a whale-lance they are made of a hard wood highly polished. The spears were headed with bone, or the sting rays of the raia (*pastinea*), a custom which once existed at Otaheite, and now extends to many of the low islands The antiquity of this practice is traced to very remote periods, as it is said that the head of the spear presented by Circe to Telegonus, and with which he unceremoniously slew his father Ulysses, was of this kind At Gambier Island they remove the heads of the spears when not required, a square piece being left at the end of the staff to receive it. Besides these weapons, they always carry large sticks.

Contrary to the general custom, no canoes are seen at Gambier Islands, but rafts or katamarans are used instead. They are from forty to fifty feet in length, and will contain upwards of twenty persons They consist of the trunks of trees fastened together by rope and cross-beams upon this a triangular sail is hoisted, supported by two poles from each end; but it is only used when the wind is very favourable, at which time, if two or three katamarans happen to be going the same way, they fasten on and perform their voyage

together   At other times they use very large paddles made of a
dark hard wood, capable of a good polish, and neatly executed.
Some of them had a hand or foot, carved at the extremity of the
handles, very well finished.   They are above five feet and a half in
length, including two feet eight inches of blade, which is about a foot
in width, curved, and furnished with a small point or nail at the extremity.   In shallow water they make use of long poles for punting,
in preference to their paddles

CHAPTER VII

On the morning of the 13th of January we weighed from Gambier Islands, and deepened the water so much that, after quitting our anchorage, we could get no soundings with the hand-lines until near the bar, which was plainly distinguished by its colour long before we came upon it   There was not less than seven fathoms where we passed, and yet the sea, which rolled in heavily from the S. W., all but broke, notwithstanding the wind had been blowing strong in the opposite direction for a week before   This effect of the prevalent south-westerly gales in the high latitudes, which is felt many hundred miles from the place whence it proceeds, occasions a material obstacle to landing upon the low islands, by rolling in upon the shore in an opposite direction to the trade-wind, and thereby making it more dangerous to land on the lee-side of the island than on the other   In the Gambier groupe there are several small sandy islands at the S. W extremity of the chain that surrounds it, over which the sea broke so heavily that they were entirely lost amidst the foam.   I named them Wolfe Islands, after Mr Wolfe, one of the midshipmen of the ship.   We passed them tolerably close, admiring the grand scene which they presented, and then stood on a northerly course with the intention of visiting Lord Hood's Island

In the forenoon of the following day several white tern, noddies, and black gulls came about us, and gradually increased in numbers as we proceeded on our course   A few hours afterwards Lord Hood's Island was reported from aloft   On nearing it, we found it to consist of an assemblage of small islets, rising from a chain of coial, even with, or a little above the water's edge   Upon these grew a variety of evergreen trees thickly intertwined, among which the broad leaves and clusters of fruit of the pandanus were conspicuous, and beneath them a matted surface of moss and grass, so luxuriant and invitingly cool, that we were almost tempted to land at any risk.   The sea, however, broke so heavily upon all parts of the shore that the attempt would have been highly dangerous, and we consequently collected all the information that was required, and hastened our departure   Krusenstern states in his " Memoire sur la Pacifique," that this island is inhabited . such must undoubtedly have been the case once, as we saw a square stone hut, similar to those described at Crescent Island, on one of its angles ; but there are no human beings upon it at present, which indeed we conjectured to be the case before our boats made the circuit of it, from the number of sea birds in the vicinity, and also from the shoals of sharks which followed the boats, and even bit at the oars ; for these animals, like most others, seem to have learned by experience to avoid the haunts of man.   The only living thing seen upon the shore was a grey heron gorging itself with black star-fish.

Lord Hood's Island was discovered by Mr. Wilson in the Missionary ship Duff, it is 11 2 miles in length, and 4 7 miles in width, in a north and south direction ; and like almost all the coral islands it contains a lagoon, and is steep on all its sides

After quitting it, we looked in vain, the next day, for an island which Mr. Wilson supposed he saw, but not finding it in or near the situation assigned, and he being himself doubtful whether it might not have been a cloud, I did not bestow longer time in the search, but steered for the island of Clermont Tonnere, which was seen on the 18th.   This island bore a very close resemblance to Hood's Island, but was inhabited, and clothed with cocoanut trees   The sea broke so heavily upon all parts of the shore that there was no possibility of landing in our boats, yet the natives put off in their canoes and paddled to us   They were a very inferior race to those of the Gambier Islands, and seemed more nearly allied in feature to those of Mangea and New Caledonia ; yet here also there was among them a great diversity of complexion   In one of the canoes there was a man nearly as dark as an African negro, with woolly hair. tied in a knot like the Radackers, and another with a light complexion, sandy hair, and European features.

About forty of the natives came down to the beach when we approached it, with bunches of feathers and leaves fastened upon sticks, and with bludgeons in their hands   Both sexes were naked with the exception of their maros, and without any ornaments or tattooing.   Iron, which they called " toki," was the most marketable article, but the surf was so high that there was very little communication with them. The men, who came off to us in their canoes, would not suffer our boats to approach them. After having made a number of presents to one of them, we thought we might at least examine his canoe; but he and his comrades paddled away with the greatest precipitation, and were so terrified at the approach of the boat that they jumped overboard and swam towards the shore

The canoe was constructed with small pieces of wood well put together and sewed with the bark of a tree, and, like all the single canoes of Polynesia, was provided with an outrigger. She carried two men, but was propelled almost entirely by one, the other being fully occupied in throwing out the water, which came in plentifully at both sides and over the stern. Could they have avoided this and applied the efforts of both to the paddles, her rapidity would have surpassed that of our boat; but as it was, she was soon overtaken. We did not keep these poor fellows longer in the water than we could help, but quitted the canoe as soon as we had examined its construction, and had the satisfaction to observe them return to it, and get in, one at a time, at the stern, and then paddled ashore.

The dialect of the people of Clermont Tonnere was quite different from that of the Gambier Islanders, though, from a few words which we distinguished, there is no doubt of the language being radically the same According to our calculation, the whole population did not exceed two hundred.

The island is ten miles in length, but very narrow, particularly at the extremities, and, when seen at a distance, does not appear to be half a mile wide. It is of the same formation as Lord Hood's Island, but more perfect With the exception of a few breaks in the southern shore, by which the sea, when high, may at times communicate with the lagoon, it is altogether above water At the extremities and angles the soil is more elevated than in other parts, as if the influence of the sea had been more felt upon them, and heaped up the coral higher They are, also, better provided with shrubs, and particularly cocoa-nut trees, the soil resting upon the debris being, I suppose, deeper The lagoon had several small islets in it, and the shores all round are steep, and abound with fish, but we did not see any sharks.

Captain Duperrey, in his voyage round the world in the Coquille, visited this island, and, supposing it to be a new discovery, named it Clermont Tonnere, after the French minister of marine. It is evident, however, from its situation agreeing very nearly with that of an island discovered by the Minerva, that it must be the same; no other being found sufficiently near to answer the description. Captain Duperrey has, no doubt, been misled by the dimensions given of the island by the Minerva, but that may be easily accoun-

ted for, by supposing the island to have been seen from the Minerva lengthwise, and at a distance

While we were off Clermont Tonnere, we had a narrow escape
from a water-spout of more than ordinary size   It approached us
amidst heavy rain, thunder, and lightning, and was not seen until it
was very near to the ship.   As soon as we were within its influence,
a gust of wind obliged us to take in every sail, and the topsails,
which could not be furled in time, were in danger of splitting.
The wind blew with great violence, momentarily changing its direction, as if it were sweeping round in short spirals ; the rain which
fell in torrents, was also precipitated in curves with short intervals
of cessation.   Amidst this thick shower the water-spout was discovered, extending in a tapering form from a dense stratum of cloud,
to within thirty feet of the water where it was hid, by the foam of
the sea being whirled upwards with a tremendous giration.   It
changed its direction after it was first seen, and threatened to pass
over the ship, but being diverted from its course by a heavy gust
of wind, it gradually receeded   On the dispersion of this magnificent phenomenon, we observed the column to diminish gradually,
and at length to retire to the cloud, from whence it had descended,
in an undulating form

Various causes have been assigned for these formations, which
appear to be intimately connected with electricity   On the present occasion a ball of fire was observed to be precipitated into the
sea, and one of the boats, which was away from the ship, was so
surrounded by lightning, that Lieutenant Belcher thought it advisable to get rid of the anchor, by hanging it some fathoms under water,
and to cover the seamen's muskets   From the accounts of this officer and Mr. Smyth, who were at a distance from the ship, the
column of the water-spout first descended in a spiral form, until it
met the ascending column a short distance from the sea ; a second
and a third were afterwards formed, which subsequently united
into one large column, and this again separated into three small
spirals, and then dispersed   It is not impossible that the highly
rarified air confined by the woods encircling the lagoon islands may
contribute to the formation of these phenomena

A canoe near the ship very wisely hastened on shore at the approach of the bad weather, for had it been drawn within the vortex
of the whirlwind it must have perished   We had the greatest apprehension for our boats, which were absent during the storm, but
fortunately they suffered no injury

Neither the barometer nor sympeisometer were sensibly affected
by this partial disturbance of the atmosphere, but the temperature
underwent a change of eight degrees, falling from 82° to 74°, at
midnight it rose to 78°   On the day succeeding this occurrence,

several water-spouts were seen in the distance, the weather being
squally and gloomy.

After examining the vicinity of Clermont Tonnere for the island
of the Minerva, and seeing no other land, we steered for Serle Isl-
and, which was discovered at daylight on the 21st January, bearing
west.   Its first appearance was that of a low strip of land with a
hillock at each extremity, but these, on a near approach, proved to
be clumps of large trees   Admiral Krusenstern, in his valuable
Memoir on the South Pacific,[*] observes, that Serle Island is higher
than any other island of the low archipelago ; that it has two hills
at its extremities, and a third near its centre , and on this account
recommends it as a place of reconnoissance for ships entering the
archipelago.   In this, however, he has been misled by some navigator who mistook the the trees for hills, and over-estimated the
height of them, as the tallest does not exceed fifty feet.

Some columns of smoke rising from the island showed that it was
inhabited, and on rounding the N. W   extreme we perceived several men and women running along the beach, dragging after them
long poles or spears.   The population altogether cannot exceed a
hundred   The men were entirely naked, but the women had the
usual covering   They were of the same dark swarthy colour with
the natives of Clermont Tonnere, with the hair tied in a similar
knot on the top of the head, and like them they were deficient in
tattooing and ornaments.   Their weapons were poles about twenty
feet in length, similar to those of the Friendly Islanders, and heavy
clubs.   We could not perceive any canoes.

This island is seven miles and a half in length, in a N W. direction, and two and a quarter miles in width in its broadest part   It
is of coral formation, and very similar to that just described ; its
windward side is the most perfect · the southern side of the chain,
however, differs in being wider, and having a barren flat full an
eighth of a mile outside the trees.   On this account it is necessary
for a ship to be cautious in approaching it during the night, as it is
so low that the breakers would be the first warning of the danger of
her situation.   The lagoon is very narrow, and apparently shallow,
with several islands in the middle.   Besides the clumps of trees at
the extremities, which at a distance have the appearance of banyan
trees, there are several clusters of palms ; a distinction which I
would recommend to the attention of commanders of vessels : as, besides assisting them in identifying the islands, it will enable them to
estimate their distance from them with tolerable precision

We left Serle Island on the morning of the 22d, and at sunset
hove-to in the parallel of Whitsunday Island.   This island, discov-

* Page 276, 4to edition.

ered, by Captain Wallis in 1767, is situated forty miles to the westward of the place he has assigned to it, and we consequently ran to the westward all the next day, in expectation of seeing it, but it was not reported from the masthead until late in the evening In the morning of the 23d the boats succeeded in landing, though with some difficulty ; and found indubitable proofs of the island having been inhabited, but no natives were seen.   Under a large clump of trees we observed several huts, eight feet by three, thatched with dried palm leaves, the doors of which were so low that it was necessary to crawl upon the ground to enter the apartments within Near these dwellings were some sheds and several piles of chewed pandanus nuts.

The island was traversed in various directions by well-trodden pathways : not far from the huts were several reservoirs of water cut about eighteen inches into the coral, and about five feet from the general surface of the soil, the water in them was fresh, but from neglect the reservoirs were nearly filled with decayed leaves, and emitted a putrid smell In another direction we saw several slabs of coral placed erect, to denote burial places, and near the opening to the lagoon there were several rows of stakes driven into the ground for the purpose of taking fish But what most attracted our attention was a heap of fish bones, six feet by five, neatly cleaned, and piled up very carefully with planks placed upon them to prevent their being scattered by the wind.

We found the island only a mile and a half in length, instead of four miles, as stated by Captain Wallis; steep all round; of coral formation ; well wooded, and containing a lagoon.   The general height of the soil was six feet above the level of the sea, of which nearly two feet were coral rock ; from the trees to the surf there was a space of hard rock nearly 150 yards in length, covered with about a foot of water, beyond which it descended rapidly, and at 500 yards distance no bottom could be found with 1500 feet of line. On the inner side from the trees to the lake, there was a gentle declivity of muddy sand filled with shells of the cardium, linedo, tridacnæ, gigas, and a species of trochus.   The trees, which formed a tolerably thick wood round the lagoon, were similar to those at Clermont Tonnere, consisting principally of pandanus and cocoanut, interwoven with the tournefortia, scœvola, and lepidium piscidium.

On the south side of the island there was a very narrow entrance to the lagoon, too shallow for the passage of boats, even had the water been smooth.   It was of this opening, I presume, that Captain Wallis observes that the surf was too high upon the rocks for his boats to attempt the passage.

The lagoon was comparatively shallow; the edges, for a consid-

erable distance, sloped gradually toward the centre, and then deepened suddenly . the edge of the bank being nearly perpendicular
This bank, as well as numerous islets in the lagoon, were formed
of coral and dead and live tridacnæ shells   The space between the
islets was very rugged, and full of deep holes.

In the lagoon there were several kinds of brilliantly coloured
fish , on the reef, some fistularia , and in the surf a brown and black
chætodon with a black patch at the junction of the tail with the
body   Upon the land were seen a few rats and lizards, a white heron, a curlew, some sandpipers, and a species of columba resembling the columba australis

In the evening we bore up for Queen Charlotte's Island, another coral formation also discovered by Captain Wallis, and so
grown up that we could not see any lagoon in its centre, as we had
done in all the others   Several huts and sheds similar to those at
Whitsunday Island occur in a bay on its northern shore, but there
were no inhabitants   It may be remembered that when Captain
Wallis visited this island, the natives took to their canoes and fled
to the next island to the westward   whether they did so on the
present occasion we could not determine, but in all probability we
should have seen them if they had   Queen Charlotte's Island afforded Captain Wallis a plentiful supply of cocoa-nuts, but at present not a tree of that description is to be seen.   The shore is more
steep than either Whitsunday or Clermont Tonnere, and the huts
more numerous

At two o'clock in the afternoon we quitted Queen Charlotte's Isl-
and, and in two hours afterwards saw Lagoon Island, which was
discovered by Captain Cook, the former bearing S 6° W. true,
the latter due north, by which an excellent opportunity occurred of
comparing the longitudes of those celebrated navigators.

The next morning we coasted the north side of Lagoon Island
very closely, while the barge navigated the other   It is three miles
in length in a W by S direction, and a mile and a quarter in width.
Its general figure has been accurately described by Captain Cook :
the southern side is still the low reef of breakers which he saw, and
the three shallow openings on the north shore still exist, though one
of them has almost disappeared   Two cocoa-nut trees in the centre of the island, which Cook observes had the appearance of flags,
are still waving , "the tower" at the western end is also there, but
has increased to a large clump of cocoa-nut trees. a similar clump
has sprung up at the eastern end.   The lagoon is, in some parts,
very shallow and contracted, and has many dry islets upon it   The
shore is steep, as at the other coral islands, excepting on the south
side, which should not be approached within a quarter of a mile

We brought-to off a small village at at the N. W extremity of the island, and sent two boats on shore.   The natives seeing them approach came down to the beach armed with poles from twenty to twenty-five feet in length, with bone heads, and short clubs shaped like a bill-hook ; but before they reached the surf they laid down their weapons   At first they beckoned our people to land, but seeing the breakers too high, they suffered themselves to be bribed by a few pieces of iron, and swam off to them   A brisk traffic soon began, and all the disposable articles of the natives were speedily purchased for a few nails, broken pieces of iron, and beads   they then brought down cocoa-nuts, and exchanged six of them for a nail or a bit of iron, which is known here, as at Clermont Tonnere, by the name of " toki "   The strictest integrity was observed by these people in all their dealings.   If one person had not the number of cocoa-nuts demanded for a piece of iron, he borrowed from his neighbour, and when any of the fruit fell overboard in putting it into the boat, they swam after it, and restored it to the owner   Such honesty is rare among the natives of Polynesia, and the Lagoon Islanders consequently ingratiated themselves much with us.   We got from them nearly two hundred cocoa-nuts, and several ornamental parts of their dress, one of which consisted of thin bands of human hair, very neatly plaited, about five feet in length, with four or five dozen strings in each.   To some of these were attached a dried doodoe-nut (*aleurites triloba*), or a piece of wood   We also got some of their mats and sinnet made of the porou bark (*hibiscus tiliaceas*)

The men were a fine athletic race, with frizzled hair, which they wore very thick   In complexion they were much lighter than the islanders of Clermont Tonnere : one man, in particular, and the only one who had whiskers, was so fair, and so like an European, that the boat's crew claimed him as a countryman   No superfluous ornaments were worn by either sex, nor were any of them tattooed   the dress of the males was simply a maro of straw, and sometimes a straw sack hung over their shoulders to prevent the sun from scorching their backs : two of them were distinguished by crowns of white feathers   The women had a mat wrapped about their loins as their only covering   some wore the hair tied in a bunch upon one side of the head, others had a plaited band tied round it   They were inferior to the men in personal appearance, and mostly bowlegged ; but they exercised an authority not very common among uncivilized people, by taking from the men whatever articles they received in exchange for their fruit, as soon as they returned to the shore. The goodnatured countenances of these people, the honesty observed in all their dealings, and the great respect they paid their women, bespeak them a more amiable race than the avaricious Gambier Islanders.

We quitted them about three o'clock in the afternoon, and in a few hours after saw Thrum Cap Island, bearing N 56° 54' W ; the clump on Lagoon Island at the same time bearing S. 58° 14' E , thirteen miles distant   This island, discovered and so named by Captain Cook, is also of coral, three-quarters of a mile in length, well wooded, and steep all round   At a mile distant from it we could get no bottom with 400 fathoms   We could perceive no lagoon ; and the surf ran too high to admit of landing   Some slabs placed erect, and a hut, showed it had once been inhabited ; but the only living things we saw were birds and turtle.   M. Bougainville gave this island the name of Les Lanciers, in consequence of the men whom he saw on it, being armed with long spears, and who probably were visiters from the island we had just left

From Thrum Cap we steered for Egmont Island, the second discovery of Captain Wallis, which we shortly saw from the masthead, and by sunset were close to it.   The next morning the shore was very carefully examined, and we found the reef so low toward the centre that in high tides there can be no communication with the extremities.   The island is steep, like all the other coral islands, and well wooded with cocoa-nut and pandanus-trees, and has one of the large clumps at its N W extremity

Upon the windward island we perceived about fifty inhabitants collected upon the beach , the men in one groupe, armed in the same manner as the Lagoon Islanders, and the women in another place more inland.   No boat could land on this or on any other part of the island. to leeward the S W. swell rolled even more heavily upon the shore than that occasioned by the trade-wind on the opposite side . we were in consequence obliged to trade with the natives in the manner pursued at Lagoon Island   Two of the islanders, when they thought we were going to land, advanced with slow strides, and went through a number of pantomimic gestures, which we could not understand, except that they were of a friendly nature   This lasted until the boats anchored outside the reef, and they were invited to accept some pieces of " toki."   Gold and silver are not more valued in European countries, than iron, even in its rudest form, is by the islanders of Polynesia   At the sound of the word, the two spokesmen, and all the natives who had before been seated under the shade of the trees, ran off to their huts, and brought down whatever they thought likely to obtain a piece of the precious substance,—mats, bands, nets, oyster-shells, hooks, and a variety of small articles similar to those before described were offered for sale. The only article they would not part with, though we offered a higher price than it seemed to deserve, was a stick with a bunch of black tern feathers suspended to it.   At Lagoon, and other islands which we visited both before and afterwards, the natives carried one or more of these sticks   they are mentioned as being seen by the earliest voyagers, and are probably marks of distinction or of amity.

These people so much resemble the Lagoon Islanders in person, manners, language and dress, as to need no description   the island is also of the same formation, and has apparently the same productions.   We noticed only one canoe, but no doubt they have others, as a constant communication is kept up with the islands to windward It may be recollected that it was upon this island Captain Wallis found all the natives collected who had deserted Queen Charlotte's Island on his approach   Though these two places are many miles out of sight of each other, yet their canoes took the exact direction which, being afterwards followed by Captain Wallis, led to the discovery of the island

Next morning we saw land to the S by E, which proved to be a small coral island, answering in situation nearly to that of Carysfort Island, discovered by Captain Edwards, but so small as to render it very unlikely that it should be the same   Though we ranged the shore very closely, we did not perceive any inhabitants   It was well wooded, and had several clusters of cocoa-nut trees.   The next morning parties were sent to cut down some of the trees for fire-wood. The surf ran high upon the shore, but, with the assistance of a small raft, a disembarkation was effected without any serious accident.   Several of the officers, anxious to land upon this our first discovery in these seas, joined the party in spite of a sound ducking, which was the smallest penalty attached to the undertaking.   In one of these attempts the Naturalist was unfortunately drawn into a deep hole in the coral by the recoil of the sea, and, but for prompt assistance, would in all probability have lost his life.

The island proved to be only a mile and three-quarters in length, from north to south, and a mile and three-tenths in width.   It consisted of a narrow strip of land of an oval form, not more than two hundred yards wide in any part, with a lagoon in its centre, which the colour of the water indicated to be of no great depth   In places this lake washed the trunks of the trees, in others it was separated from them by a whitish beach, formed principally of cardium and venus-shells.   Shoals of small fish of the chætodon genus, highly curious and beautiful in colour, sported along the clear margin of the lake, and with them two or three species of fistularia; several moluscous animals and shell-fish occupied the hollows of the coral (principally madrepora cervi-cornis); and the chama giganteus was found so completely overgrown by the coral, that just sufficient space was left for it to open its shell; a fact which tends to show the rapidity with which coral increases.

Upon the shores of the lagoon, the pandanus, cocoa-nut, toufano, scœvola kœnigii, the suriana (whose aroma may be perceived at the distance of several miles), the large clump-tree, pemphis acidula, tournefortia sericea, and other evergreens common to these formations, constituted a thick wood, and afforded a cool retreat from the scorching rays of a vertical sun, and the still greater annoyance arising from the reflection of the bright white sand; a luxury which until our arrival was enjoyed only by a few black and white tern, tropic and frigate birds, and some soldier-crabs which had taken up their abode in the vacated turbo-shells.

Under these trees were three large pits containing several tons of fresh water, and not far from them some low huts similar to those described at the other islands, and a tomb-stone shaped like that at Whitsunday Island. We judged that the huts had been long deserted, from the circumstance of the tern and other aquatic birds occupying some calabashes which were left in them. Among several things found in this deserted village were part of a scraper used by merchants-ships, and a large fish-hook, which we preserved, without suspecting that they would at a future day clear up the doubt that these articles were calculated to throw upon the merit of discovering this island, to which we otherwise felt an indisputable claim. Our suspicions on this head were also strengthed by noticing that a cocoa-nut tree had been cut down with an instrument sharper than the stone axes of the Indians. We had, however no direct proof that the island had been before visited by any ship; and we consoled ourselves with the possibility of the instruments having been brought from a distance by the natives, who might be absent on a temporary visit, and several of whose canoes we found in the lagoon: the largest of these was eighteen feet in length by fifteen inches in breadth, hollowed out of the large-tree (which we at first mistook for a banyan-tree,) and furnished with outriggers similar to the canoes of Clermont Tonnere.

This island, the north end of which is situated in latitude 20° 45' 07' S., and longitude 4° 07' 48'' West, of Gambier Island, I named Barrow Island, in compliment to the Secretary of the Admiralty, whose literary talents and zeal for the promotion of geographical science have been long known to the world.

The party on shore succeeded in the course of a few hours in collecting a tolerable supply of hard wood, very well adapted for fuel, and some brooms, after which we beat to the windward in search of Carysfort Island; and at four o'clock in the afternoon had the satisfaction to see land in that direction, but in consequence of a strong current setting to the southward, we did not get near it until the afternoon of the following day. It answered in every respect to Captain Edwards's description of Carysfort Island. The strip of land is so low, that the sea, in several places, washes into the lagoon. Like all the other islands of this formation we had visited, the

weather side and the points of the island were most wooded, but
the vegetation was on the whole scanty   There is no danger near
this island   The outer part of the bank descends abruptly as follows. at sixty yards from the breakers, 5 fathoms water

Eighty yards . . .	13	ditto
One hundred and twenty do . .	18	ditto
Two hundred yards . .	24	ditto

On the edge of the bank immediately after, no bottom with 35
fathoms

During the night we stood quietly to the southward in search of
Matilda Rocks and Osnaburgh Island   At daylight we saw flocks
of tern, and at eleven o'clock land was reported bearing W. by S.
The barge and the ship circumnavigated this island before dark,
and then kept under easy sail during the night   I learnt from Mr
Belcher, who passed round the eastern side of the island, that he
had found an opening into the lagoon in that direction, and had discovered near it two anchors lying high up on the reef

At daylight next morning land was seen to the southward, which
on examination proved to be another small coral island, three miles
and three quarters in length, by three in width   its form is nearly
an oblong with the southern side much curved.   The lagoon in the
centre was deep, its boundary very low and narrow, and in places
it overflowed.   Several ripplings were observed about these islands,
but we passed through them without obtaining soundings

As soon as the plan of this island was completed we returned to
that upon which the anchors were observed, and spent the whole
day in its examination.   The lagoon was entered in the boats by a
channel sufficiently wide and deep for a vessel of the class of the
Blossom, and proved in every respect an excellent harbour · in entering, however, it is necessary to look out carefully for rocks, which
rise suddenly to the surface, or within a very short distance of it

On landing at the back of the reef, we perceived unequivocal
signs of a shipwreck—part of a vessel's keel and fore-foot, broken
casks, a number of staves, hoops, a ship's hatch marked VIII,
some copper, lead, &c, and the beach strewed with broken iron
hoops, and in their vicinity the anchors which were discovered the
preceding day   there were also broken harpoons, lances, a small
cannon, cast metal boilers, &c. &c., and a leaden pump which had
a crown and the date 1790 raised upon it   All the iron-work was
much corroded, and must have been a considerable time exposed to
the action of the sea and air, but it was not overgrown in the least
by the coral   Two of these anchors weighed about a ton each;
the other was a stream anchor, and with one of the bowers, was at
the break of the sea . the other bower, together with the boiler, and
all the before-mentioned materials, were lying about two hundred

yards from it The situation in which they were found, the size of
the anchors, the harpoons, staves, &c and the date of the pump,
render it highly probable that they belonged to the Matilda, a whaler which was wrecked in 1792, in the night-time, upon a reef of
coral rocks in latitude 22° S, and longitude 138° 34' W But
whether they had been washed up there by some extraordinarily
high tide and sea, or the reef had since grown upward, and raised
them beyond the present reach of the waves, we could not decide;
the former is most probable; though it is evident, if the above-mentioned remains be those of the Matilda, of which there can be very
little doubt, that a considerable alteration has taken place in the island, as the crew of that vessel describe themselves to have been
lost on *a reef of rocks*, whereas the island on which these anchors
are lying extends fourteen miles in length, and has one of its sides
covered nearly the whole of the way with high trees, which, from
the spot where the vessel was wrecked, are very conspicuous, and
could not fail to be seen by persons in the situation of her crew.

The island differs from the other coral formations before described, in having a greater disproportion in growth of its sides The
one to the windward is covered with tall trees as before mentioned,
while that to the leeward is nearly all under water. The dry part
of the chain enclosing the lagoon is about a sixth of a mile in width,
but varies considerably in its dimensions the broad parts are furnished with low mounds of sand, which have been raised by the
action of the waves, but are now out of their reach, and mostly covered with vegetation. The violence of the waves upon the shore,
except at low water, forces the sea into the lake at many points,
and occasions a constant outset through the channel to leeward.

On both sides of the chain the coral descends rapidly. on the
outer part there is from six to ten fathoms close to the breakers,
the next cast is thirty to forty, and at a little distance there is no
bottom with two hundred and fifty fathams On the lagoon side
there are two ledges· the first is covered about three feet at high
water at its edge the lead descends to three fathoms to the next
ledge, which is about forty yards in width, it then slopes to about
five fathoms at its extremity, and again descends perpendicularly
to ten after which there is a gradual descent to twenty fathoms,
which is the general depth of the centre of the lagoon The lake
is dotted with knolls or columns of coral, which rise to all intermediate heights between the bottom and the surface, and are dangerous
even to boats sailing in the lagoon with a fresh breeze, particularly
in cloudy weather, as at that time it is difficult to distinguish even
those which are close to the surface

No cocoa-nut or other fruit-trees have yet been planted on the
isolated shore, nor are there any vestiges of its ever having been in-

habited, excepting by the feathered tribe, a few lizards, soldier-crabs, and occasionally by turtle   The birds, unaccustomed to molestation, were so ignorant of their danger that we lifted them off their nests, and the fish suffered as much by our sticks and boat-hooks, as by our fishing-lines   The sharks, as in almost all unin-habited islands within the tropics, were so numerous and daring, that they took the fish off our lines as we were hauling them in, and the next minute were themselves taken by a bait thrown over for them, a happy thought of our fishermen, who by that means not only recovered many of their hooks, but got back the stolen fish in a tolerably perfect state.

In several small lakes, occasioned by the sea at times overflow-the land, we saw an abundance of fish of the chætodon and sparus genera, of the same beautiful colours as those at Barrow Island, and in one of them caught a species of gymnothorax about two feet in length   There were but few echini upon the reef, but an abund-ance of shell-fish, consisting of the arca, ostrea, cardium, turbo, he-lix, conus, cypræa, voluta, harpa, haliotis, patella, &c , also seve-ral aphroditæ holuthuriæ (biche la mer) and asteriæ, &c

The position of this island differed so considerably from that of Osnaburgh Island, discovered by Captain Carteret, that I beat two days to the eastward in the parallel of 22° S in the expectation of finding another, but when the view from the mast-head extended half a degree beyond the longitude he had assigned to his discove-ry, and we had not even any indication of land, I gave up further search   The probability, therefore, is, that the island upon which we found the wreck is the Osnaburgh of Captain Carteret, and as it is equally probable, from what has been said, that the remains are those of the Matilda, it will be proper henceforward to affix to it the name of both Osnaburgh and Matilda

A doubt might have arisen with respect to the island discovered to the southward being Osnaburgh Island, had Captain Carteret not expressly said in his journal, that the island he saw was to the *south* of him, but this bearing put such a supposition out of the question, as in that case he must have seen the island to the northward also I have, in consequence, considered it a new discovery, and honour-ed it with the name of Cockburn Island, in compliment to the Right Honourable Sir George Cockburn, G C B , one of the Lords of the Admiralty.

After we gave up the search to the eastward for the island of Captain Carteret, we pursued the same parallel of 22° S some dis-tance to the westward without being more successful, and then steered for the Lagoon Island of Captain Bligh, which was seen the following day   On our approach several large fires were kindled in different parts.   The natives were darker than those of Lagoon

Island of Cook, were nearly naked, and had their hair tied in a knot on the top of the head, they were all provided with stones, clubs, and spears. As the sea ran very high, we did not land, and consequently had no further communication with them. The island is larger than is exhibited upon Arrowsmith's Charts, but agrees in situation very closely with the position assigned to it by Captain Bligh.

Two days afterwards we discovered a small island in lat 19° 40′ S and long 140° 29′ W, which, as it was not before known, I named Byam Martin Island, in compliment to Sir Thomas Byam Martin, K. C B, the Comptroller of the Navy.

As we neared the shore the natives made several fires. Shortly afterwards three of them launched a canoe, and paddled fearlessly to the barge, which brought them to the ship. Instead of the deep-coloured uncivilized Indians inhabiting the coral islands in general, a tall well-made person, comparatively fair, and handsomely tattooed, ascended the side, and, to our surprise, familiarly accosted us in the Otaheitan manner. The second had a hog and a cock tattooed upon his breast—animals almost unknown among the islands of Eastern Polynesia; and the third wore a turban of blue nankeen. Either of these were distinctions sufficient to excite considerable interest, as they convinced us they were not natives of the island before us, but had either been left there, or drifted away from some other island the latter supposition was the most probable, as they described themselves to have undergone great privation and suffering, by which many of their companions had lost their lives, and their canoe to have been wrecked upon the island; and that they and their friends on shore were anxious to embark in the ship, and return to Otaheite. A little suspicion was at first attached to this account, as it seemed impossible for a canoe to reach their present asylum without purposely paddling towards it; as Byam Martin Island, unlike Wateo, upon which Omai found his countrymen, is situated six hundred miles from Otaheite, in the direction of the trade-wind. We could not doubt, however, that they were natives of that place, as they mentioned the names of the missionaries residing there, and proved that they could both read and write.

To their solicitation to return in the ship to Otaheite, as their numbers on shore amounted to forty persons I could not yield, and I pointed out to them the impossibility of doing so; but that we might learn the real history of their adventures, I offered a passage to the man who first ascended the side, as he appeared the most intelligent of the party. The poor fellow was at first quite delighted, but suddenly became grave, and inquired if his wife and children might accompany him, as he

could on no account consent to a separation Our compliance with
this request appeared to render him completely happy ; but still
fearful of disappointment, before quitting the ship he sent to ask if
I was in earnest.

The next morning, on landing, we found him, his wife, and family, with their goods and chattels, upon the beach, ready to embark,
and all the islanders assembled to take leave of them ; but as we
wished to examine the island first, we postponed this ceremony until the evening. The little colony gave us a very friendly reception, and conducted us to their village, which consisted of a few
low huts, similar to those at Barrow Island ; but they had no fruit
to offer us, excepting pandanus-nuts, which they disliked almost as
much as ourselves, and told us they had been accustomed to better
fare.

In their huts we found calabashes of water suspended to the roof,
mats, baskets, and every thing calculated for a sea-voyage ; and not
far from them a plentiful store of fish, raised about four feet above
the ground, out of the reach of the rats, which were very numerous.
They had clothing sufficient for the climate, and were in every respect stout and healthy , there was therefore no immediate necessity for removing them, though I offered to take them as far as the
next island, which was larger and inhabited, and where—concluding, from what we saw, that these people were auxiliary missionaries—they would have an opportunity of prosecuting their pious intentions in the conversion of the natives This proposal, however, after a little consultation. was declined, from an apprehension
of being killed and eaten, as they supposed the greater part of the
inhabitants of the eastern islands of Polynesia to be cannibals

We very soon discovered that our little colony were Christians ;
they took an early opportunity of convincing us that they had both
Testaments, hymn-books, &c printed in the Otaheitan language :
they also showed us a black-lead pencil, and other materials for
writing Some of the girls repeated hymns, and the greater part
evinced a reverence and respect for the sacred books, which reflects
much credit upon the missionaries, under whose care we could no
longer doubt they had at one time been.

Tuwarri, to whom I offered a passage, we found was not the
principal person on the island, but that their chief was a man
who accompanied him in the boat, with his legs dreadfully enlarged
with the elephantiasis it was he who directed their course, rebuilt
their canoe after it had been stranded, and who appeared also to be
their protector, being the only one who possessed fire-arms. His
importance in this respect was, however, a little diminished by the
want of powder and shot. and by an accident which had deprived
him of the hammer of his gun—a misfortune he particularly regret-

ted, as it had been given him by King Pomarree, His anxiety on this head was relieved by finding our armourer could supply the defect, and that we could furnish him with the necessary materials for the defence of his party

The canoe in which this extraordinary voyage had been made was found hauled up at a different part of the island from that on which we landed, and placed under a shed very neatly built, with the repairs executed in a workmanlike manner, and in every respect ready for sea   She was a double canoe, upwards of thirty feet long by nine broad, and three feet nine inches deep ; each vessel having three feet three inches beam · one was partly decked, and the other provided with a thatched shed : they were sharp at both ends, each of which was fitted for a rudder, and the timbers were sewed together with strong plaited cord, after the manner of the canoes of Chain Island, where they are brought to great perfection

We remained the whole day upon the island, contributing to the comfort of the inhabitants by the distribution of useful presents , and at the same time making our own observations, and endeavouring to learn something of their history, and at sunset we assembled upon the beach to embark   Poor Tuwarri was quite overwhelmed at separating from his companions and fellow-sufferers.   The whole village accompanied him to the boat, to the last testifying their regard by some little act of civility   When the moment of departure arrived, the men gathered about him, shed abundance of tears, and took their leave in a solemn manner with a very few words   The women, on the other hand, clung about his wife and children, and indulged a weakness that better become their sex.

The island upon which we found them is nearly an oval of three miles and three-quarters diameter   It is of coral formation, and has a lagoon and productions very similar to the other islands recently described   One species of coral not noticed before was seen in the lagoon, growing above water   it was a millepore extending itself in vertical plates parallel to the shore   Among the vegetable productions, the *polypodium vulgare*, seen at Whitsunday Island, was found here , and also a small shrub, which we afterwards ascertain to be an achyranthus   From the pemphis we procured a large supply of firewood, to which use it is well adapted, as it burns a long time, gives great heat, and occupies comparatively little room   The wood of this tree is hard as lignum vitæ, and equally good for tools , its specific gravity much greater than sea water   its colour is deep red, but the inner bark more strongly tinged ; and if properly prepared, would perhaps afford a good dye

From Byam Martin Island we steered for Gloucester Island of Captain Wallis, and early the next morning were close to it.   The appearance of the island has been accurately described by its dis-

coveied, but its present form and extent differ materially   At the
S E. angle of the island we noticed a morai built of stones, but
there were no inhabitants upon the shore,   In passing to windward
of the island, the currant unexpectedly set so strong upon it, that
the ship was for a considerable time in imminent danger of being
thrown upon the rocks, and her escape is entirely attributable to the
rapid descent of the coral reef, which at times was almost under
her bottom,   She, however, fortunately cleared the reef, and was
immediately in safety   After collecting the necessary information,
we steered for Bow Island, which was seen from the mast-head at
three o'clock the same afternoon,

CHAPTER VIII.

Boat sent to examine the Channel into Bow Island Lagoon—Unexpected Interview
between Tuwarri and his Brother—A Pearl Brig at anchor in the Lagoon—Mystery attached to the Byam Martin Islanders dispelled—Their interesting History,
extensive Wanderings and Sufferings—Sequel of Tuwarri's History—Ship enters
the Lagoon—Description of the Island—A short Account of the Natives—Visit
several other coral Islands, and discover Melville and Croker Islands—Remarks
on the Discoveries of Cook, Wallis, Carteret, &c.—Peculiarities of the coral Islands
—Arrival at Otaheite.

Bow Island was discovered by M. Bougainville in 1768, and the
following year was visited by Captain Cook, who gave it its present name from the resemblance its shape bore to a bow.   Its figure
protracted upon paper, however, is very irregular, and bears but
small resemblance to the instrument after which it was named, but
to a person viewing it as Captain Cook did, the mistake is very
likely to occur.   It is of coral formation, thirty-four miles long, and
ten broad ; well wooded on the weather side, but very scantily so on
the other ; and so low in this half, that the sea in places washes into the lagoon.   We sailed close along what may be considered the
string of the bow, which the barge navigated the arch, and thus,
between us, in a few hours made the circuit of the island
   Previous to quitting England, Captain Charlton, the consul at
the Sandwich Islands, among other useful matter which he obligingly communicated, informed me of an opening through the coral reef
of this island into the lagoon ; and as I was desirous, at this period
of the survey, of having a point astronomically fixed to correct the
chronometrical measurements, I determined, if possible, to enter the
lagoon with the ship.   When we reached the supposed opening, a
boat was lowered to examine it ; and Tuwarri was sent in her to
conciliate the natives, should any be seen in the course of the service   As she drew near the shore, several men were observed
among the trees, and the officer in charge of the boat, acting under
my general orders of being always prepared for an attack, desired
the muskets to be loaded   Tuwarri, who had probably never possessed much courage, at the sight of these preparations, wished him-

self anywhere else than in his present situation, and, to judge from
his countenance, calculated at least upon being killed and eaten by
cannibals   he was in the greatest agitation as the boat advanced,
until she came within speaking distance of the strangers, when, instead of the supposed monsters ready to devour him, he recognised,
to his surprise, his own brother and several friends whom he had
left at Chain Island three years before, all of whom had long given
him up as lost, and whom he never expected to see again.

The two brothers met in a manner which did credit to their feelings, and after the first salutation sat down together upon the beach
with their hands firmly locked, and entered into serious conversation,
consisting no doubt of mutual inquiries after friends and relations,
and Tuwarri's account of his perilous adventure.   They continued
with their hands grasped until it was time for the boat to return to
the ship, when they both came on board.   This affecting interview
increased our impatience to have the mystery which overhung the
fate of our passenger cleared up, and an opportunity fortunately
happened for doing so

The gig, on entering the lagoon, had been met by a boat from an
English brig (the Dart, employed by the Australian Pearl Company) at anchor there, with a number of divers, natives of Chain Island, hired into her service   among these men there was one who
acted as interpreter, and who was immediately engaged to communicate to us the particulars of Tuwarri's adventures, which possess
so much interest, that the reader will not, I am sure, regret the relation of them.

Tuwarri was a native of one of the low coral formations discovered by Captain Cook in his first voyage, called Anaa by the natives, but by him named Chain Island, situated about three hundred
miles to the eastward of Otaheite, to which it is tributary.   About
the period of the commencement of his misfortunes, old Pomarree
the king of Otaheite died, and was succeeded by his son, then a
child.   On the accession of this boy, several chiefs and commoners
of Chain Island, among whom was Tuwarri, planned a voyage to
Otaheite, to pay a visit of ceremony and of homage to their new
sovereign   The only conveyance these people could command was
double canoes, three of which, of the largest class, were prepared for
the occasion   To us, accustomed to navigate the seas in ships of
many tons burthen, provided with a compass and the necessary instruments to determine our position, a canoe with only the stars for
her guidance, and destined to a place whose situation could be at
the best but approximately known, appears so frail and uncertain a
conveyance, that we may wonder how any persons could be found
sufficiently resolute to hazard the undertaking.   They knew, however, that similar voyages had been successfully performed, not only

to mountainous islands to leeward, but to some that were scarcely six feet above the water, and were situated in the opposite direction, and as no ill omens attended the present undertaking, no unusual fears were entertained   The canoes being accordingly prepared, and duly furnished with all that was considered necessary, the persons intending to proceed on this expedition were embarked, amounting in all to a hundred and fifty souls.   What was the arrangement of the other two canoes is unknown to us, but in Tuwairi's there were twenty-three men, fifteen women, and ten children and a supply of water and provision calculated to last three weeks

On the day of departure all the natives assembled upon the beach to take leave of our adventurers, the canoes were placed with scrupulous exactness in the supposed direction which was indicated by certain marks upon the land, and then launched into the sea, amidst the good wishes and adieus of their countrymen.   With a fair wind and full sail they glided rapidly over the space without a thought of the possibility of the miseries to which they were afterwards exposed

It happened, unfortunately, that the monsoon that year* began earlier than was expected, and blew with great violence, two days were, notwithstanding, passed under favourable circumstances, and the adventurers began to look for the high land of Maitea, an island between Chain Island and Otaheite, and to anticipate the pleasures which the successful termination of their voyage would afford them, when their progress was delayed by a calm, the precursor of a storm, which rose suddenly from an unfavourable quarter, dispersed the canoes, and drove them away before it   In this manner they drifted for several days, but on the return of fine weather, having a fortnight's provision remaining, they again resolutely sought their destination, until a second gale drove them still farther back than the first, and lasted so long that they became exhausted.   Thus many days were passed; their distance from home hourly increasing, the sea continually washing over the canoe, to the great discomfiture of the women and children, and their store of provision dwindled to the last extremity   A long calm, and, what was to them even worse, hot dry weather, succeeded the tempest, and reduced them to a state of the utmost distress   They described to us their canoe alone and becalmed on the ocean, the crew, perishing with thirst, beneath the fierce glare of a tropical sun, hanging exhausted over their paddles, children looking to their parents for support, and mothers deploring their inability to afford them assistance.   Every

* In the South Pacific the monsoons are occasionally felt throughout all the islands of Eastern Polynesia

means of quenching their thirst were resorted to, some drank the
sea-water, and others bathed in it, or poured it over their heads;
but the absence of fresh water in the torrid zone cannot be compen-
sated by such substitutes   Day after day those who were able extended their gourds to heaven in supplication for rain, and repeated
their prayers, but in vain; the fleecy cloud floating high in the air
indicated only an extension of their suffering   distress in its most
aggravated form had at length reached its height, and seventeen persons fell victims to its horrors

The situation of those who remained may readily be imagined,
though their fate would never have been known to us, had not
Providence at this critical moment wrought a change in their favour.   The sky, which for some time had been perfectly serene,
assumed an aspect which at any other period would have filled our
sufferers with aprehension, but, on the present occasion, the tropical storm, as it approached, was hailed with thankfulness, and welcomed as their deliverer.   All who were able came upon the deck
with blankets, gourds, and cocoa-nut shells, and held them toward
the black cloud, as it approached, pouring down torrents of rain, of
which every drop was of incalculable value to the sufferers, they
drank copiously and thankfully, and filled every vessel with the
precious element.   Thus recruited, hope revived, but the absence
of food again plunged them into the deepest despair   We need
not relate the dreadful alternative to which they had recourse until
several large sharks rose to the surface and followed the canoe;
Tuwarri, by breaking off the head of an iron scraper, formed it into
a hook, and succeeded in catching one of them, which was instantly
substitued for the revolting banquet which had hitherto sustained
life.

Thus refreshed, they again worked at their paddles or spread
their sail, and were not long before their exertions were repaid with
the joyful sight of land, on which clusters of cocoa-nuts crowned
the heads of several tufts of palm-trees · they hurried through the
surf and soon reached the much wished-for spot, but being too fee-
ble to ascend the lofty trees, they were obliged to fell one of them
with an axe

On traversing the island to which Providence had thus conducted them, they discovered by several canoes in the lagoon and pathways intersecting the woods, that it had been previously inhabited,
and knowing the greater part of the natives of the low islands to be
cannibals, they determined to remain no longer upon it than was
absolutely necessary to recruit their strength, imagining that the
islanders, when they did return, would not rest satisfied with merely dispossessing them of their asylum.

It was necessary, while they were allowed to remain, to seek shelter from the weather, and to exert themselves in procuring a supply of provision for their further voyage, huts were consequently built, pools dug for water, and three canoes added to those which were found in the lake. Their situation by these means was rendered tolerably comfortable, and they not only provided themselves with necessaries sufficient for their daily consumption, but were able to dry and lay by a considerable quantity of fish for sea stock.

After a time, finding themselves undisturbed, they gained confidence, and deferred their departure till thirteen months had elapsed from the time of their landing. At the expiration of which period, being in good bodily health and supplied with every requisite for their voyage, they again launched upon the ocean in quest of home.

They steered two days and nights to the northwest, and then fell in with a small island, upon which, as it appeared to be uninhabited, they landed, and remained three days, and then resumed their voyage. After a run of a day and a night they came in sight of another uninhabited island. In their attempt to land upon it their canoe was unfortunately stove, but all the party got safe on shore. The damage which the vessel had sustained requiring several weeks to repair, they established themselves upon this island, and again commenced storing up provision for their voyage. Eight months had already passed in these occupations, when we unexpectedly found them thus encamped upon Byam Martin Island; with their canoe repaired, and all the necessary stores provided for their next expedition. The other two canoes were never heard of.

Several parts of this curious history strongly favoured the presumption that the island upon which the party first landed and established themselves was Barrow Island. and, in order to have it confirmed, the piece of iron that had been brought from thence, and had fortunately been preserved, was produced. Tuwarri, when he saw it, immediately exclaimed that it was the piece of iron he had broken in two to form the shark-hook, which was the means of preserving the lives of his party, and said that the tree we found cut down with some sharp edged tool was that which his party felled before their strength enabled them to climb for fruit: and hence the huts, the pools of water, the canoes, &c. were the remains of their industry.

This curious discovery enabled us to form a tolerably accurate idea of the distance the canoe had been drifted by the gale, as Barrow Island is 420 miles in a direct line from Chain Island, their native place; and if to this be added 100 miles for the progress they made during the first two days toward Maitea, and the distance they went on their return before they reached Barrow Island, the whole cannot amount to much less than 600 miles.

. Before Tuwairi could be restored to his home, we visited in succession several low islands to which he was a stranger. While we were cruising among them, he entertained the greatest apprehension lest we had lost our way, and perhaps pictured to himself a repetition of his disastrous voyage. He could not imagine our motive for pursuing so indirect a course, and frequently inquired if we were going to his native island, and if we knew where it was, occasionally pointing in the direction of it. He always boasted of a knowledge of the islands lying between Bow Island (He-ow) and Chain Island (Anaa), but never informed us right when we came to any of them. He had, it is true, reason to be anxious; for his wife, almost the whole of the passage, was very sea-sick, which gave him great concern; and when the sea was much agitated, he appeared inconsolable. When he at length arrived within sight of Chain Island, his joy at the certainty of again setting foot on his native soil, and meeting friends who had long supposed him lost, may readily be imagined. His gratitude to us for having given him a passage, and for our attention to his comfort, was expressed in tears of thankfulness; and he testified his regret at parting in a manner which showed him to be sincere; and as he was going away, he expressed his sorrow that the ship would not remain long enough off the island for him to send some little token of his gratitude. These feelings, so highly creditable to Tuwairi, were not participated by his wife, who, on the contrary, showed no concern at her departure, expressed neither thanks nor regrets, nor turned to any person to bid him farewell; and while Tuwairi was suppressing his tears, she was laughing at the exposure which she thought she should make going into the boat without an accommodation-ladder. Tuwairi, while on board showed no curiosity, knew nothing of our language, or evinced any desire to learn it; took very little interest in any thing that was going forward, and was very dull of comprehension. He appeared to be a man whose energies had been worn down by hardship and privation, and whom misfortune had taught to look on the worst side of every thing. But with all these weak points, he had many good qualities. He lent a willing hand to pull at a rope, was cleanly and quiet, punctually attended church on Sundays, and had a strong sense of right and wrong, which, as far as his abilities enabled him, governed his actions. He had a warm heart, and his attachment to his wife and children amounted even to weakness. He had a tolerable knowledge of the relative situation of the islands of the archipelago, and readily drew a chart of them, assigning to each its name, though, as I have said before, he never could recognise them. Some of these we were able to identify, and perhaps should have done so with others, had there not been so much sameness in all the coral islands.

Mr Belcher, who was in command of the barge which put him on shore, says, he was not received by his countrymen with the surprise and pleasure which might have been expected, but this may, perhaps, be explained by there being no one on the beach to whom he was particularly attached   Before the barge quitted the island, he put on board some shells as a present, in gratitude for the assistance which had been rendered him.

Reverting to the occurrences of the ship off Bow Island. Mr. Elson, the officer who was sent to examine the channel into the lagoon, returned with the supercargo of the Dart, Mr Hussey, and made a favourable report of the depth of water in the passage, but said its width was so very contracted that it could not be passed without hazard.   The exact distance from reef to reef is 115 feet, and there is a coral knoll in the centre ; the trade-wind does not always allow a ship to lie well through it, and there is, at times, a tide running out at the rate of four knots an hour   It was, however, necessary to incur this risk, and, on the information of Mr Hussey that the morning was the most favourable time for the attempt, shortly after daylight on the next day (15th), under Mr. Elson's skilful pilotage, we shot through the passage, at the rate of seven knots, and were instantly in a broad sheet of smooth water   We found the lagoon studded with coral knolls, which it was necessary to avoid by a vigilant look out from aloft, as the lead gave no warning of their vicinity , we beat among them at some risk, and at ten o'clock anchored at the N E angle of the lake, in ten fathoms water on a broad patch of sand, about a quarter of a mile from the shore, and in as secure a harbour as could be required

Nearly opposite to our anchorage, the natives, about fifty in number, had erected temporary huts during the stay of the Dart, their permanent residences being at the opposite end of the island. They were in appearance the most indolent ill-looking race we had yet seen ; broad flat noses, dull sunken eyes, thick lips, mouths turned down at the corners, strongly wrinkled countenances, and long bushy hair matted with dirt and vermin   Their stature was above the middle size, but generally crooked , their limbs bony, their muscles flaccid, and their covering a maro   But hideous as the men were, their revolting appearance was surpassed by the opposite sex of the same age   The males were all lolling against the cocoa-nut trees, with their arms round each other's necks, enjoying the refreshing shade of a thick foilage of palm-trees , while the women, old and young, were labouring hard in the sun, in the service of their masters for they did not merit the name of husbands   The children, quite naked, were placed upon mats, crying and rolling to and fro, to displace some of the myriads of house-flies, which so speckled their bodies that their real colour was scarcely discernible.

Amidst this scene I was introduced to the chief, who was distinguished from his subjects by his superior height and strength, and probably maintained his authority solely by those qualities He gave me a friendly reception, and suffered us to cut down what wood we wanted, confining us only to those trees which produced no edible fruits In return for some presents made him, he drew from his canoe several pearl fishing-hooks and bundles of turtle-shell, and begged my acceptance of them , but his extreme poverty was such, that I could not bring myself to do so, though I do not know to what material use the last-mentioned article could be applied by him

We availed ourselves of the areghe's permission, and sent a party to cut as many trees as we required, consisting principally of the pemphis acidula, as at Byam Martin Island Mr Marsh endeavoured to engage some of the natives in this implyment, by offering shirts, tobacco, &c. but, notwithstanding the munificence of the reward, the areghe alone could be roused from his lethargy , and even he quitted the axe before the first tree was felled.

A party of seamen was at the same time sent, under the direction of Lieutenant Wainwright, to dig wells; in which their success was so satisfactory, that in less than three days we procured thirty tons of fresh water The wells were about four feet deep, dug through the sand into the coral rock Into two of these the water flowed as fast as we could fill the casks , and when allowed to stand, rose eighteen inches This water was drunk by all the ship's company for several weeks, and proved tolerably good, though it did not keep as well as spring water.* It is important to navigators to know, that even as good water as this may be procured on the coral islands by means of wells In digging them, the choice of situation should be given to the most elevated part of the island, and to a spot distant from the sea; perhaps in the vicinity of cocoa-nut trees It is a curious fact that, in Bow Island, the water that flowed into holes dug within a yard of the sea was fresh enough to be drunk by the sailors, and served the purpose of the natives while they remained in our vicinity ; though I do not think Europeans could have used it long with impunity

Not far from the temporary residence of the natives, there was a level spot of ground, overgrown with grass, upon which the observ-

* Mr Collie observes, in his Journal, that a "solution of nitrate of soda detected in it a moderate proportion of muriatic acid, embodied in the soda. It had no brackish taste With an alcoholic solution of soap it formed a copious white precipitate with oxalate of ammonia it formed slowly, but after some time a dense white cloud with nitrate of silver an abundant purplish-white precipitate, it remained unchanged with nitrate of barytes Thus showing that it contained no sulphuric acid, but that it was impregnated with muriatic acid and magnesia, most likely muriate of soda and magnesia, the component parts of sea water "

atory was erected, and I had in consequence frequent intercourse
with them, and, through the medium of the interpreter of the Dart,
learned many interesting particulars concerning them   By this account they have not long desisted from cannibalism.   On questioning the chief, he acknowldged himself to have been present at several feasts of human bodies, and on expatiating on the excellence
of the food, particularly when it was that of a female, his brutal
countenance became flushed with a horrible expression of animation
Their enmies, those slain in battle, or those who die violent deaths,
and murderers, were, he said, the only subjects selected for these
feasts, the latter, whether justified or not, were put to death, and
eaten alike with their victims   They have still a great partiality
for raw food, which is but one remove from cannibalism, and when
a canoe full of fish was brought one day to the village, the men, before it could be drawn to the shore, fell upon its contents, and devoured every part of the fish except the bones and fins.   The women, whose business it was to unload the boat, did the best they
could with one of them between their teeth, while their hands were
employed portioning the contents of the canoe into small heaps
But even in this repast we were glad to observe some indication of
feeling in putting the animal speedily out of torture by biting its
head in two, the only proof of humanity which they manifested   In
like manner, cleanliness was not overlooked by them, for they carefully rinsed their mouths after the disgusting meal.

It appeared that the chief had three wives, and that polygamy
was permitted to an unlimited extent, any man of the community,
we were told, might put away his wife whenever it was his pleasure
to do so, and take another, provided she were disengaged.   No ceremony takes place at the wedding; it being sufficient for a man to
say to a woman, "You shall be my wife;" and she becomes so

The offspring of these unions seemed to be the objects of the only
feelings of affection the male sex possessed, as there were certainly
none bestowed on the women.   Indeed the situation of the females
is much to be pitied, in no part of the world, probably, are they
treated more brutally.   While their husbands are indulging their
lethargic disposition under the shade of the cocoa-nut trees, making
no effort toward their own support beyond that of eating when their
food is placed before them, the women are sent to the reefs to wade
over the sharp-pointed coral in search of shell-fish, or the woods to
collect pandanus-nuts.   We have seen them going out at day-light
on these pursuits, and returning quite fatigued with their morning
toil   In this state, instead of enjoying a little repose on reaching
their home, they are engaged in the laborious occupation of preparing what they have gathered for their hungry masters, who, immediately the nuts are placed before them, stay their appetites by extrac-

ting the pulpy substance contained in the outside woody fibres of the
fruit, and throw the remainder to their wives, who further extract
what is left of the pulp for their own share, and proceed to extricate
the contents of the interior, consisting of four or five small kernels
about the size of an almond. To perform this operation, the nut is
placed upon a flat stone endwise, and with a block of coral, as large
as the strength of the women will enable them to lift, is split in pieces,
and the contents again put aside for their husbands - As it requires
a considerable number of these small nuts to satisfy the appetites of
their rapacious rulers, the time of the women is wholly passed upon
their knees pounding nuts, or upon the sharp coral collecting shells
and sea eggs   On some occasions the nuts are baked in the ground,
which gives them a more agreeable flavour, and facilitates the ex-
traction of the pulp; it does not, however, diminish the labour of
the females, who have in either case to bruise the fibres to procure
the smaller nuts

The superiority of sex was never more rigidly enforced than
among these barbarians, nor were the male part of the human species ever more despicable   On one occasion an unfortunate women
who was pounding some of these nuts, which she had walked a great
distance to gather, thinking herself unobserved, ate two or three of
the kernels as she extracted them, but this did not escape the vigilance of her brutal husband, who instantly rose and felled her to the
ground in the most inhuman manner with three violent blows of his
fist   Thus tyrannised over, debased, neglected by the male sex, and
strangers to social affection, it is no wonder all those qualities which
in civilized countries constitute the fascination of woman are in these
people wholly wanting

The supercargo of the Dart, to forward the service he was engaged in, had hired a party of the natives of Cham Island to dive for
shells   Among these was a native missionary,* a very well-behaved man, who used every effort to convert his new acquaintances
to Christianity   He persevered amidst much silent ridicule, and at
length succeeded in persuading the greater part of the islanders to
conform to the ceremonies of Christian worship.   It was interesting to contemplate a body of savages, abandoning their superstitions,
silently and reverently kneeling upon the sandy shore, and joining
in the morning and evening prayers to the Almighty   Though
their sincerity may be questioned, yet it is hoped that an impression
may be made upon these neophytes, which may tend to improve
their moral condition

Previous to the arrival of the missionary, every one had his peculiar deity, of which the most common was a piece of wood with a

* We were told that at Cham Island there were thirteen houses of prayer under
the direction of native missionaries

tuft of human hair inserted into it ; but that which was deemed most efficacious, when it could be procured, was the thigh bone of an enemy, or of a relation recently dead   Into the hollow of this they inserted a lock of the same person's hair, and then suspended the idol to a tree.   To these symbols they address their prayers as long as they remained in favour, but, like the girl in China, who when disappointed by her lover, pulled down the brazen image and whipped it, these people, when dissatisfied with their deity, no longer acknowledged his power, and substituted some other idol   There were times, however, when they feared its anger, and endeavoured to appease it with cocoa-nuts; but I did not hear of any human sacrifices being offered   They appeared to entertain the Pythagorean doctrine of the transmigration of the soul, and supposed the first vessel which they saw to be the spirit of their relations lately deceased. The compartments allotted to the dead are here tabooed   and the bodies, first wrapped in mats, are placed under ground   As the soul is supposed for a time to frequent these places, provision and water are placed near the spot for its use, and it would be thought unkind, or that some evil would befal the person whose business it is to provide them if these supplies were neglected

The manufactures of those people are the same with those of all the other islanders, and are only such as nature renders necessary, consisting of mats, maros, baskets, fishing-tackle, &c   They have no occupation beyond the manufacture of these few articles, and providing for their daily support.   On interrogating the chief how he passed the day, he said he rose early and ate his breakfast   he then invoked his deity, sometimes he went to fish or catch turtle, but more generally passed his time under the shade of the cocoa-nut trees. in the evening he ate again, and went to sleep

The natives of this island, according to information obtained by the interpreter on board the Dart, amount altogether to about a hundred souls

As my stay at the island was limited to four days, my time was much occupied at the observatory, and I am indebted to the journals of the officers for many interesting particulars relating to other parts of it, and to its natural productions

By our trigonometrical survey, Bow Island is thirty miles long by an average of five miles broad   It is similar to the other coral islands already described, confining within a narrow band of coral a spacious lagoon, and having its windward side higher and more wooded than the other, which indeed, with the exception of a few clusters of trees and heaps of sand, is little better than a reef. The sea in several places washes into the lagoon, but there is no passage even for a boat, except that by which the ship entered which is sometimes dangerous to boats, in consequence of the overfalls from the lagoon, especially a little after the time of high water.   It is to be hoped that the rapid current which sets through the channel will prevent the growth of the coral, and leave the lagoon always accessible to shipping   It lies at the north side of the island, and may be known by two straggling cocoa-nut trees near it, on the western side, and a clump of trees on the other

The bottom of the lagoon is in parts covered with a fine white sand, and it is thickly strewed with coral knolls   the upper parts of which overhang the lower, though they do not at once rise in this form from the bottom, but from small hillocks.   We found comparatively few beneath the surface, though there are some; at the edge of such as are exposed, there is usually six or seven fathoms water, receeding from it, the lead gradually decends to the general level of about twenty fathoms   The lagoon contains an abundance of shell-fish, particularly those of the pearl-oyster kind.   The party in the employ of the Dart sometimes collected seventeen hundred of these shells in one day.

The height of the lagoon is subject to the variations of the tides of the ocean , but it suffers so many disturbances from the waves which occasionally inundate the low parts of the surrounding land, that neither the rise of the tide nor the time of high water can be estimated with any degree of certainty.   Were the communication between the lake and the sea larger, so as to admit of the water finding its level, the period of low water might be determined, as there is a change of tide in the entrance.

The strip of low land enclosing the lagoon is nearly seventy miles in extent, and the part that is dry is about a quarter of a mile in width   On the inner side, a few yards from the margin of the lake, there is a low bank formed of finely broken coral , and, at the outer edge, a much higher bank of large blocks of the same material, long since removed from the reach of the waves, and gradually preparing for the reception of vegetation.   Beyond this high bank there is a third ridge, similar to that skirting the lagoon · and outside it again, as well as in the lagoon, there is a wide shelf three or four feet under water, the outer one bearing upon its surface huge masses of broken coral . the materials for an outer bank, similar to the large one just described.   These appearances naturally suggest the idea of the island having risen by slow degrees   Thus the sand dispersed over the lagoon indicates a period when the sea rolled entirely over the reef, tore up blocks of coral from its margin and by constant trituration ground them to powder, and finally deposited the particles where they now rest   The bank near the lake must have originated at a subsequent period, when the outer edge becoming nearer to the surface, moderated the strength of the waves, and the wash of the sea reached only far enough to deposit the

broken coral in the place described   At a still less distant period,
when the island became dry, and the violence of the sea was wholly spent upon its margin, the coral, which had before escaped by
being beneath the surface, gave way to the impetuous wave, and
was deposited in broken masses, which formed the high ridge.
Here the sea appears to have broken a considerable time, until a
second ledge gradually extending seaward, and approaching the surface, so lessened the effect of the waves upon this ledge also, that
they were again only capable of throwing up an inferior heap similar to the one first mentioned   In process of time this outer ledge will
become dry, and many large blocks of coral now lying near its edge will,
probably, form another heap similar to the large one, and thus the
island will continue to increase by a succession of ledges being
brought to the surface, while, by the same process, the lagoon will
gradually become more shallow and contracted

The ridges are particularly favourable to the formation of a soil,
by retaining within them whatever may be there deposited until it decays, and by protecting the tender shrubs during their
early growth   Near our observatory the soil had attained a depth
of about eight inches before we came to broken coral.

"In the central and sheltered parts of the plain between the
ridges the pandanus spreads its divergent roots and rears its fruitful
branches; the pemphis also takes root in the same situation.   The
loose dry stones of the first ridge are penetrated by the hard roots of
the tetano, which expands its branches into a tall spreading tree,
and is attended by the fragrant suriana, and the sweet-scented tournefortia, in the shelter of whose foilage the tender achyranthus and
lepidium seem to thrive best.   Beyond the first high stony ridge
the hardy scævola extends its creeping roots and procumbent verdure towards the sea, throwing its succulent leaves round the sharp
coral stones."

"On the windward side, wherever the pandanus was devoid of
the protection of the more hardy trees, the brown and decayed
leaves showed it had advanced beyond its proper boundary."*

We quitted Bow island on the 20th of February, and continued
the survey of the archipelago, until the period had arrived when it
was necessary to proceed direct to Otaheite, to prepare the ship
for her voyage to the northward.   We were greatly retarded toward the close of our operations by the rainy season, which was
attended with calms, and hot, sultry, wet weather, and perhaps,
had we continued at sea, would have prevented any thing more
being done.   The dysentary about this time began to make its appearance among the ship's company, owing no doubt to the rains

*Mr Collie's Journal

and closeness of the atmosphere, combined with the harassing duty arising from the navigation of a sea so thickly strewed with islands, and to the men having been a long time on a reduced allowance of salt provisions

The islands which were visited between Bow Island and Otaheite were all of the same character and formation as those already described, and furnished us with no additional information beyond the correct determination of their size and position ; which, with some remarks that may be useful to navigation, are given in the Appendix to the 4to ed. Among the number there were two which were previously unknown , the largest of these which was also the most extensive of our discoveries in the archipelago I named Melville Island, in honour of the first lord of the Admiralty , and the other, Croker Island, in compliment to the right honourable secretary.

The discoveries of Cook and Wallis in this track are relatively correctly placed; but those of the latter are as much as forty miles in error in longitude, and several miles in latitude, which has occasioned two of them to be mistaken for each other by Bellinghausen, and one to be considered as a new discovery by Captain Duperrey. It would not have been easy to detect these errors, had we not visited the discoveries of Wallis in succession, beginning with Whitsunday and queen Charlotte's Islands, which are so situated that no mistake in them could possibly occur   Moreover, we always searched the vicinity narrowly for the existence of other islands.

The mistakes have arisen from placing too much confidence in the longitude of the early navigator. The true place of Cumberland Island lying much nearer the alleged position of Wallis's Prince William-Henry Island than any other, has occasioned Bellinghausen's mistake ; and the true position of Prince William-Henry being so remote from any of Wallis's discoveries, as placed by himself, has made Captain Duperrey think the one which he saw could not possibly be one of them, and he in consequence bestowed upon it the new name of L'Ostange.

There can be no doubt that the island which I consider Prince William-Henry Island is the L'Ostange of Captain Duperrey, as we had an opportunity of comparing longitudes with him at Moller Island , and it is equally certain that this island is the same with that discoverd by Wallis, as at its distance from Queen Charlotte's Island and his other discoveries to the eastward, each of which we visited, exactly coincides.   Wallis has certainly erred ten miles in latitude, but it should be recollected that the position of the island was fixed by reckoning from noon, the island having been seen at daybreak " far to windward," and it should not be overlooked that his latitude at Cumberland Island the day before was eight miles in error the same way, which makes it very probable that either his observations were indifferent, or that he had incorrect tables of declination.

In forming this conclusion, I am aware that I am depriving Captain Duperrey of the merit of a discovery, but he will, it is hoped, admit the justice of my opinion.

All the islands seen by Cook, Wallis, and Carteret, lying within the limit of our survey, have been found to be accurately described, excepting that their size has always been overrated; a mistake very likely to arise with low strips of land deficient in familiar objects to direct the judgment where actual measurement is not resorted to.

The discoveries of Mr. Turnbull are so loosely related in his entertaining Voyage, that their situation cannot be entertained; and unless some better clue to them is given, they will always be liable to be claimed by subsequent navigators.

Of the thirty-two islands which have thus been visited in succession, only twelve are inhabited, including Pitcairn Island, and the amount of the population altogether cannot possibly exceed three thousand one hundred souls · of which one thousand belong to the Gambier groupe, and twelve hundred and sixty to Easter Island, leaving eight hundred and forty persons only to occupy the other thirty islands.

All the natives apparently profess the same religion; all speak the same language, and are in all essential points the same people. There is a great diversity of features and complexion between those inhabiting the volcanic islands and the natives of the coral formations, the former being a taller and fairer race   This change may be attributed to a difference of food, habits, and comfort; the one having to seek a daily subsistence upon the reefs, exposed to a burning sun and to the painful glare of a white coral beach, while the other enjoys plentifully the spontaneous produce of the earth, reposes beneath the genial shade of palm or bread-fruit groves, and passes a life of comparative ease and luxury

It has hitherto been a matter of conjecture how these islands, so remote from both great continents, have received their aborigines. The intimate connexion between the language, worship, manners, customs, and traditions of the people who dwell upon them, and those of the Malays and other inhabitants of the great islands to the westward, leaves no doubt of frequent emigrations from thence, and we naturally look to those countries as the source from which they have sprung. The difficulty, however, instantly presents itself of proceeding so vast a distance in opposition to the prevailing wind and current, without vessels better equipped than those which are in possession of the above-mentioned people   This objection has so powerfully influenced the minds of some authors that they have had recourse to the circuitous route through Tartary, across Beering's Strait, and over the American continent, to bring the emigrants to a situation whence they might be drifted by the ordinary course of the winds to the lands in question   But had this been the case, a more intimate resemblance would surely be found to exist between the American Indians and the natives of Polynesia.

All agreed as to the manner in which these migrations between the islands have been effected, and some few instances have actually been met with , but they have been in one direction only, and have rather favoured the opinion of migration from the eastward   The accident which threw in our way Tuwarri and his companions, who, it may be recollected, were driven six hundred miles in a direction contrary to the trade-wind in spite of their utmost exertions, has fortunately enabled us to remove the objections, which have been urged against the general opinion.   The fact being so well attested, and the only one of the kind upon record, is, consequently, of the highest interest, both as regards its singularity, and as it establishes the *possibility* of the case.   Though this is the only instance that has come to our knowledge, there is no reason why many other canoes may not have shared a similar fate , and some few of many thousands, perhaps, may have drifted to the remotest island of the archipelago, and thus peopled them

The navigation of canoes between the islands in sight of each other was, and is still, very general : and it was not unusual, in early times, for warriors, after a defeat, to embark, careless of the consequences, in order to escape the persecution of their conquerors To remain, was certain death and ignominy ; to fly, was to leave their fate to chance.

The temporary obstruction of the trade wind in these seas, by the westerly monsoons, has not been duly considered by those who represent the difficulties as insurmountable   At the period of the year corresponding with our spring these gales commence, and blow with great violence during the rainy season   As they arise very suddenly, any canoes at sea must have difficulty in escaping them, and would, in all probability, be driven so far as never to be able to regain their native country, or be drifted to islands upon which their crews might be contented to dwell, in preference to encountering farther risks.

The traces of inhabitants upon almost all the islands of the low archipelago, many of which are at present uninhabited, show both the frequency with which these migrations have occurred, and the extent to which they have been made   some of these isolated spots where remains have been found, Pitcairn Island for instance, are 400 miles from any land whence inhabitants were likely to be derived ; and the circumstance of their having abandoned that island

is a fair presumption that the people who landed there knew of other
lands which there was a probability of their reaching, and which
certainly could not be the coast of America, at least 2000 miles
against the trade-wind.

I shall now bring together a few facts connected with the formation of these islands, which it is hoped may be useful to those persons who are interested in the subject, observing, in extenuation of
the absence of more detailed information, that our time did not admit
of more than was actually essential to the purposes of a correct delineation of their outline, and that in general the islands were so surrounded by breakers that it was dangerous to approach the shore, in
the ship in particular, which alone was calculated to obtain very deep
soundings.   To windward this could not be done of course, and to
leeward there was not unfrequently a heavier swell setting upon the
island than in other parts of it

In speaking of the coral islands hereafter, my observations will
be confined to the thirty-two islands already stated to have fallen
under our examination. The largest of them was thirty miles in
diameter, and the smallest less than a mile: they were of various
shapes, were all formed of living coral, except Henderson's Island,
which was partly surrounded by it and they all appeared to be increasing their dimensions by the active operations of the lithophytes,
which appeared to be gradually extending and bringing the immersed parts of their structure to the surface

Twenty-nine of the number had lagoons in their centres, which
is a proportion sufficiently large, when coupled with information
supplied from other parts of the globe where such formations abound,
to render it almost certain that the remainder also had them in the
early period of their formation, and that such is the peculiar structure of the coral islands.   And, indeed, these exceptions can scarcely be considered objections, as two of them—Thrum Cap, which
is only seventeen hundred yards long by twelve hundred broad;
and Queen Charlotte's Island, which is not more than three quarters of a mile wide in its broadest part, and less than half a mile in
other places—are so circumstanced, that, had their lagoons existed,
they would have been filled in the course of time with the masses
of coral and other substances which the sea heaps upon such
formations as they rise above the surface, they have, besides,
long been wooded and inhabited, though deserted at the present
moment, both of which would tend to efface the remains of a lagoon of such small dimensions The sea, however, prevented our
boats from landing upon either of these islands, to ascertain the fact
of the early existence of lagoons The other exception, Henderson's Island, though of coral formation, appears to have been raised
to its present height above the sea by a subterraneous convulsion,

and has its centre so incumbered and overgrown with bushes that we could not determine whether it ever had a lagoon

In the above-mentioned twenty-nine islands the strips of dry coral enclosing the lagoons, divested of any loose sandy materials heaped upon them, are rarely elevated more than two feet above the level of the sea, and were it not for the abrupt descent of the external margin, which causes the sea to break upon it, these strips would be wholly inundated · this height of two feet is continued over a small portion only of the width of the island, which slopes on both sides, by an almost imperceptible inclination to the first ledge, where, as I said before, its descent is very steep, but this is greatly altered by circumstances, and the growth or age of the island. Those parts of the strip which are beyond the reach of the waves are no longer inhabited by the animals that reared them, but have their cells filled with a hard calcareous substance, and present a brown rugged appearance The parts still immersed, or which are dry at low water only, are intersected by small channels, and are so full of hollows, that the tide as it recedes leaves small lakes of water upon them The width of the plain or strip of dead coral, in the islands which fell under our observation, in no instance exceeded half a mile from the usual wash of the sea to the edge of the lagoon, and in general was only about three or four hundred yards. Beyond these limits, on the lagoon side in particular, where the coral was less mutilated by the waves, there was frequently a ledge, two or three feet under water at high tide,* thirty to fifty yards in width. after which the sides of the island descended rapidly, apparently by a succession of inclined ledges formed by numerous columns united at their capitals, with spaces between them in which the sounding lead descended several fathoms. This formation, though not clearly established as applying to all the islands, was so conspicuous in some as to justify the conclusion with regard to others At Bow and Matilda Islands, I have been tolerably minute in my descriptions of them, and it will be unnecessary here to repeat what has been said there, but these two, as also Henderson's Island, afford good examples of what I have been describing.

All these islands are situated within the trade-wind, with the exception of Oeno, which is only on the verge of it. and follow one general rule in having their windward sides higher and more perfect than the others, and not unfrequently well wooded while the opposite ones are only half-drowned reefs, or are wholly under water. At Gambier and Matilda Islands this inequality was very conspicuous, the weather side of both being wooded, and of the former, in-

* At Bow Island, on the sea side, it was more

habited, while the other sides were from twenty to thirty feet under water, where they might be perceived equally narrow, and well defined   It is on the leeward side also that the entrances into the lagoons generally occur, though they are sometimes situated in a side that runs in the direction of the wind, as at Bow Island, but I do not know of any one being to windward   The fact, if it be found to be general with regard to other coral islands, is curious, and is not fully accounted for by the continued operation of the tradewind upon its side, as the coincidence would suggest.   After the reef has arrived at the surface of the sea, it is easy to conceive what would be the effect of the trade-wind, but it does not seem possible that its influence could be felt so far under water as some of the reefs are situated

All the points or angles of these islands descend into the sea with less abruptness than the sides, and, I think, with more regularity   The wedge-shaped space that the meeting of the two sides would form in the lagoon is filled up by the ledges there being broader, in such places, as well as in the narrow parts of the lake, the coralline are in greater numbers, though, generally speaking, all the lagoons are more or less incumbered with them   They appear to arise to the surface in the form of a truncated cone, and then, their progress being arrested, they work laterally, so that if several of them were near each other they would unite and form a shelf similar to that which has been described round the margins of some of the lagoons

The depth of these lagoons is various. in those which we entered it was from twenty to thirty-eight fathoms, but in others, to which we had no access, by the light-blue colour of the water it appeared to be very small   It is, however, tolerably certain that the coral forms the bases of them, and consequently, unless depositions of sand or other substances, obnoxious to the coral insects, take place, their depth must depend upon their age.

Very little offered itself to our notice, by which we could judge of the rapidity of the growth of the coral, as the islands which we examined had never been described with the accuracy necessary for this purpose; and there were, consequently, no means of comparing the state in which they were found by us, with that which was presented to our predecessors; but from the report of the natives, the coral bordering the volcanic islands does not increase very fast, as we never heard of any channels being filled up, but, on the contrary, that the passages through the reefs were apparently always in the same condition   The only direct evidence, however, which I could obtain of this fact was that of the Dolphin reef off Point Venus in Otaheite.   This reef, when first examined by Captain Wallis in 1769, had "two fathoms water upon it"   Cook sounded upon it a few years afterwards, and gave its depth fifteen feet.   In

our visit to this place, we found, upon the shallowest part of it, thirteen feet and a half   These measurements, though at variance,
from the irregularity of the surface of the reef, are sufficiently exact
to warrant the conclusion that it has undergone no very material alteration during an interval, it should be recollected, of fifty-six years
But the Dolphin, as well as the above-mentioned reefs and channels, are within the influence of rivers, which, in my opinion, materially retard their increase, and their growth must not be taken as
a criterion of that of the islands of which I have been speaking
With regard to them, there is one fact worthy of consideration, and
upon which every person must form his own judgment   I allude
to the remains of the Matilda, a ship which a few pages back is stated to have been cast away upon one of these coral islands.   In my
description of Matilda Island, it is stated, that one of the anchors of
this ship, a ton in weight, a four-pounder gun, her boilers and iron-
work, are lying upon the top of the reef, two hundred yards from
the present break of the sea, and are dry at low water *   The nature of these articles and the quantity of iron bolts and other materials lying with them renders it probable that the vessel went to pieces in that spot, for had the sea been heavy enough to wash the anchor from deeper water, the boiler must have been carried much be
yond it; and the question is, whether the hull of a vessel of the Matilda's tonnage could be washed upon a reef dry at low water, and
be deposited two hundred yards within the usual break of the sea
The circumstance of the hatches, staves of casks, and part of the
vessel, being deposited in parts of the dry land not far distant, and
scarcely more than four feet from the present level of the sea, offers a presumption that the sea did not rise more than that height
above its ordinary level, or it would have washed the articles further and left them in the lagoon, whence they would have been carried to sea by the current
    The materials were not in the least overgrown with coral, nor
had they any basin left round them by which the progress of the
coral could be traced , and yet, in other parts of this reef, we noticed the chama gigas of seven or eight inches in diameter so overgrown by it, that there was only a small aperture of two inches left
for the extremity of the shell to open and shut
    When the attention of men of science was called to these singu-
lar formations by the voyages of Captain Cook, one opinion, among
others respecting their formation was, that they sprung from a small
base, and extended themselves laterally as they grew perpendicularly towards the surface of the sea ; and that they represented upon
a large scale the form which is assumed by some of the corallines.

* The rise of the tide is about two feet

In particular this theory was entertained by Mr John R. Forster, who accompanied Captain Cook on his second voyage and visited several of the coral islands, and was founded, no doubt, upon the experience which he had derived, upon that voyage.   But considering the extent of some of these islands, it is evident that if this be their form, the lithophytes, the animals which construct them, must commence their operations at very great depths, a fact which is doubted by naturalists.   The general opinion now is, that they have their foundations upon submarine mountains, or upon extinguished volcanoes, which are not more than four or five hundred feet immersed in the ocean: and that their shape depends upon the figure of the base whence they spring   It would be immaterial which of these theories were correct, were it not that in the latter instance the lagoon that is formed in all the islands of this description might be occasioned by the shape of the crater alone, whereas, in the former, it must result from the propensity of the coral animals, and this, if true, forms a remarkable and interesting feature in their natural history   Mr Forster[*] thought this peculiarity might arise from the instinct of the animacules forming the reefs, which from a desire to shelter their habitation from the impetuosity of the winds, and the power and rage of the ocean, endeavoured to construct a ledge, within which was a lagoon entirely screened against the power of the elements, and where a calm and sheltered place was by these means afforded to the animals in centre of the island

Another reason why the consideration of the nature of their foundation is not immaterial is, that if the form of the islands arose from the peculiar shape of the craters, and it be admitted that the lithophytes are unable to exist at greater depths than those above-mentioned, we shall have examples of craters of considerably larger dimensions and more complete in their outline, than any that are known upon the land, which, if true, is a curious fact.   Until the voyage of the Blossom, it was not generally known that the lagoons in these islands were of such depths, or that the wall of coral which encircles them was so narrow and perfect, as in almost every instance it has been found ; nor that the islands were of such dimensions, as they were designated groupes, or chains of islands, in consequence of the wall being broken by channels into the lagoon ; but on examination, the chain is found continuous under water ; and as in all probability it will in time reach the surface and become dry, the whole groupe may be considered as one island.

The subject of the formation of these islands is one of great interest, and will require a numerous and careful collection of facts before any entirely satisfactory conclusion can be arrived at.   I re-

[*] Forster's Observations, 4to, page 150

gret that my time did not permit me to inquire more particularly
into this curious matter, but having to survey about fifty islands,
some of which were of great extent, in the space of about four
months, I could not accomplish more than was absolutely necessary
to the purposes of a safe navigation of the Archipelago   We were,
however, not inattentive to the subject, and when opportunity offered, soundings were tried for at great depth, and the descent of the
islands was repeatedly ascertained as far as the common lines would
extend.

In considering the subject of these coral formations, my attention
was drawn to the singularity of the occurrence of openings in them,
either opposite to, or in the direction of some stream of fresh water
from the mountains, and on searching several charts, I find so many
corroborations of the fact, that I have no doubt of the truth of it
as far as my own observations extended. it was always so.   The
aversion of the lithophytes to fresh water is not singular, as, independent of its not being the natural element of those animals, it
probably supplies no materials with which they can work

It has been suggested, that these openings being opposite to valleys, the continuation of them under water is the cause of the break
in the reef   But when we consider the narrowness of these openings, compared with the width of the valleys, and that the latter
are already filled up to the surface and furnished with a smooth
sandy beach, many obstacles will be found to the confirmation of
such an opinion, and it appears to me more reasonable to attribute
it to the nature of the element   The depth of these channels
rarely exceeds twenty-five feet, the greatest limit probably to which
the influence of fresh water would be felt

Henderson Island, one of the exceptions mentioned in the early
part of this discussion, is among the rare instances of its kind in
these seas   It is an island composed of dead coral, about eighty
feet above the sea, with perpendicular cliffs nearly all the way
round it, as if after being formed in the ocean it had been pushed
up by a subterraneous convulsion.   These cliffs are undermined at
the base, as though the sea had beaten against them considerable
time in their present position   There are no marks upon them indicative of the island having risen by degrees; but on the contrary,
a plain surface indicating its ascent by one great effort of nature.
On examining the volcanic islands near Henderson Island, no traces appeared of the sea having retired, and we may, therefore,
presume it to have risen as. described   Its length is five miles.
and breadth one mile   it is nearly encompassed by a reef of living
coral, so wide that the cliffs, which were at first subjected to the
whole force of the waves, are now beyond the reach even of their
spray.

The navigation of this archipelago was made at a period of the year when the westerly monsoon was about to commence, and toward the end of which it had actually begun, and materially retarded our operations, but previous to that time, or about the beginning of March, the trade was fresh and steady, blowing between S E by E and E N E, which is more northerly than the direction of the same trade between corresponding parallels in the Atlantic In consequence of this opposition to the trade wind the currents were very variable, sometimes setting to the eastward, and others in the opposite direction, and on the whole, the body of water at that period is not drifted to the westward with the same rapidity that it is in other parts of the ocean within the influence of the tropical winds The mean temperature for the above-mentioned period, the weight and humidity of the atmosphere, with other meteorological observations, are given in the Appendix to the 4to ed under their respective heads.

For the information of persons who may traverse this archipelago, it is evident from the account of Tuwarri, that there is a small island situated about half way between Byam Martin and Barrow Islands, which was not seen by us, and hence it is possible that there are other low islands lying between the tracks of the Blossom which were not seen; and ships ought in consequence to keep a vigilant look out during the night, or adopt the precaution of lying to when the weather is dark or thick. The lead is no guide whatever in these seas, and the islands are so low that in the night the white line of the surf or the roar of the breakers would give the first warning Fallacious as the appearance of birds is generally considered, and in some parts of the globe justly so, in this archipelago, when seen in flocks, it is an almost certain indication of land They range about forty miles from the islands, and consist principally of black and white tern This, however, applies particularly to uninhabited islands; for when they become peopled, the birds generally quit them, and resort to those where they are less molested

At day-light on the 15th the Island of Maitea was seen in the north-west, and soon afterwards the mountains of Otaheite appeared five minutes above the horizon at the distance of ninety miles, from which its height may be roughly estimated at 7000 feet As we passed Maitea we had an opportunity of verifying its position and ascertaining its height to be 1432 feet Baffling winds prevented us from reaching our port until the evening of the 18th, when at the suggestion of Captain Charlton, his Majesty's consul for the Society and Sandwich Islands, from whom we had the pleasure of receiving a visit, we anchored in the outer harbor of Toanoa, about four miles to the westward of Matavai Bay

CHAPTER IX.

Proceedings at Otaheite—The Ship visited by the Queen Regent, the Royal Family, and several Chiefs—Short Account of the former since Captain Cook's Visit—Successful Issue of a Dispute with the Government respecting the Detention of a trading Vessel—Visit to the Queen Regent's House—Present Condition of the Chiefs and of the Inhabitants—Superstitions—Trial of Natives for Theft of the Ship's Stores—The King visits the Ship—Lake and Morai of Mirapaye—Dance exhibited by a Party of New Zealanders—Considerations on the Effect of the Introduction of Christianity

The diversity of feature of the romantic Island of Otaheite formed a strong contrast with the monotonous appearance of the coral formations, the variety of hill and valley, and of woods and rivers in the one, after the sameness of flat, sterile, parched-up surface in the other, and the glassy smoothness of the harbours around us, opposed to the turbulent shores we had recently quitted, were gratifying in the extreme, and impressed us most forcibly with the truth of the observations of our predecessors, who have spoken of the scenery of this island in the highest terms of commendation.

As I proposed to remain here a few weeks to recruit the health of the crew, who were somewhat debilitated, and to prepare the ship for her voyage to the northward, she was moved to an inner anchorage opposite a small village called Toanoa, and there secured by a cable fastened to some trees on one side, and by a bower anchor dropped at the edge of a coral reef on the other. This reef forms one side of the harbour; which, though small, possesses several advantages over the more spacious one of Papiete generally resorted to, and of which the superior freshness and salubrity of its atmosphere are not the most inconsiderable.

Previous to entering upon a relation of our proceedings with the natives, it must be understood that the short time we remained, and our various occupations necessarily rendered our intercourse with them very limited compared with that of many of our predecessors. Still, it is hoped, the remarks which I shall offer will be sufficient to present a candid and faithful picture of the existing state of society in the island; a feature by no means unimportant in the history of the country, which is otherwise complete.   To exceed this, by dwelling upon the beauties of the scenery, the engaging manners of the inhabitants, their mythology, superstitions, and legends, &c. would be only to recapitulate what has been detailed in the interesting voyages of Wallis, Cook, Vancouver, Wilson, Turnbull, and others, and very recently by Mr. Ellis, in his valuable work entitled "Polynesian Researches," compiled after ten years' residence in the Pacific, and from the journals of other missionary gentlemen in those parts.   In this useful work Mr Ellis has traced the history of some of the islands through all their various stages ; he has explained the origin of many of their barbarous customs, has elucidated many hitherto obscure points and has shown the difficulties which opposed themselves to the introduction of Christianity, the hardships, dangers, and privations, which were endured by himself and his brethren, who, actuated by religious motives, were induced to sacrifice their own health, comfort, and worldly advantages in the attempt to ameliorate the condition of their fellow-creatures   But complete as that work is in many respects, it is nevertheless deficient in some essential points.   The author, with a commendable feeling of charity, consonant with his profession, has by his own admission in the account of the biography of Pomarree, glossed over the failings and dwelt upon the better qualities of the subject of his memoir ; and pursuing the same course throughout, he has impressed the reader with a more elevated idea of their moral condition, and with a higher opinion of the degree of civilization to which they have attained, than they deserve, or, at least, than the facts which came under our observation authorize   There seems to be no doubt that he has drawn the picture, generally, as it was presented to him ; but he has unconsciously fallen into an error almost inseparable from a person of his profession, who, when mixing with society, finds it under that restraint which respect for his sacred office and veneration for his character create.   As in our intercourse with these people they acted more from the impulse of their natural feelings, and expressed their opinions with greater freedom, we were more likely to obtain a correct knowledge of their real disposition and habits.

To convey to the reader, who has not perused the above-mentioned work, an idea of the political state of the island, in which there has been a material alteration since the period alluded to in the early voyages, it will be necessary to state briefly that since 1815 a code of laws has been drawn up by Pomarree II., with the assistance of the missionaries, which has subsequently been extended from time to time ; and that since 1825 a house of parliament has been established, to which representatives of the several districts in the island are returned by popular election.   The penalties proposed by Pomaree were very severe, but that of death has as yet been enforced upon four culprits only

The limit thus imposed on the arbitrary power of the monarch, and the security thus afforded to the liberties and properties of the people, reflect credit upon the missionaries, who were very instrumental in introducing these laws , at the same time, had they been better informed in the history of mankind, they would have been less rigid upon particular points, and would have more readily produced those benefits which they no doubt hoped would ensue Magistrates are appointed to try cases, and conduct their judicial proceedings in open court, and the police are continually on the alert both day and night to prevent irregularities, and to suppress the amusements of the people, whom, from mistaken views of religion, they wish to compel to lead a life of austere privation

We found the consul in possession of a small but comfortable house opposite the anchorage, which had been hastily run up by the natives for his use ; and took the earliest and most favourable opportunity of impressing the importance of his situation upon the inhabitants, by the salute due to his rank. Besides the missionary gentlemen, we found that several other Europeans were residing in our vicinity; and as some of these, as well as the consul, had their wives and female relatives with them, we looked forward to the pleasure of varying our intercourse with the uncouth natives by more agreeable society—an anticipation which was fully realised by their unremitting attention, especially on the part of the consul, whose house was the general resort of all the officers

Our arrival was immediately communicated, through the proper channel, to the queen regent, who lived about a mile from the anchorage, and we received an intimation of her intention of paying an early visit to the ship

The arrival of a man-of-war at Otaheite is still an event of much interest, and brings a number of the inhabitants from the districts adjoining the port, some in canoes, others on foot   The little hamlet opposite the ship was almost daily crowded with strangers, and a vast number of canoes skimmed the smooth surface of the harbour, or rather the narrow channel of water which is tied to the shores of this luxuriant island by reefs of living coral   A remarkable exception to this scene of bustle occurred on the day of our arrival, which, although Saturday, according to our mode of reckoning, was here observed as the Sabbath, in consequence of the missionaries having proceeded round by the Cape of Good Hope, and having thereby gained a day upon us   Next morning, however, a busy scene ensued   Canoes laden with fruit, vegetables, and articles of curiosity, thronged as closely round the ship as their slender outriggers would allow, while such of the inhabitants as wanted these means of approaching us awaited their harvest on the shore

We soon found that the frequent intercourse of Europeans with the islanders had effected an alteration in the nature of the currency, and that those tinselled ornaments with which we had provided ourselves were now objects of desire only as presents, the more substantial articles of clothing and hard dollars being required for the purposes of the market, except, perhaps, where a ring or a jew's harp happened for the moment to attract the attention of some capricious individual.   However gratified we might be to observe this advance towards civilization, we experienced considerable inconvenience from its effects ; for on leaving the coast of Chili, very few of us had provided dollars, under an impression that they would not be necessary , and those which we had were principally of the republican coinage, and as useless in the Otaheitan market as they would have been in New Zealand   No dollars bear their full value here, unless the pillars on the reverse are clearly distinguishable, and a greater degree of value is attached to such as are bright than to others   So ignorant, indeed, were these simple people of the real worth of the coin, that it was not unusual for them to offer two that were blemished in exchange for one that was new, and in the market a yard of printed calico, a white shirt, new or old, provided it had not a hole in it (even a threadbare shirt that is whole being whimsically preferred to one which might have been eaten through by a mouse), or a Spanish dollar that had two pillars upon it, were in the ordinary way equivalent to a club, a spear, a conch shell, a paddle, or a pig.   Deviations, of course, occurred from this scale, founded on the superior quality or size of the article, and occasionally on the circumstances of the vendor, who, when he anticipated a better bargain, would accommodate his price to his preconceived opinion of the disposition of the purchaser   We were not more conveniently circumstanced in regard to the clothing which we could offer in exchange, as we had a long voyage before us, and little to spare without subjecting ourselves to future inconvenience.   We, consequently, found ourselves at first surrounded with plenty, without the means of purchase, or obliged to part in payment with what we could very ill spare   and we incurred the additional risk of being charged with parsimony, which the good people of Otaheite are very apt to attach to those who may not meet their ideas of generosity   " Taata paree," or stingy people, is an epithet which they always affix to such persons, with a feeling of contempt, although they are themselves equally open to the charge, never offering a present without expecting a much larger one in return   It is very desirable to secure a favourable impression by liberality on your first arrival at this island ; it being a constant custom with the natives to mark those who have any peculiarity of person or manner by a nickname, by which alone the person will be known as long

as any recollection of his visit may remain   Among the many instances which occurred of this, was one of a brother officer, who,
when we quitted England, begged to be remembered to his old acquaintances in Otaheite; but we found they had lost all memory of
his name, and we at last only brought him to their recollection by
describing his person, and mentioning that he had lost an eye by a
wound received in service; on which they at once exclaimed
" "Tapane Matapo !" or "Captain Blind-eye."   We were the more
anxious to avoid aquiring a distinction of this kind for ourselves, as
a Russian ship had just preceded us, the crew of which, according
to the natives, purchased every thing that was offered without regard to price, at whom they laughed heartily, because one of the
officers had given a blue jacket in exchange for a pearl which had
been ingeniously made out of an oyster shell.

Some of us, therefore, had recourse to the European residents,
and fortunately obtained what cloth and specie we wanted; while
others preferred bartering such portions of their wardrobes as they
considered unnecessary for their approaching change of climate

On the Monday succeeding our arrival, all the stores of the ship
that required removal were landed and placed under a shed; the observatory was erected close to the consulate, a rope-walk was constructed, and the forge was put under the shade of some trees   Thus,
as the shore was so near, all the duties of the ship were carried on
under our own immediate superintendence far more expeditiously
than the confined space on board would have allowed.   The sick
were also landed, and provided with a place better adapted to their
situation.

The state of our provisions rendered it necessary to observe the
strictest economy, for we had been confined to our own resources
during several months, and Otaheite afforded nothing except beef
and pork, nor had we any certainty of an opportunity of replenishing them.   The bread fruit was, fortunately, at this time excellent,
and was substituted for the daily allowance of flour, at first in moderate proportions, that no bad effects might arise from such a change
of diet, but, latterly, the crew were allowed as much as they could
consume, by which necessary piece of economy we saved during
our stay about 2,000 pounds of flour, the most valuable articles of
sea store, a measure which subsequently proved of the utmost importance to us.   I do not think that this fruit, though very delicious
and more farinaceous than potatoes, is a satisfactory substitute for
bread, but it is by no means a bad one

Foreseeing the possibility of being obliged to cure our own meat,
we fortunately provided a quantity of salt for that purpose at Chili,
an article which we found very scarce at Otaheite, and the consul
made arrangements for salting both beef and pork for our future use,

which succeeded uncomomonly well , and he materially forwarded
the object of our voyage by exerting himself to satisfy all our demands, so far as their resources would admit   Before our arrival articles of food were sufficiently cheap , but the great demand which we
occasioned materially enhanced their prices, and there appeared to
be a great dislike to competition   The resources of the island, fruit
excepted, are considerably diminished from what they formerly were,
notwithstanding the population at one time exceeded its present
amount twenty-fold

On the day appointed for the visit of the royal party, the duty
of the ship was suspended, and we were kept in expectation of their
arrival until four o'clock in the afternoon, when I had the honour of
receiving a note, couched in affectionate terms, from the queen regent, to whom, as well as to her subjects, the loss of time appears
to be immaterial, stating her inability to fulfil her engagement, but
that she would come on board the following day.   Scarcely twenty
minutes had elapsed, however, from the receipt of this note, when
we were surprised by the appearance of the party, consisting of the
queen regent, the queen dowager and her youthful husband, and
Utamme and his wife   Their dress was an incongruous mixture of
European and native costumes; the two queens had wrappers of
native cloth wound loosely round their bodies, and on their heads
straw poked bonnets, manufactured on the island, in imitation of
some which had been carried thither by European females, and
trimmed with black ribands.   Their feet were left bare, in opposition to the showy covering of their heads, as if purposely to mark
the contrast between the two countries whose costumes they united ;
and neatly executed blue lines formed an indelible net-work over
that portion of the frame which in England would have been covered with silk or cotton   Utamme, who, without meaning any in-
sinuations to the disadvantage of the queen, appeared to be on a
very familiar footing with her majesty, (notwithstanding he was accompanied by his own wife), was a remarkably tall and comely
man , he wore a straw hat, and a white shirt, under which he had
taken the necessary precaution of tying on his native maro, and
was provided with an umbrella to screen his complexion from the
sun.   This is the common costume of all the chiefs, to whom an
umbrella is now become almost as indispensable as a shirt ; but by
far the greater part of the rest of the population are contented with
a mat and a maro

It may be desirable, in this early period of our communications
with the court of Otaheite, to state the relationship which exists between the reigning family and Otoo, who was king of the larger
peninsula at the period of Captain Cook's last visit.

Otoo, after Cook's departure, was surnamed Pomarree, from a

hoarseuss that succeeded a sore throat which he caught in the mountains, and this afterwards became the royal patronymic His son, Pomarree II, who was a child at that period, succeeded him in 1803, and reigned until December, 1821, when, having effected many most important changes in the customs of the island, and having, under the zealous exertions of the missionaries, converted the chief part of the population to Christianity, he expired in a fit of apoplexy, accelerated no doubt, by frequent excesses. Of this man it may be lamented that his exertions in the cause of Christianity were not seconded in the fullest extent by a rigid adherence to its precepts in his own person. He had two wives, or rather a wife and a mistress, who were sisters, named Tene-moe-moe, and Pomarree Waheine This woman, daughter of the King of Ulietea, had been sent for from Huaheine to be married to the king, but being accompanied by her sister, Tene-moe-moe, who was very superior in personal attractions, the latter captivated his majesty at first sight, and received the honour of his hand, while Pomarree Waheine was retained in the more humble capacity of mistress Each sister bore a child, Terre-moe-moe giving birth to Pomaree III., and the mistress presenting him with a daughter named Aimatta, the present queen Pomaree III. was only six years old at the time we arrived. and the regency was administered by his aunt Pomarree Waheine, who I suppose was considered a more fit person to manage the affairs of the state than her sister, who had doubtless the greater claim to the office. We found that the queen mother, widow of Pomaree II., had married a chief of Bora Bora, a finelooking lad of ten or eleven years of age, and that Aimatta was united to a chief of Huaheine, a short corpulent person, who, in consequence of his marriage, was allowed to bear the royal name of Pomaree, to which, however, in allusion to his figure, and in conformity with their usual custom, they had added the appropriate but not very elegant surname of "Aboo-rai," or big-belly

We treated the royal party with a few good things which remained, and they landed at night, highly delighted with a display of fire works purposely prepared for them. Next morning the party repeated their visit, somewhat better dressed, and accompanied by Aimatta and Aboo-rai. They were followed by a large double canoe and many small single ones, bearing upon their gunwales heaps of fruit and roots, and four enormous hogs, at the imminent risk of upsetting the whole The double canoe was the "last of her race," and had been used for the nobler purposes of war, but, like the inhabitants, was now devoted to humbler but more useful occupations.

As soon as the queen reached the deck she tendered the present to me in the name of the young king, then at the missionary school at Eimeo, and I returned the compliment that was due to her for

this mark of her attention, as well as for the munificence of the gift
As soon as the remainder of the party were assembled, it was proposed that we should adjourn to the breakfast prepared in the cabin ; but the regent desired that every part of the present should
previously be set out on a particular part of the deck, pigs and all,
in order to impress us more fully with an idea of her liberality ; and
when the whole was collected, she led me to the pile, and expatia-
ted on the superior quality of the fruit.

Having at length assembled at breakfast, which by this time was
cold, a difficulty arose, I was informed, in consequence of Aimatta,
the king's sister, being unwilling to relinquish the distinction she had
enjoyed under the former custom of the island, which rendered it
indecorous for some of her countrywomen, who were of the party,
to presume to eat in the presence of so exalted a personage   As
these distinctions, however. had been removed upon the introduction of Christianity, there was an evident apprehension of giving offence to the assembled chiefs by such a display of ambition on the
present occasion.   The inconvenience which it was suggested would
attend the observance of the custom in this instance, and the opposition afforded by the precepts of the missionaries to any such mode
of displaying the royal prerogative, relieved us from our dilemma.
A cloud of discontent hung for a time on the countenance of our
royal guest, but it was dispelled by the first breeze of mirth, and
the party appeared to enjoy greatly the remainder of their visit.

It is by no means surprising that the chiefs should wish to adhere
to such of their old customs as constituted the principal if not the
only distinction between them and their vassals.   Should they be
deprived of these, and should the superstitions, by means of which
they awed the lower classes of the community, be brought into contempt, they would be left with no other superiority than that conferred by bodily strength ; for in education, and not unfrequently
even in wealth, their advantages were very limited   Pomaree, in
framing his laws to meet the new circumstances of his subjects,
seems to have been too zealous in pressing his reforms in this as
well as in many other points   It would be ridiculous to advocate
the perpetuation of customs fit only for the darkest ages of barbarism ; but it might probably not be unwise to retain in the earlier
progress towards improvement such as are least objectionable ; particularly in a country like Otaheite, where their observance had
been enforced with the greatest rigour   The effect produced by
the abolition of that most detestable of all their pagan rites, human
sacrifice, is noticed by Mr Ellis in his Polynesian Researches, to
have endangered the royal authority.*

*He says (vol ii p 378,) that "many, free from the restraint it (human sacrifice)
had imposed, seemed to refuse almost all lawful obedience and rightful support to
the king"

In the course of the day several chiefs came on board, dressed in white shirts and straw hats, and were all remarkable for their extraordinary height and noble appearance. Whether this superiority of stature is the result of the better quality of their food, or whether, by the commission of infanticide, their parents have preserved only the largest or most healthy children, and bestowed upon them a more careful nursing than may have fallen to the lot of their vassals, I cannot say, but it is beyond a doubt that the advantage which their chiefs enjoyed in this respect had a strong influence on the minds of the simple Otaheitans, who were with difficulty convinced that the size of the purser (who was the largest man in the ship) did not confer on him the best claim to be the Ratira-rai, or captain of the Blossom.

The arrival of the chiefs was an event very favourable to the wishes of the consul, who availed himself of the opportunity it afforded of urging, with some prospect of success, the repeal of an order issued by the regent, which had occasioned serious mischief to one of our merchant ships, and which, if not speedily rescinded, must have endangered not only the property, but even the lives of individuals trading to these islands. The consul had already appealed against the obnoxious decree, but it was at a time when he was not supported by the presence of a king's ship, and the short-sighted policy of the regent did not anticipate the probability of the consul soon receiving such a strong support to his negotiation. She had ventured, therefore, to dismiss his remonstrance, intimating that she was fully aware of his defenceless situation. The case under discussion was as follows.

The queen, seeing the estimation in which the pearl oyster-shells were held by Europeans, imagined that by levying a duty on them she would greatly increase her revenue. Orders were accordingly issued to all the tributary islands to seize every vessel trading in shells, which had not previously obtained the royal licence to procure them. The Chain Islanders, who, from their enterprising and maurauding habits, may be considered the buccaneers of the eastern South Sea archipelago, were too happy to find themselves fortified with a plea for a proceeding of this nature, and instantly sent one of their double canoes to Tiokea, where they found the Dragon, an English brig, taking in pearl shells. These people behaved in a very friendly manner to her crew, and allowed her quietly to take her cargo on board, but the Dragon was no sooner ready to put to sea, than several of the islanders went on board with the ostensible purpose of taking leave, but suddenly possessing themselves of the vessel, overpowering the master and crew, binding their hands, and sending them on shore as prisoners. A general plunder of the vessel ensued, in which every thing moveable was carried away.

The natives, after this atrocious act, went to church to return thanks
for their victory; and to render their prayers more acceptable, removed the bell of the ship to their place of worship.   During several days
they detained the master bound hand and foot, and debated whether he should be put to death and eaten; a fate which we were informed he would in all probability have encountered but for the interference of one of their chiefs, for the Tiokeans are still reputed to be cannibals, notwithstanding they have embraced the christian
religion.   The crew, more fortunate than their commander, very
soon obtained their release, upon condition of fitting the brig for sea,
the natives imagining they could navigate her themselves   The vessel being ready, the master, under some pretext, obtained permission to go on board, and having speedily established an understanding with his crew, he cut the cables and carried her out to sea.

The stolen property was of course never recovered, and the
vessel was so plundered of her stores that the object of her voyage
was lost   When she reached Otaheite the master stated the case
to the consul, whose representation of the outrage to the queen was,
as has already been said, treated with derision.   The consul availed
himself of the present occasion to obtain restitution of the stolen
property, or remuneration for the owners, and a repeal of the ob-
jetionable order, the execution of which it is evident could not be safely confided to a barbarous people, at all times too prone to appropriate to themselves whatever might fall within their reach.   Her
majesty was exceeding unwilling to abandon this source of revenue,
and strenuously urged her indubitable right to levy taxes within her
own dominions, maintaining her arguments with considerable shrewd-
ness, appealing finally to the chiefs.   Finding them, however, disposed to accede to the demands of the consul, she burst into tears;
but at length consented, by their advice, to send a circular to the Pa-
moutas, or Low Islands, directing that no molestation should be offered to any vessels trading in shells, or touching at those islands
for refreshment; but on the contrary that all necessary aid and assistance should be afforded to them, and that in the event of any
dispute, the matter should be referred to the authorities at Otaheite.

This concession destroyed the complacency of the queen for
some time, but she recovered her spirits in the course of the afternoon, and amused herself much by listening to the drum, which she
begged might be permitted to play on the upper deck.   As this
species of music, however, was not very agreeable in the confined
space of a ship, it was proposed that the instrument should be removed to the shade of some tall trees on the shore, whither the
whole party repaired; the drummer continuing his performance,
and marching to and fro, until he became heartily tired, to the infi-

nite delight of the assembled populace, who crowded round, and even scaled the loftiest trees, to obtain a glimpse of him

A few days after this visit the queens came again to Toanoa, and I invited them into the tent we had pitched on shore, with the view of making a present to each of them, and of confiding to their care the presents intended for Pomarree Aboo-rai, Aimatta, and Utamme, who were absent. The present for the king, which consisted of a handsome double-barrelled gun inlaid with silver, with some broad cloth and other valuables, I reserved until I should have an opportunity of seeing him. The other parcels were apportioned according to what I considered to be the rank of the parties, and the name of each person was placed on his destined share. The regent, however, opened them all, and very unceremoniously transferred a portion of each to her own, and huddling the whole together, she sent them off to her canoe. Then finishing half a bottle of brandy between them, the regent and her sister despatched the remainder of the spirits after the presents, and took their leave.

In the course of the day we received an invitation to pass the evening at the regent's house at Papiete, a very romantic spot about a mile from the place where the ship was anchored. After a delightful walk along the shore in the refreshing coolness which succeeds a tropical day, we arrived at the royal residence, which was in one of those spacious sheds frequently mentioned by my predecessors. It was about a hundred feet in length, by thirty-five in width, of an oval form, with a thatched roof, supported upon small poles placed close together. By the light of the moon we discovered a small door about mid-way between the extremities, which we entered, and immediately found ourselves in darkness. On groping our way, our shins came in contact with several bamboo partitions dividing the area into various compartments. In one of these we distinguished by the rays of moonlight which fell through the interstices of the dwelling, that it was occupied by toutous, or common people, of both sexes. We, therefore turned to the opposite direction, which soon led us to the royal saloon, which we found illuminated by a yellow and melancholy light proceeding from a rag hung over the edge of a broken cocoa-nut shell half filled with oil; The apartment, to our surprise, was quite still, but we were soon greeted with the salutation of "Euranna-poy" (How do you do?) from a number of athletic men, her majesty's favourites, as they awoke in succession from their nap.

We at length discovered the queen regent extended upon a mat spread upon dried grass, with which the whole apartment was strewed, around her, upon mats also, were several interesting young females, and occupying a wooden bedstead, placed against a slight partition, which contained numerous cases filled with cocoa-nut oil, we found Pomaree Aboo-iai, and Aimatta. Our entiy thiew this numerous party into a state of activity and bustle, some to piocuie a second light, and some to accommodate us with mats ; while Pomaiiee, diawing his tappa round him, led forward his piincess, Aimatta, and extended his politeness much beyond what we could possibly have anticipated from so young a husband

Fearful that we might have misundeistood the morning invitation, oi that we were later than we had been expected, we began to offer apologies, and to excuse ourselves for bieaking in upon the repose of the paity , but the indisposition of the queen appeared to be the cause, as she was suffering fiom repletion, and, foigetting all about the invitation, had retiied earliei than usual   She had scarcely had sufficient iest when we arrived to engage in any amusement herself, but gave us a fiiendly reception, and desired that a dance might be performed for our enteitainment   This was an indulgence we hardly expected, such perfoimances being piohibited by law, under severe penalties, both against the perfoimers, and upon those who should attend such exhibitions , and for the same reason it was necessary that it should be executed quietly, and that the *vivo*, or reed pipe, should be played in an undei tone, that it might not reach the eais of an aava, oi policeman, who was parading the beach, in a soldier's jacket, with a rusty sword , foi even the use of this melodious little instrument, the delight of the natives, from whose nature the dance and the pipe aie inseparable, is now stiictly piohibited   None of us had witnessed the dances of these people before they were restrained by law, but in that which was exhibited on the present occasion, there was nothing at which any unprejudiced person could take offence ; and it confirmed the opinion I had often heaid expressed, that Pomariee, or whoevei fiamed the laws, would have more effectually attained his object had these amusements been restricted within proper limits, rather than entirely suppiessed. To some of us, who had formed our opinion of the native dance of this island fiom the fascinating iepresentation of it by Mr Webber, who accompanied Captain Cook, that which we saw gieatly disappointed our expectation, and we turned from it to listen to the simple airs of the females about the queen, who sang very well, and were ieady *improvisatiices*, adapting the woids of the song to the paiticulai case of each individual.

While these amusements engaged the attention of oui party, scenes of a veiy diffeient natuie were passing in the same apaitment, which must have convinced the greatest sceptic of the thoioughly immoral condition of the people , and if he ieflected that he was in the royal residence, and in the piesence of the individual at the head of both chuich and state, he would have either concluded, as Tuinbull did many yeais before, that theii inteicouise with Europeans had tend-

ed to debase rather than to exalt their condition, or that they were
wilfully violating and deriding laws which they considered ridicu-
lously severe

In our intercourse with the chiefs and middle classes of society,
the impression left by this night's entertainment was in some measure removed; and especially as regards the former, who are, on the
whole, a well-behaved class of men, though they are much addicted
to intemperance. A party of them, among which were Utammee
and Pa-why, came on board one day, and having received a present
of a bottle of rum from the cabin, went to pay a visit to the gun-
room officers, who politely offered them a glass of wine, but evincing some reluctance to this beverage, rum was placed upon the
table, upon which the chiefs manifested their approbation, and
Utammee seizing the bottle requested it as a present, and then
emptying their glasses, which had been filled with wine, to the toast
of *Eurannapoy*, they bowed politely and withdrew This partiality
for spirits seems to be an incorrigible vice, and it is a fortunate circumstance that their means of indulging in it are so very limited.
Some of them have materially benefited by the residence of the
missionaries, and, in particular, two who resided at Matavai, about
four miles to the eastward of our anchorage They piqued themselves on their imitation of European customs, and had neat little
cottages, built after the European style, with whitewashed fronts,
which, peeping through some evergreen foliage, had a most agreeable effect, and being the only cottages of this description upon the
island in the possession of the natives, were the pride of their owners.
The apartments contained chests, chairs, a table, and a knife and
fork for a guest; and nothing gave these chiefs greater pleasure than
the company of some of the officers of the ship. Each of them
could read and write their own language, and the elder, Pa-why,
had, I believe, been useful to the missionaries in translating some
part of the Scriptures. He was the more learned of the two brothers, but Hetotte was the more esteemed, and was an exception to
almost all his countrymen in not asking for what was shown to him
His inquiries concerning the use of every thing which offered itself
to his notice, on coming on board the ship, surprised and interested
us, while his amiable disposition and engaging manners won him
the esteem of almost all on board An anecdote illustrative of his
character will be read with interest The missionaries had for several years endeavoured to produce a change of religion in the island,
by explaining to the natives the fallacy of their belief, and assuring
them that the threats of their deities were absurd Hetotte at
length determined to put their assertions to the test, by a breach of one
of the strictest laws of his religion, and resolved either to die under
the experiment or embrace the new faith.

A custom prevailed of offering pigs to the deity, which were brought to the morai and placed upon whattas, or fantus, for the purpose From that moment they were considered sacred, and if afterwards any human being, the priests excepted, dared to commit so great a sacrilege as to partake of the offering, it was supposed that the offended god would punish the crime with instant death. Hetotte thought a breach of this law would be a fair criterion of the power of the deity, and accordingly stole some of the consecrated meat, and retired with it to a solitary part of the wood to eat it, and perhaps to die   As he was partaking of the food, he expected at each mouthful to experience the vengeance he was provoking; but having waited a considerable time in the wood in awful suspense, and finding himself rather refreshed, than otherwise by his meal, he quitted the retreat and went quietly home   For several days he kept his secret, but finding no bad effects from his transgression he disclosed it to every one, renounced his religion, and embraced Christianity.   Such instances of resolution and good sense, though they have been practised before, are extremely rare in Otaheite, and in this sketch of two brothers a highly favourable picture is presented of the class to which they belong, though there are others, particularly Taate, the first and most powerful chief upon the island, who are equally deserving of favourable notice.

Of the rest of the population, though their external deportment is certainly more guarded than formerly, in consequence of the severe penalties which their new laws attach to a breach of decorum, yet their morals have in reality undergone as little change as their costume   Notwithstanding all the restrictions imposed, I do not believe that I should exceed the bounds of truth in saying, that, if opportunity offered, there is no favour which might not be obtained from the females of Otaheite for the trifling consideration of a Jew's harp, a ring, or some other bauble

Their dwellings, with the exception of doors to some, and occasionally latches and locks, are precisely what they were when the island was first discovered.   The floor is always strewed with grass, which they are not at all careful to preserve clean or dry, and it consequently becomes extremely filthy and disagreeable and when it can be no longer endured, it is replaced by fresh material.   Their household furniture has been increased by the introduction of various European articles . and a chest, or occasionally a bedstead, may be seen occupying the corner of an apartment, but these are not yet in great demand, the natives having little to put into the former, and esteeming such of the latter as have found their way to Otaheite scarcely more desirable places of repose than their mats spread upon straw   The extreme mildness of the climate, however, sufficiently accounts for the contented state of the population in this respect

Their occupations are few, and in general only such as are necessary to existence or to the gratification of vanity. In our repeated visits to their huts we found them engaged either in preparing their meals, plaiting straw-bonnets, stringing the smallest kinds of beads to make rings for the fingers or the ears, playing the Jew's harp, or lolling about upon their mats; the princess excepted, whose greatest amusement consisted in turning a hand-organ. The indolence of these people has ever been notorious, and has been a greater bar to the success of the missionaries than their previous faith The fate of the experiment on the cotton in Eimeo is an exemplification of this It is well known that the land was cleared, and the cotton planted and grown, but the perseverance to clean the crop, to make it marketable, was wanting, and finding no sale for the articles in its rude state, they forbore to cultivate it the next year. A small portion, however, was picked by way of experiment the missionaries taught the girls to spin, and even furnished them with a loom, and instructed them in the use of it, upon condition that they should weave fifty yards of cloth for the king, and fifty for themselves. The novelty of the employment at first brought many pupils, but they would not persevere, and not one was found who fulfilled the engagement The proportion due to the king was wove, but not as much more as would make a single gown, and the pupils, after a dispute regarding their wages, abandoned the employment about the period of our arrival " Why should we work ?" they would say to us; " have we not as much bread-fruit, cocoa-nuts, bananas, vee-apples, &c. as we can eat? It is very good for you to work who require fine clothes and fine ships; but,' looking around their apartment with evident satisfaction, " we are contented with what we possess." And in disposition they certainly appeared to be so ; for a more lively, goodnatured, inoffensive people it is impossible to conceive. The only interruption to their general serenity appears to be occasioned by the check which the laws have placed upon their amusements ; a feeling which became very apparent the moment the missionaries were mentioned They have in general, however, a great respect for those gentlemen, and are fearful of the consequences of offending them

Some of the natives had an indistinct notion of this philanthropic society, and were not a little surprised at being told that we were not missionaries, and in answer to their inquiry " King George missionary ?" their astonishment was greatly increased at being informed that he was not ; for as they had an idea that King George was at the head of the missionary society, they naturally imagined that his officers must of course also belong to it. This misconception had been so generally entertained before our arrival, that we were told they had threatened to complain to the society of the master of a merchant ship who had by some means incurred their displeasure

The Otaheitans were always a very superstitious people, and notwithstanding their change of religion, still entertain most absurd notions on several points. Though they have ceased to give credit to any recent prophecies, many firmly believe they have seen the fulfillment of some of the predictions that were made before their conversion to Christianity, of which the invasion of the island by the natives of Bora Bora was one. This event was foretold by a little bird called Oomamoo, which had the gift of speech, and used to warn persons of any danger with which they were threatened. On many occasions, when persons have taken refuge in the mountains to avoid a mandate for a victim for the morai, or to escape from some civil commotion, this little bird has been their guardian spirit, has warned them when danger was near, and directed them how to escape pursuit I used to laugh at Jim, our interpreter, a good-natured intelligent fellow, for his belief in these tales, but he was always very earnest in his relation of them, and never allowed himself to join in our ridicule Though he confessed that this little monitor had been dumb since the introduction of Christianity, yet it would evidently have been as difficult to make him believe it never had spoken, as that the danger of which it warned him had never existed, and this feeling is, I believe, common to all his countrymen. Nothing is more difficult than the removal of early impressions, particularly when connected with superstitions I was one evening returning with him round the shore of the bay from Papiete, a favourite route, and was conversing on the superstitions of his countrymen, when we came to a retired spot crowned with tall cocoanut trees, with a small glen behind it. Night was fast approaching, and the long branches of the palm, agitated by the wind, produced a mournful sound, in unison with the subject of our conversation. As we passed I observed Jim endeavouring to get on the outside, and latterly walking in the wash of the sea, and found that he never liked to pass this spot after dark for fear of the spirits of his unfortunate countrymen who were hanged there between the cocoa-nut trees. The popular belief, before the introduction of our faith, was, that the spirit of the deceased visited the body for a certain time, and for this reason many of them would on no account approach this place in the night time.

A few days after our arrival some offenders were brought to trial, and as we were desirous of witnessing the proceedings of the court, it was removed from its usual site, to the shade of some trees in our immediate vicinity. The court was ranged upon benches placed in successive rows under the trees, with the prisoners in front, under the charge of an officer with a drawn sabre, and habited in a volunteer's jacket and a maio. The aava-rai of the district in which the crimes had been committed took his place between the court and the prisoners, dressed in a long straw mat, finely plaited, and edged with fringe, with a slit cut in it for the head to pass through, a white oakum wig, which, in imitation of the gentlemen of our courts of law, flowed in long curls over his shoulders, and a tall cap surmounting it, curiously ornamented with red feathers, and with variously coloured tresses of human hair. His appearance without shoes, stockings, or trousers, the strange attire of the head, with the variegated tresses of hair mingling with the oakum curls upon his shoulders, produced, as may be imagined, a ludicrous effect, and I regret that the limits of this work prevent my subjoining an admirable representation of it by Mr. Smyth.

The prisoner being brought up, the aava read certain passages from the penal code, and then accused the prisoner of having stolen a gown from a European resident. He instantly pleaded guilty to the charge, and thereby saved a great deal of trouble. He was then admonished against the repetition of evil practices, and fined four hogs, two to the king, and two to the person from whom the property had been stolen. Bail is not necessary in Otaheite; and the prisoner, consequently, was allowed to go where he pleased, which of course was to such of his friends as were most likely to supply him with a hog. Three other persons were then put to the bar, and fined for a breach of our seventh commandment. The young lady, who had sinned with several persons, but two of whom only were detected, smilingly heard herself sentenced to make twenty yards of cloth, and the two men to furnish six posts each, for a building that was about to be erected at Papiete. In default of payment, transgressors are condemned to labour.

Before we sailed, a more serious theft was committed on the stores of the ship, which had been placed under a shed, and likewise on the wearing apparel of one of the officers who was ill on shore. Immediately the aavas (policemen) heard of it, they were on the alert, and arrested two men, on whom suspicion fell, from their having slept in the place the night of the robbery, and absconded early in the morning. The news of the offence spread with its accustomed rapidity among uncivilized tribes, and various were the reports in circulation, as to the manner in which I intended to visit the misdemeanour. The prisoners at first acknowledged their guilt, but afterwards denied it; and declared they had been induced to make the confession from the threats of the aavas who apprehended them. Nothing was found upon them, and no person could be brought forward as direct witness of the fact, so that their guilt rested on circumstantial evidence alone. I was, however, anxious to

bring the offenders to trial, as all the sails and stores of the ship
were on shore, and at the mercy of the inhabitants, and unless severe measures were pursued in this instance, successive depredations would in all probability have occurred. The chiefs were in
consequence summoned, and at an early date the prisoners were
brought to trial opposite the anchorage   As it was an extraordinary case, I was invited to the tribunal, and paid the compliment of
being allowed to interrogate the prisoners, but nothing conclusive
was elicited, though the circumstantial proof was so much against
them that five out of the six of the chiefs pronounced them guilty
The penalty in the event of conviction in a case of this nature is,
that the culprit shall pay fourfold the value of the property stolen
in this instance, however, as the articles could not be replaced, and
the value was far beyond what the individuals could pay, I proposed, as the chiefs referred the matter to me, that, by way of an example, and to deter others from similar acts, the prisoners should
suffer corporal punishment. Their laws, however, did not admit
of this mode of punishment, and the matter concluded by the chiefs
making themselves responsible for the stores, and directing Pa-why
to acquaint the people that they had done so, promising to make
further inquiry into the matter; which was never done, and the
prisoners escaped. but the investigation answered our purpose
equally well, as the stores afterwards remained untouched   The
various reports which preceeded the trial, the assembling of the
chiefs, and other circumstances, had brought together a great concourse of people. Pa-why, raising himself above the multitude,
harangued them in a very energetic and apparently elegant manner, much to the satisfaction of the inhabitants, who all dispersed
and went quietly to their homes   The consideration which the
chiefs gave to the merits of this question, and the pains they took
to elicit the truth, reflect much credit upon them. The case was
a difficult one, and Hetotte, not being able to make up his mind to the
guilt of the prisoners, very honestly differed from his colleagues,
and his conduct, while it afforded a gratifying instance of the integrity of the man, showed a proper consideration for the prisoners,
which in darker ages would have been sacrificed to the interested
motive of coinciding in opinion with the majority. If we compare
the fate which would have befallen the prisoners, supposing them
innocent, had they been arraigned under the early form of government, with the transactions of this day, we cannot but congratulate
the people on the introduction of the present penal code, and acknowledge that it is one of the greatest temporal blessings they have
derived from the introduction of Christianity   At the same time
it is just to observe, that had a similar depredation been committed
under those circumstances, there is every reason to believe from

former expeiience, that the real offender would have been detected, and the propeity restored.

On the 3rd Apiil the young king landed at Otaheite from Eimeo, and was received with the most enthusiastic shouts of his subjects, who weie assembled in great numbers on the beach to welcome his arrival The following day he paid a visit to the ship, attended by the queen, a numerous retinue, and Mi. Pritchard, the principal missionary upon the island   I saluted the king on the occasion with nine guns, much to the delight of his subjects , and presented him with the fowling-piece which was sent out by the government foi that purpose.   The stock was inlaid with silver, and the case handsomely lined, and fitted up in a manner which made a deep impression on the minds of the Otaheitans, who aie extremely fond of display, and who expiessed then approbation by repeated exclamations of " My-tie ! mia my-tie Pretannee !" as each article was exhibited The king was a well-behaved boy, of slender make, uniting with the iudiments of an European education much native shiewdness , and the chiefs weie consideiably interested in him, as they consideied his education would give him advantages over his piedecessois . and his succession to the thione would iemove the reins of goveinment fiom the hands of the present possessor, whose measuies were not always the most disinteiested or beneficial to her country . and who, in consequence of her influence with the Booiatiras, the most powerful body of men upon the island, often caiiied hei plans into execution in spite of the wishes of the chiefs to the contiaiy.   But the object of their hopes unfoitunately died the following yeai, and the sceptre passed to the hands of Aimatta, his sister, of whom the missionaiies speak well

Beiore we sat down to dinnei, I was amused at Jim, the interpreter, bringing me the queen dowadger's compliments, and " she would be much obliged by a little rum," to qualify a iepast she had been making on raw fish, by way, I suppose, of provoking an appetite for dinner. We had missed her majesty a few minutes before fiom the cabin, and on looking over the stern of the ship, saw her seated in a native boat finishing her crude repast.

A few days previous to this visit Lieutenant Belcher was despatched in the barge to Mnapaye, in the district of Papara, to bring round a quantity of beef which had been piepared theie for the ship's use by Mr Henry, the son of one of the early missionaries. In this district there is a lake and a moiai, of which it will be proper to give a short notice, as the former is consideied curious, and foreigners are often led. by the exaggerated account of the natives, to visit the place, which really does not repay the trouble it involves. To convey some idea of the difficulty of reaching this lake, Lieutenant Belchei and Mr. Collie, who accompanied him, ciossed a

stream which ran through the valley leading to it twenty-nine times
in their ascent, sometimes at a depth considerably above their
knees; and after it was passed it was necessary to climb the mountain upon hands and knees, and to maintain their position by grasping the shrubs in their way, which indeed were, for the most part,
weak and treachrous, consisting principally of the *musa sapientum*,
spondias dulcis, and some ferns.

"In this manner," says Mr Collie, "after tracing a zigzag and
irregular course, losing our way once or twice, we reached the highest part of the activity; and then descending a short distance, the
puny lake burst upon our disappointed view." Its dimensions were
estimated at three quarters of a mile in circumference; and it was
stated by the natives to be fourteen fathoms deep. The water of
the lake was muddy, and appeared to receive its supplies from several small streams from the mountains, and the condensation of the
vapour around, which fell in a succession of drops, and, bounding
off the projecting parts of the cliff, formed here and there thin and
airy cascades. Though there is a constant accession of water, there
has not yet been found any outlet to the lake; and what renders it
still more curious is, that when heavy rains descend, the water, instead of rising and overflowing its margin, is carried off by some
subterraneous channel. The natives say, when these rains occur
there is a great rush of water from a large cavern beneath the bed
of the lake. The temperature of the lake at seven A. M. was 72°,
and that of the atmosphere 71°. During a shower of rain it rose to
74°: a thermometer at the level of the sea at the same time stood
at 77°. One side of the lake was bounded by lofty perdendicular
precipices, the other by a gentle slope covered with the varied verdure of trees, shrubs, and ferns, with a few herbaceous plants. The
general appearance of the country suggested the idea of an enormous avalanche, which stopped up the valley, and intercepted the
streams that heretofore found their way along its bed to the sea.

The lake was estimated at 1500 feet above the level of the sea,
and the cliffs from which this avalanche appeared to have been
precipitated were considered to be eight hundred feet more.
Though at so great a height, and so far from any large tract of land,
this extraordinary basin is said to abound in fresh water eels of an
enormous size. On the margin of the basin, blocks of columnar
basalt, with poros and vesicular lava, were heaped in great confusion.

On the eastern side, Mr Belcher found great quantities of vesicular shaggy lava, which led him to suppose a volcano existed in
the vicinity, and he remarks that many persons who visited the
lake were of the opinion that it was a crater filled with water. In
other parts he collected some very perfect crystals of basaltic horn-

blend, and found one or two of olvine on the surface of the vesicular lava.   The lake appeared to be falling rapidly when they saw it, at a place where Mr Belcher was obliged to cross it there were eighteen inches of water, some time after, at sunset, there were only six inches, and the next morning the rock was dry.   On examining this place he noticed a large chasm beneath a rock, through which it appeared the water had found an outlet ; and favoured the opinion of the basin being caused by an avalanche.

The moral is the same as that exhibited in the voyage of Mr. Wilson, and mentioned by Captain Cook   Its measurements have been given in those voyages, and perhaps more correctly than the present dilapated state of the edifice admits   But its history is interesting, as it was told by a desendant of the chief who erected it, and whose family, as well as himself, were priests of the god to whom it was consecrated   It differs in several respects from the account given by Mr Ellis, but I insert it as related to Mr Belcher by the chief.

The great-grandfather of Taati, the present chief, whose name holds a conspicuous place in the wars of Pomaree, was defeated in a pitched battle by the king   The chief, incensed at the god under whose protection he fought, went to Uhetea, and by devotion, presents, and promises, induced the god of that place, Oroo, to accompany him to Otaheite   On his return, the new and, as it was supposed, powerful god, so inspired the refugee party with courage, that they again rallied around their chief, and so forcibly did the superstition of those dark ages operate, that the king, before victorious, was now repeatedly beaten and driven to the opposite side of the island   The chief, having secured tranquility to his district, began to construct the moral above alluded to, which was of such magnitude as to require two years for its completion.   It was then dedicated to the god whose presence had achieved for him such repeated victories.

The change effected in the circumstances of the chief of Papara by the introduction of this new god, acquired for the deity a reputation beyond any thing that had been known in Otaheite ; and the king determined to obtain possession of it   By bribing the priests, he was allowed to pay his devotions to the deity, and afterwards to fight under its auspices, which he did so successfully that he ultimately obtained possession of the idol   A moral was then built for it in the valley of Atehuru, situated between Muapaye and Papiete ; memorable as the place where the last battle was fought which decided the cause between Christianity and pagarism, and crowned with success the labours of the missionaries, who for eighteen years had been unremitting in their endeavours to accomplish this great end ; this valley is also celebrated in consequence of a strong-hold

on an eminence near it, where the old men and women used to retire in all cases of attack upon the district In this last and important battle Taati's brother lost his life, supporting to the last the
cause of idolatry. Taati himself had been converted to the new
faith, and was joined with Pomarree in opposition to his relation

While we were at anchor, a whale-ship arrived from New Zealand, with a party of natives of that country on board, whom the
master permitted to exhibit their war-dance for our diversion After
the duty of the day was over, the party assembled in front of the
consul's house and the Otaheitans, anxious for an opportunity of
comparing the dances of other countries with their own, crowded
round in great numbers to witness the performance.

The exhibition took place by torch-light, and began by the party
being drawn up in a line with their chief in advance, who regulated
their motions, which, though very numerous, were all simultaneous,
and showed that they were well practised in them They began
by stamping their feet upon the ground, and then striking the palms
of the hands upon the thighs for about a minute, after which they
threw their bodies into a variety of contortions, twisted their heads
about, grinned hideously, and made use of all kinds of imprecations
and abuse on their supposed enemy, as if to defy him to battle :
having at length worked themselves into a complete frenzy, they
uttered a yell, and rushed to the conflict ; which, from what we saw
represented, must in reality be horrible, the effect upon the peaceable Otaheitans was such that long before they came to the charge
some of them ran away through fear, and all, no doubt, congratulated themselves that there was so wide an expanse of water between their country and New Zealand A dirge over the fallen
enemy concluded the performance, which it is impossible adequate-
ly to describe We learned from the whaler, that Shonghi, the
New Zealand chief who was educated in England, was availing
himself of the superiority he had acquired. and was making terrible
ravages among his countrymen, whose heads, when dried, furnished
him with a lucrative trade

On the 24th we prepared for our departure : during our stay we
visited the natives almost daily in their habitations, and became well
acquainted with their habits and manner of living : but in this intercourse there was so little novelty, that, considering how many volumes have been written upon the country. by persons whose stay
far exceeded ours, it would be both tiresome and useless to detain
the reader with their description The conclusion generally arrived at was, that the people retain much of their original character
and many of their habits, and appear to have been particularly described by Turnbull ; but if early historians err not, they have lost

25

much of their cheerfulness, and the women a great deal of their beauty.

Considering the advances the country had made toward the formation of a government by the election of a parliament, and by the promulgation of laws, we certainly expected to find something in progress to meet approaching events, yet in none of our excursions did we see any manufactures beyond those which were in use when the island was first discovered, but on the contrary, it was evident that they had neglected many which then existed. We were sorry to find that none of those in operation could be materially useful to the state; that there were no dawnings of art, nor did there appear to be any desire on the part of the people to improve their condition; but so far from it, we noticed a feeling of composure and indifference which will be the bane of their future prosperity

The island is nevertheless imperceptibly entering into notice · it is advantageously situated for various purposes of commerce, and, consequently, in the event of a war between England and other powers, it might be subjected to many annoyances from the most insignificant force—from and armed vessel indeed which might think it her duty to annoy the island on the ground of its reputed alliance with England. There are no works of defence to obviate such a possibility the natives have not yet thought of the precaution, much less have they commenced any preparation, and the island throughout is in a perfectly defenceless condition. The weapons with which their battles were formerly fought are now in disuse, and the inhabitants have lost the skill necessary to employ them to advantage. A number of muskets distributed amongst the population creates an imaginary security, but the bad condition of the arms, and the want of powder, would render them unavailable At all events they are deficient in an organized body of men; a species of defence which seems necessary for the security of every country that does not wish her shores to be invaded, or to have her internal tranquillity disturbed by feuds; which in Otaheite have frequently occurred, and are very likely to do so again, either from the differences of opinion in the affairs of the government, or from the jealousies between the chief and the great landholders, the *Boo Raturas* Their tranquillity besides may have hitherto depended upon their obscurity, or on the equally defenceless condition of their neighbours with themselves, but the extension of navigation has removed the one, and an advancement of civilization and of power has destroyed the balance of the other

Religious books are distributed among the huts of such of the natives as are converted, or who are, as they term themselves, *missi-norees;* but many of the inhabitants are still tooti-ouris or bad characters, an old expression signifying literally rusty iron, and now indiscriminate-

ly used for a dissenter from the Christian religion and a low character.   These persons are now of no religion, as they have renounced their former one, and have not embraced that which has been
recently introduced

Ignorance of the language prevented my obtaining any correct
information as to the progress that had been made generally towards
a knowledge of the Scriptures by those who were converted ; but
my impression was, and I find by the journals of the officers it was
theirs also, that it was very limited, and but few understood the
simplest parts of them   Many circumstances induced me to believe
that they considered their religious books very much in the same
light as they did their household gods ; and in particular their conduct on the occasion of a disturbance, which arose from some false
reports at the time of the robbery on the stores of the ship, when
they deposited these books in the mission, and declared themselves
to be indifferent about their lives and property, so long as the sacred
volume, which could be replaced at any time for a bamboo of oil,
was in safety.   In general those who were *missi-narees* had a proper respect for the book, but associating with it the suppression of
their amusements, their dances, singing, and music, they read it with
much less good will than if a system had been introduced which
would have tempered religion with cheerfulness, and have instilled
happiness into society

The Otaheitans, passionately fond of recreation, require more re-
laxation than other people ; and though it might not have been possible at once to clear the dances from the immoralities attending
them, still it would have been good policy to sanction these diversions under certain restrictions, until laws which were more important began to sit easy on the shoulders of the people.   Without
amusements, and excessively indolent, they now seek enjoyment in
idleness and sensuality, and too much pains cannot be bestowed to
arouse them from their apathy, and to induce them to emerge from
their general state of indifference to those occupations which are
most essential to their welfare.   Looking only to the past, they at
present seem to consider that they can proceed in the same easy
manner they have hitherto done , forgetting that their wants, formerly gratified by the natural produce of the earth, have lately been
supplied by foreign commodities, which, by indulgence, have become essential to their comfort ; and that as their wants increase, as
in all probability they will, they will find themselves at a loss to
meet the expenses of the purchase   They forget also that being
dependent upon the casual arrival of merchant vessels for the supplies, they are liable to be deprived of them suddenly by the occurrence of a war, or some other contingency, and this at a period perhaps when by disuse they will not have the power of falling back
upon those which have been discontinued.

The country is not deficient in the productions adapted to commerce   The sugar-cane grows so luxuriantly that from two small enclosurses five tons of white sugar are annually manufactured under the superintendence of an Englishman , cotton has been found to succeed very well , arrow-root of good quality is plentiful : they have some sandal-wood, and other ornamental woods suitable for furniture, and several dyes   Besides these, coffee and other grain might no doubt be grown, and they might salt down meat, which, with other articles I have mentioned, would constitute a trade quite sufficient to procure for the inhabitants luxuries which are in a gradual course of introduction, and to make it desirable for merchant vessels to touch at the island.   It is not from the poverty of the island, therefore, from which they are likely to feel inconvenience, but from their neglect to avail themselves of its capabilities, and employ its productions to advantage.

It seemed as if the people never had these things revealed to them, or had sunk into an apathy, and were discouraged at finding each year burdened with new restrictions upon their liberties and enjoyments, and nothing in return to sweeten the cup of life   I cannot avoid repeating my conviction, that had the advisers of Pomaree limited the penal code at first, and extended it as it became familiar to the people , had they restricted instead of suppressed the amusements of the people, and taught them such parts of the Christian religion as were intelligible to their simple understandings, and were most conducive to the moral improvement and domestic comfort, these zealous and really praiseworthy men would have made greater advances towards the attainment of their object

If in offering these remarks it should be thought I have been severe upon the failings of the people, or upon the conduct of the missionary gentlemen, I have only to say, that I have felt myself called upon to declare the truth, which I trust has been done without any invidious feeling to either ; indeed, I experienced nothing during my stay that could create such a feeling, but very much to the contrary, as both my officers and myself received every possible kindness from them.   And if I have pourtrayed their errors more minutely than their virtues, it has been done with a view to show, that although the condition of the people is much improved, they are not yet blessed with that state of innocence and domestic comfort of which we have read   It would have been far more agreeable to have dwelt on the fair side of their character only, but that has already been done, and by following the same course I should only have increased the general misconception

At the time of our arrival, the rainy season, which had been somewhat protracted, was scarcely over.   Its proper period is December, January, and February.   So much wet weather in the height of summer is always the occasion of fevers, and together with the abundance of vee-apples (*spondias dulcus*), which ripen about that period, produce dysentary and sickness among the poorer class of inhabitants, several of whom were labouring under these and other complaints during our stay. Miserable indeed was the condition of many of them. They retired from their usual abode and the society of their friends, and erected huts for themselves in the woods, in which they dwelt, until death terminated their sufferings. The missionaries and resident Europeans strove as much as was in their power to alleviate these distresses; but the natives were so improvident and careless that the medicine often did them harm rather than good, and many preferred their own simple pharmacopœia, and thus fell victims to their ignorance. Our own ship's company improved upon the abundance of fish and vegetable diet, but from what afterwards occurred, I am disposed to think the change from their former food to so much vegetable substance was very injurious. Regard to this subject ought not to be overlooked in vessels circumstanced as the Blossom was

The winds during our stay were principally from the eastward, freshening in the forenoon, and moderating toward sun-set to a calm, or giving place to a light breeze off the land, which sometimes prevailed through the night. This effect upon the trade-wind, by comparatively so small a tract of coast, shows the powerful influence of the land upon the atmosphere

In the height of summer, or during the rainy season, the winds fly round to the W and N W and blow in gales or hard squalls, which it is necessary to guard against in anchoring upon the north-western coast, particularly at Matavai Bay, which is quite open to those quarters. The mean temperature of the atmosphere during our stay was 79° 98, the minimum 75°, and maximum 87°.

The many excellent ports in Otaheite have been enumerated by Captain Cook, though he only made use of one, Matavai Bay, and that which was most exposed; in consequence, probably, of the facility of putting to sea. Those on the north-western coast are the most frequented, as some difficulty of getting out and in attends most of the others, particularly those in the south-western side of the island, which are subject to a constant heavy swell from the higher latitudes, and in the long calms that prevail under the lee of the island, are apt to endanger vessels approaching the reefs. Of the four on the north-western coast, viz Matavai, Papawa, Toanoa, and Papiete, the last is the common anchorage, and were it not that it is subject to long calms and very hot weather, in consequence of being more to leeward than others, it would certainly be the best Toanoa is very small, but conveniently adapted to the refit of one or two ships. The best port however lies between this anchorage and Matavai, and is called Papawa: several ships may anchor there in perfect safety quite close to the shore, and if a wharf were constructed, might land their cargoes upon it without the assistance of boats   It may be entered either from the east or west, and it has the additional advantage of having Matavai Bay for a stopping place, should circumstances render it inconvenient to enter at the moment, but this channel which communicates with Matavai Bay must be approached with attention to two coral knolls that have escaped the notice of both Cook and Bligh   I have given directions for avoiding them in my nauctical remarks.

The tides in all harbours formed by coral reefs are very irregular and uncertain, and are almost wholly dependant upon the sea-breeze.   At Toanoa it is usually low water about six every morning, and high water half an hour after noon.   To make this deviation from the ordinary course of nature intelligible, it will be better to consider the harbour as a basin, over the margin of which, after the breeze springs up, the sea beats with considerable violence, and throws a larger supply into it than the narrow channels can carry off in the same time, and consequently during that period the tide rises. As the wind abates the water subsides, and the nights being generally calm, and the water finds its lowest level by the morning.

CHAPTER X.

On the 26th of April, we left this delightful island in which we had passed many very pleasant days, in the enjoyment of the society of the residents, and of the scenery of the country   We put to sea in the morning, and about noon reached the low island of Te- thoroa, the watering place of the Otaheitans   It is a small coral island, distant about seven leagues from Otaheite . from the hills of which it may be distinctly seen, and is abundantly provided with cocoa-nut trees.   The salubrity of this little island, which was for- merly the resort of the chiefs, arreoys, and others, for the purpose if recruiting their health after their debaucheries, is still proverbial at Otaheite   Spare diet and fresh air were the necessary conse- quences of a visit to this place, and for a good constitution were the only restoratives required, and, as these seldom failed in their ef- fects, it obtained a reputation in Otaheite, no less famous than that of the celebrated spring of eternal youth, which Ponce de Leon so long sought in vain.   From the proximity of the islands of Tethoroa Otaheite, and Eimeo, we were enabled to connect them trigonome- trically.   Upon the latter there is a peak with a hole through it to which a curious history is attached, connected with the superstition of early times   It is asserted that the great god, Oroo, being one day angry with the Tu, or the little God of Eimeo, he threw his spear across the water at him, but the activity of the Tu evaded the blow, and the spear passed through the mountain, and left the hole which we saw   The height of this peak is 4041 feet

On the 27th, we were within six miles of the situation in which Arrowsmith has placed Roggewein's high Island of Recreation; but nothing was in sight from the mast-head.   In all probability this island, which answers so well in its description, excepting as to its size, is the Maitea of Mr Turnbull, situated nearly in the same latitude. From this time we endeavoured to get to the eastward, and to cross the equator in about 150° W longitude, so that when we met the N E trade-wind, we might be well to windward There is otherwise, some difficulty in rounding Owyhee, which should be done about forty miles to the eastward to ensure the breeze

The passage between the Society and Sandwich groupes differs from navigation between the same parallels in the Atlantic, in the former being exempt from long calms which sometimes prevail about the equator, and in the S E. trade being more easterly. The westerly current is much the same in both ; and if not attended to in the Pacific, will carry a ship so far to leeward, that by the time she reaches the parallel of the Sandwich Islands, she will be a long way to the westward, and have much difficulty in beating up to them

Soon after leaving Otaheite, the officers and ship's company generally were afflicted with dysentery, which, at one time, assumed an alarming appearance On the 3d of May, we had the misfortune to lose Mr Crawley, one of the midshipmen, a young gentleman of very good abilities, and much regretted by all who knew him, and on the 6th, William Must, my steward, sunk under the same complaint On the 7th, great apprehensions were entertained for Mr. Lay, the naturalist, but fortunately, his complaint took a favourable turn and he ultimately recovered The disease, however, continued among us some time, threatening occasionally different portions of the ship's company

As we approached the Sandwich Islands, our view was anxiously directed to the quarter in which Owyhee* was situated, in the hope of obtaining a sight of the celebrated Mouna Roa, but the weather was so unfavourable for this purpose, that the land at the foot of the hills was the only part of the coast which presented itself to our view. On the 18th, we passed about thirty miles to windward of the eastern points of the island, and in the afternoon of the following day, as it was too late to fetch the anchorage off Woahoo, we rounded to under the lee of Morotoi, the next island The following morning we came to an anchor in nineteen fathoms outside the reefs of Honoruro, the principal port of the Sandwich Islands, and the residence of the king This anchorage is very much exposed, and during the N. W monsoon, unsafe; but as there is great difficulty attending a large ship going in and out of the harbour, it is the general stopping place of such vessels as make but a short stay at the island

Our passage from Otaheite to this place had been so rapid, that the contrast between the two countries was particularly striking.

* More recently written Hawaii

At Woahoo, the eye searches in vain for the green and shady forests skirting the shore, which enliven the scene at Otaheite   The whole country has a parched and comparatively barren aspect , and it is not until the heights are gained, and the extensive ranges of taro plantations are seen filling every valley, that strangers learn why this island was distinguised by the name of the garden of the Sandwich Islands.

The difference betwixt the appearance of the natives of Woahoo and Otaheite is not less conspicuous than that of the scenery.   Constant exposure to the sun has given them a dark complexion and a coarseness of feature which do not exist in the Society Islands ; and their countenances, moreover, have a wildness of expression which at first misleads the eye; but this very soon wears off, and I am not sure whether this manliness of character does not create a respect which the effeminacy of the Otaheitians never inspires.

As we rowed up the harbour, the forts, the cannon, and the ensign of the Tamahamaha, displayed upon the ramparts of a fort mounting forty guns, and at the gaff of a man-of-war brig, and of some other vessels, rendered the distinction between the two countries still more evident ; and on landing, the marked attention to etiquette, and the respect shown by the subjects to their chiefs, offered a similar contrast.   In every way this country seemed far to surpass the other in civilization—but there were strong indications of a close connexion between the natives of both

It was not long since Lord Byron in the Blonde had quitted these islands ; the appearance of a man-of-war was, therefore, no novelty , but the beach was thronged to excess with people of all distinctions, who behaved in a very orderly manner, helped us out of the boats, and made a passage as we advanced   In our way, nothing more strikingly marked the superiority of this country over that we had recently quitted than the number of wooden houses, the regularity of the town laid out in squares, intersected by streets properly fenced in, and the many notices which appeared right and left, on pieces of board, on which we read " An Ordinary at one o'clock, Billiards, the Britannia, the Jolly Tar, the Good Woman," &c. After a short walk, we came to a neatly built wooden house, with glass windows, the residence of Krimakoo, or, as he was commonly called, Pitt, whom I found extended upon the floor of his apartment, suffering under a dropsical complaint, under which he ultimately sunk   This disease had so increased upon him of late that he had undergone five operations for it since the departure of the Blonde. Though unable to rise from his bed, his mind was active and unimpaired ; and when the conversation turned upon the affairs of the island, he was quite energetic, regretting that his confinement prevented his looking more into them ; and his greatest annoyance

26

seemed to be his inability to see every thing executed himself. He expressed his attachment strongly to the British Government, and his gratitude for the respect that had been shown the descendant of his illustrious patron, and his queen, by sending their bodies to the Sandwich Islands in so handsome a manner, and also for the footing upon which the affairs of the state had been placed by Lord Byron in command of the Blonde. He was anxious to requite these favours, and pressed his desire to be allowed to supply all the demands of the ship himself, in requital for the liberty with which his countrymen were treated in England I could not accede to this effusion of the chief's gratitude, as the expense attending it would have been considerably felt by him, and more particularly as Lord Byron had previously declined the same offer.

The young king, who had been taking an airing, arrived at this moment, and repeated the sentiments of his protector, making, at the same time, many inquiries for his friends in the Blonde. Boki was absent at Owyhee, attending his sister, who was dangerously ill. Madam Boki, Kuanoa, Manuïa, and the other chiefs who were of the party in England, were all anxious to show us civility, and spoke of England in such high terms, that they will apparently never forget the kind treatment they experienced there but they had a great dread of the diseases of our country, and many of them considered it very unhealthy. My impression was, that those who had already been there had had their curiosity satisfied to feel in no way disposed to risk another visit The want of their favourite dish Poe was, besides, so serious an inconvenience, that when allusion was made to England, this privation was always mentioned.

Our reception was friendly in the extreme , all our wants, as far as possible, were supplied, but unfortunately there was this year a scarcity of almost every kind of production ; the protracted rainy season and other circumstances having conspired to destroy or lessen the crops, and the whole population was in consequence suffering from its effects There was also a scarcity of dried provision, our visit having proceeded the usual time of the arrival of the whalers, who discharge all they can spare at this place previous to their return home. Our expectation of replenishing the ship's provisions was consequently disappointed, and it therefore became necessary to reduce the daily allowance of the ship's company, and to pursue the same economical system here, with regard to taro and yams, as was done at Otaheite with the bread-fruit.

The few days I had to remain here were devoted to astronomical and other observations, and I had but little opportunity of judging of the state of the island ; but from a letter which I received from Boki, it was evident that he did not approve of the system of religious restraint that had been forced into operation, which was

alike obnoxious to the foreigners residing upon the island and to the
natives.

At the time of our departure the health of Mr. Lay was by no
means restored, and as it appeared to me that his time during the
absence of the ship could be more profitably employed among the
islands of the Sandwich groupe than on the frozen shores of the
north, he was left behind, under the protection of Pitt, whose kindness on the occasion nothing could exceed. Mr. Collie took upon
himself the charge of the naturalist, and acquitted himself in a highly creditable manner.

On the 31st of May we took our leave of Woahoo and proceeded to Oneehow, the westernmost island of the Sandwich groupe,
famous for its yams, fruit, and mats. This island is the property of
the king, and it is necessary, previous to proceeding thither, to make
a bargain with the authorities at Woahoo for what may be required,
who in that case send an agent to see the agreement strictly fulfilled. On the 1st of June we hauled into a small sandy bay on the
western side of the island, the same in which Vacouver anchored
when he was there on a visit of a similar nature to our own; and I
am sorry to say that like him we were disappointed in the expected supplies; not from their scarcity, but in consequence of the indolence of the natives.

Oneehow is comparatively low, and, with the exception of the
fruit trees, which are carefully cultivated, it is destitute of wood.
The soil is too dry to produce taro, but on that account it is well
adapted to the growth of yams, &c. which are very excellent and
of an enormous size. There is but one place in this bay where the
boat of a man of war can effect a landing with safety when the sea
sets into the bay, which is a very common occurrence; this is on
its northern shore, behind a small reef of rocks that lies a little way
off the beach, and even here it is necessary to guard against sunk-
en rocks; off the western point these breakers extend a mile and a
half. The soundings in the bay are regular, upon a sandy bottom,
and there is good anchorage, if required, with the wind from the
eastward; but it would not be advisable to bring up under any other
circumstances. The natives are a darker race of people than those
of Woahoo, and reminded us strongly of the inhabitants of Bow Isl-
and. With the exception of the house of the Earee, all the huts
were small, low, and hot; the one which we occupied was so close
that we were obliged to make a hole in its side to admit the sea
breeze.

We took on board as many yams as the natives could collect before sun-set, and then shaped our course for Kamschatka. In doing
this I deviated from the tracks of both Cook and Clerke, which I
think was the occasion of our passage being shorter than either of

theirs.   Instead of running to the westward in a low latitude, we
passed to the eastward of Bird Island, and gained the latitude of
27° N   In this parallel we found the trade much fresher, though
more variable, and more subject to interruption, than within the
tropic ; we had also the advantage of a more temperate climate, of
which we stood in need, as the sickness among the ship's company
was so far from being removed, that on the 13th we had the misfortune to lose one of the marines.   On this day we spoke the Tuscan, an English whaleship, and found that on quitting the Sandwich
Islands her crew had suffered in the same way as our own, but had
since quite recovered.   In all probability the sudden change of diet
from the usual seafare to so much vegetable food, added to the heat
and humidity of the atmosphere at the season in which our visits
were made to those islands, was the cause of the sickness of both
vessels.   The master of the Tuscan informed me that the preceding year his ship's company had been so severely afflicted with
disease that he found it necessary to put into Loo Choo, where he
was well received, and his people were treated with the greatest
kindness   He was supplied with fresh meat and vegetables daily,
without being allowed to make any other payment than that of a chart
of the world, which was the only thing the natives would accept.
It was, however, not without the usual observance of narrow-minded
Chinese policy, that himself and his invalid crew were allowed to
set their feet on shore, and even then they were always attended by
a party of the natives, and had a piece of ground bordering on the
beach fenced off for them   The salute which the Alceste and Lyra
had fired on the 25th of October, was well remembered by these
people, and they had an idea that it was an annual ceremony performed in commemoration of something connected with the king of
England.   On the return of this day, during the Tuscan's visit, they
concluded that the ship would observe the same ceremony, and
looked forward with such anxiety and delight to the event, that the
master of the whaler was obliged to rub up his four pateieros, and
go through the salute without any intermission, as the Loochooans
counted the guns as they were fired.

A few hours after we parted with the Tuscan, we fell in with two
other whale ships, neither of which could spare us any provisions.
These ships were no doubt fishing down a parallel of latitude, which
is a common custom, unless they find a continued scarcity of whales,
The 30th degree, I believe, is rather a favourite one with them.

Ten days after our departure from Oneehow we lost the trade
wind in latitude 30° N. and longitude 195° W   it had been variable before this, but had not fairly deserted us.   Its failure was of little consequence, as in three days afterwards we were far enough to
the westward to ensure the remainder of the passage ; and indeed

from the winds which ensued, a course might as well have been shaped for Kamschatka on the day we lost the wind

On the 3d of June, the day after leaving Oneehow, in latitude
25° N and longitude 160° 15′ W., we saw large flocks of tern and
noddies, and a few gannets and tropic birds, also boneta, and shoals
of flying-fish ; and on the 5th, in latitude 28° 10′ N and longitude
172° 20′ W , we had similar indications of the proximity of land.
Though such appearances are by no means infallible, yet as so many
coral islands have recently been discovered to the W N. W. of the
Sandwich Islands, ships in passing these places should not be regardless of them.   On this day we observed an albatross (*diomedia ex-
ulans*), the first we had seen since quitting the coast of Chili   It is
remarkable that Captain King, in his passage to Kamschatka, first
met these birds within thirty miles of the same spot.   We noticed
about this time a change in the colour of the wings of the flying-
fish, and on one of the species being caught it was found to differ
from the common *exocætus volitans*.   We continued to see these
fish occasionally as far as 30° N , about which time the tern also
quitted us   In 33° N we first met the birds of the northern regions,
the *procellaria puffinus*, but it was not until we were within a hundred miles of the coast of Kamschatka that we saw the lumme, do-
vekie, rotge, and other alca, and the shag.   The tropic birds accompanied us as far as 36° N

On the 18th and 19th, in latitude 35° N., longitude 194° 30′ W.,
we made some experiments on the temperature of the sea at intermediate depths, as low as 760 fathoms, where it was found to be
twenty-eight degrees colder than at the surface ; two days afterwards
another series was obtained, by which it appeared that the temperature at 180 fathoms was as cold as that at 500 fathoms on the former occasion, and it was twenty degrees colder at 380 fathoms on
this, than it was at 760 fathoms on the other.   Between these experiments we entered a thick fog, which continued until we were
close off the Kamschatka coast ; and we also experienced a change
of current, both of which, no doubt contributed towards the change
of temperature of the sea, which was much greater than could have
been produced by the alteration in the situation of the ship : the fog
by obstructing the radiation of heat, and the current by bringing a
colder medium from higher latitudes.   About this period we began
to see drift wood, some of which passed us almost daily   The sea
was occasionally strewed with moluscous animals, principally beroes
and nereis, among which on the 19th were a great many small crabs of
a curious species   Whether it was that these animals preferred the
foggy weather, or that we more narrowly scrutinized the small space
of water around us to which our view was limited, I cannot say, but
it appeared to us that they were much more numerous while the
fog lasted than before or afterwards.

In the afternoon of the 23d, in latitude 44° N , the wind, which had been at S W , drew round to the west, and brought a cold atmosphere, in which the thermometer fell fourteen degrees , it is remarkable that sixteen hours before this change occurred, the temperature of the sea fell six degrees, while that of the atmosphere was affected only four hours previous In my remarks on our passage round Cape Horn, I have mentioned the frequency with which the temperature of the surface of the sea was affected before that of the atmosphere when material changes of wind were about to occur.

On the 26th, in latitude 49° N , after having traversed nearly seven hundred miles in so thick a fog that we could scarcely see fifty yards from us, a north-east wind cleared the horizon for a few hours this change again produced a sensible diminution of the temperature, which was thirty-one degrees lower than it had been thirteen days previous The next day we had the satisfaction of seeing the high mountains of Kamschatka, which at a distance are the best guides to the port of Awatska The eastern mountain, situated twenty-five miles from Petropaulski, is 7 375 feet high by my trigonometrical measurment : another, which is the highest, situated N. 5° E from the same place, and a little to the northward of a short range upon which there is a volcano in constant action, is 11.500 feet high. At eight o'clock we distinguished Cape Gavarea, the southern point of a deep bay in which the harbour of Petropaulski is situated, and the same evening we were becalmed within six miles of our port Nothing could surpass the serenity of the evening or the magnificence of the mountains capped with perennial snows, rising in majestic array above each other The volcano emitted smoke at intervals, and from a sprinkling of black dots on the snow to leeward of the crater, we concluded there had been a recent eruption

At two o'clock the following afternoon we anchored off the town of Petropaulski, and found lying in the inner harbour his imperial majesty's ship Modeste, commanded by Baron Wrangel, an enterprising officer, well known to the world as the commander of a hazardous expedition on sledges over the ice to the northward of Schelatskoi Noss

I found despatches awaiting my arrival, communicating the return of the expedition under Captain Parry, and desiring me to cancel that part of my instructions which related to him The officers, on landing at the little town of Petropaulski, met with a very polite reception from the governor, Stanitski, a captain in the Russian navy, who, during our short stay in port, laid us under many obligations for articles of the most acceptable kind to seamen after a long voyage I regretted extremely that confinement to my cabin at this time prevented my having the pleasure of making either his acquaintance or that of the pastor of Paratounka, of whose ancestor such honourable mention has been made in the voyages of Captain Cook, a pleasure which was reserved for the following year. The worthy pastor, in strict compliance with the injunctions of his grandfather, that he should send a calf to the captain of every English man of war that might arrive in the port, presented me with one of his own rearing, and sent daily supplies of milk, butter, and curd. Had our stay in this excellent harbour permitted, we should have received a supply of oxen, which would have been most acceptable to the ship's company; but the animals had to be driven from Bolcheresk, and, pressed as we were for time, too great a delay would have been incurred in waiting for them. The colony at this time was as much distressed for provisions as ourselves, and was even worse off, in consequence of the inferior quality of the articles.

On the 1st of July we weighed and attempted to put to sea, but after experiencing the difficulties of which several navigators have complained, were obliged to anchor again, and that at too great a distance from the town to have any communication.

On the 2nd, as well as on the 3rd, we also weighed, but were obliged to anchor as before, and it was not until the 5th, after weighing and anchoring twice that morning, to prevent going ashore, that the ship reached the outside of the harbour, this difficulty arises from counter currents, which prevent the steerage of the ship. After clearing the harbour there was a strong wind against us, but it soon died entirely away, and left us exposed to a heavy swell, which rolled with great violence upon the shore, so much so, that for some time the boats were insufficient to prevent the ship nearing the land, and there was no anchorage, in consequence of the great depth of water: fortunately, towards night a light air favoured our departure, and we succeeded in getting an offing.

My object was now to make the best of my way to Kotzebue Sound, as there were but fourteen days left before the arrival of the appointed time of rendezvous there, and every effort was directed towards that end. As we sailed across the wide bay in which Petropaulski is situated, we connected the capes at its extremities with the port and intermediate objects, by which it appears that Cape Gavarea has hitherto been erroneously placed with regard to Chepoonski Noss; but I shall not here interrupt the narrative by the insertion of the particulars of the operations.

At day-light the following morning, Chepoonski Noss was seen N 19° W, and in the afternoon of the next day high land was discerned from the mast-head in the direction of Krotnoi Mountain. This was the last view we had of Kamschatka, as a thick fog came on, and attended us to Beering's Island.

At day-light on the 10th a high rock was seen about nine miles off, and shortly afterwards Beering's Island appeared through the fog When we had reached close in with the land the mist partially dispersed, and exposed to our view a moderately high island, armed with rocky points.   The snow rested in ridges upon the hills, but the lower parts of the island were quite bare, and presented a green mossy appearance, without a single shrub to relieve its monotony   Its dreary aspect, associated with the recollection of the catastrophe that befel Beering and his shipmates, who were cast upon its shores on the approach of winter with their own resources exhausted, produced an involuntary shudder.   The bay in which this catastrophe occurred is on the north side of the island, on a part of the coast which fortunately afforded fresh water, and abounded in stone foxes, sea otters, and moor-hens , and where there was a quantity of drift wood washed upon the shore, which served for the construction of huts , but notwithstanding these resources, the commander Vitus Beering, and twenty-nine of the crew, found their graves on this desolate spot.   The island is now visited occasionally by the Russians for the skins of the sea otter and black fox.   The highest part of the island which we saw was towards its N. W extremity, from whence the shore slopes gradually to the coast, and is terminated by cliffs   At the foot of these are low rocky flats, which can only be seen when quite close to them, and outside again are breakers   Off the western point these reefs extend about two miles from the shore, and off the northern, about a mile and a quarter, so that on the whole it is a dangerous coast to approach in thick weather.   The rock first seen was situated five miles and a half off shore, and was so crowded with seals basking upon it, that it was immediately named Seal Rock.*

To the northward of this there were several small bays in the coast, which promised tolerably good anchorage, particularly one towards the eastern part of the indentation in the coast line, off which there was a small low island or projecting point of land.   This, in all probability, is the harbour alluded to by Krenitzen, as there were near it " two small hillocks like boats with their keels upwards."

We did not see the south-eastern part of this island, as it was obscured by fog, but sailed along the southern and western shores as circumstances permitted until seven in the evening, when we got out of the region of clear weather, which usually obtains in the vicinity or leeward of land in these seas, and entered a thick fog With the summer characteristics of this latitude—fine weather and a thick fog—we advanced to the northward, attended by a great

* Kotzebue observes in his narrative that " this rock has not been laid down in any chart " I presume he alludes to those which are modern, as on a reference to the map of Captain Krenitzen's discoveries in 1768, it will be found occupying its proper place

many birds, nearly all of the same kind as those which inhabit the
Greenland Sea, sheerwaters, lummes, puffins, parasitic gulls, stormy
petrel, dusky albatross, a larus resembling the kittiwake, a small
dove-coloured tern, and shags.   In latitude 60° 47' N. we noticed
a change in the colour of the water, and on sounding found fifty-four
fathoms, soft blue clay   From that time until we took our final departure from this sea the bottom was always within reach of our
common lines.   The water shoaled so gradually that at midnight on
the 16th, after having run a hundred and fifty miles, we had thirty-
one fathoms.   Here the ground changed from mud to sand, and apprized us of our approach to the Island of St. Lawrence, which on
the following morning was so close to us that we could hear the surf
upon the rocks   The fog was at the same time so thick that we
could not see the shore, and it was not until some time afterwards,
when we had neared the land by means of a long ground swell, for
it was quite calm, that we discerned the tops of the hills.

It is a fortunate circumstance that the dangers in these seas are
not numerous, otherwise the prevalence of fogs in the summer time
would render the navigation extremely hazardous.   About noon we
were enabled to see some little distance around us ; and, as we expected, the ship was close off the western extremity of St. Lawrence Island.   In this situation the nearest hills, which were about
five hundred feet above the sea, we observed to be surmounted by
large fragments of rock having the appearance of ruins.   These hills
terminate to the southward and south-westward in bold rocky cliffs,
off which are situated three small islands, the hills have a gradual
slope to the coast line to the northward and westward ; but at the
north-western extremity of the island they end in a remarkable
wedge-shaped promontory—particulars which may be found useful
to navigators in foggy weather.   The upper parts of the island were
buried in snow ; but the lower, as at Beering's Island, were bare and
overgrown with moss or grass.   We stood close into a small bay at
the S W. angle of the island, where we perceived several tents,
and where, from the many stakes driven into the ground, we concluded there was a fishing-station.   The natives soon afterwards
launched four baidars,* of which each contained eight persons, males
and females.   They paddled towards the ship with great quickness,
until they were within speaking distance, when an old man who
steered the foremost boat stood erect, and held up in succession nets,
walrus teeth, skin shirts, harpoons, bows and arrows and small birds,
he then extended his arms, rubbed and patted his breast,† and came

* This boat, called by the natives oomiac, is the same in every respect as the oomiac, or woman boat, of the Esquimaux   It is here used by the men instead of the
women

† This is the ususal Esquamaux indication of friendship

fearlessly alongside.   We instantly detected in these people the features of the Esquimaux, whom in appearance and manners also, and indeed in every particular, they so much resembled, that there cannot, I think, be the least doubt of their having the same origin They were if any thing less dirty, and somewhat fairer, and their implements were better made.   Their dress, though Esquimaux, differed a little from it in the skin shirts being ornamented with tassels, after the manner of the Oonalashka people, and in the boots fitting the leg, instead of being adapted to the reception of either oil or infants.

The old men had a few gray hairs on their chins, but the young ones, though grown up, were beardless.   Many had their heads shaved round the crown, after the fashion of the Tschutschi, the Otaheitans, or the Roman Catholic priesthood in Europe, and all had their hair cut short.   Their manner of salutation was by rubbing their noses against ours, and drawing the palms of their hands over our faces, but we were not favoured as Kotzebue was, by their being previously spit upon.   In the stern of one of the baidars there was a very entertaining old lady, who amused us by the manner in which she tried to impose upon our credulity.   She was seated upon a bag of peltry, from which she now and then cautiously drew out a skin, and exhibited the best part of it, with a look implying that it was of great value ; she repeatedly hugged it, and endeavoured to coax her new acquaintances into a good bargain, but her furs were scarcely worth purchasing   She was tattooed in curved lines along the sides of the cheek, the outer one extending from the lower jaw, over the temple and eyebrow.

Our visiters on board were not less accomplished adepts at bartering than the old woman, and sold almost every thing they had With the men, " tawac," as they called our tobacco, was their great object ; and with the women, needles and scissors, but with both, blue beads were articles highly esteemed   We observed, that they put some of these to the test, by biting them to ascertain whether they were glass, having, perhaps, been served with wax ones by some of their former visiters

Their implements were so similar to those of the Esquimaux as to need no description ; except that their bows partook of the Tschutschi form.   They had a great many small birds of the alca crestatella, strung upon thongs of hide, which were highly acceptable to us, as they were very palatable in a pie.   These birds are, I believe, peculiar to St. Lawrence Island, and in proceeding up the strait their presence is a tolerably certain indication of the vicinity of the island   They are very numerous, and must be easily taken by the natives, as they sold seven dozen for a single necklace of blue glass beads

About seven o'clock in the evening, the natives quitted us rather abruptly, and hastened toward the shore, in consequence of an approaching fog, which their experience enabled them to foresee sooner than us, who, having a compass to rely upon, were less anxious about the matter.   We soon lost sight of every distant object, and directed our course along the land, trying the depth of water occasionally.   The bottom was tolerably even; but we decreased the soundings to nine fathoms, about four miles off the western point, and changed the ground from fine sand, to stones and shingle. When we had passed the wedged-shaped cliff at the north-western point of the island, the soundings again deepened, and changed to sand, as at first.

At night the fog cleared away for a short time, and we saw the Asiatic coast about Tschukutskoi Noss, but it soon returned, and with it a light air in the contrary direction to our course.   The next day, as we could make no progress, the trawl was put overboard, in the hope of providing a fresh meal for the ship's company; but after remaining down a considerable time, it came up with only a sculpen (*cottus scorpius*), a few specimens of moluscæ, and crustaceæ, consisting principally of maias.   In the evening, Lieutenant Peard was more successful in procuring specimens with the dredge, which supplied us with a great variety of invertebral animals, consisting of asterias holothurias, echini, amphitrites, ascidias, actinias, euryales, murex, chiton crinitus, nereides, maias, gammarus, and pagurus, the latter inhabiting chiefly old shells of the murex genus.   This was in seventeen fathoms over a muddy bottom, several leagues from the island.

About noon the fog dispersed, and we saw nearly the whole extent of the St Lawrence Island, from the N. W. cape we had rounded the preceding night to the point near which Cook reached close in with, after his departure from Norton Sound   The middle of this island was so low, that to us it appeared to be divided, and I concluded, as both Cook and Clerke had done before, that it was so; circumstances did not, however, admit of my making this examination, and the connexion of the two islands was left for the discovery of Captain Schismareff of the Russian navy   The hills situated upon the eastern part of the island, to which Cook gave the name of his companion Captain Clerke, are the highest part of St. Lawrence Island, and were at this time deeply buried in snow.

The current off here, on one trial, ran N. E. five-eighths of a mile per hour, and on another, N. 60° E seven-eigtths of a mile per hour; as observations on this interesting subject were repeatedly made

Favoured with a fair wind, on the 19th we saw King's Island, which, though small, is high and rugged, and has low land at its base, with apparrently breakers off its south extreme

We had now advanced sufficiently far to the northward to carry on our operations at midnight, an advantage in the navigation of an unfrequented sea which often precludes the necessity of lying to.

We approached the strait which separates the two great continents of Asia and America, on one of those beautiful still nights, well known to all who have visited the arctic regions, when the sky is without a cloud, and when the midnight sun, scarcely his own diameter below the horizon, tinges with a bright hue all the northern circle. Our ship, propelled by an increasing breeze, glided rapidly along a smooth sea, startling from her path flocks of lummes and dovekies, and other aquatic birds, whose flight could, from the stillness of the scene, be traced by the ear to a considerable distance. Our rate of sailing, however, by no means kept pace with our anxiety that the fog, which usually succeeds a fine day in high latitudes, should hold off until we had decided a geographical question of some importance, as connected with the memory of the immortal Cook. That excellent navigator, in his discoveries of these seas, placed three islands in the middle of the strait (the Diomede Islands). Kotzebue, however, in passing them, fancied he saw a fourth, and conjectured that it must have been either overlooked by Cook and Clerke, or that it had been since raised by an earthquake *

As we proceeded, the land on the south side of St Lawrence Bay made its appearance first, and next the lofty mountains at the back of Cape Prince of Wales, then hill after hill rose alternately on either bow, curiously refracted, and assuming all the varied forms which that phenomenon of the atmosphere is known to occasion. At last, at the distance of fifty miles, the Diomede Islands, and the eastern Cape of Asia, rose above the horizon of our mast-head. But, as if to teach us the necessity of patience in the sea we were about to navigate, before we had determined the question, a thick fog enveloped every thing in obscurity. We continued to run on, assisted by a strong northerly current, until seven o'clock the next morning, when the western Diomede was seen through the fog close to us.

In our passage from the St. Lawrence Island to this situation, the depth of the sea increased a little, until to the northward of King's Island, after which it began to decrease; but in the vicinity of the Diomede Islands, where the strait became narrowed, it again deepened, and continued between twenty-five and twenty-seven fathoms. The bottom, until close to the Diomedes, was composed of fine sand, but near them it changed to course stones and

* Some doubt, it appears, was created in the minds of the Russians themselves as to this supposed discovery, as we understood at Petropaulski, that a large wager depending upon it,

gravel, as at St. Lawrence Island, transitions which, by being attended to, may be of service to navigators in foggy weather.

During the day we saw a great number of whales, seals, and birds; but none, I believe, that are not mentioned in Pennant's Arctic Zoology.

We noticed upon the island abreast of us, which we conjectured to be the westernmost Diomede, several tents and youits, and also two or three baidars, hauled upon the beach. On the declivity of the hill were several frames, apparently for drying fish and skins, and depositing canoes and sledges upon It was nearly calm when we were off this place, but the current, which still ran to the northward carried us fast along the land. I steered for the situation of the supposed additional island, until by our reckoning we ought to have been upon it, and then hauled over towards the American shore In the evening the fog cleared away, and our curiosity was at last satisfied. The extremities of the two great continents were distinctly seen, and the islands in the strait clearly ascertained to be only three in number, and occupying nearly the same situations in which they were placed in the chart of Captain Cook

The south-eastern of the three islands is a high square rock, the next, or middle one, is an island with perpendicular cliffs, and a flat surface; and the third, or north-western, which is the largest, is three miles long, high to the southward, and terminates, in the opposite direction, in low cliffs with small rocky points off them. East Cape, in almost every direction, is so like an island, that I have no doubt it was the occasion of the mistake which the Russian navigator has committed.

For the sake of convenience, I named each of these islands. The eastern one I called Fairway Rock, as it is an excellent guide to the eastern channel, which is the widest and the best, the centre one I named after the Russian Admiral Krusenstern; and to the north-western island I transferred the name of Ratmanoff, which had been bestowed upon the supposed discovery of Kotzebue. we remarked that the Asiatic shore was more buried in snow than the American The mountains in the one were entirely covered, in the other, they were streaked, and partly exposed. The low land of both on the coast was nearly bare.

Near the Asiatic coast we had a sandy bottom, but, in crossing over the strait, it changed to mud, until well over on the American side, where we passed a tongue of sand and stones in twelve fathoms which, in all probability, was the extremity of a shoal, on which the ship was nearly lost the succeeding year. After crossing it, the water deepened, and the bottom again changed to mud, and we had ten and a half fathoms within two and a half miles of the coast.

We closed with the American shore, a few miles to the northward of Cape Prince of Wales, and found the coast low, with a ridge of sand extending along it, on which we noticed several Esquimaux habitations.   Steering along this shore to the northward, in ten and eight fathoms water, a little before noon we were within four and a half miles of Schismareff Inlet   Here we were becalmed, and had leisure to observe the broadsheet of water that extends inland in an E. S. E direction beyond the reach of the eye *   The width of the inlet between the two capes is ten miles ; but Saritcheff Island lies immediately before the opening, and we are informed by Kotzebue, that the channel, which is on the northern side of it, is extremely intricate and narrow, and that the space is strewed with shoals The island is now low and sandy, and is apparently joined under water, to the southward, to the strip of sand before mentioned as extending along the coast · we noticed upon it a considerable village of yourts, the largest of any that had as yet been seen.   The natives appear to prefer having their dwellings upon this sandy foundation to the main land, probably on account of the latter being swampy, which is the case every where in the vicinity of this inlet and Kotzebue Sound.   Several of them, taking advantage of the calm, came off in baidais, similar to those used by the St Lawrence islanders, though of inferior workmanship.   The people, however, differed from them in many respects ; their complexion was darker, their features were more harsh and angular, they were deficient in the tattooing of the face ; and what constituted a wider distinction between them was a custom, which we afterwards found general on the American coast, of wearing ornaments in their under lips   Our visitors were noisy and energetic, but good-natured ; laughed much, and humorously apprized us when we were making a good bargain

They willingly sold every thing they had, except their bows and arrows, which they implied were required for the chase on shore ; but they could not resist " tawac" (tobacco) and iron knives, and ultimately parted with them.   These instuments differed from those of the islanders to the southward, in being more slender, but they were made upon the same principle, with drift pine, assisted with thongs of hide, and occasionally with pieces of whalbone placed at the back of them neatly bound round with small cord   Their arrows were tipped with bone, flint, or iron, and they had spears or lances headed with the same materials   Their dress was the same as that worn by the whole tribe inhabiting the coast.   It consisted of a shirt which reached half way down the thigh, with long sleeves and a hood to it, made generally of the skin of the reindeer and

---

* Mountains were seen at the back of it, but the coast was not visible—probably it is low.

edged with the fur of the gray or white fox, and sometimes with dog's skin. The hood is usually edged with a longer fur than the other parts, either of the wolf or dog. They have besides this a jacket made of eider drakes' skins sewed together, which, put on underneath their other dress, is a tolerable protection against a distant arrow, and is worn in times of hostility. In wet weather they throw a shirt over their fur dress made of the entrails of the whale, which, while in their possession, is quite water tight, as it is then, in common with the rest of their property, tolerably well supplied with oil and grease; but after they had been purchased by us and became dry, they broke into holes and let the water through. They are on the whole as good as the best oil-skins in England. Besides the shirt, they have breeches and boots, the former made of deer's hide, the latter of seal's skin, both of which have drawing strings at the upper part, made of sea-horse hide. To the end of that which goes round the waist they attach a tuft of hair, the wing of a bird, or sometimes a fox's tail, which, dangling behind as they walk, gives them a ridiculous appearance, and may probably have occasioned the the report of the Tschutschi, recorded in Muller, that the people of this country have " tails like dogs "

It was at Schismareff Inlet that we first saw the lip ornaments which are common to all the inhabitants of the coast thence as far as Point Barrow. These ornaments consist of pieces of ivory, stone, or glass, formed with a double head, like a sleeve-button, one part of which is thrust through a hole bored in the under lip. Two of these holes are cut in a slanting direction about half an inch below the corners of the mouth. The incision is made when about the age of puberty, and is at first the size of a quill; as they grow older the natives enlarge the orifice, and increase the dimensions of the ornament accordingly, that it may hold its place: in adults, this orifice is about half an inch in diameter, and will, if required, distend to three quarters of an inch. Some of these ornaments were made of granite, others of jade-stone, and a few of large blue glass beads let into a piece of ivory which formed a white ring round them. These are about an inch in diameter, but I afterwards got one of a finely polished jade that was three inches in length, by an inch and a half in width.

About noon, a breeze springing up, the natives quitted us for the shore, and we pursued our course to the northward without waiting to explore further this deep inlet, which has since been a subject of regret, as the weather afterwards in both years prevented its being done. I could not, however, consistently with my instructions, wait to examine it at this moment, as the appointed time of rendezvous at Chamisso Island was already past.* While becalmed off it, we

* It has since been surveyed by the Russians.

were carried slowly to the north-eastward by a current which had been running in that direction from the time of our quitting St. Lawrence Island. With a fair wind we sailed along the coast to the northward, which was low and swampy, with small lakes inland The ridge of sand continued along the coast to Cape Espenburg, and there terminated

We entered Kotzebue Sound early in the morning of the 22d of July, and plied against a contrary wind, guided by the soundings; the appearance of the land was so distorted by mirage, and in parts so obscured by low fog, that it was impossible to distinguish where we were The naturalist who accompanied Kotzebue in his voyage particularly remarks this state of the atmosphere in the vicinity of the sound, and suggests that it may be occasioned by the swampy nature of the country, in which opinion I fully concur. When it cleared off we were much surprised to find ourselves opposite a deep inlet in the northern shore, which had escaped the observation of Captain Kotzebue I named it Hotham Inlet, in compliment to the Hon. Sir Henry Hotham, K C B, one of the lords of the Admiralty. We stood in to explore it, but found the water too shallow, and were obliged to anchor in four fathoms to pervent being carried away by a strong tide which was setting out of the sound, the wind being light and contrary

As it would be necessary to remain three or four days at Chamisso Island to increase our stock of water, previous to proceeding to the northward, the barge was hoisted out and sent to examine the inlet, with directions to meet the ship at Chamisso Island. She was again placed under the command of Mr. Elson, and equipped in every way necessary for the service required.

We were visited by several baidars, containing from ten to thirteen men each, whose object was to obtain articles in exchange. They were in every respect similar to the natives of Schismareff Inlet, though rather better looking, and were all, without exception, provided with labrets, either made of ivory and blue beads, as before described, of ivory alone, or of different kinds of stone, as steatite, porphyry, or greenstone; they readily disengaged these from their lips, and sold them, without minding the inconvenience of the saliva that flowed through the badly cicatriced orifice over the chin; but on the contrary derided us when we betrayed disgust at the spectacle, by thrusting their tongues through the hole, and winking their eyes. One or two had small strings of beads suspended to their ears

The articles they brought off were, as before, skins, fish, fishing implements, and nic-nacs. Their peltry consisted of the skins of the seal, of the common and arctic fox, the common and musk-rat, the marten, beaver, three varieties of ermine, one white, one with a light brown back and yellow belly, and the third with a gray back spotted white and yellow; the American otter, the white hare, the polar bear, the wolf, the deer, and the badger   Their fish were salmon and herrings · their implements, lances, either of stone or of a walrus tooth fixed to the end of a wooden staff · harpoons precisely similar to the Esquimaux, arrows, drills, and an instrument, the use of which was at first not very evident.   It was part of a walrus tooth shaped something like a shoehorn, with four holes at the small end, communicating with a trough that extended along the middle of the instrument and widened as it neared the broad part.   From the explanation given of it by the natives, it was evidently used to procure blood from dying animals, by inserting the end with the holes into the wound, and placing the mouth at the opposite end of the trough to receive the liquid as it flowed.   From the satisfaction that was evinced by the describer during the explanation, it is evident that the blood of animals is as much esteemed by these people as by the eastern Esquimaux *   On the outside of this and other instruments there were etched a variety of figures of men, beasts, and birds, &c , with a truth and character which showed the art to be common among them   The reindeer were generally in herds : in one picture they were pursued by a man in a stooping posture in snow-shoes ; in another he had approached nearer to his game, and was in the act of drawing his bow   A third represented the manner of taking seals with an inflated skin of the same animal as a decoy; it was placed upon the ice, and not far from it a man was lying upon his belly with a harpoon ready to strike the animal when it should make its appearance   Another was dragging a seal home upon a small sledge ; and several baidars were employed harpooning whales which had been previously shot with arrows , and thus, by comparing one device with another, a little history was obtained which gave us a better insight into their habits than could be elicited from any signs or intimations

The natives also offered to us for sale various other articles of traffic, such as small wooden bowls and cases, and little ivory figures, some of which were not more than three inches in length, dressed in clothes which were made with seams and edgings precisely similar to those in use among the Esquimaux

The staves of the harpoons and spears were made of pine or cypress, in all probability from drift wood, which is very abundant upon the shores ; and yet the circumstance of their having lumps of the resin in small bags, favoured the supposition that they had access to the living trees   They had also iron pyrites, plumbago, and red ochre, with which the frame of the baidar was coloured

* See Captain Parry's Second Voyage, 4to , p 510

The people themselves, in their persons as well as in their manners and implements, possessed all the characteristic features of the Esquimaux, large fat round faces, high cheek bones, small hazel eyes, eyebrows slanting like the Chinese, and wide mouths   They had the same fashion with their hair as the natives of Schismareff Inlet, cutting it close round the crown of the head, and thereby leaving a bushy ring round the lower part of it.   Ophthalmia was very general with them, and obliged some to wear either some kind of shade or spectacles, made of wood, with a wide slit for each eye to look through.   At Schismareff Inlet diseases of this nature were, also, prevalent among those who visited us

The salutation of our visiters was, as before, by a contact of noses, and by smoothing our faces with the palms of their hands, but without any disgusting practice

When they had parted with all they had for sale, they quitted the ship, well pleased with their excursion, and having pushed off to a little distance, clapped their hands, extended their arms, and stroked their bodies repeatedly ; which we afterwards found to be the usual demonstration of friendship among all their tribe   They then pointed to the shore, and with one consent struck the water with their paddles, and propelled their baidars with a velocity which we were not prepared to witness   These boats are similar in construction to the oomiaks of Hudson's Bay , but the model differs in being sharp at both ends   They consist of a frame made of drift wood, covered with the skins of walruses which are strained over it, and are capable of being tightened at any time by a lacing on the inside of the gunwale ; the frame and benches for the rowers are fastened with thongs, by which the boat is rendered both light and pliable ; the skin, when soaked with water, is translucent ; and a stranger placing his foot upon the flat yielding surface at the bottom of the boat fancies it a frail security ; but it is very safe and durable, especially when kept well greased

In Hudson's Strait the oomiak is principally used by the women and children   here it is the common conveyance of the men, who, without them, would not be able to collect their store of provisions for the winter   They are always steered by the elderly men, who have also the privilege of sitting in the stern of the boat when unemployed   The starboard paddles of those which we saw were stained with black stripes, and the larboard with red, as were also the frames of some of the baidars.

We formed a favourable opinion of our visiters from the strict integrity which they evinced in all their dealings, even when opportunities offered of evading detection, which I notice the more readily, as we afterwards experienced very different behaviour from the same tribe

Light winds kept us at anchor for twenty-four hours, during which time the current ran almost constantly to the south-westward, at the rate of from two fathoms to two miles per hour ; and the water was nearly fresh (1.0089 to 1 0096 sp gr) this stratum, however, was confined to a short distance from the surface, as a patent log, which was sunk for three hours at the depth of three fathoms, showed only a fifth of a mile in that time.   These facts left no doubt of our being near the estuary of a considerable river, flowing, in all probability. through the large opening abreast of us, which the boat had been sent to explore.

We weighed in the afternoon of the 23d, but in consequence of light winds and counter currents made very little progress ; indeed, a great part of the time the ship would not steer, even with a moderate breeze and two boats a-head, and it was necessary to keep carrying out the kedge anchors on the bow to maintain the ship's head in the right direction.   This was occasioned by some large rivers emptying themselves into the sound, the fresh water of which remained at the surface, and flowed in a contrary direction to the tide of the ocean.   Had this occured in an intricate channel it might have been dangerous, but in Kotzebue Sound the bottom is quite even and there is plenty of room to drift about.

At four o'clock in the morning of the 25th we reached our appointed rondezvous at Chamisso Island, ten days later than had been agreed upon by Captain Franklin and myself, but which, it appeared, was quite early enough, as there were no traces of his having arrived   On approaching the island we discovered, through our telescopes, a small pile of stones upon its summit ; and as every object of this kind which was likely to be the work of human hands was interesting, from the possibility that it might be the labour of the party we were in search of, it was not long in undergoing an examination, there was nothing however to lead to its history, but conjecture attributed it to Captain Kotzebue, who visited that spot in 1816.

The ship was anchored nearly as far up in Kotzebue Sound as a vessel of her class can go, between Chamisso Island on the south, and Choris peninsula on the north, with Escholtz Bay on the east, and an open space on the west, in which the coast was too distant to be seen.   The land about this part of the Sound is generally characterised by rounded hills from about six hundred feet to a thousand above the sea, with small lakes and rivers ; its surface is rent into deep furrows, which, until a very late period in the summer, are filled with water, and being covered with a thick swampy moss, and in some places with long grass or bushes, it is extremely tedious to traverse it on foot.   Early in the summer myriads of moskitos infest this swampy shore, and almost preclude the possibility of continuing any pursuit, but in August they begin to die off, and soon afterwards entirely disappear.

Chamisso Island, the highest part of which is 231 feet above the sea, is steep, except to the eastward, where it ends in a low sandy point, upon which are the remains of some Esquimaux habitations; it has the same swampy covering as the land just described, from which, until late in the summer, several streams descend, and are very convenient for procuring water. Detached from Chamisso, there is a steep rock which by way of distinction we named Puffin Island, composed of mouldering granite, which has been broken away in such a manner that the remaining part assumes the form of a tower. During the period of incubation of the aquatic birds, every hole and projecting crag on the sides of this rock is occupied by them. Its shores resound with the chorus of thousands of the feathery tribe; and its surface presents a curiously mottled carpet of brown, black, and white.

In a sandy bay upon the western side of the peninsula we found a few Esquimaux who had hauled up their baidars, and erected a temporary hut; they were inferior in every respect to those we had seen before, and furnished us with nothing new. In this bay we caught enough salmon and other fish to give a meal to the whole of the ship's company, which was highly acceptable; but we had to regret that similar success did not attend our subsequent trials.

By my instructions, I was desired to await the arrival of Captain Franklin at this anchorage; but in a memoir drawn up by that officer and myself, to which my attention was directed by the Admiralty, it was arranged that the ship should proceed to the northward, and survey the coast, keeping the barge in shore to look out for the land party, and to erect posts as signals of her having been there, and also to leave directions where to find the ship.

I was also desired to place a small party in occupation of Chamisso Island during the absence of the ship; but this spot proved to be so different from what we imagined, being accessible in almost every quarter, instead of having only one landing place, that a a small party would have been of no use if the natives were inclined to be hostile, and the numerical strength of the crew did not admit of a large detachment being spared from her. But in order that Captain Franklin should not want provision in the event of his missing the ship along the coast, and arriving at the island in her absence, a tight barrel of flour was buried upon Puffin Rock, which appeared to be the most unfrequented spot in the vicinity, and directions for finding it were deposited in a bottle at Chamisso Island, together with such other information as he might require, and the place where it was deposited was pointed out by writing upon the cliffs with white paint. It was further arranged, that a party should proceed overland in a northerly direction, in the hope of falling in with Captain Franklin, as it was possible the shore of the

Polar Sea might be more to the southward than the general trending of that part of its coast which had been explored led us to expect But as the ship was likely to be absent several weeks, and we were unacquainted with the disposition of the people or with the country, further than that from its swampy nature, it seemed to present almost insurmountable difficulties to the journey, I deferred the departure of the party, and afterwards wholly abandoned the project, as the coast was found to extend so far to the northward as to render it quite useless.

As I wished to avail myself of the latitude afforded by this memoir, to survey and examine as much of the coast as possible before Captain Franklin arrived, no time was lost in preparing the ship for sea, which it required only a little time to effect.

On the 28th Mr Elson returned from the examination of the opening we discovered on the north side of Kotzebue Sound, and reported the water at the entrance to be shallow, that the barge could not enter The inlet was of considerable width, and extended thirty or forty miles in a broad sheet of water, which some distance up was fresh This was ascertained by landing in the sound to the eastward of the opening, at which place it was found that the inlet approached the sea within a mile and a half The time to which it was necessary to limit Mr Elson, prevented his doing more than ascertaining that this opening was navigable only by small boats ; and by the water being quite fresh, that it could not lead to any sea beyond

The Esquimaux in the inlet were more numerous than we supposed, but were very orderly and well behaved. When the barge anchored off a low sandy point, on which they had erected their summer habitations and fishing stakes, she was surrounded by fourteen baidars, containing 150 men ; which, considering the crew of the barge only amounted to eight men and two officers, was a superiority of strength that might well have entitled them to take liberties, had they been disposed, armed as they usually are with bows and arrows, spears, and a large knife strapped to their thigh but so far from this being the case, they readily consented to an arrangement, that only one baidar at a time should come alongside to dispose of her goods, and then make way for another : the proposal was made while the baidars were assembled round our boat, and was received with a shout of general applause.

Blue beads, cutlery, tobacco, and buttons, were the articles in request, and with which almost any thing they had might have been purchased . for these they sold their implements, ornaments, and some very fine salmon , also a small canac very similar to those of Greenland and Hudson's Strait.

While the duties of the ship were being forwarded under my first lieutenant, Mr. Peard, I took the opportunity to visit the extraordinary ice-formation in Escholtz Bay, mentioned by Kotzebue as being "covered with a soil half a foot thick, producing the most luxuriant grass," and containing an abundance of mammoth bones. We sailed up the bay, which was extremely shallow, and landed at a deserted village on a low sandy point, where Kotzebue bivouacked when he visited the place, and to which I afterwards gave the name of Elephant Point, from the bones of that animal being found near it.

The cliffs in which this singular formation was discovered begin near this point and extend westward in nearly a straight line to a rocky cliff of primitive formation at the entrance of the bay, whence the coast takes an abrupt turn to the southward. The cliffs are from twenty to eighty feet in height ; and rise inland to a rounded range of hills between four and five hundred feet above the sea. In some places they present a perpendicular front to the northward, in others a slightly inclined surface ; and are occasionally intersected by valleys and water-courses generally overgrown with low bushes. Opposite each of these valleys, there is a projecting flat piece of ground, consisting of the materials that have been washed down the ravine, where the only good landing for boats is afforded. The soil of the cliffs is a bluish-coloured mud, for the most part covered with moss and long grass, full of deep furrows, generally filled with water or frozen snow. Mud in a frozen state forms the surface of the cliff in some parts ; in others the rock appears, with the mud above it, or sometimes with a bank half way up it, as if the superstratum had gradually slid down and accumulated against the cliff. By the large rents near the edges of the mud cliffs, they appear to be breaking away, and contributing daily to diminish the depth of the water in the bay.

Such is the general conformation of this line of coast. That particular formation, which, when it was first discovered by Captain Kotzebue, excited so much curiosity, and bore so near a resemblance to an iceberg as to deceive himself and his officers, when they approached the spot to examine it, remains to be described. As we rowed along the shore, the shining surface of small portions of the cliffs attracted our attention, and directed us where to search for this curious phenomenon, which we should otherwise have had difficulty in finding, notwithstanding its locality had been particularly described, for so large a portion of the ice cliff has thawed since it was visited by Captain Kotzebue and his naturalist, that only a few insignificant patches of the frozen surface now remain. The largest of these, situated about a mile to the westward of Elephant Point, was particularly examined by Mr. Collie, who, on cutting through the ice in a horizontal direction, found that it formed only a casing to the cliff which was composed of mud and gravel in a frozen state

On removing the earth above, it was also evident, by a decided line of separation between the ice and the cliff, that the Russians had been deceived by appearances. By cutting into the upper surface of the cliff three feet from the edge, frozen earth, similar to that which formed the face of the cliff, was found at eleven inches' depth, and four yards further back the same substance occurred at twenty-two inches' depth.

The glacial facing we afterwards noticed in several parts of the sound . and it appears to me to be occasioned either by the snow being banked up against the cliff, or collected in its hollows in the winter, and converted into ice in the summer by partial thawings and freezings—or by the constant flow of water during the summer over the edges of the cliffs, on which the sun's rays operate less forcibly than on other parts, in consequence of their aspect. The streams thus become converted into ice, either while trickling down the still frozen surface of the cliffs, or after they reach the earth at their base, in which case the ice rises like a stalagmite, and in time reaches the surface But before this is completed, the upper soil, loosened by the thaw is itself projected over the cliff, and falls in a heap below, whence it is ultimately carried away by the tide We visited this spot a month later in the season, and found a considerable alteration in its appearance, manifesting more clearly than before the deception under which Kotzebue laboured

The deserted village upon the low point consisted of a row of huts, rudely formed with drift-wood and turf, about six feet square and four feet in height In front of them was a quantity of drift-wood raised upon rafters , and around them there were several heaps of bones and skulls of seals and grampuses, which in all probability had been retained conformably with the superstitions of the Greenlanders, who carefully preserve these parts of the skeleton.*
A rank grass grew luxuriantly about these deserted abodes, and also about the edges of several pools of fresh water, in which there were some wild fowl We returned to the ship late at night, and found her ready for sea

* Crantz Greenland, Vol. 1.

CHAPTER XI.

Quit Kotzebue Sound, and proceed to survey the Coast to the Northward—Interviews with the Natives—Cape Thomson Point Hope—Current—Capes Sabine and Beaufort—Barrier of Ice—Icy Cape—Advanced Position of the Ship—Discover Cape Franklin, Wainwright Inlet, Shoals off Icy Cape, &c.—Boat sent on an Expedition along the Coast—Return of the Ship to Kotzebue Sound—Interviews with the Esquimaux—Boat rejoins the Ship—Important Results of her Expedition

On the 30th of July we weighed from Chamisso Island, attended by the barge, and steered out of the sound. The day was very fine, and as we sailed along the northern shore, the sun was reflected from several parts of the cliff, which our telescopes discovered to be cased with a frozen surface, similar to that just described in Escholtz Bay. We kept at six or seven miles distance from the land, and had a very even bottom, until near Hotham Inlet, when the soundings quickly decreased, and the ship struck upon a shoal before any alteration of the helm had materially changed her position. The water was fortunately quite smooth and she grounded so easily, that, but for the lead-lines, we should not have known any thing had occurred. We found, upon sounding, that the ship had entered a bight in the shoal, and that there was a small bank between her and deep water, so that it became necessary to carry out the stream anchor in the direction of her wake, by means of which, and a little rise of the tide, she soon got off.

This shoal, which extends eight miles off the land, is very dangerous, as the soundings give very short warning of its proximity, and there are no good landmarks for avoiding it. The distance from the shore, could it be judged of under ordinary circumstances, would on some occasions be a most treacherous guide, as the mirage in fine weather plays about it and gives the land a very different appearance at one moment from that which it assumes at another.

As soon as we were clear of the shoal, we continued our course for Cape Krusenstern, near which place we the next day buried a letter for Captain Franklin, and erected a post to direct him to the spot. The cape is a low tongue of land, intersected by lakes, lying at the foot of a high cluster of hills not in any way remarkable. The land slopes down from them to several rocky cliffs, which, until the low point is seen at the foot of them, appear to be the entrance to the sound, but they are nearly a mile inland from it   The coast here takes an abrupt turn to the northward, and the current sets strong against the bend , which is probably the reason of there being deep water close to the beach, as also the occasion of a shoal in a north-westerly direction from the point, which appears to have been thrown up by the eddy water.

The boat landed about two miles to the northward of this point, upon a shingly beach, sufficiently steep to afford very good landing when the water is smooth , behind it there was a plain about a mile wide, extending from the hills to the sea, composed of elastic bog earth, intersected by small streams, on the edges of which the buttercup, poppy, blue-bell, pedicularis, vaccinium, saxifrages, and some cruciform plants* throve very well ; in other parts, however, the vegetation was stinted, and consisted only of lichens and mosses.   There were here some low mud cliffs frozen so hard that it required considerable labour to dig fifteen inches to secure the end of the post that was erected.

Mr Elson, in command of the barge, was now furnished with a copy of the signals drawn up by Captain Franklin and myself, and directed to proceed close along the shore to the northward, vigilantly looking out for boats, and erecting posts and landmarks in the most conspicuous places for Captain Franklin's guidance, and to trace the outline of the beach   He was also desired to explore the coast narrowly, and to fill in such parts of it as could not be executed in the ship, and instructed where to rendezvous in case of separation

We then steered along the coast, which took a north-westerly direction, and at midnight passed a range of hills terminating about four miles from the sea, which must be the Cape Mulgrave of Captain Cook, who navigated this part of the coast at too great a distance to see the land in front of the hills, which is extremely low, and after passing the Mulgrave Range, forms an extensive plain intersected by lakes near the beach ; these lakes are situated so close together that by transporting a small boat from one to the other, a very good inland navigation, if necessary, might be performed. They are supplied by the draining of the land and the melting snow, and discharge their water through small openings in the shingly beach, too shallow to be entered by any thing larger than a baidar, one of them excepted, through which the current ran too strong for soundings to be taken.

* The botany of this part of the coast is published in the Flora Americana of Dr Hooker

On the 1st of August we did little more than drift along the coast with the current—which was repeatedly tried, and always found setting to the north-west—from half a mile to a mile and a half per hour The Esquimaux, taking advantage of the calm, came off to the ship in three baidars, and added to our stock of curiosities by exchanging their manufactures for beads, knives, and tobacco.

On the 2d, being favoured with a breeze, we closed with a high cape, which I named after Mr. Deas Thomson, one of the commissioners of the navy.* It is a bold promontory 450 feet in height, and marked with differently-coloured strata, of which there is a representation in the geological memorandum. As this was a fit place to erect a signal-post for Captain Franklin, we landed, and were met upon the beach by some Esquimaux, who eagerly sought an exchange of goods Very few of their tribe understood better how to drive a bargain than these people ; and it was not until they had sold almost all they could spare, that we had any peace. We found them very honest, extremely good natured, and friendly. Their features, dress, and weapons were the same as before described in Kotzebue Sound, with the exception of some broad-headed spears, which they had probably obtained from the Tschutschi. They had more curiosity than our former visiters, and examined very minutely every part of our dress; from which circumstance, and their being frightened at the discharge of a gun, and no less astonished when a bird fell close to them, we judged they had had a very limited intercourse with Europeans. The oldest person we saw among the party was a cripple about fifty years of age. The others were robust people above the average height of Esquimaux : the tallest man was five feet nine inches, and the tallest woman five feet four inches All the women were tattooed upon the chin with three small lines, which is a general distinguishing mark of the fair sex along this coast ; this is effected by drawing a blackened piece of thread through the skin with a needle, as with the Greenlanders. Their hair was done up in large blaits on each side of the head, as described by Captain Parry at Melville Peninsula We noticed a practice here amongst the women, similar to that which is common with the Arabs, which consisted of blacking the edges of the eyelids with plumbago rubbed up with a little saliva upon a piece of slate. All the men had labrets, and both sexes had their teeth much worn down, probably by the constant application of them to hard substances, of which their dresses, implements, and canoes are made.

They had several rude knives, probably obtained from the Tschutschi, some lumps of iron pyrites, and pieces of amber strung

* A cape close to this has been named Cape Ricord by the Russians

round their neck; but I could not learn where they had procured them.

As soon as we finished the necessary observations with the artificial horizon, to the no small diversion and surprise of our inquisitive companions, we paid a visit to the next valley, where we found a small village situated close upon a fine stream of fresh water flowing from a large bed of thawing snow. The banks of the brook were fertile, but vegetation was more diminutive here than in Kotzebue Sound; notwithstanding which, several plants were found which did not exist there The tents were constructed of skins loosely stretched over a few spars of drift-wood, and were neither wind nor water tight They were, as usual, filthy, but suitable to the taste of their inhabitants, who no doubt saw nothing in them that was revolting. The natives testified much pleasure at our visit, and placed before us several dishes, among which were two of their choicest—the entrails of a fine seal, and a bowl of coagulated blood. But, desirous as we were to oblige them, there was not one of our party that could be induced to partake of their hospitality. Seeing our reluctance, they tried us with another dish, consisting of the raw flesh of the narwhal, nicely cut into lumps, with an equal distribution of black and white fat; but they were not more successful here than at first

An old man then braced a skin upon a tambourine frame, and striking it with a bone gave the signal for a dance, which was immediately performed to a chorus of Angna aya! angna aya! the tambourine marking time by being flourished and twirled about against a short stick instead of being struck. The musician, who was also the principal dancer, jumped into the ring, and threw his body into different attitudes until quite exhausted, and then resigned his office to another, from whom it passed to a lad, who occasioned more merriment by his grimaces and ludicrous behaviour than any of his predecessors His song was joined by the young women, who until then had been mute and almost motionless, but who now acquitted themselves with equal spirit with their leader, twisting their bodies, twirling their arms about, and violently rubbing their sides with their garments, which, from some ridiculous association no doubt, occasioned considerable merriment.

Against an obscure part of the cliff near the village we noticed a broad iron-headed halberd placed erect, with several bows and quivers of arrows; and near them a single arrow, with a tuft of feathers attached to it, suspended to the rock. The Esquimaux were reluctant to answer our inquiries concerning this arrangement, and were much displeased when we approached the place. From the conduct of the natives at Schismareff Inlet toward Captain Kotzebue, it is not impossible that the shooting of this arrow may be a signal of hostility, as those people, after eying him attentively and suspiciously, paddled quickly away, and threw two arrows with bunches of feathers fastened to them toward their habitations, whence shortly afterwards issued two baidars, who approached Captain Kotzebue with very doubtful intentions

Upon an eminence beyond this cliff we found several dogs tethered to stakes, and all the little children of the village, who had perhaps been sent out of the way, and who, on seeing us, set up a general lamentation

After viewing this village, we ascended Cape Thomson, and discovered low land jutting out from the coast to the W. N W as far as the eye could reach   As this point had never been placed in our charts, I named it Point Hope, in compliment to Sir William Johnstone Hope

Having buried a bottle for Captain Franklin upon the eminence, we took leave of our friends, and made sail towards the ship, which, in consequence of a current, was far to leeward, although she had been beating the whole day with every sail set   We continued to press the ship during the night, in order to maintain our position, that the barge might join; but the current ran so strong, that the next morning, finding we lost rather than gained ground, I bore away to trace the extent of the low point discovered from Cape Thompson   On nearing it, we perceived a forest of stakes driven into the ground for the purpose of keeping the property of the natives off the ground; and beneath them several round hillocks, which we afterwards found to be the Esquimaux yourts, or underground winter habitations.   The wind fell very light off this point, and I went in the gig to pay a visit to the village, leaving directions to anchor the ship in case the wind continued light   After rowing a considerable time, we found a current running so strong that we did not make any progress, and it was as much as we could do to get back to the ship, which had in the mean time been anchored with the bower, having previously parted from the kedge

The current was now running W. by N at the rate of three miles an hour.   About five o'clock the next morning, however, it slackened to a mile and a half, and the boats were sent to creep for the kedge anchor, but it could not be found   A thick fog afterwards came on, which kept us at anchor until the next day   During this time signal guns were fired every two hours, as well on account of Captain Franklin as of our own boat.

On the fifth we weighed, and set the studding-sails, but the ship would not steer, and came broadside to the tide, in spite of the helm and three boats ahead, and continued in this position until a fresh breeze sprang up from the northward.

It is necessary here to give some further particulars of this curient, in order that it may not be supposed that the whole body of water between the two great continents was setting into the Polar Sea at so considerable a rate. By sinking the patent log first five fathoms, and then three fathoms, and allowing it to remain in the first instance six hours, and in the latter twelve hours, it was clearly ascertained that there was no current at either of those depths, but at the distance of nine feet from the surface the motion of the water was nearly equal to that at the top. Hence we must conclude that the current was superficial, and confined to a depth between nine and twelve feet

By the freshness of the water alongside, there is every reason to believe that the current was occasioned by the many rivers which, at this time of the year, empty themselves into the sea in different parts of the coast, beginning with Schismareff Inlet. The specific gravity of the sea off that place was 1.02502, from which it gradually decreased, and at our station off the point was 1.0173, the temperature at each being 58°. On the other hand, the strength of the stream had gradually increased from half a mile an hour to three miles, which was its greatest rapidity. So far there is nothing extraordinary in the fact, but why this body of water should continually press to the northward in preference to taking any other direction, or gradually expending itself in the sea, is a question of considerable interest

In the afternoon the barge was discovered at anchor, close inshore, and being favoured with a breeze the ship was brought close to the point. This enabled me to land, accompanied by Mr. Collie, who, while I was occupied with my theodolite, went toward the huts, which at first appeared to be deserted, but as he was examining them several old women and children made their appearance, and gave him a friendly reception. He brought them to me, and we underwent the full delights of an affectionate Esquimaux salutation

The persons of our new acquaintance were extremely diminutive, dirty, and forbidding. Some were blind, others decrepit, and, dressed in greasy worn-out clothes, they looked perfectly wretched. Their hospitality, however, was even greater than we could desire, and we were dragged away by the wrists to their hovels, on approaching which we passed between heaps of filth and ruined habitations, filled with stinking water, to a part of the village which was in better repair. We were then seated upon some skins placed for the purpose, and bowls of blubber, walrus, and unicorn flesh (*monodon monoceros*), with various other delicacies of the same kind, were successively offered as temptations to our appetite, which nevertheless, we felt no inclination to indulge

After some few exchanges, the advantage of which was on the side of our acquaintances, who had nothing curious to part with, an old man produced a tambourine, and seating himself upon the roof of one of the miserable hovels, threw his legs across, and commenced a song, accompanying it with the tambourine, with as much apparent happiness as if fortune had imparted to him every luxury of life.   The vivacity and humour of the musician inspired two of the old hags, who joined chorus, and threw themselves into a variety of attitudes, twisting their bodies, snapping their fingers, and smirking from behind their seal-skin hoods, with as much shrewd meaning as if they had been half a century younger   Several little chubby girls, roused by the music, came blinking at the daylight through the greasy roofs of the subterranean abodes, and joined the performance ; and we had the satisfaction of seeing a set of people happy, who did not appear to possess a single comfort upon earth.

The village consisted of a number of "yourts," excavated in a ridge of mud and gravel, which had been heaped up in a parallel line with the beach   Their construction more nearly approached to the habitations of the Tschutschi than those of the Esquimaux of Greenland   They consisted of two pits about eight feet deep, communicating by a door at the bottom.   The inner one had a dome-shaped roof, made with dry wood or bones ; it was covered with turf, that rose about four feet above the surface of the earth   In the centre of this there was a circular hole or window, covered with a piece of skin (part of the intestine of the whale), which gave, however, but very little light.   The outer pit had a flat roof, and was entered by a square hole, over which there was a shed to protect it from the snow and the inclemency of the weather.   A rude ladder led to a floor of loose boards, beneath which our noses as well as our eyes were greeted by a pool of dirty green water.   The inner chamber was the sleeping and cooking room.

Another yourt, to which a store of provision was attached by a low subterraneous passage, was examined by Lieutenant Belcher the ensuing year   it was in other respects very similar, and needs no particular description.   Of these yourts, one was of much larger dimensions than the others, which, it was intimated by the natives, was constructed for the purpose of dancing and amusing themselves.   Mr Belcher was particularly struck with the cleanliness of the boards and sleeping places in the interior of the yourt he examined , whereas the passage and entrance were allowed to remain in a very filthy condition   The air was too oppressive to continue in them for any length of time.   Every yourt had its rafters for placing sledges, skins of oil, or other articles upon in the winter time, to prevent their being buried in the snow.   The number of these frames, some bearing sledges, and others the skeletons of boats, formed a complete wood, and had attracted our notice, at the distance of six or seven miles.   Of the many yourts which composed the village, very few were occupied; the others had their entrances blocked up with logs of drift-wood and the ribs of whales. From this circumstance, and the infirm condition of almost all who remained at the village, it was evident that the inhabitants had gone on a sealing excursion, to provide a supply of food for the the winter. The natives, when we were about to take our leave, accompanied us to the boat, and, as we pushed off, they each picked up a few pebbles, and carried them away with them, but for what purpose we could not guess, nor had we ever seen the custom before.

The point upon which this village stands, projects almost sixteen miles from the general line of coast, it is intersected by several lakes and small creeks, the entrances of which are on the north side. There is a bar across the mouth of the opening, consisting of pebbles and mud, which has every appearance of being on the increase; but when the water is smooth a boat may enter, and she will find very excellent security within from all winds. It is remarkable that both Cook and Clerke, who passed within a very short distance of this point, mistook the projection for ice that had been driven against the land, and omitted to mark in their chart

The next morning we communicated with the barge, and found she had been visited daily by the natives, who were very friendly. The current in-shore was more rapid than in the offing, and the water more fresh. After replenishing her provisions, we steered to the northward, and endeavoured to get in with the land on the northern side of Point Hope; but the wind was so light that we could not hold our ground against the current, and were drifted away slowly to the northward. In the morning, the wind being still unfavourable for this purpose, we steered for the farthest land in sight to the northward, which answered to cape Lisburn of Captain Cook. As we approached it, the current slackened, and the depth and specific gravity of the sea both increased We landed here, and ascended the mountain to obtain a fair view of the coast, which we found turned to the eastward, nearly at a right angle, and then to the north-eastward, as far as the eye could trace Our height was 850 feet above the sea, and at so short a distance from it on one side, that it was fearful to look down upon the beach below. We ascended by a valley which collected the tributary streams of the mountain, and poured them in a cascade upon the beach. The basis of the mountain was flint of the purest kind, and limestone, abounding in fossil shells, enchinites, and marine animals

There was very little soil in the valley: the stones were covered with a thick swampy moss, which we traversed with great difficulty, and were soon wet through by it. Vegetation was, however, as luxuriant as in Kotzebue Sound, more than a hundred miles to the southward, or, what is of more consequence, more than that distance

farther from the great barrier of ice   Several reindeer were feeding
on this luxuriant pasture . the cliffs were covered with birds ; and
the swamps generated myriads of moskitos, which were more persevering, if possible, than those at Chamisso Island

After depositing a bottle at this place, and leaving proper directions upon the cliff for finding it, we pursued our course to the eastward, accompanied by the barge   The wind was light, and we made
so little progress, that on the 9th Cape Lisburn was still in sight.
Before it was entirely lost I landed at a small cape, which I named
Cape Beaufort, in compliment to Captain Beaufort, the present
hydrographer to the Admiralty   The land northward was low and
swampy, covered with moss and long grass, which produced all the
plants we had met with to the southward, and two or three besides.
Cape Beaufort is composed of sandstone, enclosing bits of petrified
wood and rushes, and is traversed by narrow veins of coal lying in
an E. N. E and W S W direction   That at the surface was dry
and bad, but some pieces which had been thrown up by the burrow-
ing of a small animal, probably the ermine, burned very well.

As this is a part of the coast hitherto unexplored, I may stand
excused for being a little more particular in my description   Cape
Beaufort is situated in the depth of a great bay, formed between Cape
Lisburn and Icy Cape, and is the last point where the hills come
close down to the sea, by reason of the coast line curving to the northward, while the range of hills continues its former direction   From
the rugged mountains of limestone and flint at Cape Lisburn, there
is an uniform descent to the rounded hills of sandstone at Cape
Beaufort just described   The range is however, broken by extensive valleys, intersected by lakes and rivers.   Some of these lakes
border upon the sea, and in the summer months are accessible to
baidars, or even large boats ; but as soon as the current from the beds
of thawing snow inland ceases, the sea throws up a bar across the
mouths of them, and they cannot be entered   The beach, at the
places where we landed, was shingle and mud, the country mossy
and swampy, and infested with moskitos.   We noticed recent tracks
of wolves, and of some cloven-footed animals, and saw several ptar-
migans, ortolans, and a lark.   Very little drift-wood had found its
way upon this part of the coast

We reached the ship just after a thick fog came in, from seaward,
and only a short time before the increasing breeze obliged her to
quit the coast   During my absence the boats had been sent to examine a large floating mass which excited a good deal of curiosity
at the time, and found it to be the carcass of a dead whale.   It had
an Esquimaux harpoon in it, and a drag attached, made of an inflated sealskin, which had no doubt worried the animal to death.   Thus,
with knowledge just proportioned to their wants, do these untutored

barbarians, with their slender boats and limited means, contrive to take the largest animal of the creation   In the present instance, certainly, their victim had eluded their efforts, but the carcass was not yet " too high" for an Esquimaux palate, and would, no doubt, ere long, be either washed upon the shore, or discovered by some of the many wandering baidars along the coast.

Some very extensive flocks of eider ducks had also been seen from the ship   They consisted entirely of females and young ones, the greater part of which could not fly, but they nevertheless contrived to evade pursuit by diving

On the morning of the 10th we were under treblereefed topsails and foresail, with short head sea, in which we pitched away the jibboom. We had a thick fog, with the wind at N N E. A little after noon, being in lat 70° 09' N., and 165° 10' W., we had twenty-four fathoms hard bottom we then stood toward the shore, and again changed the bottom to mud, the depth of water gradually decreasing. On the 11th it was calm; by the observations at noon there had been a current to the S W., but this had now ceased, as upon trial it ran west one-third of a mile per hour, and three hours afterward N E. five-eighths per hour, which appeared to be the regular tide. In the evening the wind again blew from the northward and brought a thick fog with it. We stood off and on, guided by the soundings.

In the morning of the 12th we saw a great many birds, walrusses, and small white whales; from which I concluded that we were near a stream of ice, but only one peice was seen in the evening aground. We tacked not far from it in ten fathoms   As we stood in-shore, the temperature of the sea always decreased ; the effect, probably, of the rivers of melting snow mingling with it.

As it was impossible to determine the continuity of coast, with the weather so thick, farther than by the gradual decrease of the soundings, I stood to the northward to ascertain the position of the ice, the wind having changed to E N E and become favourable for the purpose. At eight o'clock in the morning of the 13th, the fog cleared off, and exhibited the main body of ice extending from N. 79° E. to S 29° W (true) At nine we tacked amongst the *brash*, in twenty-three fathoms water, in lat. 71° 08' N , long 163° 40' W. The wind was blowing along the ice, and the outer part of the *pack* was in streams, some of which the ship might have entered, and perhaps have proceeded up them two or three miles, but as this would have served no useful purpose, and would have occasioned unnecessary delay, I again stood in for the land, which at eight o'clock at night was seen in a low unbroken line, extending to the westward as far as Icy Cape and to the eastward as far as the state of the weather would permit. We tacked at nine, in five fathoms wa-

tei, within two miles of the shore ; and Lieutenant Belcher was
despatched in the cutter to examine some posts that were erected
upon it, thinking they might possibly have been placed there by
the land expedition   The boat found a heavy surf breaking upon
a sand bank at a little distance from the beach, which prevented her
landing, and a fog coming on, she was recalled before the attempt
could be made in another place   There was a thick wetting fog during the night   The next morning a boat was again sent on shore,
with Lieutenant Belcher, Messrs Collie and Wolfe, to make observations, collect plants, and erect a mark for Captain Franklin   They
had nearly the same difficulty in reaching the beach, on account of
shoals, as at the former place, but there was less swell

Shortly after noon I landed myself, and found that at the back of
the beach there was a lake two miles long, in the direction of the
coast, it had a shallow entrance at its south-west end, sufficiently
deep for baidars only   The main land at the back of it presented
a range of low earth cliffs, behind which there were some hills, a-
bout two hundred feet high   Near the entrance to the lake there
were two youts, inhabited by some Esquimaux, who sold us two
swans and four hundred pounds of venison, which being divided
amongst the crew, formed a most acceptable meal   These swans
were without their feet, which had been converted into bags, after
the practice of the eastern Esquimaux ; and it is remarkable, that
although so far from Kamschatka and the usual track of vessels,
these people expressed no surprise at the appearance either of the
ship or the boat, and that they were provided both with knives and
iron kettles

In our way to the huts we saw several human bones scattered a-
bout, and a skull which had the teeth worn down nearly to the
gums.   There appeared to be no place of interment near, and the
body had probably decayed where the bones were lying   So little
did the natives care for these mouldering remains that springs for catching birds were set amongst them   The beach upon which we landed
was shingle and sand, interspersed with pieces of coal, sandstone, flint,
and porphyritic granite   Vegetation was very luxuriant, and supplied
Mr Collie with three new species   The drift wood was here more
abundant than at any place we before visited   it was forced high
upon the beach, probably by the pressure of the ice when driven a-
gainst the coast

It was high water at this station at noon.   The tide fell three
feet and a half in four hours, and ebbed to the south-west   A post
was here put up for the land expedition, and a bottle buried near it
We then embarked and got on board, just as a thick fog obscured
every thing, and obliged the ship to stand off the coast   In the
course of the afternoon the dredge was put over, and supplied us with

some specimens of shells of the arca, murex, venus, and buccinum genus, and several lumps of coal. We stood to the N W , and at midnight tacked amongst the loose ice at the edge of the pack in so thick a fog that we could not see a hundred yards around us

At half past five in the morning a partial dispersion of the fog discovered to us the land, bearing N. 86° E . extending in a N. E direction as far as we could see. At six we tacked in eleven fathoms within three miles of it, and not far from an opening into a spacious lake, which appeared to be the estuary of a considerable river. There was a shoal across the mouth connected with the land on the northern side, but with a channel for boats in the opposite direction A large piece of ice was aground near it The country around was low, covered with a brown moss, and intersected by water-courses To the northward of the entrance of the lake the coast became higher, and presented an extensive range of mud cliffs, terminating in a cape, which, as it afterwards proved the most distant land seen from the ship, I named after Captain Franklin, R. N., under whose command I had the pleasure to serve on the first Polar expedition . but as this cape was afterwards found to be a little way inland, I transferred the name to the nearest conspicuous point of the coast.

The natives, taking advantage of this elevated ground, had constructed their winter residences in it · they were very numerous, and extended some way along the coast. The season, however, was not yet arrived at which the Esquimaux take up their abode in their subterranean habitations, and they occupied skin tents upon a low point at the entrance of the lake. We had not been long off here before three baidars from the village paddled alongside and bartered their articles as usual. Some of the crew ascended the side of the ship without any invitation, and showed not the least surprise at any thing they beheld, which I could not help particularly remarking, as we were not conscious of any other vessel having been upon the coast since Kotzebue's voyage, and he did not reach within two hundred miles of the residence of these people There was nothing in our visiters different to what we had seen before except that they were better dressed. One of them, pointing to the shore, drew his hand round the northern horizon as far as the south west, by which he no doubt intended to instruct us that the ice, occupied that space It would, however, have answered equally well for the land, supposing the coast beyond what we saw to have taken a circuitous direction. With the view of having this explained, I took him to the side of the ship on which the land was, and intimated a desire that he would delineate the coast ; but he evidently did not understand me, as he and his companions licked their hands, stroked their breasts, and then went into their boats and paddled on shore.

The apparently good-natured disposition of these people, and indeed of the whole of their tribe upon the coast to this advanced position, was a source of the highest gratification to us all, as it regarded Captain Franklin's welfare, for it was natural to conclude, that the whole race, which we had reason to think extended a considerable distance to the eastward, would partake of the same friendly feeling, and what was by many considered a material obstacle to his success, would thereby be removed   At this place in particular, where the natives appeared to be so numernus that they could have overpowered his party in a minute, it was gratifying to find them so well disposed.

After the natives were gone, we stood to the north-westward, in the hope that the wind, which had been a long time in the north-eastern quarter, would remain steady until we ascertained the point of conjunction of the ice and the land, which, from its position when seen in the morning, there was much reason to suppose would be near the extreme point of land in view from the mast-head.   Unfortunately, while we were doing this, the wind fell light, and gradually drew round to the north-westward; and apprehending it might get so far in that direction as to embay the ship between the land and the ice, it became my duty to consider the propriety of awaiting the result of such a change, knowing the necessity of keeping the ship in open water, and at all times, as far as could be done, free from risk, in order to insure her return to the rendezvous in Kotzebue Sound.   There was at this time no ice in sight from the ship, except a berg that was aground in-shore of her, and though a blink round the northern horizon indicated ice in that direction, yet the prospect was so flattering that a general regret was entertained that an attempt to effect the north-eastern passage did not form the object of the expedition   We all felt the greatest desire to advance, but considering what would be the consequences of any accident befalling the ship, which might either oblige her to quit these seas at once, or prevent her returning to them a second year, it was evident that by her being kept in open water was paramount to every other consideration; particularly as she had been furnished with a decked launch, well adapted by her size to prosecute a service of this nature   It was one of those critical situations in which an officer is sometimes unavoidably placed, and had further discovery depended upon the Blossom alone, it is probable I should have proceeded at all hazards. My orders, however, being positive to avoid the chance of being beset in the ship, I considered only how I could most beneficially employ both vessels, and, at the same time, comply with the spirit of my instructions. Thus circumstanced, I determined to get hold of the barge as soon as possible, and to despatch her along the coast, both with a view of rendering Captain

Franklin's party the earliest possible assistance, and of ascertaining how far it was possible for a boat to go Not a moment was to be lost in putting this project in execution, as the middle of August was arrived, and we could not calculate on a continuance of the fine weather with which we had hitherto been favoured. We accordingly returned towards Icy Cape, in order to join the barge which was surveying in that direction.

We passed along the land in about eight fathoms water until near Icy Cape, when we came rather suddenly into three fathoms and three quarters, but immediately deepened the soundings again to seven . the next cast, however, was four fathoms , and not knowing how soon we might have less, the ship was immediately brought to an anchor Upon examination with the boats, several successive banks were found at about three quarters of a mile apart, lying parallel with the coast line Upon the outer ones, there were only three and a half or four fathoms, and upon the inner bank, which had hitherto escaped notice from being under the sun, so little water that the sea broke constantly over it Between the shoals there were nine and ten fathoms, with very irregular casts. These shoals lie immediately off Icy Cape, where the land takes an abrupt turn to the eastward, and are probably the effect of a large river, which here empties itself into the sea , though they may be occasioned by heavy ice grounding off the point, and being fixed to the bottom, as we found our anchor had so firm a hold, that in attempting to weigh it the chain cable broke, after enduring a very heavy strain.

This cape, the farthest point reached by Captain Cook, was at the time of its discovery very much encumbered with ice, whence it received its name , none, however was now visible. The cape is very low, and has a large lake at the back of it, which receives the water of a considerable river, and communicates with the sea through a narrow channel much encumbered with shoals There are several winter habitations of the Esquimaux upon the cape, which were afterwards visited by Lieutenant Belcher. The main land on both sides of Icy Cape, from Wainwright Inlet on one side to Cape Beaufort on the other, is flat, and covered with swampy moss. It presents a line of low mud cliffs, between which and a shingly beach that every where forms the coast-line there is a succession of narrow lakes capable of being navigated by baidars or small boats. Off here we saw a great many black whales—more than I remember ever to have seen, even in Baffin's Bay.

After the boats had examined the shoal outside the ship, we attempted to weigh the anchor, but in so doing we broke first the messenger, and afterwards the chain, by which the anchor was lost, as I before mentioned, and the buoy-rope having been carried away in letting it go, it was never recovered.

We passed over two shoals in three and four fathoms, deepening the water to ten and eleven fathoms between them, and then held our ground for the night. A thick fog came on towards morning, which lasted until noon, when it cleared away, and we had the satisfaction to be joined by the barge.

Since our separation, Mr. Elson had kept close along the beach, and ascertained the continuity of the land from the spot where the ship quitted the coast to this place, thereby removing all doubts on that head, and proving that Captain Franklin would not find a passage south of the cape to which I had given his name. The soundings were every where regular, and the natives always friendly, though not numerous Their habitations were invariably upon low strips of sand bordering upon some brackish lakes, which extended along the coast in such a manner, that in case the ice was driven against it, a good inland navigation might be performed, transporting a small boat across the narrow necks that separate them

Drift-wood was every where abundant, though least so on such parts of the coast as had a western aspect, but without any apparent reason for this difference. After supplying the barge with water, we beat to the northward together, but found so strong a south westerly current running round Icy Cape, that, the ship being light, we could gain nothing to the windward; and observing that the barge had the advantage of us by keeping in-shore, and that we were only a hindrance to her, I made her signal to close us, and prepared her for the interesting service in view. My intentions were no sooner made known than I had urgent applications for the command of the barge from the superior officers of the ship, who, with the ardour natural to their profession when any enterprise is in view, came forward in the readiest manner, and volunteered their services, but Mr Elson, the master, who had hitherto commanded the boat, had acquitted himself so much to my satisfaction, that I could not in justice remove him, more especially at a moment when the service to be performed was inseparable from risk. Mr. Smyth the senior mate of the ship, was placed with Mr Elson, who had besides under his command a crew of six seamen and two marines

My instructions to Mr. Elson were to trace the shore to the northeastward as far as it was possible for a boat to navigate, with a view to render the earliest possible assistance to Captain Franklin, and to obtain what information he could of the trending of the coast and of the position of the ice He was also directed to possess himself of facts which, in the event of the failure of the other expedition, would enable us to form a judgment of the probable success which might attend an attempt to effect a north-eastern passage in this quarter and further, he was to avoid being beset in the ice, by returning immediately the wind should get to the north-west or westward, and not to prolong his absence from the ship beyond the first week in September. He was at the same time ordered to place landmarks and directions in conspicuous places for Captain Franklin's guidance ; and if possible, on his return, to examine the shoals off Icy Cape.

We steered together to the northward with foggy weather until midnight on the 17th, when I made Mr. Elson's signal to part company, and he commenced his interesting expedition with the good wishes of all on board. We continued our course to the northward until four o'clock in the morning of the 18th, when the fog, as is ususal in the neighbourhood of the ice, cleared away, and we saw the main body in latitude 71° 07' N. nearly in the same position we had left it some days before. It was loose at the edge, but close within, and consisted of heavy floes. We tacked near it, and found it trending from E to S W (mag.) There were no living things near it, except a few tern and kittiwakes, which was rather remarkable, as the edge of the ice is usually frequented by herds of amphibious animals. As we receded from the ice, the fog again thickened, and latterly turned to small snow. The temperature was about the freezing point. At noon the sun broke through, and we found ourselves in latitude 70° 18' N , and by the soundings about twelve miles from the land, which was not seen. By this we discovered that instead of gaining twenty miles to the eastward, we had lost four. by which it was evident that a current had been running S 58° W. a mile an hour; off this place, however, it was found upon trial to run S 60° W only half a mile per hour. The fog afterwards came on very thick and remained so during the day.

Finding the inconvenience from the current off Icy Cape, I steered to the westward, to ascertain how near the ice approached the coast in that direction, and on the 20th, I stood in for the land which is about midway between Cape Beaufort and Icy Cape, to verify some points of the survey. About this time immense flocks of ducks, consisting entirely of young ones and females, were seen migrating to the southward. The young birds could not fly : and not having the instinct to avoid the ship in time, one immense flock was run completly over by her. They, however, were more wary when the boats were lowered. and successfully avoided our attempts to shoot them, by diving. At the place where we landed, there was a long lake between us and the main land , and our walk was confined to a strip of shingle and sand, about 150 yards wide, and about six feet above the level of the sea. In the sheltered parts of it there were a few flowers, but no new species. The lake was connected with the sea at high tide, and was consequently salt ; but we obtained some water sufficiently fresh to drink by digging at a distance of less than a yard from its margin. a resource of which the natives appeared to be well aware.

An abundance of drift wood was heaped upon the upper part of the shingle. The trees were torn up by the roots, and some were worm-eaten, but the greater part appeared to have been only a short time at sea, and all of it, that I examined, was pine

From the desolate appearance of the coast where we landed, I scarcely expected to find a human being, but we had no sooner put our foot ashore than a biadar full of people landed a short distance from us. Her crew consisted of three grown-up males and four females, besides two infants. They were as ready as their neighbours to part with what they had in exchange for trifles; esteeming our old brass buttons above all other articles, excepting knives There was a blear-eyed old hag of the party, who separated from her companions, and seated herself upon a piece of drift wood at a little distance from the baidar, and continued there, muttering an unintelligible language, and apparently believing herself to be holding communion with that invisible world to which she was fast approaching. Though in her dotage, her opinion was consulted, and on more than one occasion in a mysterious manner. We afterwards witnessed several instances of extremely old women exercising great influence over the younger part of the community. On this occasion I purchashed a bow and quiver of arrows for a brooch. The man who sold them referred the bargain to the old woman above-mentioned, who apparently disapproved of it, as the brooch was returned, and the bow and arrows re-demanded

The males of this party were all provided with lip ornaments; and we noticed a gradation in the size, corresponding to the ages of the party who wore them, as well as a distinction in the nature of them Two young lads had the orifices in their lips quite raw they were about the size of a crow-quill, and were distended with small cylindrical pieces of ivory, with a round knob at one end to prevent their falling out. For some time after the operation has been performed, it is necessary to turn the cylinders frequently, that they may not adhere to the festering flesh: in time this action becomes as habitual with some of them as that of twirling the mustachois is with a Musulman. In the early stage it is attended with great pain, the blood sometimes flowing, and I have seen tears come into the boys' eyes while doing it. Lip ornaments, with the males, appear to correspond with the tattooing of chins of the females; a mark which is universally borne by the women throughout both the eastern and western Esquimaux tribes: the custom of wearing the labrets, however, does not extend much beyond the Mackenzie River. The children we saw to-day had none of these marks; a girl, about eleven, had one line only; and a young woman, about twenty-three years of age, the mother of the infants, had the three perfect. One of her children was rolling in the bottom of the bai-

dar, with a large piece of seal-blubber in its mouth, sucking it as an
European child would coral   The mother was rather pretty, and
allowed her portrait to be taken   At first she made no objection to
being gazed at as steadfastly as was necessary for an indifferent artist to accomplish his purpose, but latterly she shrunk from the
scrutiny with a bashfulness that would have done credit to a more
civilized female, and on my attempting to uncover her head, she
cast a look of inquiry at her husband, who vociferated "naga," when
she very properly refused to comply.   The young men were very
importunate and curious, even to annoyance, and there is little
doubt that if any persons in our dress had fallen in with a powerful
party of these savages, they would very soon have been made to exchange their suit of broad cloth for the more humble dress of furs.
Their honesty was not more conspicuous than their moderation, as
they appropriated to themselves several articles belonging to Mr.
Collie

Dunng three hours that we were on shore, the tide fell one foot;
it had subsided eighteen inches from its greatest height when we
first landed, and when we put off was still ebbing to the S. S. W. at
the rate of half a mile an hour   Four hours afterwards, when by
our observations on shore it must have changed, it ran N 1-2 E.
at the same rate, and afforded another instance of the flood coming
from the southward

A thick fog came on after we returned on board.   The next
morning we closed with the land near Cape Beaufort, with a view
of trying the veins of coal in its neighbourhood, as we were very
short of that article, but the wind veered round to the N. N. W,
and by making it a lee shore prevented the boats landing, and rendered it expedient for the ship. which was very light, and hardly
capable of beating off, to get an offing.   The bay was fine, and
afforded an opportunity of verifying some of our points, which we
had the satisfaction to find quite correct.   The next day the wind
veered to S. S. W and then to the westward.   Throughout the
23d, 24th, and part of the 25th, it blew hard, with a short head sea,
thick weather, and latterly with snow showers, which obliged the
ship to keep at so great a distance that the land expedition would
have passed her unobserved, had they been in progress along the
coast   With these winds we kept off the coast.   The night of the
25th was clear and cold, with about four hours' darkness, during
which we beheld a brilliant display of the aurora borealis, which
was the first time that phenomenon had been exhibited to us in this
part of the world.   It first appeared in an arch extending from W.
by N to N E mag. (by the north), passing through benetnasch,
$\beta. \gamma$. Ursæ Maj. and β Aurigæ, decidedly dimming their lustre.
The arch, shortly after it was formed, broke up, but united again,

threw out a few coruscations, and then entirely disappeared. Soon after, a new display began in the direction of the western foot of the first arch, preceded by a bright flame, from which emanated coruscations of a pale straw-colour. An almost simultaneous movement occurred at both extremities of the arch, until a complete segment was formed of wavering perpendicular radii. As soon as the arch was complete, the light became greatly increased; and the prismatic colours, which had before been faint, now shone forth in a very brilliant manner. The strongest colours, which were also the outside ones, were pink and green, the centre colour was yellow, and the intermediate ones on the pink side purple and green, all of which were as imperceptibly blended as in the rainbow. The green was the colour nearest the zenith. This magnificent display lasted a few minutes; and the light had nearly vanished, when the N E quarter sent forth a vigorous display, and nearly at the same time a corresponding coruscation emanated from the opposite extremity. The western foot of the arch then disengaged itself from the horizon, crooked to the northward, and the whole retired to the N. E. quarter, where a bright spot blazed for a moment, and all was darkness. I have been thus particular in my description, because the appearance was unusually brilliant, and because very few observations on this phenomenon have been made in this part of the world. There was no noise audible during any part of our observations, nor were the compasses perceptibly affected. The night was afterwards squally, with cumuli and nimbi, which deposited showers of sleet and snow as they passed over us, the wind being rather fresh throughout.

On the 26th the weather was moderate, and being off Point Hope, on which there were several lakes and a great abundance of driftwood, the boats were sent to endeavour to procure a supply of fuel and water. We had completed only one turn, and buried a bottle for Captain Franklin, when the wind freshened from the S W and prevented a second landing. During the afternoon we turned to windward, with the wind blowing fresh from the westward.

From the time of our passing Beering's Strait up to the 23d instant, we enjoyed an almost uninterrupted series of fine weather; during which we had fortunately surveyed the whole of the coast from Cape Prince of Wales as far to the northward as I deemed it proper to go, consistent with the necessity of keeping the ship, at all times, in open water and in safety. Now, however, there appeared to be a break up, and a commencement of westerly winds, which made the whole of this coast a lee shore, and together with several hours of darkness, rendered it necessary to keep the ship at a distance from the land. In doing this the chances were equal that the land expedition, in the event of its success, would pass her.

I therefore determined to repair to the rendezvous in Kotzebue Sound, and, as nothing further was to be done at sea, to await there the arrival of our boat and of Captain Franklin's expedition Accordingly on the 27th we made Cape Krusenstern, and on the following evening anchored at Chamisso Island nearly in our former situation.

Directly the ship was secured, two boats were despatched to the islands to examine the state of the rivulets, and ascertain whether the cask of flour, that had been buried for Captain Franklin's use, had been molested: our suspicion of its safety having been excited by observing six baidars upon the beach opposite the anchorage, none of which ventured off to the ship as was usual.   On the return of the boat from Chamisso Island we learned that there was not a drop of water to be had, in consequence of the streams at which we had formerly filled our casks being derived from beds of thawing ice and snow which were now entirely dissolved

By the other boat, we found, as we expected, that the cask of flour had been dug up and broken open, that the hoops had been taken away, and that the flour had been strewed about the ground, partly in a kneaded state.   Suspicion immediately fell upon the natives encamped upon the peninsula, which was strengthened by the manner in which they came off the next morning, dancing and playing a tambourine in the boats, a conciliatory conduct with which we had never before been favoured   When they came alongside, they were shown a handful of flour, and were referred to the island upon which the cask had been buried   Their guilty looks showed that they perfectly understood our meaning; but they strongly protested their innocence, and as a proof that they could not possibly have committed the theft, they put their fingers to their tongues, and sp   with disgust, to show us how much they disliked t   little considering that the fact of their   of their having tasted it but   as I wished as much as   of the land expedition

The baidars of these people   seen, excepting those of the St Lawrence   resembled in having a flap made of walrus skin attached   wale for the purpose of keeping their bows and arrows dry. The natives had a great variety of articles for sale, all of which they readily parted with, except their bows, arrows, and spears, and these they would on no account sell.   Several old men were among their party, all of whom sat in the stern of the boat, a deference which, as I have already said, we everywhere observed to be paid to age by the younger part of this tribe.   When they had sold all they intended to part with, and had satisfied their curiosity, they paddled on shore, well satisfied, no doubt, at having escaped detection

The next morning the boats were sent to find water and to dig wells upon Chamisso Island, as we had but nine days' supply on board at very reduced allowance. In the mean time I paid a visit to the Esquimaux, who were on their travels towards home with cargoes of dried salmon, oil, blubber, and skins, which they had collected in their summer excursion along the coast When they perceived our boat approaching the shore, they despatched a baidar to invite us to their encampment, and as we rowed towards the place together, observing with what facility they passed our boats, they applied their strength to their paddles, and, exulting on the advantage they possessed, left us far behind. It was perfectly smooth and calm, or this would not have been the case, as their boats have no hold of the water, and are easily thrown back by a wave, and when the wind is on the side, they have the greatest difficulty in keeping them in the right direction.

The shallowness of the water obliged our boat to land a short distance from the village; and the natives, who by this time had hauled up their baidair, walked down to meet us with their arms drawn in from their sleeves, and tucked up inside their frocks They were also very particular that every one should salute us, which they did by licking their hands, and drawing them first over their own faces and bodies, and then over ours. This was considered the most friendly manner in which they could receive us, and they were officiously desirous of ingratiating themselves with us, but they would on no account suffer us to approach their tents, and, when we urged it, seemed determined to resist, even with their weapons, which were carefully laid out upon the low piece of ground near them They were resolved, nevertheless, that we should partake of their hospitality, and seating us upon a rising ground, placed before us strips of blubber in wooden bowls, and whortle-berries mashed up with fat and oil, or some such heterogeneous stuff   c, b we did not taste it   seeing   id not partake of their fare,   commenced a brisk   of   'n   facls and   such re word ed a great quan   lly speaking, they were ho   in their dealings, exc g their goods with us when they were in doubt about a bargain, until they had   it to a second person, or more commonly to some of the old women. If they approved of it, our offer was accepted; if not, they took back their goods. On several occasions, however, they tried to impose upon us with fish-skins, ingeniously put together to represent a whole fish, though entirely deprived of their original contents · but this artifice succeeded only once The natives, when detected in other attempts, laughed heartily, and treated the matter as a fair practical joke. Their cunning and inven-

tion were farther exhibited in the great pains which they took to
make us understand, before we parted, that the flour had been
stolen by a party who had absconded on seeing the ship.   Their
gestures clearly intimated to us that the attention of this party had
been attracted to the spot by the newly-turned earth, though we
had replaced it very carefully, on which, it appears, they began to
dig, and, to their great surprise and joy no doubt they soon discovered the cask.   They knocked off the hoops with a large stone,
and then tasted the contents, which they intimated were very nau-
scous.   The thieves then packed up the hoops, and carried them
over the hills to another part of the country.

We patiently heard the whole of this circumstantial account, which
we had afterwards great reason to believe was an invention of their
own, and that they had some of the flour secreted in their tents,
which, no doubt, was the reason of their dislike to our approaching
them

In the forenoon one of our seamen found a piece of board upon
Chamisso Island, upon which was written, in Russian characters,
"Rurick, July 28th, 1816," and underneath it "Blaganome erin-
oy, 1820."   The former was, of course, cut by Kotzebue when he
visited the island; and the latter, I suppose, by Captain Von Ba-
silief Schismareff, his lieutenant, who paid this island a second visit
in 1820

Upon the low point of this island there was another party of Esquimaux, who differed in several particulars from those upon the
peninsula.   I was about to pay them a visit, but early in the morning our peninsular friends came off to say they were going away;
and as I wished to see a little more of them before they left us, I
deferred going there until the next day, by which I lost the opportunity of seeing those upon Chamisso, as they decamped in the evening unobserved   Like the party on the peninsula, they were on
their return to winter quarters, with large heaps of dried fish, seals,
flesh, oil, skins, and all the necessary appurtenances to an Esquimaux residence.   They had four tents and several baidars, which
were turned over upon their nets and fishing-tackle for protection,
In one of their tool-chests was found a part of an elephant's tooth,
of the same species as those which were afterwards collected in
Escholtz Bay.   They had the same aversion to our officers approaching their habitations as the party before described on the peninsula,
and in all probability it proceeded from the same cause, as Mr. Osmer detected a young girl eating some of our flour mixed up with
oil and berries.   On seeing him she ran hastily into her tent, and
in so doing spilt some of the mixture, which led to the discovery.

The women of this party differed from the females we had hitherto
seen, in having the septum of the nose pierced, and a large blue bead

strung upon a strip of whalebone passed through the orifice, the bead hanging as low as the opening of the mouth   One of them, on receiving a large stocking needle, thrust it into the orifice, or as some of the seamen said, "spritsail-yarded her nose."   A youth of the party, who had not yet had his lips perforated, wore his hair in bunches on each side of the head, after the fashion of the women, which I notice as being the only instance of the kind we had met with, and which I trust does not indicate a nearer resemblance to a class of individuals mentioned by Langsdorff as existing in Oonalashka under the denomination of Schopans.

Red and blue beads, buttons, knives, and hatchets were as usual the medium through which every thing they would part with was purchased.   The men were more excited than usual by a looking-glass, which, after beholding their own features in it, and admiring alternately the reflection of their head and lip ornaments, they very inconsiderately carried it to one of their party who was perfectly blind, and held before his face.   As this was done rather seriously, certainly without any appearance of derision, it is possible that they imagined it might produce some effect upon his sight

On landing at the encampment on the peninsula, I was received in a more friendly manner even than the day before.   Each of the natives selected a friend from among our party, and, like the Gambier islanders, locked their arms in ours, and led us to a small piece of rising ground near their tents, where we sat down upon broad planks and deer-skins.   A dried fish was then presented to each of us, and a bowl of cranberries mashed up with sorrel and rancid train-oil was passed round, after the manner of the Kraikees on the Asiatic shore ; but, however palatable this mixture might have been to our hosts, it was very much the reverse to us, and none of our party could be induced to partake of it, except Mr. Osmer, who did so to oblige me at the expense of his appetite for the rest of the day. The Esquimaux were surprised at our refusal of this offer, and ridiculed our squeamishness ; and by way of convincing us what bad judges we were of good cheer, five of them fell to at the bowl, and with their two fore fingers very expeditiously transferred the contents to their own mouths, and cleansing their fingers upon the earth, gave the vessel to one of the women

The whole village then assembled, better dressed than they had been on our first visit, and ranged themselves in a semicircle in front of us, preparatory to an exhibition of one of their dances, which merits a description, as it was the best of the kind we saw.   A double ring was formed in front of us by men seated upon the grass, and by women and children in the background, who composed the orchestra   The music at the beginning was little better than a buzz of " Ungna-aya, Amna-aya !"—words which always constitute the burthen of an Esquimaux song.   The leader of the party, a strong athletic man, jumped into the ring and threw himself into various attitudes, which would have better become a pugilist than a performer on the light fantastic toe!   As his motions became violent, he manifested his inspiration by loud exclamations of Ah! Ah! until he became exhausted, and withdrew, amidst shouts of approbation from all present, and the signal was given for new performers   Five younger men then leaped into the area, and again exhibited feats of activity, which, considering the heavy clothing that encumbered their limbs were very fair   A simple little girl about eight years of age, dressed for the occasion, joined the jumpers, but did not imitate their actions.   Her part consisted in waving her arms and inclining her body from side to side   The poor little thing was so abashed that she did not even lift her head or open her eyes during the whole of her performance, and seemed glad when it was over, though she was not unmindful of the praise bestowed upon her exertions

The violent action of the male performers required that they should occasionally take breath, during which time the music was lowered, but as soon as the ring was re-furnished it again became loud and animated   A grown-up female now formed one of the party, and appeared to be the prize of contention among several young men, who repeatedly endeavoured to ingratiate themselves with her, but she as often rejected their offers and waved them away. At last an old man, all but naked, jumped into the ring, and was beginning some indecent gesticulations, when his appearance not meeting with our approbation, he withdrew, and the performance having been wrought to its heighest pitch of noise and animation ceased.

Such is the rude dance of these people, in which, as may be seen from the above description, there was neither elegance nor grace ; but on the contrary it was noisy, violent, and as barbarous as themselves.   The dancers were dressed for the occasion in their best clothes, which they considered indispensable, as they would not sell them to us until the performance was over   In addition to their usual costume, some had a kind of tippet of ermine and sable skins thrown over their shoulders, and others wore a band on their heads, with strips of skin suspended to it at every two inches, to the end of which were attached the nails of seals.

When the dance was over, they presented us with dried salmon, , and each person brought his bag of goods, which produced a brisk barter, with great fairness on all sides, and with a more than ordinary sense of propriety on theirs, in never raising or lowering their prices, and by their testifying their disapprobation of it by a groan, when it was attempted by one of our party.   But though so strict in this particular, they were not exempt from that failing so unaccountably innate in all uncivilized people, which they endeavoured to gratify in various ways, by engaging our attention at a moment when some of our trinkets were exposed to them for the purpose of selection. Suspecting their designs, however, we generally detected their thefts, and immediately received back our goods, with a hearty laugh in addition. They understood making a good bargain quite as well as ourselves, and were very wary how they received our knives and hatchets, putting their metal to the test by hacking at them with their own. If they stood the blow, they were accepted, but if, on the contrary, they were notched, they were refused. A singular way of deciding a bargain was resorted to by one of their party, almost equivalent to that of tossing up a coin. We had offered an adze for a bundle of skins, but the owner, who at first seemed satisfied with the bargain, upon reflection became doubtful whether he would not be the looser by it; and to decide the doubtful point he caught a small beetle, and set it at liberty upon the palm of his hand, anxiously watching which direction the insect should take. Finding it run towards him, he concluded the bargain to be disadvantageous to him, and took back his goods

On this day they admitted us to their habitations, and all restrictions were removed, except that upon writing in our remark books, to which they had such an objection, that they refused us any information while they were open, and with great good-nature closed them, or if we persisted, they dodged their heads and made off.

Our new acquaintances, amounting to twenty-five in number, had five tents, constructed with skins of sea-animals, strained upon poles, and for floors they had some broad planks two feet in the clear. I was anxious to learn where they obtained these, knowing that they had themselves no means of reducing a tree to the form of a plank, but I could get no information on this point: in all probability they had been purchased from the Tschutschi, or the Russians. Each tent had its baidar, and there were two to spare, which were turned upside down, and afforded a convenient house for several dogs, resembling those of Baffin's Bay, which were strapped to logs of wood to prevent their straying away. In front of these baidars there were heaps of skins filled with oil and blubber, &c., and near them some very strong nets full of dried salmon, suspended to frames made of drift wood these frames also contained, upon stretchers, the intestines of whales, which are used for a variety of purposes, particularly for the kamlaikas, a sort of shirt which is put over their skin dresses in wet weather

More provident than the inhabitants of Melville Peninsula, these people had collected an immense store of provision, if intended only for the number of persons we saw. Besides a great many skins of oil, blubber, and blood, they had about three thousand pounds of dried fish.

On the first visit to this party, they constructed a chart of the coast upon the sand, of which I took very little notice at the time. To-day, however, they renewed their labour, and performed their work upon the sandy beach in a very ingenious and intelligible manner The coast line was first marked out with a stick, and the distances regulated by the days' journeys. The hills and ranges of mountains were next shown by elevations of sand or stone, and the islands represented by heaps of pebbles, their proportions being duly attended to. As the work proceeded, some of the bystanders occasionally suggested alterations, and I removed one of the Diomede Islands which was misplaced . this was at first objected to by the hydrographer , but one of the party recollecting that the islands were seen *in one* from Cape Prince of Wales, confirmed its new position and made the mistake quite evident to the others, who seemed much surprised that we should have any knowledge of such things When the mountains and the islands were erected, the villages and fishing stations were marked by a number of sticks placed upright, in imitation of those which are put upon the coast wherever these people fix their abode. In time, we had a complete topographical plan of the coast from Point Darby to Cape Krusenstern. In this extent of coast line they exhibited a harbour and a large river situated to the southward of Cape Prince of Wales, of neither of which we had any previous knowledge. The harbour communicated with an inner basin, named Imaurook, which was very spacious, and where the water was fresh. The entrance to the outer one was so narrow, that two baidars could not paddle abreast of each other. This they explained by means of two pieces of wood, placed together, and motioning with their hands that they were paddling They then drew them along till they came to the channel, when they were obliged to follow one another, and, when through, they took up their position, as before. The river was between this harbour and the cape, and by their description it wound among lofty mountains, and between high rocky cliffs, and extended further than any of the party had been able to trace in their baidars. Its name was Youp-nut, and its course must he between the ranges of mountains, at the back of Cape Prince of Wales At this last mentioned cape, they placed a village, called Iden-noo ; and a little way inland another, named Kmk-a-ghee, which was their own winter residence. Beyond Imau-rook there was a bay, of which we have no knowledge, named I-art-so-rook. A point ,beyond this, which I took to be the entrance to Norton Sound, was the extent of their geographical knowledge in that direction.

To the Diomede Islands they gave the names of Noo-nar-boak ; Ignailook, and Oo-ghe-eyak ; King's Island, Oo-ghe-a-book ; and Sledge Island, Ayak. It is singular that this island, which was named Sledge Island by captain Cook, from the circumstance of one of these implements being found upon it, should be called by a word signifying the same thing in the Esquimaux language. For East Cape they had no name, and they had no knowledge of any other part of the Asiatic coast. Neither Schismareff Bay nor the inlet -in the Bay of Good Hope was delineated by them, though they were not ignorant of the former when it was pointed out to them. It has been supposed that these two inlets communicate, and that the Esquimaux, who intimated to Kotzebue that a boat could proceed nine days up the latter and would then find the sea, alluded to this junction ; but our rude hydrographers knew of no such communication ; which I think they certainly would, had it existed, as by pursuing that course they would have avoided a passage by sea or round Cape Espenburg, which in deep-laden boats is attended with risk, from the chance of their not being able to land upon the coast. They would, at all events, have preferred an inland navigation had it not been very circuitous

We passed the greater part of the day with these intelligent people, who amused us the whole time in some way or other. The chief, previous to embarkation examined every part of our boat, and was highly pleased with the workmanship, but he seemed to regret that so much iron had been expended where thongs would have served as well. He was more astonished at the weight of a sounding lead than at any thing in the boat, never having felt any metal so heavy before ; iron pyrites being the heaviest mineral among this tribe.

When we were about to embark, all the village assembled and took leave of us in the usual manner of the Esquimaux tribes ; and as it was probable we should never meet again, the parting much to our annoyance, was very affectionate. A middle-aged man, who had taken the lead throughout, and who was probably their *neakoa* (or head-man) recommended us to depart from these regions, but I signified my intention of waiting some time longer, and sleeping at least twenty nights where we were, on which he shivered, and drew his arms in from his sleeves to apprise us of the approaching cold. I thanked him for his advice, and making them each a parting present we took our leave. The next morning they embarked every thing, and paddled over to Escholtz Bay. After they were gone, we found some of our flour where the tents had stood, and a quantity of it secreted in a bush near the place; so that their cautious behaviour with regard to our approachinging their tents the first day was no doubt occasioned by fear of this discovery : and they afterwards secreted their plunder in a manner probably not likely to meet detection.

Among this party there was a man so crippled that he went on all fours; how it occurred we could not learn, but it was probably

in some hunting excursion, as several of his companions had deep
scars, which they intimated had been inflicted by walrusses, which
in the following year we found in great numbers off the coast   In
this party we detected a difference of dialect from what we had
heard in general, which made their objection to our writing in our
books the more provoking, as it prevented us recording any of the
variations, except in regard to the negative particle *no*, which with
other parties was *naga*, and with these *aun-ga*   The females were
provided with broad iron bracelets, which we had not seen before;
and by their having four or five of them upon each wrist, it appeared that this metal, so precious with the tribes to the northward, was
with them less rare; nevertheless it is very probable that they intended to appropriate to this purpose the iron hoops they had stol-
en from us

I have said nothing of the dress or features of these people, as,
with the exception of two of them, they so nearly resemble those
already described as to render it unnecessary.   These two persons,
in the tattooing of the face, and in features, which more nearly resembled those of the Tschutschi, seemed to be allied to the tribes
on the Asiatic coast, with whom they no doubt have an occasional intercourse

On the first of September our sportsmen succeeded in bagging
several braces of ptarmigan and wild ducks, but game was not so
plentiful as might have been expected at this season of the year, in
a country so abundantly provided with berries and so scantily inhabited.   It was a pleasure to find that we could now pursue this and
other occupations free from the annoyance of moskitos; a nuisance
which, whatever it may appear at first, is in reality not trifling.   Dr.
Richardson fixes the departure of these insects from Fort Franklin
on the 11th of September: here, however, it takes place at least a
fortnight earlier.

On the 5th I visited the northern side of Escholtz Bay, and found
the country almost impassible from swamp, notwithstanding the season was so far advanced.   It seemed as if the peaty nature of
the covering obstructed the drainage of the water, which the
power of the sun had let loose during the summer, and that
the frozen state of the ground beneath prevented its escape in
that direction.   The power of the sun's rays upon the surface was
still great, and large stones and fragments of rock that had been split
by the frost were momentarily relinquishing their hold and falling
down upon the beach.   A thermometer exposed upon a piece of
black cloth rose to 112°, and in the shade stood at 62°.   On the
side of the hill that sloped to the southward the willow and the birch
grew to the height of eighteen feet, and formed so dense a wood
that we could not penetrate it.   The trees bordering upon the beach

were quite dead, apparently in consequence of their bark having been rubbed through by the ice, which had been forced about nine feet above high-water mark, and had left there a steep ridge of sand and shingle.   The berries were at this time in great perfection and abundance, and proved a most agreeable addition to the salt diet of the seamen, who were occasionally permitted to land and collect them

The cliffs on this side of Choris Peninsula were composed of a green-coloured mica slate, in which the mica predominated, and contained garnets, veins of felspar, enclosing chrystals of schorl, and had its fissures filled with quartz ; but I shall avoid saying any thing on geological subjects here.

On the 6th our curiosity was excited by the appearance of two small boats under sail, which, when first seen through a light fog, were so different from the sails of the Esquimaux, that our imagination, which had latterly converted every unusual appearance in the horizon into the boats of Captain Franklin, really led us to conclude he had at length arrived , but as they rounded the point, we clearly distinguished them to be two native baidars   We watched their landing, and were astonished at the rapidity with which they pitched their tents, settled themselves, and transferred to their new habitation the contents of the baidars, which they drew out of the sea and turned bottom upwards   On visiting their abode an hour after they landed, every thing was in as complete order as if they had been established there a month, and scarcely any thing was wanting to render their situation comfortable   No better idea could have been conveyed to us of the truly independent manner in which this tribe wander about from place to place, transporting their houses. and every thing necessary to their comfort, than that which was afforded on this occasion.   Nor were we less struck with the number of articles which their ingenuity finds the means of disposing in their boats, and which, had we not seen them disembarked, we should have doubted the possibility of their having been crammed into them   From two of these they landed fourteen persons, eight tent poles, forty deer skins, two kyacks, many hundred weight of fish, numerous skins of oil, earthen jars for cooking, two living foxes, ten large dogs, bundles of lances, harpoons, bows and arrows, a quantity of whalebone, skins full of clothing, some immense nets, made of hide, for taking small whales and porpoises, eight broad blanks, masts, sails, paddles, &c , besides sea-horse hides and teeth, and a variety of nameless articles always to be found among the Esquimaux.

They received us in the most friendly and open manner, and their conduct throughout was so different from that of their predecessors, that had we had no proof of the latter being guilty of the theft on oui flour, this difference of conduct would have afforded a strong presumption against them. The party consisted of two families, each of which had its distinct property, tents, baidai, &c They were in feature and language nearly connected with the King-a-ghee party, and from what they told us, resided near them ; but to judge from their dresses and establishment they were of much lower condition. However, the women had the same kind of beads in their ears, and sewn upon their dresses, and had evidently been to the same market We remarked, however, in two of the young ladies a custom which, when first discovered, created considerable laughter. When they moved, several bells were set ringing, and, on examining their persons, we discovered that they had each three or four of these instruments under their clothes, suspended to their waists, hips, and one even lower down, which was about the size of a dustman's bell, but without a clapper. Whether they had disposed of them in this manner as charms, or through fear, it was impossible to say ; but by their polished surface, and the manner in which they were suspended, they appeared to have long occupied these places. They were certainly not hung there for convenience, as the large one, in particular, must have materially incommoded the ladies in their walking. One of our party suggested that this large bell might, perhaps, be appropriated to the performance of a ceremony mentioned by Muller, in his " Voyages from Asia to America," &c. p 28., where he states that the bond of friendship or enmity depends upon a guest rinsing his mouth with the contents of the cup, which formed an indispensable part of a very singular custom among the Tschutschi, the people of Cashemir, and some other countries.*

Among other things, this party had small bags of resin, which appeared to be the natural exudation of the pine From their constantly chewing it, it did not seem difficult to be had ; and as no trees of this nature, that we were acquainted with, grew upon the coast, we were anxious to learn whence they had procured it, but we could not make our acquaintances understand our wishes

An old lady, who was the mother of the two girls with the bells, invited me into her tent, where I found her daughters seated amidst a variety of pots and pans, containing the most unsavoury messes, highly repugnant to both the sight and smell of a European, though not at all so to the Esquimaux. These people are in the habit of collecting certain fluids for the purposes of tanning , and that, judging from what took place in the tent, in the most open manner, in the presence of all the family.

The old matron was extremely good-natured, lively, and loqua-

* M. Paulus venetus, Witsen, and Trigaut.

cious; and took great pleasure in telling us the name of every thing, by which she proved more useful than any of our former visiters; and had she but allowed us time to write down one word before she furnished another, we should have greatly extended our vocabularies; but it appeared to her, no doubt, that we could write as fast as she could dictate, and that the greater number of words she supplied, the more thankful we should be. So far from this party having any objection to our books, to which the former one had manifested the greatest repugnance, they took pleasure in seeing them, and were very attentive to the manner in which every thing was committed to paper.

The daughters were fat good-looking girls; the eldest, about thirteen years of age, was marked upon the chin with a single blue line; but the other, about ten, was without any tattooing. I made a sketch of the eldest girl, very much to the satisfaction of the mother, who was so interested in having her daughter's picture, and so impatient to see it finished, that she snatched away the paper several times to observe the progress I was making. The father entered the tent while this was going forward, and observing what I was about, called to his son to bring him a piece of board that was lying outside the tent, and to scrape it clean, which indeed was very necessary. Having procured a piece of plumbago from his wife, he seated himself upon a heap of skins, threw his legs across, and very good-humouredly commenced a portrait of me, aping my manner and tracing every feature with the most affected care, whimsically applying his finger to the point of his pencil instead of a penknife, to the great diversion of his wife and daughters. By the time I had finished my sketch, he had executed his, but with the omission of the hat, which, as he never wore one himself, he had entirely forgotten; and he was extremely puzzled to know how to place it upon the head he had drawn.

On meeting with the Esquimaux, after the first salutation is over an exchange of goods invariably ensues, if the party have any thing to sell, which is almost always the case, and we were no sooner seated in the tent than the old lady produced several bags, from which she drew forth various skins, ornamental parts of the dress of her tribe, and small ivory dolls, allowing us to purchase whatever we liked. Our articles of barter were necklaces of blue beads, brooches, and cutlery, which no sooner came into the possession of our hostess than they were transferred to a stone vessel half filled with train-oil, where they underwent an Esquimaux purification.

We found amongst this party a small Russian coin of the Empress Catherine, and the head of a halberd, which had been converted into a knife; both of which were evidence of the communication that must exist between their tribe and those of the Asiatic coasts opposite.

We returned on board with a boat full of dried salmon, and the next day the party visited the ship. Notwithstanding the friendly treatment they had experienced the day before, it required much persuasion to induce them to come upon deck; and even when some of them were prevailed upon to do so, they took the precaution of leaving with their comrades in the boat whatever valuable articles they had about their persons. They were shown every thing in the ship most likely to interest them, but very few objects engaged them long, and they passed by some that were of the greatest interest, to bestow their attention upon others which to us were of none, thus showing the necessity of fully understanding the nature of any thing before the mind can properly appreciate its value. The sail-maker sewing a canvass bag, and the chain cable, were two of the objects which most engaged their attention: the former from its being an occupation they had themselves often been engaged in, and the latter as exhibiting to them the result of prodigious labour, as they would naturally conclude that our chains—though so much larger and of so much harder a material than their own—were made in the same manner. The industry and ingenuity of the Esquimaux are, however, displayed in nothing more than in the fabrication of chains, two or three of which we met with cut out of a solid piece of ivory. On showing these people the plates of natural history in Rees's Cyclopædia, they were far more intelligent than might have been expected from the difficulty that naturally occurs to uncivilized people in divesting their minds of the comparative size of the living animal and its picture. But the Esquimaux are very superior in this respect to the South Sea Islanders, and immediately recognized every animal they were acquainted with that happened to be in the book, and supplied me with the following list of them:—

English Names.	Esquimaux Names.	English Names.	Esquimaux Names.
Squirrel	*Tsey-kereck.*	Porpoise	*Agh-bee-zeeak*
Fox	*Kiock-toot.*	Dog	*Koo-neak.*
Musk rat	*Paoona.*	Owl	*Igna-zee-wyuck.*
Rein-deer	*Tootoot.*	Falcon	*Kje-goo-ut.*
Musk ox	*Mign-ugne.*	Grouse	*A-hag-ghi-uck.*
White bear	*Tsu-nark*	Snipe	*Nuck-too-o-lit.*
Walrus	*Ei-bwo-ak*	Vulture	*Keegli-aght.*
Seal	*Kasi-goo-ak.*	Swan	*Tadi-dracht.*
Otter	*Te-ghe-ak-book*	Duck	*Ew-uck.*
Porcupine	*Igla-koo-sok.*	Puffin	*Kooli-nockt.*
Mouse	*Koobla-ook*	Plover	*Tud-gluct*
Beaver	*Ka-boo-ek*	Pelican	*Peebli-ark-took.*
Hare	*Oo-good-ligh.*	Salmon	*Ish-allook*
Goat	*Ip-na-uck.*	Flounder	*Ek-anee-luk.*

Sheep	*Ok-shulk.*	Guard fish	*Iz-nee-a-ook.*
Bull (musk ?)	*Moong-mak.*	Crab	*Edloo-azrey-uk.*
White horse	*Izoo-kar-uck.*	Shrimp	*Nowd-lennok*
Narwhal	*Tse-doo-ak.*	Lobster	*Poo-cœ-o-tuk*
Whale	*Ah-ow-look*	Butterfly	*Tai-dle-oot-zuk.*

Among which there are three animals—the goat, the sheep, and the horse—hitherto unknown upon this coast. probably the sheep may refer to the argali, which has been seen near Cook's River. By the time I had collected these names, our visiters had become impatient to join their comrades, who in like manner, finding them a long time absent, had become equally anxious on their account, and had quitted the boat in search of them, and both parties met upon deck, to their mutual satisfaction Previous to their going away we made them several useful presents of axes, knives, combs, &c. for which they seemed thankful, and offered in return a few skins, pointing at the same time to the south side of the sound, where their habitations probably were, intimating that if we went there they would give us more They then pushed off their baidars, rested on their paddles for a minute, and made off as fast as they could, to give us an idea of the swiftness of their boat, which seems to be a favourite practice.

Next day we revisited their abode, and found that the price of every article had been raised several hundred per cent, and that nothing of reasonable value would induce them to part with either bows or arrows, so that our generosity of the preceding day had not left any durable impression.

Every visit to these parties furnished some new insight into their manners, though it was but trifling. on this occasion we witnessed a smoking party in which the women and children partook equally with the men. The pipe used on this occasion was small, and would contain no more tobacco than could be consumed at a whiff. To these instruments there were attached a pricker and a strip of dog's skin, from the last of which they tore off a few hairs, and placed them at the bottom of the bowl of the pipe to prevent the tobacco, which was chopped up very fine, being drawn into the mouth with smoke The tobacco which they used had pieces of wood cut up fine with it, a custom which is no doubt derived from the Tschutschi, who use the bark of the birch-tree in this manner, and imagine it improves the quality of the herb * The pipe being charged with about a pinch of this material, the senior person present took his whiff and passed the empty pipe to the next, who replenished it and passed it on, each person in his turn inflating himself to the fullest

* Dobell's Travels in Siberia,

extent, and gradually dissipating the fumes through the nostrils. The pungency of the smoke, and the time necessary to hold the breath, occasioned considerable coughing with some of the party, but they nevertheless appeared greatly to enjoy the feast

On the 8th, Spafarief Bay, which had been but little explored by Captain Kotzebue, underwent a satisfactory examination, and was found to terminate in a small creek navigable a very short distance, and that by boats only. Its whole extent inland is about three miles, when it separates into a number of small branches communicating with several lakes, which, in the spring, no doubt, discharge a large quantity of fresh water into the sound, though at this dry season of the year they were of inconsiderable size. A little to the northward of the creek there is a pointed hill just 640 feet high by measurement, from whence we surveyed the surrounding country, and found that this side of the sound also was covered with a deep swampy moss. The summit of this hill, and indeed of all the others that were ascended in the sound, was the only part destitute of this covering. The beach was strewed with a great quantity of drift wood, some of which was in a very perfect state, and appeared to have been recently split with wedges by the natives, who had carried away large portions of the trunks to make their bows, arrows, and fishing implements. They were all pine-trees except one, which by the bark appeared to be a silver birch.

On the 10th we had the satisfaction to see the barge coming down to us under a press of canvass, and the most lively expectations were formed until she approached near enough to discover that the appointed signal of success was wanting at her mast-head. Though unfortunate in accomplishing what we most anxiously desired, her voyage was attended with advantage. We had the satisfaction to learn from her commander when he came on board that he had discovered a large extent of coast beyond the extreme cape which we had seen from the mast-head of the ship on the 15th ultimo, and which I had named after Captain Franklin; and had proceeded to the latitude of 71° 23′ 31″ N and to 156° 21′ 30″ W, where the coast formed a low narrow neck beyond which it was impossible to proceed to the eastward, in consequence of the ice being attached to the land, and extending along the horizon to the northward.

The boat had not been at this point many hours, before the wind changed to south-west, and set the whole body of ice in motion toward the land. This was a case in which Mr Elson had received strict orders to return immediately, and he accordingly began to retrace his route; but in so doing he found that, in addition to the disadvantage of a contrary wind he had to contend with a current running to the north-east at the rate of three miles and a half an hour, and with large pieces of floating ice which he found it very difficult to avoid, until he was at last obliged to anchor to prevent being carried back. It was not long before he was so closely beset in the ice, that no clear water could be seen in any direction from the hills, and the ice continuing to press against the shore, his vessel was driven upon the beach, and there left upon her broadside in a most helpless condition ; and to add to his cheerless prospect, the disposition of the natives, whom he had found to increase in numbers as he advanced to the northward, was of very doubtful character. At Point Barrow, where they were extremely numerous, their overbearing behaviour, and the thefts they openly practiced, left no doubt of what would be the fate of his little crew in the event of its falling into their power. They were in this dilemma several days, during which every endeavour was made to extricate the vessel, but without effect ; and Mr Elson contemplated sinking her secretly in a lake that was near, to prevent her falling into the hands of the Esquimaux, and then making his way along the coast in a baidar, which he had no doubt he should be able to purchase from the natives At length, however, a change of wind loosened the ice ; and after considerable labour and toil, in which the personal strength of the officers was united to that of the seamen, our shipmates fortunately succeeded in affecting their escape

The farthest tongue of land which they reached is conspicuous as being the most northerly point yet discovered on the continent of America ; and I named it Point Barrow, to mark the progress of northern discovery on each side the American continent which has been so perseveringly advocated by that distinguished member of our naval administration It lies 126 miles to the north-east of Icy Cape, and is only 146 miles from the extreme of Captain Franklin's discoveries in his progress westward from the Mackenzie River The bay which appeared to be formed to the eastward of this point I named Elson's Bay, in compliment to the officer in command of the barge ; and the extreme point of our discoveries after Captain Franklin, the commander of the land expedition. I could have wished that this point had been marked by some conspicuous headland worthy of the name bestowed upon it, but my hope is that the officer who may be so fortunate as to extend our discoveries will do him the justice to transfer his name to the first object beyond it more deserving of the honour. To the nearest conspicuous object to the southward of Point Barrow I attached the name of Smyth, in compliment to the second officer of the barge ; and to the points and inlets to the southward, I with pleasure affixed the names of the officers of the ship, whose merits entitled them to this distinction.

I will no longer anticipate the journal of these interesting proceedings, in which are recorded several particulars relating to the natives, the currents, and the geography of these regions , and by which it

is evident that the officers and crew acquitted themselves in the most
persevering and zealous manner, equally honourable to themselves
and to their country   I shall merely remark upon the facts which
the journal sets forth, that it was fortunate the ship did not continue
near the ice, as she would have been unable to beat successfully
against the current, and the violence of the gale would probably
have either entangled her amongst the ice, or have driven her on
shore

The narrative was kept by Mr Smyth, under the superintendence
of his commander, whose more important duties of surveying prevented his recording more than the necessary detail of a log-book.
In publishing it I have given the most important parts of it in Mr.
Smyth's own words, and have only compressed the matter where it
could be done with propriety and advantage.

CHAPTER XII.

NARRATIVE OF THE PROCEEDINGS OF THE BARGE OF H. M. SHIP
BLOSSOM IN QUEST OF CAPTAIN FRANKLIN, AND TO EXPLORE
THE COAST N. E. OF ICY CAPE.

After the signal was made by the Blossom on the night of the 17th of August, to carry orders into execution, the barge stood inshore, and the next morning was off Icy Cape. Having a contrary wind, she beat up along the land to the N. E., and shortly after noon the officers landed opposite a village of yourts, which was found to be deserted, and the houses to be closed up for the summer. These habitations closely resembled those of the Esquimaux, which have been already described. The country here was covered with a thick peat, which retained the water and made it very swampy and almost impassable. Upon the beach there was found an abundance of coal and drift-wood. Working to the north-eastward from this village, they discovered a shoal with only eight feet water upon it lying about 150 yards from the beach, which having deep water within it, offered a security against the ice in the event of its closing the shore, and they did not fail to bear in mind the advantage it might afford in a moment of necessity. About midnight they were visited by four baidars containing about sixty persons, from whom they expected to obtain a supply of venison, as this kind of provision is, generally speaking, abundant to the northward of Cape Lisburn, but being disappointed, they continued their progress along the land. On the morning of the 20th there was a fall of snow,

and the weather turned very cold.   They found themselves off a
village, and were visited by several baidars, the crews of which were
very anxious to get alongside the barge, and in so doing one of the
baidars was upset.   An Esquimaux dress is very ill adapted to
aquatic exercises, and persons acquainted with it would think there
was considerable danger in being plunged into the sea thus habited ;
but the natives in the other baidars did not seem to reflect upon these
consequences, and laughed most immoderately at the accident ; they,
however, went to the assistance of their friends, and rescued them
all.   It must have been a cold dip for these people, as the rigging
and masts were partially covered with ice.

About noon they landed to procure observations, and found the latitude of this part of the coast to be 70° 43′ 47″ N., and longitude from
the bearings of Wainwright Inlet, 159° 46′ W.   Here a post was erected for Capt Franklin, on which the following inscription was painted·
" Blossom's tender, Sunday, August 20th, latitude 70° 43′ N , bound
alon the coast to the N E   If Captain Franklin should pass this
place, he will probably leave some memorandum "   The coast was
here low, and more dry than that in the vicinity of Wainwright Inlet, with a beach of sand and gravel mixed, upon which there was
an abundance of coal and drift-wood.   In the the evening they
passed several yourts, but saw no inhabitants until nine o'clock, when
several came off and annoyed the crew with their importunities and
disorderly conduct.   The coast was here more populous than any
where to the southward, which their visiters probably thought a
good protection against the small force of our boat, and they were
not easily driven away

On the 21st they arrived off a chain of sandy islands lying some
distance from the main land, which I have distinguished by the name
of the Sea Horse Islands.   As the wind was light and baffling, they
landed upon several of these for observation , and tracking the boat
along the shore, at eight in the evening they arrived at the point to
which I transferred the name of Captain Franklin, from the cliff on
the main land to which I had originally given that name, as I found
by the discoveries of Mr Elson that the cliff was not actually the
coast line   From Cape Franklin, the coast, still consisting of a
chain of sandy islands lying off the main land, turned to the south-
east and united with the main land, forming a bay, on which I bestowed the name of my first lieutenant, Mr Peard   Two posts
were found erected on Cape Franklin, upon which another notice
was painted   The surface of the beach was a fine sand, but by
digging a few inches down it was mixed with coal there was here
also, as at their former station, a great quantity of drift-wood   Off
these islands they were visited by several baidars, the people in
which behaved in a very disorderly manner, attempted several de-

predations, and even cut a piece out of one of the sails of the boat, while it was lying upon the gunwale   Finding the natives inclined to part with one of their baidars, she was purchased for two hatchets, under the impression that she might be useful to the boat hereafter.   Having run twenty-nine miles along the coast to the N E , they again landed, and obtained some lunar observations   The coats here assumed a different aspect, and consisted of clay cliffs, about fifty feet high, and presented an ice formation resembling that which has been described in Escholtz Bay   The interior of the country was flat, and only partially covered with snow   A short distance to the northward of them a river discharged itself into a lake within the shingly beach, which was about twenty yards wide, and the water being perfectly fresh, they obtained a supply, and pursued their course to the north-east   Their latitude was 70° 58' 43 ' N ; and no ice had as yet been seen, even from the hills.   This excited the greatest hopes in our adventurous shipmates, who advanced quite elated at the prospect ; but they had not proceeded many miles further before some bergs were seen in the offing nearly in the same parallel in which the margin of the ice had been found by the ship ; and from the number of bergs increasing as they advanced, the sanguine expectations in which they had indulged gradually diminished. These bergs were seen off a point of land to which I gave the name of Smyth, in compliment to the officer who accompanied the boat expedition, and very deservedly obtained his promotion for that service   In the course of their run they passed a village, where the inhabitants, seeing them so near, came out of their yourts, and men, women, children, and dogs set up a loud hallooing until they were gone.   Upon Cape Smyth there was also a village, the inhabitants of which accosted them with the same hooting noises as before.

Advancing to the northward with the wind off the land, they saw the main body of ice about seven miles distant to the westward, and were much encumbered by the icebergs, which they could only avoid by repeatedly altering the course   The land from Cape Smyth, which was about forty-five feet in height, sloped gradually to the northward, and terminated in a low point which has been named Point Barrow.   From the rapidity with which the boat passed the land, there appears to have been a current setting to the north-east. The water, about half a mile from the cape, was between six and seven fathoms deep.

Wednesday, 23rd Aug.   "Arriving about two A. M off the low point, we found it much encumbered with ice, and the current setting N. W. (mag) between three and four miles an hour.   Opening the prospect on its eastern side, the view was obstructed by a barrier of ice which appeared to join with the land.   This barrier seemed high ; but as there was much refraction, in this we might

possibly have been deceived   The weather assuming a very unsettled appearance in the offing, (and the S E breeze dying away,)
we had every reason to expect the wind from the westward, and
knowing the ice to extend as far south as 71°, the consequences that
would attend such a shift were so evident, that we judged it prudent
not to attempt penetrating any farther, especially in this advanced
state of the season   Accordingly we anchored within the eighth of
a mile of the point, under shelter of an iceberg about fourteen feet
high, and from fifty to sixty feet in length, that had grounded in
four fathoms water   On the eastern side of the point there was a
village, larger than any we had before seen, consisting entirely of
yourts   The natives, on seeing us anchor, came down opposite the
boat in great numbers, but seemed very doubtful whether to treat us
as friends or enemies   We made signs of friendship to them, and
a couple of baidars reluctantly ventured off and accepted a few beads
and some tobacco, which on their return to the shore induced several others to visit us   These people were clothed like the Esquimaux we had seen on the other parts of the coast   their implements were also the same, except that we thought they were more
particular in constructing the bow, the spring of which was strengthened with whalebone

Many of the men wore, as lip ornaments, slabs of bone and stone
in an oblong shape, about three inches in length and one in breadth.
They were much more daring than any people we had before seen,
and attempted many thefts in the most open manner   Tobacco was
the most marketable article, but excepting their implements, ornaments, or dress, they had nothing worth purchasing   They were
exceedingly difficult to please, and not at all satisfied with what was
given in exchange, insisting, after a bargain had been transacted, on
having more for their articles   One of them who came alongside in
a *caiack*, having obtained some tobacco that was offered for a lance,
was resolute in not delivering up either ; and Mr Elson considering
that if such conduct was tamely submitted to they would be still
more inclined to impose, endeavoured by threats to regain the tobacco, but without effect   More boats coming off, and proving by
their audacity equally troublesome, we thought it would be most
advantageous to keep the barge under sail, which in all probability
would prevent any thing serious occurring   Before weighing, the
baidar was broken up, as her weight would materially impede our
progress in working to windward on our return, the hides were tak-
en as a covering for the deck, and the frame-work destroyed for fire-
wood.   During the time we were at anchor, the wind shifted to S
W, and we stood to the N W with a light breeze ; but finding
ourselves drifting rapidly to the northward by current, we were
again obliged to anchor, Point Barrow bearing S by E. 1-2 E two

and a half miles　　Here we remained till eight o'clock.　This point
is the termination to a spit of land, which on examination from the
boat's mast-head seemed to jut out several miles from the more regular coast line.　The width of the neck did not exceed a mile and
a half, and apparently in some places less　The extremity was
broader than any other part, had several small lakes of water on it,
which were frozen over, and the village before spoken of is situated
on its eastern shore　The eastern side of this neck trended in a S.
S. W. (mag) direction until it became lost to the eye being joined
with a body of ice that encircled the horizon in the N. E　This
union scarcely left us room to hazard an opinion which direction it
afterwards took, but from the circumstance of the current setting at
the rate of three miles and a half an hour N. E. (true), and the ice
all drifting to that quarter, we were induced to conjecture that its
continuation led well to the eastward

It was our original intention to have remained at the point till
noon, landed, and obtained if possible all the necessary observations,
besides depositing instructions for Captain Franklin; but the character of the natives entirely frustrated our plans, and obliged us, to
avoid an open rupture, to quit the anchorage—a circumstance we
greatly regretted, as we had anticipated gathering much information
respecting the coast to the eastward, and on other points of importance.　The nights had hitherto been beautifully clear and fine, and
we were very sanguine of obtaining a number of lunar distances
with the sun, being the only means we had of ascertaining correctly
our farthest easting, as the patent log, we knew, from the strength
of current, could in no way be depended on　At nine we weighed,
and, stemming the current, stood in for the low point, off which
there was an iceberg aground, on which we resolved to wait till
noon for the latitude.　On our way thither we passed another extensive iceberg aground in six fathoms water, and not more than
eight or ten feet above the surface.　At noon we were favoured
with a clear sun, and determined our lattitude to be 71° 24′ 59″ N.
Lunar anchorage bearing from the place of observation one mile
north (true); and the north-eastern part of Point Barrow S. E. 3-4
E (mag) 1 1-2′.　From which the position of Point Barrow, the
most northern part known of the American continent, is latitude
71° 23′ 31″ N., longitude 156° 21′ 30″ W　The azimuth sights
made the variation 41° east

The breeze still continuing light from the S. E. (although the
clouds were approaching from the westward), we made all sail to
the southward, and with great reluctance left this remarkable point
without being able to leave any traces of our having visited it for
Captain Franklin　The wind about one P M began gradually to
fall, and at two it was perfectly calm.　Unfortunately we were now

in too much water to anchor, and were, without the possibility of helping it, being set to the N E by the current at the rate of three miles and a half an hour. By four o'clock we had lost all we had made during the day, with a prospect, if it continued calm, of being drifted quite off the land—an accident that, had it occurred, would have placed our little vessel in a very serious situation. We were not, however, long in this state of suspense ; for an air came again from the eastward, which strengthening a little, and with the boat ahead towing, we made good progress towards the land, where, if it once more fell calm, we could retain our position with the anchor When we had by towing and pulling got within a mile of the beach (and about two miles west of the point), nineteen of the natives came down opposite us armed with bows, arrows, and spears, and im- agining that it was our intention to land, motioned us to keep off, and seemed quite prepared for hostilities Some of them were strip- ped almost naked They preserved a greater silence than we found customary among them, one only speaking at a time, and apparently interrogating us Notwithstanding this show of resistance, we still advanced nearer to the shore, as being more out of the current and favourable to our views, at the same time having the arms in read- iness in case of an attack.

When within about thirty yards of the beach, we lost the wind, and continued pulling and towing along shore, the natives walking abreast of us upon the beach. At eight P M we passed a village of eight tents and four boats, but saw neither women nor children. Whilst approaching this village, we perceived the men hauling their baidars higher up on the beach, fearful, as we supposed, that we should molest them Their dogs, as usual, set up a most abomina- ble yelling. About eleven our pedestrians began to lag, and shortly after made a general halt, watched us for a little while, and then turned back At midnight we reached Cape Smyth, and considering our- selves tolerably well secure from the ice (not having seen any until our arrival off this point on the evening before,) and the crew being much tired, we anchored, hoping that a few hours would bring a breeze—not caring from which quarter, as we felt confident that, before the ice could approach near enough to block us, we should be able to reach the Sea Horse Islands, where we made certain of being clear The night dark and cloudy.

Thursday, 24th August. At two A M , a fine breeze rising at E S. E , we weighed, but found the current so strong against us that we lost ground and anchored again the current setting north (mag) three miles and a half an hour At three we were alarmed at the sudden appearance of the ice which was drifting fast down on us No time was to be lost. The crew were instantly sent on shore with a warp We got up the anchor, and hauled within eight

34

or ten yards of the beach, it being steep enough to admit our proceeding thus close. We now began tracking the boat along, and proceeded for a short time without much difficulty , but the ice increasing fast, and the pieces getting larger, she received some violent blows   The main body nearing the shore to the distance of about 100 yards left this space less incumbered, and occasioned an increase in the rapidity of the current one knot an hour   To add to our perplexities, at five the wind freshened up at south (directly against us), and we also had the mortification to observe the ice speedily connecting with the beach, scarcely leaving an open space visible   Nothing now but the greatest exertion could extricate the boat ; and the crew, willing to make the most of every trifling advantage, gave a hearty cheer, and forced her through thick and heavy ice until we rounded a projecting point that had hitherto obstructed our view   This, however, could only be accomplished with considerable labour and risk ; for here, as in many other places, we had to track-line up cliffs, frequently covered with hard snow and ice, which, hanging a considerable distance over the water, prevented the possibility of getting round beneath   The rope was then obliged to be thrown down, and the upper end held fast, until the crew hauled themselves up one by one ; and in this manner we continued along the cliff until the beach again made its appearance   But here even we found it no easy task to walk, on account of small loose shingle, in which we often sunk to the knees ; and having the weight of the boat at the same time, it became excessively fatiguing

On opening the prospect south of this point, our spirits were greatly enlivened at perceiving the channel clear for a long way, and hoping that by constant tracking we should do much towards getting clear of the ice, we divided the crew into two parties, gave each man a dram, and sent one division on board to rest, whilst the other laboured at the line.   About eight A. M the wind freshened so heavily against us, that we contemplated whether or not it would be advantageous to make a trial with the canvass, particularly as the main body of ice was a little more distant from the shore ; but remembering our position at two P M on the preceding day, we agreed that the current was too strong, and that if we should get encircled by the ice we must inevitably be separated from the shore, carried back with the stream, or forced to sea   The difficulty of drawing the boat against so strong a wind and current became now very great, and we began to seek a place where she might be laid free of the ice.   But the straight line of coast offered us no prospect of such an asylum , we therefore determined to prosecute our first intention of persevering in our endeavours *as long as possible*   By eleven A. M. we reached a village of nine tents, and trusted through the influence of tobacco, beads, &c to receive some assis-

tance from the inhabitants. Two of them approached us at first
with some diffidence, but Mr Elson throwing the presents on shore,
and myself going to meet them, after much gesticulation denoting
peaceable intentions, we joined company. The ratification of rubbing noses and cheeks being over, a leaf of tobacco given to each
soon gained their confidence. One of them, an old man, seemed
very thankful for his present, offering me any part of his garment as
a reimbursement, which I declined accepting. Seeing so friendly
an interview, several more ventured towards us, and learning from
their companions the treasures I possessed, were very eager to obtain some. By a few signs I easily made them understand that their
assistance at the track-line would be amply rewarded. Six or seven
directly took hold of the rope, and our people relaxing a little in
their exertions, though continuing at the line, we proceeded along
gaily; but I was frequently obliged to have recourse to the presents
to keep them pulling. We had not passed the tents more than half
a mile when a new and a very serious difficulty presented itself—
the mouth of a river into which the current set with great velocity,
carrying with it large masses of ice. After many attempts we succeeded in getting a line across, but had no sooner accomplished it,
than it broke, and our repeated trials for a long time were unsuccessful. Eventually we managed to overcome this obstacle, and
had just got the boat to the opposite shore when she grounded;
and the current setting strong against her, all our exertions to get
her afloat were ineffectual. A few minutes before this accident,
Mr Elson, who was on board, hailed me, saying that the channel
after crossing the river looked more favourable than ever. Cheered
by this report, we worked harder, but so quick was the ice in its
movement, that in a few moments we were enclosed on all sides.
Nothing more towards freeing the boat could now be done, therefore we carried out her anchors to the shore and secured her, con-
templating a retreat by land should we not be so fortunate as to get
clear. On looking to the southward, we found the ice perfectly
compact, and connected with the shore, not leaving visible a space
of water three yards in diameter. The crew now enjoyed a little
rest, and Mr Elson decided that we should remain by the boat
until the 1st of September, on which day, should no chance appear
of liberating her, we were to start by land for Kotzebue Sound.

Some large ice grounding to windward partially sheltered the boat;
but as her situation was on the southern bank of the entrance to the
the river, the current swept with force round, bringing occasionally
some heavy ice in contact with the boat, the violence of which hove
her into a foot and a half less water than she drew; and the sand
soon formed a bank on the outside, leaving her quite bedded. At
six P M the current had almost subsided. A most cheerless pros-

pect presented itself, the whole sea being covered with ice sufficiently compact to walk upon, and the clouds becoming heavy and flying swiftly from the S W, offered not the smallest hope of our escape The water had likewise fallen a foot and a half, leaving the boat nearly dry. Our feelings now were indescribable, as it appeared very evident that we should be obliged to abandon our little vessel, and perform the journey to Chamisso Island on foot—an undertaking we were by no means adequate to, and which the advanced state of the season would render extremely fatiguing. At eight we ascended a hill, but saw not the slightest chance of an opening, the ice to the southward being very compact as far as the eye could reach, and varying in its height from twelve to two feet above the level of the sea. At midnight the weather was cold, dark, and foggy, and seemed to indicate a S W gale

Friday, 25th Aug At four this morning the current appeared to resume something of its former rapidity, causing the ice to move to the northward, and leaving small openings This gave us faint hopes of a release, but the wind springing up as we had anticipated, soon extinguished them. After breakfast we again visited the hill, but with no better success than before. The tide returning or ebbing from the river brought back with it a quantity of the ice, almost every piece of which drifted athwart the boat; so that we determined on getting her afloat, and shifting her to a better berth, where we should be ready to avail ourselves of the smallest prospect of getting clear. Having laid out an anchor astern, we with much difficulty got her through the sand bank that had formed itself round us, and finding that at her own length farther out a channel was left for the ice to drive either out or into the river, we secured her to a large berg that had grounded and afforded us much shelter. Towards noon a number of natives visited us, and were presented with tobacco, &c Among them was the old man spoken of the day before; who on receiving his present, offered up what we concluded to be a prayer, at the same time blowing with his mouth, as if imploring an east wind and the dispersion of the ice —In the afternoon the wind had increased to a gale We went to the hill, and there observed the line of ice within the horizon, and the sea breaking very heavily outside : we saw also a number of large bergs drifting down At four, fresh gales with heavy squalls—the ice around us became closely wedged, the pieces being forced one over another, forming a solid mass The body of ice in the offing was still drifting to the northward. This day Mr Elson determined, if we should be compelled to quit the boat, to take every thing out of her except the gun, to remove her into the deepest part of the river, and there sink her, so as to prevent the natives from destroying or breaking her up to obtain the iron ; from which situation, should we visit this coast next

year, she might with little trouble be raised	The stores and rigging
also we resolved to bury, and to leave directions where they might
be found.	On visiting the village (which was about half a mile dis-
tant), the natives were uncommonly civil	They resided in tents,
the frames of which were made with poles, and covered with seal-
skins	the bottom or floor was merely a few logs laid sidewise on the
ground : inside there was a second lining of reindeer skin, which
did not reach quite to the top : this constituted the whole of their
dwelling	Their principal food appeared to be reindeer and seal's
flesh , and having procured more than sufficient of these animals for
present use, they had buried the overplus in the sand, to be kept
until required.	They very generously led us to a seal that had
been thus deposited.	The flesh and blubber which had been sepa-
rated were wrapped in the skin, and were in a most disgusting oily
state.	One of the natives put in his hand, stirred up the contents,
and offered us some, the sight of which alone was enough to turn
one's stomach.	He seemed to pity our want of taste, and sucked
his fingers with the greatest relish.	Each of the crew having
provided himself with native boots, &c , for travelling in, return-
ed to the boat	During the night the gale abated, and the wind fell
almost calm, and it began to freeze hard.	Wherever there was any
opening before, the water was covered with young ice	The tide
here rose and fell from eighteen to twenty inches —the time of
change very irregular, probably influenced by the ice

Saturday, 26th Aug	Our chance of getting clear seemed more
remote now than ever, and we commenced making preparation for
the land journey	The crew were sent on shore to exercise their
limbs, and train themselves for walking	We traced the winding of
the river for some distance , the banks were high on each side.	It
seemed deep, and its turnings frequent and sudden	The only an-
imal we saw was a red fox, which avoided our pursuit	In the eve-
ning we returned to the boat—the weather still frosty.

Sunday, 27th Aug	We had a sharp frost during the night, attended
with frozen particles, which fell like dust, and covered our clothes
The wind light from the S W , with a thick fog	The fresh water
ponds were frozen to the thickness of half an inch.	After eight A.
M., Mr Elson and myself walked along the beach to reconnitre the
state of the ice	We found that if we could cut the boat through
a quarter of a mile of ice, we should get into about double that distance of clear water, and returned on board with the determination
to accomplish this	Having got the boat afloat, we began our ar-
duous task of cutting and hauling her through the ice.	The natives,
seeing us thus employed, very kindly came (unasked) and lent their
assistance	We persevered in our labours till half past three, by
which time we had moved the boat a mile and a half south of her for-

mer position. Another and more formidable barrier was now opposed to us, consisting of extensive pieces of ice aground, closely wedged together by smaller masses, under which we anchored. After dinner Mr. Elson and myself again visited the cliffs, and thought we could perceive a zigzag channel, which afforded a hope of liberation, provided we could force her through the present obstacle Immediately we got on board, we commenced cutting a passage ; but had no sooner made an opening, than it was filled by the current drifting smaller pieces of ice down. These we for some time kept cutting and clearing away ; but after two hours and a half of hard work, we found our exertions endless, and relinquished the attempt. In the evening the wind veered to the S E , and the breeze, though light from this quarter, put some of the smaller pieces of ice in motion off the land. We remained up till midnight, although fatigued with the toils of the day, and the wind having increased to a fresh breeze, had the consolation to witness the moving of several of the larger pieces. The collision that now took place, owing to the shift of the wind (the ice in the offing still holding its former course, whilst that in-shore was opposed to it), occasioned a grinding noise not unlike to that of a heavy roaring surf Having fully satisfied ourselves of the departure of the ice, if the wind should hold its present direction and force, we returned to rest, anxiously waiting the following morning.

Monday, 28th Aug Rising early, we had the great satisfaction to see that the formidable barrier which yesterday afternoon had been proof against our attempts, had nearly all drifted to sea, and that the coast, as far as we could discern, was fast clearing of ice The wind blew strong at S. S. E , and every preparation being made for weighing, after a hasty breakfast the anchor was got up, and our little vessel again bounded through the waters. Our tacking now was very uncertain, as in some places the ice still remained thick, and obliged us to perform that evolution twice or thrice in the space of a few minutes , and as we made it a rule not to bear up for any thing, we had some close rubs. By two P. M we could see the southern termination of the main body of ice There were still a number of large pieces aground, and much drift about us ; the current setting to the northward at the rate of a mile and half an hour At three the wind fell light A heavy swell from the S.W. occasioned a furious surf along the beach, and obliged us to keep well out to sea The ice still extending far to windward made our situation very critical should the wind blow hard from the S W. It now fell calm, with heavy clouds in the S W ; and being in want of water, we procured a supply from the bergs that were near us We watched every cloud with the greatest anxiety, and at eight observed them coming steadily from the westward, bringing with them

a thick fog.   We then stood to the northward until we reached the
ice, when we tacked to the southward, and sailed along its margin.
There were several walruses upon it, which at our approach bund-
led into the water   We had scarcely got clear of this field or body
of ice, when it again fell calm, the clouds very heavy, and a thick fog.
Finding that the current was again setting us to the northward at the
rate of two miles and a half an hour, we anchored, and had no sooner done so, than several large detached bergs were seen driving rapidly down in our hawse.   We again got up the anchor, and towed
the boat in-shore, where we anchored again, and kept a vigilant
look-out.

Tuesday, 29th Aug.   In the course of the night the S W. swell
went down, and at one this morning a light air sprang up from the
S E   Weighed and stood in-shore, the wind gradually freshening.
In running along the land, passed a quantity of drift ice.   At noon,
saw another body of ice about two miles distant, extending about
eleven miles N and S , and as we were not yet far enough south to
see Cape Franklin, we were apprehensive the ice might join it, in
which case we should be again beset   In the afternoon, with great
pleasure, we passed between it and the southern extremity of the
ice at the distance of a mile and a half   At three, it again fell calm
—Cape Franklin, W. S W one mile   We were preparing to go
on shore to deposit a bottle for Captain Franklin, which we had not
done on our way to the northward, when a fresh gale suddenly rising
at W. S W. obliged us to abandon the project, as not a moment was
to be lost in getting out of the bight, lest the ice (which experience
had now taught us was quick in its motion) might again enclose us.
The weather continued very unsettled during the night.

Wednesday, 30th Aug   Having rounded the point, we ran fifty
miles on a S W. course.   The wind then suddenly shifted to the
S W , blew very strong   We shortened sail to the close-reefed
mainsail and storm-jib, and stood off and on shore   In the evening we had showers of snow and sleet, and at midnight strong
gales with squalls of snow

Thursday, 31st Aug   At two A. M. a heavy squall came on
which split the mainsail, and a little before four the staysail shared
the same fate   Towards the morning the weather was more moderate, accompanied with rain.   Shortly after eight the wind suddenly veered to W N W. and blew strong.   Set the close-reefed
foresail, and furled the other sails, steering S S. W.   Noon, more
moderate.   Latitude observed 70° 23′ N.   The remainder of the
day was fine

Friday, 1st Sept.   Our stock of wood and water being expended,
we hauled towards the land and made all sail, but as we drew in,
the wind gradually decreased in strength, and before we obtained

the shore, on that part where the high land recedes from the coast The boat was soon despatched to procure what we wanted ; but in our thirsty moments we did not perceive that the pool from which we procured the water was brackish, having however filled our casks with it, and obtained some fuel, we again put to sea, with the wind from the southward

Saturday, 2d Sept Working along-shore Noon calm and fine. Sent the boat on shore to get a supply of better water. Found all the pools near the beach very brackish, from which we concluded that the recent westerly gales had thrown the surf so high that it became mingled with the water of the lakes, and we determined to have recourse to the first running stream we should come to. About two the wind again came from the southward, and at four we had every prospect of a gale from that quarter It therefore became necessary to carry a heavy press of sail all night to obtain an anchorage as near Cape Lisburn as possible, so that in the event of the wind shifting to the westward we might be able to get out of the bay.

On Sunday, as had been anticipated, it blew a strong gale, but the boat made good weather of it until eight P. M , when the bowsprit broke, and obliged us to anchor. Cape Lisburn W. N W. six leagues. Strong gales, with heavy gusts of wind off the land continued until four P. M., at which time the weather being more moderate, we weighed under close-reefed sails, and stood towards the cape, Mr. Elson wishing to be near an entrance to a lake which was situated a mile or two east of Cape Lisburn, in which he thought the boat might find shelter, should it blow hard from the westward. On arriving at this spot, we found, to our surprise, that the entrance which Mr Elson had sounded and examined in the barge's little boat was quite filled up, and that there was not the slightest appearance of there ever having been one. In the evening the wind became light and variable Anchored—the cape W. S W four miles.

Monday, 4th Sept It again blew strong from the southward, and at nine A M the wind increased so much as obliged us to let go another anchor to prevent being driven to sea. In the afternoon it again relaxed, but by midnight resumed its former violence

Tuesday, 5th Sept The wind somewhat subsiding this morning, completed our wood and water. Whilst thus employed, a native came over the hills and trafficked with us. Afterwards he stole from one of the crew some tobacco, and made off The theft was not discovered until he was a long way distant and running, being evidently aware of the crime he had committed At noon a baidar with eleven natives came round the cape and visited us. The wind continued strong from the southward, but being anxious to proceed, as our provisions were beginning to grow short, weighed and stood towards the cape under the foresail and staysail only   At two we got within the influence of the variable winds, occasioned by the steep and high land of the cape.   The bubble and violent agitation of the sea exceeded any idea of the kind we had formed, and broke over the boat in every direction.   We had no method of extricating her.   The gusts of wind that came from every quarter lasting but a moment, left us no prospect of getting clear.   We were at this time about two miles from the land.   The wind inshore of us blew with astonishing violence; the eddies from the hills making whirlwinds which carried up the spray equal in height to the mountain.   However, by four P. M., what with a slight current, and taking advantage of every flaw, we gained an offing of four miles, and, to prevent being set farther to the northward, anchored .—a heavy sea running, but little wind.   We had not been more than half an hour in this situation when it blew again from the same point with redoubled violence.   With some difficulty we lifted our anchor and made sail in for the land   As we approached it, the gusts came very strong off the hills, notwithstanding which we carried a press of sail to regain an anchorage.   For an hour and a half we were literally sailing through a sea of spray.   At six, having closed well with the land, we anchored and rode out the gale   This evening Mr. Elson put the crew on half an allowance of provisions.

Wednesday, 6th Sept   Early in the morning we observed an alteration in the weather.   The clouds collecting fast from the N. W. led us to expect the wind from that quarter.   At ten A. M., the wind becoming variable and moderate, weighed, and by three in the afternoon, to our inexpressible joy, got round the windy promontory of Cape Lisburn.   The crew were again put on their former allowance, and we made all sail, with an increasing breeze, to the southward   Passing the cape, we observed five baidars hauled up and one tent, but saw few of the natives.   It had been Mr. Elson's intention to look into the bight on the northern side of Point Hope; but the sea was so high and the weather so threatening that we kept well off, in order to weather the point.   We noticed the water, whilst off Marryat Creek, to be of a very muddy colour, as if some river discharged itself there.   By nine P. M we rounded the point and steered S S. E , to have a good offing in case the wind should again come from the westward.

Thursday, 7th Sept.   The weather seemed determined to persecute us to the last.   The wind strengthened to a gale, and raised a short, high, dangerous sea.   We hauled in for the land as much as it would allow   At nine A. M. it blew extremely hard; and, considering it dangerous to scud, rounded to on the larboard tack, took in the foresail, and set balanced-reefed mainsail and storm-jib Found the boat behave uncommonly well and continue tolerably dry. At noon our latitude was 67° 19' N. In the afternoon it moderated, and we made sail in for the land. At four p. m. saw Cape Mulgrave on the weather-bow, and altered our course for Kotzebue Sound. The wind dying away left us at midnight becalmed a few miles from Cape Krusenstern

Friday, 8th. After a few hours' calm, a breeze came from the S. E., and we worked along shore. In the forenoon several baidars came off to us We procured in exchange for a few beads, a large quantity of salmon, in hopes we should be able to keep enough to supply the ship. While sailing along the land, many more of these boats came off; but on waving them to return, they left us unmolested. We saw immense quantities of fish drying on shore, and concluded that the natives assembled at this inlet to lay in their winter stock.

Saturday, 9th Owing to the light winds, we made but small progress during the night, and this morning were off Hotham Inlet. At eleven anchored Sent the boat on shore to obtain wood and water. Noon, the latitude observed (with false horizon) was 66° 58' N. The spot abreast where we anchored had, when Mr. Elson visited this inlet before, been the site of an Esquimaux village; but there was not a single tent left. In the evening we weighed from here, and the next morning had the pleasure of seeing the ship at anchor off Chamisso Island, and the gratification to find all on board of her well.

(Signed)   WILLIAM SMYTH,
                            Mate of H. M S Blossom

By this expedition about seventy miles of coast, in addition to those discovered by the Blossom—making in the whole 126 miles—have been added to the geography of the polar regions, and the distance between Captain Franklin's discoveries and our own has been brought within so small a compass as to leave very little room for further speculation on the northern limits of the continent of America. The actual distance left unexplored is thus reduced to 146 miles, and there is much reason to believe, from the state of the sea about Point Barrow, and along that part of the coast which was explored by Captain Franklin, that the navigation of the remaining portion of unknown coast in boats is by no means a hopeless project.

Having now the assistance of the barge, I embarked in her to examine narrowly the shores of Kotzebue Sound Proceeding to survey the head of Escholtz Bay, shallow water obliged the boat to anchor off Elephant Point, where I left Mr Collie with a party to examine again the cliffs in which the fossils and ice formation had been seen by Kotzebue, and proceeded to the head of the bay in a small boat.   We landed upon a flat muddy beach, and were obliged to wade a quarter of a mile before we could reach a cliff for the purpose of having a view of the surrounding country.   Having gained its summit, we were gratified by the discovery of a large river coming from the southward, and passing between our station and a range of hills   At a few miles distance the river passed between rocky cliffs, whence the land on either side became hilly, and interrupted our further view of its course.   The width of the river was about a mile and a half ; but this space was broken into narrow and intricate channels by banks—some dry, and others partly so The stream passed rapidly between them, and at an earlier period of the season a considerable body of water must be poured into the sound, though, from the comparative width of the channels, the current in the latter is not much felt.

The shore around us was flat, broken by several lakes, in which there were a great many wildfowl   The cliff we had ascended was composed of a bluish mud and clay, and was full of deep chasms lying in a direction parallel with the front of the eminence   In appearance this hill was similar to that at Elephant Point, which was said to contain fossils ; but there were none seen here, though the earth, in parts, had a disagreeable smell, similar to that which was supposed to proceed from the decayed animal substances in the cliff near Elephant Point.

Returning from this river, we were joined by three caiacs from some tents near us, and four from the river, who were very troublesome, pestering us for *tawack*, and receiving the little we had to give them in the most ungracious manner, without offering any return.

I found Mr Collie had been successful in his search among the cliffs at Elephant Point, and had discovered several bones and grinders of elephants and other animals in a fossil state.   Associating these two discoveries, I bestowed the name of Elephant upon the point, to mark its vicinity to the place where the fossils were found ; and upon the river that of Buckland, in compliment to Dr. Buckland, the professor of geology at Oxford, to whom I am much indebted for the above mentioned description of the fossils

The cliff in which these fossils appear to have been imbedded is part of the range in which the ice formation was seen in July. During our absence (a space of five weeks) we found that the edge of the cliff in one place had broken away four feet, and in another two feet and a half, and a further portion of it was on the eve of being precipitated upon the beach.   In some places where the icy shields had adhered to the cliff nothing now remained, and frozen earth formed the front of the cliff.   By cutting through those parts of the ice which were still attached, the mud in a frozen state presented itself as before, and confirmed our previous opinion of the nature of the cliff.   Without putting it to this test, appearances might well have led to the conclusion come to by Kotzebue and M. Escholtz ; more especially if it happened to be visited early in the summer, and in a season less favourable than that in which we viewed it.   The earth, which is fast falling away from the cliffs—not in this place only, but in all parts of the bay—is carried away by the tide ; and throughout the summer there must be a tendency to diminish the depth of the water, which at no very distant period will probably leave it navigable only by boats   It is now so shallow off the ice cliffs, that a bank dries at two miles, distance from the shore ; and it is only at the shingly points which occur opposite the ravines that a convenient landing can be effected with small boats.*

In consequence of this shallow water there was much difficulty in embarking the fossils, the tusks in particular, the largest of which weighed 160lbs , and it took us the greater part of the night to accomplish it.   In our way on board we met several native caiacs, and had an exhibition of one of the Esquimaux in throwing his dart, which he placed in a slip, a small wooden instrument about a foot in length, with a hole cut in the end to receive the forefinger, and a notch for the thumb.   The stick being thus grasped, the dart was laid along a groove in the slip, and embraced by the middle finger and thumb.   The man next propelled his caiac with speed in order to communicate greater velocity to the dart, and then whirled it through the air to a considerable distance.   As there was no mark, we could not judge of his skill in taking aim   His party lived a long distance up Buckland river, and were acquainted with the musk ox, which I am the more particular in remarking, as we had never seen that animal on the coast.

About eight o'clock at night we had a brilliant display of the aurora borealis, a phenomenon of the heavens so beautiful that it has been justly thought to surpass all description.

In our return to the ship to deposit the fossils, a calm obliged us to anchor on the north side of the bay, where we landed with difficulty, in consequence of the shallowness of the beach, and of several ridges of sand thrown up parallel with it, too near the surface for the boat to pass over, and with channels of water between them too deep to wade through without getting completely wet.   The country abounded in lakes, in which were many wild ducks, geese, teal, and widgeon ; and was of the same swampy nature before described : it was covered with moss, and occasionally by low bushes of

* This difficulty of approaching the shore, even in a boat, will, I trust, convince the reader of the impracticability of trying the effect of a cannon shot upon the mud cliff with a view of bringing down some part of its surface, as has been suggested since the publication of the quarto edition.

juniper, cranberry, whortleberry, and cloudberry. Near this spot, two days before, we saw a herd of eleven reindeer, and shot a musk rat.

Hence westward, to the neck of Choris Peninsula, the shore was difficult of access, on account of long muddy flats extending into the the bay, and at low water drying in some places a quarter of a mile from the beach.

Bad weather and the duties of the ship prevented my resuming the examination of the sound until the 20th, when we ran across in the barge to Spafarief Bay, and explored the coast from thence to the westward; passing close along the beach, anchoring at night, and landing occasionally during the day for observations, and to obtain information of the nature of the country.

This part of the sound appeared to have so few temptations to the Esquimaux, that we saw only two parties upon it; and one of these, by having their dogs harnessed in the boat, appeared to be only on an excursion. the other was upon Cape Deceit, a bold promontory, with a conspicuous rock off it, so named by Captain Kotzebue. At two places where we landed there were some deserted yourts, not worthy of description, and at the mouth of two rivers in the first and second bays to the eastward of Cape Deceit, there were several spars and logs of drift-wood, placed erect, which showed that the natives had occupied these stations for catching fish, but they were now all deserted. Both these rivers had bars across the entrances, upon which the sea broke, so as to prevent a boat from entering them.

The land on the south side of the sound, as far as the Bay of Good Hope, is higher, more rocky, and of a bolder character than the opposite shore, though it still resembles it in its swampy superficial covering, and in the occurrence of lakes wherever the land is flat. Under water also, it has a bolder character than the northern side, and has generally soundings of four and five fathoms quite close to the promontories. There are two or three places under these headlands which, in case of necessity, will afford shelter to boats, but each with a particular wind only; and in resorting thither the direction of the wind and the side of the promontory must be taken into consideration

In a geological point of view this part of the coast is interesting, as being the only place in the sound where volcanic rocks occurred. Near the second promontory, to the eastward of Cape Deceit, we found slaty limestone, having scales of talc between the layers, and in those parts of the cliff which were most fallen down a talcaceous slate, with thin layers of limestone, and where the rocks were more abrupt, limestone of a more compact nature   In this cliff there was also an alum slate of a dark bluish colour. We could not land at the next cliff, but, on a close view of the rock, conjectured it to con-

sist of compact limestone, dipping to the E. N. E at an angle of
30°   Cape Deceit, the next headland, appeared to be compact
limestone also, in large angular blocks, devoid of any distinct stratafication   Proceeding on to Gullhead, which is a narrow rocky peninsula, stretching a mile into the sea, we found it chiefly composed
of slaty limestone, of a blackish and grayish colour, containing particles of talc in larger or smaller quantities, as it was elevated above
or on a level with the sea, but without any visible stratafication
A bed of slate to the eastward of the promontory, bore strong
marks of its having been subjected to the action of fire.   The slaty
limestone of the cliff on the eastern side of this, dips at an angle of
65° to the eastward.   The neck or isthmus is either unstratafied, or
its beds are perpendicular, beyond it the strata dip to the west at
nearly a right angle

Eight miles farther along the coast, we landed at the first of a
series of low points, with small bays between them, which continue
about four miles, beyond which the coast assumes a totally different
character.   On these low points, as well as upon the shores of the
bay, we were surprised to find large blocks of porous vesicular lava
and more compact lava, containing portions of olivine   These blocks
are accumulated in much larger quantities on the points, and in the
bays form reefs off the coast which are dangerous to boats passing
close along the shore   The country here slopes gradually from
some hills to the beach, and is so well overgrown that we could not
examine its substrata, but they do not in outward formation exhibit any indication of volcanic agency.

Further on we landed in a small bay formed by a narrow wall of
volcanic stones—some wholly above water, others only slightly immersed.   These reefs were opposite a low mud cliff, similar in its
nature to those in which the fossils were found in Escholtz Bay,
and though they did not furnish any bones, yet it is remarkable that
a piece of a tusk was picked up on the beach near them.   It must,
however, be observed that its edges were rounded off by the surf, to
which it had been a long time exposed; and it might have been
either washed up from some other place, or have been left on the
beach by the natives

To the westward of these rocky projections the coast is low,
swampy, and intersected by lakes and rivers.   The rounded hills
which thus far bound the horizon of the sound to the southward here
branch off inland, and a distant range of a totally different character
rises over the vast plain that extends to Cape Espenburg, and forms
the whole of the western side of the sound.   In the angle which it
makes, we discovered a river, which, we were informed by a few
natives who came off to us in a miserable baidar, with dogs looking
as unhappy as themselves, extended inland five days' journey for

their baidars; but on examination it proved so shallow at the mouth, that even the gig could not enter it.   A few miles to the north-westward of this river, we arrived off the inlet which Captain Kotzebue meditated to explore in baidars, and was very sanguine that it would lead to some great inland discovery   We consequently approached the spot with interest, and as soon as the mud capes through which the river has made its way to the ocean opened to our view, bore up, with the intention of sailing into the inlet, which runs in a westerly direction; but we were here again obliged to desist, in consequence of the shallowness of the water   At two miles and more from the shore, we had less than a fathom water, and we observed the sea breaking heavily upon a bank which extended from shore to shore across the mouth of the inlet.   Thinking, however, these breakers might be occasioned by the overfall of the tide, the gig was despatched to endeavour to effect a passage through them, but the water shoaling gradually, she could not approach within even a cable's length of the breakers.   At the top of the tide, probably, when the water is smooth, small boats may enter the inlet; but if the bar is attempted under other circumstances, the crew will probably be subjected to a similar ducking to that which Captain Kotzebue himself experienced in repassing it.   Seeing these difficulties I did not deem any further examination necessary; and as it could never lead to any useful purpose of navigation, I did not even contemplate a return to it under more favourable circumstances.   The inlet occurs in a vast plain of low ground, bounded on the north by Cape Espenburg, on the east by the Bay of Good Hope, on the west by Beering's Strait, and on the south by ranges of mountains There are also several lakes and creeks in the plain, some of which may probably communicate with the inlet; or they may all. Schismareff Inlet included, be the mouths of a large river.   It is, however, very improbable that there should be any direct communication between these two inlets, as the natives would, in that case, have informed us of it when they drew their chart of the sound.

While we were off here, we noticed a parhelion so bright that it was difficult to distinguish it from the sun : a circumstance the more deserving of remark, in consequence of the naturalist of Kotzebue's expedition having observed that this phenomenon is very rare in these seas, and that a Russian grown old in the Aleutean Islands never saw it more than once   Quitting this inlet, we directed our course along the land toward Cape Espenburg, and found that the bar was not confined to the mouth of the inlet alone, but extended the whole way to the cape. and was not passable in any part; having tried ineffectually in those places which afforded the best prospect of success.

On landing at Cape Espenburg, we found that the sea penetrated to the southward of it, formed it into a narrow strip of land, upon which were some high sand-hills   The point had a great many poles placed erect upon it, and had evidently been the residence of the Esquimaux ; but it was now entirely deserted.   Near these poles there were several huts and native burial-places, in which the bodies were disposed in a very different manner to that practised by the eastern Esquimaux   The corpse was here enclosed in a sort of coffin formed of loose planks, and placed upon a platform of drift-wood, covered over with a board and several spars, which were kept in their places by poles driven into the ground in a slanting direction, with their ends crossing each other over the pile.   The body was found lying with the head to the westward, and had been inter-red in a double dress, the under one made of the skins of eider-drakes, and the upper one of those of reindeer.   It had been ex-posed a considerable time, as the skeleton only was left, but enough of the dress remained to show the manner in which the body had been clothed

The beach was in a great measure composed of dark-coloured volcanic sand, and was strewed with dead shells of the cardium, Ve-nus, turbo, murex, solen, trochus, mytilus, mya, lepas, and tellina genera : there were also some large asterias   The sand-hills were partly covered with elymus grass, the vaccinium vitis idæa empe-trum nigrum, and some shrubs, while the carex preferred the hollow moist places ; the rest of the surface was occupied by lichens.   On the border of the lakes there were several curlew, sanderlings, and gulls; while small flocks of ptarmigan alighted upon those parts which produced berries.   A red fox prowling among the deserted huts and the graves was the only quadruped seen.   Nearly the whole of the day was passed at this place in making astronomical ob-servations, after which we embarked, and were obliged by bad weather to return to the ship.

The day after my departure, a new cutter, which had been built of some wood of the porou-tree, grown upon Otaheite, was com-pleted and launched, and upon trial found to answer under canvas beyond our expectations, doing great credit to Mr Garnet, the car-penter, who built her almost entirely himself   I placed her under the charge of Lieutenant Belcher, who was afterwards almost daily employed in surveying.

On the 22nd the aurora borealis was seen in the W N. W.; from which quarter it passed rapidly to the N. E., and formed a splendid arch, emitting vivid and brilliantly coloured coruscations.

On the 25th the wind, which had blown strong from the northward the day before changed to the southward, and had such an effect upon the tide that it ebbed twenty hours without intermission.

In another excursion which I made along the north side of the sound, I landed at a cape which had been named after the ship, and had the satisfaction of examining an ice formation of a similar nature to that in Escholtz Bay, only more extensive and having a contrary aspect The ice here, instead of merely forming a shield to the cliff, was imbedded in the indentations along its edge, filling them up nearly even with the front. A quantity of fallen earth was accumulated at the base of the cliff, which uniting with the earthy spaces intervening between the beds of ice, might lead a person to imagine the ice formed the cliff, and supported a soil two or three feet thick, part of which appeared to have been precipitated over the brow. But on examining it above, the ice was found to be detached from the cliff at the back of it ; and in a few instances so much so, that there were deep chasms between the two. These chasms are no doubt widened by the tendency the ice must have towards the edge of the cliff; and I have no doubt the beds of ice are occasionally loosened, and fall upon the beach, where if they become covered with the earthy materials from above. and perhaps remain some time immured In some places the cliff was undermined, and the surface in general was very rugged ; but it was evident in this, as in the former instance, that the ice was lodged in the hollow places in the cliff. While we continued here we had an example of the manner in which the face of the cliff might obtain an icy covering similar to that in Escholtz Bay. There had been a sharp frost during the night, which froze a number of small streams that were trickling down the face of the cliff, and cased those parts of it with a sheet of ice, which, if the oozings from the cliff and the freezing process were continued, would without doubt form a thick coating to it

Upon the beach, under the cliffs, there was an abundance of drift birch and pine wood, among which there was a fir-tree three feet in diameter. This tree, and another, which by the appearance of its bark had been recently torn up by the roots, had been washed up since our visit to this spot in July ; but from whence they came we could not even form a conjecture, as we had frequently remarked the absence of floating timber, both in the sound and in the strait.

We found some natives at this place laying out their nets for seals, who, perceiving we were about to take up our quarters near them, struck their tents expeditiously, threw every thing into their baidars, to which they harnessed their dogs, and drove off for about half a mile, where they encamped again. We procured from them about two bushels of whortle berries, which they had collected for their own consumption. and learnt that they had been unsuccessful in fishing. We noticed that at their meals they stripped their dried fish of its skin, and gave it to the women and children, who ate it very contentedly, while the men regaled themselves upon the flesh.

During the night we had a brilliant display of the aurora borealis, remarkable for its masses of bright light. It extended from N E to W , and at one time formed three arches. As we were taking our departure we were visited by a baidar, from which we procured some fine fresh salmon and trout. The coxswain of this boat wore unusually large labrets, consisting of blue glass beads fixed upon circular pieces of ivory, a full inch in diameter. He drew us a chart of Hotham Inlet, which resembled one that had been traced upon the beach by some natives the day before ; both of which represented it as an arm of the sea in the form of an hour-glass, which was not far from the truth. The Esquimaux seem to have a natural talent for such delineations ; and though their outlines may serve no essential purpose of navigation, they are still useful in pointing out the nature of a place that has not been visited : an information which may sometimes save a useless journey. It is, however, to be observed, that not unfrequently they appear to trace the route which a boat can pursue, rather than the indentations of the coast, by which rivers and bays not frequented would be overlooked. Such charts are further useful in marking the dwellings and fishing stations of the natives.

From hence we bore away to examine Hotham Inlet, and found it so encumbered with shoals that it was necessary to run seven miles off the land to avoid striking upon them ; it had but one small entrance, so very narrow and intricate, that the boats grounded repeatedly in pursuing it. In the middle of the channel there were only five feet water at half-flood , and the tide ebbed so strong through it, that the boat could not stem it ; and as there was but a small part of the coast of this inlet that we had not seen, and finding the examination of it would be attended with difficulty, and would occupy a long time, the boats did not ascend it. The shoal which is off the entrance has no good land-marks for it ; the bearings from its extremity in two fathoms and a half of water are Cape Blossom, S 66° 40' E (true), Western High Mount, N. 17° 30' W. (true), and the west extreme, a bluff cape, near Cape Krus-eastern, N 37° 0' W (true.) But the best way to avoid it is to go about directly the soundings decrease to six fathoms, as after that depth they shoal so rapidly to two fathoms and a quarter that there is scarcely room to put the ship round.

On the 1st of October we landed upon a sandy point at the western limit of the inlet, and were joined by a few Esquimaux who had their tents not far off to the westward , they had communicated with the boat two months before, and came again in the expectation of getting a few more blue beads and foreign articles for some nets and fish. They immediately recognised such of the officers as they had seen before, and were delighted at meeting them. Some of the beads which they had obtained were now suspended to different parts of their dress, in the same manner as was practised by the Esquimaux of Melville Peninsula, and round their necks, or were made into bracelets. They corroborated the former account of the inlet, the length of which they estimated a long day's paddle, our observations made it thirty-nine miles. At the back of the point where we landed there was another inlet, to the end of which they said their baidars could also go, notwithstanding we saw a bar across its mouth so shallow that the gulls waded over from shore to shore. Near us, there was a burying ground, which, in addition to what we had already observed at Cape Espenburg, furnished several examples of the manner in which this tribe of natives dispose of their dead. In some instances a platform was constructed of drift-wood, raised about two feet and a quarter from the ground, upon which the body was placed with its head to the westward, and a double tent of drift-wood erected over it, the inner one with spars about seven feet long, and the outer one with some that were three times that length. They were placed close together, and at first no doubt sufficiently so to prevent the depredations of foxes and wolves; but they had yielded at last; and all the bodies, and even the hides that covered them, had suffered by these rapacious animals.

In these tents of the dead there were no coffins or planks, as at Cape Espenburg; the bodies were dressed in a frock made of eider-duck skins, with one of deer-skin over it, and were covered with a sea-horse hide, such as the natives use for their baidars. Suspended to the poles, and on the ground near them, were several Esquimaux implements, consisting of wooden trays, paddles, and a tambourine, which, we were informed, as well as signs could convey, were placed there for the use of the deceased, who, in the next world, (pointing to the western sky) ate drank, and sang songs. Having no interpreter, this was all the information I could obtain; but the custom of placing such implements around the receptacles of the dead is not unusual, and in all probability the Esquimaux may believe that the soul has enjoyments in the next world similar to those which constitute happiness in this.

The people whom we saw here were very inquisitive about our fire-arms, and to satisfy one of them I made him fire off a musket, that was loaded with ball, towards a large tree that was lying upon the beach. The explosion and the recoil which succeeded the simple operation of touching the trigger so alarmed him, that he turned pale and put away the gun. As soon as his fear subsided he laughed heartily, as did all his party, and went to examine the wood which was found to be perforated by the ball, and afforded them a fair specimen of the capability of our arms; but he could not be prevailed upon to repeat the operation

They had some skins of ravens with them, upon which they place a high price, though being of no use to us, they did not find a purchaser. On several occasions we had noticed the beaks and claws of these birds attached to ornamental bands for the head and waist, and they were evidently considered valuable. On our return to the ship we fell in with another party of natives, among whom there were two men whose appearance and conduct again led us to conclude that the large blue glass labrets indicated a superiority of rank, and found, as before, that no reasonable offer would induce them to part with these ornaments

On the 3rd, we reached the ship, and were informed that she had been visited by several baidars in our absence, and had procured from them a quantity of dried salmon, which was afterwards served to the ship's company These boats were the last that visited the ship, as the season was evidently arrived for commencing their preparations for winter. About this time we had sharp frosts at night; some snow fell, and on the 5th all the lakes on shore were frozen. The hares and ptarmigan were quite white, and all the birds had quitted their abodes in the rocks to seek a milder atmosphere. These unequivocal symptoms of the approach of winter excited great anxiety for the safety of the land expedition.

On the 7th, Mr. Elson went up Escholtz Bay with two boats for the purpose of sounding and obtaining further information of Buckland River, but returned on the 10th, without having been able to effect it, on account of the hostile disposition of the natives, whom he met in the bay When the small boat was detached from the barge, three baidars approached her; and their crews, consisting of between thirty and forty men, drew their knives and attempted to board her, and, on the whole, behaved in so daring and threatening a manner, that Mr. Elson, fearing he should be compelled to resort to severe measures, if he proceeded with the examination of the river, desisted, and returned to the ship This was the first instance of any decidedly hostile conduct of the natives in the sound, whose behaviour in general had left with us a favourable impression of the disposition of their tribe The barge brought us down a valuable addition to our collection of fossils, the cliff having broken away considerably since the first specimens were obtained.

On the 8th, we had the misfortune to lose one of the marines, by dysentery and general inflammation of the abdomen. On the 10th, having selected a convenient spot for a grave, on the low point of Chamisso Island, his body was interred in the presence of almost all his shipmates, and a stone properly inscribed put up to mark the spot, but the earth was replaced over the grave as evenly as possible, in order that no appearance of excavation might remain to attract the attention of the natives.

We had hitherto remained in the sound, in the expectation of being able to wait till the end of October, the date named in my instructions, but the great change that had recently occurred in the atmosphere, the departure of all the Esquimaux for their winter habitations, the migration of the birds, the frozen state of the lakes, and the gradual cooling down of the sea, were symptoms of approaching winter too apparent to be disregarded, and made it evident that the time was not far distant when it would be necessary to quit the anchorage, to avoid being shut up by the young ice On every account I was anxious to remain until the above-mentioned period ; but as my instructions were peremptory in desiring me not to incur the risk of wintering, it was incumbent upon me seriously to consider how late the ship could remain without encountering that risk By quitting the rendezvous earlier than had been agreed upon, the lives of Captain Franklin's party might be involved; by remaining too long, those of my own ship's company would be placed in imminent hazard, as but five weeks' provision at full allowance remained in the ship, and the nearest place where we could replenish them was upwards of 2000 miles distant.   Thus circumstanced, I was desirous of having the advice of the officers of the ship before I made up my own mind, and accordingly addressed an official letter to them, requesting they would take every circumstance into their consideration, and furnish me with their opinion on the propriety of remaining longer in these seas

Their answer, which I received the next day, conveyed an unanimous opinion that the ship could not continue longer at her present anchorage without incurring the risk of wintering, and suggested her removal to the entrance of the sound, where the majority of the officers thought she might remain a few days longer ; but previous to our taking up our station there, it was considered advisable that the strait should be ascertained to be navigable, lest the ice should have been drifted down from the northward, and the retreat of the ship be cut off.   I fully concurred in with them, that if the frost continued the ship could not remain at her anchorage ; but as there was a possibility of its yielding, I resolved to wait a day or two or longer upon the chance, determined, if it did not give way, to quit the sound ; and in the event of Beering's Strait being found clear, to return, as had been proposed, and to wait a few days off Cape Krusenstern, in the hope of meeting the party.   Considering, however, the lateness of the season and the long nights, there did not appear to be much chance of the ship being able to maintain an advantageous position at the mouth of the sound ; still, as I was unwilling to relinquish the smallest chance of falling in with the party, I purposed making the attempt.   In so doing, however, it was necessary to insure our departure by the 23rd instant, which considering our distance from any new supplies, and that at that period there would be but nine weeks' provision remaining at half allowance, was as late as I thought it prudent to continue

We were now made sensible of the great advantage arising from the economical system that had been adopted at the Society and Sandwich Islands, and also from the reduction of an eleventh part of the ship's company at Portsmouth, without which the provision before this period would have been wholly expended, as the allowance from the time of leaving Chili had been reduced as low as it conveniently could, for a continuance, consistent with the strength of the ship's company, who for several months had been on half allowance.

It now remained for me to consider how Captain Franklin could be most benefitted in the event of his party arriving after our departure. It was evident that we could do no more than put him in possession of every information we had obtained, and leave him a temporary supply of provisions and bartering articles, with which he could procure others from the natives. To this end a barrel of flour was buried for him upon the sandy point of Chamisso, a place which, from the nature of the ground, was more likely to escape observation than the former one, where the newly turned turf could not be concealed. A large tin case, containing beads and a letter, was deposited with it, to enable him to purchase provisions from the natives, and to guide his conduct. Ample directions for finding these were both cut and painted on the rock; and to call the attention of the party to the spot, which they might otherwise pass, seeing the ship had departed, her name was painted in very large letters on the cliffs of Puffin Island, accompanied with a notice of her departure, and the period to which she had remained in the sound. Beneath it were written directions for finding the cask of flour, and also a piece of drift-wood which was deposited in a hole in the cliff. This billet had been purposely bored and charged with a letter containing all the useful information I could impart to the party, and then plugged up in such a manner that no traces of its being opened were visible. In fact, nothing was left undone that appeared to me likely to prove useful.

Having thus far performed our duty, we prepared the ship for sea, in order that she might start at an hour's notice. On the 13th the temperature fell to 27°, the lakes on shore had borne two or three days, and the sea had cooled down 8°; in short, there was every appearance of a settled frost. The next day the edges of the sound began to freeze, and it was evident that it needed only calm weather to skin it entirely over. I therefore desired the anchor to be weighed, and having taken on board a large supply of drift-wood, the last thing we procured from the shore, we steered out of the sound

We passed Cape Krusenstein about midnight and then shaped a course for the strait. The night, though cold, was fine, and furnished me with eighteen sets of lunar distances, east and west of the moon, which I was very anxious to obtain, in order to fix more accurately the position of Chamisso Island, never having been able to succeed in getting fine weather with the moon to the east of the sun, until his declination was too far south for the lunars to be of any value.

We had no observation at noon the next day, and the land was so refracted that we scarcely recognised it; we, however, continued to run for the strait, anxious to reach it before sunset. The breeze increased as we advanced, and before the Diomede Islands came in sight it blew so violently that there was no alternative but to endeavour to push through them before dusk. At this time there was a very thick haze, with a bright setting sun glaring through it, which with the spray around us prevented any thing being seen but the tops of the mountains near Cape Prince of Wales. It was consequently with great pleasure we perceived Fairway Rock, and found the strait quite free from ice.

Having no choice, we passed through it at a rapid rate; and as the night set in dark and thick, with snow showers, we were glad to find ourselves with sea-room around us. A little before midnight the lee-bow port was washed away, and so much water came in that was necessary to put before the wind to free the ship. In half an hour, however, we resumed our course, and about two o'clock in the morning passed King's Island.

We were now in a situation where, by rounding to, we might have awaited fine weather to return to Cape Krusenstern, and execute the whole of the plan that had been contemplated; but considering that our being able to do so was uncertain, as the barometer, which had fallen to 28,7, afforded no prospect of a change of weather, and that the period I had fixed for my departure might expire before I could repass the straits: together with the state of our provisions, and the improbability of meeting with Captain Franklin after all, it appeared to me that the risks which it involved were greater than the uncertainty of the result justified, and painful as it was to relinquish every hope of this successful issue of our voyage, it became my duty to do so. In the execution of this necessary resolution, it was some consolation to reflect, that from the nature of Captain Franklin's instructions, it was almost certain that by this time he had either commenced his return or taken up his winter abode. He had been directed to return to his winter quarters on the 15th of August, if he found the prospect of success was not such as to ensure his reaching Icy Cape that season, and if it should prove impracticable to winter at an advanced station on the coast.

We were justified, therefore, in supposing that he had already been either compelled to pause or to turn back, as, in the event of the successful prospect anticipated in his instructions, it could hardly happen, considering the open state in which we had found the sea to the northward, that he should not have reached Kotzebue sound by the time the Blossom left it

In taking our departure from these seas, some general observations on the country, natives, the currents, meteorology, and other subjects, naturally present themselves ; but as we returned to the same place the following year, and extended our experience, I shall defer them until a future opportunity.

Up to this period of the voyage, my instructions had been a safe guide for my proceedings, but between our departure from these seas, and our return to them the following year, with the exception of touching at the Sandwich Islands, there were no specific directions for my guidance, and it became me seriously to consider how the time could be most usefully employed   It was necessary to repair to some port to refit and caulk the ship, to replenish the provisions and stores, and, what was equally important, to recruit the health of the people, who were much debilitated from their privations, having been a considerable time on short allowance of salt provision, and in the enjoyment of only seven weeks' fresh meat in the last ten months

From the favourable account I had herd of Saint Francisco in California, it appeared to be the most desirable place to which a ship under our circumstances could resort ; and as the coast between that port and Cape St. Lucas was very imperfectly known, that the time could not be more usefully employed than in completing the survey of it.   I therefore directed our course to that place, and determined to enter the Pacific by the Strait of Oonemak ; which, if not the safest of those formed by the Aleutian Islands, is certainly the best known

After passing King's Island on the 16th, we saw some very large flocks of ducks migrating to the southward, and fell in with the lummes, which had deserted us more than a month before at Chamisso Island.   As we approached St. Lawrence Island, the little crested auks flew around us, and some land birds took refuge in our rigging   We passed to the eastward of this island in very thick weather, and had only a transient view of its eastern extremity, and thence pursued a course to the southward, passing between Gore's Island and Nunevack, an island recently discovered by the Russians, but not known to us at that time   The soundings increased, though not always regularly ; and we had thick misty weather which prevented and thing drying   The barometer fluctuated a little on either side of 28,6.   On the 18th, the temperature, which had risen gradually as we advanced to the southward, was twenty degrees higher than it was the day we left Kotzebue Sound—a change which was sensibly felt,

On the 21st we came within sight of the island of St Paul, the northern island of a small groupe, which, though long known to English geographers, has been omitted in some of our most esteemed modern charts. The groupe consists of three islands named St. George's, St. Paul's, and Sea-otter. We saw only the two latter in this passage, but in the following year passed near to the other, and on the opposite side of St Paul's to that on which our course was directed at this time. The islands of St. Paul and St George are both high, with bold shores, and without any port, though there is said to be anchoring-ground off both, and soundings in the offing at moderate depths. At a distance of twenty-five miles from Sea-otter Island, in the direction of N 37° W. (true), and in latitude 59° 22' N, we had fifty-two fathoms hard ground; after this, proceeding southward, the water deepens. St Paul's is distinguished by three small peaks, which, one of them in particular, have the appearance of craters; St George's consists of two hills, united by moderately high ground, and is higher than St Paul's; both were covered with a brown vegetation. Sea-otter Island is very small, and little better than a rock. The Russians have long had settlements upon both the large islands, subordinate to the establishment at Sitka, and annually send thither for peltry, consisting principally of the skins of amphibious animals, which, from their fine furry nature, are highly valued by the Chinese and Tartar nations.

At sunset we lost sight of St. Paul's Island, and being at that time ignorant of the position of St. George's, further than what knowledge was derived from a rough notice of it in the geological account of Kotzebue's Voyage, we pursued our course with some anxiety, as the night was dark and unsettled, and the morning came without our obtaining a sight of the island. On approaching the Aleutian Islands, we found them obscured by a dense white haze, which hung to windward of the land; and the wind increasing with every appearance of a gale, our situation became one of great difficulty. Early in the morning, a peak was seen for so short a time that it only served to show us that we were not far from the land, without enabling us to determine which of the islands we were near; and as in this part of the Aleutian Chain there are several passages so close together, that one may easily be mistaken for the other, an accurate knowledge of the position of the ship is of the greatest importance. Under our circumstances, I relied on the accuracy of Cook's chart, and steered due east, knowing that if land were seen in that parallel, it could be no other than the island of Oonemak;

37

and that then, should the fog not clear away, the course might still be directed along that island to the southward

This is a precaution I strongly recommend to any person who may have to seek a channel through this chain in foggy weather, particularly as these passages are said to be rendered dangerous by the rapid tides which set through them.   It was no doubt these tides, added to the prevalence of fogs, that caused many of the misfortunes which befel the early Russian navigators   Shelekoff, in speaking of the strait to the westward of Oonemak, through which we passed, observes that it is free from the danger of rocks and shoals, but is troubled with a strong current   In our passage through it, however, we did not remark that this was the case ; but no doubt there are just grounds for the observation *

After running five miles, breakers were seen upon both bows, and, at the same time, very high cliffs above them.   We stood on a little further, and then, satisfied that the land must be that of Oonemak, bore up along it, and passed through the strait.   We had no soundings with forty fathoms of line until we were about four miles off the S W. end of the island , and there we found thirty fathoms on a bank of dark-coloured lava, pebbles and scoriæ, but immediately lost it again, and had no bottom afterwards   The south-west angle of Oonemak is distinguished by a wedge-shaped cape, with a pointed rock off it   This cape and the island of Coogalga form the narrowest part of the strait, which is nine miles and a half across   Coogalga is about four miles long, and rendered very conspicuous by a peak on its N. E extremity   Acouan, the island to the northward of this, which also forms part of the strait, is high and remarkable ; but on this occasion we did not see it, in consequence of the bright haze that hung over the hills on the northern part of the chain

Oonemak was the only island upon which snow was observed. Its summit was capped about one-third down, even with a line of clouds which formed a canopy over the northern half of the groupe The limits of this canopy were so well defined, that in passing through the strait on one side of us there was a dense fog, while on the other the sun was shining bright from a cloudless sky

As soon as we had fairly entered the Pacific the wind abated, and we had a fine clear night, as if in passing through the chain that divides the Kamschatka Sea from the Pacific we had left behind us the ungenial climate of the former   Shortly after dark flashes were observed in the heavens, in the direction of the burning mountain of Alaska, sometimes so strong as to be mistaken for

---

* I afterwards learned from a very respectable master of an American brig, that in passing through the strait to the westward of Oonalaska, he experienced a current running to the northward at the rate of six miles an hour, and was unable to stem it.

sheet lightning, at others very confined ; viewed with a telescope, they appeared to consist entirely of bright sparks.   They seemed to proceed from different parts of a long narrow cloud elevated 8°, and lying in the direction of the wind.   Our distance from the volcano at this time was about seventy miles, and as similar flashes were observed in this place the following year, it is very probable they were caused by an eruption   This mountain, I am informed, has burnt lately with great activity, and has been truncated much lower than is represented in the drawings of it in Captain Cook's Voyage.*

After clearing the Aleutian Chain, we had the winds from the westward, and made rapid progress towards our port.   The first part of the passage was remarkable for heavy rolling seas, misty weather, and a low barometer, which varied a little each side of 28,5 ; in the latter part of the passage we had dry foggy weather, and the barometer was at 30,5.

On the 5th of November we made the high land of New Albion about Bodega, and soon afterwards saw Punta de los Reyes, a remarkable promontory, from which the general line of coast turns abruptly to the eastward, and leads to the port of St Francisco

We stood to the southward during the night, and about three o'clock in the morning unexpectedly struck soundings upon a clayey bank in 35 fathoms very near the Farallones, a dangerous cluster of rocks, which, until better known, ought to be avoided.   The ship was put about immediately ; but the next cast was 25 fathoms in so stiff a clay that the line was broken   The weather was very misty, and a long swell rolled towards the reefs, which, had there been less wind, would have obliged us to anchor ; but we increased our distance from them, and deepened the water.   This cluster of rocks is properly divided into two parts, of which the south-eastern is the largest and the highest, and may be seen nine or ten leagues in clear weather.   The most dangerous part is apparently towards the north-west.

The next evening we passed Punta de los Reyes, and awaited the return of day off some white cliffs, which, from their being situated so near the parallel of 38° N are in all probability those which induced Sir Francis Drake to bestow upon this country the name of New Albion   They appear on the eastern side of a bay too exposed to authorize the conjecture of Vancouver, that it is the same in which Sir Francis refitted his vessel.

* See also Kotzebue's Voyage, vol iii p 283

CHAPTER XIII.

Arrive at San Francisco—Description of the Harbour, Presidio, and the missions—Occupations—Dissatisfied State of the Garrison and the Priesthood—Contemplated Plan of settling the Indians in the Missions—Occupations of the converted Indians—Manner of making converts—Expedition against the Tribe of Cosemenes—Official Despatch—Overland Journey to Monterey—Scarcity of Provisions at that place—Plan of the voyage altered in consequence—Departure.

When the day broke, we found ourselves about four miles from the land. It was a beautiful morning, with just sufficient freshness in the air to exhilarate without chilling The tops of the mountains, the only part of the land visible, formed two ranges, between which our port was situated; though its entrance, as well as the valleys and the low lands, were still covered with the morning mist condensed around the bases of the mountains We bore up for the opening between the ranges, anxious for the rising sun to withdraw the veil, that we might obtain a view of the harbour, and form our judgment of the country in which we were about to pass the next few weeks. As we advanced, the beams of the rising sun gradually descended the hills, until the mist, dispelled from the land, rolled on before the refreshing sea wind, discovering cape after cape and exhibiting a luxuriant country apparently abounding in wood and rivers. At length two low promontories, the southern one distinguished by a fort and a Mexican flag, marked the narrow entrance of the port.

We spread our sails with all the anxiety of persons who had long been secluded from civilized society, and deprived of wholesome aliment; but after the first effort of the breeze, it died away and left us becalmed in a heavy N. W swell.

Off the harbour of San Francisco there is a bar which extends from the northern shore, gradually deepening its water until it approaches the peninsula on the opposite side *, where nine fathoms may be carried over it. Of this bar, however, we were ignorant, and naturally steered directly for the harbour, in doing which the

* The best part for crossing is with the island of Alcatrasses in one with the fort

depth of water gradually diminished to five fathoms. This would have been of no consequence, had it not been for a swell which rolled so heavily over the bank that it continually broke ; and though our depth of water was never less than four and a half fathoms, the ship on two or three occasions disturbed the sand with her keel. The tide was unfortunately against us, and the swell propelled the ship just sufficiently fast for her to steer without gaining any ground, so that we remained in this unpleasant situation several hours.

At length a breeze sprung up and we entered the port, and dropped our anchor in the spot where Vancouver had moored his ship thirty-three years before.   As we passed the entrance, a heavy sea rolling violently upon a reef of rocks on our left * bespoke the danger of approaching that side too close in light or baffling winds ; while some scattered rocks with deep water round them skirting the shore on our right, marked that side also as dangerous ; so that the entrance may be justly considered difficult   Beyond these rocks, however, near the fort, there is a bay in which if necessary, ships may drop their anchor

The fort, which we passed upon our right, mounts nine guns, and is built upon a promontory on the south side of the entrance, apparently so near to the precipice, that one side will, before long, be precipitated over it by the gradual breaking away of the rock.   Its situation, nevertheless, is good, as regards the defence of the entrance ; but it is commanded by a rising ground behind it.   As we passed, a soldier protruded a speaking-trumpet through one of the embrasures, and hailed us with a stentorian voice, but we could not distinguish what was said.   This custom of hailing vessels has arisen from there being no boat belonging to the garrison, and the inconvenience felt by the governor, in having to wait for a report of arrivals, until the masters of the vessels could send their boats on shore.

The port of San Francisco does not show itself to advantage until after the fort is passed, when it breaks upon the view, and forcibly impresses the spectator with the magnificence of the harbour. He then beholds a broad sheet of water, sufficiently extensive to contain all the British navy, with convenient coves, anchorage in every part, and, around, a country diversified with hill and dale, partly wooded, and partly disposed in pasture lands of the richest kind, abounding in herds of cattle.   In short, the only objects wanting to complete the interest of the scene are some useful establishments and comfortable residences on the grassy borders of the harbour, the absence of which creates an involuntary regret, that so fine a country, abounding in all that is essential to man, should be

---

* This reef lies three quarters of a mile from Punta Boneta.

allowed to remain in such a state of neglect.   So poorly did the place appear to be peopled that a sickly column of smoke rising from within some dilapidated walls, misnamed the presidio or protection, was the only indication we had of the country being inhabited

The harbour stretches to the S E to the distance of thirty miles, and affords a water communication between the missions of San Jose, Santa Clara, and the presidio, which is built upon a peninsula about five miles in width.   On the north the harbour is contracted to a strait, which communicates with a basin ten miles wide, with a channel across it sufficiently deep for frigates, though they cannot come near the land on account of the mud.   A creek on the N W side of this basin leads up to the new mission of San Francisco Solano, and a strait to the eastward named Estrecho de Karquines, communicates with another basin into which three rivers discharge themselves, and bring down so large a body of water that the estrecho is from ten to eleven fathoms deep.   These rivers are named Jesus Maria, El Sacramento, and San Joachin the first, I was informed, takes a northerly direction, passes at the back of Bodega, and extends beyond Cape Mendocino.   El Sacramento tends to the N. E, and is said to have its rise in the rocky mountains near the source of the Columbia.   The other, San Joachin, stretches to the southward through the country of the Bolbones, and is divided from the S. E., arm of the harbour by a range of mountains.

When Langsdorff was at this port, an expedition was undertaken by Don Louis Arguello and Padre Uria to make converts, and to enquire into the nature of the country in the vicinity of Sierra nevada, and I learned from Don Louis, I believe a son of the commander, that they traced the Sacramento seventy or eighty leagues up, and that it was there very wide and deep, but that he had no boat to ascertain its depth.   The Padre had it in contemplation to form a settlement in that direction, which he thought would become very rich in a short time by the number of Indians who would flock to it; but as it was never done, I presume he found material obstacles to his design.

As we opened out the several islands and stopping places in the harbour, we noticed seven American whalers at anchor at Sausalito, not one of which showed their colours we passed them and anchored off a small bay named Yerba Buena, from the luxuriance of its vegetation, about a league distant from both the presidio and the mission of San Francisco I immediately went on shore to pay my respects to Don Ignacio Martinez, a lieutenant in the Mexican army, acting governor in the absence of Don Louis, and to the priest, whose name was Tomaso, both of whom gave me a very hospitable and friendly reception, and offered their services in any way they might be required.   Our first inquiries naturally related to supplies, which we were disappointed to find not at all equal to what had been reported ; in short, it seemed that with the exception of flour, fresh beef, vegetables, and salt, which might be procured through the missions, we should have to depend upon American vessels for whatever else we might want, or upon what might chance to be in store at Monterey, a port of more importance than San Francisco, and from being the residence of a branch of a respectable firm in Lima, better supplied with the means of refitting vessels after a long sea voyage

It was evident from this report that the supplies were likely to be very inadequate to our wants ; but that no opportunity of obtaining them might be lost, I despatched Mr Collie the surgeon, and Mr. Marsh the pursuer, overland to Monterey, with Mr Evans as interpreter, with orders to procure for the ship what medicines, provisions, and other stores were to be had, and to negotiate government bills, on which the exchange was far more more favourable there than at the Sandwich Islands   The governor politely furnished a passport and a guard for this service ; and our hospitable friend Tomaso, the padre of the mission, provided horses for them free of any charge.   In the mean time we arranged with a relation of the governor for the daily supply of the ship's company, an arrangement which it afterwards appeared increased the jealousy that had long existed between the presidio and the missions, by transferring to the pocket of the commandant the profits that would otherwise have been reaped by the padre.

We were happy to find the country round our anchorage abounding in game of all kinds, so plentiful, indeed, as soon to lessen the desire of pursuit ; still there were many inducements to both the officers and seamen to land and enjoy themselves ; and as it was for the benefit of the service that they should recruit their health and strength as soon as possible, every facility was afforded them. Horses were fortunately very cheap, from nine shillings to seven pounds apiece, so that riding became a favourite amusement ; and the Spaniards finding they could make a good market by letting out their stud, appeared with them every Sunday opposite the ship, ready saddled for the occasion, as this was a day on which I allowed every man to go out of the ship.   Some of the officers purchased horses and tethered them near the place, but the Spaniards finding this to interfere with their market, contrived to let them loose on Saturday night, in order that the officers might be compelled to hire others on the following day.   The only obstacle to the enjoyment of this amusement was the scarcity of saddles and bridles, some of which cost ten times as much as a decent horse.   The ingenuity of the seamen generally obviated these difficulties, while some bor-

rowed or hired saddles of the natives : for my own part, I purchased a decent looking horse for about thirty-five shillings sterling, and
on my departure presented it to a Spaniard, who had lent me the
necessary accoutrements for it during my stay, which answered the
purpose of both parties, as he was pleased with his present, and I
had my ride for about a shilling a day : a useful hint to persons who
may be similarly circumstanced

Such of the seamen as would not venture on horse back made
parties to visit the presidio and mission, where they found themselves
welcome guests with the Spanish soldiers.   These two places were
the only buildings within many miles of us, and they fortunately
supplied just enough spirits to allow the people to enjoy themselves
with their friends, without indulging in much excess—a very great
advantage in a seaport

The roads leading to these two great places of attraction in a short
time became well beaten, and that to the mission very much improved, by having the boughs removed which before overhung it.
It was at first in contemplation to hire a Spaniard to lop them ; but
our pioneers, who stopped at nothing, soon tore them all away,
except one, a large stump, which resisted every attack, and unhor-
sed several of its assailants.

Martinez was always glad to see the officers at the presidio, and
made them welcome to what he had   Indeed, nothing seemed to
give him greater pleasure than our partaking of his family dinner ;
the greater part of which was dressed by his wife and daughters, who
prided themselves on their proficiency in the art of cooking.   It was
not, however, entirely for the satisfaction of presenting us with a
well-prepared repast that they were induced to indulge in this humble occupation : poor Martinez had a very numerous offspring to provide for out of his salary, which was then eleven years in arrears.
He had a sorry prospect before him, as, a short time previous to our
visit, the government, by way of paying up these arrears, sent a
brig with a cargo of paper cigars to be issued to the troops in lieu
of dollars ; but, as Martinez justly observed, cigars would not satisfy the families of the soldiers, and the compromise was refused.
The cargo was, however, landed at Monterey and placed under the
charge of the governor, where all other tobacco is contraband ; and
as the Spaniards are fond of smoking, it stands a fair chance, in the
course of time, of answering the intention of the government, particularly as the troops apply for these oftener than they otherwise
would, under the impression of clearing off a score of wages that
will never be settled in any manner.   Fortunately for Martinez and
other veterans in this country, both vegetable and animal food are
uncommonly cheap, and there are no fashions to create any expense
of dress.

The governor's abode was in a corner of the presidio, and formed one end of a row, of which the other was occupied by a chapel; the opposite side was broken down, and little better than a heap of rubbish and bones, on which jackals, dogs, and vultures were constantly preying, the other two sides of the quandrangle contained storehouses, artificer's shops, and the goal, all built in the humblest style with badly burnt bricks, and roofed with tiles. The chapel and the governor's house were distinguished by being white-washed.

Whether viewed at a distance or near, the establishment impresses a spectator with any other sentiment than that of its being a place of authority and but for a tottering flag-staff, upon which was occasionally displayed the tri-coloured flag of Mexico, three rusty field pieces, and a half accoutred centinel parading the gateway in charge of a few poor wretches heavily shakled, a visitor would be ignorant of the importance of the place The neglect of the government to its establishments could not be more thouroughly evinced than in the dilapidated condition of the building in question; and such was the dissatisfaction of the people that there was no inclination to improve their situation, or even to remedy many of the evils which they appeared to us to have the power to remove.

The plain upon which the presidio stands is well adapted to cultivation; but it is scarcely ever touched by the plough, and the garrison is entirely beholden to the mission for its resources. Each soldier has nominally about three pounds a month, out of which he is obliged to purchase his provision. If the governor were active, and the means were supplied, the country in the vicinity of the establishment might be made to yield enough wheat and vegetables for the troops, by which they would save that portion of their pay which now goes to the purchase of these necessary articles.

The garrison of San Francisco consists of seventy-six cavalry soldiers and a few artillerymen, distributed between the presidios and the missions, and consequently not more than half a dozen are at any time in one place

They appeared to us to be very dissatisfied, owing not only to their pay being so many years in arrear, but to the duties which had been imposed both on the importation of foreign articles, and on those of the Mexican territory, amounting in the first instance to forty-two and a half per cent; whereas under the old government, two ships were annually sent from Acapulco with goods, which were sold duty free, and at their original cost in that country, and then, also, their pay being regularly discharged, they were able to purchase what they wanted A further grievance has arisen by the refusal of the government to continue certain privileges which were enjoyed under the old system. At that time soldiers entered for a term of ten

years, at the expiration of which they were allowed to retire to the Pueblos—villages erected for this purpose, and attached to the missions,
where the men have a portion of ground allotted to them for the
support of their families This afforded a competency to many ;
and while it benefited them, it was of service to the government, as
the country by that means became settled, and its security increased   But this privilege has lately been witheld, and the applicants
have been allowed only to possess the land and feed their cattle
upon it, until it shall please the government to turn them off.   The
reason of this, I believe, was that Mexico was beginning to turn her
attention to California, and was desirous of having settlers there
from the southern districts, to whom it would be necessary to give
lands , and until they could see what would be required for this purpose and for the government establishments, and had the limits of
the property already allotted defined, they did not wish to make any
new grants   The real cause, however, was not explained to the
soldiers : they merely heard that they would not have the land ce-
ded to them for life as usual, and they were consequently much
dissatisfied.

The same feeling of discontent that was experienced by the garrison, pervaded the missions, in consequence of some new regulations of the republican government, the first and most grievous of
which was the discontinuance of a salary of 400 dollars per annum,
heretofore allowed to each of the padres · the support the former
government, had given to the missions amounted, according to Langsdorff, to a million piastres a year   Another grievance was, the
requisition of an oath of allegiance to the reigning authorities, which
these holy men considered so egregious a violation of their former
pledge to the king of Spain, that, until he renounced his sovereignty
over the country, they could not conscientiosly take it , and, much
as they were attached to the place in which they had passed a large
portion of their lives, and though by quitting it they would be reduced to the utmost penury—yet, so much did they regard this pledge
that they were prepared to leave the country, and to seek an asylum
in any other that would afford it them   Indeed, the Prefect, preferring his expulsion to renouncing his allegiance, had already received
his dismissal, and was ready at the seaport of Monterey to embark
in any vessel the government might appoint to receve him   A
third greivance, and one which, when duly considered, was of some
importance, not only to the missions but to the country in general,
was an order to liberate all those converted Indians from the missions who bore good characters, and had been taught the art of agriculture, or were masters of a trade, and were capable of supporting themselves, giving them portions of land to cultivate, so arranged that they should be divided into parishes, with curates to super-

intend them, subservient to the clergy of the missions, who were to
proceed to the conversion of the Indians as usual, and to train them
for the domesticated state of society in contemplation

This philanthropic system at first sight appeared to be a very
excellent one, and every friend to the rights of man would naturally
join in a wish for its prosperity, but the Mexican government could
not have sufficiently considered the state of California, and the disposition of the Indians, or they would have known it could not possibly succeed without long previous training, and then it would require to be introduced by slow degrees.

The Indians whom this law emancipated were essential to the
support of the missions, not only for conducting their agricultural
concerns, but for keeping in subordination by force and example
those whom disobedience and ignorance would exempt from the privilege: and as a necessary consequence of this indulgence the missions would be ruined before the system could be brought into
effect, even supposing the Indians capable of conducting their own
affairs.   So far from this being the case, however, they were known
to possess neither the will, the steadiness, nor the patience to provide for themselves   Accustomed, many of them from their infancy, to as much restraint as children, and to execute, mechanically,
what they were desired and no more, without even entertaining a
thought for their future welfare, it was natural that such persons,
when released from this discipline, should abandon themselves entirely to their favourite amusements, pastimes, and vices   Those
also who had been converted in later life would return to their former habits, and having once again tasted the blessings of freedom,
which confinement and discipline must have rendered doubly desirable, would forget all restraint, and then being joined by the wild
discontented Indians, they would be more formidable enemies to the
missions than before, inasmuch as they would be more enlightened.
But I will not anticipate the result, which we had an opportunity
of seeing on our return the following year; and from which the
reader will be able to judge how the system worked

The padres, however, dreading the worst, were very discontented, and many would willingly have quitted that country for Manilla.
The government appeared to be aware of this feeling, as they sent
some young priests from Mexico to supplant those who were disaffected, and desired that they should be trained up in the mission,
and should make themselves acquainted with the language and usa-
ges of the Indians, in order that they might not promote discontent
by any sudden innovation

The missions have hitherto been of the highest importance to
California, and the government cannot be too careful to promote
their welfare, as the prosperity of the country in a great measure is

dependent upon them, and must continue to be so until settlers from the mother country can be induced to resort thither.   As they are of such consequence, I shall enter somewhat minutely into a description of them   In Upper California there are twenty-one of these establishments, of which nine are attached to the presidios of Monterey and San Francisco, and contain about 7000 converts. They are in order as follow from north to south :—

					Converts.
San Francisco	San Francisco Solano, established in		1822,	about	1000
	San Raphael	-	-	1817	-	250
	San Francisco	-	-	1776	-	260
	San Jose	-	-	1797	-	1800
	Santa Clara	-	-	1777	-	1500
Monterey	Santa Cruz	-	-	1797	-	300
	San Juan	-	-	1797	-	1100
	San Carlos	-	-	1770	-	200
	La Soledad	-	-	————	-	300
					6910

San Antonio	Buena Vistura
San Miguel	San Fernando
San Luis	San Gabriel
De la Purissima	San Juan Capistram
Santa Ignes	San Luis Rey 3000
Santa Barbara	San Tomaso

I could no learn the number of Indians which are in each of the missions to the southward of Soledad, but they were stated collectively to amount to 20,000 : on this head I must observe that the padres either would not say, or did not know exactly, how many there were, even in their own missions, much less the number contained in those to the southward   and the accounts were at all times so various that the above computation can be only an approximation   Almost all these establishments cultivate large portions of land, and rear cattle, the hides and tallow of which alone form a small trade, of which the importance may be judged from the fact of a merchant at Monterey having paid 36,000 dollars in one year to a mission, which was not one of the largest, for its hide, tallow, and Indian labour   Though the system they pursue is not calculated to raise the colony to any great prosperity, yet the neglect of the missions would not long precede the ruin of the presidios, and of the whole of the district.   Indeed, with the exception of two pueblos, containing about seven hundred persons, and a few farm houses widely scattered over the country, there are no other buildings to the northward of Monterey   thus, while the missions furnish the means of subsistence to the presidios, the body of men they contain keeps the wild Indians in check, and prevents their making incursions on the settlers.

Each mission has fifteen square miles of ground allotted to it. The buildings are variously laid out, and adapted in size to the number of Indians which they contain; some are enclosed by a high wall, as at San Carlos, while others consist merely of a few rows of huts, built with sun-burnt mud-bricks, many are white-washed and tiled, and have a neat and comfortable appearance   It is not, however, every hut that has a white face to exhibit, as that in a great measure depends upon the industry and good conduct of the family who possess it, who are in such case supplied with lime for the purpose.   It is only the married persons and the officers of the establishment who are allowed these huts, the bachelors and spinsters having large places of their own, where they are sepa-rately incarcerated every night

To each mission is attached a well-built church, better decorated in the interior than the external appearance of some would lead a stranger to suppose.   they are well supplied with costly dresses for processions and feast days, to strike with admiration the sense of the gazing Indians, and on the whole are very respectable establish-ments.   In some of these are a few tolerable pictures, among many bad ones; and those who have been able to obtain them are always provided with representations of hell and paradise: the former ex-hibiting in the most disgusting manner all the torments the imagina-tion can fancy, for the purpose of striking terror into the simple Indians, who look upon the performance with fear and trembling. Such representations may perhaps be useful in exhibiting to the dull senses of the Indians what could not be conveyed in any other way, and so far they are desirable in the mission; but to an Euro-pean the one is disgusting, and the other ludicrous.   Each establish-ment is under the management of two priests if possible, who in Upper California belong to the mendicant order of San Francisco They have under them a major-domo, and several subordinate offi-cers, generally Spaniards, whose principal business is to overlook the labour of the Indians.

The object of the missions is to convert as many of the wild In-dians as possible, and to train them up within the walls of the estab-lishment in the exercise of a good life, and of some trade, so that they may in time be able to provide for themselves and become useful members of civilized society   As to the various methods employed for the purpose of bringing proselytes to the mission, there are several reports, of which some were not very creditable to the institution.   nevertheless, on the whole I am of opinion that the priests are innocent, from a conviction that they are ignorant of the means employed by those who are under them   Whatever

may be the system, and whether the Indians be really dragged from
their homes and families by armed parties, as some assert, or not,
and forced to exchange their life of freedom and wandering for one
of confinement and restraint in the missions, the change according
to our ideas of happiness would seem advantageous to them, as they
lead a far better life in the missions than in their forests, where they
are in a state of nudity, and are frequently obliged to depend solely
upon wild acorns for their subsistence.

Immediately the Indians are brought to the mission they are
placed under the tuition of some of the most enlightened of their
countrymen, who teach them to repeat in Spanish the Lord's Prayer
and certain passages in the Romish litany ; and also to cross themselves properly on entering the church   In a few days a willing
Indian becomes a proficient in these mysteries, and suffers himself
to be baptized, and duly initiated into the church   If, however, as
it not unfrequently happens, any of the captured Indians show a
repugnance to conversion, it is the practice to imprison them for a
few days, and then to allow them to breathe a little fresh air in a
walk round the mission, to observe the happy mode of life of their
converted countrymen, after which they are again shut up, and
thus continue to be incarcerated until they declare their readiness
to renounce the religion of their forefathers

I do not suppose that this apparently unjustifiable conduct would
be pursued for any length of time ; and I had never an opportunity
of ascertaining the fact, as the Indians are so averse to confinement
that they very soon become impressed with the manifestly superior
and more comfortable mode of life of those who are at liberty, and
in a few days declare their readiness to have the new religion explained to them   A person acquainted with the language of the
parties, of which there are sometimes several dialects in the same
mission, is then selected to train them, and having duly prepared
them takes his pupils to the padre to be baptized, and to receive
the sacrament   Having become Christians they are put to trades,
or if they have good voices they are taught music, and form part
of the choir of the church   Thus there are in almost every mission weavers, tanners, shoemakers, bricklayers, carpenters, black-
smiths, and other artificers   Others again are taught husbandry, to
rear cattle and horses, and some to cook for the mission   while the
females card, clean, and spin wool, weave, and sew, and those who
are married attend to their domestic concerns.

In requital of these benefits, the services of the Indian, for life,
belong to the mission, and if any neophyte should repent of his
apostacy from the religion of his ancestors and desert, an armed
force is sent in pursuit of him, and drags him back to punishment
apportioned to the degree of aggravation attached to his crime.   It

does not often happen that a voluntary convert succeeds in his attempt to escape, as the wild Indians have a great contempt and dislike for those who have entered the missions, and they will frequently not only refuse to re-admit them to their tribe, but will sometimes even discover their retreat to their pursuers. This animosity between the wild and converted Indians is of great importance to the missions, as it checks desertion, and is at the same time a powerful defence against the wild tribes, who consider their territory invaded, and have other just causes of complaint. The Indians, besides, from political motives, are, I fear, frequently encouraged in a contemptuous feeling towards their unconverted countrymen, by hearing them constantly held up to them in the degrading light of *bestias* ¹ and in hearing the Spaniards distinguished by the appellation of *gente de razon*

The produce of the land, and of the labour of the Indians, is appropriated to the support of the mission, and the overplus to amass a fund which is entirely at the disposal of the padres. In some of the establishments this must be very large, although the padres will not admit it, and always plead poverty The government has lately demanded a part of this profit, but the priests who, it is said, think the Indians are more entitled to it than the government, make small donations to them, and thus evade the tax by taking care there shall be no overplus. These donations in some of the missions are greater than in others, according as one establishment is more prosperous than another, and on this, also, in a great measure, depends the comforts of the dwellings, and the neatness, the cleanliness, and the clothing of the people In some of the missions much misery prevails, while in others there is a degree of cheerfulness and cleanliness which shows that many of the Indians require only care and proper management to make them as happy as their dull senses will admit of under a life of constraint

The two missions of San Francisco and San Jose are examples of the contrast alluded to. The former in 1817 contained a thousand converts, who were housed in small huts around the mission, but at present only two hundred and sixty remain—some have been sent, it is true, to the new mission of San Francisco Solano, but sickness and death have dealt an unsparing hand among the others. The huts of the absentees, at the time of our visit, had all fallen to decay, and presented heaps of filth and rubbish, while the remaining inmates of the mission were in as miserable a condition as it was possible to conceive, and were entirely regardless of their own comfort Their hovels afforded scarcely any protection against the weather, and were black with smoke some of the Indians were sleeping on the greasy floor; others were grinding baked acorns to make into cakes, which constitute a large portion of their food. So little attention indeed had been paid even to health, that in one hut there was a quarter of beef suspended opposite a window, in a very offensive and unwholsome state, but its owners were too indolent to throw it out   San Jose, on the other hand, was all neatness, cleanliness, and comfort, the Indians were amusing themselves between the hours of labour at their games; and the children uniformly dressed in white bodices and scarlet petticoats, were playing at bat and ball   Part of this difference may arise from the habits of the people, who are of different tribes   Langsdorff observes, that the Indians of the mission of San Jose are the handsomest tribe in California; and in every way a finer race of men; and terms the neophytes of San Francisco pigmies compared with them   I cannot say that this remark occurred to me, and I think it probable that he may have been deceived by the apparently miserable condition of the people of San Francisco.

The children and adults of both sexes, in all the missions, are carefully locked up every night in separate apartments, and the keys are delivered into the possession of the padre, and as in the daytime, their occupations lead to distinct places, unless they form a matrimonial alliance, they enjoy very little of each other's society. It, however, sometimes happens that they endeavour to evade the vigilance of their keepers, and are locked up with the opposite sex; but severe corporeal punishment, inflicted in the same manner as is practised in our schools, but with a whip instead of a rod, is sure to ensue if they are discovered   Though there may be occasional acts of tyranny, yet the general character of the padres is kind and benevolent, and in some of the missions, the converts are so much attached to them that I have heard them declare they would go with them, if they were obliged to quit the country.   It is greatly to be regretted that, with the influence these men have over their pupils, and with the regard those pupils seem to have for their masters, the priests do not interest themselves a little more in the education of their converts, the first step to which would be in making themselves acquainted with the Indian language   Many of the Indians surpass their pastors in this respect, and can speak the Spanish language, while scarcely one of the padres can make themselves understood by the Indians.   They have besides, in general, a lamentable contempt for the intellect of these simple people, and think them incapable of improvement beyond a certain point   Notwithstanding this, the Indians are, in general, well clothed and fed, they have houses of their own, and if they are not comfortable, it is, in a great measure, their own fault; their meals are given to them three times a day, and consist of thick gruel made of wheat, Indian corn, and sometimes acorns, to which at noon is generally added meat. Clothing of a better kind than that worn by the Indians is given to the officers of the missions, both as a reward for their services, and to create an emulation in others.

If it should happen that there is a scarcity of provisions, either through failure in the crop, or damage of that which is in store, as they have always two or three years in reserve, the Indians are sent off to the woods to provide for themselves, where, accustomed to hunt and fish, and game being very abundant. they find enough to subsist upon. and return to the mission when they are required to reap the next year's harvest.

Having served ten years in the mission, an Indian may claim his liberty, provided any respectable settler will become surety for his future good conduct   A piece of ground is then alloted for his support, but he is never free from the establishment, as part of his earnings must still be given to them.   We heard of very few to whom this reward for servitude and good conduct had been granted , and it is not improbable that the padres are averse to it, as it deprives them of their best scholars.   When these establishments were first founded, the Indians flocked to them in great numbers for the clothing with which the neophytes were supplied , but after they became acquainted with the nature of the institution, and felt themselves under restraint, many absconded   Even now, notwithstanding the difficulty of escaping, desertions are of frequent occurrence, owing probably, in some cases, to the fear of punishment—in others to the deserters having been originally inveigled into the mission by the converted Indians or the neophytes, as they are called by way of distinction to Los Gentiles, or the wild Indians—in other cases again to the fickleness of their own disposition

Some of the converted Indians are occasionally stationed in places which are resorted to by the wild tribes for the purpose of offering them flattering accounts of the advantages of the mission, and of persuading them to abandon their barbarous life ; while others obtain leave to go into the territory of the Gentiles to visit their friends, and are expected to bring back converts with them when they return.   At a particular period of the year, also, when the Indians can be spared from the agricultural concerns of the establishment, many of them are permitted to take the launch of the mission, and make excursions to the Indian territory.   All are anxious to go on such occasions, some to visit their friends, some to procure the manufactures of their barbarous countrymen, which, by the by, are often better than their own , and some with the secret determination never to return.   On these occasions the padres desire them to induce as many of their unconverted brethren as possible to accompany them back to the mission, of course implying that this is to be done only by persuasions , but the boat being furnished with a cannon and musketry, and in every respect equipped for war, it too often happens that the neophytes, and the gente de razon, who superintend the direction of the boat, avail themselves of their superiority, with the desire of ingratiating themselves with their masters, and of receiving a reward   There are, besides, repeated acts of aggression which it is necessary to punish, all of which furnish proselytes   Women and children are generally the first objects of capture, as their husbands and parents sometimes voluntarily follow them into captivity.   These misunderstandings and captivities keep up a perpetual enmity amongst the tribes, whose thirst for revenge is almost insatiable.

We had an opportunity of witnessing the tragical issue of one of these holyday excursions of the neophytes of the mission of San Jose   The launch was armed as usual, and placed under the superintendance of an alcalde of the mission, who it appears from one statement (for there are several,) converted the party of pleasure either into one of attack for the purpose of procuring proselytes, or of revenge upon a particular tribe for some aggression in which they were concerned   They proceeded up the Rio San Joachin until they came to the territory of a particular tribe named Cosemenes, when they disembarked with the gun, and encamped for the night near the village of *Los Gentiles*, intending to make an attack upon them the next morning ; but before they were prepared, the Gentiles, who had been apprised of their intention, and had collected a large body of friends, became the assailants, and pressed so hard upon the party that, notwithstanding they deal death in every direction with their cannon and musketry, and were inspired with confidence by the contempt in which they held the valour and tactics of their unconverted countrymen, they were overpowered by numbers, and obliged to seek their safety in flight, and to leave the gun in the woods.   Some regained the launch and were saved, and others found their way overland to the mission ; but thirty-four of their party never returned to tell their tale

There were other accounts of this unfortunate affair; one of which accused the padre of authorizing the attack, and another stated that it was made in self-defence   but that which I have given appeared to be the most probable.   That the reverend father should have sanctioned such a proceeding is a supposition so totally at variance with his character, that it will not obtain credit, and the other was in all probability the report of the alcalde to excuse his own conduct.   They all agreed, however, in the fatal termination of their excursion, and the neophytes became so enraged at the news of the slaughter of their companions, that it was almost impossible to prevent them from proceeding forthwith to revenge their deaths. The padre was also greatly displeased at the result of the excursion, as the loss of so many Indians to the mission was of the greatest

consequence, and the confidence with which the victory would inspire the Indians was equally alarming.   He, therefore, joined with
the converted Indians in a determination to chastise and strike terror into the victorious tribe, and in concert with the governor planned an expedition against them.   The mission furnished money,
arms, Indians, and horses and the presidio provided troops, headed
by the alferez, Sanchez, a veteran who had been frequently engaged with the Indians, and was acquainted with every part of the
country   The troops carried with them their armour and shields,
as a defence against the arrows of the Indians: the armour consisted
of a helmet and jerkin made of stout skins, quite impenetrable to an
arrow, and the shield might almost vie with that of Ajax in the
number of its folds

The expedition set out on the 19th of November, and we heard
nothing of it until the 27th, but two days after the troops had tak-
en the field, some immense columns of the smoke rising above the
mountains in the direction of the Cosemenes, bespoke the confla-
gration of the village of the persecuted Gentiles.   And on the day
above-mentioned, the veteran Sanchez made a triumphant entry into the mission of San Jose, escorting forty miserable women and
children, the gun that had been taken in the first battle, and other
trophies of the field   This victory, so glorious, according to the
ideas of the conqueror, was achieved with the loss of only one man
on the part of the Christians, who was mortally wounded by the
bursting of his own gun; but on the part of the enemy it was considerable, as Sanchez the morning after the battle counted forty-one
men, women and children, dead.   It is remarkable that none of the
prisoners were wounded, and it is greatly to be feared that the
Christians, who could scarcely be prevented from revenging the
death of their relations upon those who were brought to the
mission, glutted their brutal passion on all the wounded who fell into their hands.   The despatch which the alferez wrote to his commanding officer on the occasion of this successful termination of his
expedition, will convey the best idea of what was executed, and
their manner of conducting such an assault

Translation—" Journal kept by citizen Jose Antonio Sanchez,
ensign of cavalry of the presidio of San Francisco, during the enterprise against the Gentiles, called Cosemenes, for having put to
death the neophytes of the mission of San Jose." Written with
gunpowder on the field of battle!

" On the morning of the 20th the troop commenced its march,
and, after stopping to dine at Las Positas, reached the river San
Joachin at eleven o'clock at night, when it halted   This day's
march was performed without any accident, except that neighbour
Jose Ancha was nearly losing his saddle.   The next day the alfe-

iez determined to send forward the 'auxiliary neophytes' to construct balsas* for the troop to pass a river that was in advance of
them   The troop followed, and all crossed in safety, but among
the last of the horses that forded the river was one belonging to soldier Leandro Flores, who lost his bridle, threw his rider, and kick-
ed him in the face and forehead; and as poor Flores could not
swim, he was in a fair way of losing his life before he came within
sight of the field of battle. assistance was speedily rendered, and
he was saved.   As Sanchez wished to surprise the enemy, he encamped until dusk, to avoid being seen of the wild Indians, who
were travelling the country; several of whom were met and taken
prisoners.   At five they resumed their march; but neighbour Ghex-
bano Chaboya being taken ill with a pain in his stomach, there was
a temporary halt of the army: it however soon set forward again,
and arrived at the river of Yachicume at eleven at night, with only
one accident, occasioned by the horse of neighbour Leandro Flores
again throwing up his heels, and giving him a formidable fall.

"The troop lay in ambush until five o'clock the next evening,
and then set out; but here they were distressed by two horses running away; they were however both taken after a short march,
which brought them to the river San Francisco, near the rancheria
of their enemy the Cosemenes, and where the alferez commanded
his troops to prepare for battle, by putting on their cueros, or armour.
The 23d the troops divided, and one division was sent round to intercept the Cosemenes, who had discovered the Christians, and were
retreating; some of whom they made prisoners, and immediately
the firing began   It had lasted about and hour, when the musket
of soldier Jose Maria Garnez burst, and inflicted a mortal wound
in his forehead; but this misfortune did not hinder the other soldiers
from firing.   The Gentiles also opened their fire of arrows, and the
skirmishing became general   Towards noon a shout was heard in
the north quarter, and twenty Gentiles were seen skirmishing with
three Christians, two on foot and one on horseback, and presently
another shout was heard, and the Christians were seen flying,
and the Gentiles in pursuit of them, who had already captured the
horse.

" It was now four o'clock, and the alferez, seeing that the Gentiles, who were in ambush, received little injury, disposed every
thing for the retreat of the troops, and having burnt the rancheria,
and seen some dead bodies, he retreated three quarters of a league,
and encamped for the night   On the 24th the troops divided into
two parties, one charged with booty and prisoners amounting to forty-four souls, mostly women.

* These are rafts made of rushes, and are the Indian substitute for canoes.

" The other party went with the veteran Sanchez to the rancheria, to reconnoitre the dead bodies, of which he counted forty one men, women, and children. They met with an old woman there, the only one that was left alive, who was in so miserable a state that they showed their compassion by *taking no account of her*. The alferez then set out in search of the cannon that had been abandoned by the first expedition. The whole of the troop afterwards retreated, and arrived at the mission of San Jose on the night of the 27th "

This truly ludicrous account of an expedition of such trifling importance might appear to require an apology for its insertion, but it conveys so good an idea of the opposition to be expected by any power which might think proper to land upon the coast of California, that its omission might fairly be considered a neglect.

The prisoners they had captured were immediately enrolled in the list of the mission, except a nice little boy, whose mother was shot while running away with him in her arms, and he was sent to the presidio, and was, I heard, given to the alferez as a reward for his services The poor little orphan had received a slight wound in his forehead; he wept bitterly at first, and refused to eat, but in time became reconciled to his fate.

Those who were taken to the mission were immediately converted, and were daily taught by the neophytes to repeat the Lord's prayer, and certain hymns in the Spanish language. I happened to visit the mission about this time, and saw these unfortunate beings under tuition: they were clothed in blankets, and arranged in a row before a blind Indian, who understood their dialect, and was assisted by an alcalde to keep order. Their tutor began by desiring them to kneel, informing them that he was going to teach them the names of the persons composing the Trinity, and that they were to repeat in Spanish what he dictated.

The neophytes being thus arranged, the speaker began, " Santissima Trinidada, Dios, Jesu Cristo, Espiritu Santo"—pausing between each name, to listen if the simple Indians, who had never spoken a Spanish word before, pronounced it correctly, or any thing near the mark. After they had repeated these names satisfactorily, their blind tutor after a pause added, " Santos"—and recapitulated the names of a great many saints, which finished the morning's tuition I did not attend the next schooling to hear what was the ensuing task, but saw them arranged on their knees, repeating Spanish words as before.

They did not appear to me to pay much attention to what was going forward, and I observed to the padre that I thought their teachers had an arduous task; but he said they had never found any difficulty : that the Indians were accustomed to change their own

gods, and that their conversion was in a measure habitual to them.
I could not help smiling at this reason of the padre, but have no
doubt it was very true ; and that the party I saw would feel as little
compunction at apostatizing again, whenever they should have an
opportunity of returning to their own tribe.

The expenses of the late expedition fell heavy upon the mission,
and I was glad to find that the padre thought it was paying very
dear for so few converts, as in all probability it will lessen his desire to undertake another expedition ; and the poor Indians will be
spared the horrors of being butchered by their own countrymen,
or dragged from their homes into perpetual captivity.   He was also
much concerned to think the Cosemenes had stood their ground so
firmly, and he was under some little apprehension of an attack upon the mission   Impressed with this idea, and in order to defend
himself the more effectually, he begged me to furnish him with a
few fireworks, which he thought would strike terror into his enemies in case of necessity.

Morning and evening mass are daily performed in the missions,
and high mass as it is appointed by the Romish Church, at which
all the converted Indians are obliged to attend   The commemoration of the anniversary of the patroness saint took place during my
visit at San Jose, and high mass was celebrated in the church   Before the prayers began, there was a procession of the young female
Indians, with which I was highly pleased.   They were neatly
dressed in scarlet petticoats, and white bodices, and walked in a
very orderly manner to the church, where they had places assigned
to them apart from the males.   After the bell had done tolling,
several alguazils went round to the huts, to see if all the Indians
were at church, and if they found any loitering within them, they
exercised with tolerable freedom a long lash with a broad thong at
the end of it , a discipline which appeared the more tyrannical, as
the church was not sufficiently capacious for all the attendants, and
several sat upon the steps without , but the Indian women who had
been captured in the affair with the Cosemenes were placed in a
situation where they could see the costly images, and vessels of
burning incense, and every thing that was going forward.

The congregation was arranged, on both sides of the building,
separated by a wide aisle passing along the centre, in which were
stationed several alguazils with whips, canes, and goads, to preserve
silence and maintain order, and, what seemed more difficult than
either, to keep the congregation in their kneeling posture   The
goads were better adapted to this purpose than the whips, as they
would reach a long way, and inflict a sharp puncture without making any noise.   The end of the church was occupied by a guard
of soldiers under arms, with fixed bayonets , a precaution which I

suppose experience had taught the necessity of observing.   Above
them there was a choir, consisting of several Indian musicians, who
performed very well indeed on various instruments, and sang the
Deum in a very passable manner   The congregation was very attentive, but the gratification they appeared to derive from the music
furnished another proof of the strong hold this portion of the ceremonies of the Romish church takes upon uninformed minds

The worthy and benevolent priests of the mission devote almost
the whole of their time to the duties of the establishment, and have
a fatherly regard for those placed under them who are obedient and
diligent; and too much praise cannot be bestowed upon them, considering that they have relinquished many of the enjoyments of life,
and have embraced a voluntary exile in a distant and barbarous
country   The only amusement which my hospitable host of the
mission of San Jose indulged in, during my visit to that place, was
during meal times, when he amused himself by throwing pancakes
to the *nuchachos*, a number of little Indian domestics, who stood
gaping round the table.   For this purpose, he had every day two
piles of pancakes made of Indian corn . and as soon as the olla was
removed, he would fix his eyes upon one of the boys, who immediately opened his mouth, and the padre, rolling up a cake, would
say something ludicrous in allusion to the boy's appetite, or to the
size of his mouth, and pitch the cake at him, which the imp would
catch between his teeth, and devour with incredible rapidity, in
order that he might be ready the sooner for another, as well as to
please the padre, whose amusement consisted in a great measure in
witnessing the sudden disappearance of the cake   In this manner
the piles of cakes were gradually distributed among the boys, amidst
much laughter, and occasional squabbling.

Nothing could exceed the kindness and consideration of these excellent men to their guests and to travellers, and they were seldom
more pleased than when any one paid their mission a visit   we always fared well there, and even on fast days were provided with fish
dressed in various ways, and preserves made with the fruit of the
country   We had, however, occasionally some difficulty in maining our good temper, in consequence of the unpleasant remarks
which the difference of our religion brought from the padres, who
were very bigoted men, and invariably introduced this subject.   At
other times they were very conversible, and some of them were ingenious and clever men; but they had been so long excluded
from the civilized world, that their ideas and their politics, like the
maps pinned against the walls, bore date of 1772, as near as I could
read it for fly spots   Their geographical knowledge was equally
backward, as my host at San Jose had never heard of the discoveries of Captain Cook; and because Otaheite was not placed upon
the chart, he would scarcely credit its existence.

The Indians after their conversion are quiet and tractable, but extremely indolent, and given to intoxication, and other vices. Gambling in particular they indulge in to an unlimited extent they pledge the very clothes on their backs, and not unfrequently have been known to play for each other's wives. They have several games of their own, besides some with cards, which have been taught them by the Spaniards Those which are most common, and are derived from the wild indians, are tousse called by the Spaniards pares y nones, odd or even , escondido, or hunt the slipper; and takersia.

The first, though sometimes played as in England, generally consists in concealing a piece of wood in one hand, and holding out both for the guessing party to declare in which it is contained The intense interest that is created by its performance has been amusingly described by Perouse. The second, escondido, needs no description the last, takersia, requires some skill to play well, and consists in rolling a circular piece of wood with a hole in its centre along the ground, and throwing a spear through it as it rolls. If the spear pierces the hole, it counts ten towards the game ; and if it arrests the wood in such a manner that it falls upon the spear, two is reckoned. It is a sport well calculated to improve the art of throwing the spear but the game requires more practice to play it well than the Indians usually bestow upon it

At some of the missions they pursue a custom said to be of great antiquity among the aborigines, and which appears to afford them much enjoyment. A mud house, or rather a large oven, called temeschal by the Spaniards, is built in a circular form, with a small entrance, and an aperture in the top for the smoke to escape through. Several persons enter this place quite naked and make a fire near the door, which they continue to feed with wood as long as they can bear the heat. In a short time they are thrown into a most profuse perspiration, they wring their hair, and scrape their skin with a sharp piece of wood or an iron-hoop, in the same manner as coach horses are sometimes treated when they come in-heated , and then plunge into a river or pond of cold water, which they always take care shall be near the temeschal.

A similar practice to this is mentioned by Shelekoff as being in use among the Konaghi, a tribe of Indians near Cook's River, who have a method of heating the oven with hot stones, by which they avoid the discomfort occasioned by the wood-smoke ; and, instead of scraping their skin with iron or bone, rub themselves with grass and twigs.

Formerly the missions had small villages attached to them, in which the Indians lived in a very filthy state ; these have almost all disappeared since Vancouver's visit, and the converts are disposed of in huts as before described , and it is only when sickness prevails to a great extent that it is necessary to erect these habitations, in order to separate the sick from those who are in health   Sickness in general prevails to an incredible extent in all the missions, and on comparing the census of the years 1786 and 1813, the proportion of deaths appears to be increasing   At the former period there had been only 7,701 Indians baptized out of which 2,388 had died , but in 1813 there had been 37,437 deaths to only 57,328 baptisms.

The establishments are badly supplied with medicines, and the reverend fathers, their only medical advisers, are inconceivably ignorant of the use of them   In one mission there was a seaman who pretended to some skill in pharmacy, but he knew little or nothing of it, and perhaps often did more harm than good.   The Indians are also extremely careless and obstinate, and prefer their own simples to any other remedies, which is not unfrequently the occasion of their disease having a fatal termination

The Indians in general submit quietly to the discipline of the missions, yet insurrections have occasionally broken out, particularly in the early stage of the settlement, when father Tamoral and other priests suffered martyrdom *   In 1822, also, a priest was murdered in a general insurrection in the vicinity of San Luis Rey ; and in 1827, the soldiers of the garrison were summoned to quell another riot in the same quarter.

The situations of the missions, particularly that of San Jose, are in general advantageously chosen.   Each establishment has fifteen square miles of ground, of which part is cultivated, and the rest appropriated to the grazing and rearing of cattle ; for in portioning out the ground, care has been taken to avoid that which is barren. The most productive farms are held by the missions of San Jose, Santa Clara, San Juan, and Santa Cruz   That of San Francisco appears to be badly situated, in consequence of the cold fogs from the sea, which approach the mission through several deep valleys, and turn all the vegetation brown that is exposed to them, as is the case in Shetland with the top of every tree that rises above the walls. Still, with care, more might be grown in the mission than it is at present made to produce.   Santa Cruz is rich in supplies, probably on account of the greater demand by merchant vessels, whalers in particular, who not unfrequently touch there the last thing on leaving the coast, and take on board what vegetables they require ; the quantity of which is so considerable, that it not unfrequently happens that the missions are for a time completely drained.   On this

* Noticias de California, by Miguel Venegas.

account it is advisable, on arriving at any of the ports, to take an early opportunity of ordering every thing that may be required.

A quantity of grain, such as wheat and Indian corn, is annually raised in all the missions, except San Francisco, which, notwithstanding it has a farm Burri Burri, is sometimes obliged to have recourse to the other establishments. Barley and oats are said to be scarcely worth the cultivation, but beans, peas, and other leguminous vegetables are in abundance, and fruit is plentiful. The land requires no manure at present, and yields on an average twenty for one. San Jose reaps about 3,000 fanegas * of wheat annually.

Hides and tallow constitute the principal riches of the missions, and the staple commodity of the commerce of the country; a profitable revenue might also be derived from grain, were the demand for it on the coast such as to encourage them to cultivate a larger quantity than is required by the Indians attached to the missions. San Jose, which possesses 15,000 head of cattle, cures about 2,000 hides annually, and as many botas of tallow, which are either disposed of by contract to a mercantile establishment at Monterey or to vessels in the harbour. The price of these hides may be judged by their finding a ready market on the Lima coast. Though there are a great many sheep in the country, as may be seen by the mission San Jose alone possessing 3,000, yet there is no export of wool, in consequence of the consumption of that article in the manufacture of cloth for the missions.

Husbandry is still in a very backward state, and it is fortunate that the soil is so fertile, and that there are abundance of labourers to perform the work, or I verily believe the people would be contented to live upon acorns. Their ploughs appear to have descended from the patriarchal ages, and it is only a pity that a little of the skill and industry then employed upon them, should not have devolved upon the present generation. It will scarcely be credited by agriculturists in other countries, that there were seventy ploughs and two hundred oxen at work upon a piece of light ground of ten acres; nor did the overseers appear to consider that number unnecessary, as the padre called our attention to this extraordinary advancement of the Indians in civilization, and pointed out the most able workmen as the ploughs passed us in succession. The greater part of these ploughs followed in the same furrow without making much impression, until they approached the padre, when the ploughman gave the necessary inclination of the hand, and the share got hold of the ground. It would have been good policy for the padre to have moved gradually along the field, by which he would leave had it properly ploughed; but he seemed to be quite

---

* A fanega is one hundred pounds weight.

satisfied with the performance Several of the missions, but particularly that of Santa Barbara, make a wine resembling claret, though not near so palatable, and they also distil an ardent spirit resembling arrack

In this part of California, besides the missions, there are several pueblos, or villages, occupied by Spaniards and their families, who have availed themselves of the privileges granted by the old government, and have relinquished the sword for the ploughshare There are also a few settlers who are farmers, but, with these exceptions, the country is almost uninhabited Perhaps I cannot convey a better idea of the deserted state of the country, or of the capability of its soil, than by inserting a short narrative which I have compiled from the journals of three of my officers who travelled over land from San Francisco to " the famous port of Monterey '

I have already stated that it was found expedient to make this journey to learn whether any supplies could be procured for the ship and in consequence Mr. Collie the surgeon, Mr Marsh, the purser, and Mr Evans, who was well acquainted with the Spanish language, were requested to proceed on this service. As it was of importance that no time should be lost in acquiring this information, they had very little time allowed to prepare them for so long, and to seamen, so unusual a journey, but as the mode of travelling in that rude country admitted but few incumbrances, the omission of these preparations was of less consequence

In order to reach a tolerable halting-place for the night, the first day's journey was necessarily long, and consequently by daylight on the 9th November the three officers were on the road to the mission, having found horses and an escort prepared in pursuance of previous arrangements

Setting off at a round trot, they made the best of their way over three or four miles of ground so overgrown with dwarf oaks and other trees, that they were every moment in danger of being thrown from their horses, or having their eyes torn out by the branches as they passed In half an hour, however, they reached the mission of San Francisco, and soon forgot the little annoyances they had hitherto met with in the hospitable welcome of the good priest, who regaled them with excellent pears and new milk. Nor was his conversation less palatable than his cheer ; for, notwithstanding the introduction of half a dozen unnecessary *si senors* in each sentence, he contrived to amuse the vacant time with a flow of most genuine humour, for which Tomaso was always prepared, till the rattling accoutrements of a Californian dragoon announced the arrival of the passport from the governor Intrusting their baggage to the care of two vaqueros (Indian cattle drivers) who were to accompany them, and receiving each a blessing from the padre, they set off with their escort about ten o'clock in the forenoon The cavalcade consisted of three officers of the Blossom, the two vaqueros, and their champion the dragoon, proceeded by nine or ten loose horses, driven on before as a relay, to be used when those they mounted should become fatigued. These Rozinantes are not much inclined to deviate from the road, but if any thing should inspire them with a spirit of straying, the unerring lasso, the never-failing appendage to a Californian saddlebow, soon embraces their neck or their feet, and brings them back again to the right way.

I must not, however, permit the party to proceed without introducing to the notice of the reader the costume and equipments of this dragoon of California. As for his person, I do not find it described, but his dress consisted of a round blue cloth jacket with red cuffs and collar; blue velvet breeches, which being unbuttoned at the knees, gave greater display to a pair of white cotton stockings. cased more than half way in a pair of deer-skin boots. A black hat, as broad in the brim as it was disproportionably low in the crown, kept in order, by its own weight, a profusion of dark hair, which met behind, and dangled half way down the back in the form of a thick queue. A long musket, with a fox skin bound round the lock, was balanced upon the pummel of the saddle; and our hero was further provided for defence against the Indians with a bull's hide shield, on which, notwithstanding the revolution of the colony, were emblazoned the royal arms of Spain, and by a double-fold deer skin cuirass as a covering for his body. Thus accoutred he bestrode a saddle, which retained him in his seat by a high pummel in front and a corresponding rise behind. His feet were armed at the heels with a tremendous pair of iron spurs, secured by a metal chain; and were thrust through an enormous pair of wooden box shaped stirrups. Such was the person into whose charge our shipmates were placed by the governor, with a passport which commanded him not to permit any person to interfere with the party, either in its advance or on its return, and that it was to be escorted from place to place by a soldier

Leaving the mission of San Francisco, the party receded from the only part of the country that is wooded for any considerable distance, and ascended a chain of hills about a thousand feet in height, where they had an extensive view, comprehending the sea, the Farallones rocks, and the distant Punta de los Reyes, a headland so named by the expedition under Sebastian Viscaino in 1602. The ridge which afforded this wide prospect was called Sierra de San Bruno, and for the most part was covered with a burnt-up grass, but such places as were bare presented to the eye of the geologist, rocks of sandstone conglomerate, intersected by a few veins of jaspar. Winding through the Sierra de San Bruno, they crossed a river of that name, and opened out the broad arm of the

sea which leads from the port to Santa Clara, and is confined between the chain they were traversing and the Sierra de los Bolbones, distinguishable at a distance by a peaked mountain 3,783
feet high by trigonometrical measurement.   Upon the summit of
that part of the sierra bordering the arm of sea called Estrecho de
San Jose, a thick wood, named Palos Colorados from its consisting
principally of red cedar pine, stands conspicuous on the ridge   I
mention this particularly, and wish to call attention to the circumstance, as the straggling trees at the south extreme of the wood
are used as landmarks for avoiding a dangerous rock which we discovered in the harbour, and named after the Blossom

About noon they reached a small cottage named Burri Burri,
about twelve miles from San Francisco : and being unused to travelling, especially upon Californian saddles, which are by no means
constructed for comfort, they determined to rest, until the baggage
that had been left in the rear should overtake them.   The house in
which they lodged was a small miserable mud cottage full of holes,
which however, afforded them some repose and some new milk.
Its inhabitants had been engaged in tanning, in which process they
used a liquid extracted from oak bark, contained in a hide suspended by the corners.   They had also collected in great quantities a
very useful root called in that country *amoles*, which seems to answer all the purposes of soap

From Burri Burri, a continuation of the Sierra de San Bruno
passes along the centre of the peninsula formed by the sea and the
Estrecho de San Jose, and is separated from this arm of the harbour by a plain, upon which the travellers now descended from the
mountains, and journeyed at a more easy and agreeable rate than
they had done on the rugged paths among the hills.   This plain
near the sea is marshy, and having obtained the name of Las Salinas is probably overflowed occasionally by the sea.   The number
of wild geese which frequent it is quite extraordinary, and indeed
would hardly be credited by any one who had not seen them covering whole acres of ground, or rising in myriads with a clang that
may be heard at a very considerable distance.   They are said to
arrive in California in November, and to remain there until March
Their flesh in general is hard and fishy, but it was reported by padre Luis Gil, of the mission of Santa Cruz, that those which have
yellow feet are exceptions to this, and are excellent eating.   The
blackbirds are almost equally numerous, and in their distant flight
resemble clouds.   Among the marshes there were also a great many
storks and cranes, which in San Francisco have the reputation of
affording a most delicious repast.

Travelling onward, the hills on their right, known in that part as
the Sierra del Sur, began to approach the road, which passing over

a small eminence, opened out upon a wide country of meadow land, with clusters of fine oak free from underwood. It strongly resembled a nobleman's park: herds of cattle and horses were grazing upon the rich pasture, and numerous fallow-deer, startled at the approach of strangers, bounded off to seek protection among the hills. The resemblance, however, could be traced no further. Instead of a noble mansion, in character with so fine a country, the party arrived at a miserable mud dwelling, before the door of which a number of half-naked Indians were basking in the sun. Several dead geese, deprived of their entrails, were fixed upon pegs around a large pole, for the purpose of decoying the living game into snares, which were placed for them in favourable situations. Heaps of bones also of various animals were lying about the place, and sadly disgraced the park-like scenery around. This spot is named San Matheo, and belongs to the mission of San Francisco.

Quitting this spot, they arrived at a farm-house about half way between San Francisco and Santa Clara, called Las Pulgas (fleas), a name which afforded much mirth to our travellers, in which they were heartily joined, by the inmates of the dwelling, who were very well aware that the name had not been bestowed without cause. It was a miserable habitation, with scarcely any furniture, surrounded by decaying hides and bones. Still, fatigue renders repose sweet upon whatsoever it can be indulged, and our party were glad enough to stretch themselves awhile upon a creaking couch, the only one in the hut, notwithstanding that the owner had a numerous family. Here, had there been accommodation, and had the place not acquired the reputation its name conveys, they would willingly have ended their day's journey, but the idea of las pulgas, sufficiently numerous in all the houses of California, determined them to proceed as soon as they conveniently could. The plain still continued animated with herds of cattle, horses, and sheep grazing; but the noble clusters of oak were now varied with shrubberies, which afforded a retreat to numerous coveys of Californian partridges, of which handsome species of game the first specimen was brought to England by the Blossom, and is now living in the gardens of the Zoological Society. They are excellent food; and the birds, in the country now under description, are so tame that they would often not start from a stone directed with Indian skill.

The sun went down before they reached Santa Clara, which was to terminate that day's journey, and, being unaccustomed to ride, the whole party were thoroughly fatigued. Indeed, so wearying was the journey even to the animals that bore them, that but for the relays of horses, which were now brought in with a lasso, they might have been compelled to pass the night upon the plain among the geese, the jackals, and the bears, which in the vicinity of Santa

Clara are by no means scarce   The pleasure of removing from a jaded horse to one that is fresh is not unknown probably to my readers, and our party rode in comparative comfort the remainder of the journey, and reached the mission of Santa Clara at eight o'clock.

Santa Clara, distant by the road about forty miles from San Francisco, is situated in the extensive plain before described, which here, however, becomes more marshy than that part of the ground over which they had just travelled   It nevertheless continues to be occupied by herds of cattle, horses, sheep, and flocks of geese. Here, also, troops of jackals prowl about in the most daring manner, making the plain resound with their melancholy howlings ; and indeed both wild and domesticated animals seem to lose their fear and become familiar with their tyrant man   The buildings of the establishment, which was founded in 1768, consist of a church, the dwelling-house of the priests, and five rows of buildings for the accommodation of 1,400 Indians, who, since Vancouver's visits, have been thus provided with comparatively comfortable dwellings, instead of occupying straw huts, which were always wet and miserable   Attached to these are some excellent orchards, producing an abundance of apples and pears   Olives and grapes are also plentiful, and the padres are enabled to make from the latter about twenty barrels of wine annually.   They besides grow a great quantity of wheat, beans, peas, and other vegetables   On the whole this is one of the best regulated and most cleanly missions in the country   Its herds of cattle amount to 10,000 in number, and of horses there are about 300.

When our travellers visited the mission it was governed by padres Jose and Machin, two priests of the mendicant order of San Francisco, to which class belong all the priests in Upper California. They appeared to lead a comfortable life, though not over well provided with its luxuries.

We will not, however, pry too narrowly into the internal arrangements of the good fathers' dwelling, let it suffice, that they gave our travellers a cordial welcome, and entertained them at their board in a most hospitable manner.   After joining them in a dram of aquadenté, they allowed their guests to retire to their sleeping apartment, where, stretched upon couches of bull-hide, as tough and impenetrable as the cuirass of their friend the dragoon (who left them at this place), they soon fell asleep—thanks to excessive weariness—and slept as soundly as *las pulgas* would let them.

Having breakfasted the following morning with the padres, and being provided with fresh horses, a new escort and vaqueros, the party was about to start, but were delayed by the punishment of an Indian who had stolen a blanket, for which he received two dozen lashes with a leathern thong upon that part of the human frame, which, we learn from Hudibras, is the most susceptible of insult. Some other Indians were observed to be heavily shackled, but the causes of their punishment were not stated.

A beautiful avenue of trees, nearly three miles in length, leads from the mission to the pueblo of San Jose, the largest settlement of the kind in Upper California It consist of mud-houses miserably provided in every respect, and contains about 500 inhabitants —retired soldiers and their families, who under the old government were allowed the privilege of forming settlements of this nature, and had a quantity of ground allotted to them for the use of their cattle They style themselves *Gente de Razon*, to distinguish them from the Indians, whose intellectual qualities are frequent subjects of animadversion amongst these enlightened communities. They are governed by an alcalde, and have a chapel of their own, at which one of the priests of the mission occasionally officiates.

About eighteen miles from Santa Clara, the party alighted upon the banks of a limpid stream, the first they had seen in their ride. It was too favourable a spot to be passed, and placing some milk and pears, which had been furnished by the hospitable priests at the mission, under the cool shade of an aliso-tree, they regaled themselves for a few minutes, and then resumed their journey. At the distance of eight leagues from Santa Clara, they passed some remarkable hills near the coast named *El ojo del coche;* and a few miles further on, they descended into the plain of *Las Llagas,* so called from a battle which took place between the first settlers and the Indians, in which many of the former were wounded Stopping towards the extremity of this fertile plain at some cottages, named *Ranchas de les animas,* the only habitations they had seen since the morning, they dined upon some jerk beef, which, according to the old custom in this and other Spanish colonies, was served in silver dishes. Silver cups and spoons were also placed before our travellers, offering a singular incongruity with the humble wooden benches, that were substituted for chairs, and with the whole arrangement of the room, which, besides the board of smoking jerk beef, contained beds for the family, and a horse harnessed to a flour mill

Leaving Llano de las Llagas, they ascended a low range of hills, and arrived at a river appropriately named Rio de los Paxaros, from the number of wild ducks which occasionally resort thither. The banks of this river are thickly lined with wood, and being very steep in many places, the party wound, with some difficulty, round the trunks of the trees and over the inequalities of the ground; but their Californian steeds, untrammelled with shoes, and accustomed to all kinds of ground, never once stumbled. They rode for some

time along the banks of this river, though so much broken, were
very agreeable, and crossing the stream a few miles lower down,
they left it to make its way towards the sea in a south-west direction, and themselves entered upon the Llano de San Juan, an extensive plain surrounded by mountains It should have been told,
before the party reached thus far, that as they were riding peaceably over the Llano de las Animas, the clanking of their guide's
huge broadsword, which had been substituted for the long musket
of the soldier from the presidio, drew the attention of the party to
his pursuit of a wild mountain-cat, which he endeavoured to ensnare with his lasso for the sake of its skin which is said to be
valuable   Two of these cats, which in species approach the oce-
lot, were shot by our sportsmen at San Francisco   Their skins
were preserved to be brought to this country, but on opening the
collection they were not found, and we have reason to suspect that
a man who assisted the naturalist, disposed of these, as well as
other specimens, to his own advantage
     Twilight approached as the party drew near to the mission of
San Juan, where they alighted, after a ride of fifty-four miles, just
as the bell tolled for vespers, and, stiff and tired, gladly availed
themselves of the accommodation afforded by padre Arroyo who in
hospitality and good humour endeavoured to exceed even the good
father of Santa Clara   This worthy man was a native of Old
Castile, and had resided in Californian since 1804, dividing his time
between the duties of his holy avocation, and various ingenious
inventions   Supper was served in very acceptable time to the fatigued visitors, and the good-natured padre used every persusaion
to induce them to do justice to his fare , treating them to several
approprioate proverbs, such as " Un dia alegre vale cien anos de
pesadumbre," (one day of mirth is worth a hundred years of grief,)
and many more to the same purpose.   Though so many summers
had passed over his head in exile, his cheerfulness seemed in no
way diminished, and he entertained his guests with a variety of anecdotes of the Indians and of their encounters with the bears too
long to be repeated here   Nor was his patriotism more diminished
than his cheerfulness, and on learning that one of the party had
been at the siege of Cadiz, his enthusiasm broke forth in the celebrated Spanish patriotic song of " Espana de la guerra," &c   Having served them with what he termed the *viatico*, consisting of a
plentiful supply of cold fricole beans, bread, and eggs, he led the
party to their sleeping apartment amidst promises of horses for the
morrow, and patriotic songs of his country adapted to the well-known
air of Malbrook   Interrupting the good man s enthusiasm, they
endeavoured to persuade the priest to allow them to proceed early
in the morning, before the commencement of mass ; this, however,

was impossible, and he shut them into their apartment, repeating the proverb, "Oir misa y dar cebada no impede jornada" (to hear mass and bestow alms will not retard your journey)

When the morning came, it was a holiday, and the vaqueros, not at all disposed to lose their recreation, had decamped with the saddles, and the party were obliged to pass the day at San Juan   After a small cup of chocolate, and a strip of dry bread, the only meal ever served in the missions until twelve o'clock, the party strolled over the grounds, and visited about thirty huts belonging to some newly converted Indians of the tribe of Toolerayos (*bulrushes*)   Their tents were about thirty-five feet in circumference, constructed with pliable poles fixed in the ground and drawn together at the top, to the height of twelve or fifteen feet   They are then interwoven with small twigs and covered with bulrushes, having an aperture at the side to admit the inhabitants, and another at the top to let out the smoke.   The exterior appearance of these wretched wigwams greatly resembles a bee-hive   In each dwelling were nine or ten Indians of both sexes, and of all ages, nearly in a state of nudity, huddled round a fire kindled in the centre of the apartment, a prey to vermin, and presenting a picture of misery and wretchedness seldom beheld in even the most savage state of society   They seemed to have lost all the dignity of their nature , even the black birds (*oriolus niger*) had ceased to regard them as human beings, and were feeding in flocks among the wigwams   This was said to be the state in which the Indians naturally live, and the reader will not be surprised to hear that this party had voluntarily come from the mountains to be converted, and to join their civilized brethren at the mission.   Happy would it be for these savages could they be once taught to make a proper use of that freedom which ought to follow their conversion to the pure religion of Christ, even under the restrained form of Catholicism, that their minds might become by this means sufficiently improved to allow of their settling in independent Christian communities, but, judging from their present mental capacity, it must be long before so great and desirable a change can be effected   The experiment of liberating the Indians has been tried and has failed , and appearances certainly justify the assertion that the Indian is happier under control than while indulging his free soul in the wilds of his native country.

What might seem a remarkable example of this was met with on turning from the dwelling of wretchedness just described to a scene of the greatest mirth and happiness amongst some converted Indians, who were passing their holiday in amusement   Some were playing at *takersia*, a game which, as already described, consists in trundling a hoop, or rather a piece of wood with a hole in it, and in endeavouring to pierce it with a short lance as it rolls.   Another party were playing at a game resembling *hockey*, and in various parts of the plain adjoining the mission many others were engaged in pleasant recreations, passing their day in exercise, content, and enjoyment.

In the neighbouring meadows there were several large herds of cattle ; and the geese settled there in flocks, as at the mission of Santa Clara   The rocks, where they protruded, were ascertained by Mr. Collie to be sand-stone conglomerate with a calcareous basis

The welcome peals of the mission bell assembled the party at dinner, but the padre, who for some time before had been earnestly engaged in endeavouring to convert one of his heretic guests, was unwilling to quit the train of theological disquisitions which in his own opinion he had almost brought to successful issue, until reminded by his other visitors, who had not been accustomed to go so long without their breakfast, that they required something more substantial.

I will not attempt to stimulate the appetite of my reader by enumerating the various exquisite dishes which successively smoked on the board of the generous priest, suffice it that there were many good ones, as the padres in California are careful to have their table well supplied at all times of the year, and have an indulgence from the pope to eat meat even-during the greater part of Lent, in consequence of the difficulty of procuring fish

Having performed the honours of the table, padre Arroyo retired to indulge his usual siesta . this, however, caused but a brief suspension to the efforts he most industriously continued to make, for the purpose of converting his heretical opponent to the true faith, reading him innumerable lectures in refutation of the Lutheran and Calvinistic doctrines, and in favour of the pope's supremacy, infallibility, and power of remitting offences

It more than once occurred to the party—and I believe, not without good foundation for their opinion—that it was the hope of success in this conversion which occasioned all the little manœuvring to delay them, that I have before described   But having at length given his pupil over as irrevocably lost, he consented to their departure on the following morning   The padre appeared to be of an active mind, and had constructed a water-clock which communicated with a bell by his bedside, and which by being arranged at night could be made to give an alarm at any stated hour

It was here that our travellers were surprised at the intelligence of the north-west passage having been effected by a Spaniard, and were not a little amused at the idea of having stumbled upon the long-sought north-west passage in an obscure mission of California.

The padre, however, was quite in earnest, and produced a work published by the Duke of Almodobar, Director of the Royal Academy in Spain, in which was transcribed at full length the fictitious voyage of Maldonado. It was in vain they endeavoured to persuade the padre that this voyage was not real, seeing that it bore even in its detail all the marks of truth, and that it emanated from such high authority His credulity in this instance affords a curious proof of the very secluded manner in which these holy men pass their time, for it may be remembered, that it was in the very ports of California that both Vancouver and Quadra anchored, after having satisfactorily proved the voyage in question to have been a fabrication

A still greater instance of the simplicity of the priest is related at his expense by persons in the mission A youthful Indian couple who had conceived an affection for each other eloped one day, that they might enjoy each other's society without reserve in the wild and romantic scenery of the forests. Soldiers were immediately sent in pursuit, when, after a week's search, the fugitives were brought back; upon which padre Arroyo, to punish their misbehaviour, incarcerated them together, and kept them thus confined until he thought they had expiated their crime.

In addition to his other manifold accomplishments, padre Arroyo was a grammarian, and said that he had written a vocabulary and grammar of the Indian languages, but he could not be prevailed upon to show them. Such works, were they in existence, would, I believe, be the only ones of the kind; and it is a pity that they should not be given to the world as a matter of curiosity, though I cannot think they would be of much use to a traveller, as the languages of the tribes differ so materially, and in such short spaces, that in one mission there were eleven totally different dialects. I cannot omit to mention padre Arroyo's disquisition on the etymology of the name of the Peninsula of California. I shall observe first, that it was never known why Cortes gave to the bay * which he first discovered, a name which appears to be composed of the Latin words *calida* and *fornax*, signifying *heat* and *furnace*, and which was afterwards transferred to the peninsula Miguel Venegas supposed it arose from some Indian words which Cortes misunderstood, and Burney, in his history of voyages in the Pacific,† observes, that some have conjectured the name to have been given on account of the heat of the weather, and says, it has been remarked that it was the only name given by Cortes which was immediately derived from the Latin language. Without entering into

* Bernal Diaz de Castillo, in his "Conquest of Mexico," calls California a bay
† Vol. I. p. 178, 4to,

a discussion of the subject, which is not of any moment, I shall observe, that it was thought in Monterey to have arisen in consequence of a custom which prevails throughout California, of the Indians shutting themselves in ovens until they perspire profusely, as I have already described in speaking of the Temeschal. It is not improbable that the practice appeared so singular to Cortes that he applied the name of California to the country, as being one in which hot ovens were used for such singular purposes. Padre Arroyo, however, maitained that it was a corruption of *colofon*, which, in the Spanish language, signifies resin, in consequence of the pine trees which yield that material being so numerous. The first settlers, he said, at the sight of these trees would naturally exclaim, "Colofon," which, by its similarity to Californo, (in the Catalonian dialect, hot oven,) a more familiar expression, would soon become changed

Our travellers, after taking leave of the hospitable and amusing priest the proceding evening, with the intention of preceding early in the morning, experienced much delay in consequence of the refusal of the guard to start without hearing mass and receiving the benediction of the priest but at length they quitted the plain of San Juan, and ascended with difficulty some steep hills commanding a view of the spacious bay of Monterey. Then winding among valleys, one of which was well wooded and watered, they entered an extensive plain called "Llano del Rey," which until their arrival, was in the quiet possession of numerous herds of deer and jackals. This tract of land is bounded on the north, east, and southeast, by mountains which extend with a semicircular sweep from the sea at Santa Cruz, and unite with the coast line again at Point Pinos. It is covered with a rank grass, and has very few shrubs In traversing this plain, before they could arrive at some ranchos, named Las Salinas, where they proposed to dine, the party had to wade through several deep ditches and the Rio del Rey, both of which were covered with wild ducks. The cottages called Las Salinas are on the farm of an old Scotchman, to whom the land was granted in consequence of some services which he rendered to the missions They rested here, and to the provision they had brought with them very gladly added some pumpkins, procured from the Indians. Here, also, they were surprised with the novel occurrence of having water brought to them in baskets, which the Indians weave so close, that when wet they become excellent substitutes for bowls.

The remainder of the plain over which they passed toward Monterey was sandy, and covered with fragrant southernwood, broken here and there by dwarf oaks, and shrubs of the syngenesious class of plants As they approached the town, pasture lands, covered with herds of cattle, succeeded this wild scenery and riding onward, trees of luxuriant growth, houses scattered over the plain, the fort, and the shipping in the bay, announced the speedy termination of their journey   At five o'clock in the evening they alighted in the square at Monterey, and met a kind reception from Mr   Hartnell, a merchant belonging to the firm of Begg and Co in Lima, who was residing there, and who pressed them to accept the use of his house while they remained in the town—an offer of which they thankfully availed themselves

Gonzales, the governor to whom the party went to pay their respects, was an officer who had been raised by his own merit from the ranks to be captain of artillery and governor of Monterey : his family were residing with him, and having been educated in Mexico, complained bitterly of their banishment to this outlandish part of the world, where the population, the ladies in particular, were extremely ignorant, and wretched companions for the *Mexicanus instrudas*   Besides, there were no balls or bull-fights in Monterey ; and for all the news they heard of their own country, they might as well have been at Kamschatka.   To compensate for these dreadful privations, the ladies generally amused themselves in the evening by smoking and playing cards, and relating the perils they encountered in the land journey from Mexico to the shores of the Pacific. Politness and attention, however, were the characteristics of the good people, who offered our party every assistance in their power during their stay at Monterey   .

Upon inquiry after the stores and medicines the ship stood in need of, the result was highly unfavourable , as there were no medicines to be had, and some stores which were essential to the ship could nowhere be procured   The exchange on bills was favourable, but there was no specie   Mr Marsh therefore purchased what stores he could from the inhabitants and from the shipping in the roads, and arranged with a person who had come out from Ireland for the purpose of salting meat for the Lima market, to cure a quantity for the use of the ship. and to have it ready on her arrival at Monterey   They then hastened their departure ; but the same difficulties arose about horses as before, and they were much inconvenienced in consequence, being obliged to alter a plan they had contemplated of returning by a different route.   This, very unexpectedly to padre Arroyo, brought them again under his roof The padre either did not like this second tax on his hospitality, or was put out of temper by the increase of a complaint to which he was subject, as he gave them a less cordial reception, and appeared very little disposed to conversation   It was imagined, however, that he still entertained hopes of the conversion of one of the party, and that with this view he again occasioned a delay in furnishing horses for the next day's journey , offering as excuses, that some of the horses of the mission were engaged by soldiers in pursuit of a Mexican exile, who had deserted, that others had been taken by the vaqueros to look after a male and female Indian, who had likewise absconded, and that the rest were gone to join the expedition against Los Gentiles, the Cosemenes. Vexed at this delay, the party endeavoured to hire horses at their own expense, but the price demanded was so exorbitant that they determined to wait the return of those that were said to be absent

It is more than probable that some one of my readers may have been in the same predicament—in a strange town, in a strange country, with a beast fatigued to death, and an urgent necessity for proceeding, he will then easily remember the amiable and benevolent alacrity with which the inhabitants endeavoured to lighten his load of every stray crown they could obtain from him, on every pretence that ingenious cupidity can invent. So at least did the good people at San Juan, when padre Arroyo would no longer assist our poor companions. Private horses could be had, it was true, but terms were either thirteen shillings sterling for the journey, or seventeen shillings sterling for the purchase of the horse, which in California is considered so exorbitant that our shipmates did not think proper to suffer the imposition, and awaited the horses belonging to the mission.

After a day's delay during which they again heard many invectives against the new government of Mexico which had deprived the priesthood of their salaries, and obliged the missions to pay a tithe to the state, they resumed their journey, and arrived at San Francisco on the 17th of November.

In this route it will be seen that, with the exception of the missions and pueblos, the country is almost uninhabited, yet the productive nature of the soil, when it has been turned up by the missions, and the immense plains of meadow land over which our travellers passed, show with how little trouble it might be brought into high cultivation by any farmers who could be induced to settle there

The unwelcome intelligence brought by this party of the nature of the supplies to be obtained at Monterey, obliged me to relinquish the plan I had contemplated of completing the survey of that part of the coast of California which had been left unfinished by Vancouver, and rendered it necessary that I should proceed direct either to Canton or to Lima, as the most likely places for us to meet with the medicines and stores of which we were in such imminent need The western route of these two afforded the best opportunity of promoting the objects of the expedition, by bringing us into the vicinity of several groupes of islands of doubtful existence, at which, in the event of their being found, our time might be usefully employed until it should be necessary to proceed to Berring's Strait.   An additional reason for this decision was, a request which I had made to the consul of the Sandwich Islands, if possible, to purchase provision for the ship at that place.   I therefore determined, after taking on board the few stores that were purchased at Monterey, to proceed to the Sandwich Islands, searching in our way thither for some Islands said to have been discovered by an American vessel, and from thence prosecute the voyage to Canton.

While we remained at San Francisco refitting the ship, the boats were constantly employed sounding and surveying the harbour, in which the duty we received every assistance from Martinez, the governor, who allowed us to enter the forts and to take what angles and measures we pleased, requiring only in return for this indulgence a copy of the plan, when finished, for his own government, his proposal seemed so fair that I immediately acceded to it, and, on my return to the place the following year, fully complied with his request.   It is impossible to pass unnoticed the difference between this liberal conduct of Martinez and that of the former Spanish authorites, who watched all Vancouver's actions with the greatest suspicion, and whose jealousy has been the subject of animadversion of almost every voyager who has touched at this port.

On the 12th of December a salute was fired from the battery ; high mass was said in all the missions, and a grand entertainment, to which all the officers were invited, was given at the presidio, in honour of Santa Senora Gaudaloupe   There was also to have been a fight between a bear and a bull, but for some reason not known to us—probably the trouble it required to bring the animal so far, as the bears do not come within many miles of the presidio—it did not take place , and we were all greatly disappointed, as we had offered to reward the soldiers for their trouble and had heard so much of these exhibitions from every body that our curiosity had been highly excited.   This is a favourite amusement with Californians, but it is of rare occurrence, as there is much trouble in getting a bear alive to the scene of combat, and there is also some risk and expense attending it.   We were informed that when a fight is determined upon three or four horsemen are dispatched with lassos to the woods where the bears resort, and that when they come to an advantageous spot they kill a horse or a bullock as a bait, and hide themselves in the wood.   Sometimes they have to wait a whole day or more before any of these animals appear, but when they come to partake of the food, the men seize a favourable opportunity, and rush upon them at different points with their lassos, and entangle one of them until he is thrown upon the ground, when they manage to suspend him between the horsemen, while a third person dismounts and ties his feet together; he is then extended upon a hide and dragged home, during which time it is necessary, they say, to keep him constantly wet to allay his thirst and rage, which amounts almost to madness—and woe be to him who should be near if he were to break away from his fastenings. The entangling of the animal in the first instance appears to be by no means devoid of risk, as in case of the failure of a lasso it is only by speed that a rider can save himself and his horse. The bear being caught, two or three men are dispatched for a wild bull, which they lasso in an equally dexterous manner, catching him either by the horns or by whichsoever leg they please, in order to trip him up and retain him between them

It is necessary to begin the fight as soon as the animals are brought in, as the bear cannot be tempted to eat, and is continually exhausting himself in struggling for his liberty. The two animals are then tied together by a along rope, and the battle begins, sometimes to the disadvantage of the bear, who is half dead with exhaustion, but in the end almost always proves fatal to the bull. It is remarkable that all the bears endeavour to seize the bull by the tongue, for which purpose they spring upon his head or neck and first grapple with his nose, until the pain compels the bull to roar, when his adversary instantly seizes his tongue, pierces it with his sharp talons, and is sure of victory. These battles were the everlasting topic of conversation with the Californians, who indeed have very little else to talk about, and they all agreed as to the manner of the fatal termination of the spectacle.

The lasso, though now almost entirely confined to Spanish America, is of very great antiquity, and originally came from the east. It was used by a pastoral people who were of Persian descent, and of whom 8,000 accompanied the army of Xerxes *

By Christmas-day we had all remained sufficiently long in the harbour to contemplate our departure without regret. the eye had become familiar to the picturesque scenery of the bay; the pleasure of the chase had lost its fascination, and the roads to the mission and presidio were grown tedious and insipid. There was no society to enliven the hours, no incidents to vary one day from the other, and, to use the expression of Donna Gonzales, California appeared to be as much out of the world as Kamschatka.

On the 26th, being ready for sea, I was obliged to relinquish the survey of this magnificent port, which possesses almost all the requisites for a great naval establishment, and is so advantageously situated with regard to North America and China, and the Pacific in general, that it will, no doubt, at some future time, be of great importance. We completed the examination of those parts of the

* Rennell on the 20 Satrapies of Darius Hystaspes, P. 287.

harbour which were likely to be frequented by vessels for some years to come, in which it is proper to mention, in order to give as much publicity to the circumstance as possible, that we discovered a rock between Alcatrasses and Yerba Buena Islands, dangerous to both shipping and boats, in consequence of its rising suddenly from about seven fathoms, so near to the surface as to occasion strong overfalls with the tides. A shoal was also found to the eastward of the landing place off the presidio, which ought to be avoided by boats sailing along shore.

On the 28th we took leave of our hospitable and affable friends, Martinez and Padre Tomaso, full of gratitude for their kindness and attention to our wants; weighed anchor and bade adieu to the Port of San Francisco, in which we had all received material benefit from the salubrity of its climate, the refreshing product of its soil and the healthy exercise we had enjoyed there In the ship's company in particular, there was the most apparent amendment; some of them, from being so emaciated on their arrival that the surgeon could scarcely recognize them, were now restored to their former healthy appearance, and we had the satisfaction of sailing without a single case of sickness on board. We had to regret during our stay the loss of one of our best men, Joseph Bowers, a marine. He had accompanied one of the officers on a shooting excursion, and was led by his naturally ardent and bold disposition to plunge into a lake after some wild fowl that had been shot, forgetting that he could not swim. His eagerness led him beyond his depth, and in his attempt to regain his footing, he unfortunately perished before any aid could be brought. His body was interred at the burial ground near the presidio landing-place, and was followed to the grave by all the officers. As the coffin was lowering into the ground, the good understanding that existed between the ship's company and the inhabitants was testified in the most gratifying manner, by the latter approaching and performing the last office for the deceased, by dropping the earth in upon his coffin. I cannot recollect ever having met with such conduct in any other foreign port, and the act, most certainly, did not lessen our regard for the inhabitants.

CHAPTER XIV.

Observations on the Country of California and its Trade—Climate—Meteorological Remarks—Short Account of the Wild Indians—Natural Productions—Monterey —Mission of San Carlos—Departure.

The more we became acquainted with the beautiful country around San Francisco, the more we were convinced that it possessed every requisite to render it a valuable appendage to Mexico, and it was impossible to resist joining in the remark of Vancouver, "Why such an extent of territory should have been subjugated, and, after all the expense and labour bestowed upon its colonization, turned to no account whatever, is a mystery in the science of state policy not easily explained." Situated in the northern hemisphere, between the parallels of 22° and 39°, no fault can be found with its climate; its soil in general is fertile, it possesses forests of oak and pine convenient for building and contributing to the necessities of vessels, plains overrun with cattle, excellent ports, and navigable rivers to facilitate inland communication   Possessing all these advantages, an industrious population alone seems requisite to withdraw it from the obscurity in which it has so long slept under the indolence of the people and the jealous policy of the Spanish government   Indeed it struck us as lamentable to see such an extent of habitable country lying almost desolate and useless to mankind, whilst other nations are groaning under the burthen of their population

It is evident, from the natural course of events, and from the rapidity with which observation has recently been extended to the hitherto most obscure parts of the globe, that this indifference cannot continue; for either it must disappear under the present authorities, or the country will fall into other hands, as from its situation with regard to other powers upon the new continent, and to the commerce of the Pacific, it is of too much importance to be permitted to remain long in its present neglected state   Already have the Russians encroached upon the territory by possessing themselves of the Faiallones, and some islands off Santa Barbara ; and their new settlement at Rossi. a few miles to the northward of Bodega, is so near upon the boundary as to be the cause of much jealous feeling ,—not without reason it would appear, as I am informed it is well fortified, and presents to California an example of what may be effected upon her shores in a short time by industry

The tract situated between California and the eastern side of the continent of North America, having been only partially explored, has hitherto presented a formidable barrier to encroachment from that quarter ; but settlements are already advancing far into the heart of the country, and parties of hunters have lately traversed the interior, and even penetrated to the shores of the Pacific ;— not without the loss of lives from the attacks of the Indians, it is true, but with ease compared with the labour and difficulty experienced by Lewis and Clarke, who had not the benefit which more recent travellers have derived from the establishment of inland depots by the American fur companies.   One of these depots we were informed by a gentleman belonging to the establishment, whom we met at Monterey in 1827, is situated on the western side of the rocky mountains on a fork of the Columbia called Lewis River, near the source of a stream supposed to be the Colorado.

The trade of Upper California at present consists in the exportation of hides, tallow, manteca, horses to the Sandwich Islands, grain for the Russian establishments at Sitka and Kodiak, and in the disposal of provisions to whale-ships and other vessels which touch upon the coast,—perhaps a few furs and dollars are sent to China The importations are dry goods, furniture, wearing-apparel, agricultural implements, deal-boards, and salt ; and silks and fireworks from China for the decoration of the churches and celebration of the saints' days   In 1827 almost all these articles bore high prices · the former in consequence of the increased demand for them ; and the latter, partly from the necessity of meeting the expenses of the purchase of a return cargo, and partly on account of the navigation act

The missions and the inhabitants in general complained loudly of these prices, not considering that the fault was in a great measure their own, and that they were purchasing some articles which had been brought several thousand miles, when they might have procured them in their own country with moderate labour only. For example, they were actually living upon the sea-coast and amongst forests of pine, and yet were suffering themselves to buy salt and deal-boards at exorbitant prices. ·

With a similar disregard for their interest, they were purchasing sea-otter skins at twenty dollars apiece, whilst the animals were swimming about unmolested in their own harbours; and this from the Russians, who are intruders upon their coast, and are depriving them of a lucrative trade · and again, they were paying two hundred dollars for carts of inferior workmanship, which, with the exception of the wheels, might have been equally well manufactured in their own country.

With this want of commercial enterprise, they are not much entitled to commiseration   With more justice might they have complained of the navigation laws, which, though no doubt beneficial to the inhabitants on the eastern coast of Mexico, where there are vessels belonging to the state in readiness to conduct the coasting trade, are extremely disadvantageous to the Californians, who having no vessels to employ in this service are often obliged to pay the duty on goods introduced in foreign bottoms   This duty for the encouragement of the coasting trade was made seventeen per cent higher than that on cargoes brought in vessels of the state   Thus not only must the inhabitants purchase their goods on very disadvantageous terms, but, as a foreign vessel cannot break stowage without landing the whole of her cargo, they must in addition incur the expenses attending that, which will in general fall upon a few goods only, as the towns in California are not sufficiently populous, any one of them, to consume a whole cargo ; and it is to be remembered, that no foreign vessel, after breaking stowage, can proceed to another port in the same dominion without being liable to seizure by the customs

The imprudent nature of these laws, as regards California, appears to have been considered by the authorities in that country, as they overlook the introduction of goods into the towns by indirect channels, except in cases of a gross and palpable nature.   In this manner several American vessels have contrived to dispose of their cargoes, and the inhabitants have been supplied with goods of which they were much in need, but, had the navigation laws been strictly attended to, the vessels must have returned unsuccessful, and the inhabitants have continued in want

Far more liberal has been the hand of nature to this much neglected country, in bestowing upon it a climate remarkable for its salubrity   The Spanish settlers in California enjoy an almost uninterrupted state of good health   Many attain the age of eighty and ninety, and some have exceeded a hundred years   There have been periods, however, when the small pox and measles have affected the population, and particulary the Indians in the missions, who, unlike the Spaniards, appear to suffer severely from diseases of all kinds   The small pox many years ago prevailed to an alarming extent, and carried off several thousand Indians; but since the introduction of cattle into the country, and with them the cow pox, it has not reappeared.   Vaccination was practised in California as early as 1806, and the virus from Europe has been recently introduced through the Russian establisment at Rossi.   The measles have also at times seriously affected the Indians, and in 1806 proved fatal to thousands, while it is remarkable that none of the Spaniards affected with the disease died   Dysentery, the most prevalent complaint amongst the converted Indians, no doubt arises in a great measure from the coldness and dampness of their habitations, and becomes fatal through the want of proper medical assistance They are happily free from the hooping cough.

This state of ill health does not extend to the uncivilized Indians; and, notwithstanding the mortality in the missions, the climate of California must be considered salubrious.   Perouse, Vancouver, and Langsdorff were of the same opinion ; and to judge of it by the general health of the Spanish residents, and by the benefit that our seamen derived from it during their short stay, it would certainly appear not to be surpassed.   The summer and early part of the autumn are the least healthy parts of the year, in consequence of continued fogs, which occur at these periods

It is, in all probability, in consequence of these fogs during the warmest part of the year, that the coast of California has the reputation of being much colder than that of Chili in corresponding parallels of latitude.   In the month of December the mean temperature of San Francisco was 53° 2', the maximum 66°, and the minimum 46°.   We nevertheless saw hoar frost upon the grass in the mornings, and in the following year observed snow lie several hours upon the ground.   As the minimum of temperature was so many degrees above the freezing point, the former was in all probability occasioned by the radiation, which is very great in that country.

The winter of 1826 was said to be a very favourable season ; we could not judge from our own experience, therefore, of what weather was usual on the coast at that period of the year.   But there were very few days during our visit in which a vessel might not have approached the coast with safety.   The strongest and most prevalent winds were from the north-west ; but these winds, though they blew directly upon the coast, were generally attended by clear weather, which would have enabled a vessel to find a port, had it been necessary.   They were strongest about the full and change of the moon

From the prevalence of the westerly swell off the harbour, and from the wind moderating as we approached the coast in both years, I am inclined to think that these winds do not usually blow home upon the shore.

There was a curious anomaly observed in the movements of the barometer and sympeisometer during our stay at San Francisco; the former rose with the winds which brought bad weather, and fell with those which restored serenity to the sky. The maximum height was 30 46, the minimum 29 98, and the mean 30 209.

The hygrometer on the whole indicated a dry atmosphere, and ranged from 0° to 20° of dryness on the thermometric scale, the mean degree of dryness being 6°, 6'. The particulars of these observations are inserted in tables in the Appendix to the 4to edition

The clear weather occasioned by the north-west wind was favourable for astronomical observations; but many were lost in consequence of a haze overhanging the land at night, and from the inconvenience arising from a heavy deposition, which, besides occasioning much mirage, fell so profusely upon the glasses of the instruments that they were obliged to be repeatedly wiped, and sometimes at the most inconvenient moments.* Our observations, however, were very satisfactory, and are important, as the longitudes of the places between Nootka Sound and San Diego are dependent upon the situation of San Francisco and Monterey; Vancouver having, in his survey of the coast, rated his chronometers between the meridians of these places. My observatory was erected upon a small eminence near the anchorage at Yerba Buena, from whence the observations were carefully reduced to the fort at the entrance of the harbour. The results have been published in the 4to edition, where will also be found some observations on the dip and variation of the needle, the tides, and other subjects.

I shall conclude this imperfect sketch of Upper California with a short description of the Indian mode of living, and of the natural productions of the country, derived principally from the information of the priests, and from the journals of the officers who went overland to Monterey. The Indians who enter the missions with which we became acquainted are divided in their wild state into distinct tribes, and are governed by a chief whose office is hereditary, but only in the male line. The widows and daughters, however, though not allowed to partake of this privilege, are exempted from labour, and are more respected than other women. Each tribe has a different dialect. and though their districts are small, the languages are sometimes so different, that the neighbouring tribes cannot understand each other. I have before observed that in the mission of San Carlos there are eleven different dialects Their villages consist of wigwams made with poles, covered with bulrushes, and are generally placed in an open plain to avoid surprise Like the Arabs and other wandering tribes, these people move about the country, and pitch their tents wherever they find a convenient place, keeping, however within their own district.

---

* I found this in a great degree obviated by fixing a long paper tube to the field end of the telescope.

They cultivate no land, and subsist entirely by the chase, and upon the spontaneous produce of the earth. Acorns, of which there is a great abundance in the country, constitute their principal vegetable food. In the proper season they procure a supply of these, bake them, and then bruise them between two stones into a paste, which will keep until the following season. The paste before it is dried is subjected to several washings in a sieve, which they say deprives it of the bitter taste common to the acorn. We cannot but remark the great resemblance this custom bears to the method adopted by the South-Sea Islanders to keep their bread fruit, nor ought we to fail to notice the manner in which Providence points out to different tribes the same wise means of preserving their food, and providing against a season of scarcity.

The country inhabited by the Indians abounds in game, and the rivers in fish ; and those tribes which inhabit the sea-coast make use of muscles and other shell-fish, of which the haliotis gigantea is the most abundant. In the chase they are very expert, and avail themselves of a variety of devices' to ensnare and decoy their game. The artifice of deceiving the deer by placing a head of the animal upon their shoulders is very successfully practiced by them. To do this, they fit the head and horns of a deer upon the head of a huntsman, the rest of his body being painted to resemble the colour of a deer. Thus disguised the Indian sallies forth, equipped with his bow and arrows, approaches the pasture of the deer, whose actions and voice he then endeavours to imitate, taking care to conceal his body as much as possible, for which purpose he generally selects places which are overgrown with long grass. This stratagem seldom fails to entice several of the herd within reach of his arrows, which are frequently sent with unerring aim to the heart of the animal, and he falls without alarming the herd ; but if the aim should fail, or the arrow only wound its intended victim, the whole herd is immediately put to flight.

Their method of taking ducks and other wildfowl is equally ingenious. They construct large nets with bulrushes, and repair to such rivers as are the resort of their game, where they fix a long pole upright on each bank, with one end of the net attached to the pole on the opposite side of the river to themselves. Several artificial ducks made of rushes are then set afloat upon the water between the poles as a decoy ; and the Indians, who have a line fastened to one end of the net, and passed through a hole in the upper end of the pole that is near them, wait the arrival of their game in concealment. When the birds approach, they suddenly extend the net across the river by pulling upon the line, and intercept them in their flight, when they fall stunned into a large purse in the net, and are captured. They also spread nets across their rivers in the evening, in order that the buds may become entangled in them as they fly.

The occupation of the men consists principally in providing for their support, and in constructing the necessary implements for the chase and for their own defence   The women attend to their domestic concerns, and work a variety of baskets and ornamental parts of their dress, some are very ingenious, and all extremely laborious.   Their closely wove baskets are not only capable of containing water, but are used for cooking their meals.   A number of small scarlet feathers of the orilus phœniceus are wove in with the wood, and completely screen it from view on the outside; and to the rim are affixed small black crests of the Californian patridges, of which birds a hundred brace are required to decorate one basket.—they are otherwise ornamented with beads, and pieces of mother-of-pearl.   They also embroider belts very beautifully with feathers of different colours, and they work with remarkable neatness, making use of the young quills of the porcupine, in a similar manner to the Canadian Indians; but here they manufacture a fine cloth for the ground, whereas the Canadians have only the bark of the birch-tree.   They also manufacture caps and dresses for their chiefs, which are extremely beautiful; and they have a great many other feather ornaments, which it would be stepping beyond the limits of my work to describe.

The stature of the Indians which we saw in the missions was by no means diminutive.   The Alchones are of good height, and the Tuluraios were thought to be, generally, above the standard of Englishmen.   Their complexion is much darker than that of the South-sea Islanders, and their features far inferior in beauty.   In their persons they are extremely dirty, particularly their heads, which are so thatched with wiry black hair that it is only by separating the locks with the hand that it can be got at for the purposes of cleanliness.   Many are seen performing such acts of kindness upon their intimate friends; and, as the readiest means of disposing of what they find, consuming it in the manner practiced by the Tartars, who according to Hakluyt—"cleanse one anothers' heades, and ever as they take an animal do eate her, saeing thus wille I doe to our enemies "*

Their bodies are in general very scantily clothed, and in summer many go entirely naked.   The women, however, wear a deer skin or some other covering about their loins . but skin dresses are not common among any of the tribes concerning whom we would procure any information.   The women are fond of ornaments, and suspend beads and buttons about their persons, while to their ears

* Hakluyt's Selection of curious and rare Voyages, Supplement

they attach long wooden cylenders, variously carved, which serve the double purpose of ear-rings and needle-cases

Tattooing is practiced in these tribes by both sexes, both to ornament the person, and to distinguish one clan from the other It is remarkable that the women mark their chins precisely in the same way as the Esquimaux

The tribes are frequently at war with each other, often in consequence of trespasses upon their territory and property , and weak tribes are sometimes wholly annihilated, or obliged to associate themselves with those of their conquerors ; but such is their warmth of passion and desire of revenge that very little humanity is in general shown to those who fall into their power Their weapons consist only of bows and arrows , neither the tomahawk nor the spear is ever seen in their hands. Their bows are elegantly and ingeniously constructed, and if kept dry will discharge an arrow to a considerable distance They resemble those of the Esquimaux, being strengthened by sinews at the back of the bow, but here one sinew, the size of the wood, occupies the whole extent of the back, and embraces the ends, where they are turned back to receive the string , the sinew is fixed to the bow while wet, and as it becomes dry draws it back the reverse way to that in which it is intended to be used. The Indian manner of stringing these bows is precisely similar to that practiced by the lovers of archery in England; but it requires greater skill and strength, in consequence of the increased curvature of the bow, and the resistence of the sinew.

The religion of all the tribes is idolatrous. The Olchone, who inhabit the sea-coast between San Francisco and Monterey, worship the sun, and believe in the existence of a beneficent and an evil spirit, whom they occasionally attempt to propitiate Their ideas of a future state are very confined · when a person dies they adorn the corpse with feathers, flowers, and beads, and place with it a bow and arrows , they then extend it upon a pile of wood, and burn it amidst the shouts of the spectators, who wish the soul a pleasant journey to its new abode, which they suppose to be a country in the direction of the setting sun Like most other nations, these people have a tradition of the deluge , they believe also that their tribes originally came from the north.

The Indians in their wild state are said to be more healthy than those which have entered the missions They have simple remedies, derived from certain medicinal herbs, with the property of which they have previously made themselves acquainted Some of these roots are useful as emetics, and are administered in cases of sickness of the stomach: they also apply cataplasms to diseased parts of the body, and practise phlebotomy very generally, using the right arm for this purpose when the body is affected, and the left where the limbs.   But the temischal is the grand remedy for most of their diseases

The very great care taken of all who are affected with any disease ought not to be allowed to escape a remark.   When any of their relations are indisposed, the greatest attention is paid to their wants, and it was remarked by Padre Arroya that filial affection is stronger in these tribes than in any civilized nation on the globe with which he was acquainted.

Our knowledge of the natural history of this country cannot be expected to be very extensive.   In the woods not immediately bordering upon the missions, the black bear has his habitation, and when food is scarce it is dangerous to pass through them alone in the dusk of the evening ; but when the acorns abound there is nothing to apprehend.   It is said that the white bear also visits this district occasionally, from the northward.   The lion (*felis concolor?*) and the tiger (*felis onca?*) are natives of these woods, but we never saw them   the inhabitants say they are small, and that the lion is less than the tiger. but more powerful.   A large species of mountain cat (*gato del monte*) is common ·   a pole cat (*vivera putorius*) also is found in the woods · wolves and foxes are numerous, and the *cuiotas*, or jackalls, range about the plains at night, and prove very destructive to the sheep.   The fallow deer browses on the pasture land, not only in the interior, but also upon some of the islands and around the shores af the harbour ; it is sought after for its skin, of which the Spaniards make boots and shoes, &c   The rein deer also is found inland, particularly upon a large plain named Tulurayos, on account of the number of bulrushes growing there.   In the months of May and June the Spaniards resort to this plain with their lassos, and take as many of these animals as they can ensnare, for the sake of their fat, of which they will sometimes procure between four and five arobas from one animal.

The fields are burrowed by a small rat, resembling the *mus arvalis*, by a mountain rat of the *cricetus*, species, and also by the ardillo, a species of sciurus, rather a pretty little animal, said to be good to eat ; another of these species was seen among the branches of the trees   A small variety of *lepus cuniculus* is very common in the sand hills near the presidio, hares are less common, and indeed it is doubtful whether any were seen by us   Raccoons are found in the mountains at a distance from the coast   The sea-otter *mussela lutris*) is not an unfrequent visitor in the harbour of San Francisco, but very few of them are taken, notwithstanding their fur is valuable   Judging from the accounts that have been published, these animals are becoming less numerous upon the coast   in 1786 it was stated that 50'000 of them might be collected annualy, whereas at present the number is reduced to about 2'000   Porpoises and whales are numerous outside the harbour, and the common seal may occasionally be seen basking on the rocks of Yerhabuena, and other places.

The feathered tribe in San Francisco are very numerous, and have as yet been so little molested that there must be a rich harvest in store for the first naturalist who shall turn his attention to this place. We succeded in killing a great many birds of different species, several of which were found to be quite new, and will be described in the natural history which will shortly appear as a supplement to this voyage . but there are not many which delight, either by the brilliancy or beauty of their plumage, or by the melody of their note. The birds of prey are the black vulture (*vultus ann a*,) sometimes large ; several species of *falco*, one of which attacks the geese, and is in consequence called *mato gansas*, also a kite, and a sparrow hawk. The horned owl (a variety of the *strix virginiana?*) flies about after dark to the terror of the superstitious Indians, who imagine its screech forbodes evil. Several species of *oriolus* are met with in the plains, and one, the *oriolus phœniceus*, is seen in immense flocks. The natives say that this bird, which in its first year is of a greyish black colour, changes to deep black in the second, and ultimately becomes black with red shoulders , but Mr Collie thinks there is some error in this. There is another oriolus which frequents moist and rushy places, crows in great numbers,some which are white, and smaller than those of England ; and several species of finches, buntings, and sparrows,prove very destructive to the grain when sown   The magpie is also an inhabitant here, and a small blue jay frequents the woods. The California quail(*tetrao virginianus*,)wood pigeons with bronzed imbricated feathers on the back of the neck, plovers (*charadrius hiaticula ?*), snipes, several species of sanderlings (*tringa*,) razorbills (*hematopus*,) herons (*ardea*,) curlew (*scolopax linosa* and *recurvirosta*,) and two species of *rallus*, afforded amusement to our sportsmen, as did also some of the many species of the geese, ducks, widgeon, and teal, which frequent the lakes and plains. The two latter species, and one of the *anas* (*erycthropus?*) were similar to those which had been seen in Kotzebue Sound , and the natives remark that they arrive from the north in the month of September, and depart again in May. The grey geese are said to be good to eat, but we found them all fishy ; not so the ducks, the greater part of which are palatable . these birds, of which we procured about twenty species and the mallard, are so common that several were frequently killed at one shot. It was observed that some kinds of ducks always preferred salt water to the lakes, particularly a species with a dark-coloured body and a white head, which we did not obtain   Among those which frequent the fresh water there were generally and abundance of water-hens.

Pelicans (*pelicanus onorcratluns*) may be seen morning and evening winging their long line of flight across the harbour, and settling upon the little island of Alcatiasses, which they have completely covered with their exuviæ, and rendered extremely offensive to persons passing near the place. Shags (*pelicanus graculus*) also abound in the harbour. I ought to have noticed in its proper place the humming bird, which, notwithstanding the high latitude of the country, is an inhabitant of the woods, and if we may rely upon Padre Tomaso, may be seen there all the year round. We noticed several of them fluttering about some gooseberry bushes near our anchorage, and shot one in full flesh: as this was in the middle of winter, the information of the padre was probably correct.

To this list of birds several were added the succeeding year at Monterey, which, being found so near the place we are describing, may justly be classed with them: these consisted of the golden winged-wood-pecker, a goat-sucker, several species of small birds unknown to us, and a golden-crested wren. At this place there were also several species of *picus*

I shall pass rapidly over the reptiles, which are not numerous at San Francisco, and none were procured during our stay. The Spaniards assert that there is an adder in the wood which is venomous, and that there are rattlesnakes upon the island of Molate in the harbour; but we saw neither the one or the other, notwithstanding Mr. Elson and a boat's crew landed upon Molate, which is very small indeed.

Fish are not much sought after in California, in consequence of the productions of the land being so very abundant; several sorts, however, are brought to the tables of the missions. In the Bay of Monterey we noticed the scomber colias, and another kind of mackerel, the torpedo and another species of raia, achimara, and swarms of small fish resembling the sardinia. Muscles are found in considerable quantities upon the shores, and form a large portion of the food of the Indians bordering upon the coasts and rivers. At Monterey two species of *haliotis* of large size are also extremely abundant, and equally sought after by the Indians. They are found on the granite rocks forming the south-east part of the bay, which appears to be their northern limit. The natives make use of these shells for ornaments, and decorate their baskets with pieces of them. Besides these shell-fish, there were noticed a few *patella*, *limpet*, *turbo*, *cardium*, and *mya* shells, and among other *lepas*, a rare species of *l anotifera* and a chiton (*tunicatus?*)

The forests of this part of California furnish principally large trees of the pinus genus, of which the *p. rigida* and the red cedar are most abundant, and are of sufficient growth for the masts of vessels. Two kinds of oak arrive at large growth, but near the

coast they do not appear to be very numerous   There is here a
low tree with a smooth reddish-brown bark, bearing red berries,
which from the hardness of its wood, would serve the purpose of
lignum vitæ · there are also some birch and plane trees ; but there
are very few trees bearing fruit which are indigenous, the cherry
tree and gooseberry bush, however, appear to be so

The shrubs covering the sand hills and moors are principally
syngenesious, or of the order rhamnus, while those which prefer
the more fertile and humid soils are a gaudy-flowered currant bush,
and a species of honeysuckle ; but the most remarkable shrub in
this country is the yedra, a poisonous plant affecting only particular
constitutions of the human body, by producing tumours and violent
inflamation upon any part with which it comes in contact, and indeed even the exhalation from it, borne upon the wind, is said to
have an effect upon some people   It is a slender shrub, preferring
cool and shady places to others, and bears a trefoil crenated leaf
Among other useful roots in this country there are two which are
used by the natives for soap, *amole* and *jamate.*

From San Francisco we proceeded to Monterey to take in the
stores that had been purchased at that place, and to procure some
spars, which grow more conveniently for embarkation there than at
San Francisco.   Though the distance between these two places
is very little more than a hundred miles, our passage was
prolonged to two days by light winds.   On the last day
of the year we passed Punto ano nuevo, which with Punto
Pinos forms the bay of Monterey.   This is a spacious sandy
bay about twenty miles across, and according to Perouse with
anchorage near the shore in almost every part, but it is not advisable to enter it in any other place than that which is frequented as
an anchorage, in consequence of a heavy swell which almost always
rolls into it from the westward   The mission of Santa Cruz is situated at the north extremity of the bay near Punto ano nuevo, and
vessels occasionally anchor off there for fresh water and supplies of
vegetables, neither of which are to be had in any quantity at Monterey.   Care should be taken in landing at Santa Cruz, as the surf
is very heavy, and the river of St Lorenzo has a bar off it, which
it is necessary to pass.

We dropped our anchor in Monterey Bay on the first of January, and with the permission of the governor, D Miguel Gonzales,
immediately commenced cutting the spars we required, for each of
which we paid a small sum   Through the assistance of Mr Hartnell, we procured several things from the missions which we should
otherwise have sailed without, and our thanks are further due to
him for his kindness and attention during our stay

The anchorage of Monterey is about two miles south-east of
point Pinos, in the south angle of the great bay just described.   It

is necessary to lie close to the shore, both on account of the depth of water, and in order to receive the protection of point Pinos, without which ships could not remain in the bay   It presents to the eye a very exposed anchorage, but no accidents have ever occurred to any vessel properly found in cables and anchors ; in which respect it very much resembles the bay of Valparaiso, nearly in the same parallel in the southern hemisphere.

The village and presidio of Monterey are situated upon a plain between the anchorage and a range of hills covered with woods of pine and oak.   The presidio is in better condition than that at San Francisco ; still as a place of defence it is quite useless.   The fort is not much better, and its strength may be judged of from its having been taken by a small party of seamen who landed from a Buenos Ayrean pirate in 1819, destroyed the greater part of the guns, and pillaged and burnt the town.

At the distance of a league to the southward of the presidio lies the mission of San Carlos, a small establishment containing 260 Indians.   It is situated in a valley near the river St.   Carmelo , a small stream emptying itself into a deep rocky bay   The shores of this bay, and indeed of the whole of the coast near Point Pinos, is armed with rocks of granite upon which the sea breaks furiously ; and, as there is no anchorage near them on account of the great depth of water, it is dangerous to approach the coast in light or variable winds.   Fortunately some immense beds of sea weed (*fucus pyriformis*) lie off the coast, and are so impenetrable that they are said to have saved several vessels which were driven into them by the swell during calm and foggy weather.   The ride from the presidio to San Carlos on a fine day is most agreeable.   The scenery is just sufficiently picturesque to interest, while the hills are not so abrupt as to inconvenience a bold rider.   The road leads principally through fine pasture lands, occasionally wooded with tall pine, oak, and birch trees ; but without any underwood to give it a wildness, or to rob it of its park-like aspect.   Before the valley of San Carmelo opens out, the traveller is apprized of his approach to the mission by three large crosses erected upon Mount Calvary ; and further on by smaller ones placed at the side of the road, to each of which some history is attached.   In the church is a drawing of the reception of La Perouse at the mission, executed on board the Astrolabe, by one of the officers of his squadron.   I much wished to possess this valuable relic, with which however the padre was unwilling to part.

We found lying in the port of Monterey an American brig endeavouring to dispose of a cargo of dry goods, and to procure hides and tallow in return ; and we opportunely received from her a supply of spirits, as the last cask was abroach.   On the 4th a Russian brig, named the Baikal, belonging to the Russian American Fur Company, anchored in the bay. This vessel was employed upon the coast, trading between Sitka, Bodega, and several ports in California, either in carrying or arranging the supplies for the Russian settlements to the northward. She was commanded by an officer in the Russian navy, and had on board Mr Klebnekoff, the agent There are several of these vessels upon the coast carrying guns, and wearing pendants. On the 5th we took leave of our hospitable acquaintances, and put to sea on our passage to the Sandwich Islands.

CHAPTER XV.

Passage to the Sandwich Islands—Woahoo—Historical Sketch of the Islands—
Progress in Civilization—Sandal wood—Resources of the Government—Slow
Progress of Education—Efforts of the Missionaries—Unsuccessful Result of their
Zeal—Sentiments of the King and Chiefs—Entertainment given by the King—
Death of Krymakoo—Wailing Scene—Departure of Kahumana for Owyhee.

Upon leaving Monterey we steered to the southward with a fair
wind, which carried us into the trades, and attended us the whole way
to the Sandwich Islands   In our course we searched unsuccessfully
for all the islands that were marked near our route, rounding to
every night when near the position of any one, that it might not be
passed unobserved, and making sail on a parallel of latitude during
the day.   In this manner we searched for Henderson's and Coop-
er's Islands, besides several others said to lie near them, and also
for a group in the latitude of 16° N., and longitude between 130o
and 133° W., but we saw nothing of them. nor had any of the
usual indications of the vicinity of land ; so that, if any of these
islands exist, they must be in some other parallel than that assigned to them in the American Geographical Table, published in
1825.*

On the 25th, after a pleasant passage of twenty days, we saw
the Island of Owyhee , and the following day anchored in the harbour of Honoruru, the capital of the Sandwich Islands   We had
the satisfaction to meet all our former acquaintances well, and to
receive their congratulations on our return , we had also the pleasure to find Mr. Lay the naturalist ready to resume his occupations
During our absence, he had unfortunately been prevented pursuing
his researches among the islands by a severe illness.

After the usual etiquette of salutes, I visited the king and Kahumana, who appeared very glad of our arrival, and being informed

---

* I have been recently informed that an island of moderate height has been seen
by the Sultan American whaler in latitude 15° 30' N, longitude between 130° and
134° W   And that another was landed upon in latitude 18° 22' N, longitude
114° W,

that the ship was to remain a few weeks in the harbour, they very kindly appropriated three houses to the use of the officers and myself, and seemed determined to show by other acts of attention that the regard they had always expressed for our nation was not merely an empty profession

In my first visit to this place, I gave a sketch of the appearance of the town of Woahoo and of the inhabitants, with the advances which the country appeared to be making in civilization. It may not be superfluous here to insert a very concise account of the islands during the last few years, to enable my readers to judge more correctly of their progress, and to furnish information to such as may not have the history of them fresh in their memories

At the time the Sandwich Islands were discovered by Captain Cook, Owyhee was under the sovereignty of Terrecoboo, or Teriopu, who died shortly after the departure of the discovery ships Tamehameha, who afterwards became so celebrated, was the nephew of Terreoboo He is not mentioned in the official account of Cook's voyage, but in a narrative of the facts relating to the death of the great navigator, published by Mr. Samwell, the surgeon of the Discovery, Meah Meah, as he is called by that gentlemen, is represented to have slept on board that ship, and to have had with him a magnificent feather cloak, with which he would not part, except for iron daggers, six of which he procured, and returned to the shore well pleased with his bargain No doubt his intention was to wrest the sovereignty from the hands of the successor of Terrecoboo, an enterprize which he performed shortly afterwards, by assembling his forces and defeating him in a pitched battle, in which he is said to have slain him with his own hands After this victory, no other chief possessing sufficient power to oppose Tamehameha, we find that on the arrival of Vancouver in 1792 he had acquired supreme authority both in Owyhee and Mowee He soon afterwards attacked and conquered Woahoo, and, assisted by his valiant protege Krymakoo, in 1817 became sovereign of all the Sandwich group

Vancouver was very instrumental in establishing the power of this chief on a firm basis, by noticing Tamehameha in a manner which could not escape the observation of the other chiefs, and by building him a decked vessel, which gave him a decided superiority of force, and enabled him to keep them in subjection In return for these important benefits, the grateful chief, in presence of Vancouver and the Eries of the group, made a formal cession of the islands to the king of Great Britain, and the natives have ever since considered themselves under the immediate protection of this country.

In the early stage of our intercourse with these islands, several acts, such as the death of Cook, the murder of Lieutenant Hergerst, and the treacherous seizure of an American vessel, rendered merchant vessels cautious of communicating with savages of apparently so ferocious a character, but when it was known that the perpetrators of these murders were punished by Tamehamha, and when his real character was made public by the voyages of Vancouver and other navigators, every vessel employed in the Pacific was desirous of visiting his dominions   In course of time a regular market was established for the sale of the productions of the island ; the natives were instructed to accept Spanish dollars and European clothing in exchange for their goods, and several foreigners, by the king's persuasion, were induced to settle upon the islands.   The native chiefs, in imitation of their sovereign, began to dress in the European style.   A fort was built for the protection of the principal town, and a number of the natives were instructed in the use of fire-arms.   The harbour of Honoruru soon became crowded with ships of all nations, and lately the place has assumed the appearance of an European colony.

The discovery of sandal wood in the mountains opened a profitable channel of commerce ; and several adventurers, chiefly from the United States, remained to collect it from the natives.   They found a ready market for it in China, the goods of that country were brought in return to the Sandwich Islands, and thus was laid the foundation of a trade which still continues   Tamehameha having purchased several vessels with this precious wood, attempted to conduct this trade with his own resources, and sent a schooner bearing his flag to Canton ; but, owing to the forms and impositions practised in China, and other circumstances which he could not control, the speculation failed, and this advantageous trade has since been carried on by the Americans

In all these plans for the benefit of his country, for the introduction of civilization among his subjects, and for the establishments of his assumed authority, Tamehameha was greatly indebted to the advice and assistance of two respectable English seamen, Young and Davis, whom he persuaded to remain in the islands.   Their services were not unrequited by the great chief, whose generous disposition and intimate knowledge of human nature induced him to bestow upon them both rank and fortune, by raising them to the station of chiefs, and giving them estates.   They in turn proved grateful to their benefactor, and conducted themselves so properly that every visitor to the islands has spoken of them in the highest terms.   Davis died in 1808, and was buried at Woahoo, where the place of his interment is marked by a humble tombstone   Young still survives, at the advanced age of eighty-two   Besides these

advisers, Tamehameha had a faithful and wise counsellor in Kiy-
makoo, afterwards better known by the appellation of Billy Pitt

Tamehameha having seen his country emerge from barbarism
under his well-directed efforts, and having conferred upon it other
important benefits, died in May 1819, at the age of sixty-three.
His biographer will do him injustice if he does not rank him, however limited his sphere, and limited his means, among those great
men who, like our Alfred, and Peter the Great of Russia, have rescued their countries from barbarism, and who are justly esteemed
the benefactors of mankind. His loss as a governor, and as a father to his people, was universally felt by his subjects. It is painful to
relate that, though his death occurred so recently several human victims were sacrificed to his names by the priests in the morais , and, according to the custom of the islands, some who were warmly attached to him committed suicide, in order to accompany his corpse to
the grave ; while great numbers knocked out their front teeth, and
otherwise mutilated and disfigured themselves.

Tamehameha was no sooner dead than his son Rio Rio, who
succeeded him, effected the most important change the country had
yet experienced   Having held conferences with the Chiefs, and
obtained the sanction of Keopuolani, a powerful female of rank, he
ordered all the morais to be destroyed, and declared the religion of
the foreigners,—of the principles of which he was then very ignorant, should henceforth be the religion of the state   The. burning
of the idols and the abolition of the *taboo* immediately succeeded
this destruction of the morais, and put an end to many cruel and
degrading customs, both injurious to the interests of the country
and oppressive to the people, especially to the females, who were
thenceforth admitted to an equality with the men.

The prejudices of Tamehameha had always opposed this change
in the religion of his subjects, not so much, I am informed, from his
being bigoted to idolatry as from its being better adapted to his
politics.   The maxims of our religion he thought would tend to
deprive him of that despotic power which he exercised over the
lives and fortunes of his subjects.   The terror inspired by human
sacrifices, and the absolute command which the superstitions of his
idolatrous subjects gave him, suited the plan of his government better than any other religion, and he, consequently, opposed every
attempt to propagate the gospel among his people.

Up to this period no missionaries had reached the Sandwich Islands, and for nearly a year there might be said to be no religion in
the country , but at the expiration of that period (in 1820,) several missionary gentlemen arrived from the United States and immediately entered upon their vocations   Keopuolani became the first
actual convert to the Christian religion, though in 1819 both Boki

and Krymakoo were baptized by the clergymen of Captain Frey-cinet's ship. Keopuolani being a chief of powerful influence, her example was followed by a great many persons, and the missiona-ries have since added daily to the number of their converts, and have been protected by the government, particularly by Kahumana and Kapeolani, two female chiefs next in rank to Keopuolani, and probably first in power in the islands.

Keopuolani died in 1823, after having received the sacrament. She was a grandchild of Terreeoboo, and a daughter of Kevalao, who was slain at Mowee. At the time of this victory, which ad-ded Mowee to the dominion of Tamehameha, Keopuolani was only thirteen years of age She happened to be on the field at the mo-ment of the defeat of her party, and became the prisoner of the conqueror, who, in order to secure his conquest by right as well as by victory, united her to himself in marriage. She had, however, afterwards, agreeably to the custom of the country, several hus-bands, of which one was Krymakoo, who also fell into the hands of the king at Mowee, and whose life was generously spared; and an-other, Hoapili, who, though a plebeian, was admitted to the hon-our of being one of the favourites of the queen This person is the reputed father of Kiukiuli the present king, while Tamehameha is said to have been the father of Rio-Rio. The queen, however, declared both her sons to be children of the illustrious chief, and they succeeded to the throne accordingly, in cases of this nature the declaration of the mother being held sufficient

Rio-Rio is represented to have been far inferior in intellect to his predecessor, and his youth and inexperience encouraged the su-perior chiefs to plan means for recovering their independence At the moment the order was given for the destruction of the idols, a chief named Kekoakalane treacherously seized the war god, and joined by a party of rebels fled with it to Owyhee, where he hoped to excite the inhabitants in his favour, and to establish himself as an independent chief; but he was closely pursued by the gallant Kry-makoo, and slain at Lakelakee, and hence that place has become celebrated, as the spot on which the last struggle for idolatry occurred Another insurrection soon afterwards occurred at Atooi, which was quieted by the courage and promptitude of Rio-Rio, who embarked with a few faithful followers in a canoe, and in a personal conference brought the rebels back to their duty. Atooi was the last of the Sandwich Islands that was reduced to subjection by Tamehameha, and its chiefs were constantly on the watch for opportunities of recovering their independence. Russia, or at least her subjects, taking advantage of the disaffected state of Atooi, landed some guns upon that island, and erected a fort, which was taken possession of by the natives. Krymakoo, however, with a body of followers from Woahoo, overthrew the rebels. The

chief being permitted to choose the manner of his death, desired
that he might be carried to sea, and be drowned by having a weight
fastened round his neck   In addition to this attempt of the Russians to separate Atooi from the kingdom, it was supposed that
America was also desirous of forming a settlement upon one of the
islands.   Rio-Rio foreseeing that occasional rebellions might arise
in his dominions, through the interference of foreign powers, determined on a voyage to England to have a personal interview with
the king, under whose protection the islands had been placed by
Tamehameha, and also, perhaps, from a desire to see the country
which furnished articles so superior to the manufacures of his own
dominions.

   The death of Rio-Rio and his queen, it is well known, occurred
in this visit to England   Their bodies were conveyed to the Sandwich Islands by Lord Byron, in H M Ship Blonde, and lodged
in a house built for the purpose, where they still remain.*   Lord
Byron having given the Chiefs, in Boki's words, "good advice" and
having placed the crown upon the head of Krukruh, the brother of
Rio-Rio, and seen the government confided to Krymakoo as regent,
quitted the islands about ten months before our first arrival

   Previous to the death of Tamehameha, several European houses
appeared in Woahoo.   Vessels and warlike stores had been purchased with sandal wood   The navigation of the Pacific became
more general in consequence of the return of peace, and the islands
were more frequently visited   The abolition of the taboo had already produced an entire change in the state of society. and frequent interviews with foreigners created amongst the inhabitants a
desire for dress and for luxuries, which was increased by the visit
of the chiefs to England.   Thus improvement advanced, as might
have been expected under such advantageous circumstances as those
in which the Sandwich Islands were placed   At that period of our
visit there were in Woahoo several respectable American manufacture, the productions of the China market, wines, and almost
every article of sea-store   There were also two hotels, at which
a person might board respectably for a dollar a day   two billiard
rooms, one of which was the property of Boki : and ten or a dozen
public houses for retailing spirits   The houses of the chiefs were
furnished with tables and chairs, and those belonging to Kahumana
with silk and velvet sofas and cushions.   Not contented with the
comforts of life, they latterly sought its luxuries, and even indulged

_____

* In 1827, some of the Chiefs had been persuaded that it was improper to keep the
bodies above ground, and these beautiful coffins covered with crimson velvet and
silver were about to be lowered into the earth, as a commendable mortification of
pride, when they were prevented by the timely arrival of a gentleman from whom
this account was derived.

in its extravagances   Kahumana filled chests, with the most costly silks of China, and actually expended four-thousand dollars upon the cargo of one vessel.   Boki paid three thousand dollars for a service of plate as a present for the king, notwithstanding he had other services in his possession; one of which was of expensively cut glass from Pellatt and Green in London.

This progress of luxury was attended by an equally remarkable change in the civil and political arrangments of the country.   At the period of our visit the king was always attended by a guard under arms; a sentinel presented his musket when an officer entered the threshold of the royal abode · soldiers paraded the ramparts of a fort mounting forty-guns; and "all's well" was repeated throughout the town during the night.   The harbour in the spring and autumn was crowded with foreign vessels. as many even as fifty having been seen there at one time; five thousand stand of arms were said to be distributed over the island; three hundred men were embodied and dressed in regimentals, and the Sandwich Island flag was daily displayed by five brigs and eight schooners. The islands had already received consuls from Great Britian and the United States, had concluded treaties of alliance with them, and we have just heard that their spirit of enterprize has induced them to fit out and despatch an expedition to take possession of some of the islands of the New Hebrides.

This state of advancement, considering the remoteness of the situation of these islands, and the little intercourse they have hitherto held with the civilized world, could hardly have been anticipated, and we hope it may not prove too rapid to be advantageous to the country, which has now several extensive establishments to maintain, and extravagant ideas to satisfy, with means evidently diminishing, if not nearly exhausted   The treasures accumulated by Tamehameha, and the supply of that precious wood which has been so instrumental in bringing the islands into notice, have been drained to meet the expenses of ruinous purchases which have materially contributed to the apparent show of grandeur and prosperity above mentioned.   The sandal wood, it is known, requires many years to arrive at a fit state for the market, and its cultivation not having been attended to, the wood is now becoming scarce, while the debt of the nation has considerable increased   During our visit, in order to avoid the expense attending the collection of this wood it became necessary to levy a tax upon the people of a pecul, or 133lb. each, which they were required to bring from the mountains, under a penalty of four dollars, and to deposit with the authorities at Honoruru for the purpose of liquidating the debt of the nation The greater part of the wood brought in was small and crooked, and only fit for the use of the Jos houses in China, where it is

burned as incense, but the consumption of it there is diminishing
in consequence of an order for its disuse in those places of worship.
The odour of the sandal wood of the Sandwich Islands is very inferior that of Malabar, Ceylon, and other parts of India. With the
exception of the profits arising from the sale of sandal wood, of salt,
and from the port dues, and from the advantage derived from merchant vessels visiting the islands for refreshments, there is no revenue of consequence; certainly none that is at all adequate to meet
the expenses of the nation.

The chiefs, foreseeing the approaching crisis, are anxious to avail
themselves of any prospect of an increase of revenue. Thus attempts have been made to manufacture sugar from the canes which
grow very abundantly and in great luxuriance in the islands; and
I sincerely hope that Mr. Marini, who has hitherto been of the
greatest benefit to the government of Woahoo, may succeed in the
mill which he was constructing for this purpose during our visit.
But machines of this nature have already cost a very large sum,
and have not hitherto succeeded, partly, perhaps, in consequence
of the want of proper materials. A cargo of this sugar it was
hoped would be ready for exportation in 1827, which was then to
be carried to the Californian market, where, as it has already been
said, sugar attains a high price. But the Sandwich Islands, until
much more advanced in the science of cultivation, will always have
to compete with manilla in the sale of this material. Tobacco,
coffee, and spices have been introduced into the islands, and it is
to be hoped they will succeed under the fostering had of the indefatigable individual before mentioned. An attempt was made to
encourage the planting of cotton, which was tolerably successful
the first year, but for some reasons, which were ascribed to the
rigid observance of the church duties, the labourers were prevented from gathering the crop, and it rotted in the pod. It is particularly unfortunate that the attempt to cultivate this plant, which
would be of great advantage to the islands, should have failed both
in the Society and Sandwich groups, as it will probably discourage
the inhabitants from any further endeavour to produce it. Salt has
been collected from some lakes near the town, and for some time
past has produced a small revenue. Hereafter it is likely to be in
greater request, for the purpose of curing meat for sea store, or for
exportation to Kamschatka, where it is in great demand. Flax of
a good quality grows upon Owhyhee, and rope for the vessels of
the country is made from a species of *urtica*? As yet, however,
the sandal wood is the only material that has produced any revenue
of consequence.

Soon after the Christian religion had been introduced into the
Sandwich Islands, several of the chiefs were taught to read and write,

and were so delighted at the idea of being able to communicate their thoughts to friends at a distance, without the necessity of disclosing them, and free from the risk of misinterpretation, that some of the scholars laboured at their task as if the prosperity of the islands depended upon penmanship alone   Education in other respects has made much slower progress than every well-wisher of the country could desire. A few individuals who have had the advantage of continued instruction, have acquired a limited knowledge of the Scriptures, but many remain ignorant even of the nature of the prayers they repeat ; and in other subjects are entirely uninstructed.

The missionaries appear to be very anxious to difuse a due knowledge of the tenets of the Gospel among all the inhabitants, and have laboured much to accomplish their praiseworthy purpose · but the residents in Honuruu well know what little effect their tutors having mistaken the means of diffusing education.   In the Sandwich Islands, as in all other places, there is a mania for every thing new, and, with due reverence to the subject, this was very much the case with religion in Honoruru, where almost every person might be seen hastening to the school with a slate in his hand, in the hope of being able soon to transcribe some part of the *pala pala* (the Scriptures). This feeling under judicious management might have produced the greatest blessings Woahoo could have enjoyed   and the gentlemen of the mission might have congratulated themselves on having bestowed upon the inhabitants very important benefits   But they were misled by the eagerness of their hopes, and their zeal carried them beyond the limits calculated to prove beneficial to the temporal interests of a people, still in the earliest stage of civilization   The apparent thirst after scriptural knowledge in Honoruru created a belief among the missionaries that this feeling was become general, and auxiliary schools were established in different parts of the island, at which we were informed every adult was required to attend several times a day.

While this demand upon their time was confined within reasonable limits, the chiefs, generally, were glad to find their subjects listen to instruction ; but when men were obliged to quit their work, and to repair to the nearest auxiliary school so frequently during the day, so much mischief was produced by loss of labour, and such ruinous consequences threatened the country, that many of the chiefs became desirous of checking it. Kahumana and her party, however, persisted in considering it desirable, and in supporting the missionaries ; while a powerful party, at the head of which were the king and the regent, exerted themselves to counteract their endeavours. Thus dissensions arose very prejudicial both to the cause of religion and to the interests of the country   The chiefs lost their influence, the subjects neglected their work, on the one side, and intemperance on the other, became the prevailing errors of the time, the latter indulged in probably to a greater extent, with the view of bringing ridicule on the opposite party; a scheme in which it is said that Boki himself condescended to join

At length the regent and other chiefs determined to break through this rigid discipline. The ten commandments had been recommended as the sole law of the land   This proposition was obstinately opposed; a meeting was called by the missionaries to justify their conduct, at which they lost ground by a proposal that the younger part of the community only should be obliged to attend the schools, and that the men should be permitted to continue at their daily labour   The king, whose riding, bathing, and other exercises had been restricted, now threw off all restraint, and appeared in public wearing the sword and feather belonging to the uniform presented to him from this country by Lord Byron, which his preceptor had forbid him to use, under the impression that it might excite his vanity   The boys, following the example of their youthful sovereign, resumed their games, which had been suppressed: and among other acts which, though aparently trifling discovered to the common people a spirit of opposition, and an earnestness on the part of the chiefs to overthrow the system that had been brought into operation, Koanoa, who had long been enamoured of a female chief, Kenow, whom Kahumana intended for the king (although she was old enough to be his mother), being refused the marriage ceremony by the mission, carried off the object of his desire, and took her to his home

This was the state in which we found Woahoo, and from it the missionaries might exact a useful lesson while imparting religious instruction to mankind, of the necessity of combining their temporal interests with those which relate to their prospects of futurity.

It was supposed, from the manner in which Kahumana persevered in her support of the missionaries, that she was actuated by a deeper policy than appeared. Her jealousy at the investment of the sovereign power in the king and Boki was well known; and it was surmised that she entertained hopes of creating a party which in the event of the death of Pitt, then daily expected, would forward her ambitious views. Whether this surmise was just I do not pretend to say, but she certainly did not succeed, that event having passed off during our stay without any movement in her favour

Amidst this conflicting interest of parties, we were gratified to observe the cordiality between the chiefs and the English and American residents, neither of whom took part in these State quarrels. To strengthen this feeling, a public dinner was given by the officers of the Blossom and myself to the king and all the royal family, the consuls, the chiefs, and the principal merchants resident in the place. On this occasion the king was received with the honours due to his rank   He was dressed in full uniform, and altogether made a very elegant appearance.   His behaviour at table was marked with the greatest propriety, and though he seemed fully aware of the superiority of Europeans, he appeared at the same time conscious that the attentions he received were no more than a just tribute to his rank   Boki, the regent, Koanoa, the colonel of troops, and Manuia, the captain of the port, were dressed in the Windsor uniform; and Kahumana, and the two female chiefs next in rank, were arrayed in silk dresses, and had expended a profusion of lavender-water upon their cambric handkerchiefs.   Many loyal and patriotic toasts succeeded the dinner, some of which were proposed by Boki, in compliment to the king of England and the President of the United States, between both of whom and his loyal protege he expressed a hope that the warmest friendship would always subsist.   The chiefs drank to the health of several persons who had shown them attention in London, and in compliment to the ladies of England proposed as a toast, " The pretty girls of the Adelphy "   Throughout the day the islanders acquitted themselves very creditably, and their conduct showed a close observance of European manners

A few days afterwards the king gave an entertainment, at which his guests were seated at a long table spread in the European style, and furnished with some very good wines   Among other good things we had Leuhow, a dish of such delicious quality that excursions are occasionally made to the plantations for the pleasure of dining upon it; and, from this circumstance, a pic-nic and a Leuhow party have become nearly synonymous   The ingredients of the dish are generally the tops of the taro plant and mullet which have been fattened in ponds, these are wrapped in large leaves and baked in the ground, though sometimes fowls and pork are used.   In order to amuse us, the king had also assembled several dancers and the best bards in the island, and we had the pleasure of witnessing some native performances, which were the more interesting, as these entertainments will shortly lose all their originality by the introduction of foreign customs.   On the present occasion, indeed, it was difficult to procure performers of any celebrity, and both bards and dancers were sent for from a considerable distance, and even then only two of the latter were considered worth our notice   The performance opened with a song in honour of Tamehameha, to which succeeded an account of the visit of Rio Rio and his queen to England, then motives for undertaking the voyage were explained, their parting with their friends at Woahoo, their sea-sickness, their landing in England; the king's attempts to speak English; the beautiful women of this country, and the sickness and death of the youthful royal pair, were described with much humour, good-nature, and feeling.

The natives were delighted with this performance, especially with that part which exhibited the sea-sickness, and the efforts of the king to speak English; but our slight acquaintance with the language did not enable us fully to appreciate the allusions   In the next performance, however, this defect was less felt   The song was executed by three celebrated bards, whose grey beards hung down upon their breasts · they were clothed in their rude native costume, and each had the under part of his right arm tattooed in straight lines from the wrist to the armpit   They accompanied themselves upon drums made of two gourds neatly joined together, and ornamented with black devices.   Each bard had one of these instruments attached to his left wrist by a cord; the instrument was placed upon a cushion, and the performer throughout measured time by beating with his right hand upon the aperture of the gourd   The subject related to the illustrious Tamehameha, whose warlike exploits are the constant theme of these people   Occasionally the bards seemed to be inspired; they struck their left breasts violently with the palms of their hands, and performed a number of evolutions with their drums, all of which were executed simultaneously, and with ease, decision, and grace   On the whole it was an exhibition very creditable to the talents of the performers.   To this succeeded several dances . the first, performed by a native of Atooi, was recommended principally by a display of muscular energy, the next was executed by a man who was esteemed the most accomplished actor of his time in Woahoo, and the son of the most celebrated dancer the islands ever had.   He wore an abundance of native cloth, variously stained, wrapped about his waist, and grass ornaments fixed upon his legs above the ancles   A garland of green leaves passed over his right shoulder and under his left arm, and a wreath of yellow blossoms, very commonly worn in the Sandwich Islands, was wound twice round his head   Unlike the former dance, the merit of this consisted in an exhibition of graceful action, and a repetition of elegant and unconstrained movements.

The dance of the females was spoiled by a mistaken refinement, which prevented their appearing, as formerly, with no other dress than a covering to the hips, and a simple garland of flowers upon the head, instead of this they were provided with frilled chemises, which so far from taking away the appearance of indecency, produced an opposite effect, and at once gave the performance a stamp of indelicacy.   In this dance, which by the way is the only one the females of these islands have, they ranged themselves in a line, and began swinging the arms carelessly, but not ungracefully, from side to side, they then proceeded to the more active part of the dance, the principal art of which consisted in twisting the loins without moving the feet or the bust　After fatiguing themselves in accomplishing this to the satisfaction of the spectators, they jumped sidewise, still twisting their bodies, and accompanying their actions with a chorus, the words of which we supposed bore some allusion to the performance.　We had afterwards a sham-fight with short spears, wherein very little skill was exhibited, and, compared with the dexterity of the warlike Tamehameha, who is said by Vancouver to have successfully evaded six spears thrown at him at the same instant, the present representation was quite contemptible. These exercises are now seldom practised, and in a short time, no doubt, both they and the dances will cease to be exhibited.

On the 12th of February, we received the melancholy intelligence of the death of Krymakoo, who had long suffered under a dropsical complaint, for which he had undergone frequent operations. Only four days previously he went to bathe in the sea at Kairnu, in Owyhee, and on coming out of the water he was taken ill, and died very soon afterwards　He was at an advanced age, and had been present at the death of our immortal countryman in Karakakoa Bay, and perfectly recollected that fatal transaction　Krymakoo, or, as he was more generally called, Pitt, from the circumstance of his being a contemporary prime minister with our great statesman, became a protege of Tamehameha shortly after the departure of Cook's ships.　He is first introduced to our notice by Vancouver, who particularly remarks his superior manners and conduct.　His life was devoted to the advantage of his country, and to the support of his illustrious patron, in whose service he distinguished himself alike as a warrior and a counsellor　Intelligent, faithful and brave, he was confided in and beloved by his king and his countrymen, and he was a chief in whom the foreign residents place implicit reliance.　His ardent spirit and anxiety for the welfare of his country led Tamehameha on one or two occasions of insurrection to suspect his fidelity, and in order to put it to the test he is said to have deprived him for the time of his estates, an act of injustice, calculated rather to increase than to allay any dissatisfaction that might have existed in his mind.　Pitt, nevertheless, remained faithful, and fought by the side of his patron.　After the death of Tamehameha, he enjoyed almost sovereign power, which he employed to the benefit and civilization of his countrymen.　His command of temper was not less praiseworthy than his other virtues.　On the occasion of some misunderstanding between the missionaries and the seamen of an American vessel, the crew went on shore with the view of burning Mr. Bingham's house, but, mistaking the place, they set

fire to one belonging to Pitt   The natives immediately flew to protect the property of their favourite chief, and a serious quarrel was
about to take place, to the disadvantage of the Americans, when
Pitt, who had escaped the flames, harangued the mob with the
greatest composure, induced them to desist from acts of violence,
and persuaded the crew, who by this time had discovered their
mistake, to return to their vessel   It has been asserted of Pitt that
he was extremely ambitious, but his ambition seems to have had
no other object than the welfare of his country . had he aspired to
the crown, there were many favourable opportunities of which he
might have availed himself without much risk of failure, of which
the death of Tamehameha, the revolt of Kekoakalane, the insurrection of Atooi, and others, are sufficient instances.   He left one
son, whom he was very anxious to have educated in England, and
pressed his request so earnestly that I had consented to take him
on board the Blossom, but the vessel which was sent to bring him
from Owyhee returned hastily with the news of the death of the
chief, which frustrated the plan.   Immediately this event was known,
the flags of the forts and the shipping were lowered half-mast, and
the shores of the bay resounded with the wailings of the inhabitants

It had been supposed that the ambition and jealousy of Kahumana and the conflicting interests of the chiefs would have displayed themselves in insurrection on this occasion, and that the disaffected chiefs would have availed themselves of this moment to
remove the supreme power from the hands of the young king ;
but, whatever results this melancholy event might have produced
had it occurred at an earlier date, nothing was now attempted   Boki,
however, thought it prudent to assemble the troops in the fort, and
the Blossom was put in readiness to preserve order, if necessary,
and to receive the foreign residents, should their safety require it
Anxious to witness the effect of this occurrence upon the court, I
immediately paid a visit of condolence to Kahumana, who was
seated amidst a motley assemblage of attendants, looking very sor-
rowful   It appeared however, from the following incident, that
the sincerity of her grief was questionable   Happening to cast
her eye upon a Bramah inkstand which I was conveying to the
observatory, she seized it with both hands, and declared, her countenance brightening into a smile, how much she should like to have
it.   As it was the only one I possessed, I did not intend at first to
gratify her majesty's wishes, but she fairly tore it from me . so that,
making a virtue of necessity, I presented it to her   After bestowing some praise upon the invention, she passed it to Karui, a female
chief next in rank to herself, and then dismissing her pleasant looks,

she resumed her sorrow, and convinced every person present that she was quite an adept in this barbarous custom of the country.

Many of the court seemed to consider this moment one of apprehension, and every person who approached the queen's abode was at first supposed be the bearer of the news of some insurrection or other convulsion of the state. As he entered the room, therefore, there was a dead silence ; but when it was found that these visits were made merely to inquire after the health of the queen, the wailing, as if it had suffered by the disappointment, burst forth with redoubled energy Kahumana herself evidently anticipated some disturbance, for she whispered to me to be upon my guard, as there was a probability that the people would be mischievous Nothing, however, occurred to disturb the tranquillity of the town but the wailings around the royal abode.

It is unnecessary here to describe many instances of the extent to which this hypocritical affectation of grief was carried , suffice it to say, that several persons, as if determined to perpetuate the barbarous practice of self-mutilation, knocked out their front teeth with hammers.

The queen almost immediately after the death of her brother embarked for Owyhee in a native schooner, to the great satisfaction of the chiefs and the European residents in Woahoo As it was probably the last time she would see us, she was complimented with a royal salute on leaving the harbour

CHAPTER XVI.

Further Remarks on the Inhabitants—Treaty of Alliance—Climate—Medicinal Properties of the Ava—Supplies—Departure—Passage to China—Ladrone and Bashee Islands—Arrival at Macao—Transactions there—Departure—Botel Tobago Xima—Arrival at the Great Loo Choo

On the return of the ship to the Sandwich Islands the chiefs were very anxious to learn where she had been, and to be informed whether in some of the countries she had visited, the produce of their dominions might not find a favourable market. Kahumana, in particular, was so much interested in these inquiries that she condescended to direct her attention to them, and laid aside a missionary book with which she had been instructing her mind while the back part of her body was undergoing the soothing operation of being pinched by one of her female attendants The conversation happening to turn upon Bird Island, Boki, on hearing it was so near to the Sandwich group, meditated its addition to the dominions of the king, no doubt under the impression of its being similar to one of the Sandwich Islands, and was greatly disappointed when informed that the island was not worth his possession. The account of the high price of sugar in California quite put him in good humour with his sugar-mills, which for some time past had been a subject of annoyance to him, in consequence of the expense incurred by their continually breaking All parties were evidently desirous to extend their commerce, and a spirit of enterprise appeared to have diffused itself amongst them, which it is to be hoped may continue

During our absence two important political events had occurred —the negociation of a treaty of alliance between Captain Jones, of the United States' sloop Peacock, on the part of America, and Boki, the regent, on the part of the Sandwich Islands; by which the reception of the American vessels in the Sandwich Islands, on the footing of the most favoured nation, was guaranteed to America in the event of that nation being involved in hostilities with any other power. The other was the resignation of Pitt, who, being

aware of his approaching dissolution, retired to Owyhee, and left
his brother Boki to act as regent   Boki, who it may remembered,
accompanied the late king Rio-Rio to England appears to have
derived much benefit from that visit, and on his return to the Sandwich Islands to have become very desirous of improving the condition of his countrymen   He was, however, a less active govern-
or than Pitt, and less capable of effecting those changes which experience had nevertheless convinced him were necessary for their
advancement

The town of Honoruru had now a more cleanly and lively appearance than on our former visit, and the streets, occupied by
happy little children who had resumed their games, wore a more
cheerful aspect   There was an improvement also in the society
of the place, arising apparently from the arrival of some Europeans, particularly of the consul's family, which was of very great
advantage to the females of Woahoo, who seemed anxious to imitate their manners, and were so desirous of becoming acquainted
with the method of arranging their different articles of dress, that
it required an unusual share of good nature to avoid taking offence
at the rude manner in which they gratified their curiosity   The females of Woahoo are shrewd observers of these matters, and on
great occasions endeavour to imitate foreigners as nearly as they
can , but the powerful influence of fashion has not been yet able
entirely to get the better of that other powerful principle, early
habit, and the women of the Sandwich Islands in retirement still
adhere to their old customs, affording as curious an instance as
was ever beheld of barbarism walking hand in hand with civilization.

The lower class of the inhabitants of Woahoo have varied their
dress very little from its original style ; though in Honoruru some
females may be seen clothed in the cotton of Europe, and even in
the silks of China, with green and red shoes, and sometimes with
parasols   They obtain these articles as presents from the crews of
such ships as touch at the port   In every uncivilized country which
has as much foreign intercourse as Woahoo, incongruities must be
of frequent occurrence ; thus we were daily in the habit of seeing
ladies disencumber themselves of their silks, slippers, and parasols,
and swim off in fine style to different vessels, carrying their bundles
on their heads, and resuming their finery when they got on board
Nor was it less amusing to observe them jump overboard soon after
daylight, and continue sporting and swimming about the vessels in
the harbour like so many nereids ; practices to which they adhere
with as much fondness as ever.   Many, however, now think it necessary to put on a bathing gown when they take this recreation

The men make very tolerable seamen, and are particularly useful in boats   Accustomed from their infancy to the water, they are as much at home in that element as on land ; and having frequently encountered gales of wind at sea in their open canoes, they have no apprehension of them on board a strongly built ship   They are active and honest, and many of them are taken on board merchant ships visiting the islands, as part of their crews.

In the course of time it is to be hoped that they will become sufficiently enlightened to navigate their own vessels, as they at present depend upon foreigners for the performance of that service   Their vessels are now generally chartered to Americans, who bear a certain proportion of the expenses of the voyage, and have carte blanche to proceed where they please, and to collect, sell, and purchase cargoes at their discretion,·and as it may seem most advantageous for themselves and the owners, who divide the profits of the venture at the end of the voyage.   Their occupation consists principally in trading with California and the islands of the Pacific, or in making sealing voyages, in which case the skins they obtain are carried to some foreign market, and the proceeds applied to the purchase of a new cargo adapted to the wants of the Sandwich Islanders, such as horses, or furniture, and other household materials   Upon the whole, these returns are said to be by no means equal to the risk and expenses of the voyage, and the ships, being built of slight materials, require constant repair, and soon wear out   so that their navy, at present, is of no great advantage to the state

No duties have as yet been imposed on any goods, either imported or exported, and the only charges made by the government are the port dues, which are very prudently lighter on vessels touching at the islands for refreshments only, than upon those which bring cargoes of merchandize . the charge in the former case is six, and in the latter fifty cents per ton for the outer anchorage, and ten and sixty cents per ton respectively for the inner anchorage.

The Sandwich Islanders will apparently make as good soldiers as they do sailors, and are so proud of the honour of being embodied in the corps of the state, that they cannot suffer a greater disgrace than to have the regimentals taken from them and to be turned out of the ranks.   They were repeatedly drilled by our serjeant of marines, and though under the disadvantage of not understanding the language in which the word of command was given, they improved quite as much as men in general would have done who had been in the habit of seeing the exercise performed   The inhabitants appear disposed to learn any thing that does not require labour, and soldiering soon became so completely a mania, that the king had the choice of his subjects, and little boys were seen in all parts

of the town tossing up a sugar cane, with a "shoulder ump!" and
some of the troop, even after being dismissed, would rehearse the
lesson of the day by themselves The islanders have a good idea
of acting in concert, derived from their early exercise of the *palalu*,
so interestingly described by Vancouver, in which they were accustomed to form solid squares, and when engaged, presented a formidable phalanx, which it was not easy to force.

Among other services which we performed for the king was an
inspection of his cannon in the forts, some of which were so corroded, that in all probability their discharge would have been productive of serious accidents to some of his subjects. We also
furnished him with twenty tons of stones, which we had taken in
at Chamisso Island as ballast, to be used in rebuilding the wall of
his mud fort

It is unnecessary to describe further the inhabitants of a country
which has already been the subject of several volumes Enough
has been said to show that the people are fast imbiding foreign
customs, and daily improving both in their manners and dress

The harbour of Honoruru is the general rendezvous of all the
whale ships employed in the North Pacific Ocean In the spring
time these vessels assemble here to the number of forty or fifty sail
at a time, and take on board large supplies of vegetables and fruit,
as sea stock, to enable them to remain upon their fishing ground
until the autumn, when many of them return to the port The
fresh provision which they procure at these islands is of the greatest advantage to the crews of the whalers, who would otherwise be
afflicted with scurvy, and the goods which they give in exchange
are very acceptable to the inhabitants. A number of idle dissolute
seamen however, discontented with their ships, generally remain
behind, and live in the public houses until their money and clothes
are expended, or attach themselves to females, and in either way
become dependent upon the inhabitants for food These characters
do infinite mischief to the lower order of the natives, by encourag-
ing them in intemperance, debauchery, idleness and all kinds of
vice, nearly sufficient of themselves to counteract all the labours
of the missionaries in the diffusion of morality and religion.

The harbour is formed by a coral reef, which extends along the
coast from the Pearl River to Wytete Bay, but connected with the
shore at intervals, so as to impede the passage of vessels The
entrance is very narrow and intricate, and vessels are generally
towed in early in the morning, before the breeze freshens. There
is a rock nearly mid-channel upon which the sea generally breaks.
Sometimes indeed it breaks quite across the entrance, and renders
it necessary at that time, in particular, to employ a pilot. The depth
in the channel at high water is about eighteen feet, but as I did

not make a plan of this port, in consequence of Lieutenant Malden of the Blonde having so recently executed all that was necessary in that respect, I cannot speak positively.   In sailing along the reefs in boats it is necessary to keep at a considerable distance on account of the sudden rise of the sea, which is very apt to fill or upset them when it breaks ; and boats should not at any time pull for the entrance until the have gained a proper station off it

The climate of the Sandwich Islands is more refreshing than that of Otaheite ; although the group is scarcely farther from the equator.   I am not aware that any register has been kept for a whole year at Otaheite , but at Woahoo this has been done by the gentlemen attached to the missions, from which it appears that the mean temperature for 1821 was 75°, the maximum 88°, and the minimum 59°, and that the daily range on an average was about 13°.   In the last fortnight of May 1826, we found the maximum 83°, and minimum 74° ; and in the last fortnight of February 1827, maximum 80, and minimum 58°.

The N. E. trade wind, in general, blows strong to the windward of the Sandwich Islands, though for many miles to leeward of them frequent calms and light baffling winds prevail, and impede the navigation between the islands.   About the period of the rainy season these winds are interrupted by gales from north-west to south-west, but when they cease the trade resumes its usual course.   The duration of this season at Woahoo is from February to May.   In 1826 it was over on the 19th of May ; and in 1827, it began on the 17th of February   At this period the rains are occasionally very heavy ; in 1826 and 1830, I have been informed they were particularly so ; at other times, however, the reverse takes place, and from August 1821, to the same month of the following year, it appears by the register of the missionaries that there were but forty days on which rain fell

The windward sides of the islands are said to be much colder, and to be subject to more rain than those to leeward   They are also liable to fogs in the spring of the year, while those which are opposite are enjoying sunshine   The mountains, from their height, act upon the atmosphere as powerful condensers, and in particular times of the year are scarcely ever free from mists ; these are occasionally detached by gusts of wind and carried over the parts of the island, and it is not unusual in Honoruru to experience a pretty sharp sprinkling of rain without perceiving any cloud from whence it proceeds.

Water-spouts not unfrequently visit these islands, one of which I was told burst over the harbour of Honoruru, discharging such a quantity of water that the sea rose three feet   I have repeatedly seen this phenomenon on a small scale carrying a column of dust along the plains near Honoruru, and whirling hats into the air; and I once saw a native boy greatly puzzled to escape from its influence.

I shall conclude these remarks with some observations on the use and effects of the ava, a root which was formerly in much use in the Pacific, taken from the Journal of the surgeon of the Blossom. The intoxicating property of the ava root, the cutaneous eruption which succeeds its use, and the renovating effect it has upon the constitution, have been noticed ever since the discovery of the Society Islands. Mr. Collie observes, that—" a course of it is most beneficial in renovating constitutions which have been worn out by hard living, long residence in warm climates, without, however, affections of the liver, and by protracted chronic diseases; more especially if the disorder be such as by the humoral pathologists would be attributed to an attenuated or acrid state of the blood " He had an opportunity of seeing "a gentleman, a foreigner, who had undergone a course of it to remove a cutaneous affection said to have been similar to St. Anthony's fire It had affected at different times almost every part of the body, going from one place to another, but had been particularly obstinate in one leg. He took two doses a day of half a pint each, one before breakfast and one before dinner, by which his appetite was sharpened; and by the time he had finished his meal a most pleasing state of half intoxication had come on, so that he was just able to go to his couch, where he enjoyed a sound and refreshing sleep.

"About the second or third week, the eyes became suffused with blood, and the cuticle around them began to scale, when the whole surface of the body assumed the appearance above described. The first dose is continued for a week or so, according to the disease, and then gradually left off The skin clears at the same time, and the whole system is highly benefited.

" I recommended the ava, and had an opportunity of seeing the first effects upon a man affected with chronic superficial ulceration, affecting the greater part of the toes, and the anterior part of the soles of the feet The legs and feet were œdematous and swelled; the pain was very distressing, preventing any sound repose, and not permitting him even to lie down or bring them up, so as to be near a line horizontal with the body. The ulcers were covered with a tough, viscid, dark-coloured discharge that adhered to the surface, and entirely concealed it. His frame was emaciated, pulse quick and irritable, appetite gone, tongue dry and reddish; he had taken mercurial preparations at two previous periods, as he said, with considerable benefit; but for want of the medicines it was stopped, when the sores were nearly healed He had been, and I believe still was, addicted to drinking spirituous liquors. The ava was given three times a day with the same immediate effects as before mentioned, and at the end of ten days the ulcers were clean and healing From the commencement of the course he had been able to lie down, allowing his feet to hang over the bed-side . he had slept soundly, and his appetite was good. Could he have procured and applied a suitable dressing for the ulcers, with appropriate support to the œdematous extremities, I have no hesitation in saying that the plan would have succeeded Even with all these disadvantages, I am inclined to believe that a cure will be effected if he abstains from liquor "

In this account of the Sandwich Islands, I have avoided touching upon subjects connected with the mythology, traditions, and early manners and customs of the islanders, from a conviction that I could give but an imperfect sketch of them, and from a hope that they will hereafter be laid before the public by the author of Polynesian Researches, who from his intimate knowledge of the language, his long residence in the Pacific, and from the nature of his occupations, has greater opportunities of becoming acquainted with them than any other foreigner. My endeavour has been to give as faithful an account as I could of the government, and of the state of society in the islands at the time of our visit, and of the resources and commerce of the country. Had my occupations been less numerous, I might have done more justice to these subjects ; but the determination of the position of the place, and attention to other observations, occupied my time so completely, that I had very little leisure for other pursuits.

During the absence of the ship from the Sandwich Islands, Captain Charlton, the consul, had succeeded in procuring a supply of salt provision for her. This was the more opportune, as the meat which had been corned in California was found on examination to be so bad that it was necessary to throw the whole of it overboard. We at first imagined that this failure proceeded from our ignorance of the method of curing the meat, but that which had been prepared at Monterey , by a person brought up to the business, was found to be equally bad and the failure, in all probability, arose from the heated and feverish state in which the animals were slaughtered. We frequently remonstrated with the governor of San Francisco against being obliged to kill the animals in this state, and begged he would have them penned up until the following day, as they were quite wild, and had been harassed with lassos, and dragged many miles by tame bullocks. We did not however, succeed, and if the animals were not slaughtered as they were delivered into our charge they either made their escape, or, as was the case with several, broke their necks in their struggles for freedom.   The present supply of provision was consequently of the greatest importance   In addition to this we procured a few other stores, but not sufficient for the purpose, and there were no medicines to be had, so that it was still necessary to proceed to China

As soon as the ship was ready for sea, therefore, we endeavoured to sail, but the wind about this time blew from the south-west, and kept us imprisoned a fortnight , the harbour of Honoruru being so difficult of egress, that unless the wind be fair, or there be a perfect calm, a vessel cannot proceed to sea   On the 4th of March, however, we took our leave of the authorities and residents of the place, from both of whom we had received the greatest attention, and put to sea on our way to Macao

Upon leaving the Sandwich Islands I directed the course to the southward   and next day having gained the latitude of 18° 32′ N., I stood to the westward, with the intention of pursuing the above-mentioned parallel as far as the Ladrone Islands   I did this with a view of keeping fairly within the limit of the trade wind, which, at the season of the year in which this passage was made, is frequently variable in a higher latitude, and even subject to interruptions from strong north-westerly winds   I was also desirous of ascertaining the position of an island bearing the name of Wake's Island, upon Arrowsmith's chart situated directly in the route between the Sandwich Islands and China

A fresh trade wind attended us until the fifth day after our departure, when it was interrupted by a breeze from the southward The serenity of the sky which accompanied the trade, now became obscured by heavy thunder clouds, which gathered around us until the night of the 6th, when they completely blackened the sky. We had lightning frequently during the day, which increased so much towards night, that from eight o'clock to day light the following morning the sky presented an uninterrupted blaze of light   It was unusually near , the forked lightning passed between the masts several times, and the zenith occasionally presented a fiery mass of short curved lines, which shot off in different directions like as many arrows ; while the heavy peals of thunder which generally accompany these storms were subdued by crackling discharges not unlike the report of musketry from a long line of infantry.   About the commencement of this storm the temperature fell four degrees, but gradually rose again to its former height.   The sympeisometer was not sensibly affected.

On the following day fine weather was restored, the trade took its proper direction , and the sea, which had been much agitated by the changeable winds, abated. and we pursued a steady course About four days afterwards a brilliant meteor was discharged from the zenith towards the north-west, in the direction of some heavy clouds (nimbi), which were pouring down torrents of rain It presented a long bright liquid flame of a bluish cast, and was followed by a train of sparks, until it had reached within 15° of the horizon, when it exploded, and three distinct fragments, having the appearance of being red hot, were discharged. They gradually lost their brilliancy as they fell, and were quite extinguished before they came in contact with the water. With the exception of the nimbi in the north west, the sky was perfectly clear, particularly at the zenith, whence the meteor appeared first to be discharged. After these meteorological disturbances we had fine weather almost all the remainder of the passage.

At two o'clock on the 15th we were within a few leagues of the situation of Wake's Island, and the ship was brought to until daylight, but seeing no land at that time we bore away again, and at noon were exactly on the spot where the island is placed in Arrowsmith's chart A few tern and a gannet were seen about eight o'clock in the morning, but we had no other indications of land ; still in the expectation of falling in with it, we continued the course due west, and ran throughout the night, which was clear and fine, but without being more successful. I afterwards learned that the master of an American trader landed upon a coral island, nearly in the same longitude, in the latitude 19° 18′ N. which is about twenty-three miles to the northward of the island in Arrowsmith's chart and in all probability is the same place.

With fine weather and a fair wind we pursued our course, without experiencing any inconvenience except that occasioned by a long swell from the northward, which made the ship roll heavily almost all the passage. On the 25th we saw the island of Assumption, and the next day passed close to it, in order to determine its position. The island is about a league in circumference, and rises from the sea in the perfect form of a cone to the height of 2,026 feet. Time must have made an agreeable alteration in the appearance of this island since it was visited by La Perouse Instead of a cone covered with lava and volcanic glass, and presenting the forbidding aspect he describes, we traced vegetation nearly to the summit, and observed woods of palm-trees skirting its base ; particularly in the south-west side. We were more fortunate than La Perouse in obtaining a view of the crater formed at the apex of the cone ; it appeared very small and perfect, and to emit no smoke. La Perouse, in sailing to leeward of this island, experienced a strong sulphorous odour. There was none, however, when we visited the spot , but it is very probable that the volcano may have been in action when he passed, which might also account for the desolation of which he speaks

There appeared to be no danger near this island, but on the contrary, judging from the deep blue colour of the sea, there was deep water close to the base of the island. The south-west side is the least abrupt, but even in that direction La Perouse informs us ships are obliged to come very close to the shore before they can find anchorage, and then only with a very long scope of cable. This bank is formed of lava and scoriæ, and, being on the leeward side of the island, has probably been raised by frequent eruptions of the volcano. There were no projections in any part of the island, that we could perceive, sufficient to afford protection to a boat attempting to land, and the sea in consequence broke heavily against it in every direction.

The day being clear, we looked to the southward for the island of Agrigan, which on Arrowsmith's chart is placed within twelve miles of the Mangs, but no land could be discerned in that direction, and from the state of the weather, I should think there could not have been any within at least twelve leagues distance of us. This would make the channel between Assumption and Agrigan about forty miles wide, the jesuits extend it to sixty; but this cannot be the case, as it would place Agrigan near the latitude of 18° 45′ N. in which parallel Ybargottia, according to Espinosa, has placed the island of Pagon. It seems necessary, therefore, to contract the channel between Assumption and Agrigan as marked in the jesuits' plan, and to reduce the size of Agrigan in order to reconcile the position of the islands. Arrowsmith has incorrectly placed the Mangs on the south side of Assumption: by our astronomical bearings they are situated N 27° 7′ 30″ W. (true) from the south east end of this island, and are in Latitude 19° 57″ 02′ N. They consist of three high rocks, lying in a south-easterly direction.*

From what I saw of the island of Assumption it appears to be a very proper headland for ships coming from the eastward and bound to Canton to steer for. It is high, and may be safely approached in the night if the weather is clear, and there is a wide channel to the southward of it. It is far preferable to adopt this channel than to pass to the northward of the Mariana group, which is sometimes done: as I am credibly informed that there is much broken ground

* It is somewhat remarkable that in passing to the southward of the island of Assumption, at the distance of four miles and a half, we did not discover the rocks which Captain Freycinet has supposed to be the Mangs, situated in latitude 19° 32′ N. Our latitude when in the meridian of Assumption was 19° 36′ N by which it is evident that we must have passed within four miles of these rocks, provided both latitudes be correct. Had I known of their existence at the time, I should certainly have stood to the southward, in order to connect them by triangulation with the Assumption and the Mangs; but Captain Freycinet's discoveries were not then published.

47

in that direction.   We have as yet no good chart of this group of islands.

Under the lee of the island we observed a great many birds, principally of the pelican tribe, of which there was a species supposed by our naturalists to be new.   It is described as being smaller than the frigate-bird, and of a dark brown colour, with the exception of the belly and breast, which were white, and the bill, which was either white or of a light lead colour.

From the Ladrones, I directed the course for the Bashee Islands and on the 7th of April, after experiencing light and variable winds, got sight of the two northern islands of that group.   The long northerly swell, which had attended us almost all the way from the Sandwich Islands, ceased immediately we were to the westward of the Ladrones ; and indeed the sea between them and the Bashee Islands was so smooth that its heave was scarcely perceptible.   We found by our observations that the magnetic meridian intersects the channel between these two groups of islands in the meridian of 226° 48′ W in the latitude of 20° 12′ N.

The Bashee Islands, so called by the Buccaneers, in consequence of a drink of that name, which was extracted by the natives from the sugar-cane, form a long group very similar to the Ladrones, and extend in the same direction nearly from north to south.   Until these Islands were surveyed by Captain Horsburg their positions were as incorrectly determined as those of the Ladrones are at present.   A contrary wind, which rendered it necessary to beat through the channel between them and Botel Tobago Xima, afforded an opportunity of connecting these islands trigonometrically, and of obtaining transit bearings when in immediate stations between them   The longitude also was afterwards measured backwards and forwards between them and Macao, and we thus had an opportunity of examining the chart of Captain Horsburg, which appeared to be constructed with great truth and with his usual accuracy.

I regret not having seen the Cumbrian reef; we stood purposely towards it until sun-set, and were within six miles of its situation when we were obliged to go about by the approach of night

The next day we stood toward the island of Formosa, and tacked within four miles of the Vele rete rocks, the largest of which has the appearance of a vessel under sail   They lie off the south end of the island of Formosa,* and are surrounded by breakers, which in thick weather could not be approached with safety.   We observed strong ripples in the water near them ; but the wind did not permit us to enter any for the purpose of sounding ; late in the evening, however, when we were several leagues from them, the weath-

---

* The large rock bears S 29° 09′ 15″ E from the west end of Lamay Island.

er being nearly calm we were drawn into one of these ripples and continued in it several hours, during which time we tried for soundings with a hundred fathoms of line without success   Upon trial a current was found to set S. E. seven furlongs per hour ; this experiment, however, was made from the ship by mooring a buoy, and was probably incorrect, as the water was much agitated ; and had a vessel seen it, or even heard it in the night time (for it made a considerable noise), she would have taken it for breakers and put about.   A peculiar smell was detected in the atmosphere while we remained unmanageable in this local disturbance of the water, which some ascribed to sea weed, and others to dead fish, but it was never ascertained whence it arose   Some seamen have an idea, though it is not very general, that this peculiar odour precedes a change of weather, and sometimes a storm, particularly in the Mediterranean   On the present occasion nothing of the kind occurred immediately, though about twenty-six hours afterwards when crossing the channel between Formosa and the main land, the temperature fell sixteen degrees from the average height of the preceeding day, and the wind blew strong from the northward.

Before daylight on the 10th, while we were crossing the channel to the westward of Formosa. going at the rate of ten miles an hour, we found ourselves surrounded by Chinese fishing boats, and narrowly escaped running over several of them, as it was very dark, and they were so thick that in trying to escape one we endangered another, and were obliged to lie to until daylight   These boats are large vessels, and would endanger a small merchant ship were she to run foul of them   We were informed that they were upon their usual fishing ground, and vessels therefore in approaching the spot should be cautious how they proceed, as these boats carry only a large paper lanthern, which cannot be seen far off, and I believe they only show this when they perceive a strange vessel.   They were fishing in pairs, one vessel being attached by cables to each end of an enormous net, which kept them both broadside to the sea ; they were constantly covered with the spray, and being light, were washed about in so violent a manner that it scarcely appeared possible for people to stand upon their decks.   Still the crews of several which we passed consisted principally of females, who did not appear to be in the least inconvenienced by their situation.

In the forenoon we passed Piedra Branca, and in the evening entered the channel between the Great Lemma and Potoy   As no pilot offered, I stood on guided by the chart of Lieutenant Ross, which was extremely accurate, and at ten at night brought up in the Lantao passage, and at nine o'clock next morning anchored in the Typa. In entering this harbour we found less depth of water than is marked in the plan of Captain King ; and by the survey which we subsequently made, it appeared that at low water a ship cannot depend upon a greater depth than two fathoms, until after she passes the rocky head on her right

Immediately after we were anchored, I visited the late Sir William Fraser, who was then chief officer of the company's factory at Canton, and we both waited upon the Portuguese governor.   He gave us a very ungracious reception, for which we could account in no other way than by supposing he felt annoyed at our unceremonious entry of the Typa, without either pilot or permission, for the Portuguese at Macao, I understand, claim the Typa as their own, under the emperor's original grant of Macao to them for their services to China.   Some Portuguese officers who came on board during my absence, intimated that the ship would not be allowed to remain in the harbour   We heard nothing more of the matter, however, for several days, when a mandarin waited upon Sir William Fraser to inquire into the business of the man of war anchored in the Typa.   About the same time several war junks, two of which had mandarin's flags, came down the river, beating their gongs, and anchored not far from us

The mandarin received a satisfactory answer from Sir William Fraser ; but some days after, the Hoppo finding the ship did not go away, addressed the following letter to the Hong merchants —

" Wan, by imperial appointment, commissioner for foreign duties of the port of Canton, an officer of the imperial household, cavalry officer, &c. &c. &c. raised three steps, and recorded seventeen times,

" Hereby issues an order to the Hong merchants.

" The Macao *Wenguin* have reported, that on the 18th of the 13th moon, the pilot *Chinnang-Kwang* announced that on the 17th an English cruiser, Peitche,* arrived, and anchored at *Tausae.*

" On the pilot's inquiring, the said captain affirmed that he came from his own country to cruise about other parts, but gales of wind forced him in here, where he would anchor awhile till the wind was fair, and then he would take his departure.   I could only in obedience ascertain these circumstances, and also the following particulars :

" There are in the ship 120 seamen, 26 guns, 60 muskets, 60 swords, 700 catties of powder, and 700 balls

" This information is hereby communicated to higher authority

" Coming before me, the Hoppo, I have inquired into the case, and since the said vessel is not a merchant ship nor convoy to merchantmen, it is inexpedient to allow pretexts to be made for her anchoring, and creating a disturbance   I, therefore, order her to

* The Chinese call their vessels by the names of the persons who command them

be driven out of the port, and on the receipt of this order, let the merchants, in obedience thereto, enjoin the said nations, foreigners, to force her away. They will not be allowed to make glossing pretexts for her lingering about, and creating a disturbance which will implicate them in crime   Let the day of her departure be reported   Haste ! Haste ! a special order

"Taou Kwang,
"7th year, 3d month, 24 day."

The Hong Merchants transmitted this bombastic letter of the Hoppo to the British factory with the following letter · but I must observe that the pilot was incorrect in saying that he derived his information from me, or that such a pretext for putting into the Typa was made.

"We respectfully inform you that on the 23d inst we received an edict from the Hoppo concerning Peitche's cruiser anchoring at Tausae and ordering her away   We send a copy of the document for your perusal, and beg your benevolent brethren of the committee to enforce the order on the said Peitche's cruiser to go away and return home   She is not allowed to linger about

"We further beg you to inform us of her departure, that we may with evidence before us report the same to government

"We write on purpose about this matter alone, and send our compliments, wishing you well in every respect

"To the chiefs   " We the merchants
Mr. Fraser,   Wooshowchang, (Howqua's son,)
Mr Toone,   and others."
Mr Plowden."

The officers of the factory were aware of the ground upon which the Chinese founded their appeal, it being understood, I believe, that a vessel of war is not to enter the Chinese territory except for the purpose of protecting their own trading ships.   At the same time they were sufficiently acquainted with the Chinese style of writing to know that this was only a common remonstrance, however strong the language used might appear, and they amicably arrranged the business until near the time of our departure, when another letter arrived, to which they were able to give a satisfactory answer by our moving out of the Typa

As our object was to procure the stores we required, and to proceed to sea as quickly as possible, our movements were not in any way influenced by this order of the Poppo , and had it not been necessary to proceed to Canton to ascertain what was in the market there, we should have sailed before this dispatch reached its destination.   It appeared that we had arrived at an unfortunate period, as there were very few naval stores in the place, and the Chinese were either so dilatory, or so indifferent about delivering some that had been bargained for in Canton that we were obliged to sail without them. We, however, procured sufficient supplies to enable us to prosecute the voyage, and on the 30th of April took our departure

During our stay at Macao we received the greatest attention from the officers of the Company's establishment, who politely gave us apartments in their houses, and in ever way forwarded our wishes; and I am happy to join in the thanks expressed in my officers' journals for the hospitality we all experienced.

Soon after our arrival in the Typa, a febrile tendency was experienced throughout the ship, and before we sailed almost every officer and seaman on board was affected with a cold and cough, which in some cases threatened aneumonia; but the officers who resided in the town were free from complaint until they returned to the ship The probable causes of this were the humid state of the air, the cold heavy dews at night, and the oppressively hot weather during the day, added to the currents of air which made their way between the islands into the Typa, where the atmosphere, penned in on all sides by hills, was otherwise excessively close. On this account I think the Typa very objectionable, and should recommend the anchorage off Cabreta Point in preference

By a plan of the Typa, which we contrived to make during our visit, it appears that the depth of water is diminishing in the harbour, and that in some parts of the channel there is not more than ten feet and a half at low water spring tides; the rise of the tide at this time being seven feet one inch. The channel has shifted since the surveys of Captains King and Heywood, and new land-marks for entering, which I have given in my Nautical Remarks, are become necessary

On leaving Macao we hoped that the S W. monsoon would set in, and carry us expeditiously to the northward, instead of this, however, we were driven down upon the island of Leuconia in the parallel of 17° 16′ N. where we perceived the coast at a great distance Here it fell calm, and the weather, which had been increasing in temperature since our departure from Macao, became oppressively hot, the thermometer sometimes standing at 89° in the shade, and the mean height for the day being 85°, 7 of Fahrenheit.

About this time we saw several splendid meteors, which left trains of sparks as they descended On the 6th a parhelion was visible at 51° 50′ on the south side of the sun, when about 2° of altitude, and as we passed Orange Island we felt a sudden shock, accompanied by a momentary gust of wind which threatened the masts : the sky at this time was quite clear and cloudless

On the 7th we saw the south Bashee Islands, celebrated as one of the resorts of the Buccaneers, and the day following made the Island of Botel Tobago Xima   While off the Bashee Islands we noticed a great rippling in the Balingtang Channel, and during the night we experienced so strong a current to the north west that instead of passing the Cumbrian Reef ten miles to the eastward, as we expected, on the following morning we found, greatly to our surprise, that we had been set on the opposite side of it, and much closer than was consistent with security in a dark night   These currents render precaution very necessary ; that by which we were affected ran N 56° W. twenty-six miles during the night, or about two miles and a half per hour.   We continued to feel this effect until we were a full day's sail from Botel Tobago Xima, and we were obliged in consequence to beat through the channel between that island and Formosa   In doing this we had an opportunity of examining the shores of Botel Tobago Xima, and of constructing a tolerably good plan of its nothern and western sides, besides determining its position more accurately than had been done when we passed it on the former occasion

The aspect of this part of the island is both agreeable and picturesque.   The mountains are covered with wood and verdure to their summit, and are broken by valleys which open out upon plains sloping rather abruptly from the bases of the hills to the sea coast.

Almost every part of this plain is cultivated in the Chinese manner, being walled up in steep places, like the sides of Dane's Island in the Tigris.   Groves and tufts of palm trees break the stiffness which this mode of cultivation would otherwise wear, and by their graceful foliage greatly improve its appearance   In a sand bay on the north side of the island there is a large village consisting of low houses with pointed roofs.

There are several rocky points on the north-west side, and some detached rocks lie off the northern extremity, which are remarkable for their spire-like form.   The coast is rocky in almost every part, and probably dangerous to land upon, as these needle rocks are seen in many parts of the island   With the exception, however, of those off the north extreme, they are attached to the island by very low land, but the shore under water often assumes the character of that which is above, in case a vigilant look out for rocks would here be necessary in towing along the coast.   At three miles distance from the land we had no bottom with 120 fathoms of line.

After beating two days off Tobago Xima without being able to

make much progress against the current, which on the average ran
a mile and a quarter per hour, on the 10th a change of wind enabled us to steer our course. We took our departure from Sam-
sanna, an island to the northward of Tobago Xima, situated by our
observations, nearly in latitude 22° 42′ N., and exactly 8′ west of
the eastern extreme of the Little Tobago Xima.

I intended, on leaving Macao, to explore the sea to the eastward
of Loo Choo, particularly that part of it where the Yslas Arzobispo, the Malabrigos, and the Bonin Islands, are laid down in various charts. It was, however, no easy matter to reach thus far, and
what with light, variable winds, and contrary currents, our progress
was extremely slow, so that on the 15th we found ourselves not far
from the Great Loo Choo, with a contrary wind

About this time it was discovered that the water we had taken
on board at Macao was extremely bad, owing to the neglect of the
comprador in filling the casks, and as I had no object in reaching
Kamschatka for nearly two months, I determined upon proceeding to Napakiang in Loo Choo I was further induced to do this,
on account of the longitude of the places we might meet between
it and Petropaulski We therefore bore away to the westward,
and in the evening saw the island bearing W. by N. ten leagues
distant.

The following morning we were close to the reefs by which the
Island of Loo Choo is nearly surrounded, and steered along them
to the southward, remarking as we passed the excellent harbours
which appear to be formed within them, and planning a chart
of them as correctly as our distance from the shore, and other circumstances, would permit The sea rolled furiously over the reefs,
which presented a most formidable barrier to encounter in a dark
night, but we were glad to find that this danger was lessened by
soundings being found outside them, in a depth of water which
would enable a vessel to anchor in case of necessity. This depth
gradually increased to seventy-five fathoms, at four miles distance
from the reefs.

Daylight had scarcely dawned the following morning before
several fishermen paddled towards the ship, and fastened their canoes alongside They had taken several dolphins, which they exchanged for a very small quantity of tobacco, tying the fish to a
rope, and without the least mistrust contentedly waiting until the
price of it was handed to them Their canoes were capable of
holding five or six persons each, but there were seldom more than
two or three in any of them They were hollowed out of large
trees, and rather clumsily made ; but it was evident, from the neat
manner in which the inside was fitted with bambo gratings, that the

constructors of them were capable of much better workmanship
They had no outriggers, and their sail was made of grass.

After remaining alongside some time they ventured upon deck,
and saluted us in the Japanese manner, by bowing their heads very
low, and clasping their hands to their breasts They appeared to
be a very diminutive race, and were nearly all bow-legged, from the
habitual confinement of their canoes   Many of them were naked,
with the exception of a maro ; but those who were clothed wore
coarse cotton gowns with large sleeves , and almost every person
had a pipe, tobacco-pouch, and match fastened to his girdle.   As
the Loo Chooans are reputed to be descended from the Japanese,
we naturally sought in the countenances of these people features
characteristic of that nation, but found that they bore a much nearer
resemblance to those of the Malay tribe.   Their manners, however,
were very different from those of the Malays; and they were marked with a degree of courtesy and good breeding, which we certainly
should not have expected to find in persons of their humble occupation, and inferior condition in life

Having obtained permission to look over the ship, they examined
attentively those things which interested them, and when their
curiosity was satisfied they made a low bow, and returned to their
canoes, leaving us well pleased with their manners.   About this
time several dolphins swam round the ship, and the fishermen threw
over their lines, and met with tolerable success.   Our lines had for
some time been towing overboard with various devices of flying-
fish, pieces of cloth, &c attached to them, and springing from the
water with the rise of the ship, in imitation of the action of the
flying-fish, but without any success, and we were happy to take a
lesson from our new acquaintances.   Their lines were similar to
ours, but their snoeuds were made of wire, and their hooks, when
properly baited, were quite concealed in the body of a flying-fish
which had one side of the flesh cut away.   Several lines thus prepared were allowed to run out to the length of about ten fathoms,
and when the dolphins were near, speed was given to the canoe,
that the bait might have the appearance of a fish endeavouring to
escape pursuit.   In this manner several were taken at no great distance from us.   If the fish happened to be large, the line was carefully drawn in, and they were harpooned with an instrument which
every canoe carried for the purpose.

We stood towards Loo Choo, accompanied by several of these
canoes, until within a few miles of the land, when fearing to be seen
from the shore, they quitted us, first making signs for us to go round
to the other side of the island.

About sunset the wind left us close off the south extremity of the
Great Loo Choo ; and all the next day it was so light that the boats

were obliged to tow the ship toward the harbour. This slow progress would have been far less tedious had we been able to see distinctly the country we were passing, and the villages situated in the bays at the back of the reefs, but this prospect was unfortunately destroyed by a dense haze which rendered every distant object indistinct, and tantalized our expectations by the variety of fallacious appearances it created. Our course, until four o'clock in the afternoon, was along the western side of Loo Choo, between it and a reef lying about midway between this western shore and the Kirrama islands About that time we arrived off Abbey Point, and were entering the harbour of Napakiang, guided by our charts, when we were obliged to drop the anchor to avoid striking upon a coral bank, with only seven feet water on its shallowest part Upon examination we found that this bank, which had hitherto escaped observation, had a deep channel on both sides of it; we therefore weighed, and steered through the southern passage. It afterwards became necessary to beat up to the anchorage, in doing which we discovered another rock, and had a still narrower escape.* We reached our destination a little before sunset, and then came to an anchor off the town of Napa.

---

* The positions of these rocks are given in the plan of Napakiang, which we constructed during our stay here.

CHAPTER XVII

Appearance of Loo Choo—Visits of the natives—Deputation—Permission given to land—Excursions into the Country—Discover Money in Circulation—Mandarin visits the Ship—Departure of a Junk with Tribute—Visit of the Mandarin return-ed—Further Intercourse—Transactions of the Ship—Departure—Observations upon the religion, manners, and Customs of the People ; upon their Laws, Money, Weapons, and Punishments their manufactures and Trade—Remarks upon the Country, its Productions and Climate—Directions for entering the Port—Histori-cal Sketch of the Kingdom of Loo Choo.

Loo Choo from the anchorage presents a very agreeable land-scape to the admirers of quiet scenery.   The land rises with a grad-ual ascent from the sea-coast to something more than five hundred feet in height, and in almost every part exhibits a delightful picture of industry.   The appearance of formality is just removed by a due proportion of hill and valley, and the monotonous aspect of continu-ed cultivation is broken by rugged ground, neatly executed cemete-ries, or by knots of trees which mingle the foliage of the temperate zone with the more graceful vegetation of the tropics.   The most remarkable feature is a hill named Sumar, the summit of which com-mands a coup-d'œil of all the country round it, including the shores of both sides of the island.   Upon this hill there is a town appar-ently of greater importance than Napa, called Shui or Shoodi, sup-posed both by Captain Hall and ourselves to be the capital of Loo Choo.   With our telescopes it appeared to be surrounded by a wall, and it had several flags (*hattas*) flying upon tall staffs   The hous-es were numerous, but the view was so obstructed by masses of fol-iage which grew about these delightful residences that we could form no estimate of their numbers.   Upon a rise, a little above the site of the other houses of the town, there was a large building half obscured by evergreen trees, which some of us imagined might be the residence of the king, who had chosen so elevated a situation, in order to enjoy the luxury of breathing a high current of air in a country occasionally exposed to excessive heat   A rich carpet of verdure sloping to the westward connects this part of the landscape with the bustling town of Napa, or Napa-ching,* of which we could see little more than a number of red roofs turned up at the corners in Chinese style, or at most only a few feet down the chunammed walls which support them, in consequence of a high wall surrounding the town. To the right of the town a long stone causeway stretches out into the sea, with arches to allow the water a free access to the harbour at the back of it, and terminates in a large square building with loop-holes. To this causeway sixteen junks of the largest class were secured some had prows formed in imitation of animals, and georgeously coloured, others presented their sides and sterns highly painted and gilt, while, from among their clumsy cordage aloft, and from a number of staffs placed erect along the stern, were suspended variously shaped flags, some indicating, by their colour, or the armorial bearing upon them, the mandarin captain of the junk; some the tributary flag of the Celestial Empire, and others the ensign of Japan. Many of these were curiously arranged and stamped in gilt characters on silken grounds.

To the left of Napa is the public cemetry, where the horse-shoe sepulchres rise in galleries, and on a sunny day dazzle the eye with the brightness of their chunammed surfaces, and beyond them again, to the northward, is the humble village of Potsoong, with its jos-house and bridge.

The bay in every part is circumscribed by a broad coral ledge, which to seaward is generally occupied by fishermen raising and depressing nets extended upon long bamboo poles, similar to those of the Chinese. Beyond these reefs are the coral islands of Tzee, the more distant islands of Kirrama, and far, in a northern direction, the cone of Ee-goo-sacoo, said to be covered with houses rising in a spiral direction up its sides The whole, when viewed on a fine day, and when the harbour is enlivened by boats passing to and fro, with well-dressed people chanting their harmonious boat song, has a pleasing effect which it is difficult to describe

Before our sails were furled the ship was surrounded by boats of various descriptions, and the tops of the houses on shore, the walls and the forts at the entrance of the harbour, were crowded with spectators watching our operations Several persons came on board, and with a respectful salutation begged permission to be allowed to look over the ship; but they were interrupted by the approach of a boat with an officer, apparently of rank, whom they endeavoured to avoid. His person underwent a severe scrutiny through our teles-

---

* Napa is decidedly the name of the village, and the words *chang* and *keang*, which are occasionally subjoined, in all probability are intended to specify whether it is the town, or the river near it, that is intended, *chung* being in Chinese language a town, and *keang* a river, and though these substantives are differently expressed in Loo Choo, yet when thus combined, the Chinese expression may probably be used

cope long before he came on board, and we could distinctly see that he had not the *hatchee-matchee*, or low cylindrical cap worn by persons of rank in Loo Choo, in the same manner as the cap and buttons are by the mandarins of China, yet he was evidently a man of consequence, from the respect paid him by the natives in making room for his approach   When he came along side he was invited upon deck, but for some time he stood minutely examining the outside of the ship, counting the number of port-holes, and apparently forming an estimate of her length and height.   At last he ascended the side and made a low salutation on the quarter deck, bowing his head in a respectful manner, and clasping his hands to his breast, as before described   Finding we could not understand his language he waved his hand to seaward, in intimation that we should not be allowed to remain in the port   He then looked down upon the gun deck, and pursued his examination of the inside of the ship with the same rigour that he had bestowed upon the exterior, making notes of what he saw.   When he was satisfied, he expressed his thanks for our civility and returned to the shore.

Soon after his departure, several well-dressed persons, with boys holding parasols over them, were observed coming off to us · they were seated in Chinese style upon mats spread in the bottom of the boat, over neat ratan platforms, and were propelled by several persons working at a large oar as a scull, keeping time to a song, of which the chorus was *ya ha mashawdy*, or words very similar.

They were elegantly dressed in gowns made of grass cloth, of which the texture was fine and open, and being a little stiff, formed a most agreeable attire in a country which was was naturally warm. To prevent this robe being incommodious while walking, it was bound at the waist with a girdle, linen or silk, according to the rank of the wearer.   They had sandals made of straw, and one of them, whose name was An-yah, had linen stockings   None of them had any covering to the head, but wore their hair turned back from all parts, and secured in a knot upon the crown, with two silver pins, *kamesashe* and *oomesashe*, the former of which had an ornamental head resembling a flower with six petals ; the other was very similar to a small marrow-spoon.   Each person had a square silken tobacco-pouch embroidered with gold and silver, and a short pipe of which the bowl and mouth-piece were also silver, and one who was secretary to An-yah carried a massy silver case of writing materials.

They saluted us very respectfully, first in the manner of their own country and then of ours, and An-yah, by means of a vocabulary which he brought in his pocket, made several inquiries, which occasioned the following dialogue   " What for come Doo Choo ?"*

* This word is pronounced Doo-Choo by the natives, but as it is known in England as Loo Choo, I shall preserve that orthography

"To get some water, refit the ship, and recover the sick." "How many mans?" "A hundred." "Plenty mans! you got hundred ten mans?" "No, a hundred." "Plenty guns?" "Yes." "How many?" "Twenty-six." "Plenty mans, plenty guns! What things ship got?" "Nothing, ping-chuen." "No got nothing?" "No, nothing." "Plenty mans, plenty guns, no got nothing!" and turning to his secretary he entered into a conversation with him, in which it appeared almost evident that he did not wholly credit our statement. It was, however, taken down in writing by the secretary

In order more fully to explain myself I showed them some sentences written in Chinese, which informed them that the ship was an English man of war. that the king of England was a friend of the emperor of China; and that ships of our nation had frequent intercourse with the town of Canton The secretary, who read these sentences aloud, immediately wrote in elegant chinese characters† "What is your reason for coming to this place! How many men are there on board your ship?" and was both sorry and surprised to find I could not understand what he had written Indeed he appeared to doubt my sincerity, particularly after I had shown him the next question, which happened to be an answer to his question, but which naturally followed the first. stating that we were in want of water and fresh provision, and that the sick required to be landed to recover their health, and concluding by specifying our desire to be allowed to pay for every thing that was supplied to us. An-yah received this information with satisfaction, and replied, "I speakee mandarin, Doo Chooman want no pay"

These sentences were kindly furnished me by Dr. Morrison, at my own request, in case circumstances should render it necessary to put into Loo Choo, and they were written in Chinese characters, which Dr Morrison was well aware would be quite intelligible to the literati of Loo Choo, who express themselves in the same character as the Chinese, though their language is totally different They contained many interesting inquiries, and afforded the means of asking questions without the chance of misinterpretation To several of them the negative or affirmative was all that was required, and these are expressions understood by most people It happened, however, that An-yah had learned enough of the English language to say something more than these monosyllables; so that what with his proficiency, and the help of these sentences, besides a dictionary, vocabulary, and dialouges in both languages, which Dr. Morrison had also very generously given me, we had the

---

† This, as well as several other papers written by the Loo Chooans, was afterwards interpreted by Mr Hultmann of the Asiatic Society, to whom, and also to Sir William Ousely, I beg permission to be allowed to express my thanks

means of gaining a good deal of information , more, probably, than we could have done through an indifferent interpreter. As, however, opinions vary concerning the written character of China being in general use in Loo Choo, I shall hereafter offer some observations on the subject

After our visiters had satisfied their curiosity concerning our object in putting into Loo Choo, they sat down to dinner, which was ready, and with much address and good humour showed us they had learned to chin-chin, or drink healths in the English manner

I was very anxious to find out who my guest with the vocabula-ry was, as it first occurred to me that it might be Madera, of whom Captain Hall so frequently speaks in his delightful publication on Loo Choo , but then he did not seem to be so well acquainted with the English language as Madera appears to have been, and, besides, he must have been much younger   His objection to answering our inquiries on this head, and disclaiming all knowledge of any vessel having ever been at Loo Choo before, put it out of my power at first to inform myself on the point, and had not his own curiosity overcome his prudence, it would perhaps have long remained a secret

The manner in which the discovery was made is curious ; after the sackee * had gone round a few times, An-yah inquired if " ship got womans ?" and being answered in the negative, he replied, somewhat surprised, " other ships got womans handsome womans !" alluding to Mrs. Loy, with whom the Loo Chooans were so much captivated that, it is thought, she had an offer from a person of high authority in the island.   I then taxed him with having a knowledge of other ships, and when he found he had betrayed himself, he laughed heartily, and acknowledged that he recollected the visit of the Alceste and Lyra, which he correctly said was 144 moons ago, and that he was the linguist An-yah whom Captain Hall calls An-yah *Toonshoonfa,* but he disclaimed all right to this appendage to his name.   Having got thus far, I inquired after almost all the characters which so much interested me in reading the publication alluded to above ; but they either prevaricated, or disclaimed all recollection of the persons alluded to, and I found it extremely difficult to get a word in answer.

At last one of them said Ookoma was at the other end of the island, and another immediately added that he had gone to Pekin. A third stated that Madera was very ill at the capital, while it was asserted by others that he was dead, or that he was banished to Patanjun.†   They all maintained they had never any knowledge

---

* The Loo Choo name for wine or spirits
† An island situated near Ty-pingchan, upon which Captain Broughton was wrecked

of such persons as Shangfwee, and Shang Pungfwee, the names given to the king and prince of Loo Choo in Captain Hall's publication. From this conversation it was very evident that they knew perfectly well who Ookoma and Madera were, but did not intend to give us any correct information about them

I was a little vexed to find that neither An-yah nor Isaacha-Sandoo, who was also of our party, and is mentioned by Captain Hall, made the slightest inquiry after any of the officers of the Alceste or Lyra, by whom they had been treated in the most friendly manner, and for whom it might have been inferred, from the tears that were shed by the Loo Chooans on the departure of those ships, · that the greatest regard had been entertained. The only time they alluded to them was when Mrs. Loy recurred to their imagination.

When they had drank enough sackee they rose to take their leave, and, emptying the contents of the fruit dishes into their pockets, retired in great good humour; but An-yah, not quite satisfied about the number of men on board the ship, probably imagining, from the number he saw aloft, that there were many more, again asked the question, "How many mans!" and on being answered as before, replied "Not got hundred one?" which he wrote down a second time; and having satisfied himself on this knotty point shook us by the hand and said, "Well, I speakee mandarin, to-morrow come water; Doo Chooman no want pay. fife day you go away." "That," I returned, "will depend upon the health of the sick, who must be allowed to land and walk about." I then desired him to tell the mandarin, that to-morrow I should go on shore and wait on him in his own house. An-yah, alarmed lest the threat might be carried into execution, hastily exclaimed, "No, no, I speakee mandarin, mans go ashore, walk about, no go house—no go house." Thus by threatening to do more than was intended, we obtained a tacit consent to that which we wanted without much chance of giving offence Unwilling to give him any further uneasiness, I permitted him to go, requesting he would deliver to the mandarin an invitation to visit the ship, which he promised to do; and seating himself and his companions on the mat in the boat, he sculled on shore to the musical chorus of "ya-ha-me-shawdy."

Our decks were by this time crowded with spectators, who had been coming off in boat loads The place did not appear to afford many of these conveyances, and they had to go backwards and forwards between the ship and the shore a great many times, always singing their boat songs as they sculled themselves along Our visitors had paid us the compliment of putting on their best attire, all of which was made of the grasscloth in the manner before described; the colours were various, but mostly blue

The utmost good breeding was manifested by every one of them, not only in scrupulously making their bow when they entered and quitted the ship, but in not allowing their curiosity to carry them beyond what they thought perfectly correct. They all seemed determined to be pleased, and were apparently quite happy in being permitted to indulge their curiosity, which was very great, and bespoke them a people extremely desirous of information. It was amusing to observe which objects attracted the particular attention of each individual, which we thought always accorded with the trade or profession of the party; for, as we had at different times all the population of Napa on board the ship, we must have had persons of all occupations. We observed two of these people, after having gratified their curiosity about the deck, seat themselves in their canoes, and commence drawing a picture of the ship—one selected a broadside view, and the other a quarter, each setting at defiance all rules of perspective. The artist on the quarter had of course the most difficult task, and drew the stern as a continuation of the broadside, by which it appeared like an enormous quarter gallery to the ship. That they might make an exact representation, they took their station at the distance of twenty feet from the side of the ship, and commenced their drawing upon a roll of paper about six feet in length, upon which they pourtrayed not only the outline of the ship, but the heads of all the bolts, the but ends of the planks, and before it was finished, no doubt, intended to trace even the grain of the wood. Whatever merit might have been attached to the drawing, the artists were entitled to commendation for their perseverance, which overcame every difficulty, and they had some few to contend with. A little before sunset they rolled up their paper and paddled on shore.

We were scarcely up the following morning before our ears were assailed by the choruses of the boatmen bringing off new visiters to the ship, who continued to pass between her and the shore the whole of the day, carrying a fresh set at every trip, so that the harbour, if possible, presented a more lively scene than it did the day before: on shore the walls and housetops were occupied by groups who sat for hours looking towards the anchorage. Our visiters as before were well dressed and well bred people, and extremely apprehensive of giving offence or even of incommoding us.

The mandarin, however, fearful we might experience some annoyance from having so many people on board without any person to control them, sent off a trusty little man with a disproportionably long bamboo cane to keep order, and who was in consequence named Master-at-Arms by the seamen. This little man took care that the importance of his office should not escape notice, and occasionally exercised his baton of authority, in a manner which seemed to me much too severe for the occasion; and sometimes even drew forth severe though ineffectual animadversions from his peaceable countrymen. but as I thought it better that he should manage matters in his own way, I did not allow him to be interfered with

Among the earliest of our visiters were An-yah, Shtafacoo, and Shayoon, three intelligent, good-natured persons, who, I have no doubt, were deputed to watch our movements They were the bearers of a present of a pig and some vegetables. As An-yah had promised, several boats commenced supplying the ship with water, bringing it off in large tubs * In reply to my request that the officers and invalids might be allowed to walk about on shore, An-yah said he had spoken to the mandarin, who had sent off a Loo Choo physician to administer to the health of our invalids, and in fact who would see whether our statement concerning them was correct or not A consequential little man, with a huge pair of Chinese spectacles, being introduced as the Esculapius in question, begged to be permitted to visit the sick and to feel their pulse The surgeon says—" he gravely placed his finger upon the rabial artery first of one wrist and then of the other, and returned to the first again, making considerable pressure for upwards of a minute upon each. To one patient affected with a chronic liver complaint, and in whom the pulsations are very different in the two arms, in consequence of an irregular distribution of the arteries, he recommended medicine : of another person affected with dyspepsia whose pulse was natural, he said nothing ; no other part of the animal economy attracted his notice He appeared to be acquainted with quicksilver and moxa, but not with the odour of cinnamon "

After this careful examination he returned to the cabin and wrote in clumsy Chinese characters that one of the patients had an affection of the stomach and required medicine ; and inquired of another if he were costive This report, which we did not understand at the time, was satisfactory to An-yah, who immediately gave us permission to land at Potsoong and Abbey Point, but with an understanding that we were not to go into the town He then produced a list of inquiries, which he had been ordered to make, such as the dimensions of the ship. the time we had been from England, Canton, &c , and lastly, what weather we had experienced, as he said Loo Choo had been visited by a violent tyfoong in April, which unroofed the houses and did much other mischief

The permission to land was immediately taken advantage of by several of the officers, who went to Potsoong, and were received in

* This water proved to be bad, for though it had no very unpleasant taste, it was found, upon being analysed, to contain in solution a large proportion of magnesia and some salt ; a circumstance which should be borne in mind by vessels obtaining a supply at this place

a very polite manner by a great concourse of spectators, who conducted them to the house in which Sir Murray Maxwell and his officers had been entertained; and regaled them with (*tsha*) tea, and (*amasa*) sweet cakes. Some of the party, instead of entering the house, strolled inland to botanize, and to look at the country, but they had not proceeded far before two or three persons ran towards them, and intimated that their company was expected at the house where the other officers were assembled drinking tea, and were waiting for them. This was the Loo Choo polite manner of preventing their proceeding inland, or of making themselves acquainted with the country; and thus, whenever any parties landed afterwards, they were shown to this house, where there was always tea ready prepared, and kept boiling in a kettle, inclosed in a neatly japanned wooden case, there were also trays of charcoal for lighting pipes, and a box to receive the ashes when they were done with the natives endeavoured, by every possible means, to engage their attention at this place, by putting a thousand inquiries, offering pipes, and pressing them to smoke, and to drink tsha, which was always poured out in small cups, and drank without milk or sugar, which, as it was quite new, and not of the best kind, or much improved by being kept boiling, had a very insipid taste, it, however, served to quench the thirst on a hot day

On no account would these people receive any present, nor would they sell any of their property in public, but if they thought we desired to possess any thing they could spare, they would offer it for our acceptance. I one day made a present to a person who had been very civil in showing me over his grounds, which he at first refused, and when I insisted on his taking it, and placed it in his pocket, he gave it me back again; but finding I would not receive it, he threw it after me; and it was not until after I had returned it in the same manner, that he was prevailed upon to accept it. Upon doing this, he first exhibited it to the crowd around him, and then thanked me for it On another occasion one of the officers offered a man, named Komee, two Spanish dollars for his pouch, which he declined, and could not be prevailed upon to accept; but with perfect good breeding he presented to him the object he desired, and insisted upon his keeping it. In private, however, they had less objection to presents, and even asked for several things · small bargains were also effected.

From this time we visited the shore daily, and made many excursions into the country, confining our rambles within reasonable limits, to avoid giving uneasiness to our guides, who were very much distressed whenever we strayed beyond what they considered strictly within the limits prescribed by their instructions. We met many peasants and other persons in these excursions, all of whom seemed eager to show us attention, and with whom there was less reserve, and less disinclination to our proceeding inland, than was manifested by our guides from Napa, who were evidently acting under much constraint.

Lieutenant Wainwright, who, since leaving San Francisco, had been an invalid, having suffered severely from a disease of the heart, was provided with a horse by the natives, and permitted to ride every day for his health   He was attended by a guide, and received much kindness and attention, from the humane Loo Chooans, who, though they often gave us many reasons to suspect the purity of their intentions, were, by their acts, certainly entitled to our gratitude.

On the 19th we received a bullock weighing 100*lbs.*; five pigs, a bag of sweet potatoes, some firewood, and some more water.   Several of the officers landed and walked into the country, attended by the natives, who endeavoured by every species' of cunning, and even by falsehood, to prevent their going near the villages, or penetrating far inland   We had again a ship full of visiters, and the two artists were employed the greater part of the day in completing their drawing which they refused to part with.   After the strangers were gone on shore, a thermometer that was kept upon deck for the purpose of registering the temperature was missed, and the natural conclusion was, that it had attracted the attention of some of our visiters, who it must be remembered, were of all classes.

It was a curious coincidence, but I believe perfectly accidental, that the day after the instrument was missed not a single person came off to the ship, except those employed in bringing water: when Au-yah came on board the next morning I made our loss known to him; he was much distressed at hearing of it, and said he would make every inquiry about it on shore, and added—"Plenty Doo Ohoo man teef—plenty mans teef," he also advised us at the same time to look well after our watches, handkerchiefs, and particularly any of the instruments that were taken on shore   These precautions I am almost certain were unnecessary, and I am inclined to believe that An-yah painted his countrymen in such odious colours to make us take proper precautions   Though the Loo Chooans are extremely curious, and highly prize such an instrument, yet the theft is not in character with the rest of their conduct, and however appearances may condemn them I am inclined to believe them guiltless of taking the thermometer, which probably was left in the tub used for drawing up sea-water to try its temperature, and was accidentally thrown overboard.   And yet in so large a body of people there must naturally be some who are bad; however, we never heard any thing more of the thermometer.

A little before noon I landed to observe the meridional altitude,

and met Shtafacoo and several other Loo Choo gentlemen, who,
were attended by little boys holding parasols over them, and carrying small japanned cases containing smoked and dried meats, small
cups of preserves, and boiled rice, sackee, a spirit resembling the
samchew of China, and fresh water. They ordered mats to be
spread for us, and we made a good luncheon of the many nice
things in their boxes We afterwards crossed over to Potsoong,
where we were met by an elderly gentleman, who made a very low
obesiance, and pressed us to come into the house in which the
officers of Sir Murray Maxwell's squadron and of the Blossom had
been entertained, and which appeared to be set apart entirely for
our use It was situated in a square area laid out in lawn and
flower beds, and enclosed by a high wall ; the house was built of
wood, and roofed with tiles in the Chinese style ; the floor was raised about two feet from the ground, and the rooms though small,
were capable of being thrown into one by means of shifting panels.
To the right of the house there was a large brass bell, which was
struck with a wooden club, and had a very melodious tone ; at the
further end of the garden was a jos house, a place of worship, which
as it has been described by Captain Hall, I shall notice only by the
mention of a screen that was let down before the three small images on the inside. It was made of canvas stretched upon a frame
forming two panels, in each of which was a figure, one represen-
ting a mandarin with a yellow robe and hatchee matchee, seated
upon a bow and quiver of arrows and a broad sword ; the other, a
commoner of Loo Choo dressed in blue, and likewise seated upon
a bow and arrows. The weapons immediately attracted my attention, and I inquired of my attendant what they were, for the purpose of learning whether he was acquainted with the use of them,
and found that he was by putting his arms in the position of drawing the bow, and by pointing to the sword and striking his arm forward ; but he implied that that weapon belonged to the mandarins
only. A great many pieces of paper were suspended on each side
of the picture, some of them marked with Chinese characters, and
were, no doubt, invocations to the deities for some temporary benefits, as all the sects are in the habit of writing inscriptions of this
kind, and depositing them in the jos houses, or placing them upon
stones, of which there are several in Loo Choo under the name of
Karoo Under a veranda which surrounded the temple there were
several wooden forms strewed with flowers, and upon the middle
one a drum was suspended by thongs in a handsome jappaned
stand.

A building in front of this jos house, mentioned by Captain Hall
has been rebuilt, but was not quite finished at the time of our visit though so near to the temple, the panels were scrawled over

with groups of figures some of which were very inappropriate to
such a situation

After we had partaken of tea in the dwelling-house we determined upon a walk in the interior, much to the discomfiture of the old
gentleman, who used every means he could think of to induce us to
desist, and produced pipes, sweet cakes, tsha, and massa chorassa,
preserves with which they tempted us whenever they feared our
walk would be directed inland. Finding he could not detain us, he
determined to be our companion, and endeavoured to confine us to
the beach by praising the freshness of the breeze, saying how hot
we should find it inland, and what bad paths there were in that direction, every word of which proved to be false, as we found the
roads very good, and by gaining elevated situations we enjoyed more
of the breeze.

We passed some tombs excavated in the cliffs, and in one that
was broken down we discovered a corpse lying upon its back, half
decayed and covered over with a mat, a jar of tea and some cups
were placed by it, that the spirit might drink, but there was nothing to eat, and our guide informed us that it was customary to place
tea only by the side of the bodies, and that food was never left there
He turned us away from this shocking spectacle as much disgusted
as ourselves, and seemed sorry that we had hit upon it. This discovery seems to strengthen some information which I afterwards received concerning the manner in which the dead were disposed of,
namely, that the flesh is allowed to decay before the bones are placed in jars in the cemetery.

From this place we ascended a hill covered with tombs, which
were excavated in the rock in a manner very similar to those near
Canton, they had almost all of them niches, wherein bowls of tea,
lamps, and cups were placed, and appeared to be kept in good order, as they had a cleanly and decent appearance. We wandered
among these some time, without finding any open, but at last we
came to one of an inferior kind, in which the door was loosely placed before the entrance, it consisted of a large slab of red pottery,
pierced with a number of holes about an inch in diameter. Having
removed this, we saw about twenty jars of fine red pottery covered
with lids shaped like mandarins' caps, the size of the jars was about
twenty inches deep by eight in the biodest part, which was one third of
the way from the mouth, they were also perforated in several places
with holes an inch in diameter We did not remove any of the lids,
as it seemed to give offence, but were told that the jars contained the
bones of the dead after the flesh had been stripped off or had decayed, on putting the question whether they burned the bones or the
flesh off them, it was answered by surprise, and an inquiry whether
we did so in England? Therefore, unless the custom has altered,

the account of Supao Koang, a learned Chinese, who visited Loo Choo in 1719, is incorrect.

After visiting the grave of one of the crew of the Alceste who was buried in this island, we were satisfied with this tour of the tombs, and turned off inland, very much to the discomfiture of our guide, and in spite of a great many remonstrances. He was a silent companion until we came to a path that went back to the beach, and there, politely stepping forward, said it was the one that would take us where we wished to go, and, touching our elbow, he would have turned us into it had he not thought it rude; but we pursued our original path, followed by a crowd of persons, who seemed to enjoy the discomfiture of our companion, and laughed heartily as we came to every track that crossed ours, each of which our officious and polite conductor would have persuaded us to take, as being far more agreeable than the other, and as leading to our destination. The mirth of the crowd pretty well satisfied us there was no great danger in advancing, and we went on further than we should otherwise have done; but in a little time they began to drop off, and we were at last left alone with the guide, who really became alarmed. We had reached the foot of the hill on which the capital is situated, and were ascending to have a near view of the houses, when he threw himself on his knees in evident alarm, bowed his head to the dust, embracing our knees implored us to desist, assuring us that the mandarin would take his head off if we did not. Some of the officers who went in another direction were told by their guide that he would get bambooed if they did not turn back, which is more probable than that the heavy penalty apprehended by our companion should be attached to so light a crime.

To quiet the irritation of the poor old man, who trembled violently, we ascended a hill some distance to the left, which commanded an extensive view of the country, and from whence we could survey the capital with our telescopes. The country was highly cultivated, and the grounds irrigated with Chinese ingenuity and perseverance by small streams of water passing through them, keeping such as were planted with rice thoroughly wet. We noticed in our walk sweet potatoes, millet, wheat, Indian corn, potatoes, cabbages, barley, sugar-cane, tea shrubs, rice, taro, tobacco, capsicums, cucumbers, cocoa nuts, carrots, lettuces, onions, plantains, pomgranates, and oranges; but amidst this display of agricultural industry there were several eminences topped with pine trees, on which the hand of the farmer might have been advantageously employed, but which were allowed to lie waste, and to be overrun with a rank grass. Such places, however, being usually the repositories of the dead, it may have been thought indecorous by the considerate Loo Chooans to disturb the ground near it with a hoe. These eminences, like the basis of the island, being formed of a very porous calca-reous rock, are peculiarly adapted to the excavation of tombs, and the natives have taken advantage of them to dispose of their dead in them.

The capital, for such I am disposed to call the town on the hill, notwithstanding the denial of several of the natives, was surround-ed by a white wall, within which there were a great many houses, and two strong buildings like forts ; with, as already mentioned, sev-eral small masts with gaffs, bearing flags of different colours.   This space was thickly interspersed with trees, whence we conjectured the houses were furnished with gardens   There seemed to be very few people moving about the island, even between the upper and lower towns, with which it would be supposed there must necessa-rily be much intercourse.   We rested awhile on the eminence that afforded this agreeable view of a country but very little known, and were joined by several persons whom fear or indolence had pre-vented keeping pace with us.   Our guide now lighted his pipe and forgot his apprehension in the consoling fumes of tobacco, while some of the party amused themselves with viewing the capital through a telescope, each preventing the other having a quiet view by their anxiety to obtain a peep   Our clothes in the meantime were undergoing an examination from the remainder of the party, who, after looking closely into the texture of the material, ex-claimed—chooassa, chooassa ' (beautiful)

While we sat here a Japanese junk bore down from the north-ward, and according to the information of those around us, which afterwards proved to be correct, she came from an island called Ooshima, to the northward of Loo Choo, and was laden with rice, hemp, and other articles   Her sails and rigging resembled the drawing of the Japanese junks in La Perouse's voyage.   She pass-ed close to the Blossom at anchor, and from the report of the officers her crew had their heads shaved in the fashion of the Japanese   Her arrival excited general interest brought all the inhabitants to the housetops, and a number of canoes crowded round her before she reached the inner harbour, where she was towed and secured alongside several other junks bearing the same flag.

On our return we passed through a village consisting of a num-ber of square inclosures of low stone walls, separated by lanes planted on both sides, and so overgrown with bamboo and ratans that we could neither see the houses nor the sky ; several handsome creepers entwined themselves round the stems of these canes, and a variety of flowers, some of which were new to us, exhaled a de-licious fragrance from the gardens which bordered these delightful avenues.   A more comfortable residence in a hot climate could not well be imagined, but I am sorry to say that the fascination was greatly lessened by the very filthy state of the dwellings and of the people who occupied them. In one of these huts there was a spinning-wheel and a hand loom, with some glass-cloth of the country in a forward state of preparation for use.

Several little children accompanied us through these delightfully cool lanes, running before us catching butterflies, or picking flowers, which they presented with a low Chinese salam, and then ran away laughing at the idea of our valuing such things. We afterwards crossed two high roads, on which there were several horses and jack-asses bearing panniers, but we saw no carriages, nor the marks of any wheels, nor do I believe there are any in Loo Choo. The horses, like the natives, were very diminutive, and showed very little blood   Several peasants, both male and female, were working in the plantations as we passed through them, neither of whom endeavoured to avoid us, and we had an opportunity of beholding, for the first time, several Loo Choo women.   They were of the labouring class, and of course not the most attractive specimens of their sex; but they were equally good-looking with the men, and a few of them were pretty, notwithstanding the assertion of An-yah, that "Loo Choo womans ugly womans."   There was nothing remarkable about them to need particular description; they were clothed much in the same manner as the men, and generally in the same colours; their hair, however, was differently dressed, being loosely fastened at the side of the head by a pin resembling a salt-spoon with a very long handle.   Their feet were of the natural size, and without shoes or sandals   We noticed some were tattooed on the back of the hand, which we were told was done to distinguish all those who were married; An-yah said the custom prevailed equally in high life.

Upon the high road we met a man with a bundle of firewood, on his way to town, and were much pleased at the confirmation of a fact, which we had no doubt existed, though the natives took every precaution to conceal it.   None of our visiters to the ship had as yet shown us any money, and An-yah, if I understood him correctly, said there was none in Loo Choo; our meeting with this peasant, however, disclosed the truth, as he had a string of cash* (small Chinese money) suspended to his girdle, in the manner adopted by the Chinese   I examined the string with much interest, and offered to purchase it with Spanish coin, but my guide would not permit the woodman to part with it, and tucking it into his belt that it might not be seen again, he said something to him in an angry tone,

* These coins being of small value, they are strung together in hundreds, and have a knot at each end, so that it is not necessary to count them

and the poor fellow walked on with his load to the town. We afterwards got some of this money, which was exactly the same as that which is current at Canton, and found that it was also in circulation in Loo Choo Though they afterwards admitted this fact, they denied having any silver or gold coin in the country

Our subsequent excursions were nearly a repetition of what has been described, and were made nearly to the same places, with the exception of two or three, which I shall describe hereafter. In all these the same artifice was practised to induce us to confine ourselves to the beach, and particularly to prevent a near approach to the villages. Tobacco, tsha, and chorassa masa were the great temptations held out to us, but neither the tea, nor the massa, which, by the by, was seldom produced, had sufficient charms to dissuade some of our young gentleman from gratifying their curiosity, though it was at the expense of the convenience of the natives, whose dresses were very ill adapted to speed; and thus, by outrunning them, they saw many places which they would not otherwise have been permitted to enter, and got much nearer, to the town than I felt it would be right for me to do in consequence of my promise to An-yah. I shall, therefore, give such extracts from their journals as are interesting, but in a few pages in advance, that I may not disturb the order of the narrative.

On the 21st, An-yah came off to say, that the mandarin had accepted my invitation to visit the ship, and would come on board that day. we consequently made preparation to receive him. As it appeared to me that Napa-keang possessed no boat sufficiently good for so great an occasion, I offered to send one of ours to the town for his accommodation, which, in addition to obliging the mandarin, would afford an opportunity of seeing the place, but An-yah would not permit it, and fearful that we might really pursue this piece of politeness further, got out of the ship as fast as he could, saying the mandarin was at Potsoong, and not in the town About two o'clock he pushed off from that place with his party in two clumsy punts, sculled by several men singing a chorus, which differed, both in words and air, from that used by the boatmen in general The mandarin was seated in the largest of these boats, under a wide Chinese umbrella, with two or three mandarins of inferior rank by him; the other boat contained An-yah, Shtafacoo, Sandoo, and others, with whom we were well acquainted, and who rowed on before the mandarin, and announced his approach by presenting a crimson scroll of paper, exactly a yard in length, on which was elegantly written in Chinese characters, "Ching-oong-choo, the magistrate of Napā, in the Loo Choo country, bows his head to the ground, and pays a visit" By this time the other boat with the great man was alongside the ship, and four domestics with scarlet hatchee-matchees ascended the side, one of them bearing a large square hatchee-matchee box, in which there was an old comb. They pulled up the side ropes, and carefully inspected them, to see whether they were strong enough to hold their master, and let them down again for the mandarin, who, very little accustomed to such feats, ascended the side with difficulty.

He was received with a guard under arms, and a mandarin's salute was fired as he put his foot upon the deck, with which he was much gratified, and he shook every officer by the hand with unaffected pleasure. The yards had been manned as he was coming off, and when the pipe was given for the seamen to come down, the evolution produced a little surprise, and must have impressed the Loo Chooans with the decided advantage of our dress over theirs, where activity is required. Ojee, one of the party, who also styled himself Jeema, and is mentioned by Captain Hall, followed, and then the rest of the mandarins in yellow hatchee-matchees and gowns.

To persons who had visited a fine English frigate, disciplined by one of the ablest officers in the British Navy, the Blossom could have presented nothing extraordinary, and as the greater part of our visiters were familiar with the Alceste, they were very little interested in what they saw; but Ching-oong-choo had not been long from Pekin, and never, probably, having put his foot on the deck of a ship before, a Chinese junk excepted, examined every thing very attentively, and made many inquiries about the guns, powder, and shot.

None of the natives offered to seat themselves in the cabin in the presence of the mandarin until dinner was brought in, but they then dispensed with formalities, and those who were familiar with European customs chinchinned each other with wine, and reversed their glasses each time, to the great amusement of their superior. During dinner the fate of Madera was inquired into, but we got no satisfactory answer, and a mystery seemed to hang over his fate, which made us suspect he had in some way or other been disgraced. Jeema took the opportunity of showing he recollected his visit to the Alceste and Lyra, but he did not make any inquiry after his friends in either vessel.

As we had lately been at Canton, we were provided with many things which were happily to the taste of our guests, who would otherwise have fared badly, as they did not appear to relish our joints of meat; nor did some bottled porter accord better with their taste, for after occasioning many wry faces, it was put aside as being bitter: a flavour which I have observed is seldom relished for the first time. Not so some noyeau, which was well adapted to the sweet palate of the Loo Chooans; nor some effervescing draughts, which were quite new to them, and created considerable surprise. They, however, seemed to enjoy themselves a great deal; were jovial without being noisy, and with the exception of a dissagreeable practice of cructation, and even worse, they were polite people, though I cannot say I approved of their refinement upon our pocket handkerchief. An-yah often intimated to me that he thought it was a disagreeable practice to use a handkerchief and carry it about all day, and thought it would be better for us to adopt their custom of having a number of square pieces of paper in our pockets for this purpose, and one of which could be thrown away when it had been used. I did not at first think he was in earnest, and when I observed my guests pocket these pieces of paper, I sent for some handkerchiefs, but they declined using them, saying paper was much better.

While we were at dinner a large junk which we had observed taking in a cargo the day before, was towed out of the harbour by an immense number of boats, making the shores echo with her deep-toned gong. She grounded off the entrance of the harbour, but was soon got off and placed outside the reefs. A more unwieldy ark scarcely ever put to sea, and when she rolled, her masts bent to that degree that the people on her deck seemed to be in imminent danger of their lives. She was decorated with flags of all sorts and sizes; at the fore there was hoisted the white flag of the emperor, at the main, the Loo Choo colours, a triangular flag, red and yelow, with a white ball in it, denoting, I believe, a tributary state. there were besides several others, and a great many mandarins' flags upon staffs along the stern. Ching-oong choo said she was the junk with tribute which was sent every second year from Loo Choo to Fochien. Her cargo, before it was stowed, was placed upon the wharf in square piles, with small flags upon sticks stuck here and there upon bales of goods, which were apparently done up in straw matting. for it was only with our telescopes that we were allowed to see this.

After dinner was over, the mandarin went on shore, and begged to have the pleasure of our company to dinner at Potsoong the next day; but the rest of the company obtained permission to stay and enjoy a little more sackee, after which they pocketed the remains of the dessert as usual, and as a token of their friendship, they each threw down their pipe and tobacco-pouch, and begged my acceptance of them; but as I knew these articles were valuable in Loo Choo, and was conscious that with some of them it was only a matter of form, I declined accepting them.

The next day it rained heavily but An-yah came off to keep us to our engagement, saying the mandarin was at Potsoong in readiness to receive us, we accordingly went, and were met at the landing place by Jeema and a great crowd of Loo Chooans, with umbrellas, who accompanied us to the house, where we were received by the mandarin in a most cordial and friendly manner. For convenience both apartments were thrown into one, by the removal of shifting panels, and the servants were regaled upon the floor in the inner room, while we were seated at a table in the outer apartment. Our table, which had been made in Japan, was nicely lacquered, and had Chinese characters gilt upon its edges and down the sides of the legs, recording the date and place where it was made, as well as the name of the workman, &c. It was covered with dishes containing a variety of eatables, principally sweetmeats, and two sorts of spirits, sackee and moo roo fa coo. The former resembles the samscheu of China, and the other is a dark coloured cordial possessing a bitter-sweet taste. We were seated on one side of the table, myself in an old fashioned chair, and the other officers upon camp stools with japanned backs, and the host, Jeema, and the other mandarins, on the other side; and each person was provided with a small enamelled cup and a saucer with a pair of chopsticks laid across it the crowd all the while surrounding the house, and watching through its open sides every motion we made. Pipes and moo roo fa coo were first offered to us, and then each dish in succession of which we partook, according to our different tastes, without being aware of the Chinese custom of giving the sweets first and reserving the substantial part of the dinner for the last.

Among the dishes, besides some sweet cakes made very light, were different kinds of pastry, one of a circular form, called *hannaburee*, another tied in a knot, hard and disagreeable, called *matza kai*, and a third called *kooming*, which enclosed some kind of fish. There was also a marmalade, called *tsheeptang*, a dish of hard boiled eggs without the shells, painted red, and a pickle which was used instead of salt, called *dzeeseekedakoonee*, besides a small dish of sliced cold liver called *watshaingo*, which in this course was the only meat upon the table. We ate more plentifully of these sweet things than we liked, in consequence of our ignorance of what was to follow, and partly from our not being aware that their politeness prevented them from sending away any dish as long as we could be prevailed upon to partake of it—a feeling which induced them continually to press us to eat, and offer us part of every dish on the end of their chopsticks. The next course induced us to regret that we had not made the taste more a matter of form, for it consisted of several good dishes, such as roast pork, hashed fowls, and vermicelli pudding, &c. After these were removed they brought basins of rice, but seeing we would eat no more, they ordered the whole to be taken away.

During the whole time we were closely plied with sackee in

small opaque wine glasses, which held about a thimblefull, and were compelled to follow the example of our host and turn our glasses down but as this spirit was of a very ardent nature, I begged to be allowed to substitute port and madera, which was readily granted, and we became more on a footing with our hosts, who seemed to think that hospitality consisted in making every person take more than they liked, and argued that, as they had been intoxicated on board, we ought to become so on shore

After dinner was removed, Jeema favoured us with two songs, which were very passable, and much to the taste of the Loo Chooans, who seemed to enjoy them very much. Nothing could exceed the politeness and hospitality of the mandarin throughout, who begged that dinner might be sent off to one of the officers, whose health would not permit him to risk a wetting, and that all the boats crews might be allowed to come to the house and partake of the feast. Though there was a little ceremony in receiving and seating us, yet that almost immediately wore off and Ching oong choo to make every person at his ease took off his hatcee-matchee, and with the rest of the mandarins sat without it. By this piece of politeness we discovered that his hair was secured on the top of the head by a gold hair pin, called *kamesache,* the first and the only one we saw made of that precious metal.

We afterwards took a short walk in the garden, when I was surprised to find An-yah and Shtafacoo in the dress and hatchee-matchee of mandarins of the second class whether this was intended as a trick, or, following Madera's example, they preferred making their first acquaintance in disguise, is not very clear, but as they both possesed a great deal of influence, and were much respected by the lower orders of the inhabitants, it was probably their proper dress.

As soon as Ching-oon-choo permitted us, we took our leave, and were accompanied to the boat by a great crowd of persons, who opened a passage as we proceeded, and were officially anxious to be useful in some way or other, and we then parted with Jeema and the rest amidst the greetings and salutations of hundreds of voices

On the 21st, one of the officers made an excursion to the southward of Abbey Point, and was attended as usual by a concourse of of boys and young men, who were extremely polite and respectful They used every artifice and persuasion to deter him from proceeding, said they were tired, tempted him with tsha, and declared that they were hungry, but he ingeniously silenced the latter complaint by offering his guide a piece of bread which he had in his basket It was thankfully accepted, but with a smile at the artifice having failed At a village called Aseemee he surprised two females standing at a well filling their pitchers, they scrutinized him for some time, and then ran off to their homes.

The village contained about fifty houses; and was almost hid from view by a screen of trees, among which were recognised the acacia, the porou of the South Seas, and the hibiscus rosa sinensis, but the greater part of the others appeared to be new; they formed a lively green wood, and gave the village an agreeable aspect.   In one of the cottages a boy of about six years of age was seated at a machine made of bamboo resembling a small Scotch muckle wheel, spinning some very fine cotton into a small thread   Though so young, he appeared to be quite an adept at his business, and was not the least embarrassed at the approach of the strangers   A quantity of thread ready spun lay in the house; there was a loom close by, and some newly manufactured cloth, which appeared to have been recently dyed, was extended to dry outside the house.   Near this cottage there were broken parts of a mill, which indicated the use of those machines, and circular marks on the earth, showing that this one had been worked by cattle.   About a mile and a half to the southward of Abbey Point, near a steep wooded eminence, which we christened Wood Point, there was another village named Oofoonee, through which Mr. Collie passed, preceded by his guide, who warned the female part of the inhabitants of his approach in order that they might get out of his way   His guide was delighted when he directed his steps toward the ship, as he was very tired, and even had a horse brought to him before he got to the beach. This animal was eleven hands and a half in height, and would hardly have kept a moderately tall person's feet off the ground; but his guide, though there was not much necessity for bracing his feet up very high, obviated the possibility of this inconvenience by riding with his knees up to his breast   The stirrups were massy, and made of iron curiously inlaid with brass, and shaped something like a clumsy Chinese shoe   At Abbey Point he visited some sepulchres hewn out of the rock or formed of natural caverns , one of these happened to be partly open, and he discovered four large red earthen jars, one of which was fortunately broken, and exhibited its contents, consisting of bones of the human skeleton.

In another excursion made by this gentleman to the north-east of Potsoong, he visited a temple of Budh, situated in a romantic copse of trees   The approach to it was along a path paved with coral slabs, partly overgrown with grass, and under an archway in the formation of which art had materially assisted the hand of nature   After resting a short time in this romantic situation he descended the paved way, passed some tall trees, among which was a species of erethrina of large growth, and arrived at the house of a priest, who invited him to smoke and partake of tea and rice. Three young boys were in the house, who, as well as the priest, had their heads shaved according to the custom of the priesthood in China

By the 25th May, we had completed the survey of the port, replenished our water, received a little fresh stock, and obtained some interesting astronomical and magnetical observations, the day of departure was consequently near at hand. This event, after which many anxious inquiries were made by the natives, was, I believe, generally contemplated with pleasure on both sides; not that we felt careless about parting with our friends, but we could not enjoy their society without so many restrictions, and we were daily exposed to the temptation of a beautiful country without the liberty of exploring it, that our situation very soon became extremely irksome. The day of our departure, therefore, we hailed with pleasure, not only by ourselves, but by those to whom the troublesome and fatiguing duty had been assigned of attending upon our motions. and they must moreover have looked with suspicion on the operations of the survey that were daily going forward, even had they not suspected our motives for putting into their port

I was very anxious before this day arrived to possess a set of the pins that are worn by the natives in their hair. From their conduct it appeared that these ornaments had some other value attached to them than that of their intrinsic worth, or there would not have been so much difficulty in procuring them. Seeing they set so much value upon them that none of the natives could be induced to part with them, I begged An-yah would acquaint the mandarin with my desire, and, if possible, that he would procure me a set. An-yah replied that he would certainly deliver my message to the mandarin, and the next morning brought a set of the most inferior kind, made of brass. As the mandarin had received some liberal presents from me, I observed to An-yah that this conduct was ungenerous, and that I expected a set made of silver; his opinion he said very much coincided with mine, and added that he would endeavour to have them changed, but the following morning he met me on shore, and said, "Mandarin very bad man, no give you silver kamesache" but An-yah, determined that my request should be complied with, had by some means succeeded in procuring a set for me, which he presented in his own name. I rewarded his generous behaviour by making him a present of some cut glass decanters and wine glasses, which are more esteemed in Loo Choo even than a telescope.

On the 27th we made preparations for weighing, by hoisting our sails, and An-yah, Shtafacoo, and Shayoon, who had been our constant attendants, came off to take leave. These good people had been put to much trouble and anxiety on our account, and had so ingratiated themselves with us, that, as the moment approached, I

really believe the desire for our departure was proportionably lessened ; and when the day arrived, they testified their regret in a
warm but manly manner, shook us heartily by the hand, and each
gave some little token of regard, which they begged us to keep in
remembrance of them.   As we moved from the anchorage, the inhabitants assembled on the house-tops, as before, upon the tombs,
in the forts, and upon every place that would afford them a view of
our operations, some waving umbrellas and others fans

Having brought to a conclusion the sketch of our visit to Loo
Choo, I intend in the few pages that follow to embody what other
information was collected from time to time, and to offer a few remarks on the state of the country as we found it, as compared with
that which has been given by Captain Hall and the late Mr. M'Leod,
surgeon of the Alceste   In the foregoing narrative I have avoided
entering minutely into a description of the manners and persons
of the inhabitants, and I have omitted several incidents and anecdotes of the people, as being similar to those which have already been given in the delightful publications above mentioned.

Loo Choo has always been said to be very populous, particularly the southern districts, and we saw nothing in that part of the
island which could induce us to doubt the assertion   On the contrary, the number of villages scattered over the country, and the
crowds of persons whom we met whenever we landed, amply testified the justness of the observation   We were, certainly, in the
vicinity of the capital, and at the principal seaport town of the island ; but, in forming our estimate of the population, it must be
borne in mind that we were very likely to underrate its amount, in
consequence of the greater number of persons who crowd into
Chinese towns than reside in villages of the same size in countries
from which we have taken our standard

The people are of very diminutive stature, and according to our
estimation their average height does not exceed five feet five inches
As might be expected, from the Loo Chooans being descendants of
the Japanese, and numerous families from China having settled in
the island, there is a union of the disposition and of the manners,
as well as of the features of both countries   The better classes
seemed by their features to be allied to the Chinese, and the lower
orders to the Japanese ; but, in each, the manners of both countries
may be traced.   Their mode of salutation, their custom of putting
to their foreheads any thing that is given to them, their paper
pocket handkerchiefs, and some parts of their dress, are peculiarly
Japanese.   In other respects they resemble the Chinese.   The
hatchee-matchee and the hair-pins are, I believe, confined to their
own country, though smaller metal hair-pins are worn by the ladies

of Japan * On the whole they appear to be a more amiable people than either the Chinese or Japanese, though they are not without the vices natural to mankind, nor free from those which characterise the inhabitants of the above mentioned countries.   They
have all the politeness, affability, and ceremony of the Chinese,
with more honesty and ingenuousness than is generally possessed
by those people , and they are less warlike, cruel, and obsequious
than the Japanese, and perhaps less suspicious of foreigners than
those people appear to be   In their intercourse with foreigners their
conduct appears to be governed by the same artful policy as that
of both China and Japan, and we found they would likewise sometimes condescend to assert an untruth to serve their purpose ; and
so apparent was this deceitfulness, that some among us were led
to impute their extreme civility, and their generosity to strangers,
to impure motives.   They are exceedingly timorous and effeminate,
so much so that I can fancy they would be induced to grant almost
any thing they possess rather than go to war , and as one of my
officers justly observes in his journal, had a party insisted upon entering the town, they would probably have submitted in silence,
treated them with the greatest politeness, and by some plausible
pretext have got rid of them as soon as they could
     They appear to be peaceable and happy, and the lower orders
to be as free from distress as those of any country that we know
of ; though we met several men working in the fields who were in
rags, and nearly naked   The most striking peculiarity of the people is the excessive politeness of even the lowest classes of inhabitants : on no account would they willingly do any thing disagreeable to a stranger, and when compelled, by higher authorities than
themselves, to pursue a certain line of conduct, they did it in the
manner that was the least likely to give offence , and it was quite
laughable to notice the fertility of their invention in order to obtain
this end, which was seldom gained without a sad sacrifice of integrity   Their reluctance to receive remuneration for their trouble, or
for the provisions which they supply to foreigners, is equally remarkable   Captain Broughton and Captain Hall have noticed
their conduct in this respect   In the case of a whale ship which
put into Napa-keang in 1826, and received nearly two dozen bullocks and other supplies, the only remuneration they would receive
was a map of the world   And in our own instance (though we
managed by making presents to the mandarins and to the people to
prevent their being losers by their generosity,) An-yah's reply to
my question, whether we should pay for the supplies we received
in money or goods ? was, " Mandarin *give* you plenty, no want pay."

* See Langsdorff's Travels, vol ii

But with all this politeness, as is the case with the Chinese, they cannot be said to be a polished people

Our means of judging of their education were very limited : a few only of the lower orders could read the Chinese characters, and still fewer were acquainted with the Chinese pronunciation, even among the better classes there were some who were ignorant of both   Schools appear to have been established in Loo Choo as far back as the reign of Chun-tine, about the year 1187, when characters were introduced into the country, and the inhabitants began to read and write   These characters were said to be the same as those of the Japanese alphabet *yrofa.*   In the year 1372, other schools were established, and the Chinese character was substituted for that of the Japanese, and about the middle of the seventeenth century, when the Mantchui dynasty became fixed upon the throne of China, the Emperor Kang-hi built a college in Loo Choo for the instruction of youth, and for making them familiar with the Chinese character   An-yah intimated that schoolmasters had recently been sent there from China ; and one day while I was making some observations, several boys who were noticed among the crowd with books, and who seemed proud of being able to read the Chinese characters, were pointed out by An-yah as being the scholars of those people

I am of opinion that the inhabitants of Loo Choo have no written character in use which can properly be called their own, but that they express themselves in that which is strictly Chinese We certainly never saw any except that of China during our residence in the country   The manuscripts which I brought away with me were all of the same character precisely, and some were written by persons who did not know that I was more familiar with the Chinese character than with any other

It is very probable that the Japanese character was in use formerly , but it is now so long since schools have been established in Loo Choo for teaching the Chinese character, viz since 1372, and the Chinese, whose written character is easier to learn than the other, have always been the favourite nation of the Loo Choo people, that it is very probable the Japanese characters may now be obsolete   An-yah would give us no information on this subject, nor would he bring us any of the books which were in use in Loo Choo   One which I saw in the hands of a boy at Abbey Point appeared to be written in Chinese characters, which are so different from those of the Japanese that they may be readily detected.

M Grosier on this subject, quoting the Chinese authors, says

* Recueil de Pere Gaubil.

that letters, accounts, and the king's proclamations are written in Japanese characters ; and books on morality, history, medicine, astronomy, &c in those of China   One of the authors whom he quotes adds, that the priests throughout the kingdom have schools for teaching the youth to read according to the precepts of the Japanese alphabet Y-ro-fa.   As we may presume they teach morality in these schools, it would follow, as books on those subjects are all written in Chinese characters, that the boys must be taught both languages, but, had this been the case. I think we should have seen the Japanese character written by some of them   It is to be observed, that the invocations in the temples and on the kao-roo stones are all in the character of China.

While upon this subject, I must observe, that the idea of Mons P S. Du Ponceau,* " that the meaning of the Chinese characters cannot be understood alike in the different languages in which they are used," is not strictly correct, as we found many Loo Choo people who understood the meaning of the character, which was the same with them as with the Chinese, but who could not give us the Chinese pronunciation of the word   And this is an answer to another observation which precedes that above mentioned. viz. that, " as the Chinese characters are in direct connexion with the Chinese spoken words, they can only be read and understood by those who are familiar with the spoken language "   The Loo Choo words for the same things are different from those of the Chinese, the one being often a monosyllable, and the other a polysyllable, as in the instance of *charcoal*, the Chinese word for it being *tan*, and the Loo Chooan *cha-ehee-jing,* and yet the people use precisely the same character as the Chinese to express this word; and so far from its being necessary to be familiar with the language to understand the characters, many did not know the Chinese words for them.   Their language throughout is very different from that of the Chinese, and much more nearly allied to the Japanese.   The observation of M. Klaproth, in Archiv fur Asiatische Litteratur, p 152, that the Loo Choo language is a dialect of the Japanese with a good deal of Chinese introduced into it, appears to be perfectly correct, from the information of some gentlemen who have compared the two, and are familiar with both languages.   The vocabulary of Lieutenant Clifford, which we found very correct, will at any time afford the means of making this comparison.

The inhabitatns of Loo Choo are very curious on almost all subjects, and seem very desirous of information ; but we were wholly

---

* See a letter from this gentleman to Captain Basil Hall, R N. published in the Annals of Philosophy for January, 1829

unable to judge of their proficiency in any subject, in consequence
of the great disadvantages under which we visited their country

Like the Japanese, they have always shown a determination to
resist the attempts of Europeans to trade with them, partly, no
doubt, in consequence of orders to that effect from China, and partly
from their own timidity , and whenever a foreign vessel arrives it is
their policy to keep her in ignorance of their weakness, by confining the crew to their vessel, or, if they cannot do that, within a
limited walk of the beach, and through such places only as will
not enlighten them on this point , and also to supply her with
what she requires, in order that she may have no pretext for remaining.

Mr Collie in his journal has given a phrenological description of
the heads of several Loo Chooans which he examined and measured, in which proportions he thinks the lovers of that science will find
much that is in accordance with the character of the people   The
article, I am sorry to say, is too long for insertion here, and I only
mention the circumstance that the information may not be lost

We had but few opportunities of seeing any of the females of
this country, and those only of the working class.   An-yah said
they were ugly, and told us we might judge of what they were like
from the lower orders which we saw.   They dressed their hair in
the same manner as those people, and were free from the Chinese
custom of modelling their feet

The Loo Choo people dress extremely neat, and always appear
cleanly in their persons , they observe the Chinese custom of going
bareheaded, and when the sun strikes hot upon their skulls, they
avert its rays with their fans, which may be considered part of the
dress of a Loo Chooan.   In wet weather they wear cloaks and
broad hats similar to those of the Japanese, and exchange their
straw sandals for wooden clogs   They have besides umbrellas to
protect them from the rain.   Of their occupations we could not
judge   it was evident that there were a great many agriculturists
among them, and many artizans, as they have various manufactures,
of which I shall speak hereafter

They appear to be very temperate in their meals, and indulge
only in tea, sweatmeats, and tobacco, of which they smoke a great
quantity ; it is, however, of a very mild quality and pleasant flavour.
Their pipes are very short, and scarcely hold half a thimbleful , this
is done that they may be the oftener replenished, in order to enjoy
the flavour of fresh tobacco, which is considered a luxury.

For further information on the manners, the dress, and minor
points of interest belonging to these people, I must refer to the
publications of Captain Hall and Mr. Macleod, who have so interestingly described all the little traits of character of the simple Loo

Chooans, and who have pourtrayed their conduct with so much spirit, good feeling, and minuteness These descriptions, though they have been a little overdrawn from the impulse of grateful recollections, from the ignorance in which the authors were kept by the cautious inhabitants, and from their desire to avoid giving offence, by pushing their inquiries as far as was necessary to enable them to form a correct judgment upon many things, are upon the whole, very complete representations of the people

The supposition that the inhabitants of Loo Choo possessed no weapons, offensive or otherwise, naturally excited surprise in England, and the circumstance became one of our chief objects of inquiry. I cannot say the result of the investigation was as satisfactory as I could have wished, as we never saw any weapon whatever in use, or otherwise, in the island : and the supposition of their existence rests entirely upon the authority of the natives, and upon circumstantial evidence The mandarin Ching-oong-choo, and several other persons, declared there were both cannon and muskets in the island : and An-yah distinctly stated there were twenty-six of the former distributed among their junks.* We were disposed to believe this statement, from seeing the fishermen, and all classes at Napa, so familiar with the use and exercise of our cannon, and particularly so from their appreciating the improvement of the flint lock upon that of the match lock, which I understood from the natives to be in use in Loo Choo , and unless they possessed these locks it is difficult to imagine from whence they could have derived their knowledge. The figures drawn upon the panels of the jos-house, seated upon broad swords and bow and arrows, may be adduced as further evidence of their possessing weapons , and this is materially strengthened by the fact of their harbour being defended by three square stone forts, one on each side of the entrance, and the other upon a small island, so situated within the harbour, that it would present a raking fire to a vessel entering the port , and these forts having a number of loop-holes in them, and a platform and parapet formed above, with stone steps leading up to it in several places This platform would not have been wide enough for our cannon, it is true ; but unless it were built for the reception of those weapons, there is apparently no other use for which it could have been designed I presented the mandarin with a pair of pistols, which he thankfully accepted, and they were taken charge of by his domestics without exciting any unusual degree of curiosity. Upon questioning An-yah where his government procured its powder, he immediately replied from Fochien

It is further extremely improbable that these people should have

---

* There were none on board the junk which sailed for China

no weapons, considering the expeditions which have been successively fitted out by both China and Japan against Loo Choo, and the
civil wars which unfortunately prevailed in the island, more or less,
during the greater part of the time that the nation was divided into
three kingdoms *   Besides, the haughty tone of the king to the
commander of an expedition which was sent, in A D 605, to demand submission to his master the Emperor of China, viz "That he
would acknowledge no master," is not the language of a people destitute of weapons.   Loo Choo has been subdued by almost every expedition against it, yet it is not likely the country could have made
even a show of resistance against the invaders, had the inhabitants
been unarmed ; they nevertheless resisted the famous Tay-Cosama,
and though conquered, threw off the yoke of Japan soon afterwards,
and returned under the dominion of China   It was afterwards re-
taken by Kingtchang with 3,000 Japanese, who imprisoned the
king, and killed Tching-hoey, his father, because he refused to acknowledge the sovereignty of Japan †   They are, besides, said to
have sent swords as tribute to Japan   In 1454 the king Chang-tai-
keiou had to sustain a civil war against his brother, who was at first
successful, and beat Chang-tai-keiou in a battle, in which he fought
at the head of *his troops*   It is not improbable that all this warfare
and bloodshed should have transpired without the Loo Chooans being possessed of arms ; besides, it is expressly stated by Supao-Koang, that arms were manufactured in the island.   I am, therefore,
disposed to believe that the Loo Chooans have weapons, and that
they are similar to those in use in China.   And with regard to the
objection which none of them having ever been seen in Loo Choo
would offer, I can only say, that while I was in China, with the
exception of cannon in the forts, I did not see a weapon of any kind,
though that people is well known to possess them

It was also thought that the Loo Choo people were ignorant of
the use of money   But this point has now been satisfactorily de-
dermined, by our having seen it in circulation in the island, and
having some of it in our own possession   The coin was similar to
the *cash* of China.   An-yah declared that there were no gold or silver coins in the country, not even ingots, which are in use in China ;
but this will hereafter, perhaps, prove to be untrue, as he even denied the use of the cash until it was found in circulation.   There is
very little doubt that money has been long known to, if not in use
among, the Loo Chooans   About the year A. D. 1454, in the

* From its division under Yut-Ching in 1300, until it was united under Chang-
pat-chi, about a century afterwards
† Report of Supao-Koang, a learned Chinese physician, sent by the Emperor of
China to Loo Choo in 1719, to report upon the country —Lettres Edifiantes et Cri-u
euses, vol. xxviii.

reign of Chang-tai-keiou, we are told that so large a quantity of silver and brass coin was taken from China to Loo Choo, that the provinces of Tche-Kiang and of Fochien complained to the emperor of the scarcity it had occasioned in those places,* and Pere Gaub'l, quoting Supao-Koang,† after enumerating several articles of trade, says " tout cela se vende et s'achete, ou par echange ou en deniers de cuivres de la Chine "

Our countrymen were further led to believe, from what we saw of the mild and gentle conduct of the superior orders in Loo Choo towards their inferiors, that the heaviest penalty attached to the commission of a crime was a gentle tap of a fan.   Our friend with his bamboo cane, who was put on board to preserve order among his countrymen, afforded the first and most satisfactory evidence we could have had of this being an error, and had we possessed no other means of information, his conduct would have favoured the presumption of more severe chastisement being occasionally inflicted It happened, however, fortunately, that I had purchased in China a book of the punishments of that country, in which the refined cruelty of the Chinese is exhibited in a variety of ways.   By showing these to the Loo Choo people, and inquiring if the same were practiced in their country, we found that many of their punishments were very similar.   Those which they acknowledged were death by strangulation upon a cross, and sometimes under the most cruel torture; and minor punishments, such as loading the body with iron chains; or locking the neck into a heavy wooden frame ; enclosing a person in a case, with only his head out, shaved, and exposed to a scorching sun , and binding the hands and feet, and throwing quicklime into the eyes.   I was further assured that confession was sometimes extorted by the unheard-of cruelty of dividing the joints of the fingers alternately, and clipping the muscles of the legs and arms with scissors.   Isaacha Sando took pains to explain the manner in which this cruelty was performed, putting his fingers to the muscles in imitation of a pair of sheers, so that I could not be mistaken : besides, other persons at Potsoong told me in answer to my inquiry, for I was rather sceptical myself, that it was quite true, and that they had seen a person expire under this species of torture.   However, lest it should be thought I may have erred in attaching such cruelties to a people apparently so mild and humane, I shall insert some questions that were put to the Loo Chooans out of Dr. Morrison's Dictionary, and their answers to them respectively

" Do the Loo Choo people torture and interrogate with the lash ?"
" Yes."—" Do they examine by torture?" Yes."—" Do they give

false evidence through fear of torture ?" " Yes "—" Are great officers of the third degree of rank and upwards, who are degraded and
seized to be tried, subjected to torture ?" " No "—" Is torture inflicted in an illegal and extreme degree ?" " Not illegal."—" Do
you torture to death the real offender ?" ' Yes, sometimes."—
" What punishment do you inflict for murder ?" " Kill *by hanging
or strangulation* "*—" For robbery ?" " The same."—" For adul-
tery ?" " *Banish to* Pantajan " (probably Pat-chong-chan, an is-
and to the south-west of Typingsan)—" For seduction ?" " The
same " Minor offences we were told were punished with a bam-
booing or flagellation with a rod   Crimes are said to be few in number, and speaking generally there appears to be very little vice in
the people.

I was assured by An-yah that marriages in Loo Choo were contracted as they are in China, by the parents or by a friend of the
parties, without the principals seeing each other.   Only one wife, I
believe is allowed in Loo Choo, though to the question, whether a
plurality of wives was permitted? both An-yah and Shtafacoo said
that the mandarin had five, and that the king had several †   They,
however, afterwards declared that in their country it was customary
to have only one wife.   Perhaps it is the same in Loo Choo as in
China where a man may have only one lawful wife , but with her
permission he may marry as many more as he can provide for.
These wives are as much respected as the first wife, but they do
not inherit their husband's property.

In Loo Choo, as in China, there is no religion of the state, and
every man is allowed freely to enjoy his own opinion, though here,
also, a distinction is made between the sects one being considered
superior to the other   The sects in Loo Choo are Joo, Taou, and
Foo, or Budh ; but the disciples of the latter consist almost entirely of persons of the lowest order, and An-yah appeared to think very
lightly of its votaries, saying there were " no good"   It is upon record that it is 1011 years since this sect passed from China to Loo
Choo.   For several centuries its doctrines appear to have been advocated by the court as well as by the common people but with
the latter classes they have since been supplanted by those of Confucius.   We are told that in the year 1372 several families from
Fochien settled near Napa-kiang, and introduced ceremonies in honour of the great Chinese philosopher, whose memory was further
honoured by a temple being erected to him in Loo Choo, in 1663,
by the Manshur Tartar, Emperor Kang-hi.   Confucius is now
honoured and revered by all classes in Loo Choo.   The sect Taou

* The words in italics were implied by signs
† Supao-Koang says a plurality of wives is permitted

which is equally corrupt with that of Foo, has but few advocates among the better classes of society.

Like the Chinese, the Loo Chooans are extremely superstitious and invoke their deities upon every occasion, sometimes praying to the good spirit, and at others to the evil. Near the beach to the northward of Potsoong, upon the shore which faces the coast of China, there were several square stones with pieces of paper attached to them. The natives gave us to understand they were the prayers of individuals; but we could not exactly understand the nature of them. A label similarly placed to those upon the beach was carried away by Captain Hall, and found to contain a prayer for the safe voyage of a friend who had gone from Loo Choo to China, it is very probable, therefore, that those which we saw were for similar purposes. At the Jos House at Potsoong I have mentioned pieces of paper being suspended between the panels, and have also suggested the probability of their being supplications of a similar nature Indeed one of these also was taken to Macao by Lieutenant Clifford, and found to be an invocation of the Devil *

In a natural cave near Abbey Point, I found a rudely carved image, about three feet in height, of the goddess Kwan-yin (pronounced Kwan-yong by the Loo Chooans) In front of the deity there were several square stone vessels for offerings, and upon one of them short pieces of polished wood were placed, which I conjectured to be for the purpose of deciding questions, in the manner practised by the Foo sect in China, by being tossed in the air, or rattled in a bamboo case, until one falls to the ground with its mark uppermost, when it is referred to a number in the book of the priest, and an answer is given accordingly. The natives were very unwilling to allow me to approach this figure, and pulled me back when I stepped into a small stone area in front of it, for the purpose of examining these pieces of wood. In China there are fasts in honour of this goddess, and no doubt there are the same in Loo Choo.

The following answers to several questions which I put to the natives of Loo Choo will fully explain the religion of the people.

"How many religions are there in Loo Choo?" "Three"— "What are these religions?" "Joo, Shih, Taou. Shih is the same as Foo."—"Are there many persons of the religion of Joo?" "Plenty."—"Foo?" "No good."—"Taou?" "Few."—"Does the sect Joo worship images?" "Sometimes kneel down to heaven sometimes pray in heart, sometimes go priest house (temple)"— "Do they go to the temple of Kwan-yin?" "Yes"—"Do they go to the temple of Pih-chang?" "Sometimes."—"Do they go to

* Hall's Loo Choo, 4to p, 206

the temple of Ching-hwang ?' *   "No."—"Do Joo, Shih, and Taou believe that heaven will reward the good and punish the bad ?" "Yes "

To the sentence, "At heart the doctrine of the three religions is the same; and it is firmly believed that heaven will do justice by rewarding the good and punishing the bad," An-yah did not assent. To the following sentence, "Both in this life and in the life to come there are rewards and punishments; but there is regard to the offences of men, whether heinous or not. speedy punishments are in this life; those that are remote in the world to come," An-yah replied, "Priest say so "

"God created and constantly governs all things ?" " Englishman's God, yes."—"When God created the great progenitor of all men, he was perfectly holy and perfectly happy ?" "No "—"The first ancestor of the human race sinned against God, and all his descendants are naturally depraved, inclined to evil, and averse from good " "Good."—"If men's hearts be not renewed, and their sins atoned for, they must after death suffer everlasting misery in hell." "Priest say so. An-yah not think so "—"Do the three sects believe in metempsychosis ?" This was not understood —"Do they believe that all things are appointed by heaven ?' " Yes."—"Are there any atheists in Loo Choo ?" "Many "

In Loo Choo the priesthood are as much neglected and despised as in China, notwithstanding their being consulted as oracles by all classes. Several of them visited me in the garden at Potsoong, and remained while I made my magnetical observations. As these occupied a long time, I had an opportunity of particularly remarking these unfortunate beings, and certainly I never saw a more unintellectual and care-worn class of men Many persons crowded round the spot to observe what was going forward, and the poor priests were obliged to give way to every new comer, notwithstanding they were in their own garden Their heads were shaved, similar to those of the Bodzes in China I am not aware in what this practice originated, but as an observer I could not help noticing that the same operation is performed on the heads of criminals, or of persons who are disgraced in China and from l'Abbe Grosier it appears to be considered a similar disgrace in Loo Choo.†

I endeavoured to distribute amongst the inhabitants some religious books which Dr. Morrison had given me in China, but there was a very great repugnance among the better part of the community to suffer them even to be looked into, much less to being carried away ; and several that were secretly taken on shore by the lower

* Ching-hwang is the goddess of Canton.
† Description de la Chine, vol II p 143

orders were brought back the next day   However I succeeded in disposing of a few copies, and Mr. Lay, I am glad to find, was equally fortunate with some which he also obtained from the same gentleman

It has been shown, in the course of the narrative, that the present manner of disposing of the dead differs from that described by Pere Gaubil, who says they burn the flesh of the deceased, and preserve the bones   It is not improbable that the custom may have changed, and that there is no mistake in the statement, as there is no reason to doubt the veracity of the Chinese author whom he quotes

They pay every possible attention and respect to their departed friends by attending strictly to their mourning, frequently visiting the tombs, and, for a certain time after the bodies are interred, in supplying the cups and other vessels placed there with tea, and the lamps with oil, and also by keeping the tombs exceedingly neat and clean. We have frequently seen persons attending these lamps, and Lieutenant Wainwright noticed an old man strewing flowers and shells upon a newly made grave, which he said contained his son, and watching several sticks of incense as they burned slowly down to the earth in which they were fixed

The trade of this island is almost entirely confined to Japan, China, and Formosa ; Manilla is known as a commercial country, and it is recorded that a vessel has made the voyage to Malacca. In China their vessels go to Fochien, which they call Wheit-yen, and sometimes to Pekin. Commerce between Japan and Loo Choo is conducted entirely in Japanese vessels, which bring hemp, iron copper, pewter, cotton. culinary utensils, lacquered furniture, excellent hones, and occasionally rice, though this article when wanted is generally supplied from an island to the northward belonging to Loo Choo, called Ooshima . but this is only required in dry seasons   The exports of Loo Choo are salt, grain, tobacco, samschew spirit, rice, when sufficiently plentiful, grass hemp, of which their clothes are made, hemp, and cotton   In return for these they bring from China different kinds of porcelain, glass, furniture, medicines, silver, iron, silks, nails, tiles, tools, and tea, as that grown upon Loo Choo is of an inferior quality. Several other articles of both export and import are mentioned by Supao-Koang, such as gold and silver from Formosa, and iron from China, among the former, mother-of-pearl, tortoise-shell, bezoar-stone, and excellent hones. The last mentioned articles, however, if found in Loo Choo are certainly not very plentiful, as they are carried thither from Japan, and An-yah denied there being any mother-of-pearl there. This trade is conducted in two junks belonging to Loo Choo, which go annually to China : and they have besides these their trib-
vessel

The trade with Japan appears formerly to have been limited at 125 thails (tael of Canton,) beyond which nothing was allowed to be sold   The goods carried to the country consisted of silks and other stuffs, with Chinese commodities, and the produce of their own country, such as corn, rice, pulse, fruits, spirits, mother of pearl, cowries, and large flat shells, which are so transparent that they are used in Japan for windows instead of glass *

Their manufactures do not appear to be numerous, and are probably only such as are necessary for their own convenience   I have spoken of the rude hand-looms in use, the spinning-wheel, and the mills worked by cattle; these were the only machines we saw, though it may be inferred they have others   A short distance to the southward of Napia-kiang I was told there was a paper manufactory, and had a quantity of paper given me said to have been made there   It closely resembled that of China, but appeared to be more woolly   Grass-cloth, of a coarse texture, and coarse cottons, are also wove upon the island, but I believe all the finer ones come from China, as well as the broad cloth of which their cloaks are made   Red pottery moderately good, a bad porcelain, and tiles, are among their manufactures, and also paper fans, of which the skeleton is bamboo; pipes, hair pins, and wicker baskets, and two sorts of spirits distilled from grain, moroofocoo, already described; and another called sackee, resembling the samshew of China, salt, from the natural deposition of the sea, is collected in pans.

Supao-Koang mentions, among the manufactures of this country, silk, arms, brass instruments, gold and silver ornaments, a paper even thicker than that of Corea, made of *les cocons*, and another made of bamboo, besides that manufactured from the bark of the paper tree   He states they have woods fit for dyes, and particularly esteem one made from a tree, the leaves of which resemble those of the citron tree, and mentions brass, pewter, saddles, bridles, and sheaths as being manufactured with considerable taste and neatness upon the island, and as forming part of the tribute to China, from which it might be inferred that they were better executed than those in Pekin.

Previous to our departure I offered An-yah a patent coin mill and a winnowing machine, and showed him the the use of them   He was extremely thankful for them at first, but after a little consideration he declined the present, without assigning any reason   He probably imagined the introduction of foreign machinery might be disapproved by his superiors

It has been observed that drums and tambourines were the only musical instruments among these people, we saw a flute, and

* Kæmpfer's History of Japan, p 381

were told that the inhabitants possessed violins and other stringed instruments ; yet they do not appear to be a musical nation.

Among our numerous inquiries there was not one to which we got such contradictory answers as that concerning the residence of the king of Loo Choo.   It was evident that there was a person of very high authority upon the island, whom they styled *wang*, which in Dr Morrison's Dictionary is translated king, and that his residence was not far from Napa-kiang , but An-yah provoked me much by always evading this question   Sometimes he said it was four days to the north-east, at others that it was only one, and at last that it was at a place called Sheui, or Shoodi   Some of the natives whom I interrogated on this subject, declared it was at Ee-goo-see-coo, about nine leagues to the northward ; others, however, told me the name of his residence was Shoodi , therefore, Sheui, or Shoodi, is in all probability the correct name of the place   As the natives pointed out to me the town upon the hill, at the back of Napa-kiang as Shoodi, and as another party named it to Mr. Collie Shumi, we may presume that this town is the capital of Loo Choo ; and this is the conclusion, as already remarked, that Captain Hall came to, after many inquiries on the subject   Indeed I should think there could be not much doubt about it, as it answers very well both in name and position to the capital described by Supao Koang, who remarks that the king holds his court in the south-west part of the island   The ground it stands upon is called Cheuli,* and that near this place the palace of the king is situated upon a hill,   In another part he says that the space between Napa-kiang and the palace is almost one continued town †   Mr Klaproth, however, has published extracts from some Chinese documents, which place the capital twenty *lis* (ten miles ?) east of Napa-kiang.

In the journal of my officers, I find that some of them were informed by the inhabitants that tribute was sent to China only once in seven years, and others that it was paid every year   Kæmpfer also says that tribute is sent every year to the Tartarian monarch, in token of submission   By the Chinese accounts it is demanded every second year, as I have already stated.   M J. Klaproth, quoting one of these authors, says, in 1654 Loo Choo sent Chang-Chy, the king's son, with an ambassador to Pekin, when it was arranged that every second year an ambassador should be sent to that court with tribute, which should consist of 3,000 lbs of copper, 12,600 lbs. of sulphur, and 3,000 lbs. of a strong silk , and that the number of his suite should not exceed a hundred and fifty persons.

Lord macartney, when on his embassy to the court of China,

---

* Cheli by the Loo Chooans would be pronounced Cheudi, in the same way as they call Loo-Choo Doo-Choo
‡ Lettres Edifiantes, p. 340

met the mandarins from Loo Choo, who were going with this tribute to Pekin, and who informed him their chief sent delegates every *two years* to offer tribute * And when we were at Loo Choo, both Ching-oong-choo and An-yah informed me to the same effect, viz that it was sent every second year We may therefore conclude, that this is the period agreed upon between the two countries

M. Klaproth, p. 164, informs us that, notwithstanding tribute is paid to the court of China, Loo Choo is also compelled to acknowledge the sovereignty of Japan, to send ambassadors there from time to time, and to pay tribute in swords, horses, a species of perfume, ambergris, vases for perfumes, and a sort of stuff, a texture manufactured from the bark of trees, lacquered tables inlaid with shells or mother of pearl, and madder, &c. I shall merely observe upon this passage, that some of the articles which are said to be carried as tribute to Japan are actually taken from thence, and from China to Loo Choo, such as the vases and lacquered tables; and that mother of pearl is said by the natives not to be found upon the shores of their island

The highest point of Loo Choo which we saw was a hill situated at the back of Barrow's Bay, in about the latitude of $26'\,27''$ N., answering in position nearly to a mountain which appears on the chart of Mr Klaproth, under the name of Onnodake The height of this mountain is 1089 feet. The next highest point to this, which was visible from the anchorage, was the summit of the hill of Sumar, on which the capital is built, the highest point of this is 540 feet, six inches. Abbey Point is 98 feet six inches, and a bluff to the northward of Potsoong 99 feet and nine inches The Sugar Loaf (Ee-goo-see-coo) was so far distant for us to determine its height: but I think Mr Klaproth is wrong in saying it may be seen twenty-five sea leagues, as our distance from it was only ten leagues, and it was scarcely above the horizon † It is certainly not so high as Onnodake, which, to a person at the surface of the sea, would be just visible at the distance of thirty-four miles He is also mistaken in supposing it the only peak on the island

These heights appear to be gained by ascents of moderate elevation only In no part did we perceive any hills so abrupt that they could not be turned to account by the agriculturist The centre of the island, or perhaps a line drawn a little to the westward of it is the most elevated part of the country Still the island is not divided by a ridge, but by a number of rounded eminences, for the most part of the same elevation, with valleys between them; so that when viewed at a distance the island appears to have a very

* Embassy to China, by Sir George Staunton, vol. ii p. 458
† Klaproth s Memoires relatifs a l, Asic, tom. ii p. 173.

level surface   In a Chinese plan of Loo Choo, all these eminences are occupied by palaces and by courts of the king.   The higher parts of the island are, in general, surmounted by trees, generally of the pinus massoniana, and the cycas, though they are sometimes bare, or at most clothed with a diminutive and ueseless vegetation. It not unfrequently happens that small precipices occur near the summits of the hills, and that large blocks of a coral-like substance are seen lying as if the they had been left there by the sea   This substance, of which all the rocky parts of the island that we examined were composed, is a cellular or granular limestone, bearing a great resemblance to coral, for which it might easily be mistaken It has a very rugged surface, not unlike silex machere   Lieutenant Belcher found sandstone of a loose texture, enclosing balls of blue marl, and in one instance interstratified with it in alternate seams with the coral formation.   This formation constituted part of a reef, dry at low water   In the marl he found cylindrical and elongated cones, similar to the belemite, of a light colour, and occasionally crystalizations of calcareous spar

The precipices inland, as well as those which form cliffs upon the coast, are hollowed out beneath, as if they had been subjected to the action of the waves   Upon the sea-coast this has no doubt been the case, and the Capstan Rock, spoken of before, presents a curious instance of its effect, but it is not quite so evident that the sea has reached the cliffs near Abbey Point, as they are separated from it by a plain covered with vegetation, and the violence of the waves is broken by reefs which lie far outside them.

The soil in the vicinity of Napa-kiang is generally arenaceous and marly but to the south-east of Abbey Point there is a stratum of clay, which, in consequence of its retaining moisture better than other parts of the soil, is appropriated to the cultivation of rice.

The greater part of the island is surrounded by reefs of coral. These are of two sorts, one in which the animals have ceased to exist, and the other which is still occupied by them.   Both are darker-coloured than the reefs in the middle of the Pacific, owing, probably, to the various depositions which the rains have washed from the land.   The shells found upon them are very much incrusted.   About eight miles to the northward of Napa-kiang there is a deep bay, the shores of which are very flat, and have been converted into salt-pans by the natives.   A river which appears to have its rise near the capital, after passing at the back of some hills, about five miles inland, empties itself into this bay.   There is also another stream at Potsoong   The natives would not permit us to ascertain how far inland the water flowed up the harbour; nor would they inform us whether it was a division of the island, as its appearance induced us to suppose.   In the Chinese plan already alluded

to, the island is divided by such a channel, but it is doubtful whether this division may not be intended for the channel which separates
Loo Choo from the Madjico-sima group, as the island to the southward has *Ta-paingchan* written upon it, and there is a small island
close to the eastward of it called *Little Lew Kew*.* The relative
positions of these are correctly given in the plan, but, if intended
for those places, there is an egregious violation of all distance and
proportion

It has been already mentioned that the vegetable productions of
the torrid and temperate zones are here found combined. The pal-
mæe, boerhavia, scævola, tournefortia, and other trees and shrubs
recall the Coral Islands of the tropical regions to our view, while
the rosaceæ onagrariæ, etc. remind us of the temperate shores of our
own continent. The remarkable genus of clerodendrum is here peculiarly abundant. Among the trees and shrubs which adorn the
heights, the bamboo, hibiscus tiliaceus, thespesia popularia, hibiscus,
rosa sinensis, pandanus, piscidium, and several other trees and shrubs,
some of which were new to us, were found uniting their graceful foliage, while in the gardens we noticed plantain, banana, fig, and
orange trees, though the latter were apparently very scarce. We
were told that they had pomegranates, but that they had neither pine-
apples, plums, nor leches, though they were perfectly acquainted
with them all. The le-che is a fruit which is said to be peculiar to
China: indeed Pere J B Dunhalde, in his Description de la Chine,
vol 1 p. 104, says it grows only in two provinces of that great empire, Quang-tong, and Fokien. Pere Gaubil, however, affirms that
it is at Loo Choo, and that there are also there citrons, lemons, rai-
sins, plums, apples, and pears, none of which we saw

We were informed that the tea plant was tolerably abundant, and
that the mild and excellent tobacco which was brought on board
was the growth of the island. Gaubil affirms they have ginger, and
a wood which they burn as incense, as well as camphor trees, ce-
dars, laurels, and pines. Among the vegetable productions the
sweet potatoe appears to be the most plentiful; the climate seemed
so favourable to its growth, that we observed the tops rising from a
soil composed almost entirely of sand. Both the root and the leaf
are eaten by the natives

The soil appears to be cultivated entirely with the hoe, and there
are very few places on which this kind of labour has not been bestowed. Streams of water are not very abundant, and it is highly
interesting to notice the manner in which the inhabitants have turned those which they possess to the greatest advantage, by conduct-

___

* Formosa, notwithstanding it is considerably larger than Loo Choo, was called
Little Lieou-Kieou, from there being so few inhabitants upon it.—*Receueil de P*
Gaubil

ing them in troughs from place to place, and at last allowing them to overflow flat places near the beach, for the purpose of raising rice and taro, which require a soil constantly wet.

The principal animals which we saw at Loo Choo were bullocks. horses, asses, goats, pigs, and cats, all of very diminutive size a bullock which was brought to us weighed only 100lbs without the offal, and the horses were so low that a tall person had difficulty in keeping his feet off the ground ; yet these animals must be esteemed in in Japan, as they are said to have formed part of the tribute to that place   The poultry are also small   we heard dogs, but never saw any   Klaproth, p 187, asserts there are bears, wolves, and jackals. A venomous snake is also said to exist in the interior   But the only other animals we saw were mice, lizards, and frogs, the latter somewhat different to those of our own country.

The insects are grasshoppers, dragon-flies, butter-flies, honeybees, wasps, moskitos of a large size, spiders, and a mantis, probably peculiar to the island.

There appeared to be very few birds, and of these we could procure no specimens, in consequence of the great objection on the part of the natives to our firing at them, arising probably from their belief in transubstantiation   Those which we observed at a distance resembled larks, martins, wood-pigeons, beach-plovers, tringas, herons, and tern.   An-yah said there were no partridges in the island

Fish are more abundant though not large, excepting sharks and dolphins, which are taken at sea, and guard-fish, which are often seen in the harbour   Those frequenting the reefs belong principally to the genera chætodon and labrus.   A chromis, a beautiful small fish, was noticed in the waters which inundated the rice fields

Upon the reefs are several *asteriæ*.   These animals are furnished with long spiny tentaculæ, and are in the habit of concealing their bodies in the hollow parts of the coral, and leaving their tentaculæ to be washed about and partake of the waving motion of the sea ; and to a person unacquainted with the zoophytes which form the coral, they might be supposed to be the animals connected with its structure   Lieutenant Belcher remarks of these reefs that a change must have taken place in them since they were visited by the Alceste and Lyra, as he never observed any coral reefs apparently so destitute of animation as those which surround Loo Choo.   The sea anemone and other zoophytes were very scarce

We saw no shells of any value   A few cardium, trochius, and strombus were brought me by An-yah, and the haliotis was seen on the beach ; but the history of this island states that the mother of pearl, large flat shells nearly transparent, and cowries, formed part of the tribute to Japan   An-yah, however, assured me there were no pearl shells upon the coast

The Climate of Loo Choo must be very mild, from the nature of the dwelling-houses and the dress of the people, the mean temperature of the air, for the fortnight which we passed in the harbour, was 70°. Unlike the Typa, we here experienced no great transitions, but an almost uniform temperature, which dissipated all the sickness the Typa had occasioned We had, however, a good deal of rain in this time, which was about the change of the monsoon By An-yah's account this island is occasionally visited by violent ta-foongs (mighty-winds,) which unroof the houses and destroy the crops, and do other damage. They had experienced one, only the month previous to our arrival, which we were told had destroyed a great deal of rice, and was the cause of so many Japanese vessels being in the port In 1708 it appears that one of these hurricanes did incalculable mischief, and occasioned much misery The inhabitants seem to entertain a great dread of famine, and it is not improbable that these ta-foongs may occasion the evil. April, May, June, July, August, and September are the months in which these winds are liable to occur

The harbour of Napa-kiang, though open to winds from the north. by the west to south-west is very secure, provided ships anchor in the Barnpool, a bay formed by the coral, to the northward of the Capstan Rock In the outer anchorage, at high water, there is sometimes a considerable swell, and, were it to blow hard from the westward at the time of the spring tides, I have no doubt it would be sensibly felt. The reefs which afford protection to the harbour are scarcely above the sea at low water neap tides, and some remain wholly covered In general they are much broken, and have many knolls in their vicinity, which ought to make ships cautious how they stand towards them. There are two entrances to the outer harbour, one from the northward, and the other from the westward The former is narrow, and has several dangerous rocks in the channel, which, as they are not in general visible, are very likely to prove injurious to vessels; and as it can seldom happen that there is a necessity for entering the harbour in that direction, the passage ought to be avoided. The western entrance is divided into two channels by a coral bank, with only seven feet water upon it, which, as it was discovered by the Blossom, I named after that ship The passage on either side this rock may be made use of as convenient, but that to the southward is preferable with southerly winds and flood tides, and the other with the reverse A small hillock to the left of a cluster of trees on the distant land, in the direction of Mt Onnadake, open about 4° to the eastward of a remarkable headland to the northward of Potsoong, will lead through the channel; and the Captsan Rock, with the highest part of the hill over Napa-kiang, which has the appearance of a small cluster of trees, will lead close over the north end of Blossom Rock. This notice of the dangers of entering the harbour will be sufficient in this place, and, if vessels are not provided with a chart or require further directions, it will be prudent to anchor a boat upon the rock

Though the inhabitants of Loo Choo show so much anxiety for charts, they do not appear to have profited much by those which have been given to them, nor by those published in China or Japan. Their knowledge of geography is indeed extremely limited, and, with the exception of the islands and places with which they trade, they may be said to be almost ignorant of the geography of every other part of the globe   I did not omit to inquire about Ginsima, Kinsima, and Bonnisima, islands which were supposed to exist at no great distance to the eastward of Loo Choo   The two first have never been seen since their discovery, but the other group has long been known to Japan and if we can credit the charts of the Japanese, it has been inhabited some time, as several villages and temples are marked therein   The Loo Chooans, however, could give me no information of it, or of any other islands lying to the eastward of their own, and were quite surprised at hearing a Japanese vessel* had been cast away upon an island in that direction.

The groups of islands seen in the distance to the westward of Loo Choo are called by the natives Kirrama Agoo-gnee.   Kirrama consists of four islands, Zammamee, Accar, Ghirooma, and Toocastchee, of which all but the last are very small   Agoo-gnee consists of two small island, Aghee and Homar   Both groups are peopled from and are subject to Loo Choo.   Kirrama has four mandarins, one of the higher order, and three inferior, and Agoo-gnee two of the latter   The islands are very scantily peopled · in Toocastchee, which is the largest, there are but five hundred houses   The small coral islands off Napa-kiang are called Tzee.

To the northward of Loo Choo there are two islands, from which supplies are occasionally received ; Ooshima,† of which I have spoken before as being subject to Loo Choo, and Yachoo-chima, a colony of Japan   Ooshima produces an abundance of rice, and as in dry seasons in Loo Choo this valuable grain sometimes fails, Yacoo chima junks, which appear to be the great carriers to Loo Choo, go there and load.   Ya-choo-chima is said to be an island of great extent, but the chart which An-yah drew to show its situation was too rude for me even to conjecture which of the islands belonging to Japan it might be

In my narrative of Loo Choo I have made allusion to the works

* See **Kæmpfer's** History of Japan
† Probably O foushima of Supao-Koang, situated in latitude 30° N

of several Chinese and Japanese authors,* who have written upon
that island.   As their accounts generally wear the appearance of
truth, and as they are the only records we have of the early history
of a country so little visited by Europeans, I shall give a sketch of
them, that my reader may become acquainted with what is known
of the history of that remote country, without having to search different books, only one of which has as yet been published in England

The inhabitants of Loo Choo are extremely jealous of their antiquity as a nation   They trace their descent, from a male and
female, who were named Omo-mey-keiou, who had three sons and
two daughters.   The eldest of these boys was named Tien sun (or
the grandson of heaven) He was afterwards the first king of Loo Choo
and from the first year of his reign to the first of that of Chun-tien,
who ascended the throne A D 1187, they reckon a period of no
less than 17,802 years   The kings were supposed to be descended
from the eldest son, the nobility from the second, and the commoners from the youngest   The eldest daughter was named Kun-
kun, and had the title of Spirit of Heaven , the other, named Tcho-
tcho, was called the Spirit of the Ocean

We are told that five and twenty dynasties successively occupied the throne of Loo Choo, from the death of Tien-sun to the
reign of Chun-tien ; but nothing further was known of the history
of the country until the year A D 605, when the Emperor of
China, of the dynasty of Soui," being informed there were some
islands to the eastward of his dominions named Loo Choo, became
desirous of reconnoitring their situation, and of becoming acquainted with the resources of the islands   He accordingly fitted out an
expedition, but it did not effect what the emperor desired   It however, brought back a few natives · and an embassador from Japan
happening to be at the court of China at that time, informed the
emperor that these people belonged to Loo Choo, and described
their island as being poor and miserable, and the inhabitants as barbarians   Being informed that in five days a vessel could go from
his dominions to the residence of the king of these islands, the emperor, Yang-tee sent some learned men with interpreters to Loo
Choo to obtain information, and to signify to the king that he must
acknowledge the sovereignty of the emperor of China, and do him
homage   This embassy succeeded in reaching its destination, but
as might have been expected from the ruler of an independent peo-

* The works of these authors will be found in Lettres Edifiantes et Curieuses, tom
xxiii. 1811   Grosier sur la Chine, tom, ii , M J Klaproth, Memoires sur la Chine,
Kœmpfer's History of Japan, vol 1 , P J. B Duhalde   For other information on
Doo Choo, the reader is referred to the Voyages of Benyowsky, Broughton, and of
H M ships Alceste and Lyra

ple, it was badly received, and was obliged to return with the haughty answer to their sovereign, that the prince of Loo Choo would acknowledge no chief superior to himself. Indignant at being thus treated by a people who had been described as barbarians, he put ten thousand experienced troops on board his junks, and made a successful descent upon the Great Loo Choo. The king, who appears to have been a man of great courage, placed himself at the head of his troops, and disputed the ground with the Chinese; but unfortunately he was killed, his troops gave way; and the victorious invaders, after pillaging and setting fire to the royal abode, and making five thousand slaves, returned to China

It is said that at this time the Inhabitants of Loo Choo had neither letters nor characters; and that all classes of society, even the king himself, lived in the most simple manner. It does not, however, appear that the people were entitled to the appellation of barbarians, which was given to them by the ambassador of Japan in China, nor that they merited the title of *poor devils*, which the word licu-kieu implies in Japanese; as they had fixed laws for marriages and interments, and paid great respect to their ancestors and other departed friends; and they had other well regulated institutions which fully relieve them from the charge of barbarism Their country was not so poor nor so destitute of valuable production, or even of manufactures, but that Chinese merchants were glad to open a trade with it, and continue it through five dynasties which successively ruled in China after the conquest of Loo Choo notwithstanding the indifference of the emperors who, during that period, ceased to exact the tribute that had been made to their predecessors. It is not improbable, therefore, that this stigma, which ought probably to belong to Formosa—which, though a much larger island, was then called Little Loo Choo—may have been attached to the island we visited from the similarity of names.

Chun-tien was said to be descended from the kings of Japan, but it is not known at what period his family settled in Loo Choo. Before he came to the throne, he was governor of the town of Po-tien.   On his accession his title was disputed by a nobleman named Li-yong; but he being defeated and killed, Chun-tien was acknowledged King of Loo Choo by the people.   Having reigned fifty-one years, and bestowed many benefits upon his subjects, whose happiness was his principal care, he died at the age of seventy two   In this reign reading and writing are said to have been first introduced from Japan, the character being that of Y-rofa

Very little mention is made of the son and successor of Chun-tien, but the reign of his grandson Y-pen is marked by the occurrence of a famine and a plague, which nearly desolated the island, and by his abdication in favour of any person whom the people might appoint to succeed him The choice fell upon Ynt-sou, the governor of a small town ; but the king, desirous of ascertaining whether he was a competent person to succeed him, first made him prime minister , and being at length satisfied that the choice of the people was judicious, he abdicated in his favour, reserving a very moderate provision for himself and family Ynt-sou ascended the throne A D 1260, and reigned forty years He is said to have been the first to levy taxes, and to have introduced useful regulations for the cultivation of the soil. In his reign Ta-tao, Ki-ki-ai, and other islands in the north-east and north-west came under the dominion of Loo Choo. This reign was also marked by an attempt of the Emperor of China to renew his demand of tribute, which had not been made for so many generations that the Loo Chooans began to consider themselves absolved from the obligation The Emperor of China however, determining not to relinquish the advantages which had been gained by his predecessor Yang-ti, equipped a fleet for the purpose of compelling payment; but about this time China having suffered a serious defeat from the Japanese, and from the kingdoms of Tonquin and Cochin China, and lost 100,000 men in her expeditions against those places, disaffection spread throughout the troops, and the expedition returned without even having reached its destination

Ynt-sou was succeeded by his son Ta-tchin, who was followed by his son Ynt-see, two princes much esteemed for their wisdom and benevolence Not so Yut-ching, a prince of avaricious and voluptuous disposition, who ascended the throne of his father in 1314 ; during whose reign the state fell into considerable disorder. The governor of Keng-koaey-gin, revolted and declared himself King of Chanpe, the northern province of the island The governor of Ta-li also revolted, and became king of the southern province Chan-nan, leaving Yut-ching to govern only the centre of the island, which was called Tchong-chan. Thus this island, not sixty miles in length, divided into three independent kingdoms. The greatest animosity prevailed between these three principalities, and long and bloody wars ensued About sixty years after the country had been thus divided, Tsay-tou, a prince beloved by his people and esteemed for his valour, came to the throne of the middle province. It was in his reign that Hong-vou, the Emperor of China, renewed overtures of protection ; and the embassy which he sent to the court of Tsay-tou acquitted itself so creditably, that the offer was accepted. The kings of the other districts of Loo Choo were no sooner apprised of the conduct of Tsay-tou, than they also put themselves under the protection of China , and thus Loo Choo once more became tributary to the Celestial Empire.

The Emperor Hong-vou was so much pleased with this conduct

of the kings of Loo Choo, that he sent them large presents of iron, porcelain, and other articles which he knew to be scarce in their dominions, and also settled in the middle province thirty-six families from Fochien, who established themselves at a place called Kumi, a little to the nothward of Napa-kiang   These people introduced into Loo Choo the Chinese written character, and ceremonies in honour of Confucius.   On the other hand, the kings of Loo Choo sent several youths to Pekin, among whom were the sons and brothers Tsay-tou, who were educated and brought up at the expense of the emperor.   -

The best understanding now existed between the kings of Loo Choo and the court of China ; and while the emperor was receiving ambassadors from Loo Choo, that country had the satisfaction of seeing several islands to the northward and southward of its own position added to its dominions   On the death of Tsay-tou, which happened in 1396, his son Au-ning was installed king by the emperor in the place of his father   He reigned ten years, and was succeeded by his son Is-tchao.   The reigns of these two princes were not distinguished by any remarkable events; but that of their successor, Change-patche, will ever be remembered by the Loo Chooans from the advantageous union of the five provinces, for nearly a century had been agitated by a continued state of warfare ; and from the estimation in which the king of the island was held by Suent-song, then emperor of China, who made him large presents of silver, and bestowed upon him the title of *Chang*, which has ever since been the patronymic of the royal family of Loo Choo

The three following reigns present no occurrences worthy of notice.   In 1456, the Chang-tai-kieou ascended the throne amidst difficulties and disaffection   His ambitious brother disputed the elevated rank he had obtained, and enlisted in his cause so powerful a body of the islanders, that the king was defeated, his palace burned, and his magazines reduced to ashes.   In this state of affairs he solicited the protection of the emperor of China, who readily assisted him ; and not only restored tranquility to the island by his interference, but caused the king to be remunerated for all his losses.

The commerce of Loo Choo with China afterwards daily increased, and under the reign of this prince so great a trade was carried on between the two countries, that the provinces of Tche-kiang and Fochien were distressed by the quantity of silver and copper coin that was carried away to Loo Choo.   The people even complained to the Emperor of the scarcity, who ordered that in future the trade between these two places should be confined within certain limits.

After a short reign of seven years, Chang-tai-kieou was succeeded by his son Chang-te, a prince whose name was rendered odious by the acts of cruelty he committed, and who was so much detested, that after his death the people refused to acknowledge as king the person whom he had appointed to succeed him; and elected in his stead Chan-y-ven, a nobleman of the island of Yo-pi-chan Though the reign of this prince is distinguished in history only by the regulation of the number of persons who should accompany the ambassadors to Pekin, yet he is said to have been a great prince. His son, Chang-tching, was a minor at the death of his father, and his paternal uncle was chosen to be his protector In this reign Loo Choo became a comparatively great commercial nation Many vessels were sent to the Formosa, to the coasts of Bungo, Fionga, Satzuma, Corea, and other places Her vessels became the carriers of Japanese produce to China, and vice versa; and one of them even made the voyage to Malacca.

By this extensive trade, and by being the entrepot between the two empires of China and Japan, Loo Choo increased in wealth and rose into notice: especially as it was found convenient by both these two great nations to have a mediator on any differences arising between them The advantage thus derived by Loo Choo was particularly manifested on the occasion of a remonstrance on the part of China against robberies and piracies committed upon the shores of that country by a prodigious number of vessels manned by resolute and determined seamen, principally Japanese, who landed upon all parts of the coast, and spread consternation along the whole of the western shore of the yellow Sea, even down to Canton The Emperor of China on this occasion sent ambassadors to Loo Choo; and a representation was made to the Court of Japan of the numerous piracies committed in the dominions of the Emperor of China by the subjects of that country, and succeeded so far that the sovereign of Japan gave up to the King of Loo Choo a number of vessels and slaves which had been captured; but as none of these marauding vessels had been fitted out by his command, and as they were the property of individuals over whom he had no control, it was out of his power to put a stop to the depredations. The Emperor of China rewarded the King of Loo Choo for this important service by sending him large presents of silk, porcelain, and silver, and brass money; and granted to his subjects very great privileges in their commercial transactions with China

The Japanese pirates, among which there were a great many vessels manned by Chinese, continued their depredations in spite of the efforts and remonstrances of the Emperor of China, and latterly occasioned such alarm in that country, that the famous Tay-Cosama, who was then secular ruler of Japan, determined to avail himself of the panic, and premeditated an attack upon the coast of that mighty empire It was necessary to the success of this bold enterprise that the assault should be conducted with the utmost secrecy;

and Tay-Cosama, fearing that the frequent intercourse between China and Loo Choo, which country could not remain in ignorance of the preparations, might be the means of divulging his intentions to China, sent ambassadors to Chang-ning, who was then King of Loo Choo, haughtily forbidding him to pay tribute to China, and desiring him to acknowledge no other sovereign than that of Japan   It is said that he also sent similar notices to the governor of the Philippines, to the King of Siam, and to the Europeans in India

Chang-ning, however, was not easily intimidated, and remained deaf to the menaces of the Emperor of Japan.   He saw through the designs of Tay-Cosama ; and by means of a rich Chinese merchant, who happened to be at Napa-kiang at the time, he apprised Ouan-li, then Emperor of China, of his designs   Ouan-li immediately increased his army, fortified his coasts, and made every preparation for a vigorous defence against the invading army of Japan, whenever it might arrive   He also apprised Corea of the danger with which that state was threatened ; but the king, misled probably by the designing Emperor of Japan, and imagining the immense preparations making by that prince were intended for the invasion of China, neglected to strengthen his defences, and was at length surprised by the Japanese, who invaded his dominions.

Chang-ning, notwithstanding the invasion with which he was also threatened, continued his tribute to China, and Ouan-li received his ambassadors with the greatest possible respect, and rewarded their sovereign for his fidelity   Some years after, in 1610, the Japanese renewed their menaces against Chang-ning, who, as on the former occasion, acquainted the Emperor of China with his situation, and implored assistance : but China at that time was fully occupied with her own troubles, and unable to render him any service.   In this state of things, a nobleman of Loo Choo, named King-tchang, taking advantage of the situation of Chang-ning, revolted, and retired to Satzuma, where he fitted out an expedition consisting of 3000 Japanese, and took Chang-ning prisoner, killed his father, Tching-hoey, because he would not acknowledge his dependency to Japan, pillaged the royal palace, and carried away the king prisoner to Satzuma

The conduct of the King of Loo Choo throughout all these disturbances is said to have been so magnanimous and spirited, that it even appeased King-tchang, and prepossessed the Japanese so much in his favour, that after two years' captivity they restored him to his throne with honour   He was scarcely reinstated. when, always faithful to China, notwithstanding the danger he had escaped, and the helpless condition of the emperor, he sent ambassadors to that country to declare his submission as heretofore ; and to apprise the emperor of an attack which was intended to be made on Formosa by the Japanese, who had conceived the project of reinstating themselves in that country, and fortifying their settlements there.

Chang-ning left no son to succeed him, and Chang-yong, a descendant of the brother of his predecessor was installed by the Emperor of China in his stead   This prince, notwithstanding the unsettled state of affairs, and the danger he had to apprehend from Japan, paid the usual tribute to China, and introduced into his country from thence the manufacture of delft-ware, and an inferior kind of porcelain

About eighty years afterwards, A. D 1643, the famous revolution occurred in China, which fixed the Tartar dynasty on the throne of that empire; and Change-tche, who at that time was King of Loo Choo, sent ambassadors to pay homage to the new sovereign, when King Chang-tche received a sign manual from the Tartar monarch, directing that Loo Choo should not pay tribute oftener than once in two years, and that the number of the embassy should not exceed a hundred and fifty persons

In 1663 the great Emperor Kang-hi succeeded to the throne of China, and received the tribute of Chang-tche on the occasion This magnanimous prince sent large presents of his own to the King of Loo Choo, in addition to some of an equally superb quality which were intended for that country by his father   His ambassadors passed over to Loo Choo, and according to custom confirmed the king in his sovereignty, the ceremony on this occasion being distinguished by additional grandeur and solemnity

Kang-hi probably foreseeing the advantages to be derived from an alliance with Loo Choo, which had so long continued faithful to the empire of China, turned his attention to the improvement of the country with great earnestness and perseverance. He built a palace there in honour of Confucius, and a college for the instruction of youth in the use of the Chinese character, and established examinations for different branches of literature   Several natives of Loo Choo were sent to Pekin, and educated at the expense of the emperor, among whom was the king's son.   The tribute was better adapted to the means of the people, and those articles only, which were either the produce of the soil, or the manufactures of the country, were in future to be sent to Pekin for this purpose   In short Kang-hi lost no opportunity of gaining the friendship and esteem of his subjects   On the occasion of great distress in Loo Choo, which occurred in 1708, when the palace of the king was burned, and hurricanes did incalculable mischief, and when the people were dying daily with contagious diseases. Kang-hi used every endeavour to mitigate their distress, and, by his humanity and generosity secured to himself the lasting gratitude of the inhabitants of Loo Choo.

In 1719 he sent Supao-koang, a learned physician, to make himself acquainted with the nature and productions of the island, and to inform himself of every particular concerning the government and the people.   Since that period nothing is mentioned of Loo Choo in Chinese history, beyond the periodical payment of the tribute, and the arrival of ambassadors from that country at the court of Pekin.

In 1771 the well known Count Benyowsky touched at an island belonging to Loo Choo, named Usmay Liagon, where he found that almost all the inhabitants had been converted to Christianity by a jesuit missionary   If we can credit his statement, he was treated by the natives with the greatest hospitality and unreserve. Contrary to the custom of the eastern Asiatic nations, these people brought their daughters to the count and his associates, and pressed them to select wives from among them.   In short, the conduct of the inhabitants is described as being so engaging, that some of Benyowsky's crew determined to remain with them, and were actually left behind when the count put to sea.   And the natives, on the other hand are asserted to have been so attached to their visitors, that they made them promise to return and form a settlement among them, and signed a treaty of friendship with the count This veracious traveller found muskets with matchlocks in use with these people; and to add to their means of defence, on his departure he presented them with 80 muskets of his own, 600 swords, and 600 pikes, besides 20 barrels of powder and 10 barrels of musket balls.

Loo Choo in 1796 was visited by Captain Broughton, and in 1803 by the ship Frederick of Calcutta, which made an unsuccessful effort to dispose of her cargo.   The inhabitants on both these occasions were as usual, extremely civil and polite, but resisted every attempt at opening a commerce.   The next mention of this interesting island is in the well known publications of Captain Basil Hall, and Mr. M‘Cleod, the surgeon of the Alceste

Thus Loo Choo, like almost every other nation, has been disturbed by civil wars, and the state has been endangered by foreign invasion.   her towns have been plundered, her palaces consumed, and her citizens carried into captivity.   Situated between the empires of China and Japan, she has been mixed up with their quarrels, and made subservient to the interests of both, at one time suffering all the miseries of invasion, and at another acting as a mediator. Allied by preference to China, and by fear and necessity, from her proximity, to Japan, she is obliged to avoid jealousy, to pay tribute to both, though that to the latter country is said to be furnished by the merchants who are most interested in the trade to that empire   Their conduct to strangers who have touched at their ports has ever been uniformly polite and hospitable   But they would rather be exempt from such friendly visits. and though extremely desirous of obtaining European manufactures, particularly cloth, hosiery, and cutlery, they would oppose any open attempt to introduce them   The most likely means of establishing a communication with them would be through Chinese merchants at Canton, who might be persuaded to send goods there in their own names, and under the charge of their own countrymen.

Whale-ships have occasionally touched at Loo Choo when distressed for provisions.   It is satisfactory to find that these interviews have been conducted without giving offence to the natives   It is to be hoped that any vessel which may hereafter be under the necessity of putting in there will preserve the same conduct, and give the inhabitants no cause to regret having extended their hospitality to foreigners.

I have perhaps entered more minutely upon several questions connected with Loo Choo than may be considered necessary, after what has already been given to the public; but it appeared desirable to remove doubts upon several points of interest, which could not perhaps be effectually accomplished without combining my remarks with a short notice of the history of the country.

CHAPTER XVIII

Passage from Loo Choo eastward—Arrive at Port Lloyd in the Yslas del Azobispo—
Description of those Islands—Passage to Kamaschatka—Arrival at Petropaulsky
—Notice of that Place—Departure—Pass Beering's Strait—Enter Kotzebue
Sound—Prosecute the Voyage to the Northward—Stopped by the Ice—Return
to the Southward—Discover Port Clarence and Grantley Harbour—Description
of these Harbours—Return to Kotzebue Sound—Ship strikes upon a Shoal

On the 25th of May we took our departure from Loo Choo, and
steered to the eastward in search of some islands which were doubt-
fully placed in the charts.   On the third day we arrived within a
few miles of the situation of Amsterdam Island without seeing any
land, and passed it to the northward, as near as the wind would
permit   The weather was very unfavourable for discovery, being
thick and rainy, or misty, with very variable winds.   On the third
of June we regretted exceedingly not having clear weather, as the
appearance of plover, sandlings, flocks of shear-waters, and several
petrel and albatrosses, created a belief that we were near some island

Three days afterwards we were upon the spot where the Island of
Disappointment is placed on the latest charts   The weather was
tolerably clear, but no land could be seen ; and as we were so near
the situation of a group of islands which, if in existence, would occupy several days in examining, I did not wait to search for Disappointment Island, which is said to be very small   I have since
been informed that this island, which in all probability is the same
as the island of Rosario, was seen by a whaler, who, not being able
to find it a second time, bestowed upon it the name of Invisible Island.   It is said to lie ninety miles N. W. from Port Lloyd, a place
which I shall presently notice

The next evening we reached the situation of the Bonin Islands
in Arrowsmith's chart, and the following morning made sail as usual
without seeing any land.   We were almost on the point of declaring them invisible also, when after having stood to the eastward a
few hours, we had the satisfaction to descry several islands extending in a north and south direction as far as the eye could discern.

They all appeared to be small, yet they were high and very remarkable, particularly one near the centre, which I named after Captain Kater, V P R S &c

As the islands to the southward appeared to be the largest I proposed to examine them first: and finding they were fertile, and likely to afford good anchorage, Lieutenant Belcher was sent on shore with a boat to search for a harbour   In the evening he returned with a favourable report, and with a supply of fourteen large green turtle.

We stood off and on for the night with very thick weather, and at daylight, when by our reckoning the ship should have been seven miles from the land, we unexpectedly saw the fog, about a fifth of a mile distant, and had but just room to clear them by going about. The depth of the water at that time was sixty fathoms, so that had it been blowing strong and necessary to anchor, there would have been but an indifferent prospect of holding on any length of time. The great depth of water, and the strong currents which set between the islands must make the navigation near them hazardous during thick weather.   On the evening preceding this unexpected event, we found so strong a current setting to the south-west, to windward, that, though the ship was lying to, it was necessary frequently to bear away, to prevent being drifted upon the land.

When the fog cleared away on the 9th, we discovered a distant cluster of islands bearing S 5° E true   I therefore declined anchoring in the bay which Lieutenant Belcher had examined the preceding evening, in the hope of being able to examine the newly discovered islands, but, finding both current and wind against us, and that the ship could scarcely gain ground in that direction—as there was no time to be lost, I returned to those first discovered. In running along-shore we observed an opening, which, appearing to afford better security than the before-mentioned bay, the master was sent to explore ; and returned with the welcome intelligence of having found a secure harbour, in which the ship might remain with all winds

We were a little surprised, when we came back, to find two strangers in the boat, for we had no idea that these islands had been recently visited, much less that there were any residents upon them ; and we concluded that some unfortunate vessel had been cast away upon the island   They proved to be part of the crew of a whale-ship belonging to London, named the William.   This ship, which had once belonged to his majesty's service, had been anchored in the harbour in deep water, and in rather an exposed situation (the port then not being well known,) and had part of her cargo upon deck, when a violent gust of wind from the land drove her from her anchors, and she struck upon a rock in a small bay close to the entrance, where in a short time she went to pieces   All the crew escaped, and established themselves on shore as well as they could, and immediately commenced building a vessel from the wreck of the ship, in which they intended to proceed to Manilla ; but before she was completed, another whaler, the Timor, arrived, and carried them all away except our two visiters, who remained behind at their own request.   They had been several months upon the island, during which time they had not shaved or paid any attention to their dress, and were very odd-looking beings   The master, Thomas Younger, had unfortunately been killed by the fall of a tree fifteen days previous to the loss of the ship, and was buried in a sandy bay on the eastern side of the harbour.

We entered the port and came to an anchor in the upper part of it in eighteen fathoms, almost land-locked.   This harbour is situated in the largest island of the cluster, and has its entrance conspicuously marked by a bold high promontory on the southern side, and a tall quion-shaped rock on the other.   It is nearly surrounded by hills, and the plan of it upon paper suggests the idea of its being an extinguished crater   Almost every valley has a stream of water, and the mountains are clothed with trees, among which the areca oleracea and fan-palms are conspicuous   There are several sandy bays, in which green turtle are sometimes so numerous that they quite hide the colour of the shore.   The sea yields an abundance of fish ; the rocks and caverns are the resort of crayfish and other shellfish ; and the shores are the refuge of snipes, plovers, and wild pigeons.   At the upper part of the port there is a small basin, formed by coral reefs, conveniently adapted for heaving a ship down ; and on the whole it is a most desirable place of resort for a whale-ship.   By a board nailed against a tree, it appeared that the port had been entered in September, 1825, by an English ship named the Supply, which I believe to be the first authenticated visit made to the place.

Taking possession of uninhabited islands is now a mere matter of form , still I could not allow so fair an opportunity to escape, and declared them to be the property of the British government by nailing a sheet of copper to a tree, with the necessary particulars engraved upon it   As the harbour had no name, I called it Port Lloyd, out of regard to the late Bishop of Oxford   The island in which it is situated I named after Sir Robert Peel, His Majesty's Secretary of State for the Home Department

As we rowed on shore towards the basin, which, in consequence of there being ten fathoms water all over it, was named Ten Fathom Hole, we were surrounded by sharks so daring and voracious that they bit at the oars and the boat's rudder, and though wounded with the boat-hook returned several times to the attack   At the

upper end of Ten Fathom Hole there were a great many green turtle, and the boat's crew were sent to turn some of them for our sea-
stock   The sharks, to the number of forty at least, as soon as they
observed these animals in confusion, rushed in amongst them, and
to the great danger of our people, endeavoured to seize them by the
fins, several of which we noticed to have been bitten off   The turtle weighed from three to four hundred-weight each, and were so
inactive that, had there been a sufficient number of men, the whole
shoal might have been turned

Wittrein and his companion, the men whom we found upon the
island, were living on the south side of the harbour, in a house built
from the planks of the William, upon a substantial foundation of
copper bolts, procured from the wreck of the ship by burning the
timbers   They had a number of fine fat hogs, a well stocked pig-
eon-house, and several gardens, in which there were growing pumpkins, water-melons, potatoes, sweet potatoes, and fricoli beans, and
they had planted forty cocoa-nuts in other parts of the bay.   In
such an establishment Wittrein found himself very comfortable, and
contemplated getting a wife from the Sandwich Islands; but I am
sorry to find that he soon relinquished the idea, and that there is
now no person to take care of the garden, which by due management might have become extremely useful to whale-ships, the crews
of which are often afflicted with the scurvy by their arrival at this
part of their voyage   The pigs, I have since learned, have become
wild and numerous, and will in a short time destroy all the roots,
if not the cabbage-trees, which at the time of our visit were in
abundance, and, besides being a delicate vegetable, were no doubt
an excellent antiscorbutic.

We learned from Wittrein, who had resided eight months upon
the island, that in the January of 1826 it had been visited by a tremendous storm, and an earthquake which shook the island so violently, and the water at the same time rose so high, that he and his
companion, thinking the island about to be swallowed up by the sea,
fled to the hills for safety.   This gale, which resembled the typhoons in the China sea, began at the north and went round the compass by the westward, blowing all the while with great violence, and
tearing up trees by the roots: it destroyed the schooner which the
crew of the William had begun to build, and washed the cargo of
the ship, which since her wreck had been floating about the bay, up
into the country.   By the appearance of some of the casks, the water must have risen twelve feet above the usual level *

We were informed that during the winter there is much bad
weather from the north and north-west, but as summer approaches

* The seamen affirmed that it rose twenty.
55

these winds abate, and are succeeded by others from the southward and south-east-ward, which prevail throughout that season, and are generally attended with fine weather, with the exception of fogs which are very prevalent. Shocks of earthquakes are frequently felt during the winter, and Wittrein and his companion repeatedly observed smoke issuing from the summits of the hills on the island to the northward. Peel Island, in which we anchored, is entirely volcanic, and there is every appearance of the others to the northward being of the same formation. They have deep water all round them, and ships must not allow their safety to depend upon the lead, for although bottom may be gained at great depths between some of the islands, yet that is not the case in other directions.

We noticed basaltic columns in several parts of Port Lloyd, and in one place Mr. Collie observed them divided into short lengths as at the Giant's Causeway, he also remarked at the head of the bay in the bed of a small river, from which we filled our water casks, a sort of tessellated pavement, composed of upright angular columns, placed side by side, each about an inch in diameter, and separated by horizontal fissures. It was the lower part of the Giant's Causeway in miniature. Many of the rocks consisted of tuffaceous basalt of a grayish or greenish hue, frequently traversed by veins of petrosilex; and contained numerous nodules of chalcedony or of cornelian, and *psalma*? The zeolites are not wanting; and the stilbite, in the lamellar foliated form, is abundant. Olivine and hornblende are also common. The drusses were often found containing a watery substance, which had an astringent taste not unlike alum, but I did not succeed in collecting any of it.

The coral animals have raised ledges and reefs of coral round almost all the bays, and have filled up the northern part of the harbor, with the exception of Ten Fathom Hole, which appears to be kept open by streams of water running into it, for it was observed here, that the only accessible part of the beach was at the mouths of these streams.

I have before observed, that the hills about our anchorage were wooded from the water's edge nearly to their summit. There were found among these trees, besides the cabbage and fan-palms, the tamanu of Otaheite, the pandanus odoratissimus, and, a species of purau, also some species of laurus, of urtica, the terminalia, dodonæa viscosa, eleocarpus serratis, &c. We collected some of the wood for building boats, and found it answer very well for knees, timbers, &c.

We saw no wild animals of the mammalia class except the vampire bat, which was very tame. Some measured three feet across the wings when fully extended, and were eight or nine inches in length in the body. We frequently saw them flying, but they were more fond of climbing about the trees, and hanging by their hind claw, which appears to be their natural position when feeding Some were observed with their young at their breast, concealed by the wide membrane of their wing   The tongue of this animal is unusually large, and furnished with fleshy papillæ on the upper surface   Here we also found another species of vespertilio

Of birds we saw some handsome brown herons with white crests, plovers, rails, snipes, wood-pigeons, and the common black crow, a small bird resembling a canary, and a grossbeak   They were very tame, and until alarmed at the noise of a gun, suffered themselves to be approached.

The sea abounded in fish, some of which were very beautiful in colour.   We noticed the green fish mentioned at Gambier Island, and a gold-coloured fish of the same genus, both extremely splendid in their appearance.   A dentex resembling our carp, a small rayfish, and some large eels, one of which weighed twenty pounds, were caught in the fresh water.   We took forty four turtles on board for sea stock, besides consuming two a day while we remained in port, weighing each about three hundred weight.

The weather during our stay was fine, but oppressively warm ; and though we had no rain, the atmosphere was generally saturated with moisture.   There was a thick fog to windward of the islands almost the whole of the time , but it dispersed on its passage over the land, and the lee side was generally clear

While our operations at the port were in progress, Lieutenant Belcher circumnavigated Peel's Island in the cutter, and discovered a large bay at the southeast angle of the island, which afforded very secure anchorage from all winds except the south-east ; as this is the prevalent wind during the summer, it is not advisable to anchor in that season.   I named it Fitton Bay, in compliment to Dr Fitton, late president of the Geological Society   Mr Elson also was employed outside of the harbour, and discovered some sunken rocks to the southward of the entrance to the port, on which account ships should not close the land in that direction so as to shut in two paps at the north-east angle of Port Lloyd with the south bluff of the harbour.   With these objects open there is no danger.

On the 15th of June, we put to sea from Port Lloyd ; and finding the wind still from the southward, and that we could not reach the islands in that direction without much loss of time, I bore away to ascertain the northern limit of the group   We ran along the western shore, and at noon on the 16th observed the meridian altitude off the northernmost islet.   The group consists of three clusters of islands lying nearly N. by E and extending from the lat of 27° 44' 35'' N. to 26° 30' N. and beyond, but that was the utmost limit of our view to the southward.   The northern cluster consists of small islands and pointed rocks, and has much broken ground about it, which renders caution necessary in approaching it I distinguished it by the name of Parry's Group, in compliment to the late hydrographer, under whose command I had the pleasure to serve on the northern expedition. The middle cluster consists of three islands, of which Peel's Island, four miles and a fifth in length is the largest. This group is nine miles and a quarter in length and is divided by two channels so narrow that they can only be seen when abreast of them Neither of them are navigable by shipping, the northern, on account of rocks which render it impassable even by boats, and the other on account of rapid tides and eddies, which, as there is no anchoring ground, would most likely drift a ship upon the rocks. The northern island I named Stapleton, and the centre Buckland, in compliment to the Professor of Geology at Oxford. At the south-west angle of Buckland Island there is a sandy bay, in which ships will find good anchorage ; but they must be careful in bringing up to avoid being carried out of soundings by the current. I named it Walker's Bay, after Mr Walker of the Hydrographical Office. The southern cluster is evidently that in which a whale ship commanded by Mr Coffin anchored in 1823, who was the first to communicate its position to this country, and who bestowed his own name upon the port As the cluster was, however, left without any distinguishing appellation, I named it after Francis Baily, Esq late President of the Astronomical Society.

These clusters of islands correspond so well with a group named Yslas del Arzobispo in a work published many years ago in Manilla, entitled *Navigacion Especulativa y Practica*, that I have retained the name, in addition to that of Bonin Islands ; as it is extremely doubtful, from the Japanese accounts of Bonin-sima, whether there are not other islands in the vicinity, to which the latter name is not more applicable In these accounts, published by M. Klaproth in his Memoire sur la Chine, and by M Abel Remusat in the Journal des Savans for September, 1817, it is said that the islands of Bonin-sima, or Mou-nin-sima, consist of eighty-nine islands of which two are large, four are of a midling size, four small and the remainder of the group consists of rocks The two large islands are there said to be inhabited, and in the Japanese chart, published in the Journal des Savans, contain several villages and temples They are stated to be extremely fertile, to produce leguminous vegetables and all kinds of grain, besides a great abundance of pasturage and sugar-canes, and the plains to afford an agreeable retreat to man ; that there are lofty palm-trees, cocoa-nuts, and other fruits, sandal wood, camphor, and other precious trees

Setting aside the geographical inaccuracy of the chart, which the Japanese might not know how to avoid, and the disagreement of distances and proportions, their description is so very unlike any thing that we found in these islands, that if the Japanese are at all to be credited they cannot be the same, and if they are not to be believed, it may be doubted whether Bonin-sima is not an imaginary island

The group which we visited had neither villages, temples, nor any remains whatever, and it was quite evident that they had never been resided upon There were no cocoa-nut trees, no sugar canes, no leguminous vegetables, nor any plains for the cultivation of grain, the land being very steep in every part, and overgrown with tall trees. Neither in number, size, or direction will the islands at all coincide. and under such dissimilarities, it may reasonably be inquired whether it is possible for these places to be the same   If we compare the number, size, and shape of the islands, or direction of the group, there is a yet wider discrepancy, ports are placed in the Japanese map where none exist in these, rocks are marked to the full number, which seem only to create useless alarm to the navigator, and throughout there is a neglect of the cardinal points. I have therefore, on this ground, presumed to doubt the propriety of the name of Bonin-sima being attached to these islands

Were the situation of Bonin-sima dependent solely upon the account furnished by Kæmpfer, it might safely be identified with the group of Yslas del Arzo-bispo; but the recent notice of that island by the Japanese authors is so very explicit, that great doubt upon the subject is thereby created. Kæmpfer's account stands thus.—In 1675 a Japanese junk was driven out of her course by strong winds, and wrecked upon an island three hundred miles to the eastward of Fatsissio   The island abounded in ariack-trees (areca?) and in enormous crabs (turtle?), which were from four to six feet in length; and was named Bunesima, in consequence of its being uninhabited. In this statement the distance, the areca-trees, the turtle, and the island being unoccupied agree very well with the description of the island I have given above? and it is curious that Wittrein, whom we found upon the island, declared he had seen the wreck of a vessel in which the planks were put together in a manner similar to that which was noticed by Lieutenant Wainwright in the junk at Loo Choo

It is remarkable that this group should have escaped the observation of Gore, Perouse, Krusenstern, and several others, whose vessels passed to the northward and southward of its position   In the journals of the above-mentioned navigators we find that when in the vicinity of these islands they were visited by land birds, but they never saw land, the three small islands of Los Volcanos excepted, which may be considered the last of the group. The consequence of their having thus escaped notice was, that all the islands, except the three last-mentioned, were expunged from the charts; and it was not until 1823 that they re-appeared on Arrowsmith's map, on the authority of M. Abel Remusat

Near these islands we found strong currents, running principally to the northward; but none of them equalled in strength that which is said by the Japanese to exist between Bonin-Sima and Fatsissio. which indeed was so rapid that it obtained the name of Kourosi-gawa, or Current of the black Gulf, [*] nor did their directions accord as the Kou-rosi-gawa is said to set from east to west At particular periods, perhaps, these currents may be greater than we found them, and may also run to the westward, but they are certainly not constant To the southward of Jesso, Captain Broughton experienced a set in the opposite direction—that is, from west to east, and so did Admiral Krusenstern With us, as has been mentioned before, the set was to the northward.

June 16th I had spent as much time in low latitudes, fixing the positions of all those islands, as was consistent with my orders, and it became necessary to make the best of our way to the northward, which we did, in the hope of being more successful in our search for the land expedition than we were the preceding year At first we stood well to the eastward, in order to get nearly into the meridian of Petropaulski, that we might not be inconvenienced by easterly winds, which appear to be prevalent in these seas in the summer time; and having attained our object, directed the course for that port.

Our passage between corresponding latitudes was very similar to that of the preceding year. Between the parallels of 30° and 35° we experienced light and variable winds, and 39° of latitude took a southerly wind, which continued with us nearly all the way We entered the region of fog nearly in the same latitude as before, and did not lose it until the day before we made the land, when, as before, it was dispersed by strong winds off the coast The currents were similar to those of the preceding year, but when near the Kurile Islands we were impeded by a strong southerly current from the Sea of Okotsk. About this time we noticed so material a change in the colour of the sea that we were induced to try for soundings, but without gaining the bottom. Captain Clerke off the same place observed a similar change, and also tried for soundings without success. It is probable that the outset from the Sea of Okotsk, the shores of which are flat and muddy, may bring down a quantity of that substance, and occasion the alteration

As we had very little to interest us in this passage, beyond that

---

[*] Description d'un Crouppe d'Iles peu connu, par M Remusat

which always attends a material change of climate, we watched the birds which flew around us, and found that the tropic birds deserted us in 35° N. The brown albatross and shearwaters fell off in 40°. N. In 41° we saw the wandering albatross and black divers, some petrel in 45°; puffins, fulmar petrels, and gannets in 49°, and as we approached Kamschatka, lummes, dovekies, and small tern. About the latitude of 42° we saw many whales, but they did not accompany us far. We observed driftwood occasionally, but it was not so plentiful as in the preceding year.

On the 2d of July we made the snowy mountains of Kamschatka, but did not reach the Bay of Awatska before the evening of the next day, when, after experiencing the difficulties which almost always attend the entry and egress of the port. we came to an anchor off the town of Petropaulski nearly in the same situation as before

We found lying in the inner harbour the Okotsk Packet, a brig of 200 tons, commanded by a Russian sub-lieutenant, on the point of sailing with the mail for St Petersburgh, and availed ourselves of the favourable opportunity of transmitting despatches and private letters by her I received some official letters which had been too late for the ship the preceding year; but neither in them nor in the Petersburgh Gazette, which finds its way occasionally to Kamschatka, was there intelligence to influence our proceedings, and we consequently began to refit the ship for her northern cruize. While this duty was in progress, we were also employed sounding and surveying the capacious bay and the harbours of Tareinski, Rakovya, and Petropaulski, the plans of those places which had been constructed by Captain King being by no means complete.

Before the ship was at an anchor we received from the governor, Captain Stankitski, a very acceptable present of some new potatoes, fresh butter, curds, and spring water—a mark of attention and politeness for which we were very thankful On landing I had the pleasure to find all the colony in good health, but a little chagrined to learn the ship was not one of the periodical vessels from St Petersburgh As these vessels bring out every kind of supply for the inhabitants, they are most anxiously looked for, and if they are detained they occasion great inconvenience

We endeavoured to supply some of the deficiences of the place by presents of flour, rice, tea, and bottled porter, and three large turtle, with some water-melons. Both the last-mentioned were great curiosities, as they had never been brought to the place before, or indeed seen by any of the inhabitants, except those in the goverment service Much curiosity was consequently excited when the turtle were landed, and very few would at first believe such forbidding animals were intended to be eaten As no person knew how to dress them, I sent my cook on shore, and they were soon converted into an excellent soup, some of which was sent round to each of the respectable inhabitants of the place, but, as may be imagined, after having brought the animals so far, we were mortified at hearing several persons declare their preference for their own dishes made of seals' flesh   These turtle were the last of the supply we had taken on board at Port Lloyd, three having died upon the passage, and the ship's company having continued to consume two every day, which on an average was about five pounds a man. This lasted for about three weeks, during which time we saved half the usual allowance of provisions

The season at Petropaulski was more backward than the preceding year, and though it was the beginning of July, the snow lay deep upon some parts of the shore, and the inhabitants were glad to keep on their fur dresses

The little town, which has been repeatedly described since King's visit, has been removed from the spit of land which forms the harbour, to a valley at the back of it, where there are several rows of substantial log-houses, comfortably fitted up inside, and warmed with large ovens in the centre, furnished with pipes for the conveyance of hot air   Glass for windows has partly superseded the laminæ of talc, before used for that purpose   Neat wooden bridges have been thrown over the ravines which intersect the town, and a new church has been built.   A guard-house and several field-pieces command the landing ; and a little to the northward there are magazines for powder and stores.   Among other buildings in the town there is a hospital and a school.   The yourts and balagans of which Captain King speaks are now only used as store-houses for fish.

The greater part of the houses are furnished with gardens, but, being badly attended to, they produce very little.   That attached to the government-house was in better order, and was planted with peas, beans, cabbages, lettuces, potatoes, radishes, cucumbers, and a few currant-trees which were blighted, barley and a small quantity of wheat were also growing in its vicinity   Some new houses were erecting in the town in expectation of the arrival of some exiles from St Petersburgh, as it was understood that several persons concerned in the conspiracy against the emperor were to be banished to this place   The town, upon the whole, was much neater than I expected to find it ; and I by no means agree with Captain Cochrane, that it is a contemptable place, and a picture of misery and wretchedness.   Considering the number of years it has been colonized, and that it is part of the Russian Empire, it ought certainly to have become of much more importance, but it does not differ so materially from the accounts of it that have been published, as to create disappointment on visiting the place, and it appeared to me that nothing is promised in those accounts which the place itself does not afford

It was with much pleasure we noticed in the governor's garden the monument of our departed countryman Captain Clerke, which for better preservation had been removed from its former position by the late governor   It was on one side of a broad gravel walk, at the end of an avenue of trees   On the other side of the walk, there was a monument to the memory of the celebrated Beering   The former it may be recollected, was erected by the officers of Captain Krusenstein's ship, and the latter had been purposely sent from St. Petersburg   This mark of respect from the Russians toward our departed countryman calls forth our warmest gratitude, and must strengthen the good understanding which exists and is daily increasing between the officers of their service and our own   The monument will ever be regarded as one of the greatest interest, as it marks the places of interment of the companions of the celebrated Cook and Beering, and records the generosity of the much-lamented Perouse, who placed a copper plate over the grave of our departed countryman Captain Clerke, and of the celebrated Admiral Krusenstern, who erected the monument, and affixed a tablet upon it to the memory of the Abbe de la Croyere   Such eminent names, thus combined, create a regret that the materials on which they are engraved are not as imperishable as the memory of the men themselves.

Since Admiral Krusenstein visited Kamschatka, several alterations have been made, probably in consequence of the suggestions in his publication   The seat of government is now fixed at Petropaulski, the town is considerably improved, and the inhabitants are better supplied than formerly.   Still much remains to be accomplished before Petropaulski can be of consequence in any way, except in affording an excellent asylum for vessels.   In this respect it is almost unequalled, being very secure, and admirably adapted to the purpose of any vessel requiring repair ; but for this she will have to depend entirely upon her own resources, as their is nothing to be had in the country but fish, wood, water, and fresh beef.

The population of the town at the beginning of the winter of 1826 was not more than three hundred and eighty-five persons, exclusive of the government establishment , the occupation of the people consists principally in curing fish and providing for a long winter, during which, with the exception of those persons who go into the interior for furs, there is very little to occupy the inhabitants.

There are no manufactures in the country, nor any establishments which require notice   The inhabitants have an idea that the climate is to cold to produce crops of wheat and other grain, and neglect almost entirely the cultivation of the soil   The consequence of this is, that they occasionally suffer very much from scurvy, and are dependent upon the supplies which are sent from St Petersburgh every second year for all their farinaceous food, and if these vessels are lost the greatest distress ensues   Many attempts have been made to persuade them to attend to agriculture, rewards have been offered by the government for the finest productions, and seeds are distributed to the people every spring.   In the autumn there is a fair at which those persons who have received seeds are required to attend, and to bring with them specimens of the fruit of their labour.   The persons who are most deserving then receive rewards, and the day finishes with a feast and a dance   In spite of these encouragements, the gardens are very little attended to.   Hay, though it is got in at the proper season, is in such inadequate proportion to the wants of the cattle, that were it not for wild garlic they would famish before the spring vegetation commences   The flavour that is communicated to the milk and butter by the use of this herbage, appears to be so familiar to the inhabitants that they find nothing unpleasant in it, but it is very much the reverse with strangers.   Every family has one or two cows, of which great care is taken during the winter, and, strictly speaking, some of the inhabitants live under the same roof with their animals, with no other partition than a screen of single boards   There are very few oxen in the town and when required they are driven from Bolcheresk, about ninety miles off, where pasturage is more abundant.   Beef is consequently a luxury seldom enjoyed, and sheep and goats cannot exist in the country, in consequence of the savage nature of the dogs, which are very large, and occasionally break away from their fastenings. fish therefore constitutes the principle food of the inhabitants.

Necessarily frugal, and blessed with a salubrious climate, the residents in general enjoy good health, and appear to lead a contented life.   They are extremely fond of the amusement of dancing, and frequently meet for this purpose   There are several musicians, and musical instruments are manufactured by an ingenious exile   As spirituous liquors of any kind in the country are scarce, these meetings are not attended with any inebriety, and serve only to pass away the dull hours of a long winter's evening   The only refreshment we saw produced at them consisted of whortle and cran-berries : these were piled up in two or three plates with a dessert-spoon to each, and passed round the company, almost every body using the same spoon   Society is necessarily very mixed, or there could be none in so small a population, and when strangers are not present it is not unusual to see exiles at the governor's parties.

In the winter sledging is a favourite occupation   The dogs are here very large and swift, and are so much esteemed that they are carried to Okotsk for sale   For a description of this amusement, and other recreations of the Kamschatdales, I must refer the reader to Cook's Voyage, to Captain Cochrane's Pedestrian Journey, and to the entertaining Travels of Mr Dobell, who quitted Kamschatka a short time before we arrived.

At present the only trade carried on at Petropaulski is in furs, which are exchanged for goods brought annually from Okotsk. Every thing is excessively dear, even the necessary article salt is in great demand, and produces a very high price.

The Bay of Awatska and the harbours which open into it leave nothing to be desired in the way of a port.   Awatska has many square miles of ground which may be appropriated to secure anchorage, and Tareinski is the beau ideal of a harbour   Petropaulski, though small, has a sufficient depth of water for a first-rate in every part of it.   The ground is good, and the smoothness of the water is never affected by any weather upon the coast   As Awatska is nearly surrounded by high land, gusts of wind are of frequent occurrence, particularly opposite Rakovya harbour   on this account it is advisable to moor or ride with a long scope of cable.   The entrance to the port is narrow and about four miles in length, and as the wind almost always blows up or down the channel, ships frequently have to beat in and out, and experience great difficulty in so doing, from the confined space to which they are limited, and the eddy currents, which in the spring-time in particular must be carefully guarded against   There are but two shoals in the harbour which it is necessary to notice ; one off Rakovya, upon which there is a buoy ; and the other off the signal station on the west side of the entrance of Awatska Bay.

Much has been said of the neglected condition of the settlement, and volumes have been written on the government, inhabitants, productions, and on the actual and prospective state of the country,[*] still there have been no exertions on the part of the government materially to improve or provide for either one or the other.   Its neglected state is probably of very little consequence at present ; but should the North Pacific ever be the scene of active naval operations, Petropaulski must doubtless become of immense importance   At present it may be said to be unfortified, but a very few guns judiciously placed would effectually protect the entrance.

On the 18th of July, having completed the survey of the bay of Awatska and its harbours, we took our leave of the hospitable inhabitants, and weighed anchor ; but, as on the former occasion, we were obliged to make several unsuccessful attempts to get out, and did not accomplish our object until the 20th, when we shaped

    *Cook's Third Voyage, vol iii Perouse's Voyage, Krusenstern's Embassy to Japan , Langsdorff's Travels , Cochrane's Journey , Dobell's Travels, &c

our course towards Chepoonski Noss   A long swell rolled in upon
the shore as we crossed this spacious bay, in the depth of which
the port of Awatska is situated, and convinced us of the difficulty
that would be experienced in getting clear of the land with a strong
wind upon the coast, and of the danger a ship would incur were
she, in addition to this, to be caught in a fog, which would prevent
her finding the port   Our winds were light from seaward, and we
made slow progress, striking soundings occasionally from sixty to
seventy fathoms, until the following morning, when we took our
departure from the Noss, and entered a thick fog, which enveloped
us until we made Beering's Island on the 22d ; when it cleared
away for the moment, we distinguished Seal Rock   We had no
observation at noon, but by comparing the reckoning with the observations of the preceding and following days, it gave the position
of the island the same as before.

We quitted the island with the prospect of a quick passage to
the Straits , and, attended by a thick fog, advanced to the northward until the 26th, at which time contrary winds brought us in
with the Asiatic coast in the parallel of 61° 58′ N   When we
were within a few leagues of the coast the fog cleared away, as it
generally does near the land, and discovered to us a hilly country,
and a coast apparently broken into deep bays and inlets , but, as
we did not approach very closely, these might have been only
valleys.   In this parallel the nearest point of land bearing N. 74°
W true, thirteen miles, the depth of water was 26 fathoms ; and it
increased gradually as we receded from the coast   The bottom
near the shore was a coarse gravel, which, as that in the offing is
mud or sand, is a useful distinctive feature.   With a northerly wind -
and a thick fog we stood towards St Lawrence Island, and on the
1st August were apprised of our approach to it, by the soundings
changing from mud to sand, and several visits from the little crested auks, which are peculiar to this island   We made the land about
the same place we had done the preceding year, stood along it to the
northward, and passed its N W extreme, at two miles and a half
distance, in 15 fathoms water, over a bottom of stones and shells,
which soon changed again to sand and mud   About midnight the
temperature of water fell to 31°, and soon after that of the air was
reduced from 42° to 34   The wind shifted to north-west, and cleared
away the fog.   On the after-noon of the 2d we passed King's Island
and the wind continuing to the northward, anchored off Point Rodney, for the purpose of hoisting out the barge   We came to anchor
in seven fathoms, three miles from the land, King's Island bearing
N. 70° 29′ W true, and Sledge Island S 65° E true.

Point Rodney is low, and the water being shallow, it is difficult
to land   From the beach to the foot of the mountains there is a

plain about two miles wide, covered with lichens and grass, upon which several herds of reindeer were feeding, but the communication is in places interrupted by narrow lakes, which extend several miles along the coast. Upon the beach there was a greater abundance of drift wood than we had noticed on any other part of the coast; some of it was perforated by the teredo, and was covered with small barnacles, but there were several trunks which appeared to have been recently torn up by the roots. Near the spot where we landed were several yourts, and a number of posts driven into the ground, and in the lake we found several artificial ducks which had been left as decoys but we saw no natives. About two miles from the coast the country becomes mountainous, and far inland rises to peaked hills of great height, covered with perennial snow

It was calm throughout the greater part of the day, with very fine weather. The temperature, which increased gradually as we left the snowy coast of Asia, at noon reached to 55°, which was twenty one degrees higher than it had been on the opposite shore, and the mean for the last twenty-four hours was seven degrees higher than that of the preceding day. Part of this difference was evidently owing to the cessation of the northerly wind and our proximity to the land, but part must also have been occasioned by one coast being naturally colder than the other.

During the time we were at anchor there was a regular ebb and flow of the tide: and there appeared by the shore to be about three or four feet rise of water. The flood came from the S E., and ran with greater strength than the ebb, which showed there was a current setting towards Beering's Strait. Captain Cook noticed the same circumstance off this part of the coast.

The equipment of our little tender was always a subject of interest, and preparations for hoisting her out seemed to give the greatest pleasure to all on board. She was again placed under the command of Mr Elson, who received orders to examine the coast narrowly between our station and Kotzebue Sound, and to search for an opening to the eastward of Cape Prince of Wales, of which the Esquimaux had apprised us the preceding year by their chart upon the sand. Mr. Elson was ordered to look into Schismareff Inlet, and afterwards to meet the ship at Chamisso Island. This little excursion was nearly being frustrated by an accident. In hoisting out the boat the bolt in the keel gave way, in consequence of the copper having corroded the iron of the clench; a circumstance which should be guarded against in coppered boats. Fortunately she was not far off the deck, or the accident might have been of a very serious nature, as her weight was as much as our yards would bear when shored up

As soon as she was equipped, Mr. Elson proceeded in shore; and a breeze springing up shortly afterwards, the ship weighed, and entered the channel between King's Island and the main. The depth of water from the anchorage off Point Rodney decreased gradually as she proceeded, until nearly mid-channel, when the soundings became very irregular; the alternate casts occasionally varying from nine to six fathoms, and vice versa. As it was blowing fresh at the time, the sudden change of soundings occasioned overfalls, and, the channel having been very indifferently explored, it was unpleasant sailing. But, although I do not think there is any danger, it would still be advisable in passing through the channel, which is full of ridges, to pay strict attention to the lead, particularly as when Captain Cook passed over the same ground, there was, according to his chart, nothing less than twelve fathoms. The wind increasing, and a thick fog approaching, the course was continued with some anxiety; but finding the same irregularity in the soundings, I hauled out due west to the northward of King's Island, which speedily brought us into twenty-eight fathoms, and showed that there was a bank, tolerably steep at its edge, extending from King's Island to the main. We now resumed our course for the strait; but the fog being very thick we had some difficulty in finding the passage, and were obliged to haul off twice before we succeeded in passing it. In doing this we crossed a narrow channel, with thirty seven fathoms water, which is deeper soundings than have been hitherto found within a great many miles of the strait. As the depth on each side of the channel is twenty-four fathoms, it may serve as a guide in future to vessels circumstanced as we were at the mouth of the strait in a thick fog. A little before noon we discerned the Fairway Rock, and passed the straits in confidence before a fresh gale of wind, which had just increased so much as to render our situation very unpleasant.

On the morning of the 5th we passed Cape Espenburg, and in the evening came to anchor off Chamisso Island, nearly in the same situation we had occupied so long the preceding year. On revisiting this island, curiosity and interest in the fate of our countrymen, of whom we were in search, were our predominant feelings; and a boat was immediately sent to ascertain whether they had been at the island. On her return we learned that no new marks had been discerned upon the rocks; no staff was erected, as had been agreed upon in the event of their arrival; and the billet of wood containing despatches was lying unopened upon the same stone on which it had been placed the preceding year, either of which facts was a conclusive answer to our inquiry.

By some chips of wood which had been recently cut, it appeared that the Esquimaux had not long quitted the island, and on exam-ning the grave of our unfortunate shipmate we found it had been disturbed by the natives, who, disappointed in their search, had again filled in the earth. It would be unfair to impute to these people any malicious intentions from this circumstance, as they must have had every reason to suppose, from their custom of concealing provisions underground, and from having found a cask of our flour buried the preceding year, that they would find a similar treasure, especially as they do not inter their dead. The cask of flour and the box of beads which had been deposited in the sand, had been unmolested ; but a copper coin which we nailed upon a post on the summit of the island was taken away

The swarms of mosquitos that infested the shore at this time greatly lessened our desire to land. However, some of our sportsmen traversed the island, and succeeded in killing a white hare, weighing nearly twelve pounds, and a few ptarmigan ; the hare was getting its summer coat, and the young birds were strong upon the wing.

For several days after our arrival the weather was very thick, with rain and squalls from the south-west, which occasioned some anxiety for the barge ; but on the 11th she joined us, and I learned from Mr. Elson that he had succeeded in finding the inlet, and that as far as he could judge, the weather being very foggy and boisterous, it was a spacious and excellent port. He was visited by several of the natives while there, one of whom drew him a chart, which corresponded with that constructed upon the sand in Kotzebue Sound the preceding year. On his putting to sea from the inlet, the weather continued very thick, so much so that he passed through Beering's Strait without seeing land ; and was unable to explore Scismareff Inlet.

The discovery of a port so near to Beering's Strait, and one in which it was probable the ship might remain after circumstances should oblige her to quit Kotzebue Sound, was of great importance ; and I determined to take an early opportunity of examining it, should the situation of the ice to the northward afford no prospect of our proceeding further than we had done the preceding year. In order that Captain Franklin's party might not be inconvenienced by such an arrangement, the barge was fitted, and placed under the command of Lieutenant Belcher, who was ordered to proceed along the coast as in the preceding year, and to use his best endeavours to communicate with the party under Captain Franklin's command, by penetrating to the eastward as far as he could go with safety to the boat ; but he was on no account to risk being beset in the ice, and in the event of separation from the ship, he was not to protract his absence from Kotzebue Sound beyond the 1st of September.

He was also to examine the shoals off Icy Cape and Cape Krusenstern, and to explore the bay to the northward of Point Hope.

Having made these arrangements, we endeavoured to put to sea, but calms and fogs detained us at Chamisso until the 14th, and it was the 16th before we reached the entrance of the sound. The barge, however, got out, and the weather afterwards being very foggy, we did not rejoin for some time. Before we left the island we were visited by several natives whom we remembered to have seen the preceding year. They brought some skins for sale, as usual, but did not find so ready a market for them as on the former occasion, in consequence of the greater part of the furs which had been purchased by the seamen at that time, having rotted and become offensive on their return to warm latitudes. Our visitors were as before, dirty, noisy, and impudent. One of them, finding he was not permitted to carry off some deep-sea leads that were lying about, scraped off the greasy arming and devoured it another, after bargaining some skins for the armourer's anvil, unconcernedly seized it for the purpose of carrying it away ; but much to his surprise, and to the great diversion of the sailors who had played him the trick, he found its weight much too great for him, and after a good laugh received back his goods A third amused the young gentlemen very much by his humourous behaviour He was a shrewd, observing, merry fellow For some time he stood eyeing the officers walking the deck, and at length appeared determined to turn them into ridicule seizing therefore a young midshipman by the hand, he strutted with him up and down the deck in a most ludicrous manner, to the great entertainment of all present. They quit us late at night, but renewed their visit at three in the morning, and that they would have an opportunity of appropriating to themselves some of the moveable articles upon deck. There was otherwise no reason for returning so soon ; and from what we afterwards saw of these people, there is every reason to believe that was their real motive.

Off the entrance of Kotzebue Sound we were met by a westerly wind, which prevented our making much progress, but on the 18th the breeze veered to the south-westward, with a thick fog, and as I had not seen any thing of the barge, I steered to the northward to ascertain the position of the ice At noon Cape Thomson was seen N 46° E (true) three leagues distant, but was immediately obscured again by fog At midnight the temperature of both air and sea fell from 43° to 39°, and rose again soon afterwards to 44° occasioned probably by some patches of ice . but the weather was so thick that we could see only a very short distance around us. We continued to stand to the north-west, with very thick and rainy weather, until half past one o'clock in the afternoon, when I hauled to the wind, in consequence of the temperature of the water having cooled down to 35°, and the weather being still very thick In half an hour afterwards we heard the ice to leeward, and had but just room to get about to clear a small berg at its edge. Our latitude at this time was 70° 01' N., and longitude 168° 50' W. or about 160 miles to the westward of Icy Cape The soundings in the last twelve hours had been very variable, increasing at one time to thirty fathoms, then shoaling to twenty-four and deepening again to thirty-two fathoms. *muddy* bottom, an hour after this we shoaled to twenty-one fathoms, *stones,* and at the edge of the ice to nineteen fathoms, *stones.* The body of ice lying to the northward prevented our pursuing this shallow water, to ascertain whether it decreased so as to become dangerous to navigation

Shortly after we tacked, the wind fell very light, and changed to west We could hear the ice plainly; but the fog was so thick that we could not see thirty yards distance , and, as we appeared to be in a bay, to avoid being beset, we stood out by the way which we had entered At nine o'clock the fog cleared off, and we returned toward the ice. At midnight, being close to its edge, we found it in a compact body, extending from W to N E and trending N 68° E. true As the weather was unsettled, I stood off until four o'clock, and then tacked, and at eight again saw the ice a few miles to the south-eastward of our position the day before. We ran along its edge, and at noon observed the latitude in 70° 06' . N.

Occasional thick weather and snow showers obliged us to keep at a greater distance from the pack, and we lost sight of it for several hours ; but finding by the increase of temperature of the water that our course led us too much from it, at nine o'clock I steered N N E. true. And at midnight was again close upon it The ice was compact as before, except near the edge, and extended from W S. W. to N.N E mag. trending N 56° E true We now followed its course closely to the eastward, and found it gradually turning to the southward At three o'clock the wind veered to south-west with snow showers and thick weather; and as this brought us upon a lee shore, I immediatly hauled off the ice, and carried a press of sail to endeavour to weather Icy Cape The edge of the packed ice at this time was in latitude 70° 47' N. trending south-eastward, and gradually approaching the land to the eastward of Icy Cape. By the information of Lieutenant Belcher, who was off the Cape at this time, though not within sight of the ship, it closed the land about twenty-seven miles east of Icy Cape

The passage that was left between it and the beach was extremely narrow , and, judging from the effect of the westerly winds off Refuge Inlet the preceding year, it must soon have closed up, as those winds blew with great strength about the time we hauled off,

From this it appears that the line of packed ice, in the meridian of icy cape, was twenty-four miles to the southward of its position the preceding year, and that it was on the whole much nearer the continent of America. With the ice thus pressing upon the American coast, and with the prevalence of westerly winds, by which this season was distinguished, there would have been very little prospect of a vessel bent upon effecting the passage succeeding even in reaching Point Barrow.

The wind continuing to blow from the S W. with thick weather and showers of snow, we endeavoured to get an offing, and at ten o'clock tacked a mile off the land near Icy Cape. In the afternoon we stood again to the southward, and the next day fetched into the bay near Cape Beaufort, and at night hove to off Cape Lisburn with thick and cold weather. The next morning, being moderate, afforded us the only opportunity we had hitherto had of depositing some information for Captain Franklin's party. The boat landed near the Cape, and buried one bottle for him and another for Lieutenant Belcher, whom we had not seen since we parted at Chamisso Island. In the evening we stretched toward Point Hope, for the purpose of depositing a bottle there also, as it was a point which could not escape Captain Franklin's observation in his route along shore; but the wind increasing from the westward occasioned a heavy surf upon the beach, and obliged the ship to keep in the offing

Seeing that we could not remain sufficiently close in shore to be of use to our friends during the westerly winds and thick weather, I determined upon the examination of the inlet discovered by Mr Elson to the eastward of Cape Prince of Wales, and made sail for Kotzebue Sound, for the purpose of leaving there the necessary information for Captain Franklin and Lieutenant Belcher, in the event of either arriving during our absence.

We passed Cape Krusenstern about sunset on the 25th; and in running along shore after dark our attention was directed to a large fire kindled as if for the purpose of attracting our notice. As this was the signal agreed upon between Captain Franklin and myself, and as we had not before seen a fire in the night on any part of the coast, we immediately brought to, and, to our great satisfaction at the moment, observed a boat pulling towards the ship. Our anxiety at her approach may be imagined, when we thought we could discover with our telescopes, by the light of the aurora borealis, that she was propelled by oars instead of paddles. But just as our expectation was at the highest, we were accosted by the Esquimaux in their usual manner, and all our hopes vanished. I fired a gun, however, in case there might be any persons on shore who could not come off to us, but the signal not being answered, we pursued our course for Chamisso

For the first time since we entered Beering's Strait the night was clear, and the aurora borealis sweeping across the heavens reminded us that it was exactly on that night twelvemonth that we saw this beautiful phenomenon for the first time in these seas. A short time before it began, a brilliant meteor fell in the western quarter. The aurora is at all times an object of interest, and seldom appears without some display worthy of admiration, though the expectation is seldom completely gratified. The uncertainty of its movements, and of the moment when it may break out into splendour, has, however, the effect of keeping the attention continually on the alert; many of us in consequence stayed up to a late hour, but nothing was exhibited on this occasion more than we had already repeatedly witnessed.

We were more fortunate the following night, when the aurora approached nearer the southern horizon than it had done on any former occasion that we had observed in this part of the globe. It commenced much in the usual manner, by forming an arch from W.N. W to E N E , and then soared rapidly to the zenith, where the streams of light rolled into each other, and, exhibited brilliant colours of purple, pink, and green. It then became diffused over the sky generally, leaving about 8° of clear space between it and the northern and southern horizons. From this tranquil state it again suddenly poured out corruscations from all parts, which shot up to the zenith, and formed a splendid cone of rays, blending pink, purple and green colours in all their varieties. This singular and beautiful exhibition lasted only a few minutes, when the light as before became diffused over the sky in a bright haze

We anchored at Chamisso on the 26th, and, after depositing the necessary information on shore, weighed the next morning to proceed to examine the inlet. We were scarcely a league from the land when our attention was again arrested by a fire kindled upon the Peninsula, and eight or ten persons standing upon the heights waving to the ship. The disappointment of the preceding night ought certainly to have put us upon our guard ; but the desire of meeting our countrymen induced us to transform every object capable of misconstruction into something favourable to our wishes, and our expectations on this occasion carried us so far that some imagined they could perceive the party to be dressed in European clothes. A boat was immediately despatched to the shore ; but, as the reader has already begun to suspect, it was a party of Esquimaux, who wished to dispose of some skins for tobacco

This disappointment lost us a favourable tide, and we did not clear the sound before the night of the 29th. After passing Cape Espenberg, a strong north-west wind made it necessary to stand off shore, in doing which the water shoaled from thirteen to nine fathoms upon a bank lying off Schismareff Inlet, and again deepened to thirteen : we then bore away for the strait, and at eleven o'clock saw the Diomede Islands, thirteen leagues distant, and about four o'clock rounded Cape Prince of Wales very close, in twenty-seven fathoms water.

This celebrated promontory is the western termination of a peaked mountain, which, being connected with the main by low ground, at a distance has the appearance of being isolated The promontory is bold, and remarkable by a number of ragged points and large fragments of rock lying upon the ridge which connects the cape with the peak. About a mile to the northward of the cape, some low land begins to project from the foot of the mountain, taking first a northerly and then a north-easterly direction to Schismareff Inlet Off this point we afterwards found a dangerous shoal, upon which the sea broke heavily. The natives have a village upon the low land near the cape called Eidannoo, and another inland, named King-a-ghe : and as they generally select the mouths of rivers for their residences, it is not improbable that a stream may here empty itself into the sea, which, meeting the current through the straight, may occasion the shoal. About fourteen miles inland from Eidannoo, there is a remarkable conical hill, often visible when the mountain-tops are covered, which, being well fixed, will be found useful at such times by ships passing through the strait. Twelve miles further inland, the country becomes mountainous, and is remarkable for its sharp ridges. The altitude of one of the peaks, which is nearly the highest on the range, is 2596 feet. These mountains, being thickly covered with snow, gave the country a very wintry aspect.

To the southward of Cape Prince of Wales the coast trends nearly due east, and assumes a totally different character to that which leads to Schismareff Inlet, being bounded by steep rocky cliffs, and broken by deep valleys, while the other is low and swampy ground The river called by the natives Youp nut must lie in one of these valleys ; and in all probability it is in that which opens out near a bold promontory, to which I have given the name of York, in honour of his late Royal Highness. On nearing that part of the coast we found the water more shallow than usual.

Having passed the night off Cape York on the 31st, we steered to the eastward, and shortly discovered a low spit of land projecting about ten miles from the coast, which here forms a right angle, and having a channel about two miles wide between its extremity and the northern shore. We sailed through this opening, and entered a spacious harbour, capable of holding a great many ships of the line. We landed first on the low spit at the entrance, and then stood across, nine miles to the eastward, and came to anchor off a bold cape, having carried nothing less than five and a half fathoms water the whole of the way.

The following morning, Sept 1st, we stood toward an opening at the north-east angle of the harbour, but finding the water get gradually shallow, came again to anchor. On examination with the boats, we found, as we expected, an inner harbour, ten miles in length by two and a quarter in width, with almost an uniform depth of two and a half and three fathoms water. The channel into it from the outer harbour is extremely narrow, the entrance being contracted by two sandy spits but the water is deep, and in one part there is not less than twelve fathoms. At the upper end of the harbour a second strait, about three hundred yards in width, was formed between steep cliffs, but this channel was also contracted by sandy points. The current ran strong through the channel, and brought down a great body of water, nearly fresh (1.0096 sp-gr.) The boats had not time to pursue this strait. but in all probability it communicates with a large inland lake, as described by the natives in Kotzebue Sound. At the entrance of the strait, called Tokshook by the natives, there is an Esquimaux village, and upon the northern and eastern shores of the harbour there are two others; the population of the whole amounted to about four hundred perons. They closely resembled the natives we had seen before, except that they were better provided with clothing and their implements were neater and more ingeniously made. Among their peltry we noticed several gray fox and land-otter skins, but they would not part with them for less than a hatchet apiece. In addition to the usual weapons of bows and arrows, these people had short iron spears neatly inlaid with brass, upon all which implements they set great value, and kept them wrapped in skins Among the inhabitants of the village on the northern shore named Choonowuck, there were several girls with massive iron bracelets. One had a curb chain for a necklace. and another a bell suspended in front in the manner described the preceding year at Choris Peninsula.

There are very few natives in the outer harbour. On the northern side there is a village of yourts, to which the inhabitants apparently resort only in the winter At the time of our visit it was in charge of an old man, his wife, and daughter, who received us civilly, and gave us some fish The yourts were in a very ruinous condition. some were half filled with water, and all were filthy. By several articles and cooking utensils left upon the shelves, and by some sledges which were secreted in the bushes, the inhabitants evidently intended to return as soon as the frost should consolidate all the stagnant water within and about their dwellings One of these yourts was so capacious that it could only have been intended as an assembly or banquetting room, and corresponded with the description of similar rooms among the eastern Esquimaux.

There was a burying ground near the village in which we noticed several bodies wrapped in skins, and deposited upon drift wood, with frames of canoes, and sledges, &c placed near them, as already described at the entrance of Hotham Inlet   The old man whom we found at this place gave the same names to the villages at the head of the inner harbour, and to the points of land at its entrance, as we had received from the natives of King-a-ghe whom we met in Kotzebue Sound

His daughter had the hammer of a musket suspended about her neck, and held it so sacred that she would scarcely submit it to examination, and afterwards carefully concealed it within her dress She was apparently very modest and bashful, and behaved with so much propriety that it was a pleasure to find such sentiments existing beneath so uncouth an exterior.

Upon the low point at the entrance of the inner harbour, called Nooke by the natives, there were some Esquimaux fishermen, who reminded us of a former acquintance at Chamisso Island, and saluted us so warmly that we felt sorry their recollection had not entirely failed them.   They appear to have established themselves on the point for the purpose of catching and drying fish : and from the number of salmon that were leaping in the channel, we should have thought they would have been more successful   They had, however, been fortunate in taking plenty of cod, and some species of salmon trout. they had also caught some herrings.

We were also recognised by a party from the southern shores of the harbour, who the preceding year, had extended their fishing excursions from this place to Kotzebue Sound   These were some of the most cleanly and well-dressed people we had seen on the coast Their residence was at King-a-ghe—a place which, judging from the respectability of its inhabitants, whom we had seen elsewhere, must be of importance among the Esquimaux establishments upon this coast.

These two ports, situated so near Beering's Strait, may at some future time be of greater importance to navigation, as they will be found particularly useful by vessels which may not wish to pass the strait in bad weather.   To the outer harbour, which for convenience and security surpasses any other near Beering's Strait with which we are acquinted, I attached the name of Port Clarence, in honour of his most gracious Majesty, then Duke of Clarence   To the inner, which is well adapted to the purposes of repair, and is sufficiently deep to receive a frigate, provided she lands her guns, which can be done conveniently upon the sandy point at the entrance, I gave the name of Grantley Harbour, in compliment to Lord Grantley To the points at the entrance of Port Clarence I attached the names of Spencer and Jackson, in compliment to Capt the Honourable

Sii Robeit Spencer and Captain Samuel Jackson, C B , two distinguished officeis in the naval service to the lattei of whom I am
indebted foi my earliest connexion with the voyages of northern
Discovery.

The noithern and eastern shores of Poit Clarence slope fiom
the mountains to the sea, and aie occasionally teiminated by cliffs
composed of fine and talcy mica slate, inteisected by veins of
calcaieous spai of a pearly lustre, mixed with grey quartz   The
soil is coveied with a thick coating of moss, among which there is
a very limited floia . the valleys and hollows are filled with dwaif
willow and birch   The country is swampy and full of ruts ; and
vegetation on the whole, even on the north side of the harbour,
which had a southern aspect, was moie backwaid than in Kotezbue
Sound , still we found here three species of plants we had not seen
before.   Plants that weie going to seed when we left that island
weie here only just in full flower, and berries that were there over
ripe were here scarcely fit to be eaten.   On the northern side of
Grantly Harbour, Mr. Collie found a bed of purple *primulas, ane-
mones,* and of *dodecatheons,* in full and fresh blossom, amidst a covering of snow that had fallen the preceding night.

The southern side of Port Clarence is a low diluvial formation,
covered with grass, and intersected by naiiow channels and lakes ;
it projects from a range of cliffs which appear to have been once
upon the coast, and sweeping round, terminates in a low shingly
point (Point Spencer.)   In one place this point is so narrow and
low, that in a heavy gale of wind the sea must almost inundate it;
to the northward, however, it becomes wider and higher, and, by
the remains of some yourts upon it, has at one time been the residence of Esquimaux.   Like the land just described, it is intersected
with lakes, some of which rise and fall with the tide, and is covered,
though scantily, with a coarse grass, *elymus,* among which we found
a species of artemesia, probably new.   Neai Point Spencei the
beach has been forced up by some extraordinaiy pressure into ridges,
of which the outer one, ten or twelve feet above the sea, is the highest.   Upon and about these ridges there is a gieat quantity of drift
timber, but more on the inner side of the point than the outer.
Some has been deposited upon the point before the ridges of sand
were formed, and is now mouldering away with the effect of time,
while other logs aie less decayed , and that which is lodged on the
outer part is in good preservation, and serves the natives for bows
and fishing staves.

We saw several reindeer upon the hilly ground ; in the lakes,
wild ducks and upon the low point of the inner harbour, golden
plover, and sanderlings, and a gull veiy much resembling the larus
sabini.

The survey of these capacious harbours occupied us until the 5th, when we had completed nearly all that was necessary, and the weather set in with such severity that I was anxious to get to Kotzebue Sound   For the three preceding days the weather had been cold, with heavy falls of snow ; and the seamen, the boat's crews in particular, suffered from their exposure to it, and from the harassing duty which was indispensable from the expeditious execution of the survey   On this day, the 5th, thermometer stood at 25 1-2°, and the lakes on shore were frozen.   We accordingly weighed, but not being able to get out, passed a sharp frosty night in the entrance ; and next morning, favoured with an easterly wind, weighed and steered for the strait   As we receded from Point Spencer, the difficulty of distinguishing it even at a short distance, accounted for this excellent point having been overlooked by Cook, who anchored within a very few miles of its entrance.

As we neared Beering's Strait the wind increased, and on rounding Cape Prince of Wales, obliged us to reduce our sails to the close reef   On leaving the port the wind had been from the eastward, but it now drew to the northward, and compelled us to carry sail, in order to weather the Diomede Islands.   Whilst we were thus pressed, John Dray, one of the seamen unfortunately fell overboard from the lookout at the masthead, and sunk alongside a boat which was sent to him, after having had his arms round two of the oars. This was the only accident of the kind that had occurred since the ship had been in commission, and it was particularly unfortunate that it should have fallen to the lot of so good a man as Dray.   Previous to his entry in the ship he resided some time at the Marquesas Islands, and was so well satisfied with the behaviour of the natives of that place that he purposed living amongst them ; but being on board a boat belonging to Baron Wrangel's ship, at a time when the islanders made a most unjustifiable attack upon her, he was afraid to return to the shore, and accompanied the Baron to Petropaulski, where I received him and another seaman, similarly circumstanced, into the ship.

Toward night the wind increased to a gale, and split almost every sail that was spread ; the weather was dark and thick, with heavy falls of snow , and suspecting there might be a current setting through the strait, we anxiously looked out for the Diomede Islands, which were to leeward, and we were not a little surprised to find, on the weather clearing up shortly after daylight the following morning, that there had been a current running nearly against the wind, at the rate of upwards of a mile an hour, in a N. 41° W. direction.

From the time we quitted Port Clarence the temperature began to rise, and this morning stood four degrees above the freezing point. Change of locality was the only apparent cause for this increase, and it is very probable that the vicinity of the mountains to Port Clarence is the cause of the temperature of that place being lower than it is at sea.

In the morning we saw a great many walrusses and whales, and observed large flocks of ducks migrating to the southward The coast on both sides was covered with snow, and every thing looked wintry   The wind about this time changed to N W , and by the evening carried us off the entrance of Kotzebue Sound, when we encountered, as usual, an easterly wind, and beat up all night with thick misty weather

In our run to this place we again passed over a shoal, with eight and a half and nine fathoms water upon it, off Schismareff inlet After beating all night in very thick weather, on the 9th of September we stood in for the northern shore of the sound, expecting to make the land well to windward of Cape Blossom, where the soundings decrease so gradually that a due attention to the lead is the only precaution necessary to prevent running on shore ; but there had unfortunately been a strong current during the night, which had drifted the ship towards Hotham Inlet, where the water shoaling suddenly from five fathoms to two and a half, the ship struck upon the sand while in the act of going about, and soon became fixed by the current running over the shoal.   In consequence of this current our small boats experienced the utmost difficulty in carrying out an anchor, but they at length succeeded, though to no purpose, as the ship was immoveable   Looking to the possible result of this catastrophe, we congratulated ourselves on having the barge at hand to convey the crew to Kamschatka, little suspecting, from an accident which had already befallen her, in what a helpless condition each party was at that moment placed.   Fortunately we were not reduced to the necessity of abandoning the ship, which appearances at one time led us to apprehend, as the wind moderated shortly after she struck, and on the rising of the next tide she went off without having received any apparent injury

CHAPTER XIX

Arri.e at Chamisso Island—Find the Barge wrecked—Lieutenant Belcher's Proceedings—Conduct of the natives—Approach of winter—Final Departure from the Polar Sea—Observations upon the probability of the North-West Passage from the Pacific—Remarks upon the Tribe inhabiting the North-West Coast of America—Return to California—Touch at San Blas, Valparaiso, Coquimbo, Rio Janeiro—Conclusion.

After having so narrowly escaped shipwreck, we beat up all night with thick weather, and the next morning steered for Chamisso Island   As we approached the anchorage we were greatly disappointed at not seeing the barge at anchor, as her time had expired several days, and her provisions were too nearly expended for her to remain at sea with safety to her crew, but on scrutinizing the shore with our telescopes, we discovered a flag flying upon the south-west point of Choris Peninsula, and two men waving a piece of white cloth to attract attention.   Amidst the sensations of hope and fear, a doubt immediately arose, whether the people we saw were the long looked for land expedition, or the crew of our boat, who had been unfortunate amongst the ice, or upon the coast, in the late boisterous weather   The possibility of its being the party under Captain Franklin arrived in safety, after having accomplished its glorious undertaking, was the first, because the most ardent, wish of our sanguine minds, but this was soon contradicted by a nearer view of the flag, which was clearly distinguished to be the ensign of our own boat, hoisted with the union downwards, indicative of distress   The boats were immediately sent to the relief of the sufferers, with provisions and blankets, concluding, as we saw only part of the crew stirring about, and others lying down within a small fence erected round the flag-staff, that they were ill, or had received hurts.

On the return of the first boat our conjectures as to the fate of the barge were confirmed; but with this difference, that instead of having been lost upon the coast to northward, she had met her fate in Kotzebue Sound, and we had the mortification to find that three of the crew had perished with her.   Thus, at the very time that we were consoling ourselves, in the event of our misfortunes of the preceding day terminating disastrously, that we should receive relief from our boat, her crew were anticipating assistance from us

From the report of Lieutenant Belcher, who commanded the barge, it appears that, after quiting Chamisso Island on the 12th ultimo, he proceeded along the northern shore of the Sound, and landed upon Cape Krusenstern, where he waited a short time, and not seeing the ship, the weather being very thick, he stood on for Cape Thomson, where he came to an anchor, and replenished his stock of water   He met some natives on shore who informed him that the ship had passed to the northward (which was not true,) and he therefore pursued his course, but finding the weather thick, and the wind blowing strong from the S E, he brought to under the lee of Point Hope, and examined the bay formed between it and Cape Lisburn, where he discovered a small cove, which afforded him a convenient anchorage in two fathoms, muddy bottom.   This cove, which I have named after his relation, Captain Murryat, R N. is the estuary of a river, which has no doubt contributed to throw up the point

After Lieutenant Belcher had constructed a plan of the cove, he proceeded to Cape Lisburn; the weather still thick, and the wind blowing at S W.   He nevertheless effected a landing upon the north side of the Cape and observed its latitude to be 68° 52′ 3″ N and the variation to be 32° 23′ E.   From thence he kept close along the shore, for the purpose of falling in with the land expedition, and arrived off Icy Cape on the 19th, when he landed and examined every place in the hope of discovering some traces of Captain Franklin   He found about twenty natives on the point living in tents, who received him very civilly, and assisted him to fill his water casks from a small well they had dug in the sand for their own use.   The yourts, which rendered this point remarkable at a distance, were partly filled with water, and partly with winter store of blubber and oil

From Icy Cape he stood E N E. ten miles, and then N. E twenty-seven, at which time, in consequence of the weather continuing thick and the wind beginning to blow hard from the south-west, he hauled off shore and shortly fell in with the main body of ice, which arrested his course and obliged him to put about.   It blew so strong during the night that the boat could only show her close-reefed mainsail and storm-jib, under which she plied, in order to avoid the ice on one side and a lee-shore on the other. the boat thus pressed leaked considerably, and kept the crew at the pumps

On the 21st August, the weather being more moderate, he again made the ice, and after keeping along it some time, returned to Icy Cape, and found that the edge of the packed ice was in latitude

70° 41 N. in a N N W direction from the cape, extending east and west (true)

On the 23d August another landing was made upon Icy Cape, and its latitude, by artificial horizon, ascertained to be 70° 19′ 28″ N, and variation by Kater's compass 32° 49′ E. Lieutenant Belcher's curiosity was here greatly awakened by one of the natives leading him to a large room used by the Esquimaux for dancing and by searching for a billet of wood, which his gestures implied had been left by some Europeans, but not finding it, he scrutinised several chips which were in the apartment, and intimated that some person had cut it up. This was very provoking, as Lieutenant Belcher naturally recurred to the possibility of Captain Franklin having returned by the same route. Nothing, however, was found, and Lieutenant Belcher, after depositing a notice of his having been there, embarked and passed the night off the Cape in heavy falls of snow, hail and sleet. The next day he again fell in with ice in latitude 70° 40′ N which determined him to stand back to the cape and examine the shoals upon which the ship lost her anchor the preceding year.

On the 26th, the ice was again found in 70° 41′ N. and the next day was traced to the E S E to within five or six miles of the land, and at the distance of about twenty miles to the eastward of Icy Cape. The ice appeared to be on its passage to the southward, and the bergs were large and scattered. Under these circumstances, Lieutenant Belcher, to avoid being beset, stood back to the cape, and had some difficulty in maintaining his station off there, in consequence of the severity of the weather, which cased his sails, and the clothes of the seamen exposed to the spray, with ice.

Three of his crew at this time became invalids with chilblains and ulcers occasioned by the cold and the necessity of carrying a press of sail strained the boat to such a degree that she again leaked so fast as to require the pumps to be kept constantly at work. It became necessary, therefore, to seek shelter, and he bore up for Point Hope, but before he reached that place the sea broke twice over the stern of the boat, and nearly swamped her. Upon landing at the point he was met by the natives, who were beginning to prepare their yourts for the winter. His crew here dried their clothes for the first time for several days, and Lieutenant Belcher having obtained the latitude, again put to sea, but finding the weather still so bad that he could not keep the coast with safety, and the period of his rendezvous at Chamisso Island having arrived, he pursued his course for that place, where he found the instructions I had left for him before I proceeded to examine Port Clarence.

Among other things he was desired to collect a quantity of drift-timber, and to erect an observatory upon Choris Peninsula; in which he was engaged, when the wind coming suddenly in upon the shore where the barge had anchored, the crew were immediately ordered on board   It unfortunately happened that the weather was so fine in the morning that only two persons were left in the vessel, and the boat belonging to the barge being small could take only four at a time   One boat load had joined the vessel, but the surf rose so suddenly that in the attempt to reach her a second time, the oars were broken, and the boat was thrown back by the sea, and rendered nearly useless.

Several persevering and unsuccessful efforts were afterwards made to communicate with the vessel, which being anchored in shallow water struck hard upon the ground, and soon filled.   Some Esquimaux happened to have a baidar near the spot, and Mr Belcher compelled them to assist him in reaching the barge, but the sea ran too high, and the natives not being willing to exert themselves the attempt again failed   The sea was now making a breach over the vessel, and Mr Belcher desired the cockswain to cut the cable, and allow her to come broadside upon the shore, but whether through fear, or that the cockswain did not understand his orders, it was not done   There were four men and a boy on board at this time, two of whom, finding no hope of relief from the shore, jumped overboard, with spars in their hands, and attempted to gain the beach, but were unfortunately drowned   The others retreated to the rigging; among them was a boy, whose cries were for some time heard on shore, but at length, exhausted with cold and fatigue, he fell from the rigging, and was never seen again.

The party of Esquimaux, who had so reluctantly rendered their personal assistance, beheld this loss of lives with the greatest composure giving no other aid than that of their prayers and superstitious ceremonies, and seeing the helpless condition of those thrown upon shore, began to pilfer every thing they could, bringing the party some fish occasionally. not from charitable motives, but for the purpose of engaging their attention, and of affording themselves a better opportunity of purloining the many articles belonging to the boat which were washed ashore   About eleven o'clock at night the sea began to subside, and at midnight, after very great exertions, a communication with the vessel was effected and the two remaining seamen were carried on shore, and laid before the fire, where they recovered sufficiently to be taken to a hut near the fatal scene

The morning after this unfortunate occurrence, part of the crew were employed collecting what was washed on shore, and preventing the natives committing further depredations   Seeing there was no chance of obtaining any thing more of consequence from the wreck, the party took up its quarters on Point Garnet, where we found them on our return from Port Clarence   Previous to this, several Esquimaux had pitched a tent in the bay close to the party and lost no opportunity of appropriating to themselves whatever they could surreptitiously obtain.   Among these were four persons whom Mr Belcher had a short time before assisted, when their baidar was thrown on shore, and one of the party drowned.   These people did not forget his kindness and brought him fish, occasionally, but they could not resist the temptation of joining their companions in plunder when it was to be had.   Mr Belcher seeing several articles amongst them which must have accompanied others in their possession, searched their bags, and recovered the boat's ensign, and many other things.   No opposition was offered to this examination but on the contrary, some of the party which had been saved from the wreck of the baidar, intimated to Mr Belcher that a man who was making off with a bag had part of his property; and on searching him, a quantity of the boat's iron and the lock of a fowling piece were discovered upon him.

Upon the whole, however, the natives behaved better than was expected, until the day on which the ship arrived.   This appears to have been a timely occurrence, for early that morning two baidars landed near the wreck, and the Esquimaux party was increased to twenty-four.   The man who had been searched the preceding evening, finding his friends so numerous and being joined by another troublesome character, came towards our people, flourishing his knife, apparently with the determination of being revenged.   It fortunately happened that there was a person of authority amongst the number, with whom Mr Belcher effected a friendship.   He expostulated with the two refractory men, and one of them went quietly away, but the other remained brandishing his weapon · and there is but too much reason to believe that, had he commenced an attack he would have been seconded by his countrymen, notwithstanding the interference of the chief.

When the ship's boat came to the relief of our party, Mr Belcher ordered the man who had been so refractory to be bound and taken on board the ship, intimating to the others that he should be kept until more of the stolen property was returned.   This they appeared perfectly to understand, as the prisoner pointed to his boat where, upon search being made, the other lock of the fowling-piece, and a haversack belonging to Lieutenant Belcher, were found.   The strength of this man was so great that it required as many of our people as could stand round to pinion his arms and take him down to the boat.   As soon as this was effected, all the other Esquimaux fled to their baidars, and did not approach the place again ; the chief excepted, who returned almost immediately, and pitched one tent for himself and another for the prisoner.   Lieutenant Belcher in concluding his account of this disastrous affair, speaks in high terms of commendation of **Mr** (now Lieutenant) Rendall, William Aldridge and George Shields, seamen and of Thomas Hazlehurst, marine; and it is with much pleasure I embrace the opportunity of giving publicity to their meritorious behaviour.

I must exonerate Lieutenant Belcher from any blame that may attach to him as commander of the vessel; for, though her loss was evidently occasioned by her being too close in shore, and by too few a number of persons being left on board, yet it is to be observed that she was only a boat, that the crew were upon the beach in readiness to assist her; and that, had it been a case of ordinary nature, they would no doubt have succeeded in their object. In place of this, however, the wind changed suddenly, and the sea rose so fast that there was no possibility of effecting what, under general circumstances. would have been perfectly practicable; the water besides, was two feet lower than usual The strenuous exertions of Lieutenant Belcher to save the crew, and his resolute conduct toward the natives, after he was thrown amongst them unprovided with arms, a brace of pistols excepted, show him to be an officer both of humanity and courage

After the loss of our favourite boat, Parties were repeatedly sent to the wreck, in the hope of being able to raise her, or to procure what they could from her cabin and holds · but she was completely wrecked and filled with sand, and a few days afterwards went to pieces Mr. Belcher was a great loser by this unfortunate accident, as he was well provided with instruments, books, papers, &c, and had some expensive fowling-pieces and pistols, all of which were lost or spoiled; and this was the more provoking, as some of them had been purchased to supply the place of those he had the misfortune to lose when upset in the cutter at Oeno Island. I am happy to say the government, on the representation of his peculiar case, made him a compensation.

On the 12th the body of one of the seamen, Thomas Uren, was found near the place where the boat was wrecked, and on the Sunday following it was attended to the grave by all the officers and ship's company The place of interment was on the low point of Chamisso Island, by the side of our shipmate who had been buried there the preceding year

On the 13th we were visited by two baidars, and among their crews discovered the party who had visited the ship so early in the morning, when she was at the anchorage in August, one of whom drew his knife upon the first Lieutenant; they were also of the party which made an attack upon our cutter in Eschscholtz Bay the preceding year. · They had with them a few skins and some fish for sale, but they were scrupulous about what they took for them, and on being ordered away late in the evening, they twanged their bows in an insolent manner, and, pushed off about a couple of yards only The officer of the watch desired them to go away, and at length presented a musket at the baidar, on which they fired an arrow into the sea in the direction of the ship, and paddled to the island, where we observed them take up their quarters.

When the boats landed the next day to fill the casks, Mr Smyth, who had charge of the party, was desired to arm his people, and to order the Esquimaux off the island if they were offensive to him, or interfered with the duty On landing, the natives met him on the beach, and were very anxious to learn whether the muskets were loaded, and to be allowed to feel the edges of the cutlasses, and were not at all pleased at having their request refused The arms were rolled up in the sail for the purpose of being kept dry, but one of the natives insisted on having the canvas unrolled, to see what it contained, and on being refused he drew his knife, and threatened the seamen who had charge of it Coupling this act with the conduct of the party on the before-mentioned occasions, Mr Smyth ordered the arms to be loaded, on which the natives fled to their baidar, and placed every thing in her in readiness to depart on a minute's warning, and then, armed with their bows and arrows and knives, they drew up on a small eminence, and twanged their bow-strings, as before, in defiance A few minutes before this occurred, five of the party, who had separated from their companions, attacked two of our seamen, who were at some distance from Mr. Smyth, digging a grave for their unfortunate shipmate, and coming suddenly upon them, while in the pit, three of the party stood over the workmen with their drawn knives, while the others rifled the pockets of their jackets, which were lying at a little distance from the grave, and carried away the contents, together with an axe. The hostile disposition of the natives on the hill, who were drawn up in a line in a menacing attitude, with their bows ready strung, and their knives in their left hands, obliged Mr Smyth to arm his people, and, in compliance with his instructions, to proceed to drive them off the island. He accordingly advanced upon them, and each individual probably had singled out his victim, when an aged man of the Esquimaux party made offers of peace, and the arms of both parties were laid aside The mediator signified that he wanted a tub, that had been left at the well, which was restored to him, and the axe that had been taken from the grave was returned to our party. The Esquimaux then embarked, and paddled towards Eschscholtz Bay. I have been thus particular in describing the conduct of these people, in consequence of a more tragical affair which occurred a few days afterwards.

Strong winds prevented the completion of our water for several days, but on the 29th it was in progress, when the same party land-

ed upon the island near our boat   The day being very fine, several of the officers had gone in pursuit of ptarmigan, which were about
this time collecting in large flocks previous to their migration ; and
I was completing a series of magnetical observations in another part
of the island.   The first lieutenant observing a baidar full of men
approach the island, despatched Lieutenant Belcher to the place
with orders to send them away, provided there were any of the
party among them who had behaved in so disorderly a manner on
the recent occasion.   On landing, he immediately recognized one of
the men, and ordered the whole party into the baidar.   They complied very reluctantly, and while our seamen were engaged pushing them off, they were occupied in preparations for hostility, by
putting on their eider-duck frocks over their usual dresses, and un-
covering their bows and arrows   They paddled a few yards from
the beach, and then rested in doubt as to what they should do ;
some menacing our party, and others displaying their weapons
Thus threatened, and the party making no attempt to depart, but
rather propelling their baidar sidewise toward the land, Mr Belcher fired a ball between them and the shore, and waved them to begone   Instead of obeying his summons, they paddled on shore instantly, and quitted their baidar for a small eminence near the beach,
from whence they discharged a flight of arrows, which wounded
two of our seamen.   Their attack was of course returned and one,
of the party was wounded in the leg by a musket ball.

Until this time they were ignorant of the effect of fire-arms, and no
doubt placed much confidence in the thickness of their clothing,
as, in addition to their eider-duck dress over their usual frock, they
each bound a deer-skin round them as they quitted their baidar ;
but seeing the furs availed nothing against a ball, they fled with
precipitation to the hills, and the commanding officer of the Blossom
observing them running towards the place where I was engaged
with the dipping needle, fired a gun from the ship, which first apprised me of anything being amiss   On the arrival of the cutter,
I joined Mr Belcher, and with a view of getting the natives into
our possession, I sent a boat along the beach, and went with a party
over land   We had not proceeded far, when suddenly four of the
marines were wounded with arrows from a small ravine, in which we
found a party so screened by long grass that it was not visible until
we were close upon it   The natives were lying upon the ground,
peeping between the blades of grass, and discharging their arrows as
opportunity offered   In return, one of them suffered by a ball from
Mr Elson : on which I stopped the firing, and endeavoured ineffectually to bring them to terms.   After a considerable time, an elderly
man came forward with his arms and breast covered with mud,
motioned us to begone, and decidedly rejected all offers of recon-

ciliation   Unwilling to chastise them further, I withdrew the party,
and towed their baidar on board, which kept them prisoners upon
the island.   I did this in order to have an opportunity of bringing
about a reconciliation, for I was unwilling to allow them to depart
with sentiments which might prove injurious to any Europeans who
might succeed us; and I thought that by detaining them we should
be able to convince them our resentment was unjustifiably provok-
'ed, and that when they conducted themselves properly, they should
command our friendship   This baidar had a large incision in her
bottom, made by the person who last quitted her when the party
landed, and must have been done either with a view of preventing
her being carried away, or by depriving themselves of the means of
escape, showing their resolution to conquer or die.   We repaired
her as well as we could, and kept her in readiness to be restored to
her owners on the first favourable opportunity that offered

The next morning a boat was sent to bring them to friendly
terms, and to return every thing that was in the baidar, except some
fish which they had brought for sale, in lieu of which some blue
beads and tobacco were left, but the natives were averse to reconciliation, and kept themselves concealed   The night was severely
cold, with snow showers; and next day. seeing nothing of the party, the baidar was returned.   The natives removed her during the
night to the opposite side of the island, where she appeared to be
undergoing an additional repair; but we saw none of the people,
who must have secreted themselves on the approach of the boat
We took every opportunity of showing them we wished to obtain
their friendship, but to no purpose, they would not make their appearance, and the next night decamped, leaving a few old skins in
return for the articles we had left them.—On examining the ravine
in which they had concealed themselves, we found one man lying
dead, with his bow and quiver, containing five arrows, placed under
his body, and clothed in the same manner as when he quitted the
baidar.   The ravine was conveniently adapted to the defence of a
party, being narrow, with small banks on each side of it, behind
which a party might discharge their arrows without much danger to
themselves until they became closely beset, to obviate which as
much as possible, and to sell their lives as dearly as they could, we
found they had constructed pits in the earth by scooping out holes
sufficiently large to contain a man, and by banking up the mud
above them.   There were five of these excavations close under
the edges of the banks, which were undermined, one at the head
of the ravine, and two on each side, about three yards lower down
the latter had a small communication at the bottom, through which
an arrow might be transferred from one person to another, without
incurring the risk of being seen by passing it over the top   The

constiuction of these pits must have occupied the man who presented himself to us with his aims covered with mud, as a defence
they weie as peifect as cncumstances would allow, and while they
show the resources of the people, they maik a deteiminaton of obstinate resistance

The effect of the aiiows was fully as great as might have been
expected, and had they been propeily directed, would have inflicted moital wounds. At the distance of a hundied yaids a flesh
wound was pioduced in the thigh, which disabled the man for a
time; and at eight oi ten yaids another fixed the right arm of a marine to his side. a third buried itself two inches an a half undei the
scalp   The wounds which they occasioned were obliged to be either enlaiged, to extract the aiiows, which wcre barbed, or to have
an additional incision made, that the aiiow might be pushed thiough
without fuither laceiation.   Most of these wounds were inflicted by
an aiiow with a bone head, tipped with a pointed piece of jaspar

We weie soiry to find our musketry had inflicted so severe a
chastisement upon these people but it was unavoidable and richly
deseived.   It was some consolation to reflect that it had fallen upon
a party from whom we had received repeated insult, and it was not
until after they had threatened our boat in Eschscholtz Bay, insulted
us along side of the ship, defied our party on shore, had twice drawn
their knives upon oui people, and had wounded several of them,
that they were made acquainted with the nature of our fire arms,
and I am convinced the example will have a good effect by teaching them that it was forbeaiance alone that induced us to tolerate
their conduct so long

For the purpose of keeping together the particulais of our transactions with the Esquimaux, I have omitted to mention several occurrences in the oidei in which they transpired   Many circumstances indicated the cailiei appioach of winter than we had experienced the preceding year   About the middle of September, therefore, we began to piepaie the ship for her depaiture, by completing
the water, taking on board stone ballast, in lieu of the piovisions
that had been expended, and refitting the iigging   These operations
weie for several days interrupted by strong westeily winds, which
occasioned much sea at the anchorage, and very unaccountably had
the effect of pioducing remaikably low tides, and of checking the
rise which on several occasions was scaicely perceptible

On the 18th a paity of the officeis landed in Eschscholtz Bay to
search for fossils, but they were unsuccessful; in consequence of an
irregularity in the tide, which was on that occasion unaccountably
high, and scarcely fell during the day.   The cliffs had broken away
considerably since the preceding yeai; and the fiozen surface of the
cliff appeared in smaller quantities than before, but the earth was

found congealed at a less depth from the top   This examination tended to confirm more steadfastly the opinion that the ice forms only a coating to the cliff, and is occasioned by small streams of water oozing out, which either become congealed themselves in their descent, or convert into ice the snow which rests in the hollows.

On the 24th and 28th the nights were clear and frosty, and the aurora borealis was seen, forming several arches   On the 28th the display was very brilliant and interesting, as it had every appearance of being between the clouds and the earth, and, after one of these displays, several meteors were observed issuing from parts of the arch, and falling obliquely toward the earth   This was also one of the rare instances of the aurora being seen to the southward of our zenith.

In the beginning of October we had sharp frosts and heavy falls of snow.   On the 4th the earth was deeply covered and the lakes were frozen. the thermometer during the night fell to 25°, and at noon on the 5th to 24°. and there was every appearance of the winter having commenced   It therefore became my duty seriously to consider on the propriety of continuing longer in these seas   We had received no intelligence of Captain Franklin's party, nor was it very probable that it could now appear, and we could only hope, as the time had arrived when it would be imperative on us to withdraw from him the only relief he could experience in these seas, that he had met with insurmountable obstacles to his proceeding, and had retraced his route up the M'Kenzie River

Anxious, however, to remain to the last, on the chance of being useful to him, I again solicited the opinions of the officers as to the state of the season, and finding them unanimous in believing the winter to have commenced, and that the ship could not remain longer in Kotzebue Sound with safety, I determined to quit the anchorage the moment the wind would permit   Weighing the probability of Captain Franklin's arrival at this late period in the season, no one on board, I believe, thought there was the smallest chance of it, for, had his prospects the preceding year been such as to justify his wintering upon the coast, the distance remaining to be accomplished in the present season would have been so short that he could scarcely fail to have performed it early in the summer in which case we must have seen him long before this date, unless, indeed, he had reached Icy Cape and found it advisable to return by his own route, a contingency authorised by his instructions   Upon the chance of his arrival after the departure of the ship, the provision that had been buried for his use, was allowed to remain, and the billet of wood was again deposited on the island, containing a statement of the behavior of the natives and of other particulars with which it was important that he should be made acquainted.

On the 6th, sharp frosty weather continuing, we weighed from Chamisso, and beat out of the sound In pasing Cape Krusenstern we perceived a blink in the N W. direction, similar to that over ice and it is not unlikely that the westerly winds which were so prevalent all the summer had drifted it from the Asiatic shore, where it rests against the land in a much lower parallel than upon the American coast

As we receded from the sound the wind freshened from the N W with every appearance of a gale ; we kept at a reasonable distance from the land until day-light and then steered towards Cape Prince of Wales, with a view of passing Beering's Strait Our depth of water thus far had been about fifteen fathoms, but at eleven o'clock in the forenoon it began to diminish and the sea being high, the course was altered, to increase our distance from the coast we had scarcely done this when the water shoaled still more and a long line of breakers was observed stretching from the land, crossing our course and extending several miles to windward The weather was so hazy that we could scarcely see the land ; but it was evident that we had run down between the coast and a shoal, and as there was no prospect of being able to weather the land on the opposite tack, the only alternative was to force the ship through the breakers, we accordingly steered for those parts where the sea broke the least and kept the ship going at the rate of seven knots, in order as the shoal appeared to be very narrow that she might not hang, in the event of touching the ground

The sea ran very high, and we entered the broken water in breathless suspense, as there was very little prospect of saving the ship, in the event of her becoming fixed upon the shoal. Four fathoms and a half was communicated from the channels, a depth in which it may be recollected we disturbed the bottom in crossing the bar of San Francisco, the same depth was again reported and we pursued our course momentarily expecting to strike Fortunately this was the least depth of water, and before long our soundings increased to twenty fathoms, when, having escaped the danger, we resumed our course for the strait

This shoal, which appears to extend from Cape Prince of Wales, taking the direction of the current through the strait, is extremely dangerous, in consequence of the water shoaling so suddenly and having deep water within it, by which a ship coming from the northward may be led down between the shoal and the land, without any suspicion of her danger Though we had nothing less than twenty-seven feet water, as near as the soundings could be ascertained in so high a sea, yet, from the appearance of the breakers outside the place where the ship crossed, the depth is probably less It is remarkable that this spit of sand, extending so far as it does from the land, should have hitherto escaped the observation of the Russians, as well as of our countrymen   Cook, in his chart, marks five fathoms close off the cape, and Kotzebue three, but this spit appeared to extend six or seven miles from it   It is true that the weather was very hazy, and we might have been deceived in our distance from the shore: but it is also probable that the spit may be extending itself rapidly

We passed Beering's Strait about one o'clock, as usual with a close reefed topsail breeze, and afterwards ran with a fresh gale until midnight, when, as I wished to see the eastern end of St Lawrence Island, we rounded to for daylight.   It was, however, of little consequence, as the weather was so foggy the next day that we could not see far around us   As we approached the island, flocks of alca crestatella and of the eider and king ducks, and several species of phalaropes, flew about us, but no land was distinguished. About noon, the water shoaling gradually to eleven fathoms, created a doubt whether we were not running upon the island, but, on altering the course to the eastward, it deepened again, and by the observations of the next day it appeared that the ship had passed over a shoal lying between St Lawrence Island and the main   It is a curious fact, that this shoal is precisely in the situation assigned to a small island which Captain Cook named after his surgeon, Mr Anderson, and as that island has never been seen since, many persons, relying upon the general accuracy of that great navigator, might suppose the island to have been sunk by some such convulsion as raised the island of Amnuk in the same sea; while others might take occasion from this fact to impeach the judgment of Cook I am happy to have an opportunity of reconciling opinions on this subject, having discovered a note by Captain Bligh, who was the master with Captain Cook, written in pencil on the margin of the Admiralty copy of Cook's third voyage, by which it is evident that the compilers of the chart have overlooked certain data collected off the eastern end of St Lawrence Island, on the return of the expedition from Norton Sound, and, that the land, named Anderson's Island, was the eastern end of the island St Lawrence, and had Cook's life been spared he would no doubt have made the necessary correction in his chart

Thick weather continued until the 10th, when, after some hard showers of snow, it dispersed, and afforded us an opportunity of determining the position of the ship, by observation, which agreed very nearly with the reckoning. and showed there had been no current of consequence   Two days afterwards we saw the island of St Paul, and endeavoured to close it, in order to examine its outline, and compare our observations with those of the preceding year, but the wind obliged us to pass at the distance of eight miles to the eastward, and we could only accomplish the latter. The next morning we passed to the eastward of St George's Island, and fixed its position also   This was the island we were anxious to see the preceding year, as its situation upon our chart was very uncertain, and in some of the most approved charts it is omitted altogether

Off here we observed a number of shags, a few albatrosses, flocks of ortolans, and a sea otter

At daylight on the 14th, we saw the Aleutian Islands, and steered for an opening which by our reckoning should have been the same strait through which we passed on a former occasion ; but, the islands being covered more than half way down with a dense fog, we were unable to ascertain our position correctly , and it was not until the latitude was determined by observation that we discovered we were steering for the wrong passage.   This mistake was occasioned by current S. 34° W true, at the rate of nearly three miles an hour, which in the last twelve hours had drifted the ship thirty-five miles to the westward of her expected position   Fortunately the wind was fair, and enabled us to correct our error by carrying a press of sail.   Before sunset we got sight of the Needle Rock in the channel of Oonemak, and passed through the strait. The strength and uncertainty of the currents about these islands should make navigators very cautious how they approach them in thick weather   whenever there is any doubt, the most certain course is to steer due east, and make the Island of Oonemak, which may be known by its latitude, being thirty miles more northerly than any other part of the chain ; and then to kept along its shores at the distance of four or five miles, until the Needle Rock, which lies nearly opposite the Island of Coogalga, is passed ; after which the coast on both sides trends nearly east and west, and a ship has an open sea before her.

The Aleutian Islands, when we passed, were covered about two-thirds of the way down with snow, and indicated an earlier winter than they had done the preceding year.

Having taken our final leave of Beering's Strait, all hope of the attainment of the principal object of the expedition in the Polar sea was at an end , and the fate of the expedition under Captain Franklin, which was then unknown to us, was a subject of intense interest   Amidst the disappointment this failure in meeting with him had occasioned us, we had the consolation of knowing that, whatever vicissitudes might have befallen his party, our efforts to maintain our station in both years had, by the blessing of Providence, been successful, so that at no period of the appointed time of rendezvous could he have missed both the boat and the ship, or have arrived at the appointed place in Kotzebue Sound without finding the anticipated relief.

The enterprising voyage of Captain Franklin down the Macken-zie, and along the northern shores of the continent of America, is now familiar to us all , and, considering that the distance between the extremities of our discoveries was less than fifty leagues, and that, giving him ten days to perform it in, he would have arrived at Point Barrow at the precise period with our boat, we must ever re-gret that he could not have been made acquainted with our advanced situation, as in that case he would have been justified in incurring a risk which would have been unwarrantable under any other circumstances. Let me not for a moment be supposed by this to detract one leaf from the laurels that have been gained by Captain Franklin and his enterprising associates, who, through obstacles which would have been insurmountable by persons of less daring and persevering minds, have brought us acquainted with an extent of country which, added to the discovery it was our good fortune to push so far along the shore to the westward of them, has left a very small portion of the coast unknown

The extent of land thus left unexplored between Point Turna-gain and Icy Cape, is comparatively so insignificant that, as regards the question of the north-west passage, it may be considered to be known ; and in this point of view both expeditions though they did not meet, may be said to have been fully successful   From the nature and similarity of the coast at Return Reef and Point Barrow, it is very probable that the land from Franklin Extreme trends gradually to the eastward to Return Reef, leaving Point Barrow in latitude 71°23′ 30″ N. the northern limit of the continent of America

The determination of this great geographical question is undoubt-edly important , but though it sets a boundary to the new continent, and so far diminishes the difficulties attending an attempt to effect a passage from the Pacific to the Atlantic, yet it leaves the practica-bility of the North-west Passage nearly as doubtful as ever ; and it it is evident that it cannot be otherwise, until the obstructions set forth in Captain Parry's voyage are removed, as it would avail little to be able to reach Hecla and Fury Strait, provided that channel were always impassable.

From what has been set forth, in the foregoing narrative of our proceedings, it is nearly certain that, by watching the opportunity, a vessel may reach Point Barrow, and in all probability proceed beyond it   Had we been permitted to make this attempt, we should no doubt be able to speak more positively upon the subject , and, as I have always been of opinion that a navigation may be performed along any coast of the Polar Sea that is *continuous*, I can see no insurmountable obstacle to the exploit.   In this attempt, however, it is evident that a vessel must be prepared to encounter very heavy pressure from the ice, and must expect, on the ice closing the coast to the westward of Point Barrow, which it unquestionably would with every strong westerly wind, to be driven on shore in the manner in which our boat was in 1826

As regards the question whether it be advisable to attempt the passage from the Atlantic to the Pacific, the advantage of being able to pursue the main land with certainty from Icy Cape is unquestionably great, and the recollection that in that route every foot gained to the eastward is an advance towards the point whence supplies and succour may be obtained, is a cheering prospect to those who are engaged in such an expedition   But while I so far advocate an attempt from this quarter, it must not be overlooked that the length of the voyage round Cape Horn, and the vicisitudes of climate to be endured, present material objections to prosecuting the enterprise by that course.

It does not appear that any preference can be given to the western route from prevailing winds or currents, as both are so variable and uncertain, that no dependence can be placed upon them   In 1826 easterly winds prevailed almost throughout the summer, both on the northern coast of America, and in the open sea to the westward of Icy cape : while in 1827, in the latter situation at least, the reverse took place.   And as the coincidence of winds experienced by Captain Franklin and ourselves in 1826 is very remarkable, there is every probability that the same winds prevailed to the eastward of Point Barrow.

The current, though it unquestionably sets to the northward through Beering's Strait, in the summer at least, does not appear to influence the sea on the northern coast of America which is navigable, as Captain Franklin, after the experience of a whole season, was unable to detect any current in either direction.   In the sea to the westward of Icy Cape, the current setting through Beering's Strait is turned off by Point Hope, and does not appear to have any perceptible influence on the water to the north-eastward of Icy Cape, for the current there, though it ran strong at times, seemed to be influenced entirely by the prevailing wind   The body of water which finds its way into the Polar Sea must undoubtedly have an outlet, and one of these appears to be the Strait of Hecla and Fury   but as this current is not felt between the ice and the continent of America, the only part of the sea that is navigable, it must rather impede than favour, the enterprise, by blocking the ice against both the strait, and the western coast of Melville Peninsula. Upon the whole, however, I am disposed to favour the western

60

route, and am of opinion that could steam vessels properly fitted, and adapted to the service, arrive in good condition in Kotzebue Sound, by the beginning of one summer they might with care and patience succeed in reaching the western shore of Melville Peninsula in the next. There, however, they would undoubtedly be stopped, and have to encounter difficulties which had repulsed three of the most persevering attempts ever made toward the accomplishment of a similar object.

I shall now offer a few remarks upon the inhabitants whom we met upon this coast.

The western Esquimaux appear to be intimately connected with the tribes inhabiting the northern and north-eastern shores of America, in language, features, manners, and customs. They at the same time, in many respects, resemble the Tschutschi, from whom they are probably descended These affinities I shall notice as I proceed with my remarks upon the people inhabiting the northwest coast of America, whom for the convenience of the reader, I shall call the western Esquimaux, in order to distinguish them from the tribes inhabiting Hudson's Bay, Greenland, Igloolik, and indeed from all the places eastward of Point Barrow. This line ought properly to be drawn at M'Kenzie River, in consequence of certain peculiarities connecting the people seen near that spot with the tribe to the westward . but it will be more convenient to confine it within the above-mentioned limits

These people inhabit the north-west coast of America, from 60º 34′ N to 71º 24′ N , and are a nation of fishermen dwelling upon or near the sea shore, from which they derive almost exclusively their subsistence.

They construct yourts or winter residences upon those parts of the shore which are adapted to their convenience, such as the mouths of rivers, the entrances of inlets, or jutting points of land, but always upon low ground. They form themselves into communities, which seldom exceed a hundred persons , though in some few instances they have amounted to upwards of two hundred Between the above mentioned limits we noticed nineteen of these villages, some of which were very small, and consisted only of a few huts, and others appeared to have been deserted a long time ; but allowing them all to be inhabited in the winter, the whole population, I should think, including Kow-ee-rock, would not amount to more than 2500 persons I do not pretend to say that this estimate is accurate, as from the manner in which the people are dispersed along the coast in the summer, it is quite impossible that it should be so ; but it may serve to show that the tribe is not very numerous

As we landed upon every part of the coast, to which these villages appear to be confined, it is not likely that many escaped our observation ; neither is it probable that there are many inland or far up the rivers, as frequent access to the sea is essential to the habits of the people   Besides, this may further be inferred, from the circumstance of no Esquimaux villages being found up either the M'Kenzie or Coppermine Rivers, and from the swampy nature of the country in general and the well known hostile disposition of the Indians towards the Esquimaux.

Their yourts or winter residences are partly excavated in the earth and partly covered with moss laid upon poles of drift-wood. There are however several kinds of habitations which seem to vary in their construction according to the nature of the ground and the taste of the inhabitants   Some are wholly above ground, others have their roof scarcely raised above it ; some resemble those of the Tschutschi, and others those of the natives near Prince William Sound ; but they all agree in being constructed with drift wood covered with peat, and in having the light admitted through a hole in the roof covered with the intestines of sea animals.   The natives reside in these abodes during the winter and when the season approaches at which they commence their wanderings they launch their baidars and taking their families with them, spread along the coast in quest of food and clothing for the ensuing winter   An experienced fisherman knows the places which are most abundant in fish and seals, and resorts thither in the hope of being the first occupier of the station.   Thus almost every point of land and the mouths of all the rivers are taken possession of by the tribe.   Here they remain, and pass their time, no doubt, very happily, in the constant occupation of taking salmon, seals, walrusses, and reindeer, and collecting peltry, of which the beaver skins are of very superior quality, or whatever else they can procure which may prove useful as winter store.

During their absence the villages are left in charge of a few elderly women and children, with a youth or two to assist them, who besides preventing depredations, are deputed to cleanse and prepare the yourts for the reception of the absentees at the approach of winter.   As long as the fine weather lasts they live under tents made of deer-skins laced upon poles , but about the middle of September, they break up these establishments load their baidars with the produce of their labour, and track them along the coast with dogs towards their yourts, in which they take up their winter station as before, and regale themselves after their success, by dancing singing and banquetting ; as appears to be the custom with the Eastern Esquimaux, and from their having large rooms appropriated to such diversions.

These winter stations may be always known at a distance by trunks of trees, and frames erected near them, some supporting sledges and skins of oil, and others the scantling of boats, caiacs, fishing implements, &c.

We had no opportunity of witnessing their occupations in the winter, which must consist in the construction of implements for the forthcoming season of activity, in making clothes and carving and ornamenting their property, for almost every article made of bone is covered with devices. They appear to have no king or governor, but, like the patriarchal tribes, to venerate and obey the aged They have sometimes a great fear of the old women who pretend to witchcraft.

It seems probable that their religion is the same as that of the Eastern Esquimaux, and that they have similar conjurers and sorcerors. We may infer that they have an idea of a future state, from the fact of their placing near the graves of their departed friends the necessary implements for procuring a subsistence in this world, such as harpoons, bows, and arrows, caiacs, &c and by clothing the body decently, and from the circumstance of musical instruments being suspended to the poles of the sepulchres, it would seem that they consider such state not to be devoid of enjoyments Their mode of burial differs from that of the Eastern Esquimaux, who inter their dead ; whereas these people dispose the corpse upon a platform of wood, and raise a pile over it with young trees. The position in which the bodies are laid also differs, the head being placed to the westward by this nation, while in the eastern tribes it lies to the north-east.

They are taller in stature than the Eastern Esquimaux, their average height being about five feet seven and a half inches. They are also a better looking race, if I may judge from the natives I saw in Baffin's Bay, and from the portraits of others that have been published. At a comparatively early age, however, they (the women in particular) soon lose this comeliness, and old age is attended with a haggard and care-worn countenance, rendered more unbecoming by sore eyes, and by teeth worn to the gums by frequent mastication of hard substances.

They differ widely in disposition from the inhabitants of Igloolik and Greenland, being more continent, industrious, and provident and rather partaking of the warlike, irascible, and uncourteous temper of the Tschutschi. Neither do they appear by any means so deficient in filial affection as the natives of Igloolik, who as soon as they commenced their summer excitions left their aged and infirm to perish in the villages ; of whom it will be recollected that one old man, in particular, must have fallen a victim to this unnatural neglect, had not his horrible fate been arrested by the timely humanity of the commander of the polar expedition.

With the Western Esquimaux, as indeed with almost all uncivilized tribes, hospitality seems to form one characteristic feature of the disposition ; as if Nature, by the gift of this virtue, had intended to check, in some measure that ferocity which is otherwise so predominant.

Smoking is their favourite habit, in which they indulge as long as their tobacco lasts   Parties assemble to enjoy the fumes of this narcotic, and the pipe passes round like the calumet of the Indians but apparently without the ceremony being binding   Their pipes are short, and the bowls of some contain no more tobacco than can be consumed in a long whiff; indeed, the great pleasure of the party often consists in individuals endavouring to excel each other in exhausting the contents of the bowl at one breath, and many a laugh is indulged at the expense of him who fails, or who, as is very frequently the case, is thrown into a fit of coughing by the smoke getting into his lungs

They seldom use tobacco in any other way than this, though some natives whom we saw to the southward of Beering's Strait were not averse to chewing it, and the St. Lawrence islanders indulged in snuff.   Their predilection for tobacco is no doubt derived from the Tschutschi, who are passionately fond of it, that they are said, by Captain Cochrane, to snuff, chew, and smoke, all at the same time.   The practice of adulterating tobacco is common with the Tschutschi, and has, no doubt, passed from them to the Esquimaux, who often adopt it from choice.   That which finds its way to the N W coast of America is of very inferior quality, and often has dried wood chopped up with it.

The ornaments worn in the lip, described in the course of this narrative, are peculiar to the males of the Western Esquimaux, and are in use only from Norton Sound, where they were seen by Captain King, to the Mackenzie River, where they were worn by the party which attacked Captain Franklin.   The practice is by no means modern, as Deschnew, as far back as 1648, describes the inhabitants of the islands opposite Tschutskoi Noss as having pieces of sea-horse tusk thrust into holes in their lips   No lip ornaments similar to these have been seen to the eastward of the Mackenzie River; and indeed we know of no other tribe which has adopted this singular custom of disfiguring the face, except that inhabiting the coast near Prince William Sound, and even there the arrangement differs   It is remarkable that the practice with them is confined to the women, while in the tribe to the northward it is limited to the men.   It is also singular, that this barbarous custom of the males is confined to so small a portion of the coast, while that by which the females are distinguished extends from Greenland, along the northern and western shores of America, down to California.

Nasal ornaments, so common with the tribes to the southward of Oonalaska, were seen by us in one instance only, and were then worn by the females of a party whose dialect differed from that in general use with the tribe to the westward of Point Barrow. The custom disappears to the northward of Alaska, and occurs again in the tribe near the Mackenzie River. A similar break in the link of fashion in the same nation may be traced in the practice of shaving the crown of the head, which is general with the Western Esquimaux, ceases at the Mackenzie River, and appears again in Hudson's Bay, and among a tribe of Greenlanders, who, when they were discovered by Captain Ross, had been so long excluded from intercourse with any other people, that they imagined themselves the only living human beings upon the face of the globe.*

It was remarked that the inhabitants of Point Barrow had copper kettles, and were in several respects better supplied with European articles than the people who resided to the southward. Captain Franklin found among the Esquimaux near the Mackenzie several of these kettles, and other manufactures, which were so unlike those supplied by the North-west Company, as to leave no doubt of their being obtained from the westward. Connecting these facts with the behaviour of the natives who visited us off Wainwright Inlet, and the information obtained by Augustus, the interpreter, it is very probable that between the Mackenzie River and Point Barrow there is an agent who receives these articles from the Asiatic coast, and parts with them in exchange for furs. Augustus learned from the Esquimaux that the people from whom these articles were procured resided up the river to the westward of Return Reef. The copper kettles, in all probability, come from the Russians, as the Tschutschi have such an aversion to utensils made of that metal, that they will not even use one when lined with tin † From the cautious manner in which the whole tribe dispose of their furs, reserving the most valuable for larger prices than we felt inclined to give, and sometimes producing only the inferior ones, we were induced to suspect that there were several Esquimaux acting as agents upon the coast, properly instructed by their employers in Kamschatka, who having collected the best furs from the natives, crossed over with them to the Asiatic coast, and returned with the necessary articles for the purchase of others.

I regret that we never had an opportunity of seeing the Esquimaux in pursuit of their game, or in any way actively employed, except in transporting their goods along the coast. One cause for this is that they relinquished all occupation on our appearance, to

---

* See a letter from Captain Edward Sabine, Journal of Science, vol. vii.
† Captain Cochrane's Journey in Siberia

obtain some of the riches that were on board the ship It may, however, be inferred, from the carvings upon their ivory implements, that their employments are numerous, and very similar to those practised by the Greenlanders Of these, rein-deer hunting appears to be the most common. If we may credit the sculptured instruments, they shoot these animals with bows and arrows, which, from the shyness of the deer, must require great skill and artifice to effect. The degree of skill may be inferred from the distance at which some of the parties are drawn shooting their arrows, and the artifice is shown by a device of a deer's head and horns placed upon the shoulders of a person creeping on all-fours towards the animal, after the manner of the Californian Indians, and of some of the inland tribes of North America We found the flint head of an arrow which had been used for this purpose broken in a haunch of venison that was purchased from the inhabitants near Icy Cape. In some of the representations the deer are seen swimming in the water, and the Esquimaux harpooning them from their caiacs, in the manner represented in the plate in Captain Parry's Second Voyage, p. 508.

As an instance of their method of killing whales, we found a harpoon in one that was dead, with a drag attached to it made of an inflated seal-skin It must be extremely difficult for these people, with their slender means, to capture these enormous animals, and it must require considerable perseverance The occupation, however, appears to be less hazardous than of killing walrusses, which, by the devices upon the instruments, occasionally attack the caiacs. The implements for taking these animals are the same as described by Captain Parry Seals are also captured in the manner described by him. Upon some of the bone implements there are correct representations of persons creeping along the ice towards their prey, which appears to have been decoyed by an inflated seal-skin placed near the edge of the ice ; an artifice frequently practised by the eastern tribes These animals are also taken in very strong nets made of walrus-hide, and another mode is by harpooning them with a dart about five feet in length, furnished with a barb, which is disengaged from its socket when it strikes the animal, and being fastened by a line to the centre of the staff, the harpoon acts as a drag. This instrument is discharged with a throwing board, which is easily used and gives very great additional force to the dart, and in the hands of a skillful person will send a dart to a considerable distance. The throwing board is mentioned also by Captain Parry, by Crantz, and others, and corresponds with the *womoru* of New Zealand

We noticed in the possession of a party to the northward of Kotzebue Sound a small ivory instrument, similar to the *keipkuttuk* of the Igloolik tribe.

Birds are likewise struck with darts which resemble the *nuguit* of Greenland; they are also caught in whalebone snares, and by having their flight arrested by a number of balls attached to thongs about two feet in length   they are sometimes shot with arrows purposely constructed with blunt heads.

The practice of firing at a mark appears to be one of the amusements of the Esquimaux, and judging from what we saw at Chamisso Island there are some extraordinary performers in this way among the tribe.   One day a diver was swimming at the distance of thirty yards from the beach, and a native was offered a reward if he would shoot it   he fired, but the bird evaded the arrow by diving   The Esquimaux watched its coming to the surface, and the instant his head appeared he transfixed both eyes with his arrow   He was rewarded for his skilfulness, and the skin was preserved as a specimen of ornithology and of Indian archery   Generally speaking, however, I do not think they are expert marksmen

Their bows are shaped differently to those of Igloolik, and are superior to any on the eastern coast of America; they are, however, made upon the same principle, with sinews and wedges at the back of the wood.   On the western coast driftwood is so abundant that the inhabitants have their choice of several trees, and are never obliged to piece their implements.   It requires some care to bring a bow to the form which they consider best, and for this purpose they wrap it in shavings soaked in water, and hold it over a fire; it is then pegged down upon the earth in the form required   If not attended to when used, the bows are apt to get out of order, and the string to slip out of its place, by which the bow bends the wrong way, and is easily broken

In these bows the string is in contact with about a foot of the wood at each end, and when used makes a report which would be fatal to secrecy   The Californians, accustomed to fight in ambush, are very careful to have that part of the string muffled with fur, but I never saw any precaution of the kind used by the Esquimaux   To protect the wrist from the abrasion which would ensue from frequent firing, the Esquimaux buckle on a piece of ivory called *mun-era*, about three or four inches long, hollowed out to the wrist or a gaurd made of several pieces of ivory or wood fastened together like an ironholder

Fishing implements are more numerous and varied with the Western Esquimaux than with the others, and some are constructed with much neatness and ingenuity; but I do not know that any of them require description except a landing net, and that only because it is not mentioned by Captain Parry.   This consists of a circular frame of wood or bone, about eight inches in diameter, worked across with whalebone like the bottoms of cane chairs, and fixed upon a long wooden handle.

Of all their manufactures, that of ivory chains is the most inge-nious   These are cut out of solid pieces of ivory, each link being separately relieved, and are sometimes twenty-six inches in length For what purpose they are used I know not , but part of the last link is frequently left solid, and formed in imitation of a whale; and these chains being strong, they may in some way or other be appropriated to the capture of that animal

Among a great many singularly shaped tools in the possession of these people, we noticed several that are not in Captain Parry's catalogue, such as instruments for breaking wood short off; small hand chisels, consisting of pieces of hard stone fixed in bone han-dles adapted to the palm of the hand , meshes for making nets , an instrument made with the claws of a seal, for cleansing skins of their fat, &c   Though I never saw the screw in use among this tribe, yet I found a worm properly cut upon the end of one of their fishing implements.   The *panna*, or double-edged knife, is also in use with these people , some of them were inlaid with brass, and undoubtedly came from the Tschutschi

The language of the Western Esquimaux so nearly resembles that of the tribes to the eastward, as scarcely to need any further mention, particularly after the fact of Augustus, who was a native of Hudson's Bay, being able to converse with the Esquimaux whom he met at the mouth of the Mackenzie River.   It may, however be useful to show, by means of a vocabulary compiled from the people we visited, how nearly it coincides with that given by Cap-tain Parry ; some allowances being made for the errors to which all collectors are liable, who can only make themselves understood by signs, and who collate from small parties, residing perhaps at a dis-tance from each other, and who, though they speak the same language, may make use of a different dialect.   It does not appear that this language extends much beyond Norton Sound, certainly not down to Oonalashka , for the natives of that island, who are sometimes employed by the Russians as interpreters, are of no use on the American coast, near Beering's Strait   The language, notwithstanding, has a great affinity, and may be radically the same

It is unnecessary to pursue further the peculiarities of these people, which are so similar to those of the eastern tribes, as to leave no doubt of both people being descended from the same stock , and, though the inhabitants of Melville Peninsula declared they knew of people to the westward of Akoolee, there is much reason to believe from the articles of Asiatic manufacture found in their possession, that there is an occasional communication between all the tribes on the north coast of America

The subject of currents in Beering's Strait has lost much of its interest by the removal of the doubt regarding the separation of the continents of Asia and America, and it is now of importance only to the navigator, and to the natural philosopher

It does not appear, from our passages across the sea of Kamschatka, that any great body of water flows towards Beering's Strait   In one year the whole amount of current from Petropaulski to St Lawrence Island was S 54° W. thirty-one miles, and in the next N 50° W fifty one miles, and from Kotzebue Sound to Oonemak N. 79°. W seventy-nine miles.   Approaching Beering's Strait, the first year, with light southerly winds, it ran north sixteen miles per day, and in the next, with strong S W. winds, north five miles, and with a strong N E wind, N 34° W twenty-three miles   Returning three different times with gales at N W there was no perceptible current. By these observations it appears that near the strait with southerly and easterly winds there is a current to the northward, but with northerly and north-westerly winds there is none to the southward, and consequently that the preponderance is in favour of the former, and of the generally received opinion of all persons who have navigated these seas   I prefer this method of arriving at the set of the current to giving experiments made occasionally with boats, as they would lead to a result, which would err according to the time of the tide at which they were made.

To the northward of Beering's Strait, the nature of the service we were employed upon confined us within a few miles of the coast, there the northerly current was more apparent   We first detected it off Schismareff Inlet, it increased to between one and two miles an hour, off Cape Krusenstern, and arrived at its maximum, three miles an hour, off Point Hope. this was with the flood tide, the ebb ran W S W half a mile an hour   Here the current was turned off to the north-west by the point. and very little was afterwards felt to the northward   The point is bold and shingly, and shows every indication of the current being prevalent and rapid.

This current as I have before remarked, was confined nearly to the surface and within a few miles of the land, at the depth of nine feet its velocity was evidently diminished, and at three and five fathoms there was none.   The upper stratum, it should be observed, was much fresher than sea water, and there is no doubt that this current was greatly accelerated, if not wholly occasioned, by rivers ; but why it took a northerly course is a question I am not prepared to answer

To the northward and eastward of Cape Lisburn we found little or no current until we arrived at Icy Cape   Off this projection it ran strong, but in opposite directions, and seemed to be influenced entirely by the winds   Near Point Barrow, with a southwesterly gale, it ran at the rate of three miles an hour and upwards to the

N E , and did not subside immediately with the wind, but the current must here have been increased by the channel between the land and the ice becoming momentarily narrowed by the *pack* closing the beach , and it must not be imagined that the whole body of water in the Polar Sea was going at the rapid rate above mentioned, which would be contrary to our experiments in the offing Another cause of this may be a bank lying to the westward of Icy Cape, upon one part of which the water shoals from thirty-two fathoms to nineteen, and the bottom is changed from mud to stones

It is evident, from the above mentioned facts, that a current prevails in a northerly direction, although we are unable to state with precision its amount, which cannot under any circumstances be great, nor, I should think, exceed a mile an hour on the average To be able to speak positively on this subject would require a vast number of trials to be made in the same place, and at a distance from the land, out of the influence of rivers.   We may however presume, that the above-mentioned direction is that of the prevailing current throughout the year , for, upon examining the shoals off the principal headlands, we find them all to extend to the northwest, as may be seen on referring to St Lawrence Island, Capes Prince of Wales, Krusenstern, and Lisburn, and also to Point Hope. This I conceive to be the most certain mode of deciding the question, without purposely stationing a vessel in the strait, and it is satisfactory to find that the result fully coincides with the experiments made near the shore by the Blossom and her boats *   Our observations, of course, apply to one season of the year only, as no experiments have as yet been made in the winter.

The course of this current, after it passes Cape Lisburn, is somewhat doubtful , we should expect it to diverge, and one part to sweep round Icy Cape and Point Barrow , but the shoals off the former place, like the currents themselves, do not furnish any satisfactory inference   These shoals lie parallel with the shore, and may be occasioned by ice grounded off the point.   It may be ob-

---

* I was in hopes that I had expressed myself clearly on this subject in the first edition of my work , but I find that I have been misunderstood, and even supposed in one place to have contradicted my statement in another   This apparrent disagreement has arisen partly, if not wholly, from an oversight in some of my readers, who have compared observations, made at the *surface* of the sea at one place, with those at *five fathoms below* it at another nearly 200 miles distant   If the reader will have the candour to compare the observations made at the *surfaces at both places*, he will find them to agree, with the exception that the current at one place ran faster than at the other, the reason of which I have endeavoured to account for in page 482 of this volume   I should observe here, that although I have not encumbered my narrative with a notice of every time the current was tried, such observations were made repeatedly, whenever the nature of the service I was employed upon would admit of it , but I wish it to be borne in mind, that the situation of the ship, necessarily close in shore, was highly unfavourable to the determination of the question under discussion

served here, that voyagers have frequently mentioned westerly currents along the northern coast of Asia and Nova Zembla, and we know from experience, that, in the summer, at least, there is a strong westerly current between Spitzbergen and Greenland. In the opposite direction, we find only a weak stream passing through the narrow strait of Hecla and Fury, and none through Barrow Strait. It seems, therefore, probable, that the principal part of the water which flows into the Polar Sea, from the Pacific, finds its way to the westward.

By many experiments made on shore at Icy Cape by Lieutenant Belcher, it appeared that southerly and westerly winds occasioned high tides, and northerly and easterly winds very low ebbs. It would seem, from this fact that the water finds some obstruction to the northward, and I think it probable that the before mentioned shoal, which closes the land toward Point Barrow, may extend to the northward, nay, it may even lie off the coast of some polar lands, too low and too far off to be seen from the margin of the ice, and which can only be ascertained by journeys over the ice, in a similar manner to that in which the mountains to the northward of Shelatskoi Noss were discovered by the Russians It was this shoaling of the water to the northward of Cape Lisburn that induced the late Captain Burney to believe the continents of Asia and Amereica were connected

To the northward of Beering's Strait the tide rises about two feet six inches at full and change, and the flood comes from the southward.

The quantity of drift wood found upon the shores of Beering's Strait has occasioned various conjectures as to the source from which it proceeds, some imagining it to be brought down the rivers; others to be drifted from the southward

We found some at almost every place where we landed, and occasionally in great quantities. There was more at Point Rodney than in any other part, a great deal upon Point Spencer; some upon Cape Espenburg, but more in Kotzebue Sound. Between Cape Krusenstern and Cape Lisburn there was very little, and in the bay to the eastward of the Cape scarcely any, but when the coast turned to the northward it became more plentiful, and it was afterwards tolerably abundant, and continued so all the way to Point Barrow. In addition to this, it should be remembered, that a great deal is used by the Esquimaux for boats, implements of all sort, houses, and fuel

These trees are principally, if not all, either pine or birch; all that we examined were of these two species. and we lost no opportunity of making inquiry on this subject The wood is often tough and good; indeed some that was taken from Chons Peninsula was

superior to the pine we procured at Monterey, but from this stage
of preservation it may be traced to old trunks crumbling to dust
Some trees still retained their bark, and appeared to have been recently uprooted, and comparatively few showed marks of having
been at sea

Some circumstances favour an opinion, by no means uncommon,
that this wood is drifted from the southward, such as its being found
in large quantities on Point Rodney, the many floating trees met
with at sea to the southward of Kamschatka, &c.; but the quantity
of this material found by Captain Franklin and Dr. Richardson at
the mouths of the rivers on the northern coast of America, and some
being found by us high up Kotzebue Sound, in Port Clarence, and
other places, where it is hardly possible for it to be drifted, considering the outset of fresh water, renders it more probable that it is
brought down from the interior of America.   Rivers quite sufficient
for this purpose will be found on an inspection of the chart, but
without this we need only advert to the before-mentioned rapid current of nearly fresh water to prove their existence.   Did the wood
come by sea from the southward, we could scarcely have failed
seeing some of it in our passage from Petropaulski, and during our
cruises to the northward of Beering's Strait, but scarcely any was
observed between Kamschatka and St Lawrence Island; none between that place and Beering's Strait, and only six or seven pieces
of short wood to the northward, notwithstanding the coast was closely navigated in both years by the ship and the barge.   Beside, the
westerly current, which is prevalent to the southward of Beering's
Strait, is very much against the probability of its being drifted from
the southward

We passed the Aleutian Islands on the night of the 14th, and as
in the preceding year entered a region of fine clear weather   The
volcano on Oonemak was still emitting flashes, which were visible
at a very considerable distance   It being my intention now to make
the best of my way to England, I directed the course towards California, for the purpose of refitting the ship, and of recruiting the
health of the ship's company   In this passage nothing remarkable
occurred until the 20th, on which day the sun was eclipsed, when
we were overtaken by a violent storm, beginning at S. E. and going
round the compass in a similar manner to the typhoons in the China Sea   As the gale increased, our sails were gradually reduced,
until a small storm staysail was the only canvass we could spread
The sea had the appearance of breakers, and the birds actually
threw themselves into the water, apparently to escape the fury of the
wind   About four in the afternoon, just before the gale was at its

highest, the wind shifted suddenly eight points, and brought the ship's head to the sea, which made a clean breach over the forecastle Anticipating a change of this nature, we fortunately wore round a few hours before it occurred, and escaped the consequences which must have attended the stern of the ship being opposed to such breakers The barometer during this gale fell an inch in eleven hours, and rose the same quantity in five hours, standing at 28 4 when at its lowest altitude The temperature of the air rose nine degrees from eight in the morning to noon, and fell again to its former altititude at eight at night

On the 24th, we were concerned to find several of the seamen afflicted with scurvy. Had this disease appeared the preceding year, in which they had been a very long time upon half allowance of salt provisions and without any vegetable diet, it would not have been extraordinary , but in this year the seamen had been on full allowance of the best kind of provision, and had been living upon fresh beef in China, turtle and fish in the Arzobispo Islands and Petropaulski, besides the full allowance of lemon juice, pickled cabbages, and other anti-scorbutics The season to the northward, it is true, had been more severe than of the preceding year, and the duty in consequence more harassing ; but this is not sufficient in my opinion to occasion the difference, and I cannot but think that the indulgence in turtle, after leaving the Arzobispo Islands, which was thought so beneficial at the moment, induced a predisposition to the complaint. The disease assumed an unusual character, by scarcely affecting the gums, while patients were otherwise so ill that a disposition to syncope attended the exertion of walking. Our cases fortunately were not numerous, being confined to six , and, after a few days' fresh provisions in California, were entirely cured

On the 29th we were apprised of our approach to the coast of California by some large white pelicans, which were fishing a few miles to the westward of Point Pinos. We soon afterwards saw the land, and at eight at night moored in the Bay of Monterey. Early the following morning I waited upon the governor, and despatched messengers to the missions of St. Carlos and St Cruz for vegetables, which were afterwards served daily in double the usual proportion to the ship's company, who benefited so much by the diet that, with one exception, they very soon recovered from all indisposition

By some English newspapers which were found in this remote part of the world, we learned the melancholy news of the death of His Royal Highness the Duke of York, and put the ship in mourning, by hoisting the flag half-mast during the time she remained in the port

In my former visit to this country I remarked that the padres

were much mortified at being desired to liberate from the missions
all the Indians who bore good characters, and who were acquainted
with the art of tilling the ground.   In consequence of their remonstrances the governor modified the order, and consented to make
the experiment upon a few only at first, and desired that a certain
number might be settled in the proposed manner   After a
few months' trial, much to his surprise, he found that these people,
who had always been accustomed to the care and discipline of
schoolboys, finding themselves then own masters, indulged freely
in all those excesses which it had been the endeavour of their tutors to repress, and that many, having gambled away their clothes,
implements, and even their land, were compelled to beg or to plunder in order to support life.   They at length became so obnoxious
to the peaceable inhabitants that the padres were requested to take
some of them back to the missions, while others who had been guilty of misdemeanors were loaded with shackles and put to hard work,
and when we arrived were employed transporting enormous stones
to the beach to improve the landing-place.

The padres, conscious that the government were now sensible
of the importance of the missions, made better terms for themselves
than they had been offered by the Republican government   They
were allowed to retain their places, and had their former salary of
four hundred dollars a year restored to them, besides a promise of
payment of arrears   In return for this a pledge was exacted from
the padres, binding them to conform to the existing laws of the country, and in every way to consider themselves amenable to them
Thus stood the missionary cause in California when we quitted that
country

We remained in Monterey until the 17th, and then sailed for
St. Francisco to complete our water, which at the former place,
besides being so scarce that we could hardly procure sufficient for
our daily consumption, was very unwholesome, being brackish and
mingled with the soapsuds of all the washerwomen in the place,
and with streams from the bathing places of the Indians, into which
they were in the habit of plunging immediately on coming out of
the Temeschal

San Francisco had undergone no visible change since 1826,
except that the presidio had suffered from the shock of an earthquake on the 22d of April, which had greatly alarmed its inhabitants.

We had here the misfortune to lose James Bailey, one of our marines, who had long been an invalid

The third of December we left the harbour of St Francisco, the
shores of which, being newly clothed with snow, had a very wintry
appearance ; and on the 13th saw Cape St. Lucas.   The next day

we were off the Tres Marias, three high islands, situated seventy-five miles to the westward of San Blas, and well known by the frequent mention of them in the history of the Buccaneers, and by other early navigators in these seas. In consequence of a current setting out of the Gulf of California we were more to leeward than we were aware, and, with a view of saving time, passed through the channel between the two northernmost islands In doing this we were becalmed several hours, and fully verified the old proverb, that the longest way round is often the shortest way home.

This channel appears to be quite safe; and in the narrowest part has from sixteen to twenty-four fathoms water, but the ground in other places is very steep, and at two miles distance from the shore to the westward there is no bottom at a hundred fathoms. When the wind is from the northward it is calm in this channel, and a current sometimes sets to the southward, which renders it advisable, on leaving the channel, to take advantage of the eddy winds which intervene between the calm and the true breeze to keep to the northward, to avoid being set down upon St George's Island We found these islands twenty miles further from San Blas than they were placed on the charts

The next morning the mountains on the mainland were seen towering above the white vapour which hangs over every habitable part of the land near San Blas The highest of these, San Juan, 6,230 feet above the sea, by trigonometrical measurement, is the best guide to the Road of San Blas, as it may be seen at a great distance and is seldom obscured by fogs, while the low lands are almost always so In my chart of this part of Mexico I have given its exact position When the Piedra de Mer can be seen, it is an equally certain guide This is a rock about ten miles west of the anchorage, a hundred and thirty feet high, with twelve fathoms water all round it

The afternoon was well advanced before we anchored in the Road of San Blas, and the refreshing seabreeze, sweeping the shores of the bay, had already dispersed the mist, which until then steamed from the hot swampy savannahs that for miles surround the little isolated rock upon which the town is built The inhabitants had not yet returned from Tepic, to which place they migrate during the *tiempo de las aguas*; the rainy season, so called from the manner in which the country is deluged with rain in the summer time

At the time of our arrival in Mexico political affairs were very unsettled, and the property of British merchants was so much endangered, that I was compelled to accede to a request of the merchants, made through the vice-consul of San Blas, that I would delay my return to England, and remain until they could collect their funds, and that I would receive them on board for conveyance to

Europe. As it would require several weeks before this specie could be got together, I proposed to visit Guaymas, and to examine the eastern coast of the Gulf of California , but this was frustrated by the revolt of Bravo, the vice-president of Mexico, and by the affairs of the state becoming so disorganized that the merchants further requested me not to quit the anchorage until they assumed a less dangerous aspect

Shortly after our arrival we began to feel the effects of the unhealthy climate of San Blas, by several of the seamen being affected with intermittent fevers and agues, the common complaints of the place, particularly with persons who reside upon low ground, or who are exposed to the night air , and I regret to add that we here lost Thomas Moore, one of our most active seamen.

On the 27th of January, 1828, the agitation occasioned by the revolt had subsided, but unfortunately to late for me to proceed to Guaymas   However, as the principle part of the specie was to be shipped at Mazatlan. we put to sea a few days earlier than was necessary for that purpose, that we might examine the Tres Marias and Issabella Islands   On the 3d February we reached Mazatlan, a very exposed anchorage, in which ships are obliged to lie so close to the shore that there would be very great difficulty in putting to sea with the wind from the W.S W. to S E.   In the course of our survey, a rock having only eleven feet of water upon it was discovered nearly in the centre of the anchorage, and occasioned no little surprise that of the many vessels which had put into the port all should have escaped being damaged upon it   Mazatlan is more healthy than San Blas, and our people here began to recover from the disorders they had contracted at that place.

February 7th.—Having embarked the specie on the 24th, we put to sea on our return to San Blas, and ran along the shore with a northerly wind which is here prevalent from November to June. Lieutenant Belcher, in the cutter, kept in shore of the ship, and filled in those parts of the coast which could not be seen by her· and we thus completed a survey of the coast from Mazatlan to several miles South of San Blas   Between these two ports the water shoals so gradually that there is no danger whatever.

In my former visit to this place I found it necessary to proceed to Tepic to meet the merchants in consultation, and on that occasion I carried with me the necessary instruments for determining its position ; by which it appears that it is only twenty-two miles direct from the port, though by the road it is fifty-two.   It is in latitude 21° 30' 42" N., and its height above the sea 2,900 feet   By a register kept there during our stay, its mean temperature was 8°.1 below that of San Blas, and the range 2° 8 greater

Tepic is the second town in importance in Xalisco, now called

Guadalaxara, and contains 8000 inhabitants; but this population is augmented to about 11,000 in the unhealthy season upon the coast, at which time the people resort to Tepic.   The town stands in the lowest part of a plain nearly surrounded by mountains, and not far from a large lake which exhales a malaria fatal to those who attempt to live upon its banks.   On hot sunny days, of which there are many the clouds as they pass often envelope the town, and strike a chill which proves fatal to hundreds of persons in the course of the year; and immediately the sun has set behind the mountains a cold deposit takes place, which is so great that it soon wets a person through Under these circumstances Tepic is itself scarcely more healthy than the sea coast, and by the records of the Church it appears that the deaths exceed the births.

About a league and a half from Tepic, at the foot of Mount San Juan, stands Xalisco, near the site of the ancient town of that name. This town, though so close to Tepic, is very salubrious   I had the curiosity to examine the parish books here, in order to compare them with those at Tepic, and found the births to exceed the deaths in the proportion eighty-four to nineteen.   In a population of only 3000, there were several persons upwards of a hundred years of age while in Tepic there are very few above seventy two   The Spaniards are fully aware of this difference of climate, and often send invalids from Tepic to Xalisco to recover their health; yet they continue to reside, and even to build new houses in the unhealthy spot their ancestors have chosen

The 1st of March was the day appointed for the embarkation of the specie at San Blas; but it was the 6th before it arrived and the 8th before we could put to sea.   On my way to the southward it became necessary to call at Acapulco for the purpose of securing the bowsprit previous to the passage round Cape Horn, as this could not be done conveniently in the open road of San Blas.   While we were at anchor we received very distressing accounts of the state of affairs at Acapulco, and several vessels arrived from that place with passengers, who had been obliged to seek their safety by flight.   It appeared that shortly after the revolt of Bravo, the Spaniards with certain exceptions, were expelled from the Mexican Territory; and that Montesdeoca, a republican general, who was deeply indebted to some Spaniards at Acapulco, took advantage of this proclamation to liquidate his debt by marching against the town with a lawless troop of half-cast Mexicans, and by obliging the Spaniards to take refuge on board the vessels in the harbour, or to secrete themselves in the woods.

On putting to sea from San Blas, we kept along the land; the next day we determined the position of Cape Corrientes, a remarkable promontory on this coast, and on the 10th were within sight of the volcano of Colima. This mountain, by our measurement from a base of forty-eight miles, is 12,003 feet above the sea , and is situated in latitude 19º 25′ 24″ N. and longitude 1º 41′ 42″ E. of the arsenal at San Blas. On the 11th, in latitude 17º 16′ N , our temperature underwent a sensible change, previous to this date the thermometer had ranged between 71° and 73°, but on this day it rose to 82°, and did not fall again below 80° until after we quitted Acapulco I notice the circumstance in consequence of Captain Hall having experienced precisely the same change in the same situation.*

Early in the morning of the 12th March we came within view of the Tetas de Coyuca, two peaked hills, which are considered by seamen the best guide to the port of Acapulco, and the next morning came to anchor in the most perfect harbour of its size that can be imagined.

The town of Acapulco was now tranquil, two Spaniards only being left in the place, and Montesdeoca having retired to Tulincinga and disbanded his troops by order of the congress. The government of Acapulco was administered by Don Jose Manuella, a tool of Montesdeoca, who received me in his shirt, seated upon a Guyaquil hammock, in which he was swinging from side to side of the apartment.

Having effected our purpose in putting into the port, and taken on board a supply of turkeys and fruit, which are finer here than in any other part of the world with which I am acquainted, we put to sea on the 18th. On the 29th March we crossed the equator in 99º 40′ W., and arrived at Valparaiso on the 29th of April, where we had the gratification to find, that his Royal Highness the Lord High Admiral had been pleased to mark his approbation of our proceedings on our voyage to the northward in 1826, by honouring the Blossom with the first commissions for promotion which had been issued under his Royal Highness's auspices. Here also, I found orders awaiting my arrival to convey to Europe the remittances of specie, part of which arrived on the 19th May, and on the 20th we proceeded to Coquimbo to take on board the remainder

On the 23d, when seven leagues S. W 1-2 W. of this port, we were surprised by the shock of an earthquake, which shook the ship so forcibly, that some of the seamen imagined the anchor had been let go by accident, and was dragging the chain-cable with it to the bottom ; while others supposed the ship had struck upon a shoal An hour afterwards we felt a second shock, but much lighter. On our arrival in Coquimbo we found that these shocks had been felt by the inhabitants and that there had been one the pre-

* Hall's South America, p. 182

ceding night, which made the churches totter until the bells rang
Several slight shocks were afterwards felt by the inhabitants, who
are very sensible to these subterraneous convulsions.

We remained several days in this port, which enjoys one of the
most delightful climates imaginable, where gales of wind are scarcely ever felt, and in which rain is a very rare occurrence Situated
between the ports of Valparaiso and of Callao, where the dews
alone irrigate the ground, it seems to partake of the advantages of
the climates of each, without the inconvenience of the rainy season
of the one, or of the heat and enervating qualities of the other.

On the 3d June all the specie was embarked, and we put to sea on
our way to Brazil; passed the meridian of Cape Horn on the 30th,
in very thick snowshowers and after much bad weather arrived at
Rio Janeiro on the 21st July. Here we received on board the
Right Hon. Robert Gordon, ambassador to the court of Brazil, and
after a passage of forty-nine days arrived at Spithead, and on the
12th October paid the ship off at Woolwich

In this voyage, which occupied three years and a half, we sailed
seventy-three thousand miles, and experienced every vicissitude
of climate It cannot be supposed that a service of such duration,
and of such an arduous nature, has been performed without the loss
of lives, particularly as our ship's company was, from the commencement, far from robust; and I have to lament the loss of eight by
sickness, of four by shipwreck, of one missing, of one drowned in a
lake, and of one by falling overboard in a gale of wind; in all fifteen
persons To individuals nothing probably can compensate for these
losses; but to the community, considering the uncertainty of life
under the most ordinary circumstances, the mortality which has attended the present undertaking will, I hope, be considered compen-
sated by the services which have been performed by the expedition

In closing this narrative I feel it my duty to the officers employed under my command, particularly to those whose immediate assistance I have acknowledged in my introduction, briefly to enumerate
these services, as they are of such a nature that they cannot
appear in a narrative, and as my professional habits have unqualified
me for executing, with justice to them, or with satisfaction to myself, the task of authorship which has devolved upon me as commander of the expedition, and which I should not have undertaken
had I not felt confident that the candid public would look more to
what has been actually done, than to the mode in which the proceedings have been detailed. In the Appendix to the quarto edition I have collected as much information as the nature of the work

would admit. Besides the interesting matter which it will be found to contain, the expedition has surveyed almost every place it touched at, and executed plans of fourteen harbours, of which two are new; of upwards of forty islands, of which six are discoveries; and of at least six hundred miles of coasts, one fifth of which has not before been delineated. There have also been executed drawings and views of headlands, two numerous to appear in one work, and I hope shortly to be able to lay before the public two volumes of natural history.

In taking my leave, it is with the greatest pleasure I reflect that the Board of Admirality again marked the sense they entertained of our exertions, by a further liberal promotion at the close of the expedition.

CPSIA information can be obtained at www.ICGtesting.com
Printed in the USA
LVOW11s0448201213

365868LV00005B/10/P